Gregory G. Dess
University of Texas at Dallas

Gerry McNamara
Michigan State University

Alan B. Eisner
Pace University

eighth edition

strategic management
creating competitive advantages

McGraw Hill Education

STRATEGIC MANAGEMENT: CREATING COMPETITIVE ADVANTAGES, EIGHTH EDITION

2 3 4 5 6 7 8 9 0 DOW/DOW 1 0 9 8 7 6

ISBN 978-1-259-303500
MHID 1-259-303500

Senior Vice President, Products & Markets: *Kurt L. Strand*
Vice President, General Manager, Products & Markets: *Michael Ryan*
Vice President, Content Design & Delivery: *Kimberly Meriwether David*
Managing Director: *Susan Gouijnstook*
Director: *Michael Ablassmeir*
Director, Product Development: *Meghan Campbell*
Lead Product Developer: *Kelly Delso*
Senior Product Developer: *Lai T. Moy*
Director, Marketing: *Robin Lucas*
Lead Digital Product Analyst: *Sanka Basu*
Director, Content Design & Delivery: *Terri Schiesl*
Program Manager: *Mary Conzachi*
Content Project Managers: *Mary E. Powers* (Core), *Danielle Clement* (Assessment)
Buyer: *Susan K. Culbertson*
Design: *Matt Diamond*
Content Licensing Specialists: *John Leland* (Image), *DeAnna Dausener* (Text)
Cover Image/pages 1, 36, 74, 108, 146, 180, 212, 248, 278, 314, 348, 380, 416: *Anatoli Styf/Getty Images*
Compositor: *SPi Global*
Printer: *R. R. Donnelley*

Library of Congress Cataloging-in-Publication Data

Dess, Gregory G.
    Strategic management : creating competitive advantages / Gregory G. Dess, Gerry McNamara, Alan B. Eisner.—Eighth edition.
        pages cm
    ISBN 978-1-259-30350-0 (alk. paper)
    1. Strategic planning. I. McNamara, Gerry. II. Eisner, Alan B. III. Title.
HD30.28.D4743 2016
658.4'012—dc23
                                                                      2015020480

mheducation.com/highered

To my family, Margie and Taylor; my parents, Bill and Mary Dess; and Michael Wood

–Greg

To my wonderful wife, Gaelen; my children, Megan and AJ; and my parents, Gene and Jane

–Gerry

To my family, Helaine, Rachel, and Jacob

–Alan

We'd like to thank Tom Lumpkin for his many valuable contributions to previous editions of *Strategic Management.* We certainly wish him the best with his scholarship, work as Co-Editor of *Strategic Entrepreneurship Journal,* and other professional endeavors.

about the authors

Gregory G. Dess

is the Andrew R. Cecil Endowed Chair in Management at the University of Texas at Dallas. His primary research interests are in strategic management, organization–environment relationships, and knowledge management. He has published numerous articles on these subjects in both academic and practitioner-oriented journals. He also serves on the editorial boards of a wide range of practitioner-oriented and academic journals. In August 2000, he was inducted into the *Academy of Management Journal*'s Hall of Fame as one of its charter members. Professor Dess has conducted executive programs in the United States, Europe, Africa, Hong Kong, and Australia. During 1994 he was a Fulbright Scholar in Oporto, Portugal. In 2009, he received an honorary doctorate from the University of Bern (Switzerland). He received his PhD in Business Administration from the University of Washington (Seattle) and a BIE degree from Georgia Tech.

Gerry McNamara

is a Professor of Management at Michigan State University. He received his PhD from the Carlson School of Management at the University of Minnesota. His research focuses on strategic decision making, organizational risk taking, and mergers and acquisitions. His research has been published in numerous journals, including the *Academy of Management Journal, Strategic Management Journal, Organization Science, Organizational Behavior and Human Decision Processes, Journal of Management,* and *Journal of International Business Studies.* Dr. McNamara's research on mergers and acquisitions has been abstracted in *The Wall Street Journal, Harvard Business Review, The New York Times, Bloomberg Businessweek, The Economist,* and *Financial Week.* He served as an Associate Editor for the *Academy of Management Journal* and currently serves on the editorial boards of the *Academy of Management Journal* and the *Strategic Management Journal.*

Alan B. Eisner

is Professor of Management and Department Chair, Management and Management Science Department, at the Lubin School of Business, Pace University. He received his PhD in management from the Stern School of Business, New York University. His primary research interests are in strategic management, technology management, organizational learning, and managerial decision making. He has published research articles and cases in journals such as *Advances in Strategic Management, International Journal of Electronic Commerce, International Journal of Technology Management, American Business Review, Journal of Behavioral and Applied Management,* and *Journal of the International Academy for Case Studies.* He is the former Associate Editor of the Case Association's peer-reviewed journal, *The CASE Journal.*

strategic
management
creating competitive advantages

preface

Welcome to the Eighth Edition of *Strategic Management: Creating Competitive Advantages!* We are all very pleased with the constructive and positive feedback that we have received on our work. Here's some of the encouraging feedback we have received from our reviewers:

The content is current and my students would find the real-world examples to be extremely interesting. My colleagues would want to know about and I would make extensive use of the following features: "Learning from Mistakes," "Strategy Spotlights," "Issues for Debate," and I especially like the "Reflecting on Career Implications" feature. Bottom line: The authors do a great job of explaining complex material and at the same time their use of up-to-date examples promotes learning.

Jeffrey Richard Nystrom, University of Colorado at Denver

The application of key strategic management concepts to real-world examples throughout the book is superb. They engage the students and provide a way for them to understand the relevance of what can sometimes be abstract and complicated. The cases are engaging and challenging, providing an excellent way for students to perform strategic analysis and gain confidence in doing so.

Krista B. Lewellyn, University of Wyoming

There are many strengths: (1) explanations of concepts are clear and concise, yet comprehensive, (2) covers new developments in the field when new editions are published, and (3) covers the strategic analysis concepts (e.g., industry analysis, resources and capabilities, etc.) very well. Great textbook. I think it is the best in the market, and that is why I have used it for over seven years.

Moses Acquaah, University of North Carolina at Greensboro

The text is thorough and all-inclusive. I don't need to refer to another book as a backup. It addresses all aspects of strategic management from the initial inspiration of a vision to the nuts and bolts of putting the plan to work. It is well structured; it is clear not only how each chapter builds on the previous ones but also how analysis, formulation, and implementation are interrelated.

Lois Shelton, California State University, Northridge

I use *Strategic Management* in a capstone course required of all business majors, and students appreciate the book because it synergizes all their business education into a meaningful and understandable whole. My students enjoy the book's readability and tight organization, as well as the contemporary examples, case studies, discussion questions, and exercises.

William Sannwald, San Diego State University

It is the best-written textbook for the undergraduate course that I have come across. Application materials tie concepts to real-world practice.

Justin L. Davis, Ohio University

The Dess book overcomes many of the limitations of the last book I used in many ways: (a) presents content in a very interesting and engrossing manner without compromising the depth and comprehensiveness, (b) inclusion of timely and interesting illustrative examples, (c) includes an excellent array of long, medium, and short cases that can be used to balance depth and variety, and (d) EOC exercises do an excellent job of complementing the chapter content.

Sucheta Nadkami, University of Cambridge

We work hard to improve our work and we are most appreciative of the extensive and constructive feedback that many strategy professionals have graciously given us. We strive to incorporate their ideas into the Eighth Edition—and we acknowledge them by name later in the Preface.

We believe we have made valuable improvements throughout our many revised editions of *Strategic Management.* At the same time, we strive to be consistent and "true" to our original overriding objective: a book that satisfies three R's: relevant, rigorous, and readable. That is, our tagline (paraphrasing the well-known Secret deodorant commercial) is "Strong enough for the professor; made for the student." And we are pleased that we have received feedback (such as the comments on the previous page) that is consistent with what we are trying to accomplish.

To continue to earn the support of strategy instructors (and students!), we try to use an engaging writing style that minimizes unnecessary jargon and covers all of the traditional bases. We also integrate some central themes throughout the book—such as globalization, technology, ethics, environmental sustainability, and entrepreneurship—that are vital in understanding strategic management in today's global economy. We draw on short examples from business practice to bring concepts to life by providing 72 Strategy Spotlights (more detailed examples in sidebars).

Unlike other strategy texts, we provide three separate chapters that address timely topics about which business students should have a solid understanding. These are the role of intellectual assets in value creation (Chapter 4), entrepreneurial strategy and competitive dynamics (Chapter 8), and fostering entrepreneurship in established organizations (Chapter 12). We also provide an excellent and thorough chapter on how to analyze strategic management cases.

In developing *Strategic Management: Creating Competitive Advantages,* we certainly didn't forget the instructors. As we all know, you have a most challenging (but rewarding) job. We did our best to help you. We provide a variety of supplementary materials that should help you in class preparation and delivery. For example, our chapter notes do not simply summarize the material in the text. Rather (and consistent with the concept of strategy), we ask ourselves: "How can we add value?" Thus, for each chapter, we provide numerous questions to pose to help guide class discussion, at least 12 boxed examples to supplement chapter material, and three detailed "teaching tips" to further engage students. For example, we provide several useful insights on strategic leadership from one of Greg's colleagues, Charles Hazzard (formerly Executive Vice President, Occidental Chemical). Also, we completed the chapter notes—along with the entire test bank—ourselves. That is, unlike many of our rivals, we didn't simply farm the work out to others. Instead, we felt that such efforts help to enhance quality and consistency—as well as demonstrate our personal commitment to provide a top-quality total package to strategy instructors. With the Eighth Edition, we also benefited from valued input by our strategy colleagues to further improve our work.

Let's now address some of the key substantive changes in the Eighth Edition. Then we will cover some of the major features that we have had in previous editions.

What's New? Highlights of the Eighth Edition

We have endeavored to add new material to the chapters that reflects the feedback we have received from our reviewers as well as the challenges that face today's managers. Thus, we all invested an extensive amount of time carefully reviewing a wide variety of books, academic and practitioner journals, and the business press.

We also worked hard to develop more concise and tightly written chapters. Based on feedback from some of the reviewers, we have tightened our writing style, tried to eliminate redundant examples, and focused more directly on what we feel is the most important content in each chapter for our audience. The overall result is that we were able to update our material, add valuable new content, and—at the same time—shorten the length of the chapters.

Here are some of the major changes and improvements in the Eighth Edition:

- **A new feature: "Insights from Executives."** We have conducted six interviews with executives from a wide variety of organizations. They have been extremely helpful in addressing issues that are salient to strategic management. We sincerely appreciate their participation, and we acknowledge each of them later in the Preface. For example, in Chapter 3, Lise Saari (Former Director of Global Employee Research, IBM) addresses some of the challenges facing organizations when it comes to recruiting and developing talent, and she considers why some human resource initiatives may fail. In Chapter 7, Terrie Campbell (Vice President of Strategic Marketing at Ricoh Americas Corporation) points out some of the challenges associated with adapting marketing strategies to local tastes and markets, and she explains how she can help ensure that managers and employees throughout Ricoh have a global perspective. And, in Chapter 8, David Drews (Executive Vice President and CFO of Project: WorldWide, a global network of marketing agencies) discusses the common drivers of new venture failures as well as the importance of social networks in creating competitive advantages.

- **A new feature: "Insights from Research."** We include this feature in six chapters of the Eighth Edition. In "Insights from Research," we summarize key research findings on a variety of issues and, more importantly, address their relevance for making organizations (and managers!) more effective. For example, in Chapter 2 we discuss findings from a meta-analysis (research combining many individual studies) to debunk several myths about older workers—a topic of increasing importance, given the changing demographics in many developed countries. In Chapter 4, we address a fascinating study that found that "dormant ties" (people we have not been in contact with for at least three years) can be extremely valuable. And, in Chapter 8, we explore useful research findings to consider when leading virtual teams.

  In each of the first 12 chapters, we include one of the two new Insights features to enrich our text.

- **Most of the 12 opening "Learning from Mistakes" vignettes that lead off each chapter are totally new.** Unique to this text, they are all examples of what can go wrong, and they serve as an excellent vehicle for clarifying and reinforcing strategy concepts. After all, what can be learned if one simply admires perfection?

- **Half of our "Strategy Spotlights" (sidebar examples) are brand new, and many of the others have been thoroughly updated.** Although we have reduced the number of Spotlights from the previous edition to conserve space, we still have a total of 72—by far the most in the strategy market. We focus on bringing the most important strategy concepts to life in a concise and highly readable manner. And we work hard to eliminate unnecessary detail that detracts from the main point we are trying to make. Also, consistent with our previous edition, many of the Spotlights focus on three "hot" issues that are critical in leading today's organizations: ethics, environmental sustainability, and crowdsourcing.

Key content changes for the chapters include:

- **Chapter 1 addresses challenges associated with making a business case for sustainability initiatives.** The ROI on sustainability projects is difficult to quantify for many reasons: Necessary data are often not available, many of the benefits are intangible, and the projects may require a longer payback period. We provide examples from three companies that have endeavored to overcome such challenges by stressing the intangible benefits the firm may attain as well as the importance of taking a broader stakeholder perspective in evaluating such initiatives.

- **Chapter 2 discusses the value of "perceptual acuity" in assessing the environment.** The term *perceptual acuity* was coined by Ram Charan, an adviser to many Fortune 500 CEOs. He defines it as "the ability to sense what is coming before the fog clears." He provides examples of how some executives have enhanced their perceptual acuity by constantly meeting with people and searching out information.

- **Chapter 3 addresses the perils and challenges associated with integrating customers into their firm's value chain.** Clearly, firms can benefit by incorporating their customers into the value creation process. For example, firms can team up with customers to design and build products to satisfy their particular needs. Or firms can leverage the power of crowdsourcing. However, there can be downsides. For example, customers can "hijack" crowdsourcing efforts, and rather than offering constructive feedback, they may address serious concerns—or even ridicule the company!

- **Chapter 4 discusses how a firm's human capital can be enhanced by redefining jobs, as well as the importance of recognizing both inherent and acquired diversity.** Many successful firms are redefining the jobs of their most valuable talent by transferring some of their less critical tasks to lower-skilled employees either inside or outside the company. Hence, by redefining high-value knowledge jobs, organizations can not only successfully address skills shortages but also lower costs and enhance job satisfaction. In this chapter, we also distinguish between two types of diversity—inherent (e.g., race and gender) and acquired (e.g., traits gained by experience). Findings indicate that companies whose leaders exhibited such "two-dimensional diversity" not only enjoyed greater market share gains but also were more likely to capture new markets.

- **Chapter 5 discusses the value of data analytics as a means to achieve an integrated overall low-cost and differentiation strategy.** While it is a challenge to pursue both differentiation and low cost simultaneously, some successful firms are finding that using data analytics allows them to better customize their product and service offerings to customers while more efficiently and fully using the resources of the company. We illustrate the potential power of data analytics with examples from Pepsi and Kaiser Permanente.

- **Chapter 6 addresses research that highlights the importance of the effective allocation of corporate capital in the portfolio management of diversified firms and presents a discussion of the concept of an "acq-hire."** Recent research has supported the contention that the effective allocation of resources is a central and important role of corporate offices in diversified firms. However, studies have also found that many firms do not adjust their capital allocations in response to changes in the performance of units or the attractiveness of the markets in which units of the corporation compete. We discuss when the need to reallocate resources is critical, and we highlight that the effective use of corporate resources can be a source of competitive advantage for diversified firms. We also discuss the concept of an acq-hire, in which a firm purchases another firm primarily to hire key personnel from the target firm. We use Apple's acquisition of Beats as a prime example of this phenomenon.

- **Chapter 7 discusses an additional motive for international expansion—learning— and outlines concerns about how the rule of law has declined in the U.S. in recent years, increasing the political risk of operating in the U.S.** Expanding into new geographic markets has, at times, been seen as an action that can distract managers from succeeding in the firm's home markets. We discuss how expansion into new markets provides a range of learning opportunities for firms, and we provide research evidence showing that international expansion often leads to improvements in home-market performance. Also, while the U.S. has long been seen as a business-friendly market, we discuss how changes in U.S. laws and regulations in recent years have made it a less attractive market for firms to enter or invest in.

- **Chapter 8 addresses two key issues associated with entrepreneurial firms: ways to deliberately search for entrepreneurial ideas and the personality traits of successful entrepreneurs.** We include a set of structured actions experienced entrepreneurs use to look for new entrepreneurial opportunities, including asking yourself questions about frustrations with current products or processes; having conversations with employees, customers, and suppliers; looking at shifts in other markets that could be translated to your market; and looking for ideas used in the past but forgotten and unexploited now. We also discuss how successful entrepreneurs differ from corporate managers on the Big Five personality traits.

- **Chapter 9 includes an extended discussion of nonmonetary incentive systems and a new discussion on the attentional focus of effective boards.** A number of studies have found that for employees who are satisfied with their base salary, nonfinancial motivators are more effective than cash incentives in building long-term employee motivation. We discuss three key ways firms can motivate their employees beyond the simple use of cash. We have also added a discussion of how the boards of directors of effective companies differ from the boards of ineffective firms in regard to the time they spend on board activities and how they focus their time.

- **Chapter 10 discusses the concept of a holacracy—an extreme version of a boundaryless organization.** To succeed in highly dynamic markets, according to some scholars and managers, firms need to ditch formal hierarchies and become more democratic. We discuss one type of structure that reflects this ideal, the holacracy. Most firms using this type of structure are small start-ups. There are obvious challenges in using a democratic structure in large firms. Zappos, the first large firm to try using a holacracy, is identified as a natural experiment to see if this new type of design has potential in larger firms.

- **Chapter 11 discusses the attributes of a learning organization. In this edition, we discuss how leadership development is a key aspect of a learning organization.** To learn and grow, firms need to continually build the leadership skills of their employees, but these efforts often go wrong. We outline four key attributes of effective leadership development programs.

- **Chapter 12 introduces the idea that firms can draw great value from failed innovations.** Failure is not fun or easy, but it can be very valuable. When firms innovate, they hope that they choose the most promising technological paths, but there is great uncertainty, and they often choose the wrong path. Interestingly, that may be the route to eventual success. We discuss why firms that initially choose the wrong technological path often turn out to be the ultimate winner in the market—if they respond well to the initial failure.

- **Chapter 13 introduces the value of asking heretical questions.** Such an approach can be valuable in case discussions because these questions help to challenge conventional wisdom. Although our discussion draws primarily on its application to environmental sustainability initiatives, the approach has useful implications for challenges faced by managers in a wide variety of firms and industries.

- **Chapter 13 updates our Appendix: Sources of Company and Industry Information.** Here, we owe a big debt to Ruthie Brock and Carol Byrne, library professionals at the University of Texas at Arlington. These ladies have graciously provided us with comprehensive and updated information for the Eighth Edition that is organized in a range of issues. These include competitive intelligence, annual report collections, company rankings, business websites, and strategic and competitive analysis. Such information is invaluable in analyzing companies and industries.

What Remains the Same: Key Features of Earlier Editions

Let's now briefly address some of the exciting features that remain from the earlier editions.

- **Traditional organizing framework with three other chapters on timely topics.** Crisply written chapters cover all of the strategy bases and address contemporary topics. First, the chapters are divided logically into the traditional sequence: strategy analysis, strategy formulation, and strategy implementation. Second, we include three chapters on such timely topics as intellectual capital/knowledge management, entrepreneurial strategy and competitive dynamics, and fostering corporate entrepreneurship and new ventures.

- **"Learning from Mistakes" chapter-opening cases.** To enhance student interest, we begin each chapter with a case that depicts an organization that has suffered a dramatic performance drop, or outright failure, by failing to adhere to sound strategic management concepts and principles. We believe that this feature serves to underpin the value of the concepts in the course and that it is a preferred teaching approach to merely providing examples of outstanding companies that always seem to get it right. After all, isn't it better (and more challenging) to diagnose problems than admire perfection? As Dartmouth's Sydney Finkelstein, author of *Why Smart Executives Fail,* notes: "We live in a world where success is revered, and failure is quickly pushed to the side. However, some of the greatest opportunities to learn—for both individuals and organizations—come from studying what goes wrong."* For example, we'll see how (and why!) Groupon's stock price went from a high of $26 a share when it debuted on NASDAQ in November 2011 to around $6 near the end of 2014. Clearly, imitation in the "daily deals" industry was creating havoc. However, CEO Andrew Mason wasn't helping the situation with the questionable accounting practices that took place under his leadership, as well as his "goofball antics" (as noted by CNBC's Herb Greenberg). We'll also explore how Stroh's Brewing Company was undone by Peter Stroh, the fifth generation of the family to lead the firm, who took over as CEO in 1980. Rather than sticking to the tried-and-true business plan of catering to the needs of the Midwest working class, he undertook a disastrous series of acquisitions. And we'll look at the recent problems faced by Tesco, a large global retailer. In addition to its failed entry into the U.S. market and increasing pressure at home from hard-discounting rivals, Tesco has been tarred in the press by accounting irregularities and flawed corporate governance.

- **"Issue for Debate"—at the end of each chapter.** We find that students become very engaged (and often animated!) in discussing an issue that has viable alternate points of view. It is an exciting way to drive home key strategy concepts. For example, in Chapter 1, Seventh Generation is faced with a dilemma that confronts its values, and the firm must decide whether or not to provide its products to some of its largest customers. At issue: While the firm sympathizes (and their values are consistent) with the striking

---

*Personal communication, June 20, 2005.

workers at the large grocery chains, should Seventh Generation cross the picket lines? In Chapter 4, some interesting trade-offs must be considered when a firm under financial duress has to make a choice: begin furloughs or lay off employees (David Cote, chairman and CEO of Honeywell, provides an insightful perspective). And, in Chapter 7, we address Medtronic's decision to acquire Covidien, an Irish-based medical equipment manufacturer, for $43 billion. Medtronic's primary motive: lower its taxes by moving its legal home to Ireland—a country that has lower rates of taxation on corporations. Some critics may see such a move as unethical and unpatriotic. Supporters would argue that the move will help the firm save on taxes and benefit its shareholders.

- **Throughout the chapters, we provide many excerpts from interviews with top executives from Adam Bryant's *The Corner Office*.** Such viewpoints provide valuable perspectives from leading executives and help to drive home the value and purpose of key strategy concepts. For example, we include the perspectives of Tim Brown (CEO of IDEO) on employee empowerment, Richard Anderson (CEO of Delta Airlines) on strategy analysis, and Gordon Bethune (former CEO of Continental Airlines) on the importance of incentive systems.

- **"Reflecting on Career Implications . . ."** We provide insights that are closely aligned with and directed to three distinct issues faced by our readers: prepare them for a job interview (e.g., industry analysis), help them with current employers or their career in general, or help them find potential employers and decide where to work. We believe this will be very valuable to students' professional development.

- **"Reflecting on Career Implications" for each chapter.** This feature—at the end of each chapter—will help instructors drive home the immediate relevance/value of strategy concepts. It focuses on how an understanding of key concepts helps business students early in their careers.

- **Consistent chapter format and features to reinforce learning.** We have included several features in each chapter to add value and create an enhanced learning experience. First, each chapter begins with an overview and a list of key learning objectives. Second, as previously noted, the opening case describes a situation in which a company's performance eroded because of a lack of proper application of strategy concepts. Third, at the end of each chapter there are four different types of questions/exercises that should help students assess their understanding and application of material:

  1. Summary review questions.
  2. Experiential exercises.
  3. Application questions and exercises.
  4. Ethics questions.

  Given the centrality of online systems to business today, each chapter contains at least one exercise that allows students to explore the use of the web in implementing a firm's strategy.

- **Key Terms.** Approximately a dozen key terms for each chapter are identified in the margins of the pages. This addition was made in response to reviewer feedback and improves students' understanding of core strategy concepts.

- **Clear articulation and illustration of key concepts.** Key strategy concepts are introduced in a clear and concise manner and are followed by timely and interesting examples from business practice. Such concepts include value-chain analysis, the resource-based view of the firm, Porter's five-forces model, competitive advantage, boundaryless organizational designs, digital strategies, corporate governance, ethics, and entrepreneurship.

- **Extensive use of sidebars.** We include 72 sidebars (or about six per chapter) called "Strategy Spotlights." The Strategy Spotlights not only illustrate key points but also increase the readability and excitement of new strategy concepts.

- **Integrative themes.** The text provides a solid grounding in ethics, globalization, environmental substainability, and technology. These topics are central themes throughout the book and form the basis for many of the Strategy Spotlights.

- **Implications of concepts for small businesses.** Many of the key concepts are applied to start-up firms and smaller businesses, which is particularly important since many students have professional plans to work in such firms.

- **Not just a textbook but an entire package.** *Strategic Management* features the best chapter teaching notes available today. Rather than merely summarizing the key points in each chapter, we focus on value-added material to enhance the teaching (and learning) experience. Each chapter includes dozens of questions to spur discussion, teaching tips, in-class group exercises, and about a dozen detailed examples from business practice to provide further illustrations of key concepts.

Teaching Resources

Instructor's Manual (IM)

Prepared by the textbook authors, along with valued input from our strategy colleagues, the accompanying IM contains summary/objectives, lecture/discussion outlines, discussion questions, extra examples not included in the text, teaching tips, reflecting on career implications, experiential exercises, and more.

Test Bank

Revised by Christine Pence of the University of California–Riverside, the test bank contains more than 1,000 true/false, multiple-choice, and essay questions. It has now been tagged with learning objectives as well as Bloom's Taxonomy and AACSB criteria.

- **Assurance of Learning Ready.** Assurance of Learning is an important element of many accreditation standards. Dess 8e is designed specifically to support your Assurance of Learning initiatives. Each chapter in the book begins with a list of numbered learning objectives that appear throughout the chapter. Every test bank question is also linked to one of these objectives, in addition to level of difficulty, topic area, Bloom's Taxonomy level, and AACSB skill area. *EZ Test,* McGraw-Hill's easy-to-use test bank software, can search the test bank by these and other categories, providing an engine for targeted Assurance of Learning analysis and assessment.

- **AACSB Statement.** The McGraw-Hill Companies is a proud corporate member of AACSB International. Understanding the importance and value of AACSB accreditation, Dess 8e has sought to recognize the curricula guidelines detailed in the AACSB standards for business accreditation by connecting selected questions in Dess 8e and the test bank to the general knowledge and skill guidelines found in the AACSB standards. The statements contained in Dess 8e are provided only as a guide for the users of this text. The AACSB leaves content coverage and assessment within the purview of individual schools, the mission of the school, and the faculty. While Dess 8e and the teaching package make no claim of any specific AACSB qualification or evaluation, we have labeled selected questions within Dess 8e according to the six general knowledge and skills areas.

- **Computerized Test Bank Online.** A comprehensive bank of test questions is provided within a computerized test bank powered by McGraw-Hill's flexible electronic testing program, *EZ Test Online* (*www.eztestonline.com*). *EZ Test Online* allows you to create paper and online tests or quizzes in this easy-to-use program. Imagine being able to create and access your test or quiz anywhere, at any time, without installing the testing software! Now, with *EZ Test Online,* instructors can select questions from multiple McGraw-Hill test banks or author their own and then either print the test for paper distribution or give it online.

- **Test Creation.**
  - Author/edit questions online using the 14 different question-type templates.
  - Create printed tests or deliver online to get instant scoring and feedback.
  - Create question pools to offer multiple versions online—great for practice.
  - Export your tests for use in *WebCT, Blackboard, PageOut,* and Apple's *iQuiz.*
  - Compatible with *EZ Test Desktop* tests you've already created.
  - Sharing tests with colleagues, adjuncts, TAs is easy.

- **Online Test Management.**
  - Set availability dates and time limits for your quiz or test.
  - Control how your test will be presented.
  - Assign points by question or question type with drop-down menu.
  - Provide immediate feedback to students or delay until all finish the test.
  - Create practice tests online to enable student mastery.
  - Your roster can be uploaded to enable student self-registration.

- **Online Scoring and Reporting.**
  - Automated scoring for most of *EZ Test*'s numerous question types.
  - Allows manual scoring for essay and other open response questions.
  - Manual rescoring and feedback are also available.
  - *EZ Test*'s grade book is designed to easily export to your grade book.
  - View basic statistical reports.

- **Support and Help.**
  - User's guide and built-in page-specific help.
  - Flash tutorials for getting started on the support site.
  - Support website: *www.mhhe.com/eztest.*
  - Product specialist available at 1-800-331-5094.
  - Online training: *http://auth.mhhe.com/mpss/workshops/.*

PowerPoint Presentation

Prepared by Pauline Assenza of Western Connecticut State University, it consists of more than 400 slides incorporating an outline for the chapters tied to learning objectives. Also included are instructor notes, multiple-choice questions that can be used as Classroom Performance System (CPS) questions, and additional examples outside the text to promote class discussion.

McGraw-Hill Connect™ Management

Less Managing. More Teaching. Greater Learning. McGraw-Hill *Connect Management* is an online assignment and assessment solution that connects students with the tools and resources they'll need to achieve success.

- **McGraw-Hill *Connect Management* Features.** *Connect Management* offers a number of powerful tools and features to make managing assignments easier, so faculty can spend more time teaching. With *Connect Management,* students can engage with their coursework anytime and anywhere, making the learning process more accessible and efficient. *Connect Management* offers you the features described below.
  - There are chapter quizzes for the first 12 chapters, consisting of 15–25 multiple-choice questions, testing students' overall comprehension of concepts presented in the chapter.
  - There are two specially crafted interactives for each of the first 12 chapters that drill students in the use and application of the concepts and tools of strategic analysis.
  - The majority of the *Connect* exercises are automatically graded, thereby simplifying the task of evaluating each class member's performance and monitoring the learning outcomes.

- **Student Progress Tracking.** *Connect Management* keeps instructors informed about how each student, section, and class are performing, allowing for more productive use of lecture and office hours. The progress-tracking function enables you to
  - View scored work immediately and track individual or group performance with assignment and grade reports.
  - Access an instant view of student or class performance relative to learning objectives.
  - Collect data and generate reports required by many accreditation organizations, such as AACSB.

- **Smart Grading.** When it comes to studying, time is precious. *Connect Management* helps students learn more efficiently by providing feedback and practice material when they need it, where they need it. When it comes to teaching, your time also is precious. The grading function enables you to
  - Have assignments scored automatically, giving students immediate feedback on their work and side-by-side comparisons with correct answers.
  - Access and review each response, manually change grades, or leave comments for students to review.
  - Reinforce classroom concepts with practice tests and instant quizzes.

- **Simple Assignment Management.** With *Connect Management,* creating assignments is easier than ever, so you can spend more time teaching and less time managing. The assignment management function enables you to
  - Create and deliver assignments easily with selectable test bank items.
  - Streamline lesson planning, student progress reporting, and assignment grading to make classroom management more efficient than ever.
  - Go paperless with online submission and grading of student assignments.

- **Instructor Library.** The *Connect Management* Instructor Library is your repository for additional resources to improve student engagement in and out of class. You can select and use any asset that enhances your lecture. The *Connect Management* Instructor Library includes
  - Instructor's Manual
  - PowerPoint® Presentations
  - Test Bank
  - Case Support (Teaching Notes, Case PowerPoints, Case financials)
  - Video Library (Video Guide and Video Links related to each chapter)

The Business Strategy Game and GLO-BUS Online Simulations

Both allow teams of students to manage companies in a head-to-head contest for global market leadership. These simulations give students the immediate opportunity to experiment with various strategy options and to gain proficiency in applying the concepts and tools they have been reading about in the chapters. To find out more or to register, please visit *www.mhhe.com/thompsonsims.*

Additional Resources for Course Design and Delivery

Create

Craft your teaching resources to match the way you teach! With McGraw-Hill *Create, www.mcgrawhillcreate.com,* you can easily rearrange chapters, combine material from other content sources, and quickly upload content you have written, like your course syllabus or teaching notes. Find the content you need in *Create* by searching through thousands of leading McGraw-Hill textbooks. Arrange your book to fit your teaching style. *Create* even allows you to personalize your book's appearance by selecting the cover and adding your name, school, and course information. Order a *Create* book and you'll receive a complimentary print review copy in three to five business days or a complimentary electronic review copy (eComp) via email in about one hour. Go to *www.mcgrawhillcreate.com* today and register. Experience how McGraw-Hill *Create* empowers you to teach *your* students *your* way.

E-Book Options

E-books are an innovative way for students to save money and to "go green." McGraw-Hill's e-books are typically 40 percent of bookstore price. Students have the choice between an online and a downloadable *CourseSmart* e-book.

Through *CourseSmart,* students have the flexibility to access an exact replica of their textbook from any computer that has Internet service, without plug-ins or special software via the version, or create a library of books on their hard drive via the downloadable version. Access to *CourseSmart* e-books is one year.

Features: *CourseSmart* e-books allow students to highlight, take notes, organize notes, and share the notes with other *CourseSmart* users. Students can also search terms across all e-books in their purchased *CourseSmart* library. *CourseSmart* e-books can be printed (5 pages at a time).

More info and purchase: Please visit *www.coursesmart.com* for more information and to purchase access to our e-books. *CourseSmart* allows students to try one chapter of the e-book, free of charge, before purchase.

McGraw-Hill Higher Education and Blackboard

McGraw-Hill Higher Education and Blackboard have teamed up. What does this mean for you?

1. **Your life, simplified.** Now you and your students can access McGraw-Hill's *Connect* and *Create* right from within your Blackboard course—all with one single sign-on. Say goodbye to the days of logging in to multiple applications.

2. **Deep integration of content and tools.** Not only do you get single sign-on with *Connect* and *Create,* you also get deep integration of McGraw-Hill content and content engines right in Blackboard. Whether you're choosing a book for your course or building *Connect* assignments, all the tools you need are right where you want them—inside Blackboard.

3. **Seamless gradebooks.** Are you tired of keeping multiple gradebooks and manually synchronizing grades into Blackboard? We thought so. When a student completes an integrated *Connect* assignment, the grade for that assignment automatically (and instantly) feeds into Blackboard grade center.

4. **A solution for everyone.** Whether your institution is already using Blackboard or you just want to try Blackboard on your own, we have a solution for you. McGraw-Hill and Blackboard can now offer you easy access to industry-leading technology and content, whether your campus hosts it or we do. Be sure to ask your local McGraw-Hill representative for details.

McGraw-Hill Customer Care Contact Information

At McGraw-Hill, we understand that getting the most from new technology can be challenging. That's why our services don't stop after you purchase our products. You can email our product specialists 24 hours a day to get product training online. Or you can search our knowledge bank of Frequently Asked Questions on our support website. For customer support, call 800-331-5094, email *hmsupport@mcgraw-hill.com,* or visit *www.mhhe.com/support.* One of our technical support analysts will be able to assist you in a timely fashion.

Acknowledgments

Strategic Management represents far more than just the joint efforts of the three co-authors. Rather, it is the product of the collaborative input of many people. Some of these individuals are academic colleagues, others are the outstanding team of professionals at McGraw-Hill/ Irwin, and still others are those who are closest to us—our families. It is time to express our sincere gratitude.

First, we'd like to acknowledge the dedicated instructors who have graciously provided their insights since the inception of the text. Their input has been very helpful in both pointing out errors in the manuscript and suggesting areas that needed further development as additional topics. We sincerely believe that the incorporation of their ideas has been critical to improving the final product. These professionals and their affiliations are:

The Reviewer Hall of Fame

Moses Acquaah,
University of North Carolina–Greensboro

Todd Alessandri,
Northeastern University

Larry Alexander,
Virginia Polytechnic Institute

Brent B. Allred,
College of William & Mary

Allen C. Amason,
University of Georgia

Kathy Anders,
Arizona State University

Peter H. Antoniou,
California State University–San Marcos

Dave Arnott,
Dallas Baptist University

Marne L. Arthaud-Day,
Kansas State University

Jay A. Azriel,
York College of Pennsylvania

Jeffrey J. Bailey,
University of Idaho

David L. Baker, *Ph.D.,*
John Carroll University

Dennis R. Balch,
University of North Alabama

Bruce Barringer,
University of Central Florida

Barbara R. Bartkus,
Old Dominion University

Barry Bayon,
Bryant University

Brent D. Beal,
Louisiana State University

Dr. Patricia Beckenholdt,
Business and Professional Programs, University of Maryland, University College

Joyce Beggs,
University of North Carolina–Charlotte

Michael Behnam,
Suffolk University

Kristen Bell DeTienne,
Brigham Young University

Eldon Bernstein,
Lynn University

David Blair,
University of Nebraska at Omaha

Daniela Blettner,
Tilburg University

Dusty Bodie,
Boise State University

William Bogner,
Georgia State University

Scott Browne,
Chapman University

Jon Bryan,
Bridgewater State College

Charles M. Byles,
Virginia Commonwealth University

Mikelle A. Calhoun,
Valparaiso University

Thomas J. Callahan,
University of Michigan–Dearborn

Samuel D. Cappel,
Southeastern Louisiana State University

Gary Carini,
Baylor University

Shawn M. Carraher,
University of Texas–Dallas

Tim Carroll,
University of South Carolina

Don Caruth,
Amberton University

Maureen Casile,
Bowling Green State University

Gary J. Castrogiovanni,
Florida Atlantic University

Radha Chaganti,
Rider University

Erick PC Chang,
Arkansas State University

Theresa Cho,
Rutgers University

Timothy S. Clark,
Northern Arizona University

Bruce Clemens,
Western New England College

Betty S. Coffey,
Appalachian State University

Wade Coggins,
Webster University–Fort Smith Metro Campus

Susan Cohen,
University of Pittsburgh

George S. Cole,
Shippensburg University

Joseph Coombs,
Texas A&M University

Christine Cope Pence,
University of California–Riverside

James J. Cordeiro,
SUNY Brockport

Stephen E. Courter,
University of Texas at Austin

Jeffrey Covin,
Indiana University

Keith Credo,
Auburn University

Deepak Datta,
University of Texas at Arlington

James Davis,
Utah State University

Justin L. Davis,
University of West Florida

David Dawley,
West Virginia University

Helen Deresky,
*State University of
New York–Plattsburgh*

Rocki-Lee DeWitt,
University of Vermont

Jay Dial,
Ohio State University

Michael E. Dobbs,
Arkansas State University

Jonathan Doh,
Villanova University

Tom Douglas,
Clemson University

Jon Down,
Oregon State University

Meredith Downes,
Illinois State University

Alan E. Ellstrand,
University of Arkansas

Dean S. Elmuti,
Eastern Illinois University

Clare Engle,
Concordia University

Mehmet Erdem Genc,
Baruch College, CUNY

Tracy Ethridge,
*Tri-County Technical
College*

William A. Evans,
*Troy State
University–Dothan*

Frances H. Fabian,
University of Memphis

Angelo Fanelli,
*Warrington College
of Business*

Michael Fathi,
*Georgia Southwestern
University*

Carolyn J. Fausnaugh,
*Florida Institute
of Technology*

Tamela D. Ferguson,
*University of Louisiana
at Lafayette*

David Flanagan,
*Western Michigan
University*

Kelly Flis,
The Art Institutes

Dave Foster,
Montana State University

Isaac Fox,
University of Minnesota

Charla S. Fraley,
*Columbus State Community
College–Columbus, Ohio*

Deborah Francis,
Brevard College

Steven A. Frankforter,
Winthrop University

Vance Fried,
Oklahoma State University

Karen Froelich,
*North Dakota State
University*

Naomi A. Gardberg,
Baruch College, CUNY

J. Michael Geringer,
Ohio University

Diana L. Gilbertson,
*California State
University–Fresno*

Matt Gilley,
St. Mary's University

Debbie Gilliard,
*Metropolitan State
College–Denver*

Yezdi H. Godiwalla,
*University of
Wisconsin–Whitewater*

Sanjay Goel,
*University of
Minnesota–Duluth*

Sandy Gough,
Boise State University

Dr. Susan Hansen,
*University of
Wisconsin–Platteville*

Allen Harmon,
*University of
Minnesota–Duluth*

Niran Harrison,
University of Oregon

Paula Harveston,
Berry College

Ahmad Hassan,
Morehead State University

Donald Hatfield,
*Virginia Polytechnic
Institute*

Kim Hester,
Arkansas State University

Scott Hicks,
Liberty University

John Hironaka,
*California State
University–Sacramento*

Anne Kelly Hoel,
*University of
Wisconsin–Stout*

Alan Hoffman,
Bentley College

Gordon Holbein,
University of Kentucky

Stephen V. Horner,
Pittsburg State University

Jill Hough,
University of Tulsa

John Humphreys,
*Eastern New Mexico
University*

James G. Ibe,
Morris College

Jay J. Janney,
University of Dayton

Lawrence Jauch,
University of Louisiana–Monroe

Dana M. Johnson,
Michigan Technical University

Homer Johnson,
Loyola University, Chicago

Marilyn R. Kaplan,
Naveen Jindal School of Management, University of Texas–Dallas

James Katzenstein,
California State University– Dominguez Hills

Joseph Kavanaugh,
Sam Houston State University

Franz Kellermanns,
University of Tennessee

Craig Kelley,
California State University–Sacramento

Donna Kelley,
Babson College

Dave Ketchen,
Auburn University

John A. Kilpatrick,
Idaho State University

Brent H. Kinghorn,
Emporia State University

Helaine J. Korn,
Baruch College, CUNY

Stan Kowalczyk,
San Francisco State University

Daniel Kraska,
North Central State College

Donald E. Kreps,
Kutztown University

Jim Kroeger,
Cleveland State University

Subdoh P. Kulkarni,
Howard University

Ron Lambert,
Faulkner University

Theresa Lant,
New York University

Ted Legatski,
Texas Christian University

David J. Lemak,
Washington State University–Tri-Cities

Cynthia Lengnick-Hall,
University of Texas at San Antonio

Donald L. Lester,
Arkansas State University

Wanda Lester,
North Carolina A&T State University

Krista B. Lewellyn,
University of Wyoming

Benyamin Lichtenstein,
University of Massachusetts at Boston

Jun Lin,
SUNY at New Paltz

Zhiang (John) Lin,
University of Texas at Dallas

Dan Lockhart,
University of Kentucky

John Logan,
University of South Carolina

Franz T. Lohrke,
Samford University

Kevin B. Lowe,
Graduate School of Management, University of Auckland

Leyland M. Lucas,
Morgan State University

Doug Lyon,
Fort Lewis College

Rickey Madden, *Ph.D.,*
Presbyterian College

James Maddox,
Friends University

Ravi Madhavan,
University of Pittsburgh

Paul Mallette,
Colorado State University

Santo D. Marabella,
Moravian College

Catherine Maritan,
Syracuse University

Daniel Marrone,
Farmingdale State College, SUNY

Sarah Marsh,
Northern Illinois University

Jim Martin,
Washburn University

John R. Massaua,
University of Southern Maine

Hao Ma,
Bryant College

Larry McDaniel,
Alabama A&M University

Jean McGuire,
Louisiana State University

Abagail McWilliams,
University of Illinois– Chicago

Ofer Meilich,
California State University– San Marcos

John E. Merchant,
California State University–Sacramento

John M. Mezias,
University of Miami

Michael Michalisin,
Southern Illinois University at Carbondale

Violina P. Rindova,
University of Texas–Austin

Ron Rivas,
Canisius College

David Robinson,
Indiana State University–Terre Haute

Kenneth Robinson,
Kennesaw State University

Simon Rodan,
San Jose State University

Patrick R. Rogers,
North Carolina A&T State University

John K. Ross III,
Texas State University–San Marcos

Robert Rottman,
Kentucky State University

Matthew R. Rutherford,
Gonzaga University

Carol M. Sanchez,
Grand Valley State University

Doug Sanford,
Towson University

William W. Sannwald,
San Diego State University

Yolanda Sarason,
Colorado State University

Marguerite Schneider,
New Jersey Institute of Technology

Roger R. Schnorbus,
University of Richmond

Terry Sebora,
University of Nebraska–Lincoln

John Seeger,
Bentley College

Jamal Shamsie,
Michigan State University

Mark Shanley,
University of Illinois at Chicago

Lois Shelton,
California State University–Northridge

Herbert Sherman,
Long Island University

Weilei Shi,
Baruch College, CUNY

Chris Shook,
Auburn University

Jeremy Short,
University of Oklahoma

Mark Simon,
Oakland University–Michigan

Rob Singh,
Morgan State University

Bruce Skaggs,
University of Massachusetts

Lise Anne D. Slattern,
University of Louisiana at Lafayette

Wayne Smeltz,
Rider University

Anne Smith,
University of Tennessee

Andrew Spicer,
University of South Carolina

James D. Spina,
University of Maryland

John Stanbury,
George Mason University & Inter-University Institute of Macau, SAR China

Timothy Stearns,
California State University–Fresno

Elton Stephen,
Austin State University

Charles E. Stevens,
University of Wyoming

Alice Stewart,
Ohio State University

Ram Subramanian,
Grand Valley State University

Roy Suddaby,
University of Iowa

Michael Sullivan,
UC Berkeley Extension

Marta Szabo White,
Georgia State University

Stephen Takach,
University of Texas at San Antonio

Justin Tan,
York University, Canada

Qingjiu Tao, *Ph.D.,*
James Madison University

Linda Teagarden,
Virginia Tech

Bing-Sheng Teng,
George Washington University

Alan Theriault,
University of California–Riverside

Tracy Thompson,
University of Washington–Tacoma

Karen Torres,
Angelo State University

Mary Trottier,
Associate Professor of Management, Nichols College

Robert Trumble,
Virginia Commonwealth University

Francis D. (Doug) Tuggle,
Chapman University

K.J. Tullis,
University of Central Oklahoma

Craig A. Turner, *Ph.D.,*
East Tennessee State
University

Beverly Tyler,
North Carolina State
University

Rajaram Veliyath,
Kennesaw State
University

S. Stephen Vitucci,
Tarleton State University–
Central Texas

Jay A. Vora,
St. Cloud State University

Valerie Wallingford, *Ph.D.,*
Bemidji State University

Jorge Walter,
Portland State University

Bruce Walters,
Louisiana Tech University

Edward Ward,
St. Cloud State University

N. Wasilewski,
Pepperdine University

Andrew Watson,
Northeastern University

Larry Watts,
Stephen F. Austin University

Marlene E. Weaver,
American Public University
System

Paula S. Weber,
St. Cloud State University

Kenneth E. A. Wendeln,
Indiana University

Robert R. Wharton,
Western Kentucky University

Laura Whitcomb,
California State
University–Los Angeles

Scott Williams,
Wright State University

Ross A. Wirth,
Franklin University

Diana Wong,
Bowling Green State
University

Beth Woodard,
Belmont University

John E. Wroblewski,
State University of New
York–Fredonia

Anne York,
University of
Nebraska–Omaha

Michael Zhang,
Sacred Heart
University

Monica Zimmerman,
Temple University

Second, we would like to thank the people who have made our two new "features" possible. The information found in our six "Insights from Research" was provided courtesy of *www. businessminded.com,* an organization founded by K. Matthew Gilley, Ph.D. (St. Mary's University) that transforms empirical management research into actionable insights for business leaders. We appreciate Matt's graciousness and kindness in helping us out. And, of course, our "Insights from Executives" would not have been possible without the participation of the six distinguished professionals who generously offered their time and insights. They are:

Melvin Alexander, CPA, Executive Director of Principled Solutions Enterprise and former CFO of three large health systems

Lise Saari, Ph.D., former director of Global Workforce Research at IBM

Archie Jones, Senior Vice President of Business Development at Kenexa

Terrie Campbell, Vice President of Strategic Marketing at Ricoh Americas Corporation

David Drews, Executive Vice President and CFO of Project: WorldWide

Michael Williams, Former CFO of Biggby Coffee

Third, the authors would like to thank several faculty colleagues who were particularly helpful in the review, critique, and development of the book and supplementary materials.

Greg's colleagues at the University of Texas at Dallas also have been helpful and supportive. These individuals include Mike Peng, Joe Picken, Kumar Nair, John Lin, Larry Chasteen, Seung-Hyun Lee, Tev Dalgic, and Jane Salk. His administrative assistant, Shalonda Hill, has been extremely helpful. Three doctoral students, Brian Pinkham, Steve Sauerwald, and Canan Mutlu, have provided many useful inputs and ideas. He also appreciates the support of his dean and associate dean, Hasan Pirkul and Varghese Jacob, respectively. Greg wishes to thank a special colleague, Abdul Rasheed at the University of Texas at Arlington, who certainly has been a valued source of friendship and ideas for us for many years. He provided many valuable contributions to the Eighth Edition. Gerry thanks all of his colleagues at Michigan State University for their help and support over the years. He also thanks his mentor, Phil Bromiley, as well as the students and former students he has had the pleasure of working with, including Becky Luce, Cindy Devers, Federico Aime, Mike Mannor, Bernadine Dykes, Mathias Arrfelt, Kalin Kolev, Seungho Choi, Rob Davison, Dustin Sleesman, Danny Gamache, Adam Steinbach, and Daniel Chaffin.

Fourth, we would like to thank the team at McGraw-Hill for their outstanding support throughout the entire process. As we work on the book through the various editions, we always appreciate their hard work and recognize how so many people "add value" to our final package. This began with John Biernat, formerly publisher, who signed us to our original contract. He was always available to us and provided a great deal of support and valued input throughout several editions. Presently, in editorial, Susan Gouijnstook, managing director, director Mike Ablassmeir, product developers Laura Griffin and Lai T. Moy, and product development coordinator Kaitlin Benson kept things on track, responded quickly to our seemingly endless needs and requests, and offered insights and encouragement. We appreciate their expertise— as well as their patience! Once the manuscript was completed and revised, content project managers Mary Powers and Danielle Clement expertly guided it through the content and assessment production process. Matt Diamond provided excellent design and artwork guidance. We also appreciate marketing manager Robin Lucas for her energetic, competent, and thorough marketing efforts. Last, but certainly not least, we thank MHE's 70-plus outstanding book reps—who serve on the "front lines"—as well as many in-house sales professionals based in Dubuque, Iowa. Clearly, they deserve a lot of credit (even though not mentioned by name) for our success.

Fifth, we acknowledge the valuable contributions of many of our strategy colleagues for their excellent contributions to our supplementary and digital materials. Such content really adds a lot of value to our entire package! We are grateful to Pauline Assenza at Western Connecticut State University for her superb work on case teaching notes as well as chapter and case PowerPoints. Justin Davis, University of West Florida, along with Noushi Rahman, Pace University, deserve our thanks for their hard work in developing excellent digital materials for *Connect*. Thanks also goes to Noushi Rahman for developing the Connect IM that accompanies this edition of the text. And, finally, we thank Christine Pence, University of California–Riverside, for her important contributions in revising our test bank and chapter quizzes, and Todd Moss, Oregon State University, for his hard work in putting together an excellent set of videos online, along with the video grid that links videos to chapter material.

Finally, we would like to thank our families. For Greg this includes his parents, William and Mary Dess, who have always been there for him. His wife, Margie, and daughter, Taylor, have been a constant source of love and companionship. He would like to acknowledge Michael Wood, his parents' caretaker. He is truly a wonderful person and his cheerfulness, kindness, and devotion have certainly added both quality and quantity to both of their lives. Gerry thanks his wife, Gaelen, for her love, support, and friendship and his children, Megan and AJ, for their love and the joy they bring to his life. He also thanks his parents, Gene and Jane, for their encouragement and support in all phases of his life. Alan thanks his family—his wife, Helaine, and his children, Rachel and Jacob—for their love and support. He also thanks his parents, Gail Eisner and the late Marvin Eisner, for their support and encouragement.

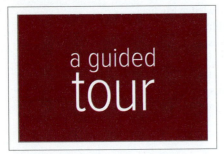

a guided
tour

After reading this chapter, you should have a good understanding of the following learning objectives:

LO1.1 The definition of strategic management and its four key attributes.

LO1.2 The strategic management process and its three interrelated and principal activities.

LO1.3 The vital role of corporate governance and stakeholder management, as well as how "symbiosis" can be achieved among an organization's stakeholders.

LO1.4 The importance of social responsibility, including environmental sustainability, and how it can enhance a corporation's innovation strategy.

LO1.5 The need for greater empowerment throughout the organization.

LO1.6 How an awareness of a hierarchy of strategic goals can help an organization achieve coherence in its strategic direction.

Learning Objectives

Learning Objectives numbered LO5.1, LO5.2, LO5.3, etc., with corresponding icons in the margins to indicate where learning objectives are covered in the text.

Learning from Mistakes

What makes the study of strategic management so interesting? Today, many new start-ups become globally recognized names seemingly overnight. At the same time, we see many of yesteryear's high-flying firms struggling to regain some of their earlier elite status or even to survive. As colorfully noted by Arthur Martinez, Sears's former chairman: "Today's peacock is tomorrow's feather duster."[1] Consider the following:[2]

- Only 74 of the original 500 companies in the S&P Index were still around 40 years later—a mortality rate of more than 10 per year. In 1935, firms in the S&P 500 would have an average lifetime of 90 years. By 2011, the average lifetime was down to 18 years.
- In March 2000, the top five stocks on the NASDAQ Stock Exchange were Cisco, Microsoft, Intel, Qualcomm, and Oracle. As of mid-2014, the top five were Apple, Google, Microsoft, Amazon.com, and Facebook.
- Until a few years ago, many customers were willing to pay more than $200 for a GPS unit. Today, most people use free navigation apps on their smartphones instead. In just 18 months, GPS makers have lost 85 percent of their market value, as noted by The Economist.
- Twenty years ago it was almost unimaginable that a South Korean firm would be a global car giant, that an Indian firm would be one of the world's largest technology outfits, or that a Chinese Internet colossus would list on an American stock exchange.

Maintaining competitive success or even surviving over long periods of time is indeed very difficult for companies of any size. As John Donahue, CEO of eBay, notes, "Almost every company has hot moments. But only great companies achieve strong, sustainable performance over time."[3] Next, let's take a look at Groupon, which, after its high-profile initial public offering (IPO) in 2011 that raised over $900 million, has struggled to live up to the initial expectations.

Andrew Mason met his earliest investor, Eric Lefkofsky, in 2003 when he was working as a web designer. Five years later, Lefkofsky provided $1 million to fund Mason's first entrepreneurial effort—a company called The Point—an interactive web platform that was originally intended to bring groups of like-minded people together behind a social cause like hunger or helping the homeless.

This idea didn't pan out; Mason and Lefkofsky pivoted into a more commercially friendly application of the same concept—Groupon. As we all know, Groupon would eventually grow into one of the most talked-about and hyped tech companies in recent history. In fact, The Wall Street Journal stated that it had "been called the fastest-growing company in history" before its 2011 IPO.

Today, Groupon has over 10,000 employees worldwide and has sold over 6 million group coupons. The company was so hot that at one point it rejected an all-cash $6 billion buyout offer from Google. The offer would have put $420 million and $1 billion in Mason's and Lefkofsky's pockets, respectively. But investors were confident that a company with as much heat and momentum as Groupon back in 2011 would certainly fetch far more value with an IPO. Unfortunately, by April 2015, Andrew Mason had

Learning from Mistakes

Learning from Mistakes vignettes are examples of where things went wrong. Failures are not only interesting but also sometimes easier to learn from. And students realize strategy is not just about "right or wrong" answers, but requires critical thinking.

Strategy Spotlight

These boxes weave themes of ethics, globalization, and technology into every chapter of the text, providing students with a thorough grounding necessary for understanding strategic management. Select boxes incorporate crowdsourcing, environmental sustainability, and ethical themes.

4.3 STRATEGY SPOTLIGHT

HOW INHERENT AND ACQUIRED DIVERSITY AFFECT INNOVATION

A study explored two kinds of diversity: *inherent* and *acquired*. Its findings were based on a nationally representative survey of 1,800 professionals, 40 case studies, and numerous focus groups and interviews. Inherent diversity involves traits one was born with, such as gender, ethnicity, and sexual orientation. On the other hand, acquired diversity involves traits gained from experience, such as working in another country to understand cultural differences and selling to both male and female consumers to develop "gender smarts." Companies whose leaders exhibited at least three inherent and three acquired traits were viewed as having two-dimensional (2-D) diversity.

The study found that companies with 2-D diversity out-innovated and outperformed the others. Employees in such companies were 45 percent likelier to report their firm's market share grew over the previous year and 70 percent likelier to report the firm captured a new market.

What explains these results? Two-dimensional diversity unlocks innovation by creating a work environment where "outside the box" ideas are heard and minorities form a critical mass. Further, leaders value differences, and all employees can find senior people to go to bat for compelling ideas and can persuade those in charge of budgets to commit resources to develop those ideas.

Inherent diversity, however, is only half of the equation. Acquired diversity provides additional benefits since employees with diverse experiences can provide insights on the needs and preferences of different groups and cultures. They are also more open to the perspectives of the other members on the team. Since acquired diversity increases openness, it also enhances the value of inherent diversity. Minority team members will be more likely to contribute to team discussions, resulting in more creative problem solving. Six behaviors spur innovation across the board: ensuring everyone is heard; making it safe to propose novel ideas; giving team members decision-making authority; sharing credit for success; giving actionable feedback; and implementing feedback from the team.

Sources: Hewlett, S. A., Marshall, M., & Sherbin, L. 2013. How diversity can drive innovation. *Harvard Business Review*, 91(12): 30; and Karlgaard, R. 2014. *The soft edge*. San Francisco: Jossey-Bass.

11.2 STRATEGY SPOTLIGHT — ETHICS

INSTILLING ETHICS AND A FIRM'S VALUES: WALKING THE TALK

Firms often draft elaborate value statements and codes of conduct, yet many firms do not live up to their own standards—or, in other words, fail to "walk the talk." Take the positive example of N. R. Narayana Murthy, chairman and one of the founders of Infosys (a giant Indian technology company). In February 1984, shortly after the firm was founded, Infosys decided to import a super minicomputer so that it could start developing software for overseas clients. When the machine landed at Bangalore Airport, the local customs official refused to clear it unless the company "took care of him"—the Indian euphemism for demanding a bribe. A delay at customs could have threatened the project. Yet, instead of caving in to the unethical customs official's demands, Murthy kept true to his values and took the more expensive formal route of paying a customs duty of 135 percent with dim chances of successfully appealing the duty and receiving a refund.

Reflecting on these events, Murthy reasons, "We didn't have enough money to pay the duty and had to borrow it. However, because we had decided to do business ethically, we didn't have a choice. We would not pay bribes. We effectively paid twice for the machine and had only a slim chance of recovering our money. But a clear conscience is the softest pillow on which you can lay your head down at night. . . . It took a few years for corrupt officials to stop approaching us for favors."

Source: Raman, A. P. 2011. "Why don't we try to be India's most respected company?" *Harvard Business Review*, 89(11): 82.

INSIGHTS

The "Insights" feature is new to this edition. "Insights from Executives" spotlight interviews with executives from worldwide organizations about current issues salient to strategic management. "Insights from Research" summarize key research findings relevant to maintaining the effectiveness of an organization and its management.

3.1 INSIGHTS FROM EXECUTIVES

LISE M. SAARI, PH.D., FORMER DIRECTOR OF GLOBAL EMPLOYEE RESEARCH, IBM

BIOSKETCH

Lise M. Saari, Ph.D., is the former director of global workforce research at IBM, where her team was responsible for researching employee attitudes and other human resource topics in over 170 countries. Before that, she was the senior manager of people research at the Boeing Company and a research scientist at Battelle Research Institute. In all of these roles, Saari had responsibility for helping design and test human resource management initiatives, such as performance management systems, teaming initiatives, and management development programs. Saari has over 100 publications and presentations and serves on a variety of editorial boards. She is a fellow in the Society for Industrial Organizational Psychology (SIOP), the Ameri-

more complex and organizationally unique than we may think they are. Some of the most interesting findings to me are from the so-called linkage research started by Ben Schneider, whereby employee attitudes are statistically related to customer and business measures to see the unique relationships for an organization. We carried out this type of research at IBM with employee attitude data across the globe. The most important employee and workplace topics that contributed value to customers and organizational performance were understanding company objectives and how the employee's own job contributes to it, receiving regular feedback, receiving pay tied to job performance, and having a challenging job with opportunities for development. These are all areas where HR can and should ensure company strategy is clear to all employees; create a performance management system

INSIGHTS FROM RESEARCH

NEW TRICKS: RESEARCH DEBUNKS MYTHS ABOUT OLDER WORKERS

Overview

People often think that older workers are less motivated and less healthy, resist change and are less trusting, and have more trouble balancing work and family. It turns out these assumptions just aren't true. By challenging these stereotypes in your organization, you can keep your employees working.

What the Research Shows

In a 2012 paper published by *Personnel Psychology*, researchers from the University of Hong Kong and the University of Georgia examined 418 studies of workers' ages and stereotypes. A meta-analysis—a study of studies—was conducted to find out if any of the six following stereotypes about older workers—as compared with younger workers—was actually true:

- They are less motivated.

employees' continued involvement in workplaces because they have much to offer in the ways of wisdom, experience, and institutional knowledge. The alternative is to miss out on a growing pool of valuable human capital.

How can you deal with age stereotypes to keep older workers engaged? The authors suggest three effective ways:

- Provide more opportunities for younger and older workers to work together.
- Promote positive attributes of older workers, like experience, carefulness, and punctuality.
- Engage employees in open discussions about stereotypes.

Adam Bradshaw of the DeGarmo Group Inc. has summarized research in addressing age stereotypes in the workplace and offers practical advice. For instance, make sure

Financial Ratio	Semiconductors	Grocery Stores	Skilled-Nursing Facilities
Quick ratio (times)	1.9	0.6	1.3
Current ratio (times)	3.6	1.7	1.7
Total liabilities to net worth (%)	35.1	72.7	82.5
Collection period (days)	48.6	3.3	36.5
Assets to sales (%)	131.7	22.1	58.3
Return on sales (%)	24	1.1	3.1

EXHIBIT 3.10

How Financial Ratios Differ across Industries

Source: Dun & Bradstreet. *Industry Norms and Key Business Ratios, 2010–2011.* One Year Edition. SIC #3600–3699 (Semiconductors); SIC #5400–5499 (Grocery Stores); SIC #8000–8099 (Skilled-Nursing Facilities). New York: Dun & Bradstreet Credit Services.

Comparing your firm with all other firms in your industry assesses relative performance. Banks often use such comparisons when evaluating a firm's creditworthiness. Exhibit 3.10 includes a variety of financial ratios for three industries: semiconductors, grocery stores, and skilled-nursing facilities. Why is there such variation among the financial ratios for these three industries? There are several reasons. With regard to the collection period, grocery stores operate mostly on a cash basis, hence a very short collection period. Semiconductor manufacturers sell their output to other manufacturers (e.g., computer makers) on terms such as 2/15 net 45, which means they give a 2 percent discount on bills

Exhibits

Both new and improved exhibits in every chapter provide visual presentations of the most complex concepts covered to support student comprehension.

Reflecting on Career Implications

This section before the summary of every chapter consists of examples on how understanding of key concepts helps business students early in their careers.

Reflecting on Career Implications . . .

- **Attributes of Strategic Management:** The attributes of strategic management described in this chapter are applicable to your personal careers as well. What are your overall goals and objectives? Who are the stakeholders you have to consider in making your career decisions (family, community, etc.)? What trade-offs do you see between your long-term and short-term goals?

- **Intended versus Emergent Strategies:** While you may have planned your career trajectory carefully, don't be too tied to it. Strive to take advantage of new opportunities as they arise. Many promising career opportunities may "emerge" that were not part of your intended career strategy or your specific job assignment. Take initiative by pursuing opportunities to get additional training (e.g., learn a software or a statistical package), volunteering for a short-term overseas assignment, etc. You may be in a better position to take advantage of such emergent opportunities if you take the effort to prepare for them. For example, learning a foreign language may position you better for an overseas opportunity.

- **Ambidexterity:** In Strategy Spotlight 1.1, we discussed the four most important traits of ambidextrous individuals. These include looking for opportunities beyond the description of one's job, seeking out opportunities to collaborate with others, building internal networks, and multitasking. Evaluate yourself along each of these criteria. If you score low, think of ways in which you can improve your ambidexterity.

- **Strategic Coherence:** What is the mission of your organization? What are the strategic objectives of the department or unit you are working for? In what ways does your own role contribute to the mission and objectives? What can you do differently in order to help the organization attain its mission and strategic objectives?

- **Strategic Coherence:** Setting strategic objectives is important in your personal career as well. Identify and write down three or four important strategic objectives you want to accomplish in the next few years (finish your degree, find a better-paying job, etc.). Are you allocating your resources (time, money, etc.) to enable you to achieve these objectives? Are your objectives measurable, timely, realistic, specific, and appropriate?

CHAPTER 1 :: STRATEGIC MANAGEMENT 29

brief contents

contents

PART 1 Strategic Analysis

PART 2 Strategic Formulation

The Strategic Management Process

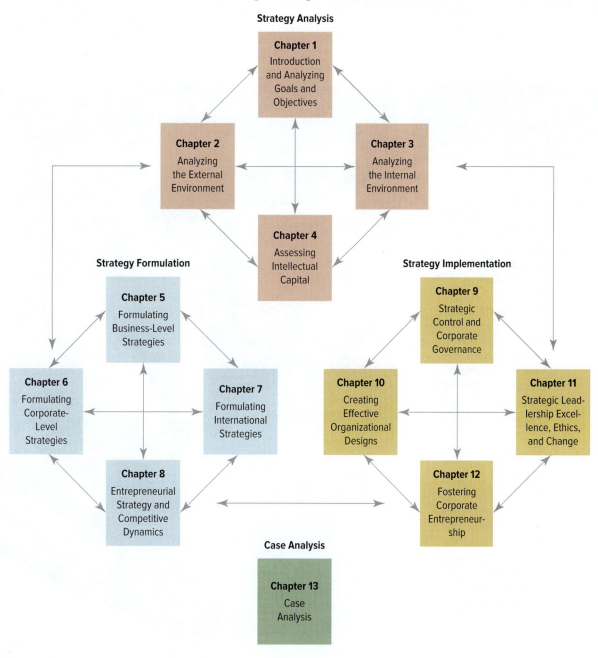

Strategy Analysis

Chapter 1
Introduction and Analyzing Goals and Objectives

Chapter 2
Analyzing the External Environment

Chapter 3
Analyzing the Internal Environment

Chapter 4
Assessing Intellectual Capital

Strategy Formulation

Chapter 5
Formulating Business-Level Strategies

Chapter 6
Formulating Corporate-Level Strategies

Chapter 7
Formulating International Strategies

Chapter 8
Entrepreneurial Strategy and Competitive Dynamics

Strategy Implementation

Chapter 9
Strategic Control and Corporate Governance

Chapter 10
Creating Effective Organizational Designs

Chapter 11
Strategic Leadership Excellence, Ethics, and Change

Chapter 12
Fostering Corporate Entrepreneurship

Case Analysis

Chapter 13
Case Analysis

Strategic Management
Creating Competitive Advantages

LO1.1 The definition of strategic management and its four key attributes.

LO1.2 The strategic management process and its three interrelated and principal activities.

LO1.3 The vital role of corporate governance and stakeholder management, as well as how "symbiosis" can be achieved among an organization's stakeholders.

LO1.4 The importance of social responsibility, including environmental sustainability, and how it can enhance a corporation's innovation strategy.

LO1.5 The need for greater empowerment throughout the organization.

LO1.6 How an awareness of a hierarchy of strategic goals can help an organization achieve coherence in its strategic direction.

Learning from Mistakes

What makes the study of strategic management so interesting? Today, many new start-ups become globally recognized names seemingly overnight. At the same time, we see many of yesteryear's high-flying firms struggling to regain some of their earlier elite status or even to survive. As colorfully noted by Arthur Martinez, Sears's former chairman: "Today's peacock is tomorrow's feather duster."[1]

Consider the following:[2]

- Only 74 of the original 500 companies in the S&P Index were still around 40 years later—a mortality rate of more than 10 per year. In 1935, firms in the S&P 500 would have an average lifetime of 90 years. By 2011, the average lifetime was down to 18 years.
- In March 2000, the top five stocks on the NASDAQ Stock Exchange were Cisco, Microsoft, Intel, Qualcomm, and Oracle. As of mid-2014, the top five were Apple, Google, Microsoft, *Amazon.com*, and Facebook.
- Until a few years ago, many customers were willing to pay more than $200 for a GPS unit. Today, most people use free navigation apps on their smartphones instead. In just 18 months, GPS makers have lost 85 percent of their market value, as noted by *The Economist*.
- Twenty years ago it was almost unimaginable that a South Korean firm would be a global car giant, that an Indian firm would be one of the world's largest technology outfits, or that a Chinese Internet colossus would list on an American stock exchange.

Maintaining competitive success or even surviving over long periods of time is indeed very difficult for companies of any size. As John Donahue, CEO of eBay, notes, "Almost every company has hot moments. But only great companies achieve strong, sustainable performance over time."[3] Next, let's take a look at Groupon, which, after its high-profile initial public offering (IPO) in 2011 that raised over $900 million, has struggled to live up to the initial expectations.

Andrew Mason met his earliest investor, Eric Lefkofsky, in 2003 when he was working as a web designer. Five years later, Lefkofsky provided $1 million to fund Mason's first entrepreneurial effort—a company called The Point—an interactive web platform that was originally intended to bring groups of like-minded people together behind a social cause like hunger or helping the homeless.

This idea didn't pan out; Mason and Lefkofsky pivoted into a more commercially friendly application of the same concept—Groupon. As we all know, Groupon would eventually grow into one of the most talked-about and hyped tech companies in recent history. In fact, *The Wall Street Journal* stated that it had "been called the fastest-growing company in history" before its 2011 IPO.

Today, Groupon has over 10,000 employees worldwide and has sold over 6 million group coupons. The company was so hot that at one point it rejected an all-cash $6 billion buyout offer from Google. The offer would have put $420 million and $1 billion in Mason's and Lefkofsky's pockets, respectively. But investors were confident that a company with as much heat and momentum as Groupon back in 2011 would certainly fetch far more value with an IPO. Unfortunately, by April 2015, Andrew Maron had been fired and the firm had lost over 70 percent of its market value since its highly successful IPO.

So what went wrong? GRPN debuted on the NASDAQ in early November 2011 at $26 a share. Investors and employees rejoiced—and Mason's shares were worth $1.196 billion and Lefkofsky's were worth $2.86 billion. Unfortunately, the opening price of $26 would be the firm's all-time high point. Groupon caught flak for questionable accounting practices that did not include marketing costs, and in the spring of 2012 it had to issue a restatement of earnings after admitting it didn't set aside enough money for refunds. In addition, few of the many acquisitions that were made were successful.

More serious was the unforeseen fact that group daily deals turned out to be much of a fad. Most people who tried Groupon (or one of the dozens of imitators) were typically not impressed. Worse, stories of small businesses losing thousands of dollars offering Groupon became common. For example, according to a recent study by Raymond James, 67 percent of merchants found Groupon users' spending habits were "lower" than those of their typical customers. And another survey indicated that just 3 percent of respondents said that these types of promotions brought them repeat business!

Other huge challenges became fending off the never-ending crop of imitator firms and needing to constantly hunt for new local businesses to offer a deal. To meet such challenges, Groupon had to hire thousands of new employees around the world. The associated costs shrunk margins at a time when revenue was dropping precipitously.

Mason, as CEO, hardly helped his own cause. He was known by many for not taking his role as CEO of a publicly traded company seriously enough. He was named "Worst CEO of the Year" by Herb Greenberg of CNBC, who wrote, in part, "Mason's goofball antics, which can come off more like a big kid than a company leader, almost make a mockery of corporate leadership—especially for a company with a market value of more than $3 billion. It would be excusable, even endearing, if the company were doing well (think Herb Kelleher of Southwest Airlines) but it's not. Sales growth is through the floor." The following would seem to support Greenberg's sentiments:

- Mason annoyed the SEC when he wrote a lengthy, profanity-laden memo that was promptly leaked to the press in the middle of the company's pre-IPO quiet period. In the memo, he touted Groupon's prospects and trashed the financial press for critical coverage of the company. The SEC ultimately forced Groupon to include the document in its IPO filing.
- In April 2012, Mason outlined the firm's corporate strategy at an all-hands meeting, which was observed via webcast by a reporter. At one point, his voice broke. "Sorry, too much beer," he said. Mason then proceeded to tell his employees that Groupon needed to grow up!
- A *Vanity Fair* piece, for which Mason posed with a cat on his head, relates how he had purchased a spotted pony named Spice that he planned to give to New York City Mayor Michael Bloomberg, who was visiting the firm. Disaster was averted only moments before Bloomberg arrived, after a Groupon employee discovered, via Google, that the mayor's daughter, Georgina, had recently suffered a concussion and a fractured spine during a horse-riding incident. Needless to say, Spice did not return to New York City with the mayor.

With mounting losses and a stock price falling through the floor, the Groupon board fired Mason in February 2013. His severance package was not what anyone would expect for a corporate CEO. Given that he had an annual salary of $756.72 (at "his own recommendation"), he walked away with just $378.36—six months' salary! He also received health coverage for 180 days. Of course, he was hardest hit when it came to his personal net worth. The value of his shares had peaked at $1.2 billion at the time of the IPO. But, at the time of his exit, they were worth $230 million—an amount that reflects the company's nearly 80 percent drop in market value from its IPO only a year and a half earlier.

Epilogue: As of April 2015 Groupon shares were hovering around $7, and it had losses of over $200 million for the years 2012-2014. Ayush Singh, an analyst, believes Groupon may again be a realistic acquisition candidate for Google. The stock is fairly cheap, and Singh believes Google would have little trouble integrating the firm into its Google Offers business, Groupon's direct competitor. This could give rise to cost synergies, which the companies would otherwise spend on outdoing each other.

Discussion Questions

1. What actions should Groupon have taken to avoid the steep drop in its stock price?
2. Is this an attactive industry? Why? Why not?

Sources: Cohen, T. 2014. Why (GRPN) stock is lower today. *www.thestreet.com*, June 2: np; Brownell, M. 2013. CEO Andrew Mason out at Groupon after stock plummets. *www.dailyfinance.com*, February 28: np; Silverman, R. E., & Gellman, L. 2014. Ice bucket challenge: Too much success? *The Wall Street Journal,* September 17: B8; Singh, A. 2014. Time to buy Groupon's terrific turnaround. *Seekingalpha .com*, July 16: np; Gustin, S. 2013. Groupon fires CEO Andrew Mason: The rise and fall of tech's enfant terrible. *business.time.com*, March 1: np; and *finance.yahoo.com.*

The recent problems faced by Groupon illustrate how even innovative firms can struggle in the marketplace if they do not anticipate and respond proactively to changes in the environment. Today's leaders face a large number of complex challenges in the global marketplace. In considering how much credit (or blame) they deserve, two perspectives of leadership come immediately to mind: the "romantic" and "external control" perspectives.[4] First, let's look at the **romantic view of leadership.** Here, the implicit assumption is that the leader is the key force in determining an organization's success—or lack thereof.[5] This view dominates the popular press in business magazines such as *Fortune, Businessweek,* and *Forbes,* wherein the CEO is either lauded for his or her firm's success or chided for the organization's demise.[6] Consider, for example, the credit that has been bestowed on leaders such as Jack Welch, Andrew Grove, and Herb Kelleher for the tremendous accomplishments when they led their firms, General Electric, Intel, and Southwest Airlines, respectively.

> **romantic view of leadership** situations in which the leader is the key force determining the organization's success—or lack thereof.

Similarly, Apple's success in the last decade has been attributed almost entirely to the late Steve Jobs, its former CEO, who died on October 5, 2011.[7] Apple's string of hit products, such as iMac computers, iPods, iPhones, and iPads, is a testament to his genius for developing innovative, user-friendly, and aesthetically pleasing products. In addition to being a perfectionist in product design, Jobs was a master showman with a cult following. During his time as CEO between 1997 and 2011, Apple's market value soared by over $300 billion!

On the other hand, when things don't go well, much of the failure of an organization can also, rightfully, be attributed to the leader.[8] Groupon's leadership clearly failed to respond effectively to important changes taking place in the daily deals industry. In contrast, Apple fully capitalized on emerging technology trends with a variety of products, including sophisticated smartphones.

The contrasting fortunes of Hewlett-Packard under two different CEOs also demonstrate the influence leadership has on firm performance.[9] When Carly Fiorina was fired as CEO of the firm in February 2005, HP enjoyed an immediate increase in its stock price of 7 percent—hardly a strong endorsement of her leadership! Her successor, Mark Hurd, led the firm to five years of outstanding financial results. Interestingly, when he abruptly resigned on August 6, 2010, the firm's stock price dropped 12 percent almost instantly! (To provide some perspective, this represents a decrease in HP's market value of about $12 billion.)

> For a more recent example, consider the announced exit of Dave Barger, chief executive of JetBlue Airways Corp. since 2007.[10] He has been highly criticized in recent years for the discount carrier's lagging performance. There is hope his replacement, Robin Hayes, a former British Airways executive, will make changes to help keep costs in line as well as enhance revenue by such actions as adding seats to aircraft (i.e., decreasing legroom) and imposing baggage fees. Perhaps not too surprising, JetBlue's shares rose nearly 40 percent between May and mid-August 2014, when speculation began circulating that Barger might be preparing to resign. And, when his resignation was announced a month later, shares immediately jumped 4 percent. (To give some perspective, even with the recent run-up, JetBlue's stock was up only 9 percent during Barger's tenure—compared to a gain of more than 140 percent for Southwest Airlines during the same period!)

However, such an emphasis on the leader reflects only part of the picture. Consider another perspective, called the **external control view of leadership.** Here, rather than making the implicit assumption that the leader is the most important factor in determining organizational outcomes, the focus is on external factors that may positively (or negatively) affect a firm's success. We don't have to look far to support this perspective. Developments in the general environment, such as economic downturns, new technologies, governmental legislation, or an outbreak of major internal conflict or war, can greatly restrict the choices that are available to a firm's executives. For example, several book retailers, such as Borders and Waldenbooks, found the consumer shift away from brick-and-mortar bookstores to online book buying (e.g., Amazon) and digital books an overwhelming environmental force against which they had few defenses.

Major unanticipated developments can often have very negative consequences for businesses regardless of how well formulated their strategies are.

Let's look at a few recent examples:[11]

- In the aftermath of BP's disastrous oil well explosion on April 20, 2010, the fishing and tourism industries in the region suffered significant downturns. BP itself was forced to pay a $20 billion fine to the U.S. government.
- On March 11, 2011, a 9.0 earthquake and tsunami devastated Japan and resulted in the loss of more than 20,000 lives. During the next two trading days, the country's stock exchange (Nikkei) suffered its biggest loss in 40 years. The disaster hit nearly every industry hard—especially energy companies. For example, Tokyo Electric Power Co., which operates a nuclear power plant that was severely damaged, fell 24.7 percent, and Toshiba Corp., a maker of nuclear power plants, slid 19.5 percent. Firms as diverse as Toyota, Honda, and Sony were forced to halt production because extensive damage to roads and distribution systems made it nearly impossible to move products.

A major piece of legislation with far-reaching consequences for businesses in the United States is the Affordable Care Act, commonly referred to as Obamacare. The Insights from Executives sidebar 1.1 provides a perspective on this law from Melvin Alexander, CPA, former chief financial officer of Kentucky One Health and other large health care systems.

Before moving on, it is important to point out that successful executives are often able to navigate around the difficult circumstances that they face. At times it can be refreshing to see the optimistic position they take when they encounter seemingly insurmountable odds. Of course, that's not to say that one should be naive or Pollyannaish. Consider, for example, how one CEO, discussed next, is handling trying times.[12]

Name a general economic woe, and chances are that Charles Needham, CEO of Metorex, is dealing with it.

- Market turmoil has knocked 80 percent off the shares of South Africa's Metorex, the mining company that he heads.
- The plunge in global commodities is slamming prices for the copper, cobalt, and other minerals Metorex unearths across Africa. The credit crisis makes it harder to raise money.
- Fighting has again broken out in the Democratic Republic of Congo, where Metorex has a mine and several projects in development.

Such problems might send many executives to the window ledge. Yet Needham appears unruffled as he sits down at a conference table in the company's modest offices in a Johannesburg suburb. The combat in northeast Congo, he notes, is far from Metorex's mine. Commodity prices are still high, in historical terms. And Needham is confident he can raise enough capital, drawing on relationships with South African banks. "These are the kinds of things you deal with, doing business in Africa," he says.

MELVIN ALEXANDER, CPA

BIOSKETCH

Melvin Alexander is presently executive director of Principled Solutions Enterprise (PSE), a management consulting firm specializing in health care. PSE's scope of services ranges from operational improvement (e.g., financial turnarounds, workflow redesigns) to strategic services (e.g., plan development and implementation, capital planning, and service line analysis). Alexander previously served as a chief financial officer of Kentucky One Health (Louisville, Kentucky), Norman Regional Health System (Norman, Oklahoma), and North Oaks Health System (Hammond, Louisiana). He also served in the U.S. Air Force as a medical service corps officer.

Alexander is a certified public accountant and a fellow of both the Healthcare Financial Management Association and the American College of Healthcare Executives. He received a bachelor of science degree in business administration (University of Texas at Dallas, 1980) and a master's of business administration (City University of Seattle, 1990), and he completed the Strategy Development for Senior Executives program (Marshall School of Business, University of Southern California, 2011).

1. *Can you explain ways in which the health care industry has responded to the ACA? Is there a difference between small and big firms in the ways in which they respond?*

    The component of the ACA that changes how Medicare pays hospitals and physicians is a major driver for the structural changes in the health care industry. The structural changes have resulted in consolidations of hospitals, increases in physicians employed by hospitals, and expanded service lines (e.g., hospitals offering health insurance). The large hospital systems (owners of multiple hospitals) have responded by acquiring other hospitals, improving quality by standardizing processes, and taking steps to prepare to become Accountable Care Organizations (ACOs) in order to optimize the changes in Medicare. The smaller organizations have not taken the same path because of resource limitations and local environmental issues (e.g., location).

    Under the ACA, Medicare beneficiaries will be assigned to an Accountable Care Organization (ACO) for health care services. The ACO will receive a single payment for each Medicare beneficiary assigned. The single payment will be divided and distributed by the ACO service providers (e.g., hospitals, physicians, ancillary care providers). The ACO essentially has the "risk" and responsibility of managing its beneficiaries' health care needs. Hospital systems are best equipped to become an ACO. The ACO concept demands comprehensive services and a continuum of services, multiple hospitals, and physicians in its network to deliver quality and timely care to assigned Medicare beneficiaries. Additionally, the ACO will need to have a good understanding of its assigned patients' health care statuses and needs, effective preventive care programs, and information technology systems that monitor patient activities. This is necessary because if the cost of care to provide services for the beneficiaries is lower than the "bundled payment" received, the ACO then makes a profit. If the cost of services is higher than payments received, the ACO loses money. The ACO concept absorbs the financial risk from the government, and this, in the long run, should reduce the amount of tax dollars spent on health care. In 2013, 25.4 percent of tax dollars paid for health care for Medicare and Medicaid patients.

2. *Environmental changes typically most often require strategic change by firms in order to survive. What strategic changes do you foresee in the next three to five years?*

    There will be new strategies to ensure success of the new law as well as to achieve projected returns on the large investments made. The new strategies will center on changing the behavior of the health care consumers (e.g., patients, insured beneficiaries). Areas ranging from preventive care to new providers of health care to improved technology will be focal points of the strategies. To ensure success and compliance, there will likely be both "carrot" and "stick" incentives for health consumers to comply.

    Preventive care will have a long-term impact on controlling costs and predictability of future service needs. The level of preventive care includes follow-up and frequent communication after major health procedures. Ensuring the patient has the appropriate medication and is following treatment plans is a form of the new model of preventive care. Health insurers and pharmaceutical companies have vested interests in preventive care as the insurer's long-term expenses could be reduced and pharmaceutical firms benefit by realizing increased revenues from their products.

    Other strategies will focus on the point of care and delivery site of health care services. This means patients may have to change physicians and receive health care services for major procedures in new locations. Health care systems as well as insurers will want their patients treated in "centers of excellence" for major health care procedures. For some patients, this may mean having

continued

procedures done in different states. This strategy will be a challenge; however, patients currently make such decisions in traveling to health care organizations such as the MD Anderson Cancer Center in Houston, Texas, and the Mayo Clinic in Rochester, Minnesota, because they are viewed as centers of excellence.

The major information technology investment encouraged by the government (through incentives to hospitals and physicians' practices in the early 2000s) will have a significant role with both preventive care and service delivery at centers of excellence.

What Is Strategic Management?

Given the many challenges and opportunities in the global marketplace, today's managers must do more than set long-term strategies and hope for the best.[13] They must go beyond what some have called "incremental management," whereby they view their job as making a series of small, minor changes to improve the efficiency of their firm's operations.[14] Rather than seeing their role as merely custodians of the status quo, today's leaders must be proactive, anticipate change, and continually refine and, when necessary, make dramatic changes to their strategies. The strategic management of the organization must become both a process and a way of thinking throughout the organization.

Defining Strategic Management

LO1.1

The definition of strategic management and its four key attributes.

strategic management
the analyses, decisions, and actions an organization undertakes in order to create and sustain competitive advantages.

strategy
the ideas, decisions, and actions that enable a firm to succeed.

competitive advantage
a firm's resources and capabilities that enable it to overcome the competitive forces in its industry(ies).

operational effectiveness
performing similar activities better than rivals.

Strategic management consists of the analyses, decisions, and actions an organization undertakes in order to create and sustain competitive advantages. This definition captures two main elements that go to the heart of the field of strategic management.

First, the strategic management of an organization entails three ongoing processes: *analyses, decisions,* and *actions.* Strategic management is concerned with the *analysis* of strategic goals (vision, mission, and strategic objectives) along with the analysis of the internal and external environments of the organization. Next, leaders must make strategic decisions. These *decisions,* broadly speaking, address two basic questions: What industries should we compete in? How should we compete in those industries? These questions also often involve an organization's domestic and international operations. And last are the *actions* that must be taken. Decisions are of little use, of course, unless they are acted on. Firms must take the necessary actions to implement their **strategies.** This requires leaders to allocate the necessary resources and to design the organization to bring the intended strategies to reality.

Second, the essence of strategic management is the study of why some firms outperform others.[15] Thus, managers need to determine how a firm is to compete so that it can obtain advantages that are sustainable over a lengthy period of time. That means focusing on two fundamental questions:

- *How should we compete in order to create* **competitive advantages** *in the marketplace?* Managers need to determine if the firm should position itself as the low-cost producer or develop products and services that are unique and will enable the firm to charge premium prices. Or should they do some combination of both?
- *How can we create competitive advantages in the marketplace that are unique, valuable, and difficult for rivals to copy or substitute?* That is, managers need to make such advantages sustainable, instead of temporary.

Sustainable competitive advantage cannot be achieved through operational effectiveness alone.[16] The popular management innovations of the last two decades—total quality, just-in-time, benchmarking, business process reengineering, outsourcing—are all about operational effectiveness. **Operational effectiveness** means performing similar activities better than rivals. Each of these innovations is important, but none lead to sustainable competitive advantage because everyone is doing them. Strategy is all about being different. Sustainable competitive advantage is possible only by performing different activities from rivals or performing similar activities in different ways. Companies such as Walmart, Southwest Airlines, and IKEA have developed unique, internally consistent, and difficult-to-imitate activity systems that have provided them with sustained competitive advantages. A company with a good strategy must make clear choices about what it wants to accomplish. Trying to do everything that your rivals do eventually leads to mutually destructive price competition, not long-term advantage.

The Four Key Attributes of Strategic Management

Before discussing the strategic management process, let's briefly talk about four attributes of strategic management.[17] It should become clear how this course differs from other courses that you have had in functional areas, such as accounting, marketing, operations, and finance. Exhibit 1.1 provides a definition and the four attributes of strategic management.

First, strategic management is *directed toward overall organizational goals and objectives.* That is, effort must be directed at what is best for the total organization, not just a single functional area. Some authors have referred to this perspective as "organizational versus individual rationality."[18] That is, what might look "rational" or ideal for one functional area, such as operations, may not be in the best interest of the overall firm. For example, operations may decide to schedule long production runs of similar products to lower unit costs. However, the standardized output may be counter to what the marketing department needs to appeal to a demanding target market. Similarly, research and development may "overengineer" the product to develop a far superior offering, but the design may make the product so expensive that market demand is minimal.

As noted by David Novak, CEO of Yum Brands:[19]

> I tell people that once you get a job you should act like you run the place. Not in terms of ego, but in terms of how you think about the business. Don't just think about your piece of the business. Think about your piece of the business and the total business. This way, you'll always have a broader perspective.

Second, strategic management *includes multiple stakeholders in decision making.*[20] **Stakeholders** are those individuals, groups, and organizations that have a "stake" in the success of the organization, including owners (shareholders in a publicly held corporation), employees, customers, suppliers, the community at large, and so on. (We'll discuss this in more detail later in this chapter.) Managers will not be successful if they focus on a single stakeholder. For example, if the overwhelming emphasis is on generating profits for the owners, employees may become alienated, customer service may suffer, and the suppliers may resent demands for pricing concessions.

Third, strategic management *requires incorporating both short-term and long-term perspectives.*[21] Peter Senge, a leading strategic management author, has referred to this need as a "creative tension."[22] That is, managers must maintain both a vision for the future of the organization and a focus on its present operating needs. However, financial markets can exert significant pressures on executives to meet short-term performance targets. Studies

stakeholders
individuals, groups, and organizations that have a stake in the success of the organization, including owners (shareholders in a publicly held corporation), employees, customers, suppliers, and the community at large.

Definition: Strategic management consists of the analyses, decisions, and actions an organization undertakes in order to create and sustain competitive advantages.

Key Attributes of Strategic Management

- Directs the organization toward overall goals and objectives.
- Includes multiple stakeholders in decision making.
- Needs to incorporate short-term and long-term perspectives.
- Recognizes trade-offs between efficiency and effectiveness.

EXHIBIT 1.1

Strategic Management Concepts

have shown that corporate leaders often take a short-term approach to the detriment of creating long-term shareholder value.

Andrew Winston addresses this issue in his recent book, *The Big Pivot:*[23]

> Consider the following scenario: It's near the end of the quarter and on your desk sits a project that you know will make money—it has a guaranteed positive net present value (NPV)—but it would reduce your earnings this quarter. Do you invest?
>
> In a study that posed this question to 400 CFOs, a majority said they would not do it. In addition, 80 percent of the executives would decrease R&D spending, advertising, and general maintenance. So what happens if you cut back on these things to prop up short-term earnings *every* quarter? Logically, you don't invest in projects with good paybacks and you under spend on initiatives that build longer-term value. Your earnings targets in future quarters actually get harder to hit.

Fourth, strategic management *involves the recognition of trade-offs between effectiveness and efficiency.* Some authors have referred to this as the difference between "doing the right thing" (**effectiveness**) and "doing things right" (**efficiency**).[24] While managers must allocate and use resources wisely, they must still direct their efforts toward the attainment of overall organizational objectives.

Successful managers must make many trade-offs. It is central to the practice of strategic management. At times, managers must focus on the short term and efficiency; at other times, the emphasis is on the long term and expanding a firm's product-market scope in order to anticipate opportunities in the competitive environment. For example, consider Kevin Sharer's perspective. He is CEO of Amgen, the giant $20 billion biotechnology firm:

> A CEO must always be switching between what I call different altitudes—tasks of different levels of abstraction and specificity. At the highest altitude you're asking the big questions: What are the company's mission and strategy? Do people understand and believe in these aims? Are decisions consistent with them? At the lowest altitude, you're looking at on-the-ground operations: Did we make that sale? What was the yield on that last lot in the factory? How many days of inventory do we have for a particular drug? And then there's everything in between: How many chemists do we need to hire this quarter? What should we pay for a small biotech company that has a promising new drug? Is our production capacity adequate to roll out a product in a new market?[25]

Some authors have developed the concept of **"ambidexterity,"** which refers to a manager's challenge to both align resources to take advantage of existing product markets and proactively explore new opportunities.[26] Strategy Spotlight 1.1 discusses ambidextrous behaviors that are required for success in today's challenging marketplace.

effectiveness

tailoring actions to the needs of an organization rather than wasting effort, or "doing the right thing."

efficiency

performing actions at a low cost relative to a benchmark, or "doing things right."

ambidexterity

the challenge managers face of both aligning resources to take advantage of existing product markets and proactively exploring new opportunities.

LO1.2

The strategic management process and its three interrelated and principal activities.

strategic management process

strategy analysis, strategy formulation, and strategy implementation.

The Strategic Management Process

We've identified three ongoing processes—analyses, decisions, and actions—that are central to strategic management. In practice, these three processes—often referred to as strategy analysis, strategy formulation, and strategy implementation—are highly interdependent and do not take place one after the other in a sequential fashion in most companies.

Intended versus Realized Strategies

Henry Mintzberg, a management scholar at McGill University, argues that viewing the strategic management process as one in which analysis is followed by optimal decisions and their subsequent meticulous implementation neither describes the strategic management process accurately nor prescribes ideal practice.[27] He sees the business environment as far from predictable, thus limiting our ability for analysis. Further, decisions are seldom based on optimal rationality alone, given the political processes that occur in all organizations.[28]

AMBIDEXTROUS BEHAVIORS: COMBINING ALIGNMENT AND ADAPTABILITY

A recent study involving 41 business units in 10 multinational companies identified four ambidextrous behaviors in individuals. Such behaviors are the essence of ambidexterity, and they illustrate how a dual capacity for alignment and adaptability can be woven into the fabric of an organization at the individual level.

They take time and are alert to opportunities beyond the confines of their own jobs. A large computer company's sales manager became aware of a need for a new software module that nobody currently offered. Instead of selling the customer something else, he worked up a business case for the new module. With management's approval, he began working full time on its development.

They are cooperative and seek out opportunities to combine their efforts with others. A marketing manager for Italy was responsible for supporting a newly acquired subsidiary. When frustrated about the limited amount of contact she had with her peers in other countries, she began discussions with them. This led to the creation of a European marketing forum which meets quarterly to discuss issues, share best practices, and collaborate on marketing plans.

They are brokers, always looking to build internal networks. When visiting the head office in St. Louis, a Canadian plant manager heard about plans for a $10 million investment for a new tape manufacturing plant. After inquiring further about the plans and returning to Canada, he contacted a regional manager in Manitoba, who he knew was looking for ways to build his business. With some generous support from the Manitoba government, the regional manager bid for, and ultimately won, the $10 million investment.

They are multitaskers who are comfortable wearing more than one hat. Although an operations manager for a major coffee and tea distributor was charged with running his plant as efficiently as possible, he took it upon himself to identify value-added services for his clients. By developing a dual role, he was able to manage operations and develop a promising electronic module that automatically reported impending problems inside a coffee vending machine. With corporate funding, he found a subcontractor to develop the software, and he then piloted the module in his own operations. It was so successful that it was eventually adopted by operations managers in several other countries.

A recent *Harvard Business Review* article provides some useful insights on how one can become a more ambidextrous leader. Consider the following questions:

- **Do you meet your numbers?**
- **Do you help others?**
- **What do you do for your peers?** Are you just their in-house competitor?
- **When you manage up, do you bring problems—or problems with possible solutions?**
- **Are you transparent?** Managers who get a reputation for spinning events gradually lose the trust of peers and superiors.
- **Are you developing a group of senior-managers who know you and are willing to back your original ideas with resources?**

Sources: Birkinshaw, J. & Gibson, C. 2004. Building ambidexterity into an organization. *MIT Sloan Management Review,* 45(4): 47–55; and Bower, J. L. 2007. Solve the succession crisis by growing inside-out leaders. *Harvard Business Review,* 85(11): 90–99.

Taking into consideration the limitations discussed above, Mintzberg proposed an alternative model. As depicted in Exhibit 1.2, decisions following from analysis, in this model, constitute the ***intended* strategy** of the firm. For a variety of reasons, the intended strategy rarely survives in its original form. Unforeseen environmental developments, unanticipated resource constraints, or changes in managerial preferences may result in at least some parts of the intended strategy remaining *unrealized.*

Consider an important trend affecting law firms:

Many of the leading corporations have reduced their need for outside legal services by increasingly expanding their in-house legal departments.[29] For example, companies and financial institutions spent an estimated $41 billion on their internal lawyers in 2014, a 22 percent increase since 2011. And a survey of 1,200 chief legal officers found that 63 percent of respondents are now "in-sourcing" legal work they used to send out to law firms or other service providers. In response, many large law firms have been forced to move away from commodity practices such as basic commercial contracts to more specialized areas like cross-border transactions and global regulatory issues.

Thus, the final **realized strategy** of any firm is a combination of deliberate and emergent strategies.

intended strategy
strategy in which organizational decisions are determined only by analysis.

realized strategy
strategy in which organizational decisions are determined by both analysis and unforeseen environmental developments, unanticipated resource constraints, and/or changes in managerial preferences.

Source: Adapted from Mintzberg, H. & Waters, J. A., "Of Strategies: Deliberate and Emergent," *Strategic Management Journal,* Vol. 6, 1985, pp. 257–272.

Next, we will address each of the three key strategic management processes—strategy analysis, strategy formulation, and strategy implementation—and provide a brief overview of the chapters.

Exhibit 1.3 depicts the strategic management process and indicates how it ties into the chapters in the book. Consistent with our discussion above, we use two-way arrows to convey the interactive nature of the processes.

Strategy Analysis

We measure, study, quantify, analyze every single piece of our business. . . . But then you've got to be able to take all that data and information and transform it into change in the organization and improvements in the organization and the formalization of the business strategy.

—*Richard Anderson, CEO of Delta Airlines*[30]

strategy analysis
study of firms' external and internal environments, and their fit with organizational vision and goals.

Strategy analysis may be looked upon as the starting point of the strategic management process. It consists of the "advance work" that must be done in order to effectively formulate and implement strategies. Many strategies fail because managers may want to formulate and implement strategies without a careful analysis of the overarching goals of the organization and without a thorough analysis of its external and internal environments.

Analyzing Organizational Goals and Objectives (Chapter 1) A firm's vision, mission, and strategic objectives form a hierarchy of goals that range from broad statements of intent and bases for competitive advantage to specific, measurable strategic objectives.

Analyzing the External Environment of the Firm (Chapter 2) Managers must monitor and scan the environment as well as analyze competitors. Two frameworks are provided: (1) The general environment consists of several elements, such as demographic and economic segments, and (2) the industry environment consists of competitors and other organizations that may threaten the success of a firm's products and services.

Assessing the Internal Environment of the Firm (Chapter 3) Analyzing the strengths and relationships among the activities that constitute a firm's value chain (e.g., operations,

EXHIBIT 1.3 The Strategic Management Process

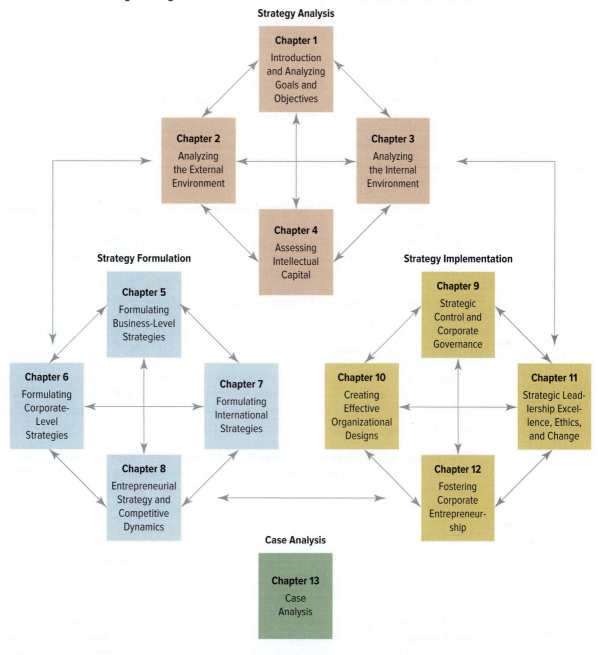

Strategy Analysis

Chapter 1
Introduction and Analyzing Goals and Objectives

Chapter 2
Analyzing the External Environment

Chapter 3
Analyzing the Internal Environment

Chapter 4
Assessing Intellectual Capital

Strategy Formulation

Chapter 5
Formulating Business-Level Strategies

Chapter 6
Formulating Corporate-Level Strategies

Chapter 7
Formulating International Strategies

Chapter 8
Entrepreneurial Strategy and Competitive Dynamics

Strategy Implementation

Chapter 9
Strategic Control and Corporate Governance

Chapter 10
Creating Effective Organizational Designs

Chapter 11
Strategic Leadership Excellence, Ethics, and Change

Chapter 12
Fostering Corporate Entrepreneurship

Case Analysis

Chapter 13
Case Analysis

marketing and sales, and human resource management) can be a means of uncovering potential sources of competitive advantage for the firm.[31]

Assessing a Firm's Intellectual Assets (Chapter 4) The knowledge worker and a firm's other intellectual assets (e.g., patents) are important drivers of competitive advantages and wealth creation. We also assess how well the organization creates networks and relationships as well as how technology can enhance collaboration among employees and provide a means of accumulating and storing knowledge.[32]

Strategy Formulation

"You can have the best operations. You can be the most adept at whatever it is that you're doing. But, if you have a bad strategy, it's all for naught."

—Fred Smith, CEO of FedEx[33]

strategy formulation
decisions made by firms regarding investments, commitments, and other aspects of operations that create and sustain competitive advantage.

Strategy formulation is developed at several levels. First, business-level strategy addresses the issue of how to compete in a given business to attain competitive advantage. Second, corporate-level strategy focuses on two issues: (a) what businesses to compete in and (b) how businesses can be managed to achieve synergy; that is, they create more value by working together than by operating as stand-alone businesses. Third, a firm must develop international strategies as it ventures beyond its national boundaries. Fourth, managers must formulate effective entrepreneurial initiatives.

Formulating Business-Level Strategy (Chapter 5) The question of how firms compete and outperform their rivals and how they achieve and sustain competitive advantages goes to the heart of strategic management. Successful firms strive to develop bases for competitive advantage, which can be achieved through cost leadership and/or differentiation as well as by focusing on a narrow or industrywide market segment.[34]

Formulating Corporate-Level Strategy (Chapter 6) Corporate-level strategy addresses a firm's portfolio (or group) of businesses. It asks: (1) What business (or businesses) should we compete in? and (2) How can we manage this portfolio of businesses to create synergies among the businesses?

Formulating International Strategy (Chapter 7) When firms enter foreign markets, they face both opportunities and pitfalls.[35] Managers must decide not only on the most appropriate entry strategy but also how they will go about attaining competitive advantages in international markets.[36]

Entrepreneurial Strategy and Competitive Dynamics (Chapter 8) Entrepreneurial activity aimed at new value creation is a major engine for economic growth. For entrepreneurial initiatives to succeed, viable opportunities must be recognized and effective strategies must be formulated.

Strategy Implementation

"We could leave our strategic plan on an airplane, and it wouldn't matter. It's all about execution."

—John Stumpf, CEO of Wells Fargo[37]

strategy implementation
actions made by firms that carry out the formulated strategy, including strategic controls, organizational design, and leadership.

Clearly, sound strategies are of no value if they are not properly implemented.[38] **Strategy implementation** involves ensuring proper strategic controls and organizational designs, which includes establishing effective means to coordinate and integrate activities within the firm as well as with its suppliers, customers, and alliance partners.[39] Leadership plays a central role to ensure that the organization is committed to excellence and ethical behavior. It also promotes learning and continuous improvement and acts entrepreneurially in creating new opportunities.

Strategic Control and Corporate Governance (Chapter 9) Firms must exercise two types of strategic control. First, informational control requires that organizations continually monitor and scan the environment and respond to threats and opportunities. Second, behavioral control involves the proper balance of rewards and incentives as well as cultures and boundaries (or constraints). Further, successful firms (those that are incorporated) practice effective corporate governance.

Creating Effective Organizational Designs (Chapter 10)   Firms must have organizational structures and designs that are consistent with their strategy. In today's rapidly changing competitive environments, firms must ensure that their organizational boundaries—those internal to the firm and external—are more flexible and permeable.[40] Often, organizations develop strategic alliances to capitalize on the capabilities of other organizations.

Creating a Learning Organization and an Ethical Organization (Chapter 11) Effective leaders set a direction, design the organization, and develop an organization that is committed to excellence and ethical behavior. In addition, given rapid and unpredictable change, leaders must create a "learning organization" so that the entire organization can benefit from individual and collective talents.

Fostering Corporate Entrepreneurship (Chapter 12)   Firms must continually improve and grow as well as find new ways to renew their organizations. Corporate entrepreneurship and innovation provide firms with new opportunities, and strategies should be formulated that enhance a firm's innovative capacity.

Chapter 13, "Analyzing Strategic Management Cases," provides guidelines and suggestions on how to evaluate cases in this course. Thus, the concepts and techniques discussed in the first 12 chapters can be applied to real-world organizations.

Let's now address two concepts—corporate governance and stakeholder management—that are critical to the strategic management process.

The Role of Corporate Governance and Stakeholder Management

Most business enterprises that employ more than a few dozen people are organized as corporations. As you recall from your finance classes, the overall purpose of a corporation is to maximize the long-term return to the owners (shareholders). Thus, we may ask: Who is really responsible for fulfilling this purpose? Robert Monks and Neil Minow provide a useful definition of **corporate governance** as "the relationship among various participants in determining the direction and performance of corporations. The primary participants are (1) the shareholders, (2) the management (led by the chief executive officer), and (3) the board of directors."[41] This relationship is illustrated in Exhibit 1.4.

The board of directors (BOD) are the elected representatives of the shareholders charged with ensuring that the interests and motives of management are aligned with those of the owners (i.e., shareholders). In many cases, the BOD is diligent in fulfilling its purpose. For

corporate governance
the relationship among various participants in determining the direction and performance of corporations. The primary participants are (1) the shareholders, (2) the management (led by the chief executive officer), and (3) the board of directors.

EXHIBIT 1.4 The Key Elements of Corporate Governance

Management
(Headed by the chief executive officer)

Shareholders
(Owners)

Board of Directors
(Elected by the shareholders
to represent their interests)

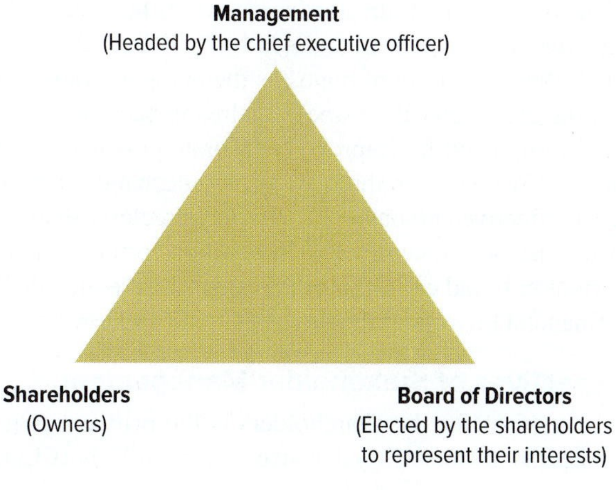

example, Intel Corporation, the giant $55 billion maker of microprocessor chips, practices sound governance. Its BOD follows guidelines to ensure that its members are independent (i.e., are not members of the executive management team and do not have close personal ties to top executives) so that they can provide proper oversight; it has explicit guidelines on the selection of director candidates (to avoid "cronyism"). It provides detailed procedures for formal evaluations of directors and the firm's top officers.[42] Such guidelines serve to ensure that management is acting in the best interests of shareholders.[43]

Recently, there has been much criticism as well as cynicism by both citizens and the business press about the poor job that management and the BODs of large corporations are doing. We only have to look at the scandals at firms such as Arthur Andersen, Best Buy, Olympus, Enron, Tyco, and ImClone Systems.[44] Such malfeasance has led to an erosion of the public's trust in corporations. For example, according to the 2014 CNBC/Burson-Marsteller Corporation Perception Indicator, a global survey of 25,000 individuals, only 52 percent of the public in developed markets has a favorable view of corporations.[45] Forty-five percent felt corporations have "too much influence over the government." More than half of the U.S. public said "strong and influential" corporations are "bad" even if they are promoting innovation and growth, and only 9 percent of the public in the United States says corporate CEOs are "among the most respected" in society. Perhaps it may be a bit reassuring to big business that a 2013 poll revealed that the public's view of Congress was significantly less positive than its view of root canals, NFL replacement referees, colonoscopies, France, and even cockroaches!

One area in which public anger is most pronounced is the excessive compensation of the top executives of well-known firms. It is now clear that much of the bonus pay awarded to executives on Wall Street in the past few years was richly undeserved.[46] In the three years that led up to the collapse of seven big financial institutions in 2008, the chief executives of those firms collected a total of $80 million in performance bonuses and raked in $210 million in severance pay and earnings from stock sales. The trend continues. 2011 was a poor year for financial stocks: 35 of the 50 largest financial company stocks fell that year. The sector lost 17 percent—compared to flat performance for the Standard & Poor's 500. However, even as the sector struggled, the average pay of finance company CEOs rose 20.4 percent. For example, JPMorgan CEO Jamie Dimon was the highest-paid banker— with $23.1 million in compensation, an 11 percent increase from the previous year. The firm's shareholders didn't do as well—the stock fell 20 percent.[47]

Of course, excessive pay is not restricted to financial institutions. Consider Staples, whose earnings fell by 43 percent in the first quarter of 2014 after a rough 2013 in which operating income fell by double digits. As expected, Staples' earnings weren't high enough for top executives to receive incentive pay. But the board decided to approve a "retention cash award" to motivate and retain the company's already well-paid executives. As a result, CEO Ron Argent was given $300,000 in cash on top of his $10.8 million total compensation package—which had already increased 40 percent in 2013. (Shareholders had lost 25 percent over the past year.) As noted by Will Becker, an analyst with Behind the Numbers, "This is the worst kind of bonus as the compensation committee essentially changed the rules of the game after the game had already been played."[48]

Clearly, there is a strong need for improved corporate governance, and we will address this topic in Chapter 9.[49] We focus on three important mechanisms to ensure effective corporate governance: an effective and engaged board of directors, shareholder activism, and proper managerial rewards and incentives.[50] In addition to these internal controls, a key role is played by various external control mechanisms.[51] These include the auditors, banks, analysts, an active financial press, and the threat of hostile takeovers.

Alternative Perspectives of Stakeholder Management

Generating long-term returns for the shareholders is the primary goal of a publicly held corporation.[52] As noted by former Chrysler vice chairman Robert Lutz, "We are here to

stakeholder management
a firm's strategy for recognizing and responding to the interests of all its salient stakeholders.

serve the shareholder and create shareholder value. I insist that the only person who owns the company is the person who paid good money for it."[53]

Despite the primacy of generating shareholder value, managers who focus solely on the interests of the owners of the business will often make poor decisions that lead to negative, unanticipated outcomes.[54] For example, decisions such as mass layoffs to increase profits, ignoring issues related to conservation of the natural environment to save money, and exerting excessive pressure on suppliers to lower prices can harm the firm in the long run. Such actions would likely lead to negative outcomes such as alienated employees, increased governmental oversight and fines, and disloyal suppliers.

Clearly, in addition to *shareholders,* there are other *stakeholders* (e.g., suppliers, customers) who must be taken into account in the strategic management process.[55] A stakeholder can be defined as an individual or group, inside or outside the company, that has a stake in and can influence an organization's performance. Each stakeholder group makes various claims on the company.[56] Exhibit 1.5 provides a list of major stakeholder groups and the nature of their claims on the company.

Zero Sum or Symbiosis?   There are two opposing ways of looking at the role of stakeholder management.[57] The first one can be termed "zero sum." Here, the various stakeholders compete for the organization's resources: the gain of one individual or group is the loss of another individual or group. For example, employees want higher wages (which drive down profits), suppliers want higher prices for their inputs and slower, more flexible delivery times (which drive up costs), customers want fast deliveries and higher quality (which drive up costs), the community at large wants charitable contributions (which take money from company goals), and so on. This zero-sum thinking is rooted, in part, in the traditional conflict between workers and management, leading to the formation of unions and sometimes ending in adversarial union–management negotiations and long, bitter strikes.

Consider, for example, the many stakeholder challenges facing Walmart, the world's largest retailer.

> Walmart strives to ramp up growth while many stakeholders are watching nervously: employees and trade unions; shareholders, investors, and creditors; suppliers and joint venture partners; the governments of the U.S. and other nations where the retailer operates; and customers. In addition many non-governmental organizations (NGOs), particularly in countries where the retailer buys its products, are closely monitoring Walmart. Walmart's stakeholders have different interests, and not all of them share the firm's goals. Each group has the ability, in various degrees, to influence the firm's choices and results. Clearly, this wasn't the case when Sam Walton built his first store in Rogers, Arkansas, in 1962![58]

There will always be conflicting demands on organizations. However, organizations can achieve mutual benefit through stakeholder symbiosis, which recognizes that stakeholders

Stakeholder Group	Nature of Claim
Stockholders	Dividends, capital appreciation
Employees	Wages, benefits, safe working environment, job security
Suppliers	Payment on time, assurance of continued relationship
Creditors	Payment of interest, repayment of principal
Customers	Value, warranties
Government	Taxes, compliance with regulations
Communities	Good citizenship behavior such as charities, employment, not polluting the environment

EXHIBIT 1.5

An Organization's Key Stakeholders and the Nature of Their Claims

are dependent upon each other for their success and well-being.[59] Consider Procter & Gamble's "laundry detergent compaction," a technique for compressing even more cleaning power into ever smaller concentrations.

P&G perfected a technique that could compact two or three times as much cleaning powder into a liquid concentration. This remarkable breakthrough has led to not only a change in consumer shopping habits but also a revolution in industry supply chain economics. Here's how several key stakeholders are affected:

> *Consumers* love concentrated liquids because they are easier to carry, pour, and store. *Retailers,* meanwhile, prefer them because they take up less floor and shelf space, which leads to higher sales-per-square-foot—a big deal for Walmart, Target, and other big retailers. *Shipping and wholesalers,* meanwhile, prefer reduced-sized products because smaller bottles translate into reduced fuel consumption and improved warehouse space utilization. And, finally, *environmentalists* favor such products because they use less packaging and produce less waste than conventional products.[60]

Although it often appears the interests of stakeholder groups are in conflict with each other, leading companies are increasingly realizing that learning to partner with governments and communities, suppliers and customers—and even longtime rivals—is essential for dealing with big, complex problems. Strategy Spotlight 1.2 discusses how firms like Nike, Walmart, and Patagonia have started working with a number of stakeholder groups through the Sustainable Apparel Coalition in order to improve the environmental impact of their products.

Social Responsibility and Environmental Sustainability: Moving beyond the Immediate Stakeholders

Organizations cannot ignore the interests and demands of stakeholders such as citizens and society in general that are beyond its immediate constituencies—customers, owners, suppliers, and employees. The realization that firms have multiple stakeholders and that evaluating their performance must go beyond analyzing their financial results has led to a new way of thinking about businesses and their relationship to society.

First, *social responsibility* recognizes that businesses must respond to society's expectations regarding their obligations to society. Second, the *triple bottom line approach* evaluates a firm's performance. This perspective takes into account financial, social, and environmental performance. Third, *making the case for sustainability initiatives* addresses some of the challenges managers face in obtaining approvals for such project—and how to overcome them.

social responsibility
the expectation that businesses or individuals will strive to improve the overall welfare of society.

LO1.4

The importance of social responsibility, including environmental sustainability, and how it can enhance a corporation's innovation strategy.

Social Responsibility   **Social responsibility** is the expectation that businesses or individuals will strive to improve the overall welfare of society.[61] From the perspective of a business, this means that managers must take active steps to make society better by virtue of the business being in existence.[62] What constitutes socially responsible behavior changes over time. In the 1970s affirmative action was a high priority; during the 1990s and up to the present time, the public has been concerned about environmental quality. Many firms have responded to this by engaging in recycling and reducing waste. And in the wake of terrorist attacks on New York City and the Pentagon, as well as the continuing threat from terrorists worldwide, a new kind of priority has arisen: the need to be vigilant concerning public safety.

Today, demands for greater corporate responsibility have accelerated.[63] These include corporate critics, social investors, activists, and, increasingly, customers who claim to assess corporate responsibility when making purchasing decisions. Such demands go well beyond product and service quality.[64] They include a focus on issues such as labor standards, environmental sustainability, financial and accounting reporting, procurement, and environmental practices.[65] At times, a firm's reputation can be tarnished by exceedingly

THE SUSTAINABLE APPAREL COALITION

The story of the Sustainable Apparel Coalition (SAC) began with a letter designed to get the attention of even a busy CEO. At the top: the logos of Walmart and Patagonia. John Fleming, Walmart's chief merchandising officer, and Yvon Chouinard, Patagonia's founder, signed the letter that invited chief executives of some of the world's biggest clothing companies—normally fierce rivals—to join together to develop an index to measure the environmental impact of their products.

Shortly thereafter, Walmart and Patagonia convened a group of 10 apparel companies in the belief that the adoption of a single, standardized index would drive efficiency and innovation across the apparel value chain and reduce environmental impact and supply chain risks. The so-called Higgs Index enabled companies to compare environmental performance outcomes in areas such as energy efficiency, material waste, water use, and sustainable raw materials. It provided benchmarks at the company, product, and factory levels. Drawing on work already done by Nike and the Outdoor Industry Association, the coalition quickly built a prototype of the index and began testing it in the fall of 2011, across more than 50 brands, retailers, and suppliers. The SAC's benchmarks have mobilized a "race to the top," in which companies that score lower than their competitors on the index are motivated to improve their ratings. (The first version of the Higgs Index was released in July 2012, and it was revised in December 2013.)

The Higgs Index has played a key role in not only driving better outcomes but also influencing capital investment decisions and changing operational behaviors. Target and other major retailers have integrated the index into their supplier scorecard, using the measures to select suppliers. Apparel brands have used the index to help reduce fabric waste through improved product design. Also, manufacturers have used it to justify investments in new capabilities such as wastewater recycling and enhanced energy efficiency. The index even improves performance within companies, as departments compare their scores and engage in productive competitions.

The SAC now has approximately 145 members, representing brands, retailers, suppliers, and other organizations that together account for more than one-third of the global apparel and footwear industry. Its vision: "an apparel and footwear industry that produces no unnecessary environmental harm and has a positive impact on the people and communities associated with its activities."

Sources: Guerin, D. (chief of staff, Sustainable Apparel Coalition). 2014. *personal communication:* October 9; Nidumolu, R., Ellison, J., Whalen, J., & Billman, E. 2014. The collaboration imperative. *Harvard Business Review,* 92(4): 76–84; Gunther, M. 2012. Behind the scenes at the Sustainable Apparel Coalition. *www.greenbix.com,* July 26, np; and *www.apparelcoalition.org.*

poor judgment on the part of one of its managers. For example, BP CEO Tony Hayward's decision to withhold information from the public about the magnitude of the oil spill in the Gulf of Mexico further damaged the firm's reputation.

A key stakeholder group that appears to be particularly susceptible to corporate social responsibility (CSR) initiatives is customers.[66] Surveys indicate a strong positive relationship between CSR behaviors and consumers' reactions to a firm's products and services.[67] For example:

- Corporate Citizenship's poll conducted by Cone Communications found that "84 percent of Americans say they would be likely to switch brands to one associated with a good cause, if price and quality are similar."[68]
- Hill & Knowlton/Harris's Interactive poll reveals that "79 percent of Americans take corporate citizenship into account when deciding whether to buy a particular company's product and 37 percent consider corporate citizenship an important factor when making purchasing decisions."[69]

Such findings are consistent with a large body of research that confirms the positive influence of CSR on consumers' company evaluations and product purchase intentions across a broad range of product categories.

The Triple Bottom Line: Incorporating Financial as Well as Environmental and Social Costs   Many companies are now measuring what has been called a **"triple bottom line."** This involves assessing financial, social, and environmental performance. Shell, NEC, Procter & Gamble, and others have recognized that failing to account for the environmental and social costs of doing business poses risks to the company and its community.[70]

> **triple bottom line**
> assessment of a firm's financial, social, and environmental performance.

The environmental revolution has been almost four decades in the making.[71] In the 1960s and 1970s, companies were in a state of denial regarding their firms' impact on the natural environment. However, a series of visible ecological problems created a groundswell for strict governmental regulation. In the U.S., Lake Erie was "dead," and in Japan, people died of mercury poisoning. More recently, Japan's horrific tsunami that took place on March 11, 2011, and Hurricane Sandy's devastation on the East Coast of the United States in late October 2012 have raised alarms. Clearly, the effects of global warming are being felt throughout the world.

Stuart Hart, writing in the *Harvard Business Review,* addresses the magnitude of problems and challenges associated with the natural environment:

> The challenge is to develop a *sustainable global economy:* an economy that the planet is capable of supporting indefinitely. Although we may be approaching ecological recovery in the developed world, the planet as a whole remains on an unsustainable course. Increasingly, the scourges of the late twentieth century—depleted farmland, fisheries, and forests; choking urban pollution; poverty; infectious disease; and migration—are spilling over geopolitical borders. The simple fact is this: in meeting our needs, we are destroying the ability of future generations to meet theirs . . . corporations are the only organizations with the resources, the technology, the global reach, and, ultimately, the motivation to achieve sustainability.[72]

Environmental sustainability is now a value embraced by the most competitive and successful multinational companies.[73] The McKinsey Corporation's survey of more than 400 senior executives of companies around the world found that 92 percent agreed with former Sony president Akio Morita's contention that the environmental challenge will be one of the central issues in the 21st century.[74] Virtually all executives acknowledged their firms' responsibility to control pollution, and 83 percent agreed that corporations have an environmental responsibility for their products even after they are sold.

For many successful firms, environmental values are now becoming a central part of their cultures and management processes.[75] And, as noted earlier, environmental impacts are being audited and accounted for as the "third bottom line." According to a recent corporate report, "If we aren't good corporate citizens as reflected in a Triple Bottom Line that takes into account social and environmental responsibilities along with financial ones—eventually our stock price, our profits, and our entire business could suffer."[76] Also, a CEO survey on sustainability by Accenture debunks the notion that sustainability and profitability are mutually exclusive corporate goals. The study found that sustainability is being increasingly recognized as a source of cost efficiencies and revenue growth. In many companies, sustainability activities have led to increases in revenue and profits. As Jeff Immelt, the CEO of General Electric, puts it, "Green is green."[77] Strategy Spotlight 1.3 provides examples of how environmental initiatives can really pay off financially, that is, increase revenues and cut costs. We mention such well-known companies as Clorox, GE, DuPont, and IBM that represent a wide range of industries. Clearly, one could argue that the benefits go far beyond "good PR"!

Many firms have profited by investing in socially responsible behavior, including those activities that enhance environmental sustainability. However, how do such "socially responsible" companies fare in terms of shareholder returns compared to benchmarks such as the Standard & Poor's 500 Index? Let's look at some of the evidence.

> SRI (socially responsible investing) is a broad-based approach to investing that now encompasses an estimated $3.7 trillion, or $1 out of every $9 under professional management in the United States.[78] SRI recognizes that corporate responsibility and societal concerns are considerations in investment decisions. With SRI, investors have the opportunity to put their money to work to build a more sustainable world while earning competitive returns both today and over time.

GOING GREEN CAN BOOST REVENUES AND CUT COSTS

Harold Sirkin, senior partner of the Boston Consulting Group (BCG), recently commented: "In days past, many sustainability efforts would have been the result of government prodding or public pressure, or would have been undertaken for PR purposes. Today's executives know better. They realize that 'green,' our convenient euphemism for sustainability, is the color of money." Let's look at how some well-known firms have benefited financially from such initiatives.

Increased Revenues

- Clorox's Green Works line of plant-based cleaning materials captured 42 percent of the natural cleaning products market in its first year.
- GE earns more than $18 billion a year from its "ecomagination" product lines, each of which contributes to solving global sustainability challenges.
- Mitsubishi expects $13.3 billion in annual sales by 2016 from clean technologies, including solar systems, heat pumps, and other energy-efficient power devices.
- DuPont expects an additional $6 billion in annual revenues through product innovation based on sustainability.

Lower Costs

- Northrup Grumman saved $2 million in energy costs at a single facility by installing reflective roofs and fluorescent lighting, replacing old equipment, and making minor temperature and humidity-level adjustments.
- IBM saved $49 million by investing $1 million in a green overhaul of one of its data centers in Kentucky; it also boosted the center's IT capacity eight times, without raising the energy footprint, through energy efficiency improvements.
- Baxter International, over the past decade, has received an average return of approximately $3 for every $1 invested in its environmental initiatives, which it has documented on its annual Environmental Financial Statement of environmental costs and benefits.
- The Fairmont Royal York in Toronto invested $25,000 in an energy conservation program to replace leaky steam traps and fix leaks, which resulted in an annual savings of over $200,000.

Sources: Sirkin, H. L. 2013. A sustainable business model pays off. *www.businessweek.com*, November 26: np; Anonymous. Why go green? The business case for sustainability. *greenhotelscombined.com*, undated, np; and Esty, D. C. & Simmons, P. J. 2011. *The green to gold business playbook*. Hoboken, NJ: Wiley.

And, as the saying goes, nice guys don't have to finish last. The ING SRI Index Fund, which tracks the stocks of 50 companies, enjoyed a 47.4 percent return in a recent year. That easily beat the 2.65 percent gain of the Standard & Poor's 500 stock index. A review of the 145 socially responsible equity mutual and exchange-traded funds tracked by Morningstar also shows that 65 percent of them outperformed the S&P 500.[79]

Making the Business Case for Sustainability Initiatives We mentioned many financial and nonfinancial benefits associated with sustainability initiatives in the previous section. However, in practice, such initiatives often have difficulty making it through the conventional approval process within corporations. This is primarily because, before companies make investments in projects, managers want to know their return on investment.[80]

The ROIs on sustainability projects are often very difficult to quantify for a number of reasons. Among these are:

1. *The data necessary to calculate ROI accurately are often not available when it comes to sustainability projects.* However, sustainability programs may often find their success beyond company boundaries, so internal systems and process metrics can't capture all the relevant numbers.
2. *Many of the benefits from such projects are intangible.* Traditional financial models are built around relatively easy-to-measure, monetized results. Yet many of the benefits of sustainability projects involve fuzzy intangibles, such as the goodwill that can enhance a firm's brand equity.
3. *The payback period is on a different time frame.* Even when their future benefits can be forecast, sustainability projects often require longer-term payback windows.

STRATEGY AND THE VALUE OF INEXPERIENCE

Peter Gruber, chairman of Mandalay Entertainment, discovered that great ideas can come from the least expected sources. During the filming of the movie *Gorillas in the Mist,* his production company faced many problems. Rwanda—the site of the filming—was on the verge of revolution, the film needed to use 200 animals, and the screenplay required the gorillas to follow a script, that is, do what the script called for and "act." If that failed, the fallback position was to use dwarfs in gorilla suits on a soundstage—a strategy that usually failed.

Gruber explains how the "day was saved" by someone with very limited experience:

> We called an emergency meeting to solve these problems. In the middle of it, a young intern asked, "What if you let the gorillas write the story?" Everyone laughed and wondered what she was doing in the meeting with experienced filmmakers. Hours later, someone casually asked her what she had meant. She said, "What if you send a really good cinematographer into the jungle with a ton of film to shoot the gorillas, then you could write a story around what the gorillas did on film." It was a brilliant idea. And we did exactly what she suggested: We sent Alan Root, an Academy Award–nominated cinematographer into the jungle for three weeks. He came back with phenomenal footage that practically wrote the story for us.

The upshot? The film cost $20 million to shoot—half the original budget. And it was nominated for five Academy Awards—including Sigourney Weaver for best actress—and it won two Golden Globe Awards.

Source: Gruber, P. 1998. My greatest lesson. *Fast Company,* 14: 88–90; and *imdb.com.*

Clearly, the case for sustainability projects needs to be made on the basis of a more holistic and comprehensive understanding of all the tangible and intangible benefits rather than whether or not they meet existing hurdle rates for traditional investment projects. For example, 3M uses a lower hurdle rate for pollution prevention projects. When it comes to environmental projects, IKEA allows a 10- to 15-year payback period, considerably longer than it allows for other types of investment. And Diversey, a cleaning products company, has employed a portfolio approach. It has established two hurdles for projects in its carbon reduction plan: a three-year payback and a cost per megaton of carbon avoided. Out of 120 possible projects ranging from lighting retrofits to solar photovoltaic systems, only 30 cleared both hurdles. Although about 60 of the other ideas could reach *one,* an expanded 90-project portfolio, all added together, met the double hurdle. Subsequently, Diversey was able to increase its carbon reduction goal from 8 to 25 percent and generated a higher net present value.

Such approaches are the result of the recognition that the intangible benefits of sustainability projects—such as reducing risks, staying ahead of regulations, pleasing communities, and enhancing employee morale—are substantial even when they are difficult to quantify. Just as companies spend large fortunes on launching advertising campaigns or initiating R&D projects without a clear quantification of financial returns, sustainability investments are necessary even when it is difficult to calculate the ROE of such investments. The alternative of not making these investments is often no longer feasible.

LO1.5

The need for greater empowerment throughout the organization.

The Strategic Management Perspective: An Imperative throughout the Organization

Strategic management requires managers to take an integrative view of the organization and assess how all of the functional areas and activities fit together to help an organization achieve its goals and objectives. This cannot be accomplished if only the top managers in the organization take an integrative, strategic perspective of issues facing the firm and everyone else "fends for themselves" in their independent, isolated functional areas. Instead, people throughout the organization must strive toward overall goals.

The need for such a perspective is accelerating in today's increasingly complex, interconnected, ever-changing, global economy. As noted by Peter Senge of MIT, the days when Henry Ford, Alfred Sloan, and Tom Watson (top executives at Ford, General Motors, and IBM, respectively) "learned for the organization are gone."[81]

To develop and mobilize people and other assets, leaders are needed throughout the organization.[82] No longer can organizations be effective if the top "does the thinking" and the rest of the organization "does the work." Everyone must be involved in the strategic management process. There is a critical need for three types of leaders:

- *Local line leaders* who have significant profit-and-loss responsibility.
- *Executive leaders* who champion and guide ideas, create a learning infrastructure, and establish a domain for taking action.
- *Internal networkers* who, although they have little positional power and formal authority, generate their power through the conviction and clarity of their ideas.[83]

Top-level executives are key in setting the tone for the empowerment of employees. Consider Richard Branson, founder of the Virgin Group, whose core businesses include retail operations, hotels, communications, and an airline. He is well known for creating a culture and an informal structure where anybody in the organization can be involved in generating and acting upon new business ideas. In an interview, he stated:

> Speed is something that we are better at than most companies. We don't have formal board meetings, committees, etc. If someone has an idea, they can pick up the phone and talk to me. I can vote "done, let's do it." Or, better still, they can just go ahead and do it. They know that they are not going to get a mouthful from me if they make a mistake. Rules and regulations are not our forte. Analyzing things to death is not our kind of thing. We very rarely sit back and analyze what we do.[84]

To inculcate a strategic management perspective, managers must often make a major effort to effect transformational change. This involves extensive communication, incentives, training, and development. For example, under the direction of Nancy Snyder, a corporate vice president, Whirlpool, the world's largest producer of household appliances, brought about a significant shift in the firm's reputation as an innovator.[85] This five-year initiative included financial investments in capital spending as well as a series of changes in management processes, including training innovation mentors, making innovation a significant portion of leadership development programs, enrolling all salaried employees in online courses in business innovation, and providing employees an innovation portal to access multiple innovation tools and data.

Many successful executives reward honesty and input and show their interest in learning what others are thinking. Methods vary and include holding town-hall meetings, seeking the advice of people at all levels of the firm, and asking employees what they would do if they were in charge. As noted by Tim Brown, CEO of the premier design consulting firm IDEO: "The best can come from anywhere in an organization. So you'd better do a good job of spotting and promoting them when they come, and not let people's positions dictate how influential their ideas are."[86]

We'd like to close with our favorite example of how inexperience can be a virtue. It further reinforces the benefits of having broad involvement throughout the organization in the strategic management process (see Strategy Spotlight 1.4).

Ensuring Coherence in Strategic Direction

Employees and managers must strive toward common goals and objectives.[87] By specifying desired results, it becomes much easier to move forward. Otherwise, when no one knows what the firm is striving to accomplish, individuals have no idea of what to work

LO1.6

How an awareness of a hierarchy of strategic goals can help an organization achieve coherence in its strategic direction.

toward. Alan Mulally, CEO at Ford Motor Company, stresses the importance of perspective in creating a sense of mission:

> I think the most important thing is coming to a shared view about what we're trying to accomplish—whether you're a nonprofit or a for-profit organization. What are we? What is our real purpose? And then, how do you include everybody so you know where you are on that plan, so you can work on areas that need special attention. And then everybody gets a chance to participate and feel that accomplishment of participating and contributing.[88]

Organizations express priorities best through stated goals and objectives that form a **hierarchy of goals,** which includes the firm's vision, mission, and strategic objectives.[89] What visions may lack in specificity, they make up for in their ability to evoke powerful and compelling mental images. On the other hand, strategic objectives tend to be more specific and provide a more direct means of determining if the organization is moving toward broader, overall goals.[90] Visions, as one would expect, also have longer time horizons than either mission statements or strategic objectives. Exhibit 1.6 depicts the hierarchy of goals and its relationship to two attributes: general versus specific and time horizon.

hierarchy of goals
organizational goals ranging from, at the top, those that are less specific yet able to evoke powerful and compelling mental images, to, at the bottom, those that are more specific and measurable.

Organizational Vision

A **vision** is a goal that is "massively inspiring, overarching, and long term."[91] It represents a destination that is driven by and evokes passion. For example, Wendy Kopp, founder of Teach for America, notes that her vision for the organization, which strives to improve the quality of inner-city schools, draws many applicants:

vision
organizational goal(s) that evoke(s) powerful and compelling mental images.

> We're looking for people who are magnetized to this notion, this vision, that one day all children in our nation should have the opportunity to attain an excellent education. And that magnetizes certain people. And so it's more about them—it's their vision, it's not my vision. It's our collective vision.[92]

Leaders must develop and implement a vision. A vision may or may not succeed; it depends on whether or not everything else happens according to an organization's strategy. As Mark Hurd, Hewlett-Packard's former CEO, humorously points out: "Without execution, vision is just another word for hallucination."[93]

In a survey of executives from 20 different countries, respondents were asked what they believed were a leader's key traits.[94] Ninety-eight percent responded that "a strong sense of vision" was the most important. Similarly, when asked about the critical knowledge skills, the leaders cited "strategy formulation to achieve a vision" as the most important skill. In other words, managers need to have not only a vision but also a plan to implement it. Regretfully, 90 percent reported a lack of confidence in their own skills and ability to conceive a vision. For example, T. J. Rogers, CEO of Cypress Semiconductor, an electronic-chip maker that faced some difficulties in 1992, lamented that his own shortsightedness caused the danger: "I did not have the 50,000-foot view, and got caught."[95]

EXHIBIT 1.6 A Hierarchy of Goals

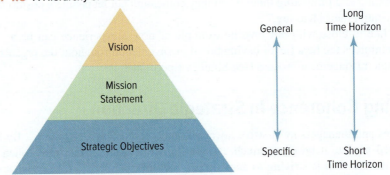

One of the most famous examples of a vision is Disneyland's: "To be the happiest place on earth." Other examples are:

- "Restoring patients to full life." (Medtronic)
- "We want to satisfy all of our customers' financial needs and help them succeed financially." (Wells Fargo)
- "Our vision is to be the world's best quick service restaurant." (McDonald's)
- "To organize the world's information and make it universally accessible and useful." (Google)
- "Connecting the world through games." (Zynga)

Although such visions cannot be accurately measured by a specific indicator of how well they are being achieved, they do provide a fundamental statement of an organization's values, aspirations, and goals. Such visions go well beyond narrow financial objectives, of course, and strive to capture both the minds and hearts of employees.

The vision statement may also contain a slogan, diagram, or picture—whatever grabs attention.[96] The aim is to capture the essence of the more formal parts of the vision in a few words that are easily remembered, yet that evoke the spirit of the entire vision statement. In its 20-year battle with Xerox, Canon's slogan, or battle cry, was "Beat Xerox." Motorola's slogan is "Total Customer Satisfaction." Outboard Marine Corporation's slogan is "To Take the World Boating."

Clearly, vision statements are not a cure-all. Sometimes they backfire and erode a company's credibility. Visions fail for many reasons, including the following:[97]

The Walk Doesn't Match the Talk An idealistic vision can arouse employee enthusiasm. However, that same enthusiasm can be quickly dashed if employees find that senior management's behavior is not consistent with the vision. Often, vision is a sloganeering campaign of new buzzwords and empty platitudes like "devotion to the customer," "teamwork," or "total quality" that aren't consistently backed by management's action.

Irrelevance Visions created in a vacuum—unrelated to environmental threats or opportunities or an organization's resources and capabilities—often ignore the needs of those who are expected to buy into them. Employees reject visions that are not anchored in reality.

Not the Holy Grail Managers often search continually for the one elusive solution that will solve their firm's problems—that is, the next "holy grail" of management. They may have tried other management fads only to find that they fell short of their expectations. However, they remain convinced that one exists. A vision simply cannot be viewed as a magic cure for an organization's illness.

Too Much Focus Leads to Missed Opportunities The downside of too much focus is that in directing people and resources toward a grandiose vision, losses can be devastating. Consider Samsung's ambitious venture into automobile manufacturing:

> In 1992, Kun-Hee Lee, chairman of South Korea's Samsung Group, created a bold strategy to become one of the 10 largest car makers by 2010. Seduced by the clarity of the vision, Samsung bypassed staged entry through a joint venture or initial supply contract. Instead, Samsung borrowed heavily to build a state-of-the-art research and design facility and erect a greenfield factory, complete with cutting-edge robotics. Samsung Auto suffered operating losses and crushing interest charges from the beginning. And within a few years the business was divested for a fraction of the initial investment.[98]

An Ideal Future Irreconciled with the Present   Although visions are not designed to mirror reality, they must be anchored somehow in it. People have difficulty identifying with a vision that paints a rosy picture of the future but does not account for the often hostile environment in which the firm competes or that ignores some of the firm's weaknesses.

Mission Statements

A company's **mission statement** differs from its vision in that it encompasses both the purpose of the company and the basis of competition and competitive advantage.

Exhibit 1.7 contains the vision statement and mission statement of WellPoint Health Network, a giant $73 billion managed health care organization. Note that while the vision statement is broad-based, the mission statement is more specific and focused on the means by which the firm will compete.

Effective mission statements incorporate the concept of stakeholder management, suggesting that organizations must respond to multiple constituencies. Customers, employees, suppliers, and owners are the primary stakeholders, but others may also play an important role. Mission statements also have the greatest impact when they reflect an organization's enduring, overarching strategic priorities and competitive positioning. Mission statements also can vary in length and specificity. The three mission statements below illustrate these issues.

- "To produce superior financial returns for our shareholders as we serve our customers with the highest quality transportation, logistics, and e-commerce." (Federal Express)
- "Build the best product, cause no unnecessary harm, use business to inspire and implement solutions to the environmental crisis." (Patagonia)
- "To be the very best in the business. Our game plan is status go . . . we are constantly looking ahead, building on our strengths, and reaching for new goals. In our quest of these goals, we look at the three stars of the Brinker logo and are reminded of the basic values that are the strength of this company . . . People, Quality and Profitability. Everything we do at Brinker must support these core values. We also look at the eight golden flames depicted in our logo, and are reminded of the fire that ignites our mission and makes up the heart and soul of this incredible company. These flames are: Customers, Food, Team, Concepts, Culture, Partners, Community, and Shareholders. As keeper of these flames, we will continue to build on our strengths and work together to be the best in the business." (Brinker International, whose restaurant chains include Chili's and On the Border)[99]

Few mission statements identify profit or any other financial indicator as the sole purpose of the firm. Indeed, many do not even mention profit or shareholder return.[100] Employees of organizations or departments are usually the mission's most important audience. For them, the mission should help to build a common understanding of purpose and commitment to nurture.

EXHIBIT 1.7

Comparing WellPoint Health Network's Vision and Mission

Vision
WellPoint *will redefine our industry:*
Through a new generation of consumer-friendly products that put individuals back in control of their future.

Mission
The WellPoint companies provide health *security* by offering a *choice* of quality branded health and related financial services *designed* to meet the *changing* expectations of individuals, families, and their sponsors throughout a *lifelong* relationship.

Source: WellPoint Health Network company records.

HOW THE JAMES IRVINE FOUNDATION REDEFINED ITS MISSION

Several years ago the James Irvine Foundation undertook its first comprehensive strategic planning effort in more than a decade. The foundation's mission is "to expand opportunity for the people of California to participate in a vibrant, successful, and inclusive society." As of 2014, it had about $1.8 billion in assets, and it awarded $69 million in grants in 2013.

Over time, however, this inspirational statement had led to a sprawling portfolio of grants, and the foundation's leaders had come to recognize that it was far too open-ended to be useful in making program and funding decisions. To decide where the foundation could have the most lasting impact, they commissioned research on a broad range of issues facing Californians, including education, health, and the environment. Through its research, the foundation found that changing demographics, technology, and audience expectations would influence dramatically how art museums, symphony orchestras, and theaters would run their establishments.

The senior team was soon flooded in data. Some findings leaped out—the significant challenges facing California's youth, for one. But given the magnitude of the state's needs, the team quickly realized that numbers alone could justify a large variety of funding decisions. So it honed in on three critical organizational values:

addressing the root causes rather than crises, enabling Californians to help themselves, and working on problems that might attract like-minded partners or funders. Guided by both values and data, the team redefined its mission and selected youths aged 14 to 24 as the primary beneficiaries of its funding, and education as the primary lever for change. For example, in 2012 the foundation approved seven grants totaling more than $1.75 million to help increase the number of low-income youth who complete high school on time and attain a postsecondary degree by the age of 25.

The Irvine Foundation had to make some hard decisions: What, for instance, should it do about its long-standing commitment to the arts? The arts did not emerge from the data as a critical challenge, but decades of investment there had given Irvine unique assets in the form of reputation and relationships. Furthermore, its exit would have a disproportionately harsh impact on the field. Thus, the foundation's leaders continued arts funding, albeit at a much lower level, and devised a new arts strategy in 2012. This new strategy offers risk capital to encourage and fuel arts engagement by local organizations.

Sources: Perry, S. 2014. James Irvine Foundation taps interim CEO for permanent post. *philanthropy.com,* September 18: np. Ditkoff, S. W. & Colby. S. J. 2009. Galvanizing philanthropy. *Harvard Business Review,* 87(11): 109; A conversation with John Jenks, Irvine's chief investment officer. Undated. *www.irvine.com,* np; Emerling, S. 2009. James Irvine Foundation rewards the innovators. *www.articles.latimes.com,* June 17: np; and Ramirez, J. 2012. Our new arts strategy's first grants. *www.irvine.com,* June 22: np.

A good mission statement, by addressing each principal theme, must communicate why an organization is special and different. Two studies that linked corporate values and mission statements with financial performance found that the most successful firms mentioned values other than profits. The less successful firms focused almost entirely on profitability.[101] In essence, profit is the metaphorical equivalent of oxygen, food, and water that the body requires. They are not the point of life, but without them, there is no life.

Vision statements tend to be quite enduring and seldom change. However, a firm's mission can and should change when competitive conditions dramatically change or the firm is faced with new threats or opportunities.

The transformation of the James Irvine Foundation is described in Strategy Spotlight 1.5. This philanthropic foundation switched from the broad mission "to expand opportunity for the people of California" to a narrow mission that focuses on the education of youths aged 14 to 24.

Strategic Objectives

Strategic objectives are used to operationalize the mission statement.[102] That is, they help to provide guidance on how the organization can fulfill or move toward the "higher goals" in the goal hierarchy—the mission and vision. Thus, they are more specific and cover a more well-defined time frame. Setting objectives demands a yardstick to measure the fulfillment of the objectives.[103]

Exhibit 1.8 lists several firms' strategic objectives—both financial and nonfinancial. While most of them are directed toward generating greater profits and returns for the owners of the business, others are directed at customers or society at large.

> **strategic objectives**
> a set of organizational goals that are used to operationalize the mission statement and that are specific and cover a well-defined time frame.

EXHIBIT 1.8
Strategic Objectives

Strategic Objectives (Financial)

- Increase sales growth 6 percent to 8 percent and accelerate core net earnings growth from 13 percent to 15 percent per share in each of the next 5 years. (Procter & Gamble)
- Generate Internet-related revenue of $1.5 billion. (AutoNation)
- Increase the contribution of Banking Group earnings from investments, brokerage, and insurance from 16 percent to 25 percent. (Wells Fargo)
- Cut corporate overhead costs by $30 million per year. (Fortune Brands)

Strategic Objectives (Nonfinancial)

- We want a majority of our customers, when surveyed, to say they consider Wells Fargo the best financial institution in the community. (Wells Fargo)
- Reduce volatile air emissions 15 percent by 2015 from 2010 base year, indexed to net sales. (3M)
- Our goal is to help save 100,000 more lives each year. (Varian Medical Systems)
- We want to be the top-ranked supplier to our customers. (PPG)

Sources: Company documents and annual reports.

For objectives to be meaningful, they need to satisfy several criteria. An objective must be:

- *Measurable.* There must be at least one indicator (or yardstick) that measures progress against fulfilling the objective.
- *Specific.* This provides a clear message as to what needs to be accomplished.
- *Appropriate.* It must be consistent with the organization's vision and mission.
- *Realistic.* It must be an achievable target given the organization's capabilities and opportunities in the environment. In essence, it must be challenging but doable.
- *Timely.* There must be a time frame for achieving the objective. As the economist John Maynard Keynes once said, "In the long run, we are all dead!"

When objectives satisfy the above criteria, there are many benefits. First, they help to channel all employees' efforts toward common goals. This helps the organization concentrate and conserve valuable resources and work collectively in a timely manner.

Second, challenging objectives can help to motivate and inspire employees to higher levels of commitment and effort. Much research has supported the notion that people work harder when they are striving toward specific goals instead of being asked simply to "do their best."

Third, as we noted earlier in the chapter, there is always the potential for different parts of an organization to pursue their own goals rather than overall company goals. Although well intentioned, these may work at cross-purposes to the organization as a whole. Meaningful objectives thus help to resolve conflicts when they arise.

Finally, proper objectives provide a yardstick for rewards and incentives. They will ensure a greater sense of equity or fairness when rewards are allocated.

A caveat: When formulating strategic objectives, managers need to remember that too many objectives can result in a lack of focus and diminished results:

> A few years ago CEO Tony Petrucciani and his team at Single Source Systems, a software firm in Fishers, Indiana, set 15 annual objectives, such as automating some of its software functions. However, the firm, which got distracted by having so many items on its objective list, missed its $8.1 million revenue benchmark by 11 percent. "Nobody focused on any one thing," he says. Going forward, Petrucciani decided to set just a few key priorities. This helped the company to meet its goal of $10 million in sales. Sometimes, less is more![104]

In addition to the above, organizations have lower-level objectives that are more specific than strategic objectives. These are often referred to as short-term objectives—essential components of a firm's "action plan" that are critical in implementing the firm's chosen strategy. We discuss these issues in detail in Chapter 9.

ISSUE FOR DEBATE

Seventh Generation's Decision Dilemma

A strike idled 67,300 workers of the United Food and Commercial Workers (UFCW) who worked at Albertsons, Ralphs, and Vons—all large grocery store chains. These stores sold natural home products made by Seventh Generation, a socially conscious company. Interestingly, the inspiration for its name came from the Great Law of the Haudenosaunee. (This Law of Peace of the Iroquois Confederacy in North America has its roots in the 14th century.) The law states that "in our every deliberation we must consider the impact of our decisions on the next seven generations." Accordingly, the company's mission is "To inspire a revolution that nurtures the health of the next seven generations," and its values are to "care wholeheartedly, collaborate deliberately, nurture nature, innovate disruptively, and be a trusted brand."

Clearly, Seventh Generation faced a dilemma: On the one hand, it believed that the strikers had a just cause. However, if it honored the strikers by not crossing the picket lines, the firm would lose the shelf space for its products in the stores it had worked so hard to secure. Honoring the strikers would also erode its trust with the large grocery stores. On the other hand, if Seventh Generation ignored the strikers and proceeded to send its products to the stores, it would be compromising its values and thereby losing trust and credibility with several stakeholders—its customers, distributors, and employees.

Discussion Questions

1. How important should the Seventh Generation values be considered when deciding what to do?
2. How can Seventh Generation solve this dilemma?

Sources: Russo, M. V. 2010. *Companies on a mission: Entrepreneurial strategies for growing sustainably, responsibly, and profitably.* Stanford: Stanford University Press: 94–96; Seventh Generation. 2012. Seventh generation's mission—Corporate social responsibility. *www.seventhgeneration.com*, np; Foster, A. C. 2004. Major work stoppage in 2003. U.S. Bureau of Labor and Statistics. Compensation and Working Conditions. *www.bls.gov*, November 23: np; Fast Company. 2008. 45 social entrepreneurs who are changing the world. Profits with purpose: Seventh Generation. *www.fastcompany*, np; and Ratical. Undated. The six nations: Oldest living participatory democracy on earth. *www.ratical.org*, np.

Reflecting on Career Implications . . .

▣ **Attributes of Strategic Management:** The attributes of strategic management described in this chapter are applicable to your personal careers as well. What are your overall goals and objectives? Who are the stakeholders you have to consider in making your career decisions (family, community, etc.)? What trade-offs do you see between your long-term and short-term goals?

▣ **Intended versus Emergent Strategies:** While you may have planned your career trajectory carefully, don't be too tied to it. Strive to take advantage of new opportunities as they arise. Many promising career opportunities may "emerge" that were not part of your intended career strategy or your specific job assignment. Take initiative by pursuing opportunities to get additional training (e.g., learn a software or a statistical package), volunteering for a short-term overseas assignment, etc. You may be in a better position to take advantage of such emergent opportunities if you take the effort to prepare for them. For example, learning a foreign language may position you better for an overseas opportunity.

▣ **Ambidexterity:** In Strategy Spotlight 1.1, we discussed the four most important traits of ambidextrous individuals. These include looking for opportunities beyond the description of one's job, seeking out opportunities to collaborate with others, building internal networks, and multitasking. Evaluate yourself along each of these criteria. If you score low, think of ways in which you can improve your ambidexterity.

▣ **Strategic Coherence:** What is the mission of your organization? What are the strategic objectives of the department or unit you are working for? In what ways does your own role contribute to the mission and objectives? What can you do differently in order to help the organization attain its mission and strategic objectives?

▣ **Strategic Coherence:** Setting strategic objectives is important in your personal career as well. Identify and write down three or four important strategic objectives you want to accomplish in the next few years (finish your degree, find a better-paying job, etc.). Are you allocating your resources (time, money, etc.) to enable you to achieve these objectives? Are your objectives measurable, timely, realistic, specific, and appropriate?

We began this introductory chapter by defining strategic management and articulating some of its key attributes. Strategic management is defined as "consisting of the analyses, decisions, and actions an organization undertakes to create and sustain competitive advantages." The issue of how and why some firms outperform others in the marketplace is central to the study of strategic management. Strategic management has four key attributes: It is directed at overall organizational goals, includes multiple stakeholders, incorporates both short-term and long-term perspectives, and incorporates trade-offs between efficiency and effectiveness.

The second section discussed the strategic management process. Here, we paralleled the above definition of strategic management and focused on three core activities in the strategic management process—strategy analysis, strategy formulation, and strategy implementation. We noted how each of these activities is highly interrelated to and interdependent on the others. We also discussed how each of the first 12 chapters in this text fits into the three core activities.

Next, we introduced two important concepts—corporate governance and stakeholder management—which must be taken into account throughout the strategic management process. Governance mechanisms can be broadly divided into two groups: internal and external. Internal governance mechanisms include shareholders (owners), management (led by the chief executive officer), and the board of directors. External control is exercised by auditors, banks, analysts, and an active business press as well as the threat of takeovers. We identified five key stakeholders in all organizations: owners, customers, suppliers, employees, and society at large. Successful firms go beyond an overriding focus on satisfying solely the interests of owners. Rather, they recognize the inherent conflicts that arise among the demands of the various stakeholders as well as the need to endeavor to attain "symbiosis"—that is, interdependence and mutual benefit—among the various stakeholder groups. Managers must also recognize the need to act in a socially responsible manner which, if done effectively, can enhance a firm's innovativeness. The "shared value" approach represents an innovative perspective on creating value for the firm and society at the same time. The managers also should recognize and incorporate issues related to environmental sustainability in their strategic actions.

In the fourth section, we discussed factors that have accelerated the rate of unpredictable change that managers face today. Such factors, and the combination of them, have increased the need for managers and employees throughout the organization to have a strategic management perspective and to become more empowered.

The final section addressed the need for consistency among a firm's vision, mission, and strategic objectives. Collectively, they form an organization's hierarchy of goals. Visions should evoke powerful and compelling mental images. However, they are not very specific. Strategic objectives, on the other hand, are much more specific and are vital to ensuring that the organization is striving toward fulfilling its vision and mission.

SUMMARY REVIEW QUESTIONS

1. How is "strategic management" defined in the text, and what are its four key attributes?
2. Briefly discuss the three key activities in the strategic management process. Why is it important for managers to recognize the interdependent nature of these activities?
3. Explain the concept of "stakeholder management." Why shouldn't managers be solely interested in stockholder management, that is, maximizing the returns for owners of the firm—its shareholders?
4. What is "corporate governance"? What are its three key elements, and how can it be improved?
5. How can "symbiosis" (interdependence, mutual benefit) be achieved among a firm's stakeholders?
6. Why do firms need to have a greater strategic management perspective and empowerment in the strategic management process throughout the organization?
7. What is meant by a "hierarchy of goals"? What are the main components of it, and why must consistency be achieved among them?

key terms

romantic view of
   leadership 5
external control view of
   leadership 6
strategic management 8
strategy 8
competitive advantage 8
operational
   effectiveness 8
stakeholders 9
effectiveness 10
efficiency 10
ambidexterity 10

strategic management
   process 10
intended strategy 11
realized strategy 11
strategy analysis 12
strategy formulation 14
strategy implementation 14
corporate
   governance 15
stakeholder
   management 16
social responsibility 18
triple bottom line 19
hierarchy of goals 24
vision 24
mission statement 26
strategic objectives 27

experiential exercise

Using the Internet or library sources, select four organizations—two in the private sector and two in the public sector. Find their mission statements. Complete the following exhibit by identifying the stakeholders that are mentioned. Evaluate the differences between firms in the private sector and those in the public sector.

Organization Name			
Mission Statement			
Stakeholders (√ = mentioned)			
1. Customers			
2. Suppliers			
3. Managers/employees			
4. Community-at-large			
5. Owners			
6. Others?			
7. Others?			

application questions & exercises

1. Go to the Internet and look up one of these company sites: *www.walmart.com*, *www.ge.com*, or *www.fordmotor.com*. What are some of the key events that would represent the "romantic" perspective of leadership? What are some of the key events that depict the "external control" perspective of leadership?

2. Select a company that competes in an industry in which you are interested. What are some of the recent demands that stakeholders have placed on this company? Can you find examples of how the company is trying to develop "symbiosis" (interdependence and mutual benefit) among its stakeholders? (Use the Internet and library resources.)

3. Provide examples of companies that are actively trying to increase the amount of empowerment in the strategic management process throughout the organization. Do these companies seem to be having positive outcomes? Why? Why not?

4. Look up the vision statements and/or mission statements for a few companies. Do you feel that they are constructive and useful as a means of motivating employees and providing a strong strategic direction? Why? Why not? (*Note:* Annual reports, along with the Internet, may be good sources of information.)

ethics questions

1. A company focuses solely on short-term profits to provide the greatest return to the owners of the business (i.e., the shareholders in a publicly held firm). What ethical issues could this raise?

2. A firm has spent some time—with input from managers at all levels—on developing a vision statement and a mission statement. Over time, however, the behavior of some executives is contrary to these statements. Could this raise some ethical issues?

references

1. Gunther, M. 2010. Fallen angels. *Fortune,* November 1: 75–78.

2. The four bulleted items are drawn from Karlgaard, R. 2014. *The soft edge.* San Francisco: Jossey-Bass; Lim, P. J. 2014. As Nasdaq rocks, don't get rolled. *CNNmoney.com*, May: 46; Downess, L. & Nunes, P. 2014. *Big bang disruption.* New York: Penguin; Anonymous. 2014. One world. *The Economist,* May 31: 16; and Colvin, G. 2014. Four things that worry business. *Fortune,* October 27: 32.

3. Donahue, J. 2012. What do CEOs admire? *Fortune,* March 19: 143.

4. For a discussion of the "romantic" versus "external control" perspective, refer to Meindl, J. R. 1987. The romance of leadership and the evaluation of organizational performance. *Academy of Management Journal,* 30: 92–109; and Pfeffer, J. & Salancik, G. R. 1978. *The external control of organizations: A resource dependence perspective.* New York: Harper & Row.

5. A recent perspective on the "romantic view" of leadership is provided by Mintzberg, H. 2004. Leadership and management development: An afterword. *Academy of Management Executive,* 18(3): 140–142.

6. For a discussion of the best and worst managers for 2008, read Anonymous. 2009. The best managers. *BusinessWeek,* January 19: 40–41; and The worst managers. On page 42 in the same issue.

7. Burrows, P. 2009. Apple without its core? *BusinessWeek,* January 26/ February 2: 31.

8. For a study on the effects of CEOs on firm performance, refer to Kor, Y. Y. & Misangyi, V. F. 2008. *Strategic Management Journal,* 29(11):1357–1368.

9. Charan, R. & Colvin, G. 2010. Directors: A harsh new reality. *money.cnn.com,* October 6: np.

10. Reed, T. 2014. Why JetBlue CEO Dave Barger was chased out by Wall Street. *www.thestreet.com,* September 18: np; and Carey, S. 2014. JetBlue chief to depart; will bag fees arrive? *The Wall Street Journal,* September 10: B1–B2.

11. Dobson, C. 2010. Global airlines lost $1.7 billion due to Iceland ash cloud. *www.theepochtimes.com,* May 23: np; and Pylas, P. 2011. Nikkei slides 11 percent on radiation fears. *www. finance.yahoo.com,* March 14: np.

12. Ewing, J. 2008. South Africa emerges from the shadows. *BusinessWeek,* December 15: 52–56.

13. For an interesting perspective on the need for strategists to maintain a global mind-set, refer to Begley, T. M. & Boyd, D. P. 2003. The need for a global mind-set. *MIT Sloan Management Review,* 44(2): 25–32.

14. Porter, M. E. 1996. What is strategy? *Harvard Business Review,* 74(6): 61–78.

15. See, for example, Barney, J. B. & Arikan, A. M. 2001. The resource-based view: Origins and implications. In Hitt, M. A., Freeman, R. E., & Harrison, J. S. (Eds.), *Handbook of strategic management:* 124–189. Malden, MA: Blackwell.

16. Porter, M. E. 1996. What is strategy? *Harvard Business Review,* 74(6): 61–78; and Hammonds, K. H. 2001. Michael Porter's big ideas. *Fast Company,* March: 55–56.

17. This section draws upon Dess, G. G. & Miller, A. 1993. *Strategic management.* New York: McGraw-Hill.

18. See, for example, Hrebiniak, L. G. & Joyce, W. F. 1986. The strategic importance of managing myopia. *Sloan Management Review,* 28(1): 5–14.

19. Bryant, A. 2011. *The corner office.* New York: Times Books.

20. For an insightful discussion on how to manage diverse stakeholder groups, refer to Rondinelli, D. A. & London, T. 2003. How corporations and environmental groups cooperate: Assessing cross-sector alliances and collaborations. *Academy of Management Executive,* 17(1): 61–76.

21. Some dangers of a short-term perspective are addressed in Van Buren, M. E. & Safferstone, T. 2009. The quick wins paradox. *Harvard Business Review,* 67(1): 54–61.

22. Senge, P. 1996. Leading learning organizations: The bold, the powerful, and the invisible. In Hesselbein, F., Goldsmith, M., & Beckhard, R. (Eds.), *The leader of the future:* 41–58. San Francisco: Jossey-Bass.

23. Winston, A. S. 2014. *The big pivot.* Boston: Harvard Business Review.

24. Loeb, M. 1994. Where leaders come from. *Fortune,* September 19: 241 (quoting Warren Bennis).

25. Hemp, P. 2004. An interview with CEO Kevin Sharer. *Harvard Business Review,* 82(7/8): 66–74.

26. New perspectives on "management models" are addressed in Birkinshaw, J. & Goddard, J. 2009. What is your management model? *MIT Sloan Management Review,* 50(2): 81–90.

27. Mintzberg, H. 1985. Of strategies: Deliberate and emergent. *Strategic Management Journal,* 6: 257–272.

28. Some interesting insights on decision-making processes are found in Nutt, P. C. 2008. Investigating the success of decision making processes. *Journal of Management Studies,* 45(2): 425–455.

29. Smith, J. 2014. Go-to lawyers are in-house. *The Wall Street Journal,* September 15: B6.

30. Bryant, A. 2009. The corner office. *nytimes.com,* April 25: np.

31. A study investigating the sustainability of competitive advantage is Newbert, S. L. 2008. Value, rareness, competitive advantages, and performance: A conceptual-level empirical investigation of the resource-based view of the firm. *Strategic Management Journal,* 29(7): 745–768.

32. Good insights on mentoring are addressed in DeLong, T. J., Gabarro, J. J., & Lees, R. J. 2008. Why mentoring matters in a hypercompetitive world. *Harvard Business Review,* 66(1): 115–121.

33. Karlgaard, R. 2014. *The soft edge.* San Francisco: Jossey-Bass.

34. A unique perspective on differentiation strategies is Austin, R. D. 2008. High margins and the quest for aesthetic coherence. *Harvard Business Review,* 86(1): 18–19.

35. Some insights on partnering in the global area are discussed in MacCormack, A. & Forbath, T. 2008. *Harvard Business Review,* 66(1): 24, 26.

36. For insights on how firms can be successful in entering new markets in emerging economies, refer to Eyring, M. J., Johnson, M. W., & Nair, H. 2011. New business models in emerging markets. *Harvard Business Review,* 89(1/2): 88–95.

37. *Fortune.* 2012. December 3: 6.

38. An interesting discussion of the challenges of strategy implementation is Neilson, G. L., Martin, K. L., & Powers, E. 2008. The secrets of strategy execution. *Harvard Business Review,* 86(6): 61–70.

39. Interesting perspectives on strategy execution involving the link between strategy and operations are addressed in Kaplan, R. S. & Norton, D. P. 2008. Mastering the management system. *Harvard Business Review,* 66(1): 62–77.

40. An innovative perspective on organizational design is found in Garvin, D. A. & Levesque, L. C. 2008. The multiunit enterprise. *Harvard Business Review,* 86(6): 106–117.

41. Monks, R. & Minow, N. 2001. *Corporate governance* (2nd ed.). Malden, MA: Blackwell.

42. Intel Corp. 2007. *Intel corporation board of directors guidelines on significant corporate governance issues. www.intel.com*

43. Jones, T. J., Felps, W., & Bigley, G. A. 2007. Ethical theory and stakeholder-related decisions: The role of stakeholder culture. *Academy of Management Review,* 32(1): 137–155.

44. For example, see: The best (& worst) managers of the year, 2003. *BusinessWeek,* January 13: 58–92; and Lavelle, M. 2003. Rogues of the year. *Time,* January 6: 33–45.

45. Baer, D. A. 2014. The West's bruised confidence in capitalism. *The Wall Street Journal,* September 22: A17; and Miller, D. 2014. Greatness is gone. *Dallas Morning News,* October 26: 1 D.

46. Hessel, E. & Woolley, S. 2008. Your money or your life. *Forbes,* October 27: 52.

47. Task, A. 2012. Finance CEO pay rose 20% in 2011, even as stocks stumbled. *www.finance.yahoo.com,* June 5: np.

48. Matthews, C. 2014. 5 companies that pay CEOs big for a job poorly done. *fortune.com,* June 17: np.

49. Some interesting insights on the role of activist investors can be found in Greenwood, R. & Schol, M. 2008. When (not) to listen to activist investors. *Harvard Business Review,* 66(1): 23–24.

50. For an interesting perspective on the changing role of boards of directors, refer to Lawler, E. & Finegold, D. 2005. Rethinking governance. *MIT Sloan Management Review,* 46(2): 67–70.

51. Benz, M. & Frey, B. S. 2007. Corporate governance: What can we learn from public governance? *Academy of Management Review,* 32(1): 92–104.

52. The salience of shareholder value is addressed in Carrott, G. T. & Jackson, S. E. 2009. Shareholder value must top the CEO's agenda. *Harvard Business Review,* 67(1): 22–24.

53. Stakeholder symbiosis. 1998. *Fortune,* March 30: S2.

54. An excellent review of stakeholder management theory can be found in Laplume, A. O., Sonpar, K., & Litz, R. A. 2008. Stakeholder theory: Reviewing a theory that moves us. *Journal of Management,* 34(6): 1152–1189.

55. For a definitive, recent discussion of the stakeholder concept, refer to Freeman, R. E. & McVae, J. 2001. A stakeholder approach to strategic management. In Hitt, M. A., Freeman, R. E., & Harrison, J. S. (Eds.), *Handbook of strategic management:* 189–207. Malden, MA: Blackwell.

56. Harrison, J. S., Bosse, D. A., & Phillips, R. A. 2010. Managing for stakeholders, stakeholder utility functions, and competitive advantage. *Strategic Management Journal,* 31(1): 58–74.

57. For an insightful discussion on the role of business in society, refer to Handy, op. cit.

58. Camillus, J. 2008. Strategy as a wicked problem. *Harvard Business Review,* 86(5): 100–101.

59. Stakeholder symbiosis. op. cit., p. S3.

60. Sidhu, I. 2010. *Doing both.* Upper Saddle River, NJ: FT Press, 7–8.

61. Thomas, J. G. 2000. Macro-environmetal forces. In Helms, M. M. (Ed.), *Encyclopedia of management* (4th ed.): 516–520. Farmington Hills, MI: Gale Group.

62. For a strong advocacy position on the need for corporate values and social responsibility, read Hollender, J. 2004. What matters most: Corporate values and social responsibility. *California Management Review,* 46(4): 111–119.

63. Waddock, S. & Bodwell, C. 2004. Managing responsibility: What can be learned from the quality movement. *California Management Review,* 47(1): 25–37.

64. For a discussion of the role of alliances and collaboration on corporate social responsibility initiatives, refer to Pearce, J. A. II. & Doh, J. P. 2005. The high impact of collaborative social initiatives. *MIT Sloan Management Review,* 46(3): 30–40.

65. Insights on ethical behavior and performance are addressed in Trudel, R. & Cotte, J. 2009. *MIT Sloan Management Review,* 50(2): 61–68.

66. Bhattacharya, C. B. & Sen, S. 2004, Doing better at doing good: When, why, and how consumers respond to corporate social initiatives. *California Management Review,* 47(1): 9–24.

67. For some findings on the relationship between corporate social responsibility and firm performance, see Margolis, J. D. & Elfenbein, H. A. 2008. *Harvard Business Review,* 86(1): 19–20.

68. Cone Corporate Citizenship Study, 2002, www.coneinc.com.

69. Refer to www.bsr.org.

70. For an insightful discussion of the risks and opportunities associated with global warming, refer to Lash, J. & Wellington, F. 2007. Competitive advantage on a warming planet. *Harvard Business Review,* 85(3): 94–102.

71. This section draws on Hart, S. L. 1997. Beyond greening: Strategies for a sustainable world. *Harvard Business Review,* 75(1): 66–76; and Berry, M. A. & Rondinelli, D. A. 1998. Proactive corporate environmental management: A new industrial revolution. *Academy of Management Executive,* 12(2): 38–50.

72. Hart, op. cit., p. 67.

73. For a creative perspective on environmental sustainability and competitive advantage as well as ethical implications, read Ehrenfeld, J. R. 2005. The roots of sustainability. *MIT Sloan Management Review,* 46(2): 23–25.

74. McKinsey & Company. 1991. *The corporate response to the environmental challenge.* Summary Report. Amsterdam: McKinsey & Company.

75. Delmas, M. A. & Montes-Sancho, M. J. 2010. Voluntary agreements to improve environmental quality: Symbolic and substantive cooperation. *Strategic Management Journal,* 31(6): 575–601.

76. Vogel, D. J. 2005. Is there a market for virtue? The business case for corporate social responsibility. *California Management Review,* 47(4): 19–36.

77. Esty, D. C. & Charnovitz, S. 2012. Green rules to drive innovation. *Harvard Business Review,* 90(3): 120–123.

78. Chamberlain, M. 2013. Socially responsible investing: What you need to know. *Forbes.com,* April 24: np.

79. Kaahwarski, T. 2010. It pays to be good. *Bloomberg Businessweek,* February 1 to February 8: 69.

80. This discussion draws on Kuehn, K. & McIntire, L. 2014. Sustainability a CFO can love. *Harvard Business Review,* 92(4): 66–74; and Esty, D. C. & Winston, A. S. 2009. *Green to gold.* Hoboken, NJ: Wiley.

81. Senge, P. M. 1990. The leader's new work: Building learning organizations. *Sloan Management Review,* 32(1): 7–23.

82. For an interesting perspective on the role of middle managers in the strategic management process, refer to Huy, Q. H. 2001. In praise of middle managers. *Harvard Business Review,* 79(8): 72–81.

83. Senge, 1996, op. cit., pp. 41–58.

84. Kets de Vries, M. F. R. 1998. Charisma in action: The transformational abilities of Virgin's Richard Branson and ABB's Percy Barnevik. *Organizational Dynamics,* 26(3): 7–21.

85. Hamel, G. 2006. The why, what, and how of management innovation. *Harvard Business Review,* 84(2): 72–84.

86. Bryant, A. 2011. *The corner office.* New York: St. Martin's/Griffin, 6.

87. An interesting discussion on how to translate top management's goals into concrete actions is found in Bungay, S. 2011. How to make the most of your company's strategy. *Harvard Business Review,* 89(1/2): 132–140.

88. Bryant, A. 2011. *The corner office.* New York: St. Martin's/Griffin, 171.

89. An insightful discussion about the role of vision, mission, and strategic objectives can be found in Collis, D. J. & Rukstad, M. G. 2008. Can you say what your strategy is? *Harvard Business Review,* 66(4): 82–90.

90. Our discussion draws on a variety of sources. These include Lipton, M. 1996. Demystifying the development of an organizational vision. *Sloan Management Review,* 37(4): 83–92; Bart, C. K. 2000. Lasting inspiration. *CA Magazine,* May: 49–50; and Quigley, J. V. 1994. Vision: How leaders develop it, share it, and sustain it. *Business Horizons,* September–October: 37–40.

91. Lipton, op. cit.

92. Bryant, A. 2011. *The corner office.* New York: St. Martin's/Griffin, 34.

93. Hardy, Q. 2007. The uncarly. *Forbes,* March 12: 82–90.

94. Some interesting perspectives on gender differences in organizational vision are discussed in Ibarra, H. & Obodaru, O. 2009. Women and the vision thing. *Harvard Business Review,* 67(1): 62–70.

95. Quigley, op. cit.

96. Ibid.

97. Lipton, op. cit. Additional pitfalls are addressed in this article.

98. Sull, D. N. 2005. Strategy as active waiting. *Harvard Business Review,* 83(9): 120–130.

99. Company records.

100. Lipton, op. cit.

101. Sexton, D. A. & Van Aukun, P. M. 1985. A longitudinal study of small business strategic planning. *Journal of Small Business Management,* January: 8–15, cited in Lipton, op. cit.

102. For an insightful perspective on the use of strategic objectives, refer to Chatterjee, S. 2005. Core objectives: Clarity in designing strategy. *California Management Review,* 47(2): 33–49.

103. Ibid.

104. Harnish, V. 2011. Five ways to get your strategy right. *Fortune,* April 11: 42.

photo credits

Analyzing the External Environment of the Firm
Creating Competitive Advantages

After reading this chapter, you should have a good understanding of the following learning objectives:

LO2.1 The importance of developing forecasts of the business environment.

LO2.2 Why environmental scanning, environmental monitoring, and collecting competitive intelligence are critical inputs to forecasting.

LO2.3 Why scenario planning is a useful technique for firms competing in industries characterized by unpredictability and change.

LO2.4 The impact of the general environment on a firm's strategies and performance.

LO2.5 How forces in the competitive environment can affect profitability, and how a firm can improve its competitive position by increasing its power vis-à-vis these forces.

LO2.6 How the Internet and digitally based capabilities are affecting the five competitive forces and industry profitability.

LO2.7 The concept of strategic groups and their strategy and performance implications.

Analyzing the external environment is a critical step in recognizing and understanding the opportunities and threats that organizations face. And here is where some companies fail to do a good job.

Consider the example of Salemi Industries and the launch of its product, Cell Zone, in 2005. Although it tried to carefully analyze its potential market, it misread the market's demand for the product and paid a steep price for its mistake.[1] Mobile phone usage was sharply increasing, and its founder observed that patrons in places such as restaurants would be annoyed by the chatter of a nearby guest having a private (but loud!) conversation. Salemi Industries interpreted this observation as an opportunity to create the Cell Zone: a "commercial sound resistant cell phone booth that provides a convenient and disturbance-free environment to place and receive phone calls . . . with a design feature to promote product or service on its curvilinear outer shell," according to the firm's website.

Salemi Industries' key error was that it failed to take into consideration an emerging technology—the increasing popularity of text messaging and other nonvoice communication technology applications and how that would affect the sales of its product. In addition to this technology shift, the target locations (restaurants) thought the price ($3,500) was too steep, and they were not interested in or willing to give up productive square footage for patrons to hold private conversations. Not surprisingly, the firm has sold only 300 units (100 of them in college libraries), and Salemi Industries has lost over $650,000 to date.

Discussion Questions

1. What is the biggest stumbling block for Cell Zone?
2. Are there other market segments where Cell Zone might work?

Successful managers must recognize opportunities and threats in their firm's external environment. They must be aware of what's going on outside their company. If they focus exclusively on the efficiency of internal operations, the firm may degenerate into the world's most efficient producer of buggy whips, typewriters, or carbon paper. But if they miscalculate the market, opportunities will be lost—hardly an enviable position for their firm. As we saw from the Cell Zone example, misreading the market can lead to negative consequences.

In *Competing for the Future,* Gary Hamel and C. K. Prahalad suggest that "every manager carries around in his or her head a set of biases, assumptions, and presuppositions about the structure of the relevant 'industry,' about how one makes money in the industry, about who the competition is and isn't, about who the customers are and aren't, and so on."[2] Environmental analysis requires you to continually question such assumptions. Peter Drucker, considered the father of modern management, labeled these interrelated sets of assumptions the "theory of the business."[3] The struggle of Groupon (Chapter 1) clearly illustrates that if a company does not keep pace with changes in the nature of competition, it becomes difficult to sustain competitive advantages and deliver strong financial results.

A firm's strategy may be good at one point in time, but it may go astray when management's frame of reference gets out of touch with the realities of the actual business situation. This results when management's assumptions, premises, or beliefs are incorrect or when internal inconsistencies among them render the overall "theory of the business" invalid.

As Warren Buffett, investor extraordinaire, colorfully notes, "Beware of past performance 'proofs.' If history books were the key to riches, the Forbes 400 would consist of librarians."

In the business world, many once-successful firms have fallen. Today we may wonder who will be the next Blockbuster, Borders, Circuit City, or Radio Shack.

Creating the Environmentally Aware Organization

LO2.1

The importance of developing forecasts of the business environment.

perceptual acuity
the ability to sense what is coming before the fog clears.

So how do managers become environmentally aware?[4] Ram Charan, an adviser to many Fortune 500 CEOs, provides some useful insights with his concept of **perceptual acuity.**[5] He defines it as "the ability to sense what is coming before the fog clears." He draws on Ted Turner as an example: Turner saw the potential of 24-hour news before anyone else did. All the ingredients were there, but no others connected them until he created CNN. Like Turner, the best CEOs are compulsively tuned to the external environment and seem to have a sixth sense that picks up anomalies and detects early warning signals which may represent key threats or opportunities.

How can perceptual acuity be improved? Although many CEOs may complain that the top job is a lonely one, they can't do it effectively by sitting alone in their office. Instead, high-performing CEOs are constantly meeting with people and searching out information. Charan provides three examples:

- One CEO gets together with his critical people for half a day every eight weeks to discuss what's new and what's going on in the world. The setting is informal, and outsiders often attend. The participants look beyond the lens of their industry because some trends that affect one industry may impact others later on.
- Another CEO meets four times a year with about four other CEOS of large, but noncompeting, diverse global companies. Examining the world from multiple perspectives, they share their thinking about how different trends may develop. The CEO then goes back to his own weekly management meeting and throws out "a bunch of hand grenades to shake up people's thinking."
- Two companies ask outsiders to critique strategy during their board's strategy sessions. Such input typically leads to spirited discussions that provide valued input on the hinge assumptions and options that are under consideration. Once, the focus was on pinpointing the risk inherent in a certain strategy. Now, discussions have led to finding that the company was missing a valuable opportunity.

We will now address three important processes—scanning, monitoring, and gathering competitive intelligence—used to develop forecasts.[6] Exhibit 2.1 illustrates relationships among these important activities. We also discuss the importance of scenario planning in anticipating major future changes in the external environment and the role of SWOT analysis.[7]

EXHIBIT 2.1 Inputs to Forecasting

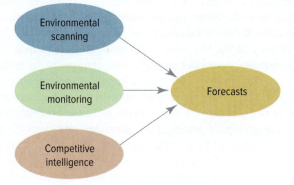

The Role of Scanning, Monitoring, Competitive Intelligence, and Forecasting

LO2.2

Environmental Scanning   **Environmental scanning** involves surveillance of a firm's external environment to predict environmental changes and detect changes already under way.[8,9] This alerts the organization to critical trends and events before changes develop a discernible pattern and before competitors recognize them.[10] Otherwise, the firm may be forced into a reactive mode.[11]

Experts agree that spotting key trends requires a combination of knowing your business and your customer as well as keeping an eye on what's happening around you. Such a big-picture/small-picture view enables you to better identify the emerging trends that will affect your business.

Leading firms in an industry can also be a key indicator of emerging trends.[12] For example, with its wide range of household goods, Procter & Gamble is a barometer for consumer spending. Any sign that it can sell more of its premium products without cutting prices sharply indicates that shoppers may finally be becoming less price-sensitive with everyday purchases. In particular, investors will examine the performance of beauty products like Olay moisturizers and CoverGirl cosmetics for evidence that spending on small, discretionary pick-me-ups is improving.

Environmental Monitoring   **Environmental monitoring** tracks the evolution of environmental trends, sequences of events, or streams of activities. They may be trends that the firm came across by accident or ones that were brought to its attention from outside the organization.[13] Monitoring enables firms to evaluate how dramatically environmental trends are changing the competitive landscape.

One of the authors of this text has conducted on-site interviews with executives from several industries to identify indicators that firms monitor as inputs to their strategy process. Examples of such indicators included:

- *A Motel 6 executive.* The number of rooms in the budget segment of the industry in the United States and the difference between the average daily room rate and the consumer price index (CPI).
- *A Pier 1 Imports executive.* Net disposable income (NDI), consumer confidence index, and housing starts.
- *A Johnson & Johnson medical products executive.* Percentage of gross domestic product (GDP) spent on health care, number of active hospital beds, and the size and power of purchasing agents (indicates the concentration of buyers).

Such indices are critical for managers in determining a firm's strategic direction and resource allocation.

Competitive Intelligence   **Competitive intelligence** (CI) helps firms define and understand their industry and identify rivals' strengths and weaknesses.[14] This includes the intelligence gathering associated with collecting data on competitors and interpreting such data. Done properly, competitive intelligence helps a company avoid surprises by anticipating competitors' moves and decreasing response time.[15]

Examples of competitive analysis are evident in daily newspapers and periodicals such as *The Wall Street Journal, Bloomberg Businessweek,* and *Fortune.* For example, banks continually track home loan, auto loan, and certificate of deposit (CD) interest rates charged by rivals. Major airlines change hundreds of fares daily in response to competitors' tactics. Car manufacturers are keenly aware of announced cuts or increases in rivals' production volume, sales, and sales incentives (e.g., rebates and low interest rates on financing). This information is used in their marketing, pricing, and production strategies.

LO2.2

Why environmental scanning, environmental monitoring, and collecting competitive intelligence are critical inputs to forecasting.

environmental scanning
surveillance of a firm's external environment to predict environmental changes and detect changes already under way.

environmental monitoring
a firm's analysis of the external environment that tracks the evolution of environmental trends, sequences of events, or streams of activities.

competitive intelligence
a firm's activities of collecting and interpreting data on competitors, defining and understanding the industry, and identifying competitors' strengths and weaknesses.

Keeping track of competitors has become easier today with the amount of information that is available on the Internet. The following are examples of some websites that companies routinely use for competitive intelligence gathering.[16]

- *Slideshare.* A website for publicly sharing PowerPoint presentations. Marketing teams have embraced the platform and often post detail-rich presentations about their firms and products.
- *Quora.* A question-and-answer site popular among industry insiders who embrace the free flow of information about technical questions.
- *Ispionage.* A site that reveals the ad words that companies are buying, which can often shed light on new campaigns being launched.
- *YouTube.* Great for finding interviews with executives at trade shows.

At times, a firm's aggressive efforts to gather competitive intelligence may lead to unethical or illegal behaviors.[17] Strategy Spotlight 2.1 provides an example of a company, United Technologies, that has set clear guidelines to help prevent unethical behavior.

A word of caution: Executives must be careful to avoid spending so much time and effort tracking the actions of traditional competitors that they ignore new competitors. Further, broad environmental changes and events may have a dramatic impact on a firm's viability. Peter Drucker, wrote:

> Increasingly, a winning strategy will require information about events and conditions outside the institution: noncustomers, technologies other than those currently used by the company and its present competitors, markets not currently served, and so on.[18]

Consider the failure of specialized medical lab Sleep HealthCenters.[19] Until recently, patients suffering from sleep disorders, such as apnea, were forced to undergo expensive overnight visits to sleep clinics, including Sleep HealthCenters, to diagnose their ailments. The firm was launched in 1997 and quickly expanded to over two dozen locations. Revenue soared from nearly $10 million in 1997 to $30 million in 2010.

However, the rapid improvements in the price and performance of wearable monitoring devices changed the business, gradually at first and then suddenly. For one thing, the more comfortable home setting produced more effective measurements. And the quick declines in the cost of wearable monitoring meant patients could get the same results at one-third the price of an overnight stay at a clinic. By 2011, Sleep HealthCenters' revenue began to decline, and the firm closed 20 percent of its locations. In 2012, its death knells sounded: Insurance companies decided to cover the less expensive option. Sleep HealthCenters abruptly closed its doors.

Environmental Forecasting   Environmental scanning, monitoring, and competitive intelligence are important inputs for analyzing the external environment. **Environmental forecasting** involves the development of plausible projections about the direction, scope, speed, and intensity of environmental change.[20] Its purpose is to predict change.[21] It asks: How long will it take a new technology to reach the marketplace? Will the present social concern about an issue result in new legislation? Are current lifestyle trends likely to continue?

Some forecasting issues are much more specific to a particular firm and the industry in which it competes. Consider how important it is for Motel 6 to predict future indicators, such as the number of rooms, in the budget segment of the industry. If its predictions are low, it will build too many units, creating a surplus of room capacity that would drive down room rates.

A danger of forecasting is that managers may view uncertainty as black and white and ignore important gray areas.[22] The problem is that underestimating uncertainty can lead to strategies that neither defend against threats nor take advantage of opportunities.

In 1977 one of the colossal underestimations in business history occurred when Kenneth H. Olsen, president of Digital Equipment Corp., announced, "There is no reason

environmental forecasting
the development of plausible projections about the direction, scope, speed, and intensity of environmental change.

LO2.3

Why scenario planning is a useful technique for firms competing in industries characterized by unpredictability and change.

ETHICAL GUIDELINES ON COMPETITIVE INTELLIGENCE: UNITED TECHNOLOGIES

United Technologies (UT) is a $65 billion global conglomerate composed of world-leading businesses with rich histories of technological pioneering, such as Otis Elevator, Carrier Air Conditioning, and Sikorsky (helicopters). UT believes strongly in a robust code of ethics. One such document is the Code of Ethics Guide on Competitive Intelligence. This encourages managers and workers to ask themselves these five questions whenever they have ethical concerns.

1. Have I done anything that coerced somebody to share this information? Have I, for example, threatened a supplier by indicating that future business opportunities will be influenced by the receipt of information with respect to a competitor?

2. Am I in a place where I should not be? If, for example, I am a field representative with privileges to move around in a customer's facility, have I gone outside the areas permitted? Have I misled anybody in order to gain access?

3. Is the contemplated technique for gathering information evasive, such as sifting through trash or setting up an electronic "snooping" device directed at a competitor's facility from across the street?

4. Have I misled somebody in a way that the person believed sharing information with me was required or would be protected by a confidentiality agreement? Have I, for example, called and misrepresented myself as a government official who was seeking some information for some official purpose?

5. Have I done something to evade or circumvent a system intended to secure or protect information?

Sources: Nelson, B. 2003. The thinker. *Forbes,* March 3: 62–64; The Fuld war room—Survival kit 010. Code of ethics (printed 2/26/01); and *www.yahoo.com.*

---

for individuals to have a computer in their home." The explosion in the personal computer market was not easy to detect in 1977, but it was clearly within the range of possibilities at the time. And, historically, there have been underestimates of the growth potential of new telecommunication services. The electric telegraph was derided by Ralph Waldo Emerson, and the telephone had its skeptics. More recently, an "infamous" McKinsey study in the early 1980s predicted fewer than 1 million cellular users in the United States by 2000. Actually, there were nearly 100 million.[23]

Obviously, poor predictions never go out of vogue. Consider some other "gems"—typically predicted by very knowledgeable people:[24]

- In a January 2014 survey by *The Wall Street Journal,* 49 economists expected oil to end 2014 at about $95 a barrel, up from about $92 at the time of the survey. *(Oil ended the year at about $54 a barrel.)*

- "Freddie Mac and Fannie Mae are fundamentally sound . . . I think they are in good shape going forward." —Barney Frank (D-Mass.), House Financial Services Committee Chairman, July 14, 2008. *(Two months later, the government forced the mortgage giants into conservatorships.)*

- "There is no chance that the iPhone is going to get any significant market share." —Steve Ballmer, former CEO of Microsoft, in 2007. *(The lineup has sold more than 500 million devices.)*

- "I think you guys are just a bunch of hippies selling food to other hippies." —a venture capitalist's response to an invitation to invest in Whole Foods, 1980.

And, going far back in time . . .

- "I don't see how it could possibly be made into a movie." —Margaret Mitchell, author of *Gone with the Wind,* on its potential as a motion picture, after selling the movie rights to producer David O. Selznick in 1936. *("GWTH," as the film would come to be known, became one of the most celebrated movies in history, won 10 Oscars, and broke all box office records.)*

- "The baseball mania has run its course. It has no future as a professional endeavor." —*Cincinnati Gazette* editorial, 1879.

Jason Zweig, an editor at *The Wall Street Journal,* provides an important cautionary note (and rather colorful example!) regarding the need to question the reliability of forecasts: "Humans don't want accuracy; they want assurance . . . people can't stand ignoring all predictions; admitting that the future is unknowable is just too frightening."[25]

The Nobel laureate and retired Stanford University economist Kenneth Arrow did a tour of duty as a weather forecaster for the U.S. Air Force during World War II. Ordered to evaluate mathematical models for predicting the weather one month ahead, he found that they were worthless. Informed of that, his superiors sent back another order: "The Commanding General is well aware that the forecasts are no good. However, he needs them for planning purposes."

scenario analysis

an in-depth approach to environmental forecasting that involves experts' detailed assessments of societal trends, economics, politics, technology, or other dimensions of the external environment.

Scenario Analysis   **Scenario analysis** is a more in-depth approach to forecasting. It draws on a range of disciplines and interests, among them economics, psychology, sociology, and demographics. It usually begins with a discussion of participants' thoughts on ways in which societal trends, economics, politics, and technology may affect an issue.[26] Scenario analysis involves the projection of future possible events. It does not rely on extrapolation of historical trends. Rather, it seeks to explore possible developments that may only be connected to the past. That is, several scenarios are considered in a scenario analysis in order to envision possible future outcomes. Strategy Spotlight 2.2 provides an example of scenario planning at PPG Industries.

SWOT Analysis

To understand the business environment of a particular firm, you need to analyze both the general environment and the firm's industry and competitive environment. Generally, firms compete with other firms in the same industry. An industry is composed of a set of firms that produce similar products or services, sell to similar customers, and use similar methods of production. Gathering industry information and understanding competitive dynamics among the different companies in your industry is key to successful strategic management.

One of the most basic techniques for analyzing firm and industry conditions is **SWOT analysis.** SWOT stands for strengths, weaknesses, opportunities, and threats. It provides "raw material"—a basic listing of conditions both inside and surrounding your company.

SWOT analysis

a framework for analyzing a company's internal and external environments and that stands for strengths, weaknesses, opportunities, and threats.

The Strengths and Weaknesses refer to the internal conditions of the firm—where your firm excels (strengths) and where it may be lacking relative to competitors (weaknesses). Opportunities and Threats are environmental conditions external to the firm. These could be factors in either the general or the competitive environment. In the general environment, one might experience developments that are beneficial for most companies, such as improving economic conditions that lower borrowing costs, or trends that benefit some companies and harm others. An example is the heightened concern with fitness, which is a threat to some companies (e.g., tobacco) and an opportunity to others (e.g., health clubs). Opportunities and threats are also present in the competitive environment among firms competing for the same customers.

The general idea of SWOT analysis is that a firm's strategy must:

- Build on its strengths.
- Remedy the weaknesses or work around them.
- Take advantage of the opportunities presented by the environment.
- Protect the firm from the threats.

Despite its apparent simplicity, the SWOT approach has been very popular. First, it forces managers to consider both internal and external factors simultaneously. Second, its emphasis on identifying opportunities and threats makes firms act proactively rather than reactively. Third, it raises awareness about the role of strategy in creating a match between

SCENARIO PLANNING AT PPG

PPG Industries, the Pittsburgh-based manufacturer of paints, coatings, optical products, specialty materials, chemicals, glass, and fiber glass, has paid dividends every year since 1899 and has maintained or increased dividends every year since 1972. With sales over $13 billion and operations in more than 60 countries, PPG is truly a global player. Although considered a very successful company, PPG has had its share of strategic errors. Realizing that business was slowing down in its core businesses, PPG acquired medical electronics businesses from Honeywell and Litton Industries in 1986 and from Allegheny International in 1987. However, these efforts at diversification proved to be failures, as the firm's competence in low-cost, standardized production in stable, mature industries was of little help in the highly volatile biomedical industry, where customization was vital. Seven years later, PPG exited the medical electronics business by selling off these units. To profit from the construction boom in China, PPG entered the Chinese market with a focus on glass. After years of losses, the company realized that it would have to focus on coatings.

These costly failures led PPG to a new emphasis on strategic planning. One of the key tools it uses today is scenario planning. PPG has developed four alternative futures based on differing assumptions about two key variables: the cost of energy (because its manufacturing operations are energy-intensive) and the extent of opportunity for growth in emerging markets. In the most favorable scenario, cost of energy will stay moderate and stable and opportunities for growth and differentiation will be fast and strong. In this scenario, PPG determined that its success will depend on having the resources to pursue new opportunities. On the other hand, in the worst-case scenario, cost of energy will be high and opportunities for growth will be weak and slow. This scenario would call for a complete change in strategic direction. Between these two extremes lies the possibility of two mixed scenarios. First, opportunity for growth in emerging markets may be high, but cost of energy may be high and volatile. In this scenario, the company's success will depend on coming up with more efficient processes. Second, cost of energy may remain moderate and stable, but opportunities for growth in emerging markets may remain weak and slow. In this situation, the most viable strategy may be one of capturing market share with new products.

Developing strategies based on possible future scenarios seems to be paying off for PPG Industries. The company's net income soared to $3.2 billion in 2013—nearly a 200 percent increase over the prior two-year period.

Sources: Camillus, J. C. 2008. Strategy as a wicked problem. *Harvard Business Review,* 86(5): 98–106; *www.ppg.com*; and *www.finance.yahoo.com.*

---

the environmental conditions and the firm's internal strengths and weaknesses. Finally, its conceptual simplicity is achieved without sacrificing analytical rigor. (We will also address some of the limitations of SWOT analysis in Chapter 3.)

While analysis is necessary, it is also equally important to recognize the role played by intuition and judgment. Steve Jobs, the legendary former chairman of Apple, took a very different approach in determining what customers *really* wanted:[27]

> Steve Jobs was convinced market research and focus groups limited one's ability to innovate. When asked how much research was done to guide Apple when he introduced the iPad, Jobs famously quipped: "None. It isn't the consumers' job to know what they want. It's hard for (consumers) to tell you what they want when they've never seen anything remotely like it."
>
> Jobs relied on his own intuition—his radarlike feel for emerging technologies and how they could be brought together to create, in his words "insanely great products, that ultimately made the difference." For Jobs, who died in 2011 at the age of 56, intuition was no mere gut call. It was, as he put it in his often-quoted commencement speech at Stanford, about "connecting the dots, glimpsing the relationships among wildly disparate life experiences and changes in technologies."

general environment
factors external to an industry, and usually beyond a firm's control, that affect a firm's strategy.

The General Environment

The **general environment** is composed of factors that can have dramatic effects on firm strategy.[28] We divide the general environment into six segments: demographic, sociocultural, political/legal, technological, economic, and global. Exhibit 2.2 provides examples of key trends and events in each of the six segments of the general environment.

LO2.4

The impact of the general environment on a firm's strategies and performance.

EXHIBIT 2.2

General Environment:
Key Trends and Events

Demographic

- Aging population
- Rising affluence
- Changes in ethnic composition
- Geographic distribution of population
- Greater disparities in income levels

Sociocultural

- More women in the workforce
- Increase in temporary workers
- Greater concern for fitness
- Greater concern for environment
- Postponement of family formation

Political/Legal

- Tort reform
- Americans with Disabilities Act (ADA) of 1990
- Deregulation of utility and other industries
- Increases in federally mandated minimum wages
- Taxation at local, state, federal levels
- Legislation on corporate governance reforms in bookkeeping, stock options, etc. (Sarbanes-Oxley Act of 2002)
- Affordable Care Act (Obamacare)

Technological

- Genetic engineering
- Three-dimensional (3D) printing
- Computer-aided design/computer-aided manufacturing systems (CAD/CAM)
- Research in synthetic and exotic materials
- Pollution/global warming
- Miniaturization of computing technologies
- Wireless communications
- Nanotechnology

Economic

- Interest rates
- Unemployment rates
- Consumer price index
- Trends in GDP
- Changes in stock market valuations

Global

- Increasing global trade
- Currency exchange rates
- Emergence of the Indian and Chinese economies
- Trade agreements among regional blocs (e.g., NAFTA, EU, ASEAN)
- Creation of WTO (leading to decreasing tariffs/free trade in services)
- Increased risks associated with terrorism

Before addressing each of the six segments in turn, consider Dominic Barton's insights in response to a question posed to him by an editor of *Fortune* magazine: *What are your client's worries right now?* (Barton is global managing director of McKinsey, the giant consulting firm.)[29]

> "They're pretty consistent around the world. The big one now is geopolitics. Whether you're in Russia, China, anywhere the assumed stability that was there for the past 20 or so years—it's not there. The second is technology, which is moving two to three times faster than management. Most CEOs I talk to are excited and paranoid at the same time. Related to that is cyber security: the amount of time and effort to protect systems and look at vulnerabilities is big.
>
> "A fourth trend is the shift in economic power, with 2.2 billion new middle-class consumers in the next 15 years, and it's moving to Asia and Africa. Do you have the right type of people in your top 100? Are you in those markets? Those are the four big ones we see everywhere."

The Demographic Segment

Demographics are the most easily understood and quantifiable elements of the general environment. They are at the root of many changes in society. Demographics include elements such as the aging population,[30] rising or declining affluence, changes in ethnic composition, geographic distribution of the population, and disparities in income level.[31]

The impact of a demographic trend, like all segments of the general environment, varies across industries. Rising levels of affluence in many developed countries bode well for brokerage services as well as for upscale pets and supplies. However, this trend may adversely affect fast-food restaurants because people can afford to dine at higher-priced restaurants. Fast-food restaurants depend on minimum-wage employees to operate efficiently, but the competition for labor intensifies as more attractive employment opportunities become prevalent, thus threatening the employment base for restaurants. Let's look at the details of one of these trends.

The aging population in the United States and other developed countries has important implications. Although the percentage of those 65 and over in the U.S. workforce bottomed in the 1990s, it has been rising ever since.[32] According to the Bureau of Labor Statistics, 59 percent of workers 65 and older were putting in full-time hours in 2013, a percentage that has increased steadily over the past decade. And, according to a 2014 study by Merrill Lynch and the Age Wave Consulting firm, 72 percent of preretirees aged 50 and over wanted to work during their retirement. "Older workers are to the first half of the 21st century what women were to the last half of the 20th century," says Eugene Steuerle, an economist at the Urban Institute.

There are a number of misconceptions about the quality and value of older workers. The Insights from Research box on page 46, however, debunks many of these myths.

The Sociocultural Segment

Sociocultural forces influence the values, beliefs, and lifestyles of a society. Examples include a higher percentage of women in the workforce, dual-income families, increases in the number of temporary workers, greater concern for healthy diets and physical fitness, greater interest in the environment, and postponement of having children. Such forces enhance sales of products and services in many industries but depress sales in others. The increased number of women in the workforce has increased the need for business clothing merchandise but decreased the demand for baking product staples (since people would have less time to cook from scratch). The health and fitness trend has helped industries that manufacture exercise equipment and healthful foods but harmed industries that produce unhealthful foods.

Increased educational attainment by women in the workplace has led to more women in upper-management positions.[33] Given such educational attainment, it is hardly surprising

demographic segment of the general environment genetic and observable characteristics of a population, including the levels and growth of age, density, sex, race, ethnicity, education, geographic region, and income.

sociocultural segment of the general environment the values, beliefs, and lifestyles of a society.

INSIGHTS FROM RESEARCH

NEW TRICKS: RESEARCH DEBUNKS MYTHS ABOUT OLDER WORKERS

Overview

People often think that older workers are less motivated and less healthy, resist change and are less trusting, and have more trouble balancing work and family. It turns out these assumptions just aren't true. By challenging these stereotypes in your organization, you can keep your employees working.

What the Research Shows

In a 2012 paper published by *Personnel Psychology,* researchers from the University of Hong Kong and the University of Georgia examined 418 studies of workers' ages and stereotypes. A meta-analysis—a study of studies—was conducted to find out if any of the six following stereotypes about older workers—as compared with younger workers—was actually true:

- They are less motivated.
- They are less willing to participate in training and career development.
- They are more resistant to change.
- They are less trusting.
- They are less healthy.
- They are more vulnerable to work-family imbalance.

After an exhaustive search of studies dealing with these issues, the investigators' meta-analytic techniques turned up some interesting results. Older workers' motivation and job involvement are actually slightly higher than those of younger workers. Older workers are slightly more willing to implement organizational changes, are not less trusting, and are not less healthy than younger workers. Moreover, they're not more likely to have issues with work-family imbalance. Of the six investigated, the only stereotype supported was that older workers are less willing to participate in training and career development.

Why This Matters

Business leaders must pay attention to the circumstances of older workers. According to the U.S. Bureau of Labor Statistics, 19.5 percent of American workers were 55 and older in 2010, but by 2020 25.2 percent will be 55 and older. Workers aged 25–44 should drop from 66.9 to 63.7 percent of the workforce during the same period. These statistics make clear that recruiting and training older workers remain critical.

When the findings of the meta-analysis are considered, the challenge of integrating older workers into the workplace becomes acute. The stereotypes held about older workers don't hold water, but when older workers are subjected to them, they are more likely to retire and experience a lower quality of life. Business leaders should attract, retain, and encourage mature employees' continued involvement in workplaces because they have much to offer in the ways of wisdom, experience, and institutional knowledge. The alternative is to miss out on a growing pool of valuable human capital.

How can you deal with age stereotypes to keep older workers engaged? The authors suggest three effective ways:

- Provide more opportunities for younger and older workers to work together.
- Promote positive attributes of older workers, like experience, carefulness, and punctuality.
- Engage employees in open discussions about stereotypes.

Adam Bradshaw of the DeGarmo Group Inc. has summarized research on addressing age stereotypes in the workplace and offers practical advice. For instance, make sure hiring practices identify factors important to the job other than age. Managers can be trained in how to spot age stereotypes and can point out to employees why the stereotypes are often untrue by using examples of effective older workers. Realize that older workers can offer a competitive advantage because of skills they possess that competitors may overlook.

Professor Tamara Erickson, who was named one of the top 50 global business thinkers in 2011, points out that members of different generations bring different experiences, assumptions, and benefits to the workforce. Companies can gain a great deal from creating a culture that welcomes workers of all ages and in which leaders address biases.

Key Takeaways

- The percentage of American workers 55 years old and older is expected to increase from 19.5 percent in 2010 to 25.2 percent in 2020.
- Many stereotypes exist about older workers. A review of 418 studies reveals these stereotypes are largely unfounded.
- Older workers subjected to negative stereotypes are more likely to retire and more likely to report lower quality of life and poorer health.
- When business leaders accept stereotypes about older workers, they lose out on these workers' wisdom and experience. And by 2020 employers may have a smaller pool of younger workers than they do today.
- Solutions include creating opportunities for younger and older workers to work together and having frank, open discussions about stereotypes.

continued

Apply This Today

The stereotypes people often hold about older workers are largely unfounded. Let's face it: The labor force is aging, and astute companies can gain a great deal by attracting and retaining these valuable employees. Train your employees to accept colleagues of all ages—and the entire organization will benefit.

Research Reviewed

Ng, T. W. H. & Feldman, D. C. 2012. Evaluating six common stereotypes about older workers with meta-analytical data. *Personnel Psychology,* 65: 821–858. We thank Matthew Gilley, Ph.D., of *businessminded.com* for contributing this research brief.

that companies owned by women have been one of the driving forces of the U.S. economy; these companies (now more than 9 million in number) account for 40 percent of all U.S. businesses and have generated more than $3.6 trillion in annual revenue. In addition, women have a tremendous impact on consumer spending decisions. Not surprisingly, many companies have focused their advertising and promotion efforts on female consumers. Consider, for example, Lowe's efforts to attract female shoppers:

> Lowe's has found that women prefer to do larger home-improvement projects with a man—be it a boyfriend, husband, or neighbor. As a result, in addition to its "recipe card classes" (that explain various projects that take only one weekend), Lowe's offers co-ed store clinics for projects like sink installation. "Women like to feel they're given the same attention as a male customer," states Lowe's spokesperson Julie Valeant-Yenichek, who points out that most seminar attendees, whether male or female, are inexperienced.[34]

Home Depot recently spent millions of dollars to add softer lighting and brighter signs in 300 stores. Why? It is an effort to match rival Lowe's appeal to women.

The Political/Legal Segment

Political processes and legislation influence environmental regulations with which industries must comply.[35,36] Some important elements of the political/legal arena include tort reform, the Americans with Disabilities Act (ADA) of 1990, the repeal of the Glass-Steagall Act in 1999 (banks may now offer brokerage services), deregulation of utilities and other industries, and increases in the federally mandated minimum wage.[37]

political/legal segment of the general environment how a society creates and exercises power, including rules, laws, and taxation policies.

Government legislation can also have a significant impact on the governance of corporations. The U.S. Congress passed the Sarbanes-Oxley Act in 2002, which greatly increases the accountability of auditors, executives, and corporate lawyers. This act responded to the widespread perception that existing governance mechanisms failed to protect the interests of shareholders, employees, and creditors. Clearly, Sarbanes-Oxley has also created a tremendous demand for professional accounting services.

Legislation can also affect firms in the high-tech sector of the economy by expanding the number of temporary visas available for highly skilled foreign professionals.[38] For example, a bill passed by the U.S. Congress in October 2000 allowed 195,000 H-1B visas for each of the following three years—up from a cap of 115,000. However, beginning in 2006 and continuing through 2015, the annual cap on H-1B visas has shrunk to only 65,000—with an additional 20,000 visas available for foreigners with a master's or higher degree from a U.S. institution. Many of the visas are for professionals from India with computer and software expertise. In 2014, companies applied for 172,500 H-1B visas. This means that at least 87,500 engineers, developers, and others couldn't take jobs in the United States.[39] As one would expect, this is a political "hot potato" for industry executives as well as U.S. labor and workers' rights groups. The key arguments against H-1B visas are that H-1B workers drive down wages and take jobs from Americans.

Strategy Spotlight 2.3 provides some facts and points out the important role immigrants have played in innovation and job creation in the United States.

IMMIGRANTS, INNOVATION, AND NEW JOB CREATION

Although there is debate about immigration in terms of the alleged threat to American jobs, the fact is quite the opposite: Those who move to the U.S. are prodigious job creators. The United States may be losing ground as a magnet for global entrepreneurs due to a huge backlog of visas that allow them to start new businesses. Last year, efforts to boost available green cards and create a new visa class for immigrant entrepreneurs failed. Hence, many foreign-born scientists and entrepreneurs are leaving the U.S., while such countries as Canada, Australia, Chile, and Singapore look to reap the benefits.

Consider the following:

- First-generation immigrants or their children had founder roles in more than 40 percent of the Fortune 500, including such marquee companies as AT&T, Procter & Gamble, Goldman Sachs, Pfizer, eBay, Google, Intel, Kraft, Cigna, and Kohl's.

- Immigrants are more than twice as likely to found a company as are native-born citizens. They started 28 percent of all new U.S. businesses in 2011, despite accounting for just 12.9 percent of the total population. And in Silicon Valley, the percentage of new companies started by foreign-born entrepreneurs was a remarkable 43.9 percent during 2006–2012.

- Immigrants contributed to more than half of the international patents filed by giant multinationals such as Qualcomm (72 percent), Merck (65 percent), General Electric (64 percent), and Cisco (60 percent).

- Immigrant-owned companies now generate more than $775 billion in annual revenue and $100 billion in income. They employ 1 of every 10 workers.

Sources: Alsever, J. 2014. Immigrants: America's job creators. *Fortune.com*, June 16: 56; and Malone, M. S. 2014. The self-inflicted U.S. brain drain. *The Wall Street Journal*, October 16: A19.

Over time, government regulations often have a tendency to become increasingly complex. For example, many would likely argue that billing requirements for Medicare reimbursements have become absurd. Consider the following from *The Economist*:[40]

> Doctors and other health professionals say it is becoming harder to stay on the right side of the rules as billing requirements grow more convoluted. In 2015, Medicare will have an astonishing 140,000 codes, including nine for injuries caused by turkeys. (Was the victim struck or pecked? Once or more often? Did he or she suffer negative after-effects? And so on).
>
> Many clinics have fallen under suspicion and had payments suspended, only to win a reprieve when the facts are examined closely. Medicare alone has a backlog of nearly a half million appeals.

technological segment of the general environment innovation and state of knowledge in industrial arts, engineering, applied sciences, and pure science; and their interaction with society.

The Technological Segment

Developments in technology lead to new products and services and improve how they are produced and delivered to the end user.[41] Innovations can create entirely new industries and alter the boundaries of existing industries.[42] Technological developments and trends include genetic engineering, Internet technology, computer-aided design/computer-aided manufacturing (CAD/CAM), research in artificial and exotic materials, and, on the downside, pollution and global warming.[43] Petroleum and primary metals industries spend significantly to reduce their pollution. Engineering and consulting firms that work with polluting industries derive financial benefits from solving such problems.

Nanotechnology is becoming a very promising area of research with many potentially useful applications.[44] Nanotechnology takes place at industry's tiniest stage: one-billionth of a meter. Remarkably, this is the size of 10 hydrogen atoms in a row. Matter at such a tiny scale behaves very differently. Familiar materials—from gold to carbon soot—display startling and useful new properties. Some transmit light or electricity. Others become harder than diamonds or turn into potent chemical catalysts. What's more, researchers have found that a tiny dose of nanoparticles can transform the chemistry and nature of far bigger things.

Another emerging technology is physioletics, which is the practice of linking wearable computing devices with data analysis and quantified feedback to improve performance.[45]

An example is sensors in shoes (such as Nike+, used by runners to track distance, speed, and other metrics). Another application focuses on people's movements in various work settings. Tesco's employees, for instance, wear armbands at a distribution center in Ireland to track the goods they are gathering. The devices free up time that employees would otherwise spend marking clipboards. The armband also allots tasks to the wearer, forecasts his or her completion time, and quantifies the wearer's precise movements among the facility's 9.6 miles of shelving and 111 loading bays.

The Economic Segment

The economy affects all industries, from suppliers of raw materials to manufacturers of finished goods and services, as well as all organizations in the service, wholesale, retail, government, and nonprofit sectors.[46] Key economic indicators include interest rates, unemployment rates, the consumer price index, the gross domestic product, and net disposable income.[47] Interest rate increases have a negative impact on the residential home construction industry but a negligible (or neutral) effect on industries that produce consumer necessities such as prescription drugs or common grocery items.

Other economic indicators are associated with equity markets. Perhaps the most watched is the Dow Jones Industrial Average (DJIA), which is composed of 30 large industrial firms. When stock market indexes increase, consumers' discretionary income rises and there is often an increased demand for luxury items such as jewelry and automobiles. But when stock valuations decrease, demand for these items shrinks.

The Global Segment

More firms are expanding their operations and market reach beyond the borders of their "home" country. Globalization provides both opportunities to access larger potential markets and a broad base of production factors such as raw materials, labor, skilled managers, and technical professionals. However, such endeavors also carry many political, social, and economic risks.[48]

Examples of key elements include currency exchange rates, increasing global trade, the economic emergence of China, trade agreements among regional blocs (e.g., North American Free Trade Agreement, European Union), and the General Agreement on Tariffs and Trade (GATT) (lowering of tariffs).[49] Increases in trade across national boundaries also provide benefits to air cargo and shipping industries but have a minimal impact on service industries such as bookkeeping and routine medical services.

A key factor in the global economy is the rapid rise of the middle class in emerging countries. The number of consumers in Asia's middle class is rapidly approaching the number in Europe and North America combined. An important implication of this trend is the dramatic change in hiring practices of U.S. multinationals. Consider:

> Thirty-five U.S.-based multinational firms have recently added jobs faster than other U.S. employers, but nearly three-fourths of those jobs were overseas, according to a *Wall Street Journal* analysis. Those companies, which include Wal-Mart Stores Inc., International Paper Co., Honeywell International, Inc., and United Parcel Service, boosted their employment at home by 3.1 percent, or 113,000 jobs, at roughly the same rate of increase as the nation's other employers. However, they also added more than 333,000 jobs in their far-flung—and faster growing—foreign operations.[50]

Relationships among Elements of the General Environment

In our discussion of the general environment, we see many relationships among the various elements.[51] For example, a demographic trend in the United States, the aging of the population, has important implications for the economic segment (in terms of tax policies to provide benefits to increasing numbers of older citizens). Another example is the emergence of information technology as a means to increase the rate of productivity gains in the

United States and other developed countries. Such use of IT results in lower inflation (an important element of the economic segment) and helps offset costs associated with higher labor rates.

The effects of a trend or event in the general environment vary across industries. Governmental legislation (political/legal) to permit the importation of prescription drugs from foreign countries is a very positive development for drugstores but a very negative event for U.S. drug manufacturers. Exhibit 2.3 provides other examples of how the impact of trends or events in the general environment can vary across industries.

Crowdsourcing: A Technology That Affects Multiple Segments of the General Environment   Before moving on, let's consider the Internet. The Internet has been a leading and highly visible component of a broader technological phenomenon—the emergence of digital technology. These technologies are altering the way business is conducted and having an effect on nearly every business domain.

One application of digital technology is **crowdsourcing,** which will be a theme throughout the text. It has affected multiple elements of the general environment, such as technology, globalization, and economics. When and where did the term originate?[52] In January 2006, open sourcing was, for most businesspeople, little more than an online curiosity. At that time, Jeff Howe of *Wired* magazine started to write an article about the phenomenon. However, he soon discovered a far more important story to be told: Large—as well as small—companies in a wide variety of industries had begun farming out serious tasks to individuals and groups on the Internet. Together with his editor, Mark Robinson, they coined a new term to describe the phenomenon. In June 2006, the article appeared in which *crowdsourcing* was defined as the tapping of the "latent talent of the (online) crowd." It has become the term of choice for a process that is infiltrating many aspects of business life.

Clearly, crowdsourcing has claimed some well-known successes, particularly on the product development front. Consider:

- The Linux operating system, created as an open-source alternative to Windows and UNIX, can be downloaded for free and altered to suit any user's needs. And with all the firepower brought to bear by the online open-source community, bugs in the system get fixed in a matter of hours.
- One of Amazon's smartest moves was to invite its customers to write online reviews. The customers are neither paid nor controlled by the company, but the content that they create adds enormous value to other customers and, therefore, to Amazon.
- Roughly 5 million users per month swear by Wikipedia. The free online encyclopedia was created and updated by Internet volunteers to the tune of roughly 2 million articles and counting.

Throughout this book, we will introduce examples of crowdsourcing to show its relevance to key strategy concepts. For example, in Chapter 3, we discuss how Procter & Gamble used it to develop social connections through digital media that enable the firm to codesign and coengineer new innovations with buyers. In Chapter 4, we discuss how SAP, the giant software company, uses crowdsourcing to tap knowledge well beyond its firm boundaries via the nearly 3 million participants in its Community Network. In Chapter 5, we explain how Unilever is using crowdsourcing to advance its sustainability initiatives. In Chapter 12, we discuss how NASA is working with Innocentive to overcome some of the technology challenges associated with deep-space missions.

Strategy Spotlight 2.4 explains how Lego has used crowdsourcing to help the toymaker strengthen its ties to customers and increase revenues.

crowdsourcing
practice wherein the Internet is used to tap a broad range of individuals and groups to generate ideas and solve problems.

Segment/Trends and Events	Industry	Positive	Neutral	Negative
Demographic				
Aging population	Health care	✓		
	Baby products			✓
Rising affluence	Brokerage services	✓		
	Fast foods			✓
	Upscale pets and supplies	✓		
Sociocultural				
More women in the workforce	Clothing	✓		
	Baking products (staples)			✓
Greater concern for health and fitness	Home exercise equipment	✓		
	Meat products			✓
Political/legal				
Tort reform	Legal services			✓
	Auto manufacturing	✓		
Americans with Disabilities Act (ADA)	Retail			✓
	Manufacturers of elevators, escalators, and ramps	✓		
Technological				
Genetic engineering	Pharmaceutical	✓		
	Publishing		✓	
Pollution/global warming	Engineering services	✓		
	Petroleum			✓
Economic				
Interest rate decreases	Residential construction	✓		
	Most common grocery products		✓	
Global				
Increasing global trade	Shipping	✓		
	Personal service		✓	
Emergence of China as an economic power	Soft drinks	✓		
	Defense			✓

EXHIBIT 2.3

The Impact of General Environmental Trends on Various Industries

LEGO'S EFFECTIVE USE OF CROWDSOURCING

Lego runs its crowdsourcing program with Cuusoo System, a Japanese company. "Both children and adults these days are used to being, and expect to be, more involved," says Mads Nipper, chief marketing officer, at Lego's headquarters in Billund, Denmark. The Lego Cuusoo site—which translates roughly to "my Lego wish" in Japanese—helps the company develop ideas that its 180 designers might not come up with on their own.

How does it work? People create a model, take photos, write a project description, and submit their idea on the Lego website (ideas.lego.com). Projects that garner more than 10,000 votes from site visitors are evaluated by designers and executives to ensure they meet such requirements as safety and playability and they fit with the Lego brand. Those whose models are chosen get 1 percent of their toy's net revenue. Plus, the Lego website asserts: "You're featured in the set materials, receive a royalty on sales, and are recognized as the product creator." Projects are reviewed about three times a year. Those scheduled for the next round include a bird, an Apple store, and a train inspired by writer Jules Verne.

A recent winner was Brent Waller, a 35-year old video game developer, who spent his childhood crafting plastic brick versions of characters from such television movies as *Teenage Mutant Turtles* and *Batman*. His miniature version of the Cadillac ambulance from Bill Murray's 1984 comedy *Ghostbusters* went into production in June 2014. Claims Waller: "It's any Lego fan's dream to have an official set they created." Brent's persistence paid off! He had struck out a few times before his big hit: His previous designs of houses, robots, and Batman's Batmobile weren't chosen.

Sources: Gustafsson, K. 2014. Who ya gonna call? Lego dials fans. *Bloomberg Businessweek,* March 19: 27–28; and *www.ideas.lego.com.*

LO2.5

How forces in the competitive environment can affect profitability, and how a firm can improve its competitive position by increasing its power vis-à-vis these forces.

industry
a group of firms that produce similar goods or services.

competitive environment
factors that pertain to an industry and affect a firm's strategies.

Porter's five forces model of industry competition
a tool for examining the industry-level competitive environment, especially the ability of firms in that industry to set prices and minimize costs.

The Competitive Environment

Managers must consider the competitive environment (also sometimes referred to as the task or industry environment). The nature of competition in an **industry,** as well as the profitability of a firm, is often directly influenced by developments in the competitive environment.

The **competitive environment** consists of many factors that are particularly relevant to a firm's strategy. These include competitors (existing or potential), customers, and suppliers. Potential competitors may include a supplier considering forward integration, such as an automobile manufacturer acquiring a rental car company, or a firm in an entirely new industry introducing a similar product that uses a more efficient technology.

Next, we will discuss key concepts and analytical techniques that managers should use to assess their competitive environments. First, we examine Michael Porter's five-forces model that illustrates how these forces can be used to explain an industry's profitability.[53] Second, we discuss how the five forces are being affected by the capabilities provided by Internet technologies. Third, we address some of the limitations, or "caveats," that managers should be familiar with when conducting industry analysis. Finally, we address the concept of strategic groups, because even within an industry it is often useful to group firms on the basis of similarities of their strategies. As we will see, competition tends to be more intense among firms *within* a strategic group than between strategic groups.

Porter's Five Forces Model of Industry Competition

The **"five forces" model** developed by Michael E. Porter has been the most commonly used analytical tool for examining the competitive environment. It describes the competitive environment in terms of five basic competitive forces:[54]

1. The threat of new entrants.
2. The bargaining power of buyers.
3. The bargaining power of suppliers.
4. The threat of substitute products and services.
5. The intensity of rivalry among competitors in an industry.

Each of these forces affects a firm's ability to compete in a given market. Together, they determine the profit potential for a particular industry. The model is shown in Exhibit 2.4. A manager should be familiar with the five forces model for several reasons. It helps you decide whether your firm should remain in or exit an industry. It provides the rationale for increasing or decreasing resource commitments. The model helps you assess how to improve your firm's competitive position with regard to each of the five forces.[55] For example, you can use insights provided by the five forces model to understand how higher entry barriers that discourage new rivals from competing with you.[56] Or how to develop strong relationships with your distribution channels. You may decide to find suppliers who satisfy the price/performance criteria needed to make your product or service a top performer.

The Threat of New Entrants   The **threat of new entrants** refers to the possibility that the profits of established firms in the industry may be eroded by new competitors.[57] The extent of the threat depends on existing barriers to entry and the combined reactions from existing competitors.[58] If entry barriers are high and/or the newcomer can anticipate a sharp retaliation from established competitors, the threat of entry is low. These circumstances discourage new competitors. There are six major sources of entry barriers.

Economies of Scale   **Economies of scale** refers to spreading the costs of production over the number of units produced. The cost of a product per unit declines as the absolute volume per period increases. This deters entry by forcing the entrant to come in at a large scale and risk strong reaction from existing firms or come in at a small scale and accept a cost disadvantage. Both are undesirable options.

Product Differentiation   When existing competitors have strong brand identification and customer loyalty, **product differentiation** creates a barrier to entry by forcing entrants to spend heavily to overcome existing customer loyalties.

threat of new entrants
the possibility that the profits of established firms in the industry may be eroded by new competitors.

economies of scale
decreases in cost per unit as absolute output per period increases.

product differentiation
the degree to which a product has strong brand loyalty or customer loyalty.

EXHIBIT 2.4 Porter's Five Forces Model of Industry Competition

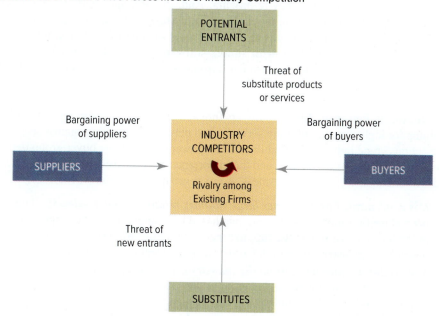

Sources: From Michael E. Porter, "The Five Competitive Forces That Shape Strategy," Special Issue on HBS Centennial. Harvard Business Review 86, No. 1 (January 2008), 78–93. Reprinted with permission of Michael E. Porter.

Capital Requirements   The need to invest large financial resources to compete creates a barrier to entry, especially if the capital is required for risky or unrecoverable up-front advertising or research and development (R&D).

Switching Costs   A barrier to entry is created by the existence of one-time costs that the buyer faces when switching from one supplier's product or service to another.

Access to Distribution Channels   The new entrant's need to secure distribution for its product can create a barrier to entry.

Cost Disadvantages Independent of Scale   Some existing competitors may have advantages that are independent of size or economies of scale. These derive from:

- Proprietary products
- Favorable access to raw materials
- Government subsidies
- Favorable government policies

Managers often tend to overestimate the barriers of entry in many industries. There are any number of cases where new entrants found innovative ways to enter industries by cleverly mixing and matching existing technologies. For example, companies, medical researchers, governments, and others are creating breakthrough technology products *without having to create any new technology.*[59] Geoff Colvin, a senior editor at *Fortune,* calls this "the era of Lego Innovation," in which significant and valuable advances in technology can be achieved by imaginatively combining components and software available to everyone. Such a trend serves to reduce entry barriers in many industries because state-of-the-art technology does not have to be developed internally—rather, it is widely available and, Colvin asserts, "we all have access to a really big box of plastic bricks."

MIT's Media Lab has created robots powered by Android smartphones. After all, those devices can see, hear, recognize speech, and talk; they know where they are, how they're oriented, and how fast they're moving. And, through apps and an Internet connection, they can do a nearly infinite number of other tasks, such as recognize faces and translate languages. Similarly, teams at the University of South Carolina combined off-the-shelf eye-tracking technology with simple software they wrote to detect whether a driver was getting drowsy; any modern car has enough computing power to handle this job easily.

The Bargaining Power of Buyers   Buyers threaten an industry by forcing down prices, bargaining for higher quality or more services, and playing competitors against each other. These actions erode industry profitability.[60] The power of each large buyer group depends on attributes of the market situation and the importance of purchases from that group compared with the industry's overall business. A buyer group is powerful when:

- *It is concentrated or purchases large volumes relative to seller sales.* If a large percentage of a supplier's sales are purchased by a single buyer, the importance of the buyer's business to the supplier increases. Large-volume buyers also are powerful in industries with high fixed costs (e.g., steel manufacturing).
- *The products it purchases from the industry are standard or undifferentiated.* Confident they can always find alternative suppliers, buyers play one company against the other, as in commodity grain products.
- *The buyer faces few switching costs.* Switching costs lock the buyer to particular sellers. Conversely, the buyer's power is enhanced if the seller faces high switching costs.

- **It earns low profits.** Low profits create incentives to lower purchasing costs. On the other hand, highly profitable buyers are generally less price-sensitive.
- **The buyers pose a credible threat of backward integration.** If buyers either are partially integrated or pose a credible threat of backward integration, they are typically able to secure bargaining concessions.
- **The industry's product is unimportant to the quality of the buyer's products or services.** When the quality of the buyer's products is not affected by the industry's product, the buyer is more price-sensitive.

At times, a firm or set of firms in an industry may increase its buyer power by using the services of a third party. FreeMarkets Online is one such third party.[61] Pittsburgh-based FreeMarkets has developed software enabling large industrial buyers to organize online auctions for qualified suppliers of semistandard parts such as fabricated components, packaging materials, metal stampings, and services. By aggregating buyers, Free-Markets increases the buyers' bargaining power. The results are impressive. In its first 48 auctions, most participating companies saved over 15 percent; some saved as much as 50 percent.

Although a firm may be tempted to take advantage of its suppliers because of high buyer power, it must be aware of the potential long-term backlash from such actions. A recent example is the growing resentment that students have toward state universities in California because of a steep 32 percent increase in tuition. Let's see why they have so little bargaining power.

> Students protested by taking over a classroom building. As noted by *Forbes* writer Asher Hawkins: "It was a futile effort. Students who are already embarked on a four-year program are something of a captive audience, and California's state coffers are empty."[62] After all, students have high exit costs, primarily because of the difficulty in transferring credits to another university. Plus, there are fewer openings at other UC campuses due to budget cuts, and there is increasing demand for them from overseas students. All these factors erode student bargaining power.
>
> After the increase, the tuition and fees for in-state undergraduate students will come to about $10,000 for the academic year (this represents a compound annual increase of nearly 10 percent over the past decade). Although this may still seem like a reasonable price for a high-quality education, there could be more price increases ahead.

The Bargaining Power of Suppliers Suppliers can exert bargaining power by threatening to raise prices or reduce the quality of purchased goods and services. Powerful suppliers can squeeze the profitability of firms so far that they can't recover the costs of raw material inputs.[63] The factors that make suppliers powerful tend to mirror those that make buyers powerful. A supplier group will be powerful when:

bargaining power of suppliers
the threat that suppliers may raise prices or reduce the quality of purchased goods and services.

- **The supplier group is dominated by a few companies and is more concentrated (few firms dominate the industry) than the industry it sells to.** Suppliers selling to fragmented industries influence prices, quality, and terms.
- **The supplier group is not obliged to contend with substitute products for sale to the industry.** The power of even large, powerful suppliers can be checked if they compete with substitutes.
- **The industry is not an important customer of the supplier group.** When suppliers sell to several industries and a particular industry does not represent a significant fraction of its sales, suppliers are more prone to exert power.
- **The supplier's product is an important input to the buyer's business.** When such inputs are important to the success of the buyer's manufacturing process or product quality, the bargaining power of suppliers is high.

- **The supplier group's products are differentiated, or it has built up switching costs for the buyer.** Differentiation or switching costs facing the buyers cut off their options to play one supplier against another.
- **The supplier group poses a credible threat of forward integration.** This provides a check against the industry's ability to improve the terms by which it purchases.

The formation of Delta Pride Catfish is an example of the power a group of suppliers can attain if they exercise the threat of forward integration.[64] Catfish farmers in Mississippi historically supplied their harvest to processing plants run by large agribusiness firms such as ConAgra and Farm Fresh. When the farmers increased their production of catfish in response to growing demand, they found, much to their chagrin, that processors were holding back on their plans to increase their processing capabilities in hopes of higher retail prices for catfish.

What action did the farmers take? About 120 of them banded together and formed a cooperative, raised $4.5 million, and constructed their own processing plant, which they supplied themselves. ConAgra's market share quickly dropped from 35 percent to 11 percent, and Farm Fresh's market share fell by over 20 percent. Within 10 years, Delta Pride controlled over 40 percent of the U.S. catfish market. Recently, Delta Pride changed its ownership structure and became a closely-held corporation. In 2014, it had revenues of $80 million, employed 600 people, and processed 80 million pounds of catfish.

The Threat of Substitute Products and Services   All firms within an industry compete with industries producing **substitute products and services.**[65] Substitutes limit the potential returns of an industry by placing a ceiling on the prices that firms in that industry can profitably charge. The more attractive the price/performance ratio of substitute products, the tighter the lid on an industry's profits.

Identifying substitute products involves searching for other products or services that can perform the same function as the industry's offerings. This may lead a manager into businesses seemingly far removed from the industry. For example, the airline industry might not consider video cameras much of a threat. But as digital technology has improved and wireless and other forms of telecommunication have become more efficient, teleconferencing has become a viable substitute for business travel. That is, the rate of improvement in the price–performance relationship of the substitute product (or service) is high.

Consider the case of hybrid cars as a substitute for gasoline-powered cars.[66] Hybrid cars, such as the Toyota Prius, have seen tremendous success since the first hybrids were introduced in the late 1990s. Yet the market share of hybrid cars has been consistently low—reaching 2.4 percent in 2009, rising to 3.3 percent (the peak) in 2013, and declining to only 3 percent in 2014. Such results are even more surprising given that the number of models almost doubled between 2009 and 2014—24 to 47. That's more choices, but fewer takers. While some may believe the hybrid car industry feels pressure from other novel car segments such as electric cars (e.g., Nissan Leaf), the primary competition comes from an unusual suspect: plain old gas combustion cars.

The primary reason many environmental and cost-conscious consumers prefer gasoline-powered over hybrid cars is rather simple. Engines of gasoline-powered cars have increasingly challenged the key selling attribute of hybrid cars: fuel economy. While hybrid cars still slightly outcompete modern gasoline cars in terms of fuel economy, consumers increasingly don't see the value of paying as much as $6,000 extra for a hybrid car when they can get around 40 mpg in a gasoline car such as the Chevrolet Cruz or Hyundai Elantra.

The Intensity of Rivalry among Competitors in an Industry   Firms use tactics like price competition, advertising battles, product introductions, and increased customer service or warranties. Rivalry occurs when competitors sense the pressure or act on an opportunity to improve their position.[67]

Some forms of competition, such as price competition, are typically highly destabilizing and are likely to erode the average level of profitability in an industry.[68] Rivals easily match price cuts, an action that lowers profits for all firms. On the other hand, advertising battles expand overall demand or enhance the level of product differentiation for the benefit of all firms in the industry. Rivalry, of course, differs across industries. In some instances it is characterized as warlike, bitter, or cutthroat, whereas in other industries it is referred to as polite and gentlemanly. Intense rivalry is the result of several interacting factors, including the following:

- **Numerous or equally balanced competitors.** When there are many firms in an industry, the likelihood of mavericks is great. Some firms believe they can make moves without being noticed. Even when there are relatively few firms, and they are nearly equal in size and resources, instability results from fighting among companies having the resources for sustained and vigorous retaliation.
- **Slow industry growth.** Slow industry growth turns competition into a fight for market share, since firms seek to expand their sales.
- **High fixed or storage costs.** High fixed costs create strong pressures for all firms to increase capacity. Excess capacity often leads to escalating price cutting.
- **Lack of differentiation or switching costs.** Where the product or service is perceived as a commodity or near commodity, the buyer's choice is typically based on price and service, resulting in pressures for intense price and service competition. Lack of switching costs, described earlier, has the same effect.
- **Capacity augmented in large increments.** Where economies of scale require that capacity must be added in large increments, capacity additions can be very disruptive to the industry supply/demand balance.
- **High exit barriers.** Exit barriers are economic, strategic, and emotional factors that keep firms competing even though they may be earning low or negative returns on their investments. Some exit barriers are specialized assets, fixed costs of exit, strategic interrelationships (e.g., relationships between the business units and others within a company in terms of image, marketing, shared facilities, and so on), emotional barriers, and government and social pressures (e.g., governmental discouragement of exit out of concern for job loss).

Rivalry between firms is often based solely on price, but it can involve other factors. Consider, for example, the intense competition between Uber Technologies Inc. and Lyft Inc., which are engaged in a fierce, ongoing battle in the taxi industry:[69]

The bitter war between Uber and Lyft has spilled into dozens of cities where they are racing to provide the default app for summoning a ride within minutes. The two rivals are busy undercutting each other's prices, poaching drivers, and co-opting innovations. These actions have increasingly blurred the lines between the two services.

The potential market for these firms may stretch far beyond rides. Investors who have bid up the value of Uber to over $18.2 billion in June 2014 are betting that it can expand into becoming the backbone of a logistics and delivery network for various services—a type of FedEx for cities.

The recruitment of drivers is the lifeblood for the services as they attempt to build the largest networks with the fastest pickup times. For example, many Uber drivers are motivated to poach Lyft's drivers in order to get a bounty—$500 for referring a Lyft driver and $1,000 for referring a Lyft "mentor," an experienced Lyft contractor who helps train new drivers.

In June 2014, another shot over the bow took place when both companies unveiled similar carpooling services within hours of each other. Lyft Line and Uber Pool let passengers ride with strangers and split the bill—lowering the cost of regular commutes. Lyft claims that it had been developing the carpooling model for several years and acquired a team to lead the effort months ago, according to John Zimmer, Lyft's president. He adds, "I think it's flattering when other companies look at how we're innovating and want to do similar things."

On the other hand, Lyft has borrowed heavily from Uber, which had originated a real-time map that showed nearby drivers. Lyft's design is quite similar. Further, Lyft's "prime time" prices for peak-demand times are a variation of Uber's surge pricing.

The ease with which both firms can imitate each other's features may lead one to believe that the ride-sharing industry has low barriers to entry. After all, since Uber and Lyft don't own cars or employ chauffeurs, they are basically matchmakers between drivers and passengers. However, investors who have poured $2 billion into the two rivals are betting the apps will have staying power. Millions of people are now used to riding with Uber, and the app is still one of the most popular programs in Apple's App Store. Says Bill Gurley, a partner at Benchmark, a large diversified financial services firm, and a member of Uber's board: "Being installed on someone's iPhone on the home page is a pretty sticky place to be."

Exhibit 2.5 summarizes our discussion of industry five-forces analysis. It points out how various factors, such as economies of scale and capital requirements, affect each "force."

How the Internet and Digital Technologies Are Affecting the Five Competitive Forces

LO2.6

How the Internet and digitally based capabilities are affecting the five competitive forces and industry profitability.

Internet
a global network of linked computers that use a common transmission format, exchange information, and store data.

The **Internet** is having a significant impact on nearly every industry. Internet-based and digital technologies have fundamentally changed the ways businesses interact with each other and with consumers. In most cases, these changes have affected industry forces in ways that have created many new strategic challenges. In this section, we will evaluate Michael Porter's five-forces model in terms of the actual use of the Internet and the new technological capabilities that it makes possible.

The Threat of New Entrants In most industries, the threat of new entrants has increased because digital and Internet-based technologies lower barriers to entry. For example, businesses that reach customers primarily through the Internet may enjoy savings on other traditional expenses such as office rent, sales-force salaries, printing, and postage. This may encourage more entrants who, because of the lower start-up expenses, see an opportunity to capture market share by offering a product or performing a service more efficiently than existing competitors. Thus, a new cyber entrant can use the savings provided by the Internet to charge lower prices and compete on price despite the incumbent's scale advantages.

Alternatively, because digital technologies often make it possible for young firms to provide services that are equivalent or superior to an incumbent, a new entrant may be able to serve a market more effectively, with more personalized services and greater attention to product details. A new firm may be able to build a reputation in its niche and charge premium prices. By so doing, it can capture part of an incumbent's business and erode profitability.

Another potential benefit of web-based business is access to distribution channels. Manufacturers or distributors that can reach potential outlets for their products more efficiently by means of the Internet may enter markets that were previously closed to them. Access is not guaranteed, however, because strong barriers to entry exist in certain industries.[70]

The Bargaining Power of Buyers The Internet and wireless technologies may increase buyer power by providing consumers with more information to make buying decisions and by lowering switching costs. But these technologies may also suppress the power of traditional buyer channels that have concentrated buying power in the hands of a few, giving buyers new ways to access sellers. To sort out these differences, let's first distinguish between two types of buyers: end users and buyer channel intermediaries.

EXHIBIT 2.5 Competitive Analysis Checklist

Threat of New Entrants Is High When:	High	Low
Economies of scale are		X
Product differentiation is		X
Capital requirements are		X
Switching costs are		X
Incumbent's control of distribution channels is		X
Incumbent's proprietary knowledge is		X
Incumbent's access to raw materials is		X
Incumbent's access to government subsidies is		X

Power of Buyers Is High When:	High	Low
Concentration of buyers relative to suppliers is	X	
Switching costs are		X
Product differentiation of suppliers is		X
Threat of backward integration by buyers is	X	
Extent of buyer's profits is		X
Importance of the supplier's input to quality of buyer's final product is		X

Power of Suppliers Is High When:	High	Low
Concentration relative to buyer industry is	X	
Availability of substitute products is		X
Importance of customer to the supplier is		X
Differentiation of the supplier's products and services is	X	
Switching costs of the buyer are	X	
Threat of forward integration by the supplier is	X	

Threat of Substitute Products Is High When:	High	Low
Differentiation of the substitute product is	X	
Rate of improvement in price–performance relationship of substitute product is	X	

Intensity of Competitive Rivalry Is High When:	High	Low
Number of competitors is	X	
Industry growth rate is		X
Fixed costs are	X	
Storage costs are	X	
Product differentiation is		X
Switching costs are		X
Exit barriers are	X	
Strategic stakes are	X	

End users are the final customers in a distribution channel. Internet sales activity that is labeled "B2C"—that is, business-to-consumer—is concerned with end users. The Internet is likely to increase the power of these buyers for several reasons. First, the Internet provides large amounts of consumer information. This gives end users the information they need to shop for quality merchandise and bargain for price concessions. Second, an end user's switching costs are potentially much lower because of the Internet. Switching may involve only a few clicks of the mouse to find and view a competing product or service online.

In contrast, the bargaining power of distribution channel buyers may decrease because of the Internet. *Buyer channel intermediaries* are the wholesalers, distributors, and retailers who serve as intermediaries between manufacturers and end users. In some industries, they are dominated by powerful players that control who gains access to the latest goods or the best merchandise. The Internet and wireless communications, however, make it much easier and less expensive for businesses to reach customers directly. Thus, the Internet may increase the power of incumbent firms relative to that of traditional buyer channels. Strategy Spotlight 2.5 illustrates some of the changes brought on by the Internet that have affected the legal services industry.

The Bargaining Power of Suppliers   Use of the Internet and digital technologies to speed up and streamline the process of acquiring supplies is already benefiting many sectors of the economy. But the net effect of the Internet on supplier power will depend on the nature of competition in a given industry. As with buyer power, the extent to which the Internet is a benefit or a detriment also hinges on the supplier's position along the supply chain.

The role of suppliers involves providing products or services to other businesses. The term "B2B"—that is, business-to-business—often refers to businesses that supply or sell to other businesses. The effect of the Internet on the bargaining power of suppliers is a double-edged sword. On the one hand, suppliers may find it difficult to hold on to customers because buyers can do comparative shopping and price negotiations so much faster on the Internet.

On the other hand, several factors may also contribute to stronger supplier power. First, the growth of new web-based business may create more downstream outlets for suppliers to sell to. Second, suppliers may be able to create web-based purchasing arrangements that make purchasing easier and discourage their customers from switching. Online procurement systems directly link suppliers and customers, reducing transaction costs and paperwork.[71] Third, the use of proprietary software that links buyers to a supplier's website may create a rapid, low-cost ordering capability that discourages the buyer from seeking other sources of supply. *Amazon.com*, for example, created and patented One-Click purchasing technology that speeds up the ordering process for customers who enroll in the service.[72]

Finally, suppliers will have greater power to the extent that they can reach end users directly without intermediaries. Previously, suppliers often had to work through intermediaries who brought their products or services to market for a fee. But a process known as *disintermediation* is removing the organizations or business process layers responsible for intermediary steps in the value chain of many industries.[73] Just as the Internet is eliminating some business functions, it is creating an opening for new functions. These new activities are entering the value chain by a process known as *reintermediation*—the introduction of new types of intermediaries. Many of these new functions are affecting traditional supply chains. For example, delivery services are enjoying a boom because of the Internet. Many more consumers are choosing to have products delivered to their door rather than going out to pick them up.

The Threat of Substitutes   Along with traditional marketplaces, the Internet has created a new marketplace and a new channel. In general, therefore, the threat of substitutes is heightened because the Internet introduces new ways to accomplish the same tasks.

Consumers will generally choose to use a product or service until a substitute that meets the same need becomes available at a lower cost. The economies created by Internet technologies have led to the development of numerous substitutes for traditional ways of doing business.

Another example of substitution is in the realm of electronic storage. With expanded desktop computing, the need to store information electronically has increased dramatically. Until recently, the trend has been to create increasingly larger desktop storage capabilities and techniques for compressing information that create storage efficiencies. But a viable

BUYER POWER IN LEGAL SERVICES: THE ROLE OF THE INTERNET

The $260 billion U.S. legal services industry, which includes about 180,000 firms, historically was a classic example of an industry that leaves buyers at a bargaining disadvantage. One of the key reasons for the strong bargaining position of law firms is high information asymmetry between lawyers and consumers, meaning that highly trained and experienced legal professionals know more about legal matters than the average consumer of legal services.

The Internet provides an excellent example of how unequal bargaining power can be reduced by decreasing information asymmetry. A new class of Internet legal services providers tries to accomplish just that and is challenging traditional law services along the way. For instance, *LawPivot.com*, a recent start-up

backed by Google Ventures and cofounded by a former top Apple Inc. lawyer, allows consumers to interact with lawyers on a social networking site. This service allows customers to get a better picture of a lawyer's legal skills before opening their wallets. As a result, information asymmetry between lawyers and consumers is reduced and customers find themselves in a better bargaining position. Another example is *LegalZoom.com*, a service that helps consumers to create legal documents. Customers familiar with *LegalZoom.com* may use their knowledge of the time and effort required to create legal documents to challenge a lawyer's fees for custom-crafted legal documents.

Sources: Jacobs, D. L. 2011. Google takes aim at lawyers. *Forbes,* August 8: np; Anonymous. 2011. Alternative law firms: Bargain briefs. *The Economist,* August 13: 64; and Anonymous. 2014. Legal services industry profile. *First Research,* August 25: np.

---

substitute has emerged: storing information digitally on the Internet. Companies such as Dropbox and Amazon Web Services are providing web-based storage that firms can access simply by leasing space online. Since these storage places are virtual, they can be accessed anywhere the web can be accessed. Travelers can access important documents and files without transporting them physically from place to place.

The Intensity of Competitive Rivalry   Because the Internet creates more tools and means for competing, rivalry among competitors is likely to be more intense. Only those competitors that can use digital technologies and the web to give themselves a distinct image, create unique product offerings, or provide "faster, smarter, cheaper" services are likely to capture greater profitability with the new technology.

Rivalry is more intense when switching costs are low and product or service differentiation is minimized. Because the Internet makes it possible to shop around, it has "commoditized" products that might previously have been regarded as rare or unique. Since the Internet reduces the importance of location, products that previously had to be sought out in geographically distant outlets are now readily available online. This makes competitors in cyberspace seem more equally balanced, thus intensifying rivalry.

The problem is made worse for marketers by the presence of shopping robots ("bots") and infomediaries that search the web for the best possible prices. Consumer websites like mySimon seek out all the web locations that sell similar products and provide price comparisons.[74] Obviously, this focuses the consumer exclusively on price. Some shopping infomediaries, such as CNET, not only search for the lowest prices on many different products but also rank the customer service quality of different sites that sell similarly priced items.[75] Such infomediary services are good for consumers because they give them the chance to compare services as well as price. For businesses, however, they increase rivalry by consolidating the marketing message that consumers use to make a purchase decision into a few key pieces of information over which the selling company has little control.

Using Industry Analysis: A Few Caveats

For industry analysis to be valuable, a company must collect and evaluate a wide variety of information. As the trend toward globalization accelerates, information on foreign markets as well as on a wider variety of competitors, suppliers, customers, substitutes, and potential new entrants becomes more critical. Industry analysis helps a firm not only to evaluate the profit potential of an industry but also to consider various ways to strengthen its position vis-à-vis the five forces. However, we'd like to address a few caveats.

First, *managers must not always avoid low-profit industries (or low-profit segments in profitable industries)*.[76] Such industries can still yield high returns for some players who pursue sound strategies. As examples, consider Paychex, a payroll-processing company, and WellPoint Health Network, a huge health care insurer:[77]

Paychex, with $2 billion in revenues, became successful by serving small businesses. Existing firms had ignored them because they assumed that such businesses could not afford the service. When Paychex's founder, Tom Golisano, failed to convince his bosses at Electronic Accounting Systems that they were missing a great opportunity, he launched the firm. It now serves nearly 600,000 clients in the United States and Germany. Paychex's after-tax-return on sales is a stunning 25 percent.

In 1986, WellPoint Health Network (when it was known as Blue Cross of California) suffered a loss of $160 million. That year, Leonard Schaeffer became CEO and challenged the conventional wisdom that individuals and small firms were money losers. (This was certainly "heresy" at the time—the firm was losing $5 million a year insuring 65,000 individuals!) However, by the early 1990s, the health insurer was leading the industry in profitability. The firm has continued to grow and outperform its rivals even during economic downturns. By 2012, its revenues and profits were $61 billion and $2.5 billion, respectively.

zero-sum game
a situation in which multiple players interact, and winners win only by taking from other players.

Second, five-forces analysis implicitly *assumes a* **zero-sum game,** *determining how a firm can enhance its position relative to the forces.* Yet such an approach can often be shortsighted; that is, it can overlook the many potential benefits of developing constructive win–win relationships with suppliers and customers. Establishing long-term mutually beneficial relationships with suppliers improves a firm's ability to implement just-in-time (JIT) inventory systems, which let it manage inventories better and respond quickly to market demands. A recent study found that if a company exploits its powerful position against a supplier, that action may come back to haunt the company.[78] Consider, for example, General Motors' heavy-handed dealings with its suppliers:[79]

In 2014, GM was already locked in a public relations nightmare as a deadly ignition defect triggered the recall of over 2.5 million vehicles.[80] At the same time, it was faced with another perception problem: poor supplier relations. GM is now considered the worst big automaker to deal with, according to a new survey of top suppliers in the car industry in the United States.

The annual survey, conducted by the automotive consultant group, Planning Perspectives Inc., asks the industry's biggest suppliers to rate the relationships with the six automakers that account for more than 85 percent of all cars and light trucks in the U.S. Those so-called "Tier 1" suppliers say GM is their least favorite big customer—less popular than even Chrysler, the unit of Fiat Chrysler Automobiles that had "earned" the dubious distinction since 2008.

The suppliers gave GM low marks on all kinds of measures, including its overall trustworthiness, its communication skills, and its protection of intellectual property. The suppliers also said that GM was the automaker least likely to allow them to raise prices to recoup unexpected materials cost increases. In return, parts executives have said they tend to bring hot new technology to other carmakers first—certainly something that makes it more difficult for GM to compete in this hotly contested industry.

Third, the five-forces analysis also has been criticized for *being essentially a static analysis.* External forces as well as strategies of individual firms are continually changing the structure of all industries. The search for a dynamic theory of strategy has led to

EXHIBIT 2.6 The Value Net

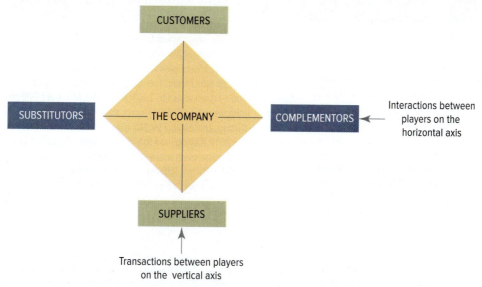

Sources: Adapted from "The Right Game: Use Game Theory Shape Strategy," by A. Brandenburger and B.J. Nalebuff, July-August 1995 Harvard Business Review.

greater use of game theory in industrial organization economics research and strategy research.

Based on game-theoretic considerations, Brandenburger and Nalebuff recently introduced the concept of the value net,[81] which in many ways is an extension of the five-forces analysis. It is illustrated in Exhibit 2.6. The value net represents all the players in the game and analyzes how their interactions affect a firm's ability to generate and appropriate value. The vertical dimension of the net includes suppliers and customers. The firm has direct transactions with them. On the horizontal dimension are substitutes and complements, players with whom a firm interacts but may not necessarily transact. The concept of complementors is perhaps the single most important contribution of value net analysis and is explained in more detail below.

Complements typically are products or services that have a potential impact on the value of a firm's own products or services. Those who produce complements are usually referred to as complementors.[82] Powerful hardware is of no value to a user unless there is software that runs on it. Similarly, new and better software is possible only if the hardware on which it can be run is available. This is equally true in the video game industry, where the sales of game consoles and video games complement each other. Nintendo's success in the early 1990s was a result of its ability to manage its relationship with its complementors. Nintendo built a security chip into the hardware and then licensed the right to develop games to outside firms. These firms paid a royalty to Nintendo for each copy of the game sold. The royalty revenue enabled Nintendo to sell game consoles at close to their cost, thereby increasing their market share, which, in turn, caused more games to be sold and more royalties to be generated.[83]

Despite efforts to create win–win scenarios, conflict among complementors is inevitable.[84] After all, it is naive to expect that even the closest of partners will do you the favor of abandoning their own interests. And even the most successful partnerships are seldom trouble-free. Power is a factor that comes into play as we see in Strategy Spotlight 2.6 with the example of Apple's iPod—an enormously successful product.

We would like to close this section with some recent insights from Michael Porter, the originator of the five-forces analysis.[85] He addresses two critical issues in conducting a

complements
products or services that have an impact on the value of a firm's products or services.

APPLE'S IPOD: RELATIONSHIPS WITH ITS COMPLEMENTORS

In 2002, Steve Jobs began his campaign to cajole the major music companies into selling tracks to iPod users through the iTunes Music Store, an online retail site. Most industry executives, after being burned by illegal file-sharing services like Napster and Kazaa, just wanted digital music to disappear. However, Jobs's passionate vision persuaded them to climb on board. He promised to reduce the risks that they faced by offering safeguards against piracy, as well as a hip product (iPod and iPad Touch) that would drive sales.

However, Apple had a much stronger bargaining position when its contracts with the music companies came up for renewal in April 2005. By then, iTunes had captured 80 percent of the market for legal downloads. The music companies, which were receiving between 60 and 70 cents per download, wanted more. Their reasoning: If the iTunes Music Store would only charge $1.50 or $2.00 per track, they could double or triple their revenues and profits. Since Jobs knew that he could sell more iPods if the music

was cheap, he was determined to keep the price of a download at 99 cents and to maintain Apple's margins. Given iTunes' dominant position, the music companies had little choice but to relent.

Apple's foray into music has been tremendously successful. Since the iPod's Introduction in 2001, Apple has sold over 300 million iPod units worldwide. And iTunes software and services are still going strong, increasing to $16 billion in 2013—a 71 percent increase over 2011! Having won the music market, Apple's success elsewhere has come even more quickly. Apple's millions of users create powerful network effects, exerting a strong gravitational pull on content providers to participate in the iTunes ecosystem. By mid-2013, the iTunes store had captured more than 65 percent of the market for digital movies and television programming—a market largely created by Apple.

Sources: Downes, L. & Nunes, P. 2014. *Big bang disruption.* New York: Penguin; Reisinger, D. 2012. Why the iPod (yes, the iPod) still matters. *Fortune,* October 8: 79; Hesseldahl, A. 2008. Now that we all have iPods. *BusinessWeek,* December 15: 36; Apple Computer Inc. 10-K, 2010; 2012 Apple, Inc. Annual Report; and Yoffie, D. B. & Kwak, M. 2006. With friends like these: The art of managing complementors. *Harvard Business Review,* 84(9): 88–98.

good industry analysis, which will yield an improved understanding of the root causes of profitability: (1) choosing the appropriate time frame and (2) a rigorous quantification of the five forces.

- ***Good industry analysis looks rigorously at the structural underpinnings of profitability. A first step is to understand the time horizon.*** One of the essential tasks in industry analysis is to distinguish short-term fluctuations from structural changes. A good guideline for the appropriate time horizon is the full business cycle for the particular industry. For most industries, a three- to five-year horizon is appropriate. However, for some industries with long lead times, such as mining, the appropriate horizon may be a decade or more. It is average profitability over this period, not profitability in any particular year, which should be the focus of analysis.

- ***The point of industry analysis is not to declare the industry attractive or unattractive but to understand the underpinnings of competition and the root causes of profitability.*** As much as possible, analysts should look at industry structure quantitatively, rather than be satisfied with lists of qualitative factors. Many elements of five forces can be quantified: the percentage of the buyer's total cost accounted for by the industry's product (to understand buyer price sensitivity); the percentage of industry sales required to fill a plant or operate a logistical network to efficient scale (to help assess barriers to entry); and the buyer's switching cost (determining the inducement an entrant or rival must offer customers).

strategic groups
clusters of firms that share similar strategies.

LO2.7

The concept of strategic groups and their strategy and performance implications.

Strategic Groups within Industries

In an industry analysis, two assumptions are unassailable: (1) No two firms are totally different, and (2) no two firms are exactly the same. The issue becomes one of identifying groups of firms that are more similar to each other than firms that are not, otherwise known as **strategic groups.**[86] This is important because rivalry tends to be greater among firms that are alike. Strategic groups are clusters of firms that share similar strategies. After all, is Kmart more concerned about Nordstrom or Walmart? Is Mercedes more concerned about Hyundai or BMW? The answers are straightforward.[87]

These examples are not meant to trivialize the strategic groups concept.[88] Classifying an industry into strategic groups involves judgment. If it is useful as an analytical tool, we must exercise caution in deciding what dimensions to use to map these firms. Dimensions include breadth of product and geographic scope, price/quality, degree of vertical integration, type of distribution (e.g., dealers, mass merchandisers, private label), and so on. Dimensions should also be selected to reflect the variety of strategic combinations in an industry. For example, if all firms in an industry have roughly the same level of product differentiation (or R&D intensity), this would not be a good dimension to select.

What value is the strategic groups concept as an analytical tool? *First, strategic groupings help a firm identify barriers to mobility that protect a group from attacks by other groups.*[89] Mobility barriers are factors that deter the movement of firms from one strategic position to another. For example, in the chainsaw industry, the major barriers protecting the high-quality/dealer-oriented group are technology, brand image, and an established network of servicing dealers.

The second value of strategic grouping is that it *helps a firm identify groups whose competitive position may be marginal or tenuous.* We may anticipate that these competitors may exit the industry or try to move into another group. In recent years in the retail department store industry, firms such as JCPenney and Sears have experienced extremely difficult times because they were stuck in the middle, neither an aggressive discount player like Walmart nor a prestigious upscale player like Neiman Marcus.

Third, strategic groupings *help chart the future directions of firms' strategies.* Arrows emanating from each strategic group can represent the direction in which the group (or a firm within the group) seems to be moving. If all strategic groups are moving in a similar direction, this could indicate a high degree of future volatility and intensity of competition. In the automobile industry, for example, the competition in the minivan and sport utility segments has intensified in recent years as many firms have entered those product segments.

Fourth, strategic groups are *helpful in thinking through the implications of each industry trend for the strategic group as a whole.* Is the trend decreasing the viability of a group? If so, in what direction should the strategic group move? Is the trend increasing or decreasing entry barriers? Will the trend decrease the ability of one group to separate itself from other groups? Such analysis can help in making predictions about industry evolution. A sharp increase in interest rates, for example, tends to have less impact on providers of higher-priced goods (e.g., Porsches) than on providers of lower-priced goods (e.g., Chevrolet Cobalt), whose customer base is much more price-sensitive.

Exhibit 2.7 provides a strategic grouping of the worldwide automobile industry.[90] The firms in each group are representative; not all firms are included in the mapping. We have identified four strategic groups. In the top left-hand corner are high-end luxury automakers that focus on a very narrow product market. Most of the cars produced by the members of this group cost well over $100,000. Some cost over twice that amount. The 2015 Ferrari California T starts at $201,940, and the 2015 Lamborghini Huracan will set you back $237,250 (in case you were wondering how to spend your employment signing bonus). Players in this market have a very exclusive clientele and face little rivalry from other strategic groups. At the other extreme, in the lower left-hand corner is a strategic group that has low-price/quality attributes and targets a narrow market. These players, Hyundai and Kia, limit competition from other strategic groups by pricing their products very low. The third group (near the middle) consists of firms high in product pricing/quality and average in their product-line breadth. The final group (at the far right) consists of firms with a

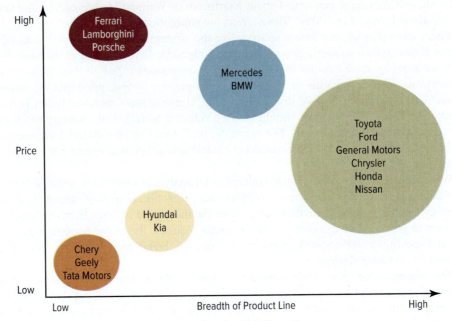

EXHIBIT 2.7 The World Automobile Industry: Strategic Groups

High

Ferrari
Lamborghini
Porsche

Mercedes
BMW

Toyota
Ford
General Motors
Chrysler
Honda
Nissan

Price

Hyundai
Kia

Chery
Geely
Tata Motors

Low

Low   Breadth of Product Line   High

Note: Members of each strategic group are not exhaustive, only illustrative.

broad range of products and multiple price points. These firms have entries that compete at both the lower end of the market (e.g., the Ford Focus) and the higher end (e.g., Chevrolet Corvette).

The auto market has been very dynamic and competition has intensified in recent years.[91] For example, some players are going more upscale with their product offerings. In 2009, Hyundai introduced its Genesis, starting at $33,000. This brings Hyundai into direct competition with entries from other strategic groups such as Toyota's Camry and Honda's Accord. And, in 2010, Hyundai introduced the Equus model. It was priced at about $60,000 to compete directly with the Lexus 460 on price. To further intensify competition, some upscale brands are increasingly entering lower-priced segments. In 2014, Audi introduced the Q3 SUV at a base price of only $32,500. And BMW, with its 1-series, is another well-known example. Such cars, priced in the low $30,000s, compete more directly with products from broad-line manufacturers like Ford, General Motors, and Toyota. This suggests that members of a strategic group can overcome mobility barriers and migrate to other groups that they find attractive if they are willing to commit time and resources.

Our discussion would not be complete, of course, without paying some attention to recent entries in the automobile industry that will likely lead to the formation of a new strategic group—placed at the bottom left corner of the grid in Exhibit 2.7. Three firms— China's Zhejiang Geely Holding Company, China's Chery Automobile Company, and India's Tata Motors—have introduced models that bring new meaning to the term "subcompact."[92] Let's take a look at these econoboxes.

Chery's 2013 QQ model sells for between $6,083 and $8,170 in the Chinese market and sports horsepower in the range of only 51 to 74. Geely's best-selling four-door sedan, the Free Cruiser, retails from $5,440 to $7,046. The firm has gone more upscale with some offerings, such as the GX7, a sports utility vehicle with a price starting at $14,910.

For low price-points, India's Tata Motors has everyone beat by the proverbial mile. In January 2008, it introduced the Nano as the "World's Cheapest Car," with an astonishing retail price of only $2,500. It is a four-door, five-seat hatchback that gets 54 miles to the gallon (but this economy originally came with a 30 horsepower motor). Initially, it was

Should Large Firms Further Delay Payments to their Suppliers?

In 2013, Mondelez International, the snack and food company recently spun off by Kraft Foods, sent a letter to its suppliers explaining its new policy: 120 days before paying a bill is now standard operating policy. It appears that this is a growing trend—companies withholding payment to suppliers after a service is performed or a product delivered. Procter & Gamble drew complaints when it started negotiating with suppliers to extend the delay in payments to 75 days, up from 45 days. Unilever is considering a similar move, and Merck has broached the subject of waiting 90 days to pay its vendors and suppliers.

One can easily understand why a large company would be tempted to hold off paying its suppliers. Holding onto millions—or even billions—of dollars for an extra month or two (or four) can free up cash to invest or generate whatever interest it can gain. In an environment in which businesses are continually scrambling to boost earnings in an uncertain economic climate, it's an easy way to hike profits.

Bill Dunkelberg, chief economist for the National Federation of Independent Businesses, has a different perspective: "It's mean. It's a pain in the butt and costly for small firms that are having this happen to them." Small companies are often very vulnerable because one large customer may make up the bulk of a small firm's sales, leaving it with little choice but to accede to the demands of a giant company—effectively financing the customer for 120 days.

In response to an inquiry by Becky Quick, a *Fortune* writer, a Mondelez spokesman emailed a statement, reading in part: "Extending our payment terms allows us to better align with industry (norms) and make sure we compete on fair grounds, while simultaneously improving transparency and predictability of payment processes." However, it may appear ironic that the company tailors its terms so that its customers are penalized if they don't pay for confections within 15 days of receipt and for snacks within 25 days, according to an industry insider.

Discussion Questions

1. Should Mondelez and other companies follow the practice of lengthening payment terms with their suppliers? Why? Or why not?
2. Do you feel that this practice can raise ethical issues?
3. What actions can suppliers take to respond to the lengthening of the payment terms?

Source: Quick, B. 2013. A snack maker's unsavory business practices. *Fortune,* September 2: 54.

a big hit in India. However, after sales peaked at about 80,000 units in 2011–2012, they crashed to only 21,000 units in 2013–2014. As noted by Girish Wagh, the man behind the Nano, "People started looking at Nano not as a low-cost innovation, but as a cheap car. This, among other factors, also hurt the chances." Needless to say, Tata has made many attempts to make the car more upscale, with a correspondingly higher price.

Not surprisingly, some automakers have recently entered the Indian market with more desirable offerings. Several have offerings that are called compact sedans, but they are actually hatchbacks with a tiny trunk tacked on. These models include Suzuki's Dzire, Honda's Amaze, and Hyundai's Xcent. Prices start at around $8,000, and with the added cachet of a sedan silhouette that adds only a few hundred dollars, these models have become very popular with Indian buyers. This niche is one of the few car segments that soared, while the country's overall car market shrunk.

Reflecting on Career Implications . . .

◼ **Creating the Environmentally Aware Organization:** Advancing your career requires constant scanning, monitoring, and intelligence gathering not only to find future job opportunities but also to understand how employers' expectations are changing. Consider using websites such as LinkedIn to find opportunities. Merely posting your résumé on a site such as LinkedIn may not be enough. Instead, consider in what ways you can use such sites for scanning, monitoring, and intelligence gathering.

◼ **SWOT Analysis:** As an analytical method, SWOT analysis is applicable for individuals as it is for firms. It is important for you to periodically evaluate your strengths and weaknesses as well as potential opportunities and threats to your career. Such analysis should be followed by efforts to address your weaknesses by improving your skills and capabilities.

◼ **General Environment:** The general environment consists of several segments, such as the demographic, sociocultural, political/legal, technological, economic, and global environments. It would be useful to evaluate how each of these segments can affect your career opportunities. Identify two or three specific trends (e.g., rapid technological change, aging of the population, increase in minimum wages) and their impact on your choice of careers. These also provide possibilities for you to add value for your organization.

◼ **Five-Forces Analysis:** Before you go for a job interview, consider the five forces affecting the industry within which the firm competes. This will help you to appear knowledgeable about the industry and increase your odds of landing the job. It also can help you to decide if you want to work for that organization. If the "forces" are unfavorable, the long-term profit potential of the industry may be unattractive, leading to fewer resources available and—all other things being equal—fewer career opportunities.

summary

Managers must analyze the external environment to minimize or eliminate threats and exploit opportunities. This involves a continuous process of environmental scanning and monitoring as well as obtaining competitive intelligence on present and potential rivals. These activities provide valuable inputs for developing forecasts. In addition, many firms use scenario planning to anticipate and respond to volatile and disruptive environmental changes.

We identified two types of environments: the general environment and the competitive environment. The six segments of the general environment are demographic, sociocultural, political/legal, technological, economic, and global. Trends and events occurring in these segments, such as the aging of the population, higher percentages of women in the workplace, governmental legislation, and increasing (or decreasing) interest rates, can have a dramatic effect on a firm. A given trend or event may have a positive impact on some industries and a negative, a neutral, or no impact on others.

The competitive environment consists of industry-related factors and has a more direct impact than the general environment. Porter's five-forces model of industry analysis includes the threat of new entrants, buyer power, supplier power, threat of substitutes, and rivalry among competitors. The intensity of these factors determines, in large part, the average expected level of profitability in an industry. A sound awareness of such factors, both individually and in combination, is beneficial not only for deciding what industries to enter but also for assessing how a firm can improve its competitive position. We discuss how many of the changes brought about by the digital economy can be understood in the context of five-forces analysis. The limitations of five-forces analysis include its static nature and its inability to acknowledge the role of complementors. Although we addressed the general environment and competitive environment in separate sections, they are quite interdependent. A given environmental trend or event, such as changes in the ethnic composition of a population or a technological innovation, typically has a much greater impact on some industries than on others.

The concept of strategic groups is also important to the external environment of a firm. No two organizations are completely different nor are they exactly the same. The question is how to group firms in an industry on the basis of similarities in their resources and strategies. The strategic groups concept is valuable for determining mobility barriers across groups, identifying groups with marginal competitive positions, charting the future directions of firm strategies, and assessing the implications of industry trends for the strategic group as a whole.

SUMMARY REVIEW QUESTIONS

1. Why must managers be aware of a firm's external environment?
2. What is gathering and analyzing competitive intelligence, and why is it important for firms to engage in it?
3. Discuss and describe the six elements of the external environment.
4. Select one of these elements and describe some changes relating to it in an industry that interests you.
5. Describe how the five forces can be used to determine the average expected profitability in an industry.

6. What are some of the limitations (or caveats) in using five-forces analysis?

7. Explain how the general environment and industry environment are highly related. How can such interrelationships affect the profitability of a firm or industry?

8. Explain the concept of strategic groups. What are the performance implications?

key terms

perceptual acuity 38
environmental
  scanning 39
environmental
  monitoring 39

competitive
  intelligence 39
environmental
  forecasting 40
scenario analysis 42
SWOT analysis 42
general
  environment 43
demographic segment
  of the general
  environment 45

sociocultural segment of the
  general environment 45
political/legal segment
  of the general
  environment 47
technological segment
  of the general
  environment 48
economic segment
  of the general
  environment 49
global segment
  of the general
  environment 49
crowdsourcing 50
industry 52
competitive
  environment 52
Porter's five-forces
  model of industry
  competition 52

threat of new
  entrants 53
economies of scale 53
product differentiation 53
switching cost 54
bargaining power of
  buyers 54
bargaining power of
  suppliers 55
threat of substitute
  products and
  services 56
substitute products and
  services 56
intensity of rivalry
  among competitors
  in an industry 56
Internet 58
zero-sum game 62
complements 63
strategic groups 64

experiential exercise

Select one of the following industries: personal computers, airlines, or automobiles. For this industry, evaluate the strength of each of Porter's five forces as well as complementors.

Industry Force	High? Medium? Low?	Why?
1. Threat of new entrants		
2. Power of buyers		
3. Power of suppliers		
4. Power of substitutes		
5. Rivalry among competitors		
6. Complementors		

application questions & exercises

1. Imagine yourself as the CEO of a large firm in an industry in which you are interested. Please (1) identify major trends in the general environment, (2) analyze their impact on the firm, and (3) identify major sources of information to monitor these trends. (Use Internet and library resources.)

2. Analyze movements across the strategic groups in the U.S. retail industry. How do these movements within this industry change the nature of competition?

3. What are the major trends in the general environment that have impacted the U.S. pharmaceutical industry?

4. Go to the Internet and look up *www.kroger.com*. What are some of the five forces driving industry competition that are affecting the profitability of this firm?

ethics questions

1. What are some of the legal and ethical issues involved in collecting competitor intelligence in the following situations?

   a. Hotel A sends an employee posing as a potential client to Hotel B to find out who Hotel B's major corporate customers are.

   b. A firm hires an MBA student to collect information directly from a competitor while claiming the information is for a course project.

   c. A firm advertises a nonexistent position and interviews a rival's employees with the intention of obtaining competitor information.

2. What are some of the ethical implications that arise when a firm tries to exploit its power over a supplier?

references

1. Schneider, J. & Hall, J. 2011. Can you hear me now? *Harvard Business Review,* 89(4): 23; Hornigan, J. 2009. Wireless Internet use—Mobile access to data and information. *www.pewinternet.org,* July 22: np; and Salemi Industries. 2012. Home page. *www.salemiindustries.com,* December 20: np.

2. Hamel, G. & Prahalad, C. K. 1994. *Competing for the future.* Boston: Harvard Business School Press.

3. Drucker, P. F. 1994. Theory of the business. *Harvard Business Review,* 72: 95–104.

4. For an insightful discussion on managers' assessment of the external environment, refer to Sutcliffe, K. M. & Weber, K. 2003. The high cost of accurate knowledge. *Harvard Business Review,* 81(5): 74–86.

5. Merino, M. 2013. You can't be a wimp: Making the tough calls. *Harvard Business Review,* 91(11): 73–78.

6. For insights on recognizing and acting on environmental opportunities, refer to Alvarez, S. A. & Barney, J. B. 2008. Opportunities, organizations, and entrepreneurship: Theory and debate. *Strategic Entrepreneurship Journal,* 2(3): entire issue.

7. Charitou, C. D. & Markides, C. C. 2003. Responses to disruptive strategic innovation. *MIT Sloan Management Review,* 44(2): 55–64.

8. Our discussion of scanning, monitoring, competitive intelligence, and forecasting concepts draws on several sources. These include Fahey, L. & Narayanan, V. K. 1983. *Macroenvironmental analysis for strategic management.* St. Paul, MN: West; Lorange, P., Scott, F. S., & Ghoshal, S. 1986. *Strategic control.* St. Paul, MN: West; Ansoff, H. I. 1984. *Implementing strategic management.* Englewood Cliffs, NJ: Prentice Hall; and Schreyogg, G. & Stienmann, H. 1987. Strategic control: A new perspective. *Academy of Management Review,* 12: 91–103.

9. An insightful discussion on how leaders can develop "peripheral vision" in environmental scanning is found in Day, G. S. & Schoemaker, P. J. H. 2008. Are you a "vigilant leader"? *MIT Sloan Management Review,* 49(3): 43–51.

10. Elenkov, D. S. 1997. Strategic uncertainty and environmental scanning: The case for institutional influences on scanning behavior. *Strategic Management Journal,* 18: 287–302.

11. For an interesting perspective on environmental scanning in emerging economies, see May, R. C., Stewart, W. H., & Sweo, R. 2000. Environmental scanning behavior in a transitional economy, Evidence from Russia. *Academy of Management Journal,* 43(3): 403–427.

12. Bryon, E. 2010. For insight into P&G, check Olay numbers. *Wall Street Journal,* October 27: C1.

13. Tang, J. 2010. How entrepreneurs discover opportunities in China: An institutional view. *Asia Pacific Journal of Management,* 27(3): 461–480.

14. Walters, B. A. & Priem, R. L. 1999. Business strategy and CEO intelligence acquisition. *Competitive Intelligence Review,* 10(2): 15–22.

15. Prior, V. 1999. The language of competitive intelligence, Part 4. *Competitive Intelligence Review,* 10(1): 84–87.

16. Hill, K. 2011. The spy who liked me. *Forbes,* November 21: 56–57.

17. Wolfenson, J. 1999. The world in 1999: A battle for corporate honesty. *The Economist,* 38: 13–30.

18. Drucker, P. F. 1997. The future that has already happened. *Harvard Business Review,* 75(6): 22.

19. Downes, L. & Nunes, P. 2014. *Big bang disruption.* New York: Penguin.

20. Fahey & Narayanan, op. cit., p. 41.

21. Insights on how to improve predictions can be found in Cross, R., Thomas, R. J., & Light, D. A. 2009. The prediction lover's handbook. *MIT Sloan Management Review,* 50(2): 32–34.

22. Courtney, H., Kirkland, J., & Viguerie, P. 1997. Strategy under uncertainty. *Harvard Business Review,* 75(6): 66–79.

23. Odlyzko, A. 2003. False hopes. *Red Herring,* March: 31.

24. Zweig, J. 2014. Lessons learned from year of shock. *The Wall Street Journal,* December 31: C1–C2; Coy, P. 2009. Worst predictions about 2008. *BusinessWeek,* January 12: 15–16; Pressman, A. 2014. Apple competitors still smarting from iPhone blow. *finance.yahoo.com,* July 17: np; Kowitt, B. Whole Foods takes over America. *Fortune.com,* April 10: 70–77; Basinger, J. 2014. "Gone with the Wind" goes Hollywood. *The Wall Street Journal,* October 4–5: C15; and *www.aarp.org.*

25. Zweig, op. cit.

26. For an interesting perspective on how Accenture practices and has developed its approach to scenario planning, refer to Ferguson, G., Mathur, S., & Shah, B. 2005. Evolving from information to insight. *MIT Sloan Management Review,* 46(2): 51–58.

27. Byrne, J. 2012. Great ideas are hard to come by. *Fortune,* April 7: 69 ff.

28. Dean, T. J., Brown, R. L., & Bamford, C. E. 1998. Differences in large and small firm responses to environmental context: Strategic implications from a comparative analysis of business formations. *Strategic Management Journal,* 19: 709–728.

29. Colvin, G. 2014. Four things that worry business. *Fortune,* October 27: 32.

30. Colvin, G. 1997. How to beat the boomer rush. *Fortune,* August 18: 59–63.

31. Porter, M. E. 2010. Discovering—and lowering—the real costs of health care. *Harvard Business Review,* 89(1/2): 49–50.

32. Farrell, C. 2014. Baby boomers' latest revolution: Unretirement. *Dallas Morning News,* October 19: 4P.

33. Challenger, J. 2000. Women's corporate rise has reduced relocations. *Lexington* (KY) *Herald-Leader,* October 29: D1.

34. Tsao, A. 2005. Retooling home improvement, *Businesssweek.com,* February 14; and Grow, B. 2004. Who wears the wallet in the family? *BusinessWeek,* August 16:10.

35. Watkins, M. D. 2003. Government games. *MIT Sloan Management Review,* 44(2): 91–95.

36. A discussion of the political issues surrounding caloric content on meals is in Orey, M. 2008. A food fight over calorie counts. *BusinessWeek,* February 11: 36.

37. For a discussion of the linkage between copyright law and innovation, read Guterman, J. 2009. Does copyright law hinder innovation? *MIT Sloan Management Review,* 50(2): 14–15.

38. Davies, A. 2000. The welcome mat is out for nerds. *BusinessWeek,* May 21: 17; Broache, A. 2007. Annual H-1B visa cap met—already. *news.cnet.com,* April 3: np; and Anonymous. Undated. Cap count for H-1B and H-2B workers for fiscal year 2009. *www.uscis.gov:* np.

39. Weise, K. 2014. How to hack the visa limit. *Bloomberg Businessweek,* May 26–June 1: 39–40.

40. Anonymous. 2014. The 140,000-code question. *The Economist,* May 31: 27.

41. Hout, T. M. & Ghemawat, P. 2010. China vs. the world: Whose technology is it? *Harvard Business Review,* 88(12): 94–103.

42. Business ready for Internet revolution. 1999. *Financial Times,* May 21: 17.

43. A discussion of an alternate energy—marine energy—is the topic of Boyle, M. 2008. Scottish power. *Fortune,* March 17: 28.

44. Baker, S. & Aston, A. 2005. The business of nanotech. *BusinessWeek,* February 14: 64–71.

45. Wilson, H. J. 2013. Wearables in the workplace. *Harvard Business Review,* 91(9): 22–25.

46. For an insightful discussion of the causes of the global financial crisis, read Johnson, S. 2009. The global financial crisis—What really precipitated it? *MIT Sloan Management Review,* 50(2): 16–18.

47. Tyson, L. D. 2011. A better stimulus for the U.S. economy. *Harvard Business Review,* 89(1/2): 53.

48. An interesting and balanced discussion on the merits of multinationals to the U.S. economy is found in Mandel, M. 2008. Multinationals: Are they good for America? *BusinessWeek,* March 10: 41–64.

49. Insights on risk perception across countries are addressed in Purda, L. D. 2008. Risk perception and the financial system. *Journal of International Business Studies,* 39(7): 1178–1196.

50. Thurm, S. 2012. U.S. firms add jobs, but mostly overseas. *wsj.com,* April 27: np.

51. Goll, I. & Rasheed, M. A. 1997. Rational decision-making and firm performance: The moderating role of environment. *Strategic Management Journal,* 18: 583–591.

52. Our discussion of crowdsourcing draws on the first two books that have addressed the concept: Libert, B. & Spector, J. 2008. *We are smarter than me.* Philadelphia: Wharton; and Howe, J. 2008. *Crowdsourcing.* New York: Crown Business. Eric von Hippel addressed similar issues in his 2005 book, *Democraticizing innovation,* Cambridge, MA.: MIT Press.

53. This discussion draws heavily on Porter, M. E. 1980. *Competitive strategy:* chap. 1. New York: Free Press.

54. Ibid.

55. Rivalry in the airline industry is discussed in Foust, D. 2009. Which airlines will disappear in 2009? *BusinessWeek,* January 19: 46–47.

56. Fryer, B. 2001. Leading through rough times: An interview with Novell's Eric Schmidt. *Harvard Business Review,* 78(5): 117–123.

57. For a discussion on the importance of barriers to entry within industries, read Greenwald, B. & Kahn, J. 2005. *Competition demystified: A radically simplified approach to business strategy.* East Rutherford, NJ: Portfolio.

58. A discussion of how the medical industry has erected entry barriers that have resulted in lawsuits is found in Whelan, D. 2008. Bad medicine. *BusinessWeek,* March 10: 86–98.

59. Colvin, G. 2014. Welcome to the era of Lego innovations (some assembly required). *Fortune,* April 14: 52.

60. Wise, R. & Baumgarter, P. 1999. Go downstream: The new profit imperative in manufacturing. *Harvard Business Review,* 77(5): 133–141.

61. Salman, W. A. 2000. The new economy is stronger than you think. *Harvard Business Review,* 77(6): 99–106.

62. Staley, O. 2011. California universities feel the squeeze. *Bloomberg Businessweek,* January 24–January 30: 20–30.

63. Mudambi, R. & Helper, S. 1998. The "close but adversarial" model of supplier relations in the U.S. auto industry. *Strategic Management Journal,* 19: 775–792.

64. Stevens, D. (vice president of Delta Pride Catfish, Inc.). 2014. *personal communication:* October 16; and Fritz, M. 1988. Agribusiness: Catfish story. *Forbes,* December 12: 37.

65. Trends in the solar industry are discussed in Carey, J. 2009. Solar: The sun will come out tomorrow. *BusinessWeek,* January 12: 51.

66. Edelstein, S. 2014. Could U.S. hybrid car sales be peaking already—and if so, why? *greencarreports.com,* June 16: np; and Naughton, K. 2012. Hybrids' unlikely rival: plain old cars. *Bloomberg Businessweek,* February 2: 23–24.

67. An interesting analysis of self-regulation in an industry (chemical) is in Barnett, M. L. & King, A. A. 2008. Good fences make good neighbors: A longitudinal analysis of an industry self-regulatory institution. *Academy of Management Journal,* 51(6): 1053–1078.

68. For an interesting perspective on the intensity of competition in the supermarket industry, refer to Anonymous. 2005. Warfare in the aisles. *The Economist,* April 2: 6–8.

69. Macmillan, D. 2014. Tech's fiercest rivalry: Uber vs. Lyft. *online.wsj.com,* August 11: np.

70. For an interesting perspective on changing features of firm boundaries, refer to Afuah, A. 2003. Redefining firm boundaries in the face of the Internet: Are firms really shrinking? *Academy of Management Review,* 28(1): 34–53.

71. Time to rebuild. 2001. *The Economist,* May 19: 55–56.

72. *www.amazon.com.*

73. For more on the role of the Internet as an electronic intermediary, refer to Carr, N. G. 2000. Hypermediation: Commerce as clickstream. *Harvard Business Review,* 78(1): 46–48.

74. *www.mysimon.com;* and *www.pricescan.com.*

75. *www.cnet.com;* and *www.bizrate.com.*

76. For insights into strategies in a low-profit industry, refer to Hopkins, M. S. 2008. The management lessons of a beleaguered industry. *MIT Sloan Management Review,* 50(1): 25–31.

77. Foust, D. 2007. The best performers. *BusinessWeek,* March 26: 58–95; Rosenblum, D., Tomlinson, D., & Scott, L. 2003. Bottom-feeding for blockbuster businesses. *Harvard Business Review,* 81(3): 52–59; Paychex 2006 Annual Report; and WellPoint Health Network 2005 Annual Report.

78. Kumar, N. 1996. The power of trust in manufacturer-retailer relationship. *Harvard Business Review,* 74(6): 92–110.

79. Welch, D. 2006. Renault-Nissan: Say hello to Bo. *BusinessWeek,* July 31: 56–57.

80. Kelleher, J. B. 2014. GM ranked worst automaker by U.S. suppliers—survey. *finance.yahoo.com,* May 12: np; and Welch, D. 2006. Renault-Nissan: Say hello to Bo. *BusinessWeek,* July 31: 56–57.

81. Brandenburger, A. & Nalebuff, B. J. 1995. The right game: Use game theory to shape strategy. *Harvard Business Review,* 73(4): 57–71.

82. For a scholarly discussion of complementary assets and their relationship to competitive advantage, refer to Stieglitz, N. & Heine, K. 2007. Innovations and the role of complementarities in a strategic theory of the firm. *Strategic Management Journal,* 28(1): 1–15.

83. A useful framework for the analysis of industry evolution has been proposed by Professor Anita McGahan of Boston University. Her analysis is based on the identification of the core activities and the core assets of an industry and the threats they face. She suggests that an industry may follow one of four possible evolutionary trajectories—radical change, creative change, intermediating change, or progressive change—based on these two types of threats of obsolescence. Refer to McGahan, A. M. 2004. How industries change. *Harvard Business Review,* 82(10): 87–94.

84. Yoffie, D. B. & Kwak, M. 2006. With friends like these: The art of managing complementors. *Harvard Business Review,* 84(9): 88–98.

85. Porter, M. I. 2008. The five competitive forces that shape strategy. *Harvard Business Review,* 86(1): 79–93.

86. Peteraf, M. & Shanley, M. 1997. Getting to know you: A theory of strategic group identity. *Strategic Management Journal,* 18 (Special Issue): 165–186.

87. An interesting scholarly perspective on strategic groups may be found in Dranove, D., Perteraf, M., & Shanley, M. 1998. Do strategic groups exist? An economic framework for analysis. *Strategic Management Journal,* 19(11): 1029–1044.

88. For an empirical study on strategic groups and predictors of performance, refer to Short, J. C., Ketchen, D. J., Jr., Palmer, T. B., & Hult, T. M. 2007. Firm, strategic group, and industry influences on performance. *Strategic Management Journal,* 28(2): 147–167.

89. This section draws on several sources, including Kerwin, K. R. & Haughton, K. 1997. Can Detroit make cars that baby boomers like? *BusinessWeek,* December 1: 134–148; and Taylor, A., III. 1994. The new golden age of autos. *Fortune,* April 4: 50–66.

90. Csere, C. 2001. Supercar supermarket. *Car and Driver,* January: 118–127.

91. For a discussion of the extent of overcapacity in the worldwide automobile industry, read Roberts, D., Matlack, C., Busyh, J., & Rowley, I. 2009. A hundred factories too many. *BusinessWeek,* January 19: 42–43.

92. McLain, S. 2014. India's middle class embraces minicars. *The Wall Street Journal,* October 9: B2; Anonymous. 2014. Geely GX7 launched after upgrading: Making versatile and comfortable SUV. *www.globaltimes.ch,* April 18: np; Anonymous. 2014. Adequate Guiyang Geely Free Cruiser higher offer 1,000 yuan now. *www.wantinews.com,* February 20: np; Anonymous. 2013. Restyled Chery QQ hit showrooms with a US$6,083 starting price. *www.chinaautoweb.com,* March 4: np; and Doval, P. 2014. Cheapest car tag hit Tata Nano: Creator. *economictimes.indiatimes.com,* August 21: np.

photo credits

Assessing the Internal Environment of the Firm

After reading this chapter, you should have a good understanding of the following learning objectives:

LO3.1 The benefits and limitations of SWOT analysis in conducting an internal analysis of the firm.

LO3.2 The primary and support activities of a firm's value chain.

LO3.3 How value-chain analysis can help managers create value by investigating relationships among activities within the firm and between the firm and its customers and suppliers.

LO3.4 The resource-based view of the firm and the different types of tangible and intangible resources, as well as organizational capabilities.

LO3.5 The four criteria that a firm's resources must possess to maintain a sustainable advantage and how value created can be appropriated by employees and managers.

LO3.6 The usefulness of financial ratio analysis, its inherent limitations, and how to make meaningful comparisons of performance across firms.

LO3.7 The value of the "balanced scorecard" in recognizing how the interests of a variety of stakeholders can be interrelated.

Learning from Mistakes

BYD (which stands for Build Your Dreams), founded by Wang Chuanfu in 1995, was originally a low-cost manufacturer of rechargeable lithium ion batteries for cell phones.[1] Wang had considerable expertise in batteries but virtually none in automotive technology. However, that didn't stop him from buying a state-owned automobile maker in 2002. He envisioned a central role for battery technologies in the rise of electric vehicles.

Although the company borrowed ideas from Japanese manufacturing (and reverse-engineered popular Japanese car designs), it shunned Japan's reliance on intensive automation and employed thousands of workers to produce not only cars but also most of the needed parts, from braking systems to CD players. And, in order to boost sales, it rapidly expanded dealerships in China, set aggressive sales targets, and pushed inventory to dealers in pursuit of those targets.

In 2008, Warren Buffett bought 10 percent of the company, dramatically enhancing its brand value and increasing BYD's sales in the United States. In 2009, its F3 model was the best-selling sedan in China, with more than 250,000 cars sold. The company's sales hit a peak of about 500,000 units in 2010. That year it was ranked as the eighth most innovative company in the world by *Businessweek*.

However, soon after, BYD began to falter. Consumer demand for electric vehicles was weak, and China Central Television questioned the company's quality standards. It was not surprising BYD ranked below the industry average on a number of J.D. Power studies, including initial quality and dependability.

Still, BYD did a few things right—from adopting a bold vision to establishing a position as a technology leader. Unfortunately, that vision was not rooted in reality. Widespread consumer adoption of battery-powered passenger vehicles is still far in the future (if it occurs at all). Further, the firm's emphasis on technology made a good start in establishing a strong competitive position, but a vehicle maker must also be known as reliable. *BYD's stumbles resulted from a failure to develop sophisticated capabilities such as new product development, demand forecasting, capacity planning, inventory management, and customer insight.* Going forward, the company may have to accept being a niche player, selling electric passenger cars and buses. And shareholders definitely haven't fared well—by the end of 2014 they had lost about half of the value that they had in 2010!

Discussion Question

1. What were BYD's key strategic mistakes? How could they have been avoided?

In this chapter we will place heavy emphasis on the value-chain concept. That is, we focus on the key value-creating activities (e.g., operations, marketing and sales, and procurement) that a firm must effectively manage and integrate in order to attain competitive advantages in the marketplace. However, firms not only must pay close attention to their own value-creating activities but also must maintain close and effective relationships with key organizations outside the firm boundaries, such as suppliers, customers, and alliance partners.

Although BYD was clearly a technology leader, it faltered because of its weaknesses in many value-creating activities. As noted earlier, these included new product development, inventory management, capacity planning, and customer insight.

LO3.1

The benefits and limitations of SWOT analysis in conducting an internal analysis of the firm.

3.1 STRATEGY SPOTLIGHT

THE LIMITATIONS OF SWOT ANALYSIS

SWOT analysis is a tried-and-true tool of strategic analysis. SWOT (strengths, weaknesses, opportunities, threats) analysis is used regularly in business to initially evaluate the opportunities and threats in the business environment as well as the strengths and weaknesses of a firm's internal environment. Top managers rely on SWOT to stimulate self-reflection and group discussions about how to improve their firm and position it for success.

But SWOT has its limitations. It is just a starting point for discussion. By listing the firm's attributes, managers have the raw material needed to perform more in-depth strategic analysis. However, SWOT cannot show them how to achieve a competitive advantage. They must not make SWOT analysis an end in itself, temporarily raising awareness about important issues but failing to lead to the kind of action steps necessary to enact strategic change.

Let's look at some of the limitations of SWOT analysis.

Strengths May Not Lead to an Advantage

A firm's strengths and capabilities, no matter how unique or impressive, may not enable it to achieve a competitive advantage in the marketplace. It is akin to recruiting a concert pianist to join a gang of thugs—even though such an ability is rare and valuable, it hardly helps the organization attain its goals and objectives! Similarly, the skills of a highly creative product designer would offer little competitive advantage to a firm that produces low-cost commodity products. Indeed, the additional expense of hiring such an individual could erode the firm's cost advantages. If a firm builds its strategy on a capability that cannot, by itself, create or sustain competitive advantage, it is essentially a wasted use of resources.

SWOT's Focus on the External Environment Is Too Narrow

Strategists who rely on traditional definitions of their industry and competitive environment often focus their sights too narrowly on current customers, technologies, and competitors. Hence they fail to notice important changes on the periphery of their environment that may trigger the need to redefine industry boundaries and identify a whole new set of competitive relationships. Consider *Encyclopaedia Britannica,* whose competitive position was severely eroded by a "nontraditional" competitor—CD-based encyclopedias (e.g., Microsoft *Encarta*) that could be used on home computers—and later by online encyclopedias (e.g., Wikipedia).

SWOT Gives a One-Shot View of a Moving Target

A key weakness of SWOT is that it is primarily a static assessment. It focuses too much of a firm's attention on one moment in time. Essentially, this is like studying a single frame of a motion picture. You may be able to identify the principal actors and learn something about the setting, but it doesn't tell you much about the plot. Competition among organizations is played out over time. As circumstances, capabilities, and strategies change, static analysis techniques do not reveal the dynamics of the competitive environment.

SWOT Overemphasizes a Single Dimension of Strategy

Sometimes firms become preoccupied with a single strength or a key feature of the product or service they are offering and ignore other factors needed for competitive success. For example, Toyota, the giant automaker, paid a heavy price for its excessive emphasis on cost control. The resulting problems with quality and the negative publicity led to severe financial losses and an erosion of its reputation in many markets.

SWOT analysis has much to offer, but only as a starting point. By itself, it rarely helps a firm develop competitive advantages that it can sustain over time.

Sources: Shapiro, C. & Varian, H. R. 2000. Versioning: The smart way to sell information. *Harvard Business Review,* 78(1): 99–106; and Picken, J. C. & Dess, G. G. 1997. *Mission critical.* Burr Ridge, IL: Irwin Professional.

Before moving to value-chain analysis, let's briefly revisit the benefits and limitations of SWOT analysis. As discussed in Chapter 2, a SWOT analysis consists of a careful listing of a firm's strengths, weaknesses, opportunities, and threats. While we believe SWOT analysis is very helpful as a starting point, it should not form the primary basis for evaluating a firm's internal strengths and weaknesses or the opportunities and threats in the environment. Strategy Spotlight 3.1 elaborates on the limitations of the traditional SWOT approach.

We will now turn to value-chain analysis. As you will see, it provides greater insights into analyzing a firm's competitive position than SWOT analysis does by itself.

Value-Chain Analysis

value-chain analysis
a strategic analysis of an organization that uses value-creating activities.

Value-chain analysis views the organization as a sequential process of value-creating activities. The approach is useful for understanding the building blocks of competitive advantage and was described in Michael Porter's seminal book *Competitive Advantage.*[2]

Value is the amount that buyers are willing to pay for what a firm provides them and is measured by total revenue, a reflection of the price a firm's product commands and the quantity it can sell. A firm is profitable when the value it receives exceeds the total costs involved in creating its product or service. Creating value for buyers that exceeds the costs of production (i.e., margin) is a key concept used in analyzing a firm's competitive position.

Porter described two different categories of activities. First, five **primary activities**—inbound logistics, operations, outbound logistics, marketing and sales, and service—contribute to the physical creation of the product or service, its sale and transfer to the buyer, and its service after the sale. Second, **support activities**—procurement, technology development, human resource management, and general administration—either add value by themselves or add value through important relationships with both primary activities and other support activities. Exhibit 3.1 illustrates Porter's value chain.

To get the most out of value-chain analysis, view the concept in its broadest context, without regard to the boundaries of your own organization. That is, place your organization within a more encompassing value chain that includes your firm's suppliers, customers, and alliance partners. Thus, in addition to thoroughly understanding how value is created within the organization, be aware of how value is created for other organizations in the overall supply chain or distribution channel.[3]

Next, we'll describe and provide examples of each of the primary and support activities. Then we'll provide examples of how companies add value by means of relationships among activities within the organization as well as activities outside the organization, such as those activities associated with customers and suppliers.[4]

Primary Activities

Five generic categories of primary activities are involved in competing in any industry, as shown in Exhibit 3.2. Each category is divisible into a number of distinct activities that depend on the particular industry and the firm's strategy.[5]

Inbound Logistics **Inbound logistics** is primarily associated with receiving, storing, and distributing inputs to the product. It includes material handling, warehousing, inventory control, vehicle scheduling, and returns to suppliers.

Just-in-time (JIT) inventory systems, for example, were designed to achieve efficient inbound logistics. In essence, Toyota epitomizes JIT inventory systems, in which parts

primary activities
sequential activities of the value chain that refer to the physical creation of the product or service, its sale and transfer to the buyer, and its service after sale, including inbound logistics, operations, outbound logistics, marketing and sales, and service.

support activities
activities of the value chain that either add value by themselves or add value through important relationships with both primary activities and other support activities, including procurement, technology development, human resource management, and general administration.

LO3.2

The primary and support activities of a firm's value chain.

inbound logistics
receiving, storing, and distributing inputs of a product.

EXHIBIT 3.1 The Value Chain: Primary and Support Activities

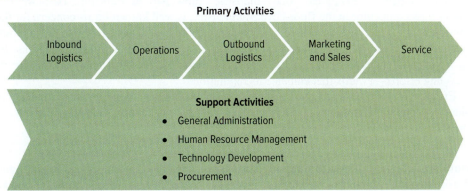

Adapted from *Competitive Advantage: Creating and Sustaining Superior Performance* by Michael E. Porter, 1985, 1998, Free Press.

Inbound Logistics

- Location of distribution facilities to minimize shipping times.
- Warehouse layout and designs to increase efficiency of operations for incoming materials.

Operations

- Efficient plant operations to minimize costs.
- Efficient plant layout and workflow design.
- Incorporation of appropriate process technology.

Outbound Logistics

- Effective shipping processes to provide quick delivery and minimize damages.
- Shipping of goods in large lot sizes to minimize transportation costs.

Marketing and Sales

- Innovative approaches to promotion and advertising.
- Proper identification of customer segments and needs.

Service

- Quick response to customer needs and emergencies.
- Quality of service personnel and ongoing training.

Source: Adapted from Porter, M. E. 1985. *Competitive Advantage: Creating and Sustaining Superior Performance.*
New York: Free Press.

deliveries arrive at the assembly plants only hours before they are needed. JIT systems will play a vital role in fulfilling Toyota's commitment to fill a buyer's new-car order in just five days.[6] This standard is in sharp contrast to most competitors that require approximately 30 days' notice to build vehicles. Toyota's standard is three times faster than even Honda Motors, considered to be the industry's most efficient in order follow-through. The five days represent the time from the company's receipt of an order to the time the car leaves the assembly plant. Actual delivery may take longer, depending on where a customer lives.

operations

all activities associated with transforming inputs into the final product form.

Operations   **Operations** include all activities associated with transforming inputs into the final product form, such as machining, packaging, assembly, testing, printing, and facility operations.

Creating environmentally friendly manufacturing is one way to use operations to achieve competitive advantage. Shaw Industries (now part of Berkshire Hathaway), a world-class competitor in the floor-covering industry, is well known for its concern for the environment.[7] It has been successful in reducing the expenses associated with the disposal of dangerous chemicals and other waste products from its manufacturing operations. Its environmental endeavors have multiple payoffs. Shaw has received many awards for its recycling efforts—awards that enhance its reputation.

Efficient operations can also provide a firm with many benefits in virtually any industry—including restaurants. Strategy Spotlight 3.2 discusses Chipotle's rather novel approach to improving its operations.

outbound logistics

collecting, storing, and distributing the product or service to buyers.

Outbound Logistics   **Outbound logistics** is associated with collecting, storing, and distributing the product or service to buyers. These activities include finished goods, warehousing, material handling, delivery vehicle operation, order processing, and scheduling.

CHIPOTLE'S EFFICIENT OPERATIONS

Peak hours at restaurants create real challenges that must be addressed. Otherwise, business may be lost and, worse yet, customers may never come back. Lines snaking out the doors have long been a bottleneck to growth at U.S. burrito chain Chipotle. However, the company has a plan—actually a four-step plan, to be exact.

The chain managed to accelerate service by six transactions per hour at peak times during a recent quarter (which is a significant increase over the mere two transactions per hour the previous quarter). "We achieved our fastest throughput ever," claims Steve Ells, co-CEO. However, some of Chipotle's fastest restaurants run more than 350 transactions per hour at lunchtime—more than three times the chainwide average.

How are such remarkable increases in productivity attained? By what the company calls "the four pillars of great throughput." These are:

- **Expediters.** An expediter is the extra person between the one who rolls your burrito and the one who rings up your order. The expediter's job? Getting your drink, asking if your order is "to go," and bagging your food.

- **Linebackers.** These are people who patrol the countertops, serving-ware, and bins of food, so the ones who are actually serving customers never turn their backs on them.

- **Mise en place.** In other restaurants, this means setting out ingredients and utensils ready for use. In Chipotle's case, it means zero tolerance for not having absolutely everything in place ahead of lunch and dinner rush hours.

- **Aces in their places.** This refers to a commitment to having what each branch considers its top servers in the most important positions at peak times. Thus, there are no trainees working at burrito rush hour.

No one can question Chipotle's success: In the past three years, it has experienced 20.5 percent annual sales growth, and its stock has soared 99 percent. And, in 2014, despite raising prices 6.5 percent in the second quarter, same-store sales grew 19.8 percent in the third quarter.

Sources: Ferdman, R. A. 2014. How Chipotle is going to serve burritos faster, and faster, and faster. www.qz.com, January 31: np; and Zillman, C. 2014. 2014's top people in business. *Fortune*, December 1: 156.

Campbell Soup uses an electronic network to facilitate its continuous-replenishment program with its most progressive retailers.[8] Each morning, retailers electronically inform Campbell of their product needs and of the level of inventories in their distribution centers. Campbell uses that information to forecast future demand and to determine which products require replenishment (based on the inventory limits previously established with each retailer). Trucks leave Campbell's shipping plant that afternoon and arrive at the retailers' distribution centers the same day. The program cuts the inventories of participating retailers from about a four- to a two-weeks' supply. Campbell Soup achieved this improvement because it slashed delivery time and because it knows the inventories of key retailers and can deploy supplies when they are most needed.

The Campbell Soup example also illustrates the win–win benefits of exemplary value-chain activities. Both the supplier (Campbell) and its buyers (retailers) come out ahead. Since the retailer makes more money on Campbell products delivered through continuous replenishment, it has an incentive to carry a broader line and give the company greater shelf space. After Campbell introduced the program, sales of its products grew twice as fast through participating retailers as through all other retailers. Not surprisingly, supermarket chains love such programs.

Marketing and Sales Marketing and sales activities are associated with purchases of products and services by end users and the inducements used to get them to make purchases.[9] They include advertising, promotion, sales force, quoting, channel selection, channel relations, and pricing.[10,11]

Consider product placement. This is a marketing strategy that many firms are increasingly adopting to reach customers who are not swayed by traditional advertising.

marketing and sales activities associated with purchases of products and services by end users and the inducements used to get them to make purchases.

A recent example is the starring role that BMW has in the film *Mission Impossible: Ghost Protocol*.[12]

> In this latest in the series of *Mission Impossible* films, the i8 concept, a next-generation supercar from BMW, helps Tom Cruise and co-star Paul Patton race through Mumbai traffic. The car's appearance highlights the brand's return to Hollywood after a hiatus of more than a decade.
>
> In addition to featuring the upcoming i8, BMW uses the film to promote its current X3 SUV, 6-series convertible, and 1-Series compact. In lieu of an up-front payment, the firm has promised to promote the film in its print and television ads, says Uwe Ellinghaus, head of brand management at BMW. As Ellinghaus claims, "*Mission Impossible* is a whole new dimension for BMW. It's what James Bond used to be."

Strategy Spotlight 3.3 discusses an example that most students are familiar with: how Frito-Lay uses crowdsourcing to create competition for ads. The best ones air during the Super Bowl.

service
actions associated with providing service to enhance or maintain the value of the product.

Service   The **service** primary activity includes all actions associated with providing service to enhance or maintain the value of the product, such as installation, repair, training, parts supply, and product adjustment.

Let's see how two retailers are providing exemplary customer service. At *Sephora.com*, a customer service representative taking a phone call from a repeat customer has instant access to what shade of lipstick she likes best. This will help the rep cross-sell by suggesting a matching shade of lip gloss. Such personalization is expected to build loyalty and boost sales per customer. Nordstrom, the Seattle-based department store chain, goes even a step further. It offers a cyber-assist: A service rep can take control of a customer's web browser and literally lead her to just the silk scarf that she is looking for. CEO Dan Nordstrom believes that such a capability will close enough additional purchases to pay for the $1 million investment in software.

Support Activities

Support activities in the value chain can be divided into four generic categories, as shown in Exhibit 3.3. Each category of the support activity is divisible into a number of distinct value activities that are specific to a particular industry. For example, technology development's discrete activities may include component design, feature design, field testing, process engineering, and technology selection. Similarly, procurement may include activities such as qualifying new suppliers, purchasing different groups of inputs, and monitoring supplier performance.

procurement
the function of purchasing inputs used in the firm's value chain, including raw materials, supplies, and other consumable items as well as assets such as machinery, laboratory equipment, office equipment, and buildings.

Procurement   **Procurement** refers to the function of purchasing inputs used in the firm's value chain, not to the purchased inputs themselves.[13] Purchased inputs include raw materials, supplies, and other consumable items as well as assets such as machinery, laboratory equipment, office equipment, and buildings.[14,15]

Microsoft has improved its procurement process (and the quality of its suppliers) by providing formal reviews of its suppliers. One of Microsoft's divisions has extended the review process used for employees to its outside suppliers.[16] The employee services group, which is responsible for everything from travel to 401(k) programs to the on-site library, outsources more than 60 percent of the services it provides. Unfortunately, the employee services group was not providing suppliers with enough feedback. This was feedback that the suppliers wanted to get and that Microsoft wanted to give.

The evaluation system that Microsoft developed helped clarify its expectations to suppliers. An executive noted: "We had one supplier—this was before the new system—that would have scored a 1.2 out of 5. After we started giving this feedback, and the supplier

FRITO-LAY'S SUPER BOWL ADS

While firms have long realized the potential of outsourcing—the practice of sending service and manufacturing jobs overseas and profiting from cheap labor—marketing and sales leaders increasingly pursue a similar concept: crowdsourcing. Although crowdsourcing does not physically send jobs abroad, it uses another pool of cheap labor: everyday people, often amateurs, using their spare time to create content and solve problems.

Take PepsiCo's Frito-Lay division, for example. Frito-Lay has been long known for its Crash the Super Bowl contest, an annual online commercial competition that invites regular consumers to create their own Doritos ads. The contest started in 2006 with a little over 1,000 entries and grew to more than 6,000 entries by 2011. Frito-Lay will air at least one of these fan-made commercials during the Super Bowl. Frito-Lay benefits from this user-generated content on multiple dimensions. The Crash the Super Bowl campaigns are a huge public relations success. In 2007, the International Public Relations Association awarded a Golden World Award to Frito-Lay because the campaign garnered 1.3 billion earned media impressions, created an enthusiastic online community of 1 million users, and helped to generate a 12 percent sales leap for the Doritos brand in January 2007.

One may think that user-generated Super Bowl ads are only a nice marketing gimmick. Think again! The low-budget ads came out on top of the *USA Today* Super Bowl Ad Meter in 2009, 2011, and 2012. The 2007 ad was even named by Time.com as the ninth best commercial of the year. Continuing the crowdsourcing success, Frito-Lay raised the challenge for the 2015 Crash the Super Bowl contest. Doritos once again looked for the best 30-second commercial that would air during Super Bowl XLIX on February 1, 2015. The grand-prize winner not only walked away with $1 million for creating the winning ad but also was invited to work on a "creative project" with Universal Pictures. In addition, the grand-prize winner and all of the finalists got all-expense-paid trips to watch the Super Bowl at the University of Phoenix Stadium in Glendale, Arizona.

The winner and finalists certainly had a good "return on their investments"! In 2014, Ryan Thomas of Scottsdale, Arizona, won $1 million after his commercial, *Time Machine,* was selected. ABC News reported that Anderson, a single dad, spent less than $300 to create the funny commercial that featured his son and their dog.

Sources: Anonymous. 2014. 2015 Doritos Crash the Super Bowl contest: Which ad will be worth $1 million? *inquisitr.com,* November 4: np. Robinson-Jacobs, K. 2012. Crunch time for contest lovers. *Dallas Morning News,* September 21: 1D; Consumer PR—Doritos crashes the Superbowl. 2007. *IPRA:* np; and Keegan, R. W. 2007. Top 10 TV ads. *www.time.com,* December 9: np.

General Administration

- Effective planning systems to attain overall goals and objectives.
- Excellent relationships with diverse stakeholder groups.
- Effective information technology to integrate value-creating activities.

Human Resource Management

- Effective recruiting, development, and retention mechanisms for employees.
- Quality relations with trade unions.
- Reward and incentive programs to motivate all employees.

Technology Development

- Effective R&D activities for process and product initiatives.
- Positive collaborative relationships between R&D and other departments.
- Excellent professional qualifications of personnel.

Procurement

- Procurement of raw material inputs to optimize quality and speed and to minimize the associated costs.
- Development of collaborative win–win relationships with suppliers.
- Analysis and selection of alternative sources of inputs to minimize dependence on one supplier.

EXHIBIT 3.3

The Value Chain: Some Factors to Consider in Assessing a Firm's Support Activities

Source: Adapted from Porter, M.E. 1985. *Competitive Advantage: Creating and Sustaining Superior Performance.* New York: Free Press.

understood our expectations, its performance improved dramatically. Within six months, it scored a 4. If you'd asked me before we began the feedback system, I would have said that was impossible."

Technology Development   Every value activity embodies technology.[17] The array of technologies employed in most firms is very broad, ranging from technologies used to prepare documents and transport goods to those embodied in processes and equipment or the product itself.[18] **Technology development** related to the product and its features supports the entire value chain, while other technology development is associated with particular primary or support activities.

> Techniq, headquartered in Paris, France, with 40,000 employees in 48 countries, is a world leader in project management, engineering, and construction for the energy industry.[19] Its manufacturing plant in Normandy, France, has developed innovative ways to add value for its customers. This division, Subsea Infrastructure, produces subsea flexible pipes for the oil and gas industry. Its technology innovations have added significant value for its customers and has led to operating margins 50 percent higher than those for the company overall.
>
> Its traditional services include installing, inspecting, maintaining, and repairing pipes in locations around the world, from the Arctic to the Arabian Gulf. However, the company now goes much further. In collaboration with oil services giant Schlumberger, Techniq has developed intelligent pipes that can monitor and regulate the temperature throughout an oil pipeline—important value-added activities for its customers, large oil producers. Fluctuating temperatures pose a major problem—they cause changes in pipe diameter, which makes the flow of oil more variable. This compromises drilling efficiency and is a significant source of costs for Techniq's customers. Using intelligent pipes not only keeps temperatures steadier but also reduces the complexity of subsea drilling layouts and shortens pipe installation times.

Human Resource Management   **Human resource management** consists of activities involved in the recruiting, hiring, training, development, and compensation of all types of personnel.[20] It supports both individual primary and support activities (e.g., hiring of engineers and scientists) and the entire value chain (e.g., negotiations with labor unions).[21]

Like all great service companies, JetBlue Airways Corporation is obsessed with hiring superior employees.[22] But the company found it difficult to attract college graduates to commit to careers as flight attendants. JetBlue developed a highly innovative recruitment program for flight attendants—a one-year contract that gives them a chance to travel, meet lots of people, and then decide what else they might like to do. It also introduced the idea of training a friend and employee together so that they could share a job. With such employee-friendly initiatives, JetBlue has been very successful in attracting talent.

Jeffrey Immelt, GE's chairman, addresses the importance of effective human resource management:[23]

> Human resources has to be more than a department. GE recognized early on—50 or 60 years ago—that in a multibusiness company, the common denominators are people and culture. From an employee's first day at GE, she discovers that she's in the people-development business as much as anything else. You'll find that most good companies have the same basic HR processes that we have, but they're discrete. HR at GE is not an agenda item; it is the agenda.

Lise Saari, Ph.D., has held executive positions in human resource management at IBM and Boeing. In addition, she is well known for her prolific academic research and publications. We are pleased that she has shared her perspectives on several issues related to human resource management, or HRM (see Insights from Executives). These include the

LISE M. SAARI, PH.D., FORMER DIRECTOR OF GLOBAL EMPLOYEE RESEARCH, IBM

BIOSKETCH

Lise M. Saari, Ph.D., is the former director of global workforce research at IBM, where her team was responsible for researching employee attitudes and other human resource topics in over 170 countries. Before that, she was the senior manager of people research at the Boeing Company and a research scientist at Battelle Research Institute. In all of these roles, Saari had responsibility for helping design and test human resource management initiatives, such as performance management systems, teaming initiatives, and management development programs. Saari has over 100 publications and presentations and serves on a variety of editorial boards. She is a fellow in the Society for Industrial Organizational Psychology (SIOP), the American Psychological Association, and the Association for Psychological Science. Saari is currently adjunct professor at New York University and Baruch College in their graduate industrial/organizational psychology and international executive programs, teaching in New York City, Singapore, and Taipei. She is also an SIOP representative to the United Nations.

1. How important is it for human resource management to coordinate its efforts with other areas of the organization?

This is extremely important and, frankly, lacking at times. In particular, human resources (HR) needs to ensure its initiatives support people as part of an organization's value-creating activities. HR needs to align to the current strategy of the organization—to ensure the organization's people practices fully support the current direction and goals of the company. This relates to HR being a true partner of the business, with a deep and up-to-date understanding of business realities and objectives, and, in turn, ensuring HR initiatives fully support them at all points of the value chain. A great human resource leader also will know how to be a true partner by being an expert and balanced voice as business strategies are being refined or changed, to ensure they take into account the people side of the business. Thus, to be successful, human resources needs to support and help carry out business strategies, yet at the same time be willing to speak up and offer sound ideas when a proposed strategy may have legitimate issues from a people perspective.

2. Based on your research and experience in the human resource area, what do you think are the most interesting findings that have important implications for organizational performance?

What makes people satisfied in their work, motivates them to perform, and makes them stay or leave are more complex and organizationally unique than we may think they are. Some of the most interesting findings to me are from the so-called linkage research started by Ben Schneider, whereby employee attitudes are statistically related to customer and business measures to see the unique relationships for an organization. We carried out this type of research at IBM with employee attitude data across the globe. The most important employee and workplace topics that contributed value to customers and organizational performance were understanding company objectives and how the employee's own job contributes to it, receiving regular feedback, receiving pay tied to job performance, and having a challenging job with opportunities for development. These are all areas where HR can and should ensure company strategy is clear to all employees; create a performance management system with a clear line of sight to that strategy; provide regular performance feedback; incorporate performance-based pay; and ensure people are challenged in their work with opportunities for learning and job movement. In many cases, managers think pay is the most important, but it is only one of many important areas.

It is also interesting that some of our long-held beliefs about people at work need continual research to understand the new realities of organizations and the people in them. What has been the case in the past may not hold up for the future of work. As an example, one supposition held for many years—based on solid research—is that employee dissatisfaction is a major cause of turnover/attrition. It was very unlikely to find extremely positive ratings on an employee survey associated with very high turnover. However, this simple truism may no longer be the case. Globalization, economic highs and lows, an elimination of the former employee contract, and a more mobile workforce probably all contribute to a need to rethink this former HR truism. My first encounter with this was looking at country employee survey data relative to turnover rates. The country with the most positive ratings on the employee survey globally also had the highest turnover rate. As it turns out, that country's economy was one of the fastest growing in the world at the time, so jobs were plentiful. As well, job movement was easy. I didn't know how easy until visiting company offices in that country and seeing that competitors were located literally in the same block of the city—it was only a few steps to a new job with a promise of more interesting work, along with likely better pay and a promotion. I now understand that simplistic conclusions about human behavior in organizations may not necessarily hold up in the complexities of the new world of work.

continued

continued

3. Based on your experience, what are the greatest challenges in implementing human resource initiatives?

HR initiatives that are *well designed, verified as effective and contributing value, fully tested before deployment, cost-effective, easy to use, and not overly time-consuming and that result in positive outcomes for the individual and the organization* should not be a challenge to implement. However, these good design features may not always be present, causing managers and employees to be wary and less than fully supportive of a "new and improved" HR initiative. Even well-designed and thoroughly tested HR initiatives may encounter resistance to implementation because people have learned new HR initiatives are not always good.

My worst story about poor HR program implementation involves an HR redesign of the online performance appraisal system at an organization. At an HR meeting after full-company deployment, the discussion turned to all the problems and what to do about them; it quickly became clear that many of those engaged in the conversation were ill-equipped to understand the problems because most of them had accessed the "old" system rather than using the new one. When asked why, the reply was, "I knew there would be problems with the new system and I didn't want the headache." Clearly these HR leaders knew it was likely to fail. Had the good design and testing principles described above been followed, many problems could

have been avoided. In contrast, in my HR work at Boeing, all HR professionals were trained on the exact same quality themes as the employees in engineering and manufacturing. Thinking about HR initiatives with the same level of rigor and testing as designing and manufacturing a new airplane went a long way toward smooth and effective implementation and, ultimately, the value of HR programs.

In addition to good design and testing of HR initiatives, having high-level line-executive endorsement can be helpful because it can signify the importance of a new HR initiative and increase manager and employee acceptance and efforts to use it effectively. This is especially the case when the initiative is due to a new company strategy and the HR initiative is in direct support of it. As an example, a company has a new strategy on a leading-edge technology and HR deploys a well-designed and tested training program to bring employees up to speed on that technology. A performance appraisal system is being redesigned, not because so many managers dislike the current one but rather because the company is undergoing an important transformation and the new performance management system aligns and supports it. High-level support helps show the importance of the initiative for more ready acceptance, and a well-designed and well-tested HR program helps ensure success of implementation and its ultimate value.

---

importance of integrating HRM with other value-creating activities in an organization, major challenges in implementing HRM initiatives, and some interesting research findings that have implications for practice.

LO3.3

How value-chain analysis can help managers create value by investigating relationships among activities within the firm and between the firm and its customers and suppliers.

general administration
general management, planning, finance, accounting, legal and government affairs, quality management, and information systems; activities that support the entire value chain and not individual activities.

General Administration   **General administration** consists of a number of activities, including general management, planning, finance, accounting, legal and government affairs, quality management, and information systems. Administration (unlike the other support activities) typically supports the entire value chain and not individual activities.[24]

Although general administration is sometimes viewed only as overhead, it can be a powerful source of competitive advantage. In a telephone operating company, for example, negotiating and maintaining ongoing relations with regulatory bodies can be among the most important activities for competitive advantage. Also, in some industries top management plays a vital role in dealing with important buyers.[25]

The strong and effective leadership of top executives can also make a significant contribution to an organization's success. As we discussed in Chapter 1, chief executive officers (CEOs) such as Herb Kelleher, Andrew Grove, and Jack Welch have been credited with playing critical roles in the success of Southwest Airlines, Intel, and General Electric.

Information technology (IT) can also play a key role in enhancing the value that a company can provide its customers and, in turn, increasing its own revenues and profits. Strategy Spotlight 3.4 describes how Schmitz Cargobull, a German truck and trailer manufacturer, uses IT to further its competitive position.

SCHMITZ CARGOBULL: ADDING VALUE TO CUSTOMERS VIA IT

Germany's truck and trailer manufacturer, Schmitz Cargobull, mainly serves customers that are operators of truck or trailer fleets. Like its rivals, the company derives a growing share of revenue from support services such as financing, full-service contracts for breakdowns and regular maintenance, and spare-parts supplies.

What sets the company apart is its expertise in telematics (the integrated application of telecommunications data) to monitor the current state of any Schmitz Cargobull–produced trailer. Through telematics, key information is continually available to the driver, the freight agent, and the customer. They can track, for instance, when maintenance is done, how much weight has been loaded, the current cargo temperature, and where the vehicle is on its route. Therefore, Schmitz Cargobull customers can better manage their trailer use and minimize the risk of breakdowns. The decision to introduce telematics, not surprisingly, derived from

management's belief that real-time sharing of data would bind the company more closely to customers.

In applying its telematic tools in its products, Schmitz Cargobull is providing clear, tangible benefits. It uses information technology only where it makes sense. On the production line, for example, workers implement statistical quality controls manually, rather than rely on an automated system, because the company found manual control improves engagement and job performance.

That strategy has helped Schmitz Cargobull become an industry leader. In 2013, the company controlled 82 percent of the sales of semitrailer reefers (refrigerated trailers) in Germany, and its market share in Europe was about 50 percent. Further, its results for the fiscal year ending March 2014 are most impressive: sales increased by 7.5 percent and pretax profit soared 66 percent.

Sources: Anonymous. 2014. Schmitz Cargobull AG announces earnings and production results for the year ending March 2014. *www.investing.businessweek.com*, July 31: np; Anonymous. 2014. Premiere at the IAA Show 2014: Increased I-beam stability and payload. *www.cargobull.com*, September: np; and Chick, S. E., Huchzermeier, A., & Netessine, S. 2014. Europe's solution factories. *Harvard Business Review*, 92(4): 11–115.

Interrelationships among Value-Chain Activities within and across Organizations

We have defined each of the value-chain activities separately for clarity of presentation. Managers must not ignore, however, the importance of relationships among value-chain activities.[26] There are two levels: (1) **interrelationships** among activities within the firm and (2) relationships among activities within the firm and with other stakeholders (e.g., customers and suppliers) that are part of the firm's expanded value chain.[27]

With regard to the first level, consider Lise Saari's interview (pages 83–84) on the strategic importance of effective human resource management practices. As she notes: "HR [must be] a true partner of the business, with a deep and up-to-date understanding of business realities and objectives, and, in turn, [must ensure] HR initiatives fully support them at all points of the value chain."

With regard to the second level, Campbell Soup's use of electronic networks enabled it to improve the efficiency of outbound logistics.[28] However, it also helped Campbell manage the ordering of raw materials more effectively, improve its production scheduling, and help its customers better manage their inbound logistics operations.

interrelationships collaborative and strategic exchange relationships between value-chain activities either (a) within firms or (b) between firms. Strategic exchange relationships involve exchange of resources such as information, people, technology, or money that contribute to the success of the firm.

Integrating Customers into the Value Chain

When addressing the value-chain concept, it is important to focus on the interrelationship between the organization and its most important stakeholder—its customers. Some firms find great value by directly incorporating their customers into the value creation process. Firms can do this in one of two ways.

First, they can employ the "prosumer" concept and directly team up with customers to design and build products to satisfy their particular needs. Working directly with customers in this process provides multiple potential benefits for the firm. As the firm develops individualized products and relationship marketing, it can benefit from greater customer satisfaction and loyalty. Additionally, the interactions with customers can generate insights that lead to cost-saving initiatives and more innovative ideas for the producing firm. In discussing this concept, Hartmut Jenner, CEO of Alfred Karcher, a German manufacturing firm, stated:

> In the future, we will be talking more and more about the "prosumer"—a customer/ producer who is even more extensively integrated into the value chain. As a consequence, production processes will be customized more precisely and individually.[29]

Second, firms can leverage the power of crowdsourcing. As introduced in Chapter 2, crowdsourcing occurs when firms tap into the knowledge and ideas of a large number of customers and other stakeholders, typically through online forums. The rise of social media has generated tremendous opportunities for firms to engage with customers.[30] In contrast to prosumer interactions, which allow the firm to gain insights on the needs of a particular customer, crowdsourcing offers the opportunity to leverage the wisdom of a larger crowd. Many companies have encouraged customers to participate in value-creating activities, such as brainstorming advertising taglines or product ideas. These activities not only enable firms to innovate at low cost but also engage customers. Clearly, a marketer's dream! At the same time, crowdsourcing has some significant risks.

Understanding the Perils of Crowdsourcing   While crowdsourcing offers great promise, in practice such programs are difficult to run. At times, customers can "hijack" them. Instead of offering constructive ideas, customers jump at the chance to raise concerns and even ridicule the company. Such hijacking is one of the biggest challenges companies face. Research has shown about half of such campaigns fail. Consider the following marketing-focused crowdsourcing examples:

- In 2006, General Motors tried a "fun" experiment, one of the first attempts to use user-generated advertising. The company asked the public to create commercials for the Chevy Tahoe—ads the company hoped would go viral. Unfortunately, some of the ads did go viral! These include: "Like this snowy wilderness. Better get your fill of it now. Then say hello to global warming. Chevy Tahoe" and "$70 to fill up the tank, which will last less than 400 miles. Chevy Tahoe."
- McDonald's set up a Twitter campaign to promote positive word of mouth. But this initiative became a platform for people looking to bash the chain. Tweets such as the following certainly didn't help the firm's cause: "I lost 50 lbs in 6 months after I quit working and eating at McDonalds" and "The McRib contains the same chemicals used to make yoga mats, mmmmm."

Research has identified three areas of particular concern:

- ***Strong brand reputation.*** Companies with strong brands need to protect them. After all, they have the most to lose. They must be aware such efforts provide consumers the opportunity to tarnish the brand. Strong brands are typically built through consistent, effective marketing, and companies need to weigh the potential for misbehaving customers to thwart their careful efforts.
- ***High demand uncertainty.*** Firms are generally more likely to ask for customer input when market conditions are changing. However, this often backfires when demand is highly uncertain, because customers in such markets often don't know what they want or what they will like. For example, Porsche received a lot of negative feedback when it announced plans to release an SUV, but it went ahead anyway, and the Porsche Cayenne was a great success.
- ***Too many initiatives.*** Firms typically benefit from working repeatedly with the same customers. Often, the quality, quantity, and variety of inputs decrease as the frequency of engagement increases. A study of the Dell IdeaStorm program (in which customers were encouraged to submit product or service ideas) discovered that the same people submitted ideas repeatedly—including submitting ones

for things the company already provided. And customers whose ideas were implemented tended to return with additional ideas that were quite similar to their initial suggestions.

Applying the Value Chain to Service Organizations

The concepts of inbound logistics, operations, and outbound logistics suggest managing the raw materials that might be manufactured into finished products and delivered to customers. However, these three steps do not apply only to manufacturing. They correspond to any transformation process in which inputs are converted through a work process into outputs that add value. For example, accounting is a sort of transformation process that converts daily records of individual transactions into monthly financial reports. In this example, the transaction records are the inputs, accounting is the operation that adds value, and financial statements are the outputs.

What are the "operations," or transformation processes, of service organizations? At times, the difference between manufacturing and service is in providing a customized solution rather than mass production as is common in manufacturing. For example, a travel agent adds value by creating an itinerary that includes transportation, accommodations, and activities that are customized to your budget and travel dates. A law firm renders services that are specific to a client's needs and circumstances. In both cases, the work process (operation) involves the application of specialized knowledge based on the specifics of a situation (inputs) and the outcome that the client desires (outputs).

The application of the value chain to service organizations suggests that the value-adding process may be configured differently depending on the type of business a firm is engaged in. As the preceding discussion on support activities suggests, activities such as procurement and legal services are critical for adding value. Indeed, the activities that may provide support only to one company may be critical to the primary value-adding activity of another firm.

Exhibit 3.4 provides two models of how the value chain might look in service industries. In the retail industry, there are no manufacturing operations. A firm such as Nordstrom adds value by developing expertise in the procurement of finished goods and by displaying them in its stores in a way that enhances sales. Thus, the value chain makes procurement activities (i.e., partnering with vendors and purchasing goods) a primary rather than a support activity. Operations refer to the task of operating Nordstrom's stores.

EXHIBIT 3.4 Some Examples of Value Chains in Service Industries

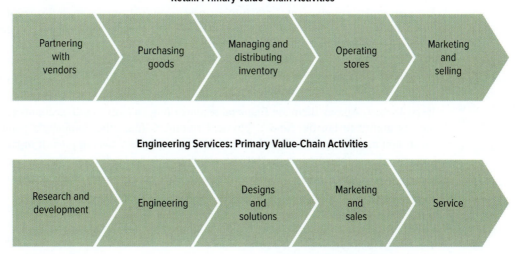

Retail: Primary Value-Chain Activities

Partnering with vendors → Purchasing goods → Managing and distributing inventory → Operating stores → Marketing and selling

Engineering Services: Primary Value-Chain Activities

Research and development → Engineering → Designs and solutions → Marketing and sales → Service

For an engineering services firm, research and development provides inputs, the transformation process is the engineering itself, and innovative designs and practical solutions are the outputs. The Beca Group, for example, is a large consulting firm with about 3,000 employees, based in 17 offices throughout the Asia Pacific region. In its technology and innovation management practice, Beca strives to make the best use of the science, technology, and knowledge resources available to create value for a wide range of industries and client sectors. This involves activities associated with research and development, engineering, and creating solutions as well as downstream activities such as marketing, sales, and service. How the primary and support activities of a given firm are configured and deployed will often depend on industry conditions and whether the company is service- and/or manufacturing-oriented.

Resource-Based View of the Firm

resource-based view (RBV) of the firm
perspective that firms' competitive advantages are due to their endowment of strategic resources that are valuable, rare, costly to imitate, and costly to substitute.

LO3.4

The resource-based view of the firm and the different types of tangible and intangible resources, as well as organizational capabilities.

The **resource-based view (RBV) of the firm** combines two perspectives: (1) the internal analysis of phenomena within a company and (2) an external analysis of the industry and its competitive environment.[31] It goes beyond the traditional SWOT (strengths, weaknesses, opportunities, threats) analysis by integrating internal and external perspectives. The ability of a firm's resources to confer competitive advantage(s) cannot be determined without taking into consideration the broader competitive context. A firm's resources must be evaluated in terms of how valuable, rare, and hard they are for competitors to duplicate. Otherwise, the firm attains only competitive parity.

As noted earlier (in Strategy Spotlight 3.1), a firm's strengths and capabilities—no matter how unique or impressive—do not necessarily lead to competitive advantages in the marketplace. The criteria for whether advantages are created and whether or not they can be sustained over time will be addressed later in this section. Thus, the RBV is a very useful framework for gaining insights as to why some competitors are more profitable than others. As we will see later in the book, the RBV is also helpful in developing strategies for individual businesses and diversified firms by revealing how core competencies embedded in a firm can help it exploit new product and market opportunities.

In the two sections that follow, we will discuss the three key types of resources that firms possess (summarized in Exhibit 3.5): tangible resources, intangible resources, and organizational capabilities. Then we will address the conditions under which such assets and capabilities can enable a firm to attain a sustainable competitive advantage.[32]

Types of Firm Resources

Firm resources are all assets, capabilities, organizational processes, information, knowledge, and so forth, controlled by a firm that enable it to develop and implement value-creating strategies.

tangible resources
organizational assets that are relatively easy to identify, including physical assets, financial resources, organizational resources, and technological resources.

Tangible Resources   **Tangible resources** are assets that are relatively easy to identify. They include the physical and financial assets that an organization uses to create value for its customers. Among them are financial resource (e.g., a firm's cash, accounts receivable, and its ability to borrow funds); physical resources (e.g., the company's plant, equipment, and machinery as well as its proximity to customers and suppliers); organizational resources (e.g., the company's strategic planning process and its employee development, evaluation, and reward systems); and technological resources (e.g., trade secrets, patents, and copyrights).

Many firms are finding that high-tech, computerized training has dual benefits: It develops more-effective employees and reduces costs at the same time. Employees at FedEx take computer-based job competency tests every 6 to 12 months.[33] The 90-minute

Tangible Resources

Financial	• Firm's cash account and cash equivalents. • Firm's capacity to raise equity. • Firm's borrowing capacity.
Physical	• Modern plant and facilities. • Favorable manufacturing locations. • State-of-the-art machinery and equipment.
Technological	• Trade secrets. • Innovative production processes. • Patents, copyrights, trademarks.
Organizational	• Effective strategic planning processes. • Excellent evaluation and control systems.

Intangible Resources

Human	• Experience and capabilities of employees. • Trust. • Managerial skills. • Firm-specific practices and procedures.
Innovation and creativity	• Technical and scientific skills. • Innovation capacities.
Reputation	• Brand name. • Reputation with customers for quality and reliability. • Reputation with suppliers for fairness, non–zero-sum relationships.

Organizational Capabilities

- Firm competencies or skills the firm employs to transfer inputs to outputs.
- Capacity to combine tangible and intangible resources, using organizational processes to attain desired end.

EXAMPLES:

- Outstanding customer service.
- Excellent product development capabilities.
- Innovativeness of products and services.
- Ability to hire, motivate, and retain human capital.

Sources: Adapted from Barney, J. B. 1991. Firm Resources and Sustained Competitive Advantage. *Journal of Management,* 17: 101; Grant, R. M. 1991. *Contemporary Strategy Analysis:* 100–102. Cambridge, England: Blackwell Business; and Hitt, M. A., Ireland, R. D., & Hoskisson, R. E. 2001. *Strategic Management: Competitiveness and Globalization* (4th ed.). Cincinnati: South-Western College Publishing.

computer-based tests identify areas of individual weakness and provide input to a computer database of employee skills—information the firm uses in promotion decisions.

Intangible Resources   Much more difficult for competitors (and, for that matter, a firm's own managers) to account for or imitate are **intangible resources,** which are typically embedded in unique routines and practices that have evolved and accumulated over time. These include human resources (e.g., experience and capability of employees, trust, effectiveness of work teams, managerial skills), innovation resources (e.g., technical and scientific expertise, ideas), and reputation resources (e.g., brand name, reputation with suppliers

intangible resources organizational assets that are difficult to identify and account for and are typically embedded in unique routines and practices, including human resources, innovation resources, and reputation resources.

for fairness and with customers for reliability and product quality).[34] A firm's culture may also be a resource that provides competitive advantage.[35]

For example, you might not think that motorcycles, clothes, toys, and restaurants have much in common. Yet Harley-Davidson has entered all of these product and service markets by capitalizing on its strong brand image—a valuable intangible resource.[36] It has used that image to sell accessories, clothing, and toys, and it has licensed the Harley-Davidson Café in New York City to provide further exposure for its brand name and products.

Social networking sites have the potential to play havoc with a firm's reputation. Consider the unfortunate situation Comcast faced when one of its repairmen fell asleep on the job—and it went viral:

> Ben Finkelstein, a law student, had trouble with the cable modem in his home. A Comcast cable repairman arrived to fix the problem. However, when the technician had to call the home office for a key piece of information, he was put on hold for so long that he fell asleep on Finkelstein's couch. Outraged, Finkelstein made a video of the sleeping technician and posted it on YouTube. The clip became a hit—with more than a million viewings. And, for a long time, it undermined Comcast's efforts to improve its reputation for customer service.[37]

Organizational Capabilities   **Organizational capabilities** are not specific tangible or intangible assets, but rather the competencies or skills that a firm employs to transform inputs into outputs.[38] In short, they refer to an organization's capacity to deploy tangible and intangible resources over time and generally in combination and to leverage those capabilities to bring about a desired end.[39] Examples of organizational capabilities are outstanding customer service, excellent product development capabilities, superb innovation processes, and flexibility in manufacturing processes.[40]

In the case of Apple, the majority of components used in its products can be characterized as proven technology, such as touch-screen and MP3-player functionality.[41] However, Apple combines and packages these in new and innovative ways while also seeking to integrate the value chain. This is the case with iTunes, for example, where suppliers of downloadable music are a vital component of the success Apple has enjoyed with its iPod series of MP3 players. Thus, Apple draws on proven technologies and its ability to offer innovative combinations of them.

Firm Resources and Sustainable Competitive Advantages

As we have mentioned, resources alone are not a basis for competitive advantages, nor are advantages sustainable over time.[42] In some cases, a resource or capability helps a firm to increase its revenues or to lower costs but the firm derives only a temporary advantage because competitors quickly imitate or substitute for it.[43]

For a resource to provide a firm with the potential for a sustainable competitive advantage, it must have four attributes.[44] First, the resource must be valuable in the sense that it exploits opportunities and/or neutralizes threats in the firm's environment. Second, it must be rare among the firm's current and potential competitors. Third, the resource must be difficult for competitors to imitate. Fourth, the resource must have no strategically equivalent substitutes. These criteria are summarized in Exhibit 3.6. We will now discuss each of these criteria. Then we will examine how Blockbuster's competitive advantage, which seemed secure a decade ago, subsequently eroded, causing the company to file for bankruptcy in 2011.

Is the Resource Valuable?   Organizational resources can be a source of competitive advantage only when they are valuable. Resources are valuable when they enable a firm to formulate and implement strategies that improve its efficiency or effectiveness. The SWOT framework suggests that firms improve their performance only when they exploit opportunities or neutralize (or minimize) threats.

EXHIBIT 3.6

Four Criteria
for Assessing
Sustainability of
Resources and
Capabilities

Is the resource or capability . . .	Implications
Valuable?	• Neutralize threats and exploit opportunities
Rare?	• Not many firms possess
Difficult to imitate?	• Physically unique • Path dependency (how accumulated over time) • Causal ambiguity (difficult to disentangle what it is or how it could be re-created) • Social complexity (trust, interpersonal relationships, culture, reputation)
Difficult to substitute?	• No equivalent strategic resources or capabilities

The fact that firm attributes must be valuable in order to be considered resources (as well as potential sources of competitive advantage) reveals an important complementary relationship among environmental models (e.g., SWOT and five-forces analyses) and the resource-based model. Environmental models isolate those firm attributes that exploit opportunities and/or neutralize threats. Thus, they specify what firm attributes may be considered as resources. The resource-based model then suggests what additional characteristics these resources must possess if they are to develop a sustained competitive advantage.

Is the Resource Rare?   If competitors or potential competitors also possess the same valuable resource, it is not a source of a competitive advantage because all of these firms have the capability to exploit that resource in the same way. Common strategies based on such a resource would give no one firm an advantage. For a resource to provide competitive advantages, it must be uncommon, that is, rare relative to other competitors.

This argument can apply to bundles of valuable firm resources that are used to formulate and develop strategies. Some strategies require a mix of multiple types of resources—tangible assets, intangible assets, and organizational capabilities. If a particular bundle of firm resources is not rare, then relatively large numbers of firms will be able to conceive of and implement the strategies in question. Thus, such strategies will not be a source of competitive advantage, even if the resource in question is valuable.

Can the Resource Be Imitated Easily?   Inimitability (difficulty in imitating) is a key to value creation because it constrains competition.[45] If a resource is inimitable, then any profits generated are more likely to be sustainable.[46] Having a resource that competitors can easily copy generates only temporary value.[47] This has important implications. Since managers often fail to apply this test, they tend to base long-term strategies on resources that are imitable. IBP (Iowa Beef Processors) became the first meatpacking company in the United States to modernize by building a set of assets (automated plants located in cattle-producing states) and capabilities (low-cost "disassembly" of carcasses) that earned returns on assets of 1.3 percent in the 1970s. By the late 1980s, however, ConAgra and Cargill had imitated these resources, and IBP's profitability fell by nearly 70 percent, to 0.4 percent.

Groupon (the company that was the focus of the Learning from Mistakes feature in Chapter 1) is a more recent example of a firm that has suffered because rivals have been able to imitate its strategy rather easily:

> Groupon, which offers online coupons for bargains at local shops and restaurants, created a new market.[48] Although it was initially a boon to consumers, it offers no lasting "first-mover" advantage. Its business model is not patentable and is easy to replicate. Not surprisingly, there are many copycats. For example, there was a tremendous amount of

churn in the industry in 2012. The number of daily deal sites in the United States rose by almost 8 percent (142 sites), according to Daily Deal Media, which tracks the industry. Meanwhile, globally, 560 daily deal sites closed over the same period!

Clearly, an advantage based on inimitability won't last forever. Competitors will eventually discover a way to copy most valuable resources. However, managers can forestall them and sustain profits for a while by developing strategies around resources that have at least one of the following four characteristics.[49]

Physical Uniqueness   The first source of inimitability is physical uniqueness, which by definition is inherently difficult to copy. A beautiful resort location, mineral rights, or Pfizer's pharmaceutical patents simply cannot be imitated. Many managers believe that several of their resources may fall into this category, but on close inspection, few do.

path dependency
a characteristic of resources that is developed and/or accumulated through a unique series of events.

Path Dependency   A greater number of resources cannot be imitated because of what economists refer to as **path dependency.** This simply means that resources are unique and therefore scarce because of all that has happened along the path followed in their development and/or accumulation. Competitors cannot go out and buy these resources quickly and easily; they must be built up over time in ways that are difficult to accelerate.

The Gerber Products Co. brand name for baby food is an example of a resource that is potentially inimitable. Re-creating Gerber's brand loyalty would be a time-consuming process that competitors could not expedite, even with expensive marketing campaigns. Similarly, the loyalty and trust that Southwest Airlines employees feel toward their firm and its cofounder, Herb Kelleher, are resources that have been built up over a long period of time. Also, a crash R&D program generally cannot replicate a successful technology when research findings cumulate. Clearly, these path-dependent conditions build protection for the original resource. The benefits from experience and learning through trial and error cannot be duplicated overnight.

causal ambiguity
a characteristic of a firm's resources that is costly to imitate because a competitor cannot determine what the resource is and/or how it can be re-created.

Causal Ambiguity   The third source of inimitability is termed **causal ambiguity.** This means that would-be competitors may be thwarted because it is impossible to disentangle the causes (or possible explanations) of either what the valuable resource is or how it can be re-created. What is the root of 3M's innovation process? You can study it and draw up a list of possible factors. But it is a complex, unfolding (or folding) process that is hard to understand and would be hard to imitate.

Often, causally ambiguous resources are organizational capabilities, involving a complex web of social interactions that may even depend on particular individuals. When Continental and United tried to mimic the successful low-cost strategy of Southwest Airlines, the planes, routes, and fast gate turnarounds were not the most difficult aspects for them to copy. Those were all rather easy to observe and, at least in principle, easy to duplicate. However, they could not replicate Southwest's culture of fun, family, frugality, and focus since no one can clearly specify exactly what that culture is or how it came to be.

Strategy Spotlight 3.5 describes Amazon's continued success as the world's largest online marketplace. Competitors recently tried to imitate Amazon's free-shipping strategy, but with limited success. The reason is that Amazon has developed an array of interrelated elements of strategy which their rivals find too difficult to imitate.

social complexity
a characteristic of a firm's resources that is costly to imitate because the social engineering required is beyond the capability of competitors, including interpersonal relations among managers, organizational culture, and reputation with suppliers and customers.

Social Complexity   A firm's resources may be imperfectly inimitable because they reflect a high level of **social complexity.** Such phenomena are typically beyond the ability of firms to systematically manage or influence. When competitive advantages are based on social complexity, it is difficult for other firms to imitate them.

A wide variety of firm resources may be considered socially complex. Examples include interpersonal relations among the managers in a firm, its culture, and its reputation with

AMAZON PRIME: VERY DIFFICULT FOR RIVALS TO COPY

Amazon Prime, introduced in 2004, is a free-shipping service that guarantees delivery of products within two days for an annual fee of $79. According to *Bloomberg Businessweek,* it may be the most ingenious and effective customer loyalty program in all of e-commerce, if not retail in general. It converts casual shoppers into Amazon addicts who gorge on the gratification of having purchases reliably appear two days after they order. Analysts describe Prime as one of the main factors driving Amazon's stock price up nearly 300 percent from 2008 to 2010. Also, it is one of the main reasons why Amazon's sales grew 30 percent during the recession, while other retailers suffered.

By 2014, Amazon had 25 million Prime members, up from 5 million two years earlier. They are practically addicted to using Amazon—and certainly don't seem to mind the annual membership price boost to $99. Scot Wingo of Channel Advisor, a company that helps online sellers, estimates that people with Prime spend about four times what others do and account for half of all spending at Amazon.

Amazon Prime has proven to be extremely hard for rivals to copy. Why? It enables Amazon to exploit its wide selection, low prices, network of third-party merchants, and finely tuned distribution system. All that while also keying off that faintly irrational human need to maximize the benefits of a club that you have already paid to join. Yet Amazon's success also leads to increased pressure from both public and private entities. For a long time, Amazon was able to avoid collecting local sales taxes because Amazon did not have a local sales presence in many states. This practice distorts competition and strains already tight state coffers. Some states have used a combination of legislation and litigation to convince Amazon to collect sales taxes; Amazon began collecting Texas state sales tax in July 2012.

Moreover, rivals—both online and off—have realized the increasing threat posed by Prime and are rushing to respond. For example, in October 2010, a consortium of more than 20 retailers, including Barnes & Noble, Sports Authority, and Toys 'R' Us, banded together to offer their own copycat $79, two-day shipping program, ShopRunner, which applies to products across their websites. As noted by Fiona Dias, the executive who administers the program, "As Amazon added more merchandising categories to Prime, retailers started feeling the pain. They have finally come to understand that Amazon is an existential threat and that Prime is the fuel of the engine."

Finally, Prime members also gain access to more than 40,000 streaming Instant Video programs and 300,000 free books in the Kindle Owners' Lending Library. And, in April 2014, Amazon paid HBO, a television company, an estimated $200 million to $250 million for a package of shows that Prime members can stream at no extra cost. As annoying as this might be to Netflix, it is not intended primarily as an assault on Netflix. Rather, CEO Jeff Bezos is willing to lose money on shipping and services in exchange for loyalty.

Sources: Anonymous. 2014. Relentless.com. *The Economist,* June 21: 23–26; McCorvey, J. J. 2013. The race has just begun. *Fast Company,* September: 66–76; Stone, B. 2010. What's in the box? Instant gratification. *Bloomberg Businessweek,* November 29–December 5: 39–40; Kaplan, M. 2011. Amazon Prime: 5 million members, 20 percent growth. *www.practicalcommerce.com,* September 16: np; Fowler, G. A. 2010. Retailers team up against Amazon. *www.wsj.com,* October 6: np; and Halkias, M. 2012. Amazon to collect sales tax in Texas. *Dallas Morning News,* April 28: 4A.

its suppliers and customers. In many of these cases, it is easy to specify how these socially complex resources add value to a firm. Hence, there is little or no causal ambiguity surrounding the link between them and competitive advantage.

The most recent Edelman Trust Barometer, a comprehensive yearly survey of public trust, found that trust and transparency are more critical than ever.[50] For the first time in the survey's history, impressions of openness, sincerity, and authenticity are more important to corporate reputation in the United States than the quality of products and services. This means trust affects tangible things such as supply chain partnerships and long-term customer loyalty. People want to partner with you because they have heard you are a credible company built through a culture of trust. In a sense, being a great company to work for also makes you a great company to work with.

Are Substitutes Readily Available? The fourth requirement for a firm resource to be a source of sustainable competitive advantage is that there must be no strategically equivalent valuable resources that are themselves not rare or inimitable. Two valuable firm resources (or two bundles of resources) are strategically equivalent when each one can be exploited separately to implement the same strategies.

Substitutability may take at least two forms. First, though it may be impossible for a firm to imitate exactly another firm's resource, it may be able to substitute a similar resource that enables it to develop and implement the same strategy. Clearly, a firm seeking to imitate another firm's high-quality top management team would be unable to copy the team exactly. However, it might be able to develop its own unique management team. Though these two teams would have different ages, functional backgrounds, experience, and so on, they could be strategically equivalent and thus substitutes for one another.

Second, very different firm resources can become strategic substitutes. For example, Internet booksellers such as Amazon.com compete as substitutes for brick-and-mortar booksellers such as Barnes & Noble. The result is that resources such as premier retail locations become less valuable. In a similar vein, several pharmaceutical firms have seen the value of patent protection erode in the face of new drugs that are based on different production processes and act in different ways, but can be used in similar treatment regimes. The coming years will likely see even more radical change in the pharmaceutical industry as the substitution of genetic therapies eliminates certain uses of chemotherapy.[51]

To recap this section, recall that resources and capabilities must be rare and valuable as well as difficult to imitate or substitute in order for a firm to attain competitive advantages that are sustainable over time.[52] Exhibit 3.7 illustrates the relationship among the four criteria of sustainability and shows the competitive implications.

In firms represented by the first row of Exhibit 3.7, managers are in a difficult situation. When their resources and capabilities do not meet any of the four criteria, it would be difficult to develop any type of competitive advantage, in the short or long term. The resources and capabilities they possess enable the firm neither to exploit environmental opportunities nor to neutralize environmental threats. In the second and third rows, firms have resources and capabilities that are valuable as well as rare, respectively. However, in both cases the resources and capabilities are not difficult for competitors to imitate or substitute. Here, the firms could attain some level of competitive parity. They could perform on par with equally endowed rivals or attain a temporary competitive advantage. But their advantages would be easy for competitors to match. It is only in the fourth row, where all four criteria are satisfied, that competitive advantages can be sustained over time. Next, let's look at Blockbuster and see how its competitive advantage, which seemed to be sustainable for a rather long period of time, eventually eroded, leading to the company's bankruptcy in 2011.

Blockbuster Inc.: From Sustainable (?) Advantage to Bankruptcy Blockbuster Video failed to recognize in time the threat posed to its brick-and-mortar business by virtual services such as Netflix.[53] At the time, few thought that consumers would trade the

EXHIBIT 3.7

Criteria for Sustainable Competitive Advantage and Strategic Implications

Is a Resource or Capability . . .				
Valuable?	Rare?	Difficult to Imitate?	Without Substitutes?	Implication for Competitiveness
No	No	No	No	Competitive disadvantage
Yes	No	No	No	Competitive parity
Yes	Yes	No	No	Temporary competitive advantage
Yes	Yes	Yes	Yes	Sustainable competitive advantage

Source: Adapted from Barney, J. B. 1991. Firm Resources and Sustained Competitive Advantage. *Journal of Management,* 17: 99–120.

convenience of picking up their videos to waiting for them to arrive in the mail. Interestingly, Blockbuster had the chance to buy Netflix for $50 million in 2000 but turned down the opportunity. Barry McCarthy, Netflix's former chief financial officer, recalls the conversation during a meeting with Blockbuster's top executives: Reed Hastings, Netflix's cofounder, "had the chutzpah to propose to them that we run their brand online and that they run (our) brand in the stores and they just about laughed us out of the office. At least initially, they thought we were a very small niche business."

Users, of course, embraced the automated self-service of Netflix's web-based interface technology that positioned the start-up to transition from mailing DVDs to streaming content over the Internet. As technologies improved broadband speed, reliability, and adoption, Netflix transitioned in just a few years to a cloud-based service.

Blockbuster tried to follow each of Netflix's strategic moves. However, it remained a perennial second in the winner-take-all market for new ways to distribute entertainment content. Blockbuster continued to lag, weighed down by the high labor costs and real estate costs of its once-dominant locations—assets that became liabilities. In 2011, after closing some 900 stores, the company declared bankruptcy.

In the end, Blockbuster's assets were acquired for only $320 million by satellite television maverick Dish Networks, which was mainly interested in Blockbuster's online channel and 3.3 million customers. Had Blockbuster sold out earlier, or found a way to shed the physical assets sooner, that price could have been much higher. In 1999, the year Netflix launched its online subscription service, Blockbuster was valued at nearly $3 billion— nearly 10 times what Dish ultimately paid. Netflix, on the other hand, had a market cap of $21 billion by the end of 2014.

The Generation and Distribution of a Firm's Profits: Extending the Resource-Based View of the Firm

The resource-based view of the firm is useful in determining when firms will create competitive advantages and enjoy high levels of profitability. However, it has not been developed to address how a firm's profits (often referred to as "rents" by economists) will be distributed to a firm's management and employees or other stakeholders such as customers, suppliers, or governments.[54] This is an important issue because firms may be successful in creating competitive advantages that can be sustainable for a period of time. However, much of the profits can be retained (or "appropriated") by a firm's employees and managers or other stakeholders instead of flowing to the firm's owners (i.e., the stockholders).*

Consider Viewpoint DataLabs International, a Salt Lake City–based company that makes sophisticated three-dimensional models and textures for film production houses, video games, and car manufacturers. This example will help to show how employees are often able to obtain (or "appropriate") a high proportion of a firm's profits:

> Walter Noot, head of production, was having trouble keeping his highly skilled Generation X employees happy with their compensation. Each time one of them was lured away for more money, everyone would want a raise. "We were having to give out raises every six months—30 to 40 percent—then six months later they'd expect the same. It was a big struggle to keep people happy."[55]

Here, much of the profits is being generated by the highly skilled professionals working together. They are able to exercise their power by successfully demanding more financial compensation. In part, management has responded favorably because they are united in their demands and their work involves a certain amount of social complexity and causal ambiguity—given the complex, coordinated efforts that their work entails.

---

*Economists define rents as profits (or prices) in excess of what is required to provide a normal return.

Four factors help explain the extent to which employees and managers will be able to obtain a proportionately high level of the profits that they generate:[56]

- **Employee bargaining power.** If employees are vital to forming a firm's unique capability, they will earn disproportionately high wages. For example, marketing professionals may have access to valuable information that helps them to understand the intricacies of customer demands and expectations, or engineers may understand unique technical aspects of the products or services. Additionally, in some industries such as consulting, advertising, and tax preparation, clients tend to be very loyal to individual professionals employed by the firm, instead of to the firm itself. This enables them to "take the clients with them" if they leave. This enhances their bargaining power.

- **Employee replacement cost.** If employees' skills are idiosyncratic and rare (a source of resource-based advantages), they should have high bargaining power based on the high cost required by the firm to replace them. For example, Raymond Ozzie, the software designer who was critical in the development of Lotus Notes, was able to dictate the terms under which IBM acquired Lotus.

- **Employee exit costs.** This factor may tend to reduce an employee's bargaining power. An individual may face high personal costs when leaving the organization. Thus, that individual's threat of leaving may not be credible. In addition, an employee's expertise may be firm-specific and of limited value to other firms.

- **Manager bargaining power.** Managers' power is based on how well they create resource-based advantages. They are generally charged with creating value through the process of organizing, coordinating, and leveraging employees as well as other forms of capital such as plant, equipment, and financial capital (addressed further in Chapter 4). Such activities provide managers with sources of information that may not be readily available to others.

Chapter 9 addresses the conditions under which top-level managers (such as CEOs) of large corporations have been, at times, able to obtain levels of total compensation that would appear to be significantly disproportionate to their contributions to wealth generation as well as to top executives in peer organizations. Here, corporate governance becomes a critical control mechanism. Consider shareholders' reaction, in April 2012, to Citigroup's proposed $15 million pay package for then-CEO Vikram Pandit.[57] It was not positive, to say the least. After all, they had suffered a 92 percent decline in the stock's price under Pandit's five-year reign. They rejected the bank's compensation proposal. In October 2012, the board ousted Pandit after the New York–based firm failed to secure Federal Reserve approval to increase its shareholder payouts and Moody's Investors Service cut the bank's credit rating two levels.

Such diversion of profits from the owners of the business to top management is far less likely when the board members are truly independent outsiders (i.e., they do not have close ties to management). In general, given the external market for top talent, the level of compensation that executives receive is based on factors similar to the ones just discussed that determine the level of their bargaining power.[58]

In addition to employees and managers, other stakeholder groups can also appropriate a portion of the rents generated by a firm. If, for example, a critical input is controlled by a monopoly supplier or if a single buyer accounts for most of a firm's sales, this supplier's or buyer's bargaining power can greatly erode the potential profits of a firm. Similarly, excessive taxation by governments can also reduce what is available to a firm's stockholders.

Evaluating Firm Performance: Two Approaches

This section addresses two approaches to use when evaluating a firm's performance. The first is financial ratio analysis, which, generally speaking, identifies how a firm is performing according to its balance sheet, income statement, and market valuation. As we will discuss, when performing a financial ratio analysis, you must take into account the firm's performance from a historical perspective (not just at one point in time) as well as how it compares with both industry norms and key competitors.[59]

The second perspective takes a broader stakeholder view. Firms must satisfy a broad range of stakeholders, including employees, customers, and owners, to ensure their long-term viability. Central to our discussion will be a well-known approach—the balanced scorecard—that has been popularized by Robert Kaplan and David Norton.[60]

Financial Ratio Analysis

The beginning point in analyzing the financial position of a firm is to compute and analyze five different types of financial ratios:

- Short-term solvency or liquidity
- Long-term solvency measures
- Asset management (or turnover)
- Profitability
- Market value

Exhibit 3.8 summarizes each of these five ratios.

financial ratio analysis
a technique for measuring the performance of a firm according to its balance sheet, income statement, and market valuation.

EXHIBIT 3.8 A Summary of Five Types of Financial Ratios

I. Short-term solvency, or liquidity, ratios

$$\text{Current ratio} = \frac{\text{Current assets}}{\text{Current liabilities}}$$

$$\text{Quick ratio} = \frac{\text{Current assets} - \text{Inventory}}{\text{Current liabilities}}$$

$$\text{Cash ratio} = \frac{\text{Cash}}{\text{Current liabilities}}$$

II. Long-term solvency, or financial leverage, ratios

$$\text{Total debt ratio} = \frac{\text{Total assets} - \text{Total equity}}{\text{Total assets}}$$

$$\text{Debt-equity ratio} = \text{Total debt/Total equity}$$

$$\text{Equity multiplier} = \text{Total assets/Total equity}$$

$$\text{Times interest earned ratio} = \frac{\text{EBIT}}{\text{Interest}}$$

$$\text{Cash coverage ratio} = \frac{\text{EBIT} + \text{Depreciation}}{\text{Interest}}$$

III. Asset utilization, or turnover, ratios

$$\text{Inventory turnover} = \frac{\text{Cost of goods sold}}{\text{Inventory}}$$

$$\text{Days' sales in inventory} = \frac{365 \text{ days}}{\text{Inventory turnover}}$$

$$\text{Receivables turnover} = \frac{\text{Sales}}{\text{Accounts receivable}}$$

$$\text{Days' sales in receivables} = \frac{365 \text{ days}}{\text{Receivables turnover}}$$

$$\text{Total asset turnover} = \frac{\text{Sales}}{\text{Total assets}}$$

$$\text{Capital intensity} = \frac{\text{Total assets}}{\text{Sales}}$$

IV. Profitability ratios

$$\text{Profit margin} = \frac{\text{Net income}}{\text{Sales}}$$

$$\text{Return on assets (ROA)} = \frac{\text{Net income}}{\text{Total assets}}$$

$$\text{Return on equity (ROE)} = \frac{\text{Net income}}{\text{Total equity}}$$

$$\text{ROE} = \frac{\text{Net income}}{\text{Sales}} \times \frac{\text{Sales}}{\text{Assets}} \times \frac{\text{Assets}}{\text{Equity}}$$

V. Market value ratios

$$\text{Price-earnings ratio} = \frac{\text{Price per share}}{\text{Earnings per share}}$$

$$\text{Market-to-book ratio} = \frac{\text{Market value per share}}{\text{Book value per share}}$$

LO3.6

The usefulness of financial ratio analysis, its inherent limitations, and how to make meaningful comparisons of performance across firms.

Appendix 1 to Chapter 13 (the Case Analysis chapter) provides detailed definitions for and discussions of each of these types of ratios as well as examples of how each is calculated. Refer to pages 441–450.

A meaningful ratio analysis must go beyond the calculation and interpretation of financial ratios.[61] It must include how ratios change over time as well as how they are interrelated. For example, a firm that takes on too much long-term debt to finance operations will see an immediate impact on its indicators of long-term financial leverage. The additional debt will negatively affect the firm's short-term liquidity ratio (i.e., current and quick ratios) since the firm must pay interest and principal on the additional debt each year until it is retired. Additionally, the interest expenses deducted from revenues reduce the firm's profitability.

A firm's financial position should not be analyzed in isolation. Important reference points are needed. We will address some issues that must be taken into account to make financial analysis more meaningful: historical comparisons, comparisons with industry norms, and comparisons with key competitors.

Historical Comparisons   When you evaluate a firm's financial performance, it is very useful to compare its financial position over time. This provides a means of evaluating trends. For example, Apple Inc. reported revenues of $171 billion and net income of $37 billion in 2012. Virtually all firms would be very happy with such remarkable financial success. These figures represent a stunning annual growth in revenue and net income of 57 percent and 43 percent, respectively, for the 2011 to 2013 time period. Had Apple's revenues and net income in 2013 been $80 billion and $20 billion, respectively, it would still be a very large and highly profitable enterprise. However, such performance would have significantly damaged Apple's market valuation and reputation as well as the careers of many of its executives.

Exhibit 3.9 illustrates a 10-year period of return on sales (ROS) for a hypothetical company. As indicated by the dotted trend lines, the rate of growth (or decline) differs substantially over time periods.

Comparison with Industry Norms   When you are evaluating a firm's financial performance, remember also to compare it with industry norms. A firm's current ratio or profitability may appear impressive at first glance. However, it may pale when compared with industry standards or norms.

EXHIBIT 3.9 Historical Trends: Return on Sales (ROS) for a Hypothetical Company

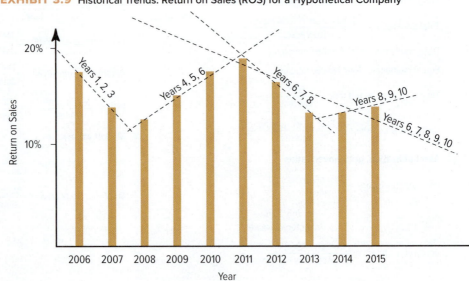

EXHIBIT 3.10

How Financial
Ratios Differ across
Industries

Financial Ratio	Semiconductors	Grocery Stores	Skilled-Nursing Facilities
Quick ratio (times)	1.9	0.6	1.3
Current ratio (times)	3.6	1.7	1.7
Total liabilities to net worth (%)	35.1	72.7	82.5
Collection period (days)	48.6	3.3	36.5
Assets to sales (%)	131.7	22.1	58.3
Return on sales (%)	24	1.1	3.1

Source: Dun & Bradstreet. *Industry Norms and Key Business Ratios, 2010–2011.* One Year Edition, SIC #3600–3699 (Semiconductors); SIC #5400–5499 (Grocery Stores); SIC #8000–8099 (Skilled-Nursing Facilities). New York: Dun & Bradstreet Credit Services.

Comparing your firm with all other firms in your industry assesses relative performance. Banks often use such comparisons when evaluating a firm's creditworthiness. Exhibit 3.10 includes a variety of financial ratios for three industries: semiconductors, grocery stores, and skilled-nursing facilities. Why is there such variation among the financial ratios for these three industries? There are several reasons. With regard to the collection period, grocery stores operate mostly on a cash basis, hence a very short collection period. Semiconductor manufacturers sell their output to other manufacturers (e.g., computer makers) on terms such as 2/15 net 45, which means they give a 2 percent discount on bills paid within 15 days and start charging interest after 45 days. Skilled-nursing facilities also have a longer collection period than grocery stores because they typically rely on payments from insurance companies.

The industry norms for return on sales also highlight differences among these industries. Grocers, with very slim margins, have a lower return on sales than either skilled-nursing facilities or semiconductor manufacturers. But how might we explain the differences between skilled-nursing facilities and semiconductor manufacturers? Health care facilities, in general, are limited in their pricing structures by Medicare/Medicaid regulations and by insurance reimbursement limits, but semiconductor producers have pricing structures determined by the market. If their products have superior performance, semiconductor manufacturers can charge premium prices.

Comparison with Key Competitors   Recall from Chapter 2 that firms with similar strategies are members of a strategic group in an industry. Furthermore, competition is more intense among competitors within groups than across groups. Thus, you can gain valuable insights into a firm's financial and competitive position if you make comparisons between a firm and its most direct rivals. Consider a firm trying to diversify into the highly profitable pharmaceutical industry. Even if it was willing to invest several hundred million dollars, it would be virtually impossible to compete effectively against industry giants such as Pfizer and Merck. These two firms have 2013 revenues of $51 billion and $44 billion, respectively, and both had R&D budgets of over $7 billion.[62]

Integrating Financial Analysis and Stakeholder Perspectives: The Balanced Scorecard

LO3.7

The value of the "balanced scorecard" in recognizing how the interests of a variety of stakeholders can be interrelated.

It is useful to see how a firm performs over time in terms of several ratios. However, such traditional approaches can be a double-edged sword.[63] Many important transactions—investments in research and development, employee training and development, and advertising and promotion of key brands—may greatly expand a firm's market potential and create significant long-term shareholder value. But such critical investments are not reflected positively in short-term financial reports. Financial reports typically measure expenses, not the value created. Thus, managers may be penalized for spending money in the short term to improve their firm's long-term competitive viability!

Now consider the other side of the coin. A manager may destroy the firm's future value by dissatisfying customers, depleting the firm's stock of good products coming out of R&D, or damaging the morale of valued employees. Such budget cuts, however, may lead to very good short-term financials. The manager may look good in the short run and even receive credit for improving the firm's performance. In essence, such a manager has mastered "denominator management," whereby decreasing investments makes the return on investment (ROI) ratio larger, even though the actual return remains constant or shrinks.

The Balanced Scorecard: Description and Benefits   To provide a meaningful integration of the many issues that come into evaluating a firm's performance, Kaplan and Norton developed a **"balanced scorecard."**[64] This provides top managers with a fast but comprehensive view of the business. In a nutshell, it includes financial measures that reflect the results of actions already taken, but it complements these indicators with measures of customer satisfaction, internal processes, and the organization's innovation and improvement activities—operational measures that drive future financial performance.

The balanced scorecard enables managers to consider their business from four key perspectives: customer, internal, innovation and learning, and financial. These are briefly described in Exhibit 3.11.

Customer Perspective   Clearly, how a company is performing from its customers' perspective is a top priority for management. The balanced scorecard requires that managers translate their general mission statements on customer service into specific measures that reflect the factors that really matter to customers. For the balanced scorecard to work, managers must articulate goals for four key categories of customer concerns: time, quality, performance and service, and cost.

Internal Business Perspective   Customer-based measures are important. However, they must be translated into indicators of what the firm must do internally to meet customers' expectations. Excellent customer performance results from processes, decisions, and actions that occur throughout organizations in a coordinated fashion, and managers must focus on those critical internal operations that enable them to satisfy customer needs. The internal measures should reflect business processes that have the greatest impact on customer satisfaction. These include factors that affect cycle time, quality, employee skills, and productivity.

Innovation and Learning Perspective   Given the rapid rate of markets, technologies, and global competition, the criteria for success are constantly changing. To survive and prosper, managers must make frequent changes to existing products and services as well as introduce entirely new products with expanded capabilities. A firm's ability to do well from an innovation and learning perspective is more dependent on its intangible than tangible assets. Three categories of intangible assets are critically important: human capital (skills, talent, and knowledge), information capital (information systems, networks), and organization capital (culture, leadership).

---

balanced scorecard a method of evaluating a firm's performance using performance measures from the customer, internal, innovation and learning, and financial perspectives.

customer perspective measures of firm performance that indicate how well firms are satisfying customers' expectations.

internal business perspective measures of firm performance that indicate how well firms' internal processes, decisions, and actions are contributing to customer satisfaction.

innovation and learning perspective measures of firm performance that indicate how well firms are changing their product and service offerings to adapt to changes in the internal and external environments.

EXHIBIT 3.11

The Balanced Scorecard's Four Perspectives

- How do customers see us? (customer perspective)
- What must we excel at? (internal business perspective)
- Can we continue to improve and create value? (innovation and learning perspective)
- How do we look to shareholders? (financial perspective)

Financial Perspective   Measures of financial performance indicate whether the company's strategy, implementation, and execution are indeed contributing to bottom-line improvement. Typical financial goals include profitability, growth, and shareholder value. Periodic financial statements remind managers that improved quality, response time, productivity, and innovative products benefit the firm only when they result in improved sales, increased market share, reduced operating expenses, or higher asset turnover.[65]

financial perspective
measures of firms' financial performance that indicate how well strategy, implementation, and execution are contributing to bottom-line improvement.

Consider how Sears, the retailer, found a strong causal relationship between employee attitudes, customer attitudes, and financial outcomes.[66] Through an ongoing study, Sears developed what it calls its total performance indicators, or TPI—a set of indicators for assessing its performance with customers, employees, and investors. Sears's quantitative model has shown that a 5 percent improvement in employee attitudes leads to a 1.3 percent improvement in customer satisfaction, which in turn drives a 0.5 percent improvement in revenue. Thus, if a single store improved its employee attitude by 5 percent, Sears could predict with confidence that if the revenue growth in the district as a whole were 5 percent, the revenue growth in this particular store would be 5.5 percent. Interestingly, Sears's managers consider such numbers as rigorous as any others that they work with every year. The company's accounting firm audits management as closely as it audits the financial statements.

A key implication is that managers do not need to look at their job as balancing stakeholder demands. They must avoid the following mind-set: "How many units in employee satisfaction do I have to give up to get some additional units of customer satisfaction or profits?" Instead, the balanced scorecard provides a win–win approach—increasing satisfaction among a wide variety of organizational stakeholders, including employees (at all levels), customers, and stockholders.

Limitations and Potential Downsides of the Balanced Scorecard   There is general agreement that there is nothing inherently wrong with the concept of the balanced scorecard.[67] The key limitation is that some executives may view it as a "quick fix" that can be easily installed. If managers do not recognize this from the beginning and fail to commit to it long term, the organization will be disappointed. Poor execution becomes the cause of such performance outcomes. And organizational scorecards must be aligned with individuals' scorecards to turn the balanced scorecards into a powerful tool for sustained performance.

In a study of 50 Canadian medium-size and large organizations, the number of users expressing skepticism about scorecard performance was much greater than the number claiming positive results. A large number of respondents agreed with the statement "Balanced scorecards don't really work." Some representative comments included: "It became just a number-crunching exercise by accountants after the first year," "It is just the latest management fad and is already dropping lower on management's list of priorities as all fads eventually do," and "If scorecards are supposed to be a measurement tool, why is it so hard to measure their results?" There is much work to do before scorecards can become a viable framework to measure sustained strategic performance.

Problems often occur in the balanced scorecard implementation efforts when the commitment to learning is insufficient and employees' personal ambitions are included. Without a set of rules for employees that address continuous process improvement and the personal improvement of individual employees, there will be limited employee buy-in and insufficient cultural change. Thus, many improvements may be temporary and superficial. Often, scorecards that failed to attain alignment and improvements dissipated very quickly. And, in many cases, management's efforts to improve performance were seen as divisive and were viewed by employees as aimed at benefiting senior management compensation. This fostered a "what's in it for me?" attitude.

The World Triathlon's Initiatives to Extend Its Brand

World Triathlon Corporation (WTC) is a Florida-based company known for recognizing athletic excellence and performance. It provides events, products, and services under the Ironman and Ironman 70.3* branded names. Since its inception, *Ironman* has been identified with ambitious and courageous individuals who aren't afraid to push their limits. Tapping into athletes' desires to pursue their dream of becoming an Ironman was a successful business strategy for WTC. Given the extreme physical challenge, disciplined training, and camaraderie it offered its clients, WTC was able to grow its revenues and profits over the years.

In 2008, Providence Equity Partners, a private equity firm, acquired WTC for an undisclosed amount. The new owners started expanding the exclusive branding of Ironman to products and events that clearly didn't represent the "spirit" of the brand. For example, those who finished Ironman 70.3 races were allowed to be called "Ironmen," regardless of the shorter length and lesser degree of difficulty. Additionally, products such as cologne, mattresses, and strollers were branded with "Ironman." In October 2010, Ironman Access was launched as a membership program wherein individuals could get preferential registration access to Ironman events for a $1,000 annual fee. The response by the triathlete community was quick and decisive—and overwhelmingly negative. The athletes felt that WTC was losing its values in its pursuit of more profits. The company was trying to expand the brand, but it was alienating its base.

Discussion Questions

1. What actions should WTC take?
2. Is the World Triathlon Corporation acting too aggressively in trying to monetize the brand?
3. What are the long-term implications of the WTC's recent strategic actions?

*Ironman 70.3 is the half triathlon; the number refers to the total distance in miles covered in the race—1.2-mile swim, 56-mile bike ride, and 13.1-mile run.

Sources: Beartini, M. & Gourville, J. T. 2012. Pricing to create share value. *Harvard Business Review,* 90(6): 96–104; and WTC. 2012. Corporate info. *www.ironman.com,* January 12: np.

Reflecting on Career Implications . . .

- **The Value Chain:** It is important that you develop an understanding of your firm's value chain. What activities are most critical for attaining competitive advantage? Think of ways in which you can add value in your firm's value chain. How might your firm's support activities (e.g., information technology, human resource practices) help you accomplish your assigned tasks more effectively? How will you bring your value-added contribution to the attention of your superiors?

- **The Value Chain:** Consider the most important linkages between the activities you perform in your organization with other activities both within your firm and between your firm and its suppliers, customers, and alliance partners. Understanding and strengthening these linkages can contribute greatly to your career advancement within your current organization.

- **Resource-Based View of the Firm:** Are your skills and talents rare, valuable, and difficult to imitate, and do they have few substitutes? If so, you are in the better position to add value for your firm—and earn rewards and incentives. How can your skills and talents be enhanced to help satisfy these criteria to a greater extent? Get more training? Change positions within the firm? Consider career options at other organizations?

- **Balanced Scorecard:** Can you design a balanced scorecard for your life? What perspectives would you include in it? In what ways would such a balanced scorecard help you attain success in life?

summary

In the traditional approaches to assessing a firm's internal environment, the primary goal of managers would be to determine their firm's relative strengths and weaknesses. Such is the role of SWOT analysis, wherein managers analyze their firm's strengths and weaknesses as well as the opportunities and threats in the external environment. In this chapter, we discussed why this may be a good starting point but hardly the best approach to take in performing a sound analysis. There are many limitations to SWOT analysis, including its static perspective, its potential to overemphasize a single dimension of a firm's strategy, and the likelihood that a firm's strengths do not necessarily help the firm create value or competitive advantages.

We identified two frameworks that serve to complement SWOT analysis in assessing a firm's internal environment: value-chain analysis and the resource-based view of the firm. In conducting a value-chain analysis, first divide the firm into a series of value-creating activities. These include primary activities such as inbound logistics, operations, and service as well as support activities such as procurement and human resource management. Then analyze how each activity adds value as well as how *interrelationships* among value activities in the firm and among the firm and its customers and suppliers add value. Thus, instead of merely determining a firm's strengths and weaknesses per se, you analyze them in the overall context of the firm and its relationships with customers and suppliers—the value system.

The resource-based view of the firm considers the firm as a bundle of resources: tangible resources, intangible resources, and organizational capabilities. Competitive advantages that are sustainable over time generally arise from the creation of bundles of resources and capabilities. For advantages to be sustainable, four criteria must be satisfied: value, rarity, difficulty in imitation, and difficulty in substitution. Such an evaluation requires a sound knowledge of the competitive context in which the firm exists. The owners of a business may not capture all of the value created by the firm. The appropriation of value created by a firm between the owners and employees is determined by four factors: employee bargaining power, replacement cost, employee exit costs, and manager bargaining power.

An internal analysis of the firm would not be complete unless you evaluate its performance and make the appropriate comparisons. Determining a firm's performance requires an analysis of its financial situation as well as a review of how well it is satisfying a broad range of stakeholders, including customers, employees, and stockholders. We discussed the concept of the balanced scorecard, in which four perspectives must be addressed: customer, internal business, innovation and learning, and financial. Central to this concept is the idea that the interests of various stakeholders can be interrelated. We provide examples of how indicators of employee satisfaction lead to higher levels of customer satisfaction, which in turn lead to higher levels of financial performance. Thus, improving a firm's performance does not need to involve making trade-offs among different stakeholders. Assessing the firm's performance is also more useful if it is evaluated in terms of how it changes over time, compares with industry norms, and compares with key competitors.

SUMMARY REVIEW QUESTIONS

1. SWOT analysis is a technique to analyze the internal and external environments of a firm. What are its advantages and disadvantages?

2. Briefly describe the primary and support activities in a firm's value chain.

3. How can managers create value by establishing important relationships among the value-chain activities both within their firm and between the firm and its customers and suppliers?

4. Briefly explain the four criteria for sustainability of competitive advantages.

5. Under what conditions are employees and managers able to appropriate some of the value created by their firm?

6. What are the advantages and disadvantages of conducting a financial ratio analysis of a firm?

7. Summarize the concept of the balanced scorecard. What are its main advantages?

key terms

value-chain analysis 76
primary activities 77
support activities 77
inbound logistics 77
operations 78
outbound logistics 78
marketing and sales 79
service 80
procurement 80
technology development 82
human resource
   management 82
general administration 84

interrelationships 85
resource-based view
   of the firm 88
tangible resources 88
intangible resources 89
organizational
   capabilities 90
path dependency 92
causal ambiguity 92
social complexity 92
financial ratio
   analysis 97
balanced scorecard 100
customer perspective 100
internal business
   perspective 100
innovation and learning
   perspective 100
financial perspective 101

experiential exercise

Caterpillar is a leading firm in the construction and mining equipment industry with extensive global operations. It has approximately 114,000 employees, and its revenues were $55 billion in 2014. In addition to its manufacturing and logistics operations, Caterpillar is well known for its superb service and parts supply, and it provides retail financing for its equipment.

Below, we address several questions that focus on Caterpillar's value-chain activities and the interrelationships among them as well as whether or not the firm is able to attain sustainable competitive advantage(s).

1. Where in Caterpillar's value chain is the firm creating value for its customers?

Value-Chain Activity	Yes/No	How Does Caterpillar Create Value for the Customer?
Primary:		
Inbound logistics		
Operations		
Outbound logistics		
Marketing and sales		
Service		
Support:		
Procurement		
Technology development		
Human resource management		
General administration		

2. What are the important relationships among Caterpillar's value-chain activities? What are the important interdependencies? For each activity, identify the relationships and interdependencies.

	Inbound logistics	Operations	Outbound logistics	Marketing and sales	Service	Procurement	Technology development	Human resource management	General administration
Inbound logistics									
Operations									
Outbound logistics									
Marketing and sales									
Service									
Procurement									
Technology development									
Human resource management									
General administration									

3. What resources, activities, and relationships enable Caterpillar to achieve a sustainable competitive advantage?

Resource/Activity	Is It Valuable?	Is It Rare?	Are There Few Substitutes?	Is It Difficult to Make?
Inbound logistics				
Operations				
Outbound logistics				
Marketing and sales				
Service				
Procurement				
Technology development				
Human resource management				
General administration				

application questions & exercises

1. Using published reports, select two CEOs who have recently made public statements regarding a major change in their firm's strategy. Discuss how the successful implementation of such strategies requires changes in the firm's primary and support activities.

2. Select a firm that competes in an industry in which you are interested. Drawing upon published financial reports, complete a financial ratio analysis. Based on changes over time and a comparison with industry norms, evaluate the firm's strengths and weaknesses in terms of its financial position.

3. How might exemplary human resource practices enhance and strengthen a firm's value-chain activities?

4. Using the Internet, look up your university or college. What are some of its key value-creating activities that provide competitive advantages? Why?

ethics questions

1. What are some of the ethical issues that arise when a firm becomes overly zealous in advertising its products?

2. What are some of the ethical issues that may arise from a firm's procurement activities? Are you aware of any of these issues from your personal experience or businesses you are familiar with?

references

1. Sheehan, M. 2014. How China's electric car dreams became a PR nightmare in America. *www.huffingtonpost.com,* April 1: np; Jullens, J. 2013. How emerging giants can take on the world. *Harvard Business Review,* 91(12): 121–125; and *finance. yahoo.com.*

2. Our discussion of the value chain will draw on Porter, M. E. 1985. *Competitive advantage:* chap. 2. New York: Free Press.

3. Dyer, J. H. 1996. Specialized supplier networks as a source of competitive advantage: Evidence from the auto industry. *Strategic Management Journal,* 17: 271–291.

4. For an insightful perspective on value-chain analysis, refer to Stabell, C. B. & Fjeldstad, O. D. 1998. Configuring value for competitive advantage: On chains, shops, and networks. *Strategic Management Journal,* 19: 413–437. The authors develop concepts of value chains, value shops, and value networks to extend the value-creation logic across a broad range of industries. Their work builds on the seminal contributions of Porter, 1985, op. cit., and others who have addressed how firms create value through key interrelationships among value-creating activities.

5. Ibid.

6. Maynard, M. 1999. Toyota promises custom order in 5 days. *USA Today,* August 6: B1.

7. Shaw Industries. 1999. Annual report: 14–15.

8. Fisher, M. L. 1997. What is the right supply chain for your product? *Harvard Business Review,* 75(2): 105–116.

9. Jackson, M. 2001. Bringing a dying brand back to life. *Harvard Business Review,* 79(5): 53–61.

10. Anderson, J. C. & Nmarus, J. A. 2003. Selectively pursuing more of your customer's business. *MIT Sloan Management Review,* 44(3): 42–50.

11. Insights on advertising are addressed in Rayport, J. F. 2008. Where is advertising going? Into 'stitials. *Harvard Business Review,* 66(5): 18–20.

12. Reiter, C. 2011. BMW gets its close-up, at Audi's expense. *Bloomberg Businessweek,* December 19–December 25: 24–25.

13. For a scholarly discussion on the procurement of technology components, read Hoetker, G. 2005. How much you know versus how well I know you: Selecting a supplier for a technically innovative component. *Strategic Management Journal,* 26(1): 75–96.

14. For a discussion on criteria to use when screening suppliers for back-office functions, read Feeny, D., Lacity, M., & Willcocks, L. P. 2005. Taking the measure of outsourcing providers. *MIT Sloan Management Review,* 46(3): 41–48.

15. For a study investigating sourcing practices, refer to Safizadeh, M. H., Field, J. M., & Ritzman, L. P. 2008. Sourcing practices and boundaries of the firm in the financial services industry. *Strategic Management Journal,* 29(1): 79–92.

16. Imperato, G. 1998. How to give good feedback. *Fast Company,* September: 144–156.

17. Bensaou, B. M. & Earl, M. 1998. The right mindset for managing information technology. *Harvard Business Review,* 96(5): 118–128.

18. A discussion of R&D in the pharmaceutical industry is in Garnier, J-P. 2008. Rebuilding the R&D engine in big pharma. *Harvard Business Review,* 66(5): 68–76.

19. Chick, S. E., Huchzermeier, A., & Netessine, S. 2014. Europe's solution factories. *Harvard Business Review,* 92(4): 111–115.

20. Ulrich, D. 1998. A new mandate for human resources. *Harvard Business Review,* 96(1): 124–134.

21. A study of human resource management in China is Li, J., Lam, K., Sun, J. J. M., & Liu, S. X. Y. 2008. Strategic resource management, institutionalization, and employment modes: An empirical study in China. *Strategic Management Journal,* 29(3): 337–342.

22. Wood, J. 2003. Sharing jobs and working from home: The new face of the airline industry. *AviationCareer. net:* February 21.

23. Green, S., Hasan, F., Immelt, J. Marks, M., & Meiland, D. 2003. In search of global leaders. *Harvard Business Review,* 81(8): 38–45.

24. For insights on the role of information systems integration in fostering innovation, refer to Cash, J. I. Jr., Earl, M. J., & Morison, R. 2008. Teaming up to crack innovation and enterprise integration. *Harvard Business Review,* 66(11): 90–100.

25. For a cautionary note on the use of IT, refer to McAfee, A. 2003. When too much IT knowledge is a dangerous thing. *MIT Sloan Management Review,* 44(2): 83–90.

26. For an interesting perspective on some of the potential downsides of close customer and supplier relationships, refer to Anderson, E. & Jap, S. D. 2005. The dark side of close relationships. *MIT Sloan Management Review,* 46(3): 75–82.

27. Day, G. S. 2003. Creating a superior customer-relating capability. *MIT Sloan Management Review,* 44(3): 77–82.

28. To gain insights on the role of electronic technologies in enhancing a firm's connections to outside suppliers and customers, refer to Lawrence, T. B., Morse, E. A., & Fowler, S. W. 2005. Managing your portfolio of connections. *MIT Sloan Management Review,* 46(2): 59–66.

29. IBM Global CEO Study, p. 27.

30. Verhoef, P. C., Beckers, S. F. M., & van Doorn, J. 2013. Understand the perils of co-creation. *Harvard Business Review,* 91(9): 28; and Winston, A. S. 2014. *The big pivot.* Boston: Harvard Business Review Press.

31. Collis, D. J. & Montgomery, C. A. 1995. Competing on resources: Strategy in the 1990's. *Harvard Business Review,* 73(4): 119–128; and Barney, J. 1991. Firm resources and sustained competitive advantage. *Journal of Management,* 17(1): 99–120.

32. For critiques of the resource-based view of the firm, refer to Sirmon, D. G., Hitt, M. A., & Ireland, R. D. 2007. Managing firm resources in dynamic environments to create value: Looking inside the black box. *Academy of Management Review,* 32(1): 273–292; and Newbert, S. L. 2007. Empirical research on the resource-based view of the firm: An assessment and suggestions for future research. *Strategic Management Journal,* 28(2): 121–146.

33. Henkoff, R. 1993. Companies that train the best. *Fortune,* March 22: 83; and Dess & Picken, *Beyond productivity,* p. 98.

34. Gaines-Ross, L. 2010. Reputation warfare. *Harvard Business Review,* 88(12): 70–76.

35. Barney, J. B. 1986. Types of competition and the theory of strategy: Towards an integrative framework. *Academy of Management Review,* 11(4): 791–800.

36. Harley-Davidson. 1993. Annual report.

37. Stetler, B. 2008. Griping online? Comcast hears and talks back. *nytimes.com,* July 25: np.

38. For a rigorous, academic treatment of the origin of capabilities, refer to Ethiraj, S. K., Kale, P., Krishnan, M. S., & Singh, J. V. 2005. Where do capabilities come from and how do they matter? A study of the software services industry. *Strategic Management Journal,* 26(1): 25–46.

39. For an academic discussion on methods associated with organizational capabilities, refer to Dutta, S., Narasimhan, O., & Rajiv, S. 2005. Conceptualizing and measuring capabilities: Methodology and empirical application. *Strategic Management Journal,* 26(3): 277–286.

40. Lorenzoni, G. & Lipparini, A. 1999. The leveraging of interfirm relationships as a distinctive organizational capability: A longitudinal study. *Strategic Management Journal,* 20: 317–338.

41. Andersen, M. M. op. cit, p. 209.

42. A study investigating the sustainability of competitive advantage is Newbert, S. L. 2008. Value, rareness, competitive advantages, and performance: A conceptual-level empirical investigation of the resource-based view of the firm. *Strategic Management Journal,* 29(7): 745–768.

43. Arikan, A. M. & McGahan, A. M. 2010. The development of capabilities in new firms. *Strategic Management Journal,* 31(1): 1–18.

44. Barney, J. 1991. Firm resources and sustained competitive advantage. *Journal of Management,* 17(1): 99–120.

45. Barney, 1986, op. cit. Our discussion of inimitability and substitution draws upon this source.

46. A study that investigates the performance implications of imitation is Ethiraj, S. K. & Zhu, D. H. 2008. Performance effects of imitative entry. *Strategic Management Journal,* 29(8): 797–818.

47. Sirmon, D. G., Hitt, M. A., Arregale, J.-L. & Campbell, J. T. 2010. The dynamic interplay of capability strengths and weaknesses: Investigating the bases of temporary competitive advantage. *Strategic Management Journal,* 31(13): 1386–1409.

48. Scherzer, L. 2012. Groupon and deal sites see skepticism replacing promise. *finance.yahoo.com,* November 30: np; The dismal scoop on Groupon. 2011. *The Economist,* October 22: 81; Slater, D. 2012. Are daily deals done? *Fast Company;* and Danna, D. 2012. Groupon & daily deals competition. *beta.fool.com,* June 15: np.

49. Deephouse, D. L. 1999. To be different, or to be the same? It's a question (and theory) of strategic balance. *Strategic Management Journal,* 20: 147–166.

50. Karlgaard, R. 2014. *The soft edge.* San Francisco: Jossey-Bass.

51. Yeoh, P. L. & Roth, K. 1999. An empirical analysis of sustained advantage in the U.S. pharmaceutical industry: Impact of firm resources and capabilities. *Strategic Management Journal,* 20: 637–653.

52. Robins, J. A. & Wiersema, M. F. 2000. Strategies for unstructured competitive environments: Using scarce resources to create new markets. In Bresser, R. F., et al. (Eds.), *Winning strategies in a deconstructing world:* 201–220. New York: Wiley.

53. Graser, M. 2013. Blockbuster chiefs lacked the vision to see how the industry was shifting under the video rental chain's feet. *www.variety.com,* November 12: np; Kellmurray, B. 2013. Learning from Blockbuster's failure to adapt. *www.abovethefoldmag.com,* November 13: np; and Downes, L. & Nunes, P. 2014. *Big bang disruption.* New York: Penguin.

54. Amit, R. & Schoemaker, J. H. 1993. Strategic assets and organizational rent. *Strategic Management Journal,* 14(1): 33–46; Collis, D. J. & Montgomery, C. A. 1995. Competing on resources: Strategy in the 1990's. *Harvard Business Review,* 73(4): 118–128; Coff, R. W. 1999. When competitive advantage doesn't lead to performance: The resource-based view and stakeholder bargaining power. *Organization Science,* 10(2): 119–133; and Blyler, M. & Coff, R. W. 2003. Dynamic capabilities, social capital, and rent appropriation: Ties that split pies. *Strategic Management Journal,* 24: 677–686.

55. Munk, N. 1998. The new organization man. *Fortune,* March 16: 62–74.

56. Coff, op. cit.

57. Anonymous. 2013. "All of them are overpaid": Bank CEOs got average 7.7% raise. *www.moneynews.com,* June 3: np.

58. We have focused our discussion on how internal stakeholders (e.g., employees, managers, and top executives) may appropriate a firm's profits (or rents). For an interesting discussion of how a firm's innovations may be appropriated by external stakeholders (e.g., customers, suppliers) as well as competitors, refer to Grant, R. M. 2002. *Contemporary strategy analysis* (4th ed.): 335–340. Malden, MA: Blackwell.

59. Luehrman, T. A. 1997. What's it worth? A general manager's guide to valuation. *Harvard Business Review,* 45(3): 132–142.

60. See, for example, Kaplan, R. S. & Norton, D. P. 1992. The balanced scorecard: Measures that drive performance. *Harvard Business Review,* 69(1): 71–79.

61. Hitt, M. A., Ireland, R. D., & Stadter, G. 1982. Functional importance of company performance: Moderating effects of grand strategy and industry type. *Strategic Management Journal,* 3: 315–330.

62. *finance.yahoo.com.*

63. Kaplan & Norton, op. cit.

64. Ibid.

65. For a discussion of the relative value of growth versus increasing margins, read Mass, N. J. 2005. The relative value of growth. *Harvard Business Review,* 83(4): 102–112.

66. Rucci, A. J., Kirn, S. P., & Quinn, R. T. 1998. The employee-customer-profit chain at Sears. *Harvard Business Review,* 76(1): 82–97.

67. Our discussion draws upon: Angel, R. & Rampersad, H. 2005. Do scorecards add up? *camagazine.com.* May: np.; and Niven, P. 2002. *Balanced scorecard step by step: Maximizing performance and maintaining results.* New York: John Wiley & Sons.

photo credits

Recognizing a Firm's Intellectual Assets

Moving beyond a Firm's Tangible Resources

After reading this chapter, you should have a good understanding of the following learning objectives:

LO4.1 Why the management of knowledge professionals and knowledge itself are so critical in today's organizations.

LO4.2 The importance of recognizing the interdependence of attracting, developing, and retaining human capital.

LO4.3 The key role of social capital in leveraging human capital within and across the firm.

LO4.4 The importance of social networks in knowledge management and in promoting career success.

LO4.5 The vital role of technology in leveraging knowledge and human capital.

LO4.6 Why "electronic" or "virtual" teams are critical in combining and leveraging knowledge in organizations and how they can be made more effective.

LO4.7 The challenge of protecting intellectual property and the importance of a firm's dynamic capabilities.

Learning from Mistakes

In September 2008, Bank of America purchased Merrill Lynch (ML) in the depths of the financial crisis for $50 billion. It seemed like a pretty good deal. However, six months later Bank of America reported $15 billion in losses due to ML's exposure in toxic mortgage-backed securities bonds. This resulted in a class-action lawsuit, with $2.43 billion going to shareholders and $150 million to the Securities and Exchange Commission.[1] Despite these early legal woes, ML has helped bolster Bank of America, contributing roughly half the bank's revenue and the bulk of its profits since 2009, according to bank analysts. From 2009 to 2011, Merrill Lynch made $164.4 billion in revenue and $31.9 billion in total profits. Bank of America over that period, as a total entity, made $326.8 billion in revenue and $5.5 billion in profits. Thus, while the bank was hemorrhaging cash and facing a struggling economy, ML was standing strong and keeping the bank afloat with its army of 16,000 brokers.

Investment bankers, senior executives, and brokers receive Bank of America stock as a significant portion of their compensation in order to align their interests with those of Bank of America. Yet hundreds of high-performing brokers and financial advisers at Merrill Lynch have recently fled the firm. What happened?

Bank of America mismanaged its most valuable asset—its human capital. While it tried to promote the corporate initiative of cross-selling Bank of America's banking products and services to ML's clients, it lost many of its star employees and, of course, their networks of high-net-worth clients in the process.

Leveraging ML's sales force was the focus of Brian Moynihan, chief executive officer. He cited cross-selling as key opportunities for growth, that is, turning brokerage clients into banking clients, and vice versa. However, as Sanford C. Bernstein analyst Brad Hintz pointed out, "The payout on banking products is less to brokers, and they're being asked to share client relationships with Bank of America. That's never a good thing for a broker." Bank of America poorly executed its cross-selling strategy. This left both clients and brokers demanding higher-quality levels of service and questioning why they were associated with Bank of America in the first place. Brokers who were managing over $1 billion in client assets were getting calls from their clients dealing with elementary banking and checking issues. For example, one high-end broker was called about misprinted checks! Additionally, the special white-glove service that ML brokers were accustomed to giving their high-value clients was falling short: Mortgages for ultra-high-net-worth individuals were taking nine months to complete, and the standard practice of charging maintenance fees to cover expenses when accounts fell below their minimum could not be waived at the discretion of the broker.

Bank of America also had some inflexible human resource practices that alienated the brokers. For example, Patrick Rush had been teaching continuing education courses focusing on retirement planning at local colleges. Although Merrill saw value in his teaching and community involvement, Bank of America told him he had to stop. Rush left in 2011 and started his own wealth management firm.

Clearly, Bank of America did not realize that its brokers are highly valuable assets (along with their high-net-worth clients). It paid the price for not fostering the environment for these employees to flourish.

Discussion Questions

1. What actions should Bank of America take to retain its top investment advisers?
2. Can it do this while still leveraging value?
3. Should Bank of America continue to cross-sell?

Managers are always looking for stellar professionals who can take their organizations to the next level. However, attracting talent is a necessary but *not* sufficient condition for success. In today's knowledge economy, it does not matter how big your stock of resources is—whether it be top talent, physical resources, or financial capital. Rather, the question becomes: How good is the organization at attracting top talent and leveraging that talent to produce a stream of products and services valued by the marketplace?

Bank of America's problems with Merrill Lynch, its brokerage division, illustrate issues related to effectively developing and retaining talent. Faced with pressures to cross-sell Bank of America products to their high-net-worth clients, many Merrill brokers have chosen to leave and, of course, taken their clients with them. Restrictive personnel policies, such as barring them from teaching continuing education courses, didn't help either. As a recent article commented, "Merrill's best assets have legs. A heavy corporate hand could send them sprinting."

In this chapter, we also address how human capital can be leveraged in an organization. We point out the important roles of social capital and technology.

The Central Role of Knowledge in Today's Economy

LO4.1

Why the management of knowledge professionals and knowledge itself are so critical in today's organizations.

Central to our discussion is an enormous change that has accelerated over the past few decades and its implications for the strategic management of organizations.[2] For most of the 20th century, managers focused on tangible resources such as land, equipment, and money as well as intangibles such as brands, image, and customer loyalty. Efforts were directed more toward the efficient allocation of labor and capital—the two traditional factors of production.

How times have changed. In the last quarter century, employment in the manufacturing sector declined at a significant rate. Today only 9 percent of the U.S. workforce is employed in this sector, compared to 21 percent in 1980.[3] In contrast, the service sector grew from 73 percent of the workforce in 1980 to 86 percent by 2012.

The knowledge-worker segment, in particular, is growing dramatically. Using a broad definition, it is estimated that knowledge workers currently outnumber other types of workers in the United States by at least four to one—they represent between a quarter and a half of all workers in advanced economies. Recent popular press has gone so far as to suggest that, due to the increased speed and competitiveness of modern business, all modern employees are knowledge workers.

knowledge economy
an economy where wealth is created through the effective management of knowledge workers instead of by the efficient control of physical and financial assets.

In the **knowledge economy,** wealth is increasingly created by effective management of knowledge workers instead of by the efficient control of physical and financial assets. The growing importance of knowledge, coupled with the move by labor markets to reward knowledge work, tells us that investing in a company is, in essence, buying a set of talents, capabilities, skills, and ideas—intellectual capital—not physical and financial resources.[4]

Consider an example. Merck didn't become the "Most Admired" company, for seven consecutive years in *Fortune*'s annual survey, because it can manufacture pills, but because its scientists can discover medicines. P. Roy Vagelos, former CEO of Merck, the $43 billion pharmaceutical giant, during its long run atop the "Most Admired" survey, said, "A low-value product can be made by any one anywhere. When you have knowledge no one else has access to—that's dynamite. We guard our research even more carefully than our financial assets."[5]

To apply some numbers to our arguments, let's ask, What's a company worth?[6] Start with the "big three" financial statements: income statement, balance sheet, and statement of cash flow. If these statements tell a story that investors find useful, then a company's

Company	Annual Sales ($ billions)	Market Value ($ billions)	Book Value ($ billions)	Ratio of Market to Book Value
Apple	182.8	641.2	112.5	5.7
Microsoft	86.8	385.4	89.8	4.3
Oracle	38.3	196.4	47.5	4.1
Intel	55.0	175.8	55.0	3.2
Nucor	21.0	15.6	7.6	2.1
General Motors	156.8	56.0	39.5	1.4

EXHIBIT 4.1

Ratio of Market Value to Book Value for Selected Companies

Note: The data on market valuations are as of January 5, 2015. All other financial data are based on the most recently available balance sheets and income statements.

Source: *finance.yahoo.com.*

market value* should roughly (but not precisely, because the market looks forward and the books look backward) be the same as the value that accountants ascribe to it—the book value of the firm. However, this is not the case. A study compared the market value with the book value of 3,500 U.S. companies over a period of two decades. In 1978 the two were similar: Book value was 95 percent of market value. However, market values and book values have diverged significantly. By April 2015, the S&P industrials were—on average—trading at 2.89 times book value.[7] Robert A. Howell, an expert on the changing role of finance and accounting, muses, "The big three financial statements . . . are about as useful as an 80-year-old Los Angeles road map."

The gap between a firm's market value and book value is far greater for knowledge-intensive corporations than for firms with strategies based primarily on tangible assets.[8] Exhibit 4.1 shows the ratio of market-to-book value for some well-known companies. In firms where knowledge and the management of knowledge workers are relatively important contributors to developing products and services—and physical resources are less critical—the ratio of market-to-book value tends to be much higher.

As shown in Exhibit 4.1, firms such as Apple, Google, Microsoft, and Oracle have very high market value to book value ratios because of their high investment in knowledge resources and technological expertise. In contrast, firms in more traditional industry sectors such as Nucor and Southwest Airlines have relatively low market-to-book ratios. This reflects their greater investment in physical resources and lower investment in knowledge resources. A firm like Intel has a market-to-book value ratio that falls between the above two groups of firms. This is because its high level of investment in knowledge resources is matched by a correspondingly huge investment in plant and equipment. For example, Intel invested $3 billion to build a fabrication facility in Chandler, Arizona.[9]

Many writers have defined **intellectual capital** as the difference between a firm's market value and book value—that is, a measure of the value of a firm's intangible assets.[10] This broad definition includes assets such as reputation, employee loyalty and commitment, customer relationships, company values, brand names, and the experience and skills of employees.[11] Thus, simplifying, we have:

intellectual capital
the difference between the market value of the firm and the book value of the firm, including assets such as reputation, employee loyalty and commitment, customer relationships, company values, brand names, and the experience and skills of employees.

$$\text{Intellectual capital} = \text{Market value of firm} - \text{Book value of firm}$$

*The market value of a firm is equal to the value of a share of its common stock times the number of shares outstanding. The book value of a firm is primarily a measure of the value of its tangible assets. It can be calculated by the formula Total assets − Total liabilities.

How do companies create value in the knowledge-intensive economy? The general answer is to attract and leverage human capital effectively through mechanisms that create products and services of value over time.

First, **human capital** is the "*individual* capabilities, knowledge, skills, and experience of the company's employees and managers."[12] This knowledge is relevant to the task at hand, as well as the capacity to add to this reservoir of knowledge, skills, and experience through learning.[13]

Second, **social capital** is "the network of relationships that individuals have throughout the organization." Relationships are critical in sharing and leveraging knowledge and in acquiring resources.[14] Social capital can extend beyond the organizational boundaries to include relationships between the firm and its suppliers, customers, and alliance partners.[15]

Third is the concept of "knowledge," which comes in two different forms. First, there is **explicit knowledge** that is codified, documented, easily reproduced, and widely distributed, such as engineering drawings, software code, and patents.[16] The other type of knowledge is **tacit knowledge.** That is in the minds of employees and is based on their experiences and backgrounds.[17] Tacit knowledge is shared only with the consent and participation of the individual.

New knowledge is constantly created through the continual interaction of explicit and tacit knowledge. Consider two software engineers working together on a computer code. The computer code is the explicit knowledge. By sharing ideas based on each individual's experience—that is, their tacit knowledge—they create new knowledge when they modify the code. Another important issue is the role of "socially complex processes," which include leadership, culture, and trust.[18] These processes play a central role in the creation of knowledge.[19] They represent the "glue" that holds the organization together and helps to create a working environment where individuals are more willing to share their ideas, work in teams, and, in the end, create products and services of value.[20]

Numerous books have been written on the subject of knowledge management and the central role that it has played in creating wealth in organizations and countries throughout the developed world.[21] Here, we focus on some of the key issues that organizations must address to compete through knowledge.

We will now turn our discussion to the central resource itself—human capital—and some guidelines on how it can be attracted/selected, developed, and retained.[22] Tom Stewart, former editor of the *Harvard Business Review,* noted that organizations must also undergo significant efforts to protect their human capital. A firm may "diversify the ownership of vital knowledge by emphasizing teamwork, guard against obsolescence by developing learning programs, and shackle key people with golden handcuffs."[23] In addition, people are less likely to leave an organization if there are effective structures to promote teamwork and information sharing, strong leadership that encourages innovation, and cultures that demand excellence and ethical behavior. Such issues are central to this chapter. Although we touch on these issues throughout this chapter, we provide more detail in later chapters. We discuss organizational controls (culture, rewards, and boundaries) in Chapter 9, organization structure and design in Chapter 10, and a variety of leadership and entrepreneurship topics in Chapters 11 and 12.

human capital

the individual capabilities, knowledge, skills, and experience of a company's employees and managers.

social capital

the network of friendships and working relationships between talented people both inside and outside the organization.

explicit knowledge

knowledge that is codified, documented, easily reproduced, and widely distributed.

tacit knowledge

knowledge that is in the minds of employees and is based on their experiences and backgrounds.

LO4.2

The importance of recognizing the interdependence of attracting, developing, and retaining human capital.

Human Capital: The Foundation of Intellectual Capital

Take away my people, but leave my factories and soon grass will grow on the factory floors. . . . Take away my factories, but leave my people and soon we will have a new and better factory.[24]

—*Andrew Carnegie, Steel industry legend*

The importance of talent to organization success is hardly new. Organizations must recruit talented people—employees at all levels with the proper sets of skills and capabilities coupled with the right values and attitudes. Such skills and attitudes must be continually developed, strengthened, and reinforced, and each employee must be motivated and his or her efforts focused on the organization's goals and objectives.[25]

The rise to prominence of knowledge workers as a vital source of competitive advantage is changing the balance of power in today's organization.[26] Knowledge workers place professional development and personal enrichment (financial and otherwise) above company loyalty. Attracting, recruiting, and hiring the "best and the brightest" is a critical first step in the process of building intellectual capital. As noted by law professor Orly Lobel, *talent wants to be free:*[27]

> Companies like Microsoft, Google, and Facebook are so hungry for talent that they acquire (or, as the tech-buzz is now calling it, acq-hire) entire start-ups only to discard the product and keep the teams, founders, and engineers.

Hiring is only the first of three processes in which all successful organizations must engage to build and leverage their human capital. Firms must also *develop* employees to fulfill their full potential to maximize their joint contributions.[28] Finally, the first two processes are for naught if firms can't provide the working environment and intrinsic and extrinsic rewards to *engage* their best and brightest.[29] Interestingly, a recent Gallup study showed that companies whose workers are the most engaged outperform those with the least engaged by a significant amount: 16 percent higher profitability, 18 percent higher productivity, and 25 to 49 percent lower turnover (depending on the industry).[30] The last benefit can really be significant: Software leader SAP calculated that "for each percentage point that our retention rate goes up or down, the impact on our operating profit is approximately $81 million."

These activities are highly interrelated. We would like to suggest the imagery of a three-legged stool (see Exhibit 4.2).[31] If one leg is weak or broken, the stool collapses.

To illustrate such interdependence, poor hiring impedes the effectiveness of development and retention processes. In a similar vein, ineffective retention efforts place additional burdens on hiring and development. Consider the following anecdote, provided by Jeffrey Pfeffer of the Stanford University Graduate School of Business:

> Not long ago, I went to a large, fancy San Francisco law firm—where they treat their associates like dog doo and where the turnover is very high. I asked the managing partner about the turnover rate. He said, "A few years ago, it was 25 percent, and now we're up to 30 percent." I asked him how the firm had responded to that trend. He said, "We increased our recruiting." So I asked him, "What kind of doctor would you be if your patient was bleeding faster and faster, and your only response was to increase the speed of the transfusion?"[32]

EXHIBIT 4.2 Human Capital: Three Interdependent Activities

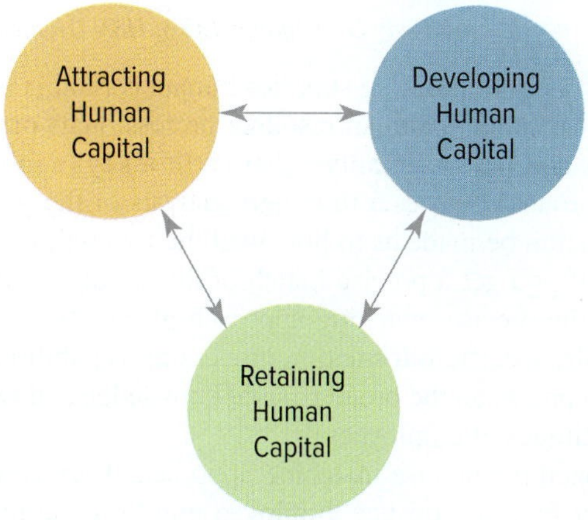

CAN GREEN STRATEGIES ATTRACT AND RETAIN TALENT?

Competing successfully for top talent and retaining high-performing employees are critical factors in an organization's success. Employee recruiting and turnover are, of course, very costly. Losing and replacing a top talent can cost companies up to 200 percent of an employee's annual salary, according to *Engaged! Outbehave Your Competition to Create Customers for Life.*

Today, some 40 percent of job seekers read a company's sustainability report, according to a survey commissioned by the Global Reporting Initiative (GRI). Prospective employees can also riffle through Google in seconds and unearth a myriad of sustainability news and accolades, including an Interbrand "Top 50 Global Green Brand" ranking. Further, a poll on green employment by MonsterTRAK.com, a job website geared toward students and entry-level hires, found that 80 percent of young professionals are interested in securing a job that has a positive impact on the environment and 92 percent would be more inclined to work for a company that is environmentally friendly.

Below, we discuss examples of green initiatives by two well-known companies that help attract and retain talent:

- Intel's "Green Intel" intranet portal, environmental sustainability network, and environmental excellence awards are beginning to yield benefits for the company. "Intel's employee engagement has resulted in increased employee loyalty, more company pride, and improved morale," according to Carrie Freeman, a sustainability strategist at the firm. Intel managers expect the next organizational health survey will show increased levels of employee pride and satisfaction with their work, which are considered to be good predictors of employee retention.

- Hewlett-Packard installed a 1.1-megawatt system of 6,256 SunPower solar panels at its San Diego facility. The system is projected to save the company $750,000 during the next 15 years, while providing more than 10 percent of the facility's power. As part of its agreement with SunPower, HP started an employee program offering joint rebates to install solar electricity for employees' homes. The program links the company's initiatives to steps employees can take and provides a unique employee benefit not available at all companies.

Sources: Earley, K. 2014. Sustainabilty gives HR teams an edge in attracting and retaining talent. *www.theguardian.com*, February 20: np; Anonymous. 2010. The business case for environmental and sustainability employee education. *National Environmental Education Foundation*, November: np; Mattioli, D. 2007. How going green draws talent, cuts costs. *Wall Street Journal*, November 13: B10; and Lederman, G. 2013. *Engaged! Outbehave your competition to create customers for life.* Ashland, OR: Evolve.

Clearly, stepped-up recruiting is a poor substitute for weak retention.[33] Although there are no simple, easy-to-apply answers, we can learn from what leading-edge firms are doing to attract, develop, and retain human capital in today's highly competitive marketplace.[34] Before moving on, Strategy Spotlight 4.1 addresses the importance of a firm's "green" or environmental sustainability strategy in attracting young talent.

Attracting Human Capital

In today's world, talent is so critical to the success of what you're doing—their core competencies and how well they fit into your office culture. The combination can be, well, extraordinary. But only if you bring in the right people.[35]

—Mindy Grossman, CEO of HSN (Home Shopping Network)

The first step in the process of building superior human capital is input control: attracting and selecting the right person.[36] Human resource professionals often approach employee selection from a "lock and key" mentality—that is, fit a key (a job candidate) into a lock (the job). Such an approach involves a thorough analysis of the person and the job. Only then can the right decision be made as to how well the two will fit together. How can you fail, the theory goes, if you get a precise match of knowledge, ability, and skill profiles? Frequently, however, the precise matching approach places its emphasis on task-specific skills (e.g., motor skills, specific information processing capabilities, and communication skills) and puts less emphasis on the broad general knowledge and experience, social skills, values, beliefs, and attitudes of employees.[37]

Many have questioned the precise matching approach. They argue that firms can identify top performers by focusing on key employee mind-sets, attitudes, social skills, and general orientations. If they get these elements right, the task-specific skills can be learned quickly. (This does not imply, however, that task-specific skills are unimportant; rather, it suggests that the requisite skill sets must be viewed as a necessary but not sufficient condition.) This leads us to a popular phrase today that serves as the title of the next section.

"Hire for Attitude, Train for Skill"   Organizations are increasingly emphasizing general knowledge and experience, social skills, values, beliefs, and attitudes of employees.[38] Consider Southwest Airlines' hiring practices, which focus on employee values and attitudes. Given its strong team orientation, Southwest uses an "indirect" approach. For example, the interviewing team asks a group of employees to prepare a five-minute presentation about themselves. During the presentations, interviewers observe which candidates enthusiastically support their peers and which candidates focus on polishing their own presentations while the others are presenting.[39] The former are, of course, favored.

Alan Cooper, president of Cooper Software, Inc., in Palo Alto, California, goes further. He cleverly *uses technology* to hone in on the problem-solving ability of his applicants and their attitudes before an interview even takes place. He has devised a "Bozo Filter," an online test that can be applied to any industry. Before you spend time on whether job candidates will work out satisfactorily, find out how their minds work. Cooper advised, "Hiring was a black hole. I don't talk to bozos anymore, because 90 percent of them turn away when they see our test. It's a self-administering bozo filter."[40] How does it work?

> The online test asks questions designed to see how prospective employees approach problem-solving tasks. For example, one key question asks software engineer applicants to design a table-creation software program for Microsoft Word. Candidates provide pencil sketches and a description of the new user interface. Another question used for design communicators asks them to develop a marketing strategy for a new touch-tone phone—directed at consumers in the year 1850. Candidates e-mail their answers back to the company, and the answers are circulated around the firm to solicit feedback. Only candidates with the highest marks get interviews.

Sound Recruiting Approaches and Networking   Companies that take hiring seriously must also take recruiting seriously. The number of jobs that successful knowledge-intensive companies must fill is astonishing. Ironically, many companies still have no shortage of applicants. For example, Google, which ranked first on *Fortune*'s 2012 and 2013 "100 Best Companies to Work For," is planning to hire thousands of employees—even though its hiring rate has slowed.[41] The challenge becomes having the right job candidates, not the greatest number of them.

GE Medical Systems, which builds CT scanners and magnetic resonance imaging (MRI) systems, relies extensively on networking. GE has found that current employees are the best source for new ones. Stephen Patscot, VP, human resources, made a few simple changes to double the number of referrals. First, he simplified the process—no complex forms, no bureaucracy, and so on. Second, he increased incentives. Everyone referring a qualified candidate receives a gift certificate from Sears. For referrals who are hired, the "bounty" increases to $2,000. Although this may sound like a lot of money, it is "peanuts" compared to the $15,000 to $20,000 fees that GE typically pays to headhunters for each person hired.[42] Also, when someone refers a former colleague or friend for a job, his or her credibility is on the line. Thus, employees will be careful in recommending people for employment unless they are reasonably confident that these people are good candidates.

Attracting Millennials   The Millennial generation has also been termed "Generation Y" or "Echo Boom" and includes people who were born after 1982. Many call them impatient, demanding, or entitled. However, if employers don't provide incentives to attract and retain young workers, somebody else will. Thus, they will be at a competitive disadvantage.[43]

Why? Demographics are on the Millennials' side—within a few years they will out-number any other generation. The U.S. Bureau of Labor Statistics projects that by 2020 Millennials will make up 40 percent of the workforce. Baby boomers are retiring, and Millennials will be working for the next several decades. Additionally, they have many of the requisite skills to succeed in the future workplace—tech-savviness and the ability to innovate—and they are more racially diverse than any prior generation. Thus, they are better able to relate rapidly to different customs and cultures.

What are some of the "best practices" to attract Millennials and keep them engaged?

- *Don't fudge the sales pitch.* High-tech sales presentations and one-on-one attention may be attractive to undergrads. However, the pitch had better match the experience. Consider that today's ultra-connected students can get the lowdown on a company by spending five minutes on a social networking site.
- *Let them have a life.* Typically, they are unenthusiastic about their parents' 70- or 80-hour workweeks. Millennials strive for more work-life balance, so liberal vacations become very important. They also want assurances that they can use the vacation time. At KPMG, 80 percent of employees used 40 hours of paid time off in the first six months of a recent year.
- *No time clocks, please.* Recent graduates don't mind long hours—if they can work them on their own schedule. Lockheed Martin allows employees to work nine-hour days with every other Friday off. And Chegg, the online textbook service, recently introduced an unlimited vacation policy—turnover rates among the younger workers dropped 50 percent. As noted by its CEO, Dan Rosensweig, "If you provide them with the right environment, they'll work forever."
- *Give them responsibility.* A chance to work on fulfilling projects and develop new ones on their own is important. Google urges entry-level employees to spend 20 percent of their time developing new ideas. PepsiCo allows promising young employees to manage small teams in six months.
- *Feedback and more feedback.* Career planning advice and frequent performance appraisals are keys to holding on to young hires. Several firms provide new hires with two mentors—a slightly older peer to help them get settled and a senior employee to give long-term guidance.
- *Giving back matters.* Today's altruistic young graduates expect to have opportunities for community service. Wells Fargo encourages its employees to teach financial literacy classes in the community. Accenture and Bain allow employees to consult for nonprofits.

A study from the Center for Work-Life Policy sums this issue up rather well: Instead of the traditional plums of prestigious title, powerful position, and concomitant compensation, Millennials value challenging and diverse job opportunities, stimulating colleagues, a well-designed communal workspace, and flexible work options. In fact, 89 percent of Millennials say that flexible work options are an important consideration in choosing an employer.

Developing Human Capital

It is not enough to hire top-level talent and expect that the skills and capabilities of those employees remain current throughout the duration of their employment. Rather, training and development must take place at all levels of the organization.[44] For example, Solectron assembles printed circuit boards and other components for its Silicon Valley clients.[45] Its employees receive an average of 95 hours of company-provided training each year. Chairman Winston Chen observed, "Technology changes so fast that we estimate 20 percent of an engineer's knowledge becomes obsolete each year. Training is an obligation we owe to our employees. If you want high growth and high quality, then training is a big part of the equation."

Leaders who are committed to developing the people who work for them in order to bring out their strengths and enhance their careers will have committed followers. According to James Rogers, CEO of Duke Energy: "One of the biggest things I find in organizations is that people tend to limit their perceptions of themselves and their capabilities, and one of my challenges is to open them up to the possibilities. I have this belief that anybody can do almost anything in the right context."[46]

In addition to training and developing human capital, firms must encourage widespread involvement, monitor and track employee development, and evaluate human capital.[47]

Encouraging Widespread Involvement Developing human capital requires the active involvement of leaders at all levels. It won't be successful if it is viewed only as the responsibility of the human resource department. Each year at General Electric, 200 facilitators, 30 officers, 30 human resource executives, and many young managers actively participate in GE's orientation program at Crotonville, its training center outside New York City. Topics include global competition, winning on the global playing field, and personal examination of the new employee's core values vis-à-vis GE's values. As a senior manager once commented, "There is nothing like teaching Sunday school to force you to confront your own values."

Similarly, A. G. Lafley, Procter & Gamble's former CEO, claimed that he spent 40 percent of his time on personnel.[48] Andy Grove, who was previously Intel's CEO, required all senior people, including himself, to spend at least a week a year teaching high flyers. And Nitin Paranjpe, CEO of Hindustan Unilever, recruits people from campuses and regularly visits high-potential employees in their offices.

Mentoring Mentoring is most often a formal or informal relationship between two people—a senior mentor and a junior protégé.[49] Mentoring can potentially be a valuable influence in professional development in both the public and private sectors. The war for talent is creating challenges within organizations to recruit new talent as well as retain talent.

Mentoring can provide many benefits—to the organization as well as the individual.[50] For the organization, it can help to recruit qualified managers, decrease turnover, fill senior-level positions with qualified professionals, enhance diversity initiatives with senior-level management, and facilitate organizational change efforts. Individuals can also benefit from effective mentoring programs. These benefits include helping newer employees transition into the organization, helping developmental relationships for people who lack access to informal mentoring relationships, and providing support and challenge to people on an organization's "fast track" to positions of higher responsibility.

Mentoring is traditionally viewed as a program to transfer knowledge and experience from more senior managers to up-and-comers. However, many organizations have reinvented it to fit today's highly competitive, knowledge-intensive industries. For example, consider Intel:

> Intel matches people not by job title and years of experience but by specific skills that are in demand. Lory Lanese, Intel's mentor champion at its huge New Mexico plant (with 5,500 employees), states, "This is definitely not a special program for special people." Instead, Intel's program uses an intranet and email to perform the matchmaking, creating relationships that stretch across state lines and national boundaries. Such an approach enables Intel to spread best practices quickly throughout the far-flung organization. Finally, Intel relies on written contracts and tight deadlines to make sure that its mentoring program gets results—and fast.[51]

Intel has also initiated a mentoring program involving its technical assistants (TAs) who work with senior executives. This concept is sometimes referred to as "reverse mentoring" because senior executives benefit from the insights of professionals who have more updated technical skills—but rank lower in the organizational hierarchy. And, not surprisingly, the TAs stand to benefit quite a bit as well. Here are some insights offered by Andy Grove (formerly Intel's CEO):[52]

> In the 1980s I had a marketing manager named Dennis Carter. I probably learned more from him than anyone in my career. He is a genius. He taught me what brands are. I had no idea—I thought a brand was the name on the box. He showed me the connection of brands to strategies. Dennis went on to be Chief Marketing Officer. He was the person responsible for the Pentium name, "Intel Inside;" he came up with all my good ideas.

Monitoring Progress and Tracking Development   Whether a firm uses on-site formal training, off-site training (e.g., universities), or on-the-job training, tracking individual progress—and sharing this knowledge with both the employee and key managers—becomes essential. Like many leading-edge firms, GlaxoSmithKline (GSK) places strong emphasis on broader experiences over longer time periods. Dan Phelan, senior vice president and director of human resources, explained, "We ideally follow a two-plus-two-plus-two for-mula in developing people for top management positions." This reflects the belief that GSK's best people should gain experience in two business units, two functional units (such as finance and marketing), and two countries.

Evaluating Human Capital   In today's competitive environment, collaboration and interdependence are vital to organizational success. Individuals must share their knowl-edge and work constructively to achieve collective, not just individual, goals. However, traditional systems evaluate performance from a single perspective (i.e., "top down") and generally don't address the "softer" dimensions of communications and social skills, val-ues, beliefs, and attitudes.[53]

To address the limitations of the traditional approach, many organizations use **360-degree evaluation and feedback systems.**[54] Here, superiors, direct reports, col-leagues, and even internal and external customers rate a person's performance.[55] Man-agers rate themselves to have a personal benchmark. The 360-degree feedback system complements teamwork, employee involvement, and organizational flattening. As organi-zations continue to push responsibility downward, traditional top-down appraisal systems become insufficient.[56] For example, a manager who previously managed the performance of 3 supervisors might now be responsible for 10 and is less likely to have the in-depth knowledge needed to appraise and develop them adequately. Exhibit 4.3 provides a portion of GE's 360-degree leadership assessment chart.

At times, a firm's performance assessment methods may get in the way of team suc-cess.[57] Microsoft is an example. For many years, the software giant employed a "stack ranking" system as part of its performance evaluation model. With this system, a certain percentage of any team's members would be rated "top performers," "good," "average," "below average," and "poor," regardless of the team's overall performance. Perhaps, in some situations, this type of forced ranking works. However, in Microsoft's case, it had (not too surprisingly!) unintended consequences. Over time, according to inside reports, the stack ranking created a culture in which employees competed with one another rather than against the firm's rivals. And "A" players rarely liked to join groups with other "A" players, because they feared they might be seen as weaker members of the team.

Strategy Spotlight 4.2 provides another cautionary note on evaluation systems: Avoid an overemphasis on internal performance measures that misses the competitive environ-ment a firm faces.

Retaining Human Capital

It has been said that talented employees are like "frogs in a wheelbarrow."[58] They can jump out at any time! By analogy, the organization can either try to force employees to stay in the firm or try to keep them from jumping out by creating incentives.[59] In other

360-degree evaluation and feedback systems
superiors, direct reports, colleagues, and even external and internal customers rate a person's performance.

"I DON'T CARE HOW MANY METRICS YOU GOT RIGHT. YOU FAILED!"

General Motors has long been obsessively inward-looking, according to a writer for *Fortune* magazine. Recently, however, GM has begun to measure success against external rather than internal standards. This represents a major shift in perspective. And it is a good example of the challenge the new CEO, Mary Barra, faces in reversing the firm's competitive position and financial performance.

Bob Lutz, who has been a top executive at all three Detroit carmakers over his 60-year career, provides a colorful example of the flaws inherent in GM's previous approach to performance evaluation. "I had a vehicle line executive come to me with his scorecard. He said, 'I've completed the most successful program in the history of the vehicle line executive system,' and he wanted to talk to me about a bonus. His scorecard had about 50 metrics on it. Each was scored red, yellow, or green, and they were solid green, top to bottom. This was the first time that feat had ever been accomplished."

"I said, 'That's nice. How's the car selling?' He said, 'Oh, it's not selling at all. The public doesn't like it.' I said, 'You failed!'" Lutz believes that the incident illustrates a larger problem—perhaps the most serious of GM's behavioral deficiencies: "Everything was internal criteria. The idiotic assumption was that if you fulfill all the internal criteria, somehow the car will be a success."

Source: Colvin, G. 2014. Mary Barra's (unexpected) opportunity. *Fortune,* September 14: 102–110.

words, either today's leaders can provide the challenges, work environment, and incentives to keep productive employees and management from wanting to bail out, or they can use legal means such as employment contracts and noncompete clauses.[60] Firms must prevent the transfer of valuable and sensitive information outside the organization. Failure to do so would be the neglect of a leader's fiduciary responsibility to shareholders. However, greater efforts should be directed at the former (e.g., challenges, good work environment, and incentives), but, as we all know, the latter (e.g., employment contracts and noncompete clauses) have their place.[61]

Vision	• Has developed and communicated a clear, simple, customer-focused vision/direction for the organization. • Forward-thinking, stretches horizons, challenges imaginations. • Inspires and energizes others to commit to Vision. Captures minds. Leads by example. • As appropriate, updates Vision to reflect constant and accelerating change affecting the business.
Customer/Quality Focus	
Integrity	
Accountability/Commitment	
Communication/Influence	
Shared Ownership/Boundaryless	
Team Builder/Empowerment	
Knowledge/Expertise/Intellect	
Initiative/Speed	
Global Mind-Set	

EXHIBIT 4.3

An Excerpt from General Electric's 360-Degree Leadership Assessment Chart

Note: This evaluation system consists of 10 "characteristics"—Vision, Customer/Quality Focus, Integrity, and so on. Each of these characteristics has four "performance criteria." For illustrative purposes, the four performance criteria of "Vision" are included.

Source: Adapted from Slater, R. 1994. *Get Better or Get Beaten:* 152–155. Burr Ridge, IL: Irwin Professional Publishing.

Gary Burnison, CEO of Korn/Ferry International, the world's largest executive search firm, provides an insight on the importance of employee retention:[62]

> How do you extend the life of an employee? This is not an environment where you work for an organization for 20 years. But if you can extend it from three years to six years, that has an enormous impact. Turnover is a huge hidden cost in a profit-and-loss statement that nobody ever focuses on. If there was a line item that showed that, I guarantee you'd have the attention of a CEO.

Identifying with an Organization's Mission and Values   People who identify with and are more committed to the core mission and values of the organization are less likely to stray or bolt to the competition. For example, take the perspective of the late Steve Jobs, Apple's widely admired former CEO:[63]

> When I hire somebody really senior, competence is the ante. They have to be really smart. But the real issue for me is: Are they going to fall in love with Apple? Because if they fall in love with Apple, everything else will take care of itself. They'll want to do what's best for Apple, not what's best for them, what's best for Steve, or anyone else.

"Tribal loyalty" is another key factor that links people to the organization.[64] A tribe is not the organization as a whole (unless it is very small). Rather, it is teams, communities of practice, and other groups within an organization or occupation.

Brian Hall, CEO of Values Technology in Santa Cruz, California, documented a shift in people's emotional expectations from work. From the 1950s on, a "task-first" relationship—"Tell me what the job is, and let's get on with it"—dominated employee attitudes. Emotions and personal life were checked at the door. In the past few years, a "relationship-first" set of values has challenged the task orientation. Hall believes that it will become dominant. Employees want to share attitudes and beliefs as well as workspace.

Challenging Work and a Stimulating Environment   Arthur Schawlow, winner of the 1981 Nobel Prize in physics, was asked what made the difference between highly creative and less creative scientists. His reply: "The labor of love aspect is very important. The most successful scientists often are not the most talented.[65] But they are the ones impelled by curiosity. They've got to know what the answer is."[66] Such insights highlight the importance of intrinsic motivation: the motivation to work on something because it is exciting, satisfying, or personally challenging.[67]

One way firms keep highly mobile employees motivated and challenged is through opportunities that lower barriers to an employee's mobility within a company. For example, Shell Oil Company has created an "open sourcing" model for talent. Jobs are listed on its intranet, and, with a two-month notice, employees can go to work on anything that interests them.

Financial and Nonfinancial Rewards and Incentives   Financial rewards are a vital organizational control mechanism (as we will discuss in Chapter 9). Money—whether in the form of salary, bonus, stock options, and so forth—can mean many different things to people. It might mean security, recognition, or a sense of freedom and independence.

Paying people more is seldom the most important factor in attracting and retaining human capital.[68] Most surveys show that money is not the most important reason why people take or leave jobs and that money, in some surveys, is not even in the top 10. Consistent with these findings, Tandem Computers (part of Hewlett-Packard) typically doesn't tell people being recruited what their salaries would be. People who asked were told that Tandem's salaries were competitive. If they persisted along this line of questioning, they would not be offered a position. Why? Tandem realized a rather simple idea: People who come for money will leave for money.

Another nonfinancial reward is accommodating working families with children. Balancing demands of family and work is a problem at some point for virtually all employees.

Below we discuss how Google attracts and retains talent through financial and nonfinancial incentives. Its unique "Google culture," a huge attraction to potential employees, transforms a traditional workspace into a fun, feel-at-home, and flexible place to work.[69]

> Googlers do not merely work but have a great time doing it. The Mountain View, California, headquarters includes on-site medical and dental facilities, oil change and bike repair, foosball, pool tables, volleyball courts, and free breakfast, lunch, and dinner on a daily basis at 11 gourmet restaurants. Googlers have access to training programs and receive tuition reimbursement while they take a leave of absence to pursue higher education. Google states on its website, "Though Google has grown a lot since it opened in 1998, we still maintain a small company feel."

Enhancing Human Capital: Redefining Jobs and Managing Diversity

Before moving on to our discussion of social capital, it is important to point out that companies are increasingly realizing that the payoff from enhancing their human capital can be substantial. Firms have found that redefining jobs and leveraging the benefits of a diverse workforce can go a long way in improving their performance.

Enhancing Human Capital: Redefining Jobs Recent research by McKinsey Global Institute suggests that by 2020, the worldwide shortage of highly skilled, college-educated workers could reach 38 to 40 million, or about 13 percent of demand.[70] In response, some firms are taking steps to expand their talent pool, for example, by investing in apprenticeships and other training programs. However, some are going further: They are redefining the jobs of their experts and transferring some of their tasks to lower-skilled people inside or outside their companies, as well as outsourcing work that requires less scarce skills and is not as strategically important. Redefining high-value knowledge jobs not only can help organizations address skill shortages but also can lower costs and enhance job satisfaction.

Consider the following examples:

- Orrick, Herrington & Sutcliffe, a San Francisco–based law firm with nine U.S. offices, shifted routine discovery work previously performed by partners and partner-tracked associates to a new service center in West Virginia staffed by lower-paid attorneys.
- In the United Kingdom, a growing number of public schools are relieving head teachers (or principals) of administrative tasks such as budgeting, facilities maintenance, human resources, and community relations so that they can devote more time to developing teachers.
- The Narayana Hrudayalaya Heart Hospital in Bangalore has junior surgeons, nurses, and technicians handle routine tasks such as preparing the patient for surgery and closing the chest after surgery. Senior cardiac surgeons arrive at the operating room only when the patient's chest is open and the heart is ready to be operated on. Such an approach helps the hospital lower the cost to a fraction of the cost of U.S. providers while maintaining U.S.-level mortality and infection rates.

Breaking high-end knowledge work into highly specialized pieces involves several processes. These include identifying the gap between the talent your firm has and what it requires; creating narrower, more-focused job descriptions in areas where talent is scarce; selecting from various options to fill the skills gap; and rewiring processes for talent and knowledge management.

Enhancing Human Capital: Managing Diversity   A combination of demographic trends and accelerating globalization of business has made the management of cultural differences a critical issue.[71] Workforces, which reflect demographic changes in the overall population, will be increasingly heterogeneous along dimensions such as gender, race, ethnicity, and nationality.[72] Demographic trends in the United States indicate a growth in Hispanic Americans from 6.9 million in 1960 to over 35 million in 2000, with an expected increase to over 59 million by 2020 and 102 million by 2050. Similarly, the Asian-American population should grow to 20 million in 2020 from 12 million in 2000 and only 1.5 million in 1970. And the African-American population is expected to increase from 12.8 percent of the U.S. population in 2000 to 14.2 percent by 2025.[73]

Such demographic changes have implications not only for the labor pool but also for customer bases, which are also becoming more diverse.[74] This creates important organizational challenges and opportunities.

The effective management of diversity can enhance the social responsibility goals of an organization.[75] However, there are many other benefits as well. Six other areas where sound management of diverse workforces can improve an organization's effectiveness and competitive advantages are (1) cost, (2) resource acquisition, (3) marketing, (4) creativity, (5) problem solving, and (6) organizational flexibility.

- *Cost argument.* As organizations become more diverse, firms effective in managing diversity will have a cost advantage over those that are not.

- *Resource acquisition argument.* Firms with excellent reputations as prospective employers for women and ethnic minorities will have an advantage in the competition for top talent. As labor pools shrink and change in composition, such advantages will become even more important.

- *Marketing argument.* For multinational firms, the insight and cultural sensitivity that members with roots in other countries bring to marketing efforts will be very useful. A similar rationale applies to subpopulations within domestic operations.

- *Creativity argument.* Less emphasis on conformity to norms of the past and a diversity of perspectives will improve the level of creativity.

- *Problem-solving argument.* Heterogeneity in decision-making and problem-solving groups typically produces better decisions because of a wider range of perspectives as well as more thorough analysis. Jim Schiro, former CEO of PricewaterhouseCoopers, explains, "When you make a genuine commitment to diversity, you bring a greater diversity of ideas, approaches, and experiences and abilities that can be applied to client problems. After all, six people with different perspectives have a better shot at solving complex problems than sixty people who all think alike."[76]

- *Organizational flexibility argument.* With effective programs to enhance workplace diversity, systems become less determinant, less standardized, and therefore more fluid. Such fluidity should lead to greater flexibility to react to environmental changes. Reactions should be faster and less costly.

Most managers accept that employers benefit from a diverse workforce. However, this notion can often be very difficult to prove or quantify, particularly when it comes to determining how diversity affects a firm's ability to innovate.[77]

New research provides compelling evidence that diversity enhances innovation and drives market growth. This finding should intensify efforts to ensure that organizations both embody and embrace the power of differences.

Strategy Spotlight 4.3 articulates two kinds of diversity, *inherent* and *acquired,* and the important role they have in driving an organization's innovation.

HOW INHERENT AND ACQUIRED DIVERSITY AFFECT INNOVATION

A study explored two kinds of diversity: *inherent* and *acquired*. Its findings were based on a nationally representative survey of 1,800 professionals, 40 case studies, and numerous focus groups and interviews. Inherent diversity involves traits one was born with, such as gender, ethnicity, and sexual orientation. On the other hand, acquired diversity involves traits gained from experience, such as working in another country to understand cultural differences and selling to both male and female consumers to develop "gender smarts." Companies whose leaders exhibited at least three inherent and three acquired traits were viewed as having two-dimensional (2-D) diversity.

The study found that companies with 2-D diversity out-innovated and outperformed the others. Employees in such companies were 45 percent likelier to report their firm's market share grew over the previous year and 70 percent likelier to report the firm captured a new market.

What explains these results? Two-dimensional diversity unlocks innovation by creating a work environment where "outside the box" ideas are heard and minorities form a critical mass. Further, leaders value differences, and all employees can find senior people to go to bat for compelling ideas and can persuade those in charge of budgets to commit resources to develop those ideas.

Inherent diversity, however, is only half of the equation. Acquired diversity provides additional benefits since employees with diverse experiences can provide insights on the needs and preferences of different groups and cultures. They are also more open to the perspectives of the other members on the team. Since acquired diversity increases openness, it also enhances the value of inherent diversity. Minority team members will be more likely to contribute to team discussions, resulting in more creative problem solving. Six behaviors spur innovation across the board: ensuring everyone is heard; making it safe to propose novel ideas; giving team members decision-making authority; sharing credit for success; giving actionable feedback; and implementing feedback from the team.

Sources: Hewlett, S. A., Marshall, M., & Sherbin, L. 2013. How diversity can drive innovation. *Harvard Business Review,* 91(12): 30; and Karlgaard, R. 2014. *The soft edge.* San Francisco: Jossey-Bass.

The Vital Role of Social Capital

LO4.3

The key role of social capital in leveraging human capital within and across the firm.

Successful firms are well aware that the attraction, development, and retention of talent *is a necessary but not sufficient condition* for creating competitive advantages.[78] In the knowledge economy, it is not the stock of human capital that is important, but the extent to which it is combined and leveraged.[79] In a sense, developing and retaining human capital becomes less important as key players (talented professionals, in particular) take the role of "free agents" and bring with them the requisite skill in many cases. Rather, the development of social capital (that is, the friendships and working relationships among talented individuals) gains importance, because it helps tie knowledge workers to a given firm.[80] Knowledge workers often exhibit greater loyalties to their colleagues and their profession than their employing organization, which may be "an amorphous, distant, and sometimes threatening entity."[81] Thus, a firm must find ways to create "ties" among its knowledge workers.

Let's look at a hypothetical example. Two pharmaceutical firms are fortunate enough to hire Nobel Prize–winning scientists.[82] In one case, the scientist is offered a very attractive salary, outstanding facilities and equipment, and told to "go to it!" In the second case, the scientist is offered approximately the same salary, facilities, and equipment plus one additional ingredient: working in a laboratory with 10 highly skilled and enthusiastic scientists. Part of the job is to collaborate with these peers and jointly develop promising drug compounds. There is little doubt as to which scenario will lead to a higher probability of retaining the scientist. The interaction, sharing, and collaboration will create a situation in which the scientist will develop firm-specific ties and be less likely to "bolt" for a higher salary offer. Such ties are critical because knowledge-based resources tend to be more tacit in nature, as we mentioned early in this chapter. Therefore, they are much more difficult to protect against loss (i.e., the individual quitting the organization) than other types of capital, such as equipment, machinery, and land.

Another way to view this situation is in terms of the resource-based view of the firm that we discussed in Chapter 3. That is, competitive advantages tend to be harder for competitors to copy if they are based on "unique bundles" of resources.[83] So, if employees are working effectively in teams and sharing their knowledge and learning from each other, not only will they be more likely to add value to the firm, but they also will be less likely to leave the organization, because of the loyalties and social ties that they develop over time.

How Social Capital Helps Attract and Retain Talent

The importance of social ties among talented professionals creates a significant challenge (and opportunity) for organizations. In *The Wall Street Journal,* Bernard Wysocki described the increase in a type of "Pied Piper effect," in which teams or networks of people are leaving one company for another.[84] The trend is to recruit job candidates at the crux of social relationships in organizations, particularly if they are seen as having the potential to bring with them valuable colleagues.[85] This is a process that is referred to as "hiring via personal networks." Let's look at one instance of this practice.

Gerald Eickhoff, founder of an electronic commerce company called Third Millennium Communications, tried for 15 years to hire Michael Reene. Why? Mr. Eickhoff says that he has "these Pied Piper skills." Mr. Reene was a star at Andersen Consulting in the 1980s and at IBM in the 1990s. He built his businesses and kept turning down overtures from Mr. Eickhoff.

However, in early 2000, he joined Third Millennium as chief executive officer, with a salary of just $120,000 but with a 20 percent stake in the firm. Since then, he has brought in a raft of former IBM colleagues and Andersen subordinates. One protégé from his time at Andersen, Mary Goode, was brought on board as executive vice president. She promptly tapped her own network and brought along former colleagues.

Wysocki considers the Pied Piper effect one of the underappreciated factors in the war for talent today. This is because one of the myths of the New Economy is rampant individualism, wherein individuals find jobs on the Internet career sites and go to work for complete strangers. Perhaps, instead of Me Inc., the truth is closer to We Inc.[86]

Another example of social relationships causing human capital mobility is the emigration of talent from an organization to form start-up ventures. Microsoft is perhaps the best-known example of this phenomenon.[87] Professionals frequently leave Microsoft en masse to form venture capital and technology start-ups, called "Baby Bills," built around teams of software developers. For example, Ignition Corporation, of Bellevue, Washington, was formed by Brad Silverberg, a former Microsoft senior vice president. Eight former Microsoft executives, among others, founded the company.

LO4.4

The importance of social networks in knowledge management and in promoting career success.

Social Networks: Implications for Knowledge Management and Career Success

Managers face many challenges driven by such factors as rapid changes in globalization and technology. Leading a successful company is more than a one-person job. As Tom Malone put it in *The Future of Work,* "As managers, we need to shift our thinking from command and control to coordinate and cultivate—the best way to gain power is sometimes to give it away."[88] The move away from top-down bureaucratic control to more open, decentralized network models makes it more difficult for managers to understand how work is actually getting done, who is interacting with whom both within and outside the organization, and the consequences of these interactions for the long-term health of the organization.[89]

Malcolm Gladwell, in his best-selling book *The Tipping Point,* used the term *connector* to describe people who have *used* many ties to different social worlds.[90] It's not the number of people that connectors know that makes them significant. Rather, it is their ability to link people, ideas, and resources that wouldn't normally bump into one another. In business, connectors are critical facilitators for collaboration and integration. David Kenny, president of Akamai Technologies, believes that being a connector is one of the most important ways in which he adds value:

> Kenny spends much of his time traveling around the world to meet with employees, partners, and customers. He states, "I spend time with media owners to hear what they think about digital platforms, Facebook, and new pricing models, and with Microsoft leaders to get their views on cloud computing. I'm interested in hearing how our clients feel about macroeconomic issues, the G20, and how debt will affect future generations." These conversations lead to new strategic insights and relationships and help Akamai develop critical external partnerships.

Social networks can also help one bring about important change in an organization—or simply get things done! Consider a change initiative undertaken at the United Kingdom's National Health Care Service—a huge, government-run institution that employs about a million people in hundreds of units and divisions with deeply rooted, bureaucratic, hierarchical systems. This is certainly an organization in which you can't rely solely on your "position power":[91]

> John wanted to set up a nurse-led preoperative assessment service intended to free up time for the doctors who previously led the assessments, reduce cancelled operations (and costs), and improve patient care. Sounds easy enough . . . after all, John was a senior doctor and near the top of the hospital's formal hierarchy. However, he had only recently joined the organization and was not well connected internally.
>
> As he began talking to other doctors and to nurses about the change, he was met with a lot of resistance. He was about to give up when Carol, a well-respected nurse, offered to help. She had even less seniority than John, but many colleagues relied on her advice about navigating hospital politics. She knew many of the people whose support John needed and she eventually converted them to the change.

Social network analysis depicts the pattern of interactions among individuals and helps to diagnose effective and ineffective patterns.[92] It helps identify groups or clusters of individuals that comprise the network, individuals who link the clusters, and other network members. It helps diagnose communication patterns and, consequently, communication effectiveness.[93] Such analysis of communication patterns is helpful because the configuration of group members' social ties within and outside the group affects the extent to which members connect to individuals who:

- Convey needed resources.
- Have the opportunity to exchange information and support.
- Have the motivation to treat each other in positive ways.
- Have the time to develop trusting relationships that might improve the groups' effectiveness.

However, such relationships don't "just happen."[94] Developing social capital requires interdependence among group members. Social capital erodes when people in the network become independent. And increased interactions between members aid in the development and maintenance of mutual obligations in a social network.[95] Social networks such as Facebook may facilitate increased interactions between members in a social network via Internet-based communications.

Let's take a brief look at a simplified network analysis to get a grasp of the key ideas. In Exhibit 4.4, the links depict informal relationships among individuals, such as communication flows, personal support, and advice networks. There may be some individuals with literally no linkages, such as Fred. These individuals are typically labeled "isolates." However, most people do have some linkages with others.

> **social network analysis**
> analysis of the pattern of social interactions among individuals.

EXHIBIT 4.4 A Simplified Social Network

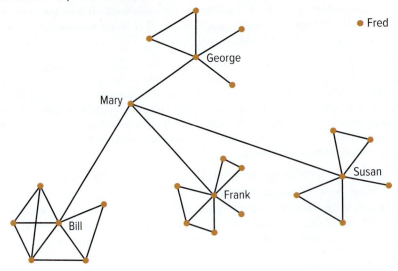

To simplify, there are two primary types of mechanisms through which social capital will flow: *closure relationships* (depicted by Bill, Frank, George, and Susan) and *bridging relationships* (depicted by Mary). As we can see, in the former relationships one member is central to the communication flows in a group. In contrast, in the latter relationships, one person "bridges" or brings together groups that would have been otherwise unconnected.

Both closure and bridging relationships have important implications for the effective flow of information in organizations and for the management of knowledge. We will now briefly discuss each of these types of relationships. We will also address some of the implications that understanding social networks has for one's career success.

closure
the degree to which all members of a social network have relationships (or ties) with other group members.

Closure   With **closure,** many members have relationships (or ties) with other members. As indicated in Exhibit 4.4, Bill's group would have a higher level of closure than Frank's Susan's, or George's groups because more group members are connected to each other. Through closure, group members develop strong relationships with each other, high levels of trust, and greater solidarity. High levels of trust help to ensure that informal norms in the group are easily enforced and there is less "free riding." Social pressure will prevent people from withholding effort or shirking their responsibilities. In addition, people in the network are more willing to extend favors and "go the extra mile" on a colleague's behalf because they are confident that their efforts will be reciprocated by another member in their group. Another benefit of a network with closure is the high level of emotional support. This becomes particularly valuable when setbacks occur that may destroy morale or an unexpected tragedy happens that might cause the group to lose its focus. Social support helps the group to rebound from misfortune and get back on track.

But high levels of closure often come with a price. Groups that become too closed can become insular. They cut themselves off from the rest of the organization and fail to share what they are learning from people outside their group. Research shows that while managers need to encourage closure up to a point, if there is too much closure, they need to encourage people to open up their groups and infuse new ideas through bridging relationships.[96]

Bridging Relationships   The closure perspective rests on an assumption that there is a high level of similarity among group members. However, members can be quite heterogeneous with regard to their positions in either the formal or informal structures of the group or the organization. Such heterogeneity exists because of, for example, vertical boundaries (different levels in the hierarchy) and horizontal boundaries (different functional areas).

Bridging relationships, in contrast to closure, stress the importance of ties connecting people. Employees who bridge disconnected people tend to receive timely, diverse information because of their access to a wide range of heterogeneous information flows. Such bridging relationships span a number of different types of boundaries.

The University of Chicago's Ron Burt originally coined the term **"structural holes"** to refer to the social gap between two groups. Structural holes are common in organizations. When they occur in business, managers typically refer to them as "silos" or "stovepipes." Sales and engineering are a classic example of two groups whose members traditionally interact with their peers rather than across groups.

A study that Burt conducted at Raytheon, a $25 billion U.S. electronics company and military contractor, provides further insight into the benefits of bridging.[97]

> Burt studied several hundred managers in Raytheon's supply chain group and asked them to write down ideas to improve the company's supply chain management. Then he asked two Raytheon executives to rate the ideas. The conclusion: *The best suggestions consistently came from managers who discussed ideas outside their regular work group.*
>
> Burt found that Raytheon managers were good at thinking of ideas but bad at developing them. Too often, Burt said, the managers discussed their ideas with colleagues already in their informal discussion network. Instead, he said, they should have had discussions outside their typical contacts, particularly with an informal boss, or someone with enough power to be an ally but not an actual supervisor.

Developing Social Capital: Overcoming Barriers to Collaboration Social capital within a group or organization develops through repeated interactions among its members and the resulting collaboration.[98] However, collaboration does not "just happen." People don't collaborate for various reasons. Effective collaboration requires overcoming four barriers:

- The not-invented-here barrier (people aren't willing to provide help).
- The hoarding barrier (people aren't willing to provide help).
- The search barrier (people are unable to find what they are looking for).
- The transfer barrier (people are unable to work with the people they don't know well).

All four barriers need to be low before effective collaboration can take place. Each one is enough to prevent people from collaborating well. The key is to identify which barriers are present in an organization and then to devise appropriate ways to overcome them.

Different barriers require different solutions. Motivational barriers require leaders to pull levers that make people more willing to collaborate. Ability barriers mean that leaders need to pull levers that enable motivated people to collaborate throughout the organization.

To be effective, leaders can choose a mix of three levers. First, when motivation is the problem, they can use the **unification lever,** wherein they craft compelling common goals, articulate a strong value of cross-company teamwork, and encourage collaboration in order to send strong signals to lift people's sights beyond their narrow interests toward a common goal.

Second, with the **people lever,** the emphasis isn't on getting people to collaborate more. Rather, it's on getting the right people to collaborate on the right projects. This means cultivating what may be called **T-shaped management:** people who simultaneously focus on the performance of their unit (the vertical part of the T) and across boundaries (the horizontal part of the T). People become able to collaborate when needed but are disciplined enough to say no when it's not required.

Third, by using the **network lever,** leaders can build nimble interpersonal networks across the company so that employees are better able to collaborate. Interpersonal networks are more effective than formal hierarchies. However, there is a dark side to networks: When people spend more time networking than getting work done, collaboration can adversely affect results.

bridging relationships
relationships in a social network that connect otherwise disconnected people.

structural holes
social gaps between groups in a social network where there are few relationships bridging the groups.

unification lever
method for making people more willing to collaborate by crafting compelling common goals, articulating a strong value of cross-company teamwork, and encouraging collaboration in order to send strong signals to lift people's sights beyond their narrow interests toward a common goal.

people lever
method for making people more willing to collaborate by getting the right people to work on the right projects.

T-shaped management
people's dual focus on the performance of their unit (the vertical part of the T) and across boundaries (the horizontal part of the T).

network lever
method for making people more willing to collaborate by building nimble interpersonal networks across the company.

PICASSO VERSUS VAN GOGH: WHO WAS MORE SUCCESSFUL AND WHY?

Vincent van Gogh and Pablo Picasso are two of the most iconoclastic—and famous—artists of modern times. Paintings by both of them have fetched over $100 million. And both of them were responsible for some of the most iconic images in the art world: Van Gogh's *Self-Portrait* (the one sans the ear-lobe) and *Starry Night* and Picasso's *The Old Guitarist* and *Guernica*. However, there is an important difference between van Gogh and Picasso. Van Gogh died penniless. Picasso's estate was estimated at $750 million when he died in 1973. What was the difference?

Van Gogh's primary connection to the art world was through his brother. Unfortunately, this connection didn't feed directly into the money that could have turned him into a living success. In contrast, Picasso's myriad connections provided him with access to commercial riches. As noted by Gregory Berns in his book

Iconoclast: A Neuroscientist Reveals How to Think Differently, "Picasso's wide ranging social network, which included artists, writers, and politicians, meant that he was never more than a few people away from anyone of importance in the world."

In effect, van Gogh was a loner, and the charismatic Picasso was an active member of multiple social circles. In social network-ing terms, van Gogh was a solitary "node" who had few connec-tions. Picasso, on the other hand, was a "hub" who embedded himself in a vast network that stretched across various social lines. Where Picasso smoothly navigated multiple social circles, van Gogh had to struggle just to maintain connections with even those closest to him. Van Gogh inhabited an alien world, whereas Picasso was a social magnet. And because he knew so many peo-ple, the world was at Picasso's fingertips. From his perspective, the world was smaller.

Sources: Hayashi, A. M. 2008. Why Picasso out earned van Gogh. *MIT Sloan Management Review,* 50(1): 11–12; and Berns, G. 2008. *A neuroscientist reveals how to think differently.* Boston: Harvard Business Press.

Implications for Career Success   Let's go back in time in order to illustrate the value of social networks in one's career success. Consider two of the most celebrated artists of all time: Vincent van Gogh and Pablo Picasso. Strategy Spotlight 4.4 points out why these two artists enjoyed sharply contrasting levels of success during their lifetimes.

Effective social networks provide many advantages for the firm.[99] They can play a key role in an individual's career advancement and success. One's social network potentially can provide three unique advantages: private information, access to diverse skill sets, and power.[100] Managers see these advantages at work every day but might not consider how their networks regulate them.

Private Information   We make judgments using both public and private information. Today, public information is available from many sources, including the Internet. However, since it is so accessible, public information offers less competitive advantage than it used to.

In contrast, private information from personal contacts can offer something not found in publicly available sources, such as the release date of a new product or knowledge about what a particular interviewer looks for in candidates. Private information can give manag-ers an edge, though it is more subjective than public information since it cannot be easily verified by independent sources, such as Dunn & Bradstreet. Consequently the value of your private information to others—and the value of others' private information to you—depends on how much trust exists in the network of relationships.

Access to Diverse Skill Sets   Linus Pauling, one of only two people to win a Nobel Prize in two different areas and considered one of the towering geniuses of the 20th century, attributed his creative success not to his immense brainpower or luck but to his diverse contacts. He said, "The best way to have a good idea is to have a lot of ideas."

While expertise has become more specialized during the past few decades, organiza-tional, product, and marketing issues have become more interdisciplinary. This means that success is tied to the ability to transcend natural skill limitations through others. Highly diverse network relationships, therefore, can help you develop more complete, creative, and unbiased perspectives on issues. Trading information or skills with people whose experiences differ from your own provides you with unique, exceptionally valuable resources. It is common for people in relationships to share their problems. If you know enough people, you will begin to see how the problems that another person is struggling with can be solved by the solutions being developed by others. If you can bring together problems and solutions, it will greatly benefit your career.

Power   Traditionally, a manager's power was embedded in a firm's hierarchy. But when corporate organizations became flatter, more like pancakes than pyramids, that power was repositioned in the network's brokers (people who bridged multiple networks), who could adapt to changes in the organization, develop clients, and synthesize opposing points of view. Such brokers weren't necessarily at the top of the hierarchy or experts in their fields, but they linked specialists in the firm with trustworthy and informative relationships.[101]

Most personal networks are highly clustered; that is, an individual's friends are likely to be friends with one another as well. Most corporate networks are made up of several clusters that have few links between them. Brokers are especially powerful because they connect separate clusters, thus stimulating collaboration among otherwise independent specialists.

In today's knowledge economy, managers must strive to develop a wide range of sources for private information. Unfortunately, we are also a very mobile society. Thus, we often lose touch with people—even those whom we may have been close to for a rather long period of time. However, making contact with such individuals can be very beneficial. Insights from Research 4.1 addresses some very interesting findings on this issue—the benefits of reconnecting with people whom managers had not been in contact with for at least three years (such people are called "dormant ties").

A Cautionary Note: Three Kinds of Network Traps   A recent study of over 300 companies explored how management teams can understand and capitalize on the formal and informal social networks of their employees.[102] Six common types of managers who get stuck in three types of network traps were identified. Such findings have important career implications:

- *The wrong structure.* The "formalist" relies too much on his firm's official hierarchy, missing out on the efficiencies and opportunities that come from informal connections. The "overloaded manager" has so much contact with colleagues and external ties that she becomes a bottleneck to progress and burns herself out.
- *The wrong relationships.* The "disconnected expert" sticks with people who keep him focused on safe, existing competencies, rather than those who push him to build new skills. The "biased leader" relies on advisers (same functional background, location, or values) who reinforce her biases, when she should instead seek outsiders to prompt more fully informed decisions.
- *The wrong behavior.* The "superficial networker" engages in surface-level interaction with as many people as possible, mistakenly believing that a bigger network is a better network. The "chameleon" changes his interests, values, and personality to match those of whatever subgroup is his audience, and winds up being disconnected from every group.

The Potential Downside of Social Capital

We'd like to close our discussion of social capital by addressing some of its limitations. First, some firms have been adversely affected by very high levels of social capital because it may breed **"groupthink"**—a tendency not to question shared beliefs.[103] Such thinking may occur in networks with high levels of closure where there is little input from people outside the network. In effect, too many warm and fuzzy feelings among group members

groupthink
a tendency in an organization for individuals not to question shared beliefs.

HELLO AGAIN! THE VALUE OF REKINDLING CONNECTIONS

Overview

Reuniting is good for you . . . and for your business. Friends, colleagues, and family members can go different directions geographically, occupationally, and otherwise, leaving those relationships on hold. This research finds dormant ties to be much more valuable than previously thought. The insights gained from reconnecting can add spark to your projects.

What the Research Shows

Researchers from Rutgers University, George Washington University, and Northwestern University published a paper in *Organization Science* in which they compared the value of executives' dormant ties to their existing ties. The research included 129 participants from executive MBA programs and a follow-up with 116 executives. In the follow-up, participants ranked 10 dormant ties (people with whom they had not had any contact for three years or more) from the most to the least preferred. It turns out those ranked low were about as useful as those ranked very high. This means the value of dormant ties is significant. Even those we think are less valuable are still worth pursuing.

Specifically, the researchers found dormant ties were often more "efficient" than current ones. This means time spent consulting with those ties was short and provided efficient access to the person's knowledge. Researchers found reconnecting dormant ties provided greater originality of ideas than consulting current ties. The knowledge accumulated during dormancy, resulting from different experiences, can provide insights if the tie is reconnected.

Finally, in dormant ties where each person was especially motivated to cooperate and had a similar understanding of a problem, trust was higher. There was more of a shared perspective, and this increased the receipt of useful knowledge even more.

Why This Matters

Have you considered reconnecting with people from your past who've changed jobs, moved away, or otherwise gone in another direction? Perhaps you've intended to reach out but have been too overwhelmed by your current obligations to do so.

This research suggests reconnecting to dormant ties is time well spent. Your current connections with customers, friends, and colleagues are valuable but may have diminishing returns. After all, you've probably already exhausted any novel insights for your business—such as marketing ideas of potential customers—from your existing circle. To gather original ideas, a reunion might be in order.

Dormant ties are efficient, so you get more bang for your buck in terms of time spent reconnecting. Because of your previous connection based on common knowledge, business arrangements, or friendship, there's a shared perspective and trust. Often, you can just pick up where you left off because emotional closeness determines a tie's strength more than frequency of communication.

So, what does this mean for management practice? Social networking websites like LinkedIn have reduced the costs of searching for dormant contacts, and such contacts are now much easier to track down. These sites provide a low-cost way to rekindle former relationships while stimulating creativity about current projects.

Top executives stand to gain from revitalizing dormant ties too. Divergent perspectives on how to navigate industry environments can benefit leaders, as can the resurgence of connections between organizations. Corporate heads sometimes even reconnect informal ties, not with individuals but with their replacements, paving the way for future collaboration or strategic alliances.

When you are reconnecting, consultant and *Harvard Business Review* blogger Jodi Glickman suggests acknowledging the lapse in time, explaining the "Why now?" question, and offering a quid pro quo. Her article and the HBR Blog Network include an enlightening example of a dormant tie that paid off, as well as practical advice for reconnecting. One post reads, "I've recently been reaching out to people in my network to build my business and I have been pleasantly surprised at how genuinely happy people are to reconnect. Your insights are spot on."

Key Takeaways

- People lose touch with one another for many reasons. Often, relationships not actively maintained, or "dormant ties," are considered worthless.

- However, reconnecting is a low-cost, high-reward way to gain insights into your business because of experiences and knowledge gained during your loss of contact.

- Dormant ties give you more bang for your buck in the form of ideas and innovations. Even contacts ranked "least preferred" were valuable.

- Former connections are generally delighted to hear from you. Catch up with old friends or associates and you might collaborate on your next big idea.

Apply This Today

Get out of your comfort zone and pursue your old contacts. Reconnecting can add to your current knowledge and give you ideas.

Research Reviewed

Levin, D. Z., Walter, J., & Murnighan, J. K. 2011. Dormant ties: The value of reconnecting. *Organization Science*, 22(4), 923–939.

prevent people from rigorously challenging each other. People are discouraged from engaging in the "creative abrasion" that Dorothy Leonard of Harvard University describes as a key source of innovation.[104] Two firms that were well known for their collegiality, strong sense of employee membership, and humane treatment—Digital Equipment (now part of Hewlett-Packard) and Polaroid—suffered greatly from market misjudgments and strategic errors. The aforementioned aspects of their culture contributed to their problems.

Second, if there are deep-rooted mind-sets, there would be a tendency to develop dysfunctional human resource practices. That is, the organization (or group) would continue to hire, reward, and promote like-minded people who tend to further intensify organizational inertia and erode innovation. Such homogeneity would increase over time and decrease the effectiveness of decision-making processes.

Third, the socialization processes (orientation, training, etc.) can be expensive in terms of both financial resources and managerial commitment. Such investments can represent a significant opportunity cost that should be evaluated in terms of the intended benefits. If such expenses become excessive, profitability would be adversely affected.

Finally, individuals may use the contacts they develop to pursue their own interests and agendas, which may be inconsistent with the organization's goals and objectives. Thus, they may distort or selectively use information to favor their preferred courses of action or withhold information in their own self-interest to enhance their power to the detriment of the common good. Drawing on our discussion of social networks, this is particularly true in an organization that has too many bridging relationships but not enough closure relationships. In high-closure groups, it is easier to watch each other to ensure that illegal or unethical acts don't occur. By contrast, bridging relationships make it easier for a person to play one group or individual off another, with no one being the wiser.[105] We will discuss some behavioral control mechanisms in Chapter 9 (rewards, control, boundaries) that reduce such dysfunctional behaviors and actions.[106]

Using Technology to Leverage Human Capital and Knowledge

LO4.5

The vital role of technology in leveraging knowledge and human capital.

Sharing knowledge and information throughout the organization can be a means of conserving resources, developing products and services, and creating new opportunities. In this section we will discuss how technology can be used to leverage human capital and knowledge within organizations as well as with customers and suppliers beyond their boundaries.

Using Networks to Share Information

As we all know, email is an effective means of communicating a wide variety of information. It is quick, easy, and almost costless. Of course, it can become a problem when employees use it extensively for personal reasons. And we all know how fast jokes or rumors can spread within and across organizations!

Strategy Spotlight 4.5 suggests an innovative approach one firm took to reduce the exorbitant number of emails it had to deal with each day.

Email can also cause embarrassment, or worse, if one is not careful. Consider the plight of a potential CEO—as recalled by Marshall Goldsmith, a well-known executive coach:[107]

> I witnessed a series of e-mails between a potential CEO and a friend inside the company. The first e-mail to the friend provided an elaborate description of "why the current CEO is an idiot." The friend sent a reply. Several rounds of e-mails followed. Then the friend sent an e-mail containing a funny joke. The potential CEO decided that the current CEO would love this joke and forwarded it to him. You can guess what happened next. The CEO scrolled down the e-mail chain and found the "idiot" message. The heir apparent was gone in a week.

YES! EMAIL CAN BE REDUCED

Typically, we all have very little control over how many email messages we receive. But we *can* control how many messages we send. That rather obvious insight sparked a huge reduction in one company's email traffic. And, after the executives reduced their output, (surprise!) other employees followed suit.

A seven-person top management team at London-based International Power wanted to increase the firm's efficiency. An analysis suggested a glut of email might be part of the problem. Although executives initially felt the volume was due to others' actions, they were astonished to learn they, themselves, were sending 56 messages a day, on average.

Rather than using email management tools to address the overflow, the firm took a page from lean manufacturing. It decided to treat communications as though they were an industrial process, targeting efficiency killers such as overproduction and defects (confusing, unnecessary, or ineffective messages, which often simply bred other messages). Believing a reduction in executive outflow would prompt a quick reduction in employee outflow, the executives aimed to cut the number of emails sent by the top team members by 20 percent within four months.

Despite a few misgivings, the executives underwent training to reduce their email output by taking more deliberate actions. These included not forwarding messages unless strictly necessary, limiting messages' recipients, and choosing the most efficient form of communication to accomplish the task at hand. A phone call, for example, provides real-time feedback on whether a message is being understood—something that is missing with the low-bandwidth email channel. Also, facial expressions and body language make in-person meetings an even richer method of communication.

The executive team received weekly reports on both their and the top management team's progress. Within three months, the team's total email output dropped by 54 percent. And even though the other 75 London-based employees received no training, their email output dropped by an even greater amount—64 percent. The result was significant: a savings of 10,400 man-hours, which translates to a 7 percent increase in productivity.

Key Lessons

- Teach executives to become more deliberate in their use of email.
- Ask them to set a goal for reducing the number of messages they send and include it in their performance goals.
- Provide weekly feedback.

Source: Brown, C., Killick, A., & Renaud, K. 2013. To reduce email, start at the top. *Harvard Business Review,* 91(9): 26.

Email can, however, be a means for top executives to communicate information efficiently. For example, Martin Sorrell, chairman of WPP Group PLC, the huge $17 billion advertising and public relations firm, is a strong believer in the use of email.[108] He emails all of his employees once a month to discuss how the company is doing, address specific issues, and offer his perspectives on hot issues, such as new business models for the Internet. He believes that it keeps people abreast of what he is working on.

Technology can also enable much more sophisticated forms of communication in addition to knowledge sharing. Cisco, for example, launched Integrated Workforce Experience (IWE) in 2010.[109] It is a social business platform designed to facilitate internal and external collaboration and decentralize decision making. It functions much like a Facebook "wall": A real-time news feed provides updates on employees' status and activities as well as information about relevant communities, business projects, and customer and partner interactions. One manager likens it to Amazon. "It makes recommendations based on what you are doing, the role you are in, and the choices of other people like you. We are taking that to the enterprise level and basically allowing appropriate information to find you," he says.

electronic teams
a team of individuals that completes tasks primarily through email communication.

LO4.6

Why "electronic" or "virtual" teams are critical in combining and leveraging knowledge in organizations and how they can be made more effective.

Electronic Teams: Using Technology to Enhance Collaboration

Technology enables professionals to work as part of electronic, or virtual, teams to enhance the speed and effectiveness with which products are developed. For example, Microsoft has concentrated much of its development on **electronic teams** (or e-teams) that are networked together.[110] This helps to accelerate design and testing of new software modules that use the Windows-based framework as their central architecture. Microsoft is able to foster specialized technical expertise while sharing knowledge rapidly throughout the firm. This helps the firm learn how its new technologies can be applied rapidly to new business ventures such as cable television, broadcasting, travel services, and financial services.

What are electronic teams (or e-teams)? There are two key differences between e-teams and more traditional teams:[111]

- E-team members either work in geographically separated workplaces or may work in the same space but at different times. E-teams may have members working in different spaces and time zones, as is the case with many multinational teams.
- Most of the interactions among members of e-teams occur through electronic communication channels such as fax machines and groupware tools such as email, bulletin boards, chat, and videoconferencing.

E-teams have expanded exponentially in recent years.[112] Organizations face increasingly high levels of complex and dynamic change. E-teams are also effective in helping businesses cope with global challenges. Most e-teams perform very complex tasks and most knowledge-based teams are charged with developing new products, improving organizational processes, and satisfying challenging customer problems. For example, Hewlett-Packard's e-teams solve clients' computing problems, and Sun Microsystems' (part of Oracle) e-teams generate new business models.

Advantages   There are multiple advantages of e-teams.[113] In addition to the rather obvious use of technology to facilitate communications, the potential benefits parallel the other two major sections in this chapter—human capital and social capital.

First, e-teams are less restricted by the geographic constraints that are placed on face-to-face teams. Thus, e-teams have the potential to acquire a broader range of "human capital," or the skills and capacities that are necessary to complete complex assignments. So e-team leaders can draw upon a greater pool of talent to address a wider range of problems since they are not constrained by geographic space. Once formed, e-teams can be more flexible in responding to unanticipated work challenges and opportunities because team members can be rotated out of projects when demands and contingencies alter the team's objectives.

Second, e-teams can be very effective in generating "social capital"—the quality of relationships and networks that form. Such capital is a key lubricant in work transactions and operations. Given the broader boundaries associated with e-teams, members and leaders generally have access to a wider range of social contacts than would be typically available in more traditional face-to-face teams. Such contacts are often connected to a broader scope of clients, customers, constituents, and other key stakeholders.

Challenges   However, there are challenges associated with making e-teams effective. Successful action by both traditional teams and e-teams requires that:

- Members *identify* who among them can provide the most appropriate knowledge and resources.
- E-team leaders and key members know how to *combine* individual contributions in the most effective manner for a coordinated and appropriate response.

Group psychologists have termed such activities "identification and combination" activities, and teams that fail to perform them face a "process loss."[114] Process losses prevent teams from reaching high levels of performance because of inefficient interaction dynamics among team members. Such poor dynamics require that some collective energy, time, and effort be devoted to dealing with team inefficiencies, thus diverting the team away from its objectives. For example, if a team member fails to communicate important information at critical phases of a project, other members may waste time and energy. This can lead to conflict and resentment as well as to decreased motivation to work hard to complete tasks.

The potential for process losses tends to be more prevalent in e-teams than in traditional teams because the geographic dispersion of members increases the complexity of establishing effective interaction and exchanges. Generally, teams suffer process loss because of low cohesion, low trust among members, a lack of appropriate norms or standard operating procedures, or a lack of shared understanding among team members about their tasks. With e-teams, members are more geographically or temporally dispersed, and the team becomes more susceptible to the risk factors that can create process loss. Such problems can be exacerbated when team members have less than ideal competencies and social skills. This can erode problem-solving capabilities as well as the effective functioning of the group as a social unit.

A variety of technologies, from email and Internet groups to Skype have facilitated the formation and effective functioning of e-teams as well as a wide range of collaborations within companies. Such technologies greatly enhance the collaborative abilities of employees and managers within a company at a reasonable cost—despite the distances that separate them.

Codifying Knowledge for Competitive Advantage

There are two different kinds of knowledge. Tacit knowledge is embedded in personal experience and shared only with the consent and participation of the individual. Explicit (or codified) knowledge, on the other hand, is knowledge that can be documented, widely distributed, and easily replicated. One of the challenges of knowledge-intensive organizations is to capture and codify the knowledge and experience that, in effect, resides in the heads of its employees. Otherwise, they will have to constantly "reinvent the wheel," which is both expensive and inefficient. Also, the "new wheel" may not necessarily be superior to the "old wheel."[115]

Once a knowledge asset (e.g., a software code or a process) is developed and paid for, it can be reused many times at very low cost, assuming that it doesn't have to be substantially modified each time. Let's take the case of a consulting company, such as Accenture (formerly Andersen Consulting).[116]

> Since the knowledge of its consultants has been codified and stored in electronic repositories, it can be employed in many jobs by a huge number of consultants. Additionally, since the work has a high level of standardization (i.e., there are strong similarities across the numerous client engagements), there is a rather high ratio of consultants to partners. For example, the ratio of consultants to partners is roughly 30, which is quite high. As one might expect, there must be extensive training of the newly hired consultants for such an approach to work. The recruits are trained at Accenture's Center for Professional Education, a 150-acre campus in St. Charles, Illinois. Using the center's knowledge-management respository, the consultants work through many scenarios designed to improve business processes. In effect, the information technologies enable the consultants to be "implementers, not inventors."

Access Health, a call-in medical center, also uses technology to capture and share knowledge. When someone calls the center, a registered nurse uses the company's "clinical decision architecture" to assess the caller's symptoms, rule out possible conditions, and recommend a home remedy, doctor's visit, or trip to the emergency room. The company's knowledge repository contains algorithms of the symptoms of more than 500 illnesses. According to CEO Joseph Tallman, "We are not inventing a new way to cure disease. We are taking available knowledge and inventing processes to put it to better

HOW SAP TAPS KNOWLEDGE WELL BEYOND ITS BOUNDARIES

Traditionally, organizations built and protected their knowledge stocks—proprietary resources that no one else could access. However, the more the business environment changes, the faster the value of what you know at any point in time diminishes. In today's world, success hinges on the ability to access a growing variety of knowledge flows in order to rapidly replenish the firm's knowledge stocks. For example, when an organization tries to improve cycle times in a manufacturing process, it finds far more value in problem solving shaped by the diverse experiences, perspectives, and learning of a tightly knit team (shared through knowledge flows) than in a training manual (knowledge stocks) alone.

Knowledge flows can help companies gain competitive advantage in an age of near-constant disruption. The software company SAP, for example, routinely taps the nearly 3 million participants in its Community Network, which extends well beyond the boundaries of the firm. By providing a virtual platform for customers,

developers, system integrators, and service vendors to create and exchange knowledge, SAP has significantly increased the productivity of all the participants in its ecosystem.

According to Mark Yolton, senior vice president of SAP Communications and Social Media, "It's a very robust community with a great deal of activity. We see about 1.2 million unique visitors every month. Hundreds of millions of pages are viewed every year. There are 4,000 discussion forum posts every single day, 365 days a year, and about 115 blogs every day, 365 days a year, from any of the nearly 3 million members."

The site is open to everyone, regardless of whether you are a SAP customer, partner, or newcomer who needs to work with SAP technology. The site offers technical articles, web-based training, code samples, evaluation systems, discussion forums, and excellent blogs for community experts.

Sources: Yolton, M. 2012. SAP: Using social media for building, selling and supporting. *sloanreview.mit.edu*, August 7: np; Hagel, J., III., Brown, J. S., & Davison, L. 2009. The big shift: Measuring the forces of change. *Harvard Business Review*, 87(4): 87; and Anonymous. Undated. SAP developer network. *sap.sys-con.com*: np.

use." The software algorithms were very expensive to develop, but the investment has been repaid many times over. The first 300 algorithms that Access Health developed have each been used an average of 8,000 times a year. Further, the company's paying customers—insurance companies and provider groups—save money because many callers would have made expensive trips to the emergency room or the doctor's office had they not been diagnosed over the phone.

The user community can be a major source of knowledge creation for a firm. Strategy Spotlight 4.6 highlights how SAP, in an example of effective crowdsourcing, has been able to leverage the expertise and involvement of its users to develop new knowledge and transmit it to SAP's entire user community.

We close this section with a series of questions managers should consider in determining (1) how effective their organization is in attracting, developing, and retaining human capital and (2) how effective they are in leveraging human capital through social capital and technology. These questions, included in Exhibit 4.5, summarize some of the key issues addressed in this chapter.

Protecting the Intellectual Assets of the Organization: Intellectual Property and Dynamic Capabilities

LO4.7

The challenge of protecting intellectual property and the importance of a firm's dynamic capabilities.

In today's dynamic and turbulent world, unpredictability and fast change dominate the business environment. Firms can use technology, attract human capital, or tap into research and design networks to get access to pretty much the same information as their competitors. So what would give firms a sustainable competitive advantage?[117] Protecting a firm's intellectual property requires a concerted effort on the part of the company. After all, employees become disgruntled and patents expire. The management of intellectual property (IP) involves, besides patents, contracts with confidentiality and noncompete clauses,

EXHIBIT 4.5 Issues to Consider in Creating Value through Human Capital, Social Capital, and Technology

Human Capital

Recruiting "Top-Notch" Human Capital

- Does the organization assess attitude and "general makeup" instead of focusing primarily on skills and background in selecting employees at all levels?
- How important are creativity and problem-solving ability? Are they properly considered in hiring decisions?
- Do people throughout the organization engage in effective networking activities to obtain a broad pool of worthy potential employees? Is the organization creative in such endeavors?

Enhancing Human Capital through Employee Development

- Does the development and training process inculcate an "organizationwide" perspective?
- Is there widespread involvement, including top executives, in the preparation and delivery of training and development programs?
- Is the development of human capital effectively tracked and monitored?
- Are there effective programs for succession at all levels of the organization, especially at the topmost levels?
- Does the firm effectively evaluate its human capital? Is a 360-degree evaluation used? Why? Why not?
- Are mechanisms in place to ensure that a manager's success does not come at the cost of compromising the organization's core values?

Retaining the Best Employees

- Are there appropriate financial rewards to motivate employees at all levels?
- Do people throughout the organization strongly identify with the organization's mission?
- Are employees provided with a stimulating and challenging work environment that fosters professional growth?
- Are valued amenities provided (e.g., flextime, child care facilities, telecommuting) that are appropriate given the organization's mission, its strategy, and how work is accomplished?
- Is the organization continually devising strategies and mechanisms to retain top performers?

Social Capital

- Are there positive personal and professional relationships among employees?
- Is the organization benefiting (or being penalized) by hiring (or by voluntary turnover) en masse?
- Does an environment of caring and encouragement rather than competition enhance team performance?
- Do the social networks within the organization have the appropriate levels of closure and bridging relationships?
- Does the organization minimize the adverse effects of excessive social capital, such as excessive costs and "groupthink"?

Technology

- Has the organization used technologies such as email and networks to develop products and services?
- Does the organization effectively use technology to transfer best practices across the organization?
- Does the organization use technology to leverage human capital and knowledge both within the boundaries of the organization and among its suppliers and customers?
- Has the organization effectively used technology to codify knowledge for competitive advantage?
- Does the organization try to retain some of the knowledge of employees when they decide to leave the firm?

Source: Adapted from Dess, G. G., & Picken, J. C. 1999. *Beyond Productivity:* 63–64. New York: AMACON.

copyrights, and the development of trademarks. Moreover, developing dynamic capabilities is the only avenue providing firms with the ability to reconfigure their knowledge and activities to achieve a sustainable competitive advantage.

Intellectual Property Rights

intellectual property rights
intangible property owned by a firm in the forms of patents, copyrights, trademarks, or trade secrets.

Intellectual property rights are more difficult to define and protect than property rights for physical assets (e.g., plant, equipment, and land). However, if intellectual property rights are not reliably protected by the state, there will be no incentive to develop new products and services. Property rights have been enshrined in constitutions and rules of law in many countries. In the information era, though, adjustments need to be made to accommodate the new realities of knowledge. Knowledge and information are fundamentally different assets from the physical ones that property rights have been designed to protect.

The protection of intellectual rights raises unique issues, compared to physical property rights. IP is characterized by significant development costs and very low marginal costs. Indeed, it may take a substantial investment to develop a software program, an idea, or a digital music tune. Once developed, though, its reproduction and distribution cost may be almost zero, especially if the Internet is used. Effective protection of intellectual property is necessary before any investor will finance such an undertaking. Appropriation of investors' returns is harder to police since possession and deployment are not as readily observable. Unlike physical assets, intellectual property can be stolen by simply broadcasting it. Recall Napster and MP3 as well as the debates about counterfeit software, music CDs, and DVDs coming from developing countries such as China. Part of the problem is that using an idea does not prevent others from simultaneously using it for their own benefit, which is typically impossible with physical assets. Moreover, new ideas are frequently built on old ideas and are not easily traceable.

Given these unique challenges in protecting IP, it comes as no surprise that legal battles over patents become commonplace in IP-heavy industries such as telecommunications. Take the recent patent battles Apple has been fighting against smartphone makers running Android, Google's mobile operating system.[118]

> In 2012, Apple and HTC, a Taiwanese smartphone maker, agreed to dismiss a series of lawsuits filed against each other after Apple accused HTC of copying the iPhone. While this settlement may be a sign that Apple's new CEO, Timothy Cook, is eager to end the distractions caused by IP-related litigation, other patent battles continue, including one between Apple and Samsung, the largest maker of Android phones. This legal battle involves much higher stakes, because Samsung shipped almost eight times as many Android smartphones as HTC in the third quarter of 2012. However, Apple's new leadership seems to be more pragmatic about this issue. In Mr. Cook's words, "It is awkward. I hate litigation. I absolutely hate it," suggesting that he is not as enthusiastic a combatant in the patent wars as was his predecessor, Steve Jobs, who famously promised to "destroy Android, because it's a stolen product."

Countries are attempting to pass new legislation to cope with developments in new pharmaceutical compounds, stem cell research, and biotechnology. However, a firm that is faced with this challenge today cannot wait for the legislation to catch up. New technological developments, software solutions, electronic games, online services, and other products and services contribute to our economic prosperity and the creation of wealth for those entrepreneurs who have the idea first and risk bringing it to the market.

Dynamic Capabilities

Dynamic capabilities entail the capacity to build and protect a competitive advantage.[119] This rests on knowledge, assets, competencies, and complementary assets and technologies as well as the ability to sense and seize new opportunities, generate new knowledge, and reconfigure existing assets and capabilities.[120] According to David Teece, an economist at the University of California at Berkeley, dynamic capabilities are related to the entrepreneurial side of the firm and are built within a firm through its environmental and technological "sensing" apparatus, its choices of organizational form, and its collective ability to strategize. Dynamic capabilities are about the ability of an organization to challenge the conventional wisdom within its industry and market, learn and innovate, adapt to the changing world, and continuously adopt new ways to serve the evolving needs of the market.[121]

dynamic capabilities
a firm's capacity to build and protect a competitive advantage, which rests on knowledge, assets, competencies, complementary assets, and technologies. Dynamic capabilities include the ability to sense and seize new opportunities, generate new knowledge, and reconfigure existing assets and capabilities.

Layoffs or Furloughs: The Action Honeywell Took

Like most companies, Honeywell was faced with severe economic challenges during the deep recession in 2008–2009. However, instead of going the usual route—massive layoffs—the firm decided to use furloughs throughout the company. In a recent *Harvard Business Review* article, David Cote, chairman and CEO of Honeywell, discussed his reasons for taking this seldom-used approach.

When Honeywell began looking at its options, it kept coming back to the idea of furloughs: Workers take unpaid leaves but remain employed. The conventional wisdom was that since furloughs spread the pain across the entire workforce, they hurt everyone's morale, loyalty, and retention, so it is actually better to lay off a smaller number, focusing on the weak performers. Also, furloughs are a challenge logistically. In order to implement them, the firm needed to comply with individual state laws as well as the laws in other countries where the firm did business.

However, Cote felt the benefits of furloughs outweighed the costs. Managers typically overestimate the savings the firm will achieve with layoffs as well as fail to understand that even bad recessions tend to end more quickly than expected. And if a firm has to pay six months of severance, for example, it will have to wait six months before there are any savings. Since recessions may last only 12 to 18 months, it is usually only about a year or so later before the firm must start hiring again. Then, of course, the firm incurs all the usual hiring costs (as well as the earlier costs associated with losing talent and experience). Also, Cote stated he had been through three recessions and seldom heard a management team talk about how choices they make during a downturn will affect performance during the recovery. He kept reiterating that point: "There will be a recovery, and we need to be prepared for it."

Discussion Questions

1. Do you think David Cote made the right decision? Why? Why not?
2. Do you think the decision was well received by the employees? What factors, changes in events, and so on, do you think would affect how employees came to accept (or reject) this decision?

Sources: Cote, D. 2013. Honeywell's CEO on how he avoided layoffs. *Harvard Business Review*, 91 (6): 43-46.

Examples of dynamic capabilities include product development, strategic decision making, alliances, and acquisitions.[122] Some firms have clearly developed internal processes and routines that make them superior in such activities. For example, 3M and Apple are ahead of their competitors in product development. Cisco Systems has made numerous acquisitions over the years. Cisco seems to have developed the capability to identify and evaluate potential acquisition candidates and seamlessly integrate them once the acquisition is completed. Other organizations can try to copy Cisco's practices. However, Cisco's combination of the resources of the acquired companies and their reconfiguration that Cisco has already achieved places it well ahead of its competitors. As markets become increasingly dynamic, traditional sources of long-term competitive advantage become less relevant. In such markets, all that a firm can strive for are a series of temporary advantages. Dynamic capabilities allow a firm to create this series of temporary advantages through new resource configurations.[123]

- ▣ **Human Capital:** Identify specific steps taken by your organization to effectively attract, develop, and retain talent. If you cannot identify such steps, you may have fewer career opportunities to develop your human capital at your organization. Do you take advantage of your organization's human resource programs, such as tuition reimbursement, mentoring, and so forth?

- ▣ **Human Capital:** As workplaces become more diverse, it is important to reflect on whether your organization values diversity. What kinds of diversity seem to be encouraged (e.g., age-based or ethnicity-based)? In what ways are your colleagues different from and similar to you? If your firm has a homogeneous workforce, there may be limited perspectives on strategic and operational issues and a career at this organization may be less attractive to you.

- ▣ **Social Capital:** Does your organization have strong social capital? What is the basis of your conclusion that it has strong or weak social capital? What specific programs are in place to build and develop social capital? What is the impact of social capital on employee turnover in your organization? Alternatively, is social capital so strong that you see effects such as "groupthink"? From your perspective, how might you better leverage social capital toward pursuing other career opportunities?

- ▣ **Social Capital:** Are you actively working to build a strong social network at your work organization? To advance your career, strive to build a broad network that gives you access to diverse information.

- ▣ **Technology:** Does your organization provide and effectively use technology (e.g., groupware, knowledge management systems) to help you leverage your talents and expand your knowledge base? If your organization does a poor job in this regard, what can you do on your own to expand your knowledge base using technology available outside the organization?

summary

Firms throughout the industrial world are recognizing that the knowledge worker is the key to success in the marketplace. However, they also recognize that human capital, although vital, is still only a necessary, but not a sufficient, condition for creating value. We began the first section of the chapter by addressing the importance of human capital and how it can be attracted, developed, and retained. Then we discussed the role of social capital and technology in leveraging human capital for competitive success. We pointed out that intellectual capital—the difference between a firm's market value and its book value—has increased significantly over the past few decades. This is particularly true for firms in knowledge-intensive industries, especially where there are relatively few tangible assets, such as software development.

The second section of the chapter addressed the attraction, development, and retention of human capital. We viewed these three activities as a "three-legged stool"—that is, it is difficult for firms to be successful if they ignore or are unsuccessful in any one of these activities. Among the issues we discussed in *attracting* human capital were "hiring for attitude, training for skill" and the value of using social networks to attract human capital. In particular, it is important to attract employees who can collaborate with others, given the importance of collective efforts such as teams and task forces. With regard to *developing* human capital, we discussed the need to encourage widespread involvement throughout the organization, monitor progress and track the development of human capital, and evaluate human capital. Among the issues that are widely practiced in evaluating human capital is the 360-degree evaluation system. Employees are evaluated by their superiors, peers, direct reports, and even internal and external customers. We also addressed the value of maintaining a diverse workforce. Finally, some mechanisms for retaining human capital are employees' identification with the organization's mission and values, providing challenging work and a stimulating environment, the importance of financial and nonfinancial rewards and incentives, and providing flexibility and amenities. A key issue here is that a firm should not overemphasize financial rewards. After all, if individuals join an organization for money, they also are likely to leave for money. With money as the primary motivator, there is little chance that employees will develop firm-specific ties to keep them with the organization.

The third section of the chapter discussed the importance of social capital in leveraging human capital. Social capital refers to the network of relationships that individuals have throughout the organization as well as with customers and suppliers. Such ties can be critical in obtaining both information and resources. With regard to recruiting, for example, we saw how some firms are able to hire en masse groups of individuals who are part of social networks. Social relationships can also be very important in the effective functioning of groups. Finally, we discussed some of the potential downsides of social capital. These include the expenses that firms may bear when promoting social and working relationships among individuals as well as the potential for "groupthink," wherein individuals are reluctant to express divergent (or opposing) views on an issue because of social pressures to conform. We also introduced the concept of social networks. The relative advantages of being central in a network versus bridging multiple networks was discussed. We addressed the key role that social networks can play in both improving knowledge management and promoting career success.

The fourth section addressed the role of technology in leveraging human capital. We discussed relatively simple means of using technology, such as email and networks where individuals can collaborate by way of personal computers. We provided suggestions and guidelines on how electronic teams can be effectively managed. We also addressed more sophisticated uses of technology, such as sophisticated management systems. Here, knowledge can be codified and reused at very low cost, as we saw in the examples of firms in the consulting, health care, and high-technology industries.

In the last section we discussed the increasing importance of protecting a firm's intellectual property. Although traditional approaches such as patents, copyrights, and trademarks are important, the development of dynamic capabilities may be the best protection in the long run.

SUMMARY REVIEW QUESTIONS

1. Explain the role of knowledge in today's competitive environment.
2. Why is it important for managers to recognize the interdependence in the attraction, development, and retention of talented professionals?
3. What are some of the potential downsides for firms that engage in a "war for talent"?
4. Discuss the need for managers to use social capital in leveraging their human capital both within and across their firm.
5. Discuss the key role of technology in leveraging knowledge and human capital.

key terms

knowledge economy 110
intellectual capital 111
human capital 112
social capital 112

explicit knowledge 112
tacit knowledge 112
360-degree evaluation
   and feedback
   systems 118
social network
   analysis 125
closure 126
bridging relationships 127
structural holes 127

unification lever 127
people lever 127
T-shaped
   management 127
network lever 127

groupthink 129
electronic teams 132
intellectual property
   rights 136
dynamic capabilities 137

experiential exercise

Pfizer, a leading health care firm with $59 billion in revenues, is often rated as one of *Fortune*'s "Most Admired Firms." It is also considered an excellent place to work and has generated high return to shareholders. Clearly, Pfizer values its human capital. Using the Internet and/or library resources, identify some of the actions/strategies Pfizer has taken to attract, develop, and retain human capital. What are their implications? (Fill in the table at bottom of the page.)

application questions & exercises

1. Look up successful firms in a high-technology industry as well as two successful firms in more traditional industries such as automobile manufacturing and retailing. Compare their market values and book values. What are some implications of these differences?
2. Select a firm for which you believe its social capital—both within the firm and among its suppliers and customers—is vital to its competitive advantage. Support your arguments.
3. Choose a company with which you are familiar. What are some of the ways in which it uses technology to leverage its human capital?
4. Using the Internet, look up a company with which you are familiar. What are some of the policies and procedures that it uses to enhance the firm's human and social capital?

ethics questions

1. Recall an example of a firm that recently faced an ethical crisis. How do you feel the crisis and management's handling of it affected the firm's human capital and social capital?
2. Based on your experiences or what you have learned in your previous classes, are you familiar with any companies that used unethical practices to attract talented professionals? What do you feel were the short-term and long-term consequences of such practices?

Activity	Actions/Strategies	Implications
Attracting human capital		
Developing human capital		
Retaining human capital		

references

1. Touryalai, H. 2011. Meddling with Merrill: Merrill Lynch's profits are bolstering BofA. What is Merrill getting in return? *Forbes,* September 26: 45–47; Benoit, D. 2012. BofA-Merrill: Still a bottom-line success. *www.wsj.com,* September 28: np; Silver-Greenberg, J. & Craig, S. 2012. Bank of America settles suit over Merrill for $2.43 billion. *www. nytimes.com,* September 28: np.

2. Parts of this chapter draw upon some of the ideas and examples from Dess, G. G. & Picken, J. C. 1999. *Beyond productivity.* New York: AMACOM.

3. Dekas, K. H., et al. 2013. Organizational citizenship behavior, version 2.0: A review and qualitative investigation of OCBs for knowledge workers at Google and beyond. *Academy of Management Perspectives,* 27(3): 219–237.

4. Stewart, T. A. 1997. *Intellectual capital: The new wealth of organizations.* New York: Doubleday/Currency.

5. Leif Edvinsson and Michael S. Malone have a similar, more detailed definition of *intellectual capital:* "the combined knowledge, skill, innovativeness, and ability to meet the task at hand." They consider intellectual capital to equal human capital plus structural capital. *Structural capital* is defined as "the hardware, software, databases, organization structure, patents, trademarks, and everything else of organizational capability that supports those employees' productivity—in a word, everything left at the office when the employees go home." Edvinsson, L. & Malone, M. S. 1997. *Intellectual capital: Realizing your company's true value by finding its hidden brainpower:* 10–14. New York: HarperBusiness.

6. Stewart, T. A. 2001. Accounting gets radical. *Fortune,* April 16: 184–194.

7. Adams, S. & Kichen, S. 2008. Ben Graham then and now. *Forbes, www. multpl.com/s-p-500-price-to-book,* November 10: 56.

8. An interesting discussion of Steve Jobs's impact on Apple's valuation is in Lashinsky, A. 2009. Steve's leave—what does it really mean? *Fortune,* February 2: 96–102.

9. Anonymous. 2007. Intel opens first high volume 45 nm microprocessor manufacturing factory. *www.intel .com,* October 25: np.

10. Thomas Stewart has suggested this formula in his book *Intellectual capital.* He provides an insightful discussion on pages 224–225,

including some of the limitations of this approach to measuring intellectual capital. We recognize, of course, that during the late 1990s and in early 2000, there were some excessive market valuations of high-technology and Internet firms. For an interesting discussion of the extraordinary market valuation of Yahoo!, an Internet company, refer to Perkins, A. B. 2001. The Internet bubble encapsulated: Yahoo! *Red Herring,* April 15: 17–18.

11. Roberts, P. W. & Dowling, G. R. 2002. Corporate reputation and sustained superior financial performance. *Strategic Management Journal,* 23(12): 1077–1095.

12. For a study on the relationships between human capital, learning, and sustainable competitive advantage, read Hatch, N. W. & Dyer, J. H. 2005. Human capital and learning as a source of sustainable competitive advantage. *Strategic Management Journal,* 25: 1155–1178.

13. One of the seminal contributions on knowledge management is Becker, G. S. 1993. *Human capital: A theoretical and empirical analysis with special reference to education* (3rd ed.). Chicago: University of Chicago Press.

14. For an excellent overview of the topic of social capital, read Baron, R. A. 2005. Social capital. In Hitt, M. A. & Ireland, R. D. (Eds.), *The Blackwell encyclopedia of management* (2nd ed.): 224–226. Malden, MA: Blackwell.

15. For an excellent discussion of social capital and its impact on organizational performance, refer to Nahapiet, J. & Ghoshal, S. 1998. Social capital, intellectual capital, and the organizational advantage. *Academy of Management Review,* 23: 242–266.

16. An interesting discussion of how knowledge management (patents) can enhance organizational performance can be found in Bogner, W. C. & Bansal, P. 2007. Knowledge management as the basis of sustained high performance. *Journal of Management Studies,* 44(1): 165–188.

17. Polanyi, M. 1967. *The tacit dimension.* Garden City, NY: Anchor.

18. Barney, J. B. 1991. Firm resources and sustained competitive advantage. *Journal of Management,* 17: 99–120.

19. For an interesting perspective of empirical research on how

knowledge can adversely affect performance, read Haas, M. R. & Hansen, M. T. 2005. When using knowledge can hurt performance: The value of organizational capabilities in a management consulting company. *Strategic Management Journal,* 26(1): 1–24.

20. New insights on managing talent are provided in Cappelli, P. 2008. Talent management for the twenty-first century. *Harvard Business Review,* 66(3): 74–81.

21. Some of the notable books on this topic include Edvisson & Malone, op. cit.; Stewart, op. cit.; and Nonaka, I. & Takeuchi, I. 1995. *The knowledge creating company.* New York: Oxford University Press.

22. Segalla, M. & Felton, N. 2010. Find the real power in your organization. *Harvard Business Review,* 88(5): 34–35.

23. Stewart, T. A. 2000. Taking risk to the marketplace. *Fortune,* March 6: 424.

24. Lobel, O. 2014. *Talent wants to be free.* New Haven, CT: Yale University Press.

25. Insights on Generation X's perspective on the workplace are in Erickson, T. J. 2008. Task, not time: Profile of a Gen Y job. *Harvard Business Review,* 86(2): 19.

26. Pfeffer, J. 2010. Building sustainable organizations: The human factor. *Academy of Management Perspectives,* 24(1): 34–45.

27. Lobel, op. cit.

28. Some workplace implications for the aging workforce are addressed in Strack, R., Baier, J., & Fahlander, A. 2008. Managing demographic risk. *Harvard Business Review,* 66(2): 119–128.

29. For a discussion of attracting, developing, and retaining top talent, refer to Goffee, R. & Jones, G. 2007. Leading clever people. *Harvard Business Review,* 85(3): 72–89.

30. Winston, A. S. 2014. *The big pivot.* Boston: Harvard Business Review Press.

31. Dess & Picken, op. cit., p. 34.

32. Webber, A. M. 1998. Danger: Toxic company. *Fast Company,* November: 152–161.

33. Martin, J. & Schmidt, C. 2010. How to keep your top talent. *Harvard Business Review,* 88(5): 54–61.

34. Some interesting insights on why home-grown American talent is going abroad are found in Saffo, P. 2009. A looming American diaspora. *Harvard Business Review,* 87(2): 27.

35. Grossman, M. 2012. The best advice I ever got. *Fortune,* May 12: 119.

36. Davenport, T. H., Harris, J., & Shapiro, J. 2010. Competing on talent analytics. *Harvard Business Review,* 88(10): 62–69.

37. Ployhart, R. E. & Moliterno, T. P. 2011. Emergence of the human capital resource: A multilevel model. *Academy of Management Review,* 36(1): 127–150.

38. For insights on management development and firm performance in several countries, refer to Mabey, C. 2008. Management development and firm performance in Germany, Norway, Spain, and the UK. *Journal of International Business Studies,* 39(8): 1327–1342.

39. Martin, J. 1998. So, you want to work for the best. . . . *Fortune,* January 12: 77.

40. Cardin, R. 1997. Make your own Bozo Filter. *Fast Company,* October–November: 56.

41. Anonymous. 100 best companies to work for. *money.cnn.com,* undated: np.

42. Martin, op. cit.; Henkoff, R. 1993. Companies that train best. *Fortune,* March 22: 53–60.

43. This section draws on: Garg, V. 2012. Here's why companies should give Millennial workers everything they ask for. *buisnessinsider.com,* August 23: np; *worklifepolicy.com*; and Gerdes, L. 2006. The top 50 employers for new college grads. *BusinessWeek,* September 18: 64–81.

44. An interesting perspective on developing new talent rapidly when they join an organization can be found in Rollag, K., Parise, S., & Cross, R. 2005. Getting new hires up to speed quickly. *MIT Sloan Management Review,* 46(2): 35–41.

45. Stewart, T. A. 1998. Gray flannel suit? Moi? *Fortune,* March 18: 80–82.

46. Bryant, A. 2011. *The corner office.* New York: St. Martin's Griffin, 227.

47. An interesting perspective on how Cisco Systems develops its talent can be found in Chatman, J., O'Reilly, C., & Chang, V. 2005. Cisco Systems: Developing a human capital strategy. *California Management Review,* 47(2): 137–166.

48. Anonymous. 2011. Schumpeter: The tussle for talent. *The Economist,* January 8: 68.

49. Training and development policy: Mentoring. *opm.gov:* undated, np.

50. Douglas, C. A. 1997. Formal mentoring programs in organizations. *centerforcreativeleadership.org:* np.

51. Warner, F. 2002. Inside Intel's mentoring movement. *fastcompany .com,* March 31: np.

52. Grove, A. 2011. Be a mentor. *Bloomberg Businessweek,* September 21: 80.

53. For an innovative perspective on the appropriateness of alternate approaches to evaluation and rewards, refer to Seijts, G. H. & Lathan, G. P. 2005. Learning versus performance goals: When should each be used? *Academy of Management Executive,* 19(1): 124–132.

54. The discussion of the 360-degree feedback system draws on the article UPS. 1997. 360-degree feedback: Coming from all sides. *Vision* (a UPS Corporation internal company publication), March: 3; Slater, R. 1994. *Get better or get beaten: Thirty-one leadership secrets from Jack Welch.* Burr Ridge, IL: Irwin; Nexon, M. 1997. General Electric: The secrets of the finest company in the world. *L'Expansion,* July 23: 18–30; and Smith, D. 1996. Bold new directions for human resources. *Merck World* (internal company publication), October: 8.

55. Interesting insights on 360-degree evaluation systems are discussed in Barwise, P. & Meehan, Sean. 2008. So you think you're a good listener. *Harvard Business Review,* 66(4): 22–23.

56. Insights into the use of 360-degree evaluation are in Kaplan, R. E. & Kaiser, R. B. 2009. Stop overdoing your strengths. *Harvard Business Review,* 87(2): 100–103.

57. Mankins, M., Bird, A., & Root, J. 2013. Making star teams out of star players. *Harvard Business Review,* 91(1/2): 74–78.

58. Kets de Vries, M. F. R. 1998. Charisma in action: The transformational abilities of Virgin's Richard Branson and ABB's Percy Barnevik. *Organizational Dynamics,* Winter: 20.

59. For an interesting discussion on how organizational culture has helped Zappos become number one in *Fortune*'s 2009 survey of the best companies to work for, see O'Brien, J. M. 2009. Zappos knows how to kick it. *Fortune,* February 2: 54–58.

60. We have only to consider the most celebrated case of industrial espionage in recent years, wherein José Ignacio Lopez was indicted in a German court for stealing sensitive product planning documents from his former employer, General Motors, and sharing them with his executive colleagues at Volkswagen. The lawsuit was dismissed by the German courts, but Lopez and his colleagues were investigated by the U.S. Justice Department. Also consider the recent litigation involving noncompete employment contracts and confidentiality clauses of *International Paper v. Louisiana-Pacific, Campbell Soup v. H. J. Heinz Co.,* and *PepsiCo v. Quaker Oats's Gatorade.* In addition to retaining valuable human resources and often their valuable network of customers, firms must also protect proprietary information and knowledge. For interesting insights, refer to Carley, W. M. 1998. CEO gets hard lesson in how not to keep his lieutenants. *The Wall Street Journal,* February 11: A1, A10; and Lenzner, R. & Shook, C. 1998. Whose Rolodex is it, anyway? *Forbes,* February 23: 100–103.

61. For an insightful discussion of retention of knowledge workers in today's economy, read Davenport, T. H. 2005. *The care and feeding of the knowledge worker.* Boston, MA: Harvard Business School Press.

62. Weber, L. 2014. Here's what boards want in executives. *The Wall Street Journal,* December 10: B5.

63. Fisher, A. 2008. America's most admired companies. *Fortune,* March 17: 74.

64. Stewart, T. A. 2001. *The wealth of knowledge.* New York: Currency.

65. For insights on fulfilling one's potential, refer to Kaplan, R. S. 2008. Reaching your potential. *Harvard Business Review,* 66(7/8): 45–57.

66. Amabile, T. M. 1997. Motivating creativity in organizations: On doing what you love and loving what you do. *California Management Review,* Fall: 39–58.

67. For an insightful perspective on alternate types of employee–employer relationships, read Erickson, T. J. & Gratton, L. 2007. What it means to work here. *Harvard Business Review,* 85(3): 104–112.

68. Pfeffer, J. 2001. Fighting the war for talent is hazardous to your organization's health. *Organizational Dynamics,* 29(4): 248–259.

69. Best companies to work for 2011. 2011. *finance.yahoo.com,* January 20: np.

70. This section draws on Dewhurst, M., Hancock, B., & Ellsworth, D. 2013. Redesigning knowledge work. *Harvard Business Review,* 91 (1/2): 58–64.

71. Cox, T. L. 1991. The multinational organization. *Academy of Management Executive,* 5(2): 34–47. Without doubt, a great deal has been written on the topic of creating and maintaining an effective diverse workforce. Some excellent, recent books include Harvey, C. P. & Allard, M. J. 2005. *Understanding and managing diversity: Readings, cases, and exercises* (3rd ed.). Upper Saddle River, NJ: Pearson Prentice-Hall; Miller, F. A. & Katz, J. H. 2002. *The inclusion breakthrough: Unleashing the real power of diversity.* San Francisco: Berrett Koehler; and Williams, M. A. 2001. *The 10 lenses: Your guide to living and working in a multicultural world.* Sterling, VA: Capital Books.

72. For an interesting perspective on benefits and downsides of diversity in global consulting firms, refer to Mors, M. L. 2010. Innovation in a global consulting firm: When the problem is too much diversity. *Strategic Management Journal,* 31(8): 841–872.

73. Day, J. C. Undated. National population projections. *cps.ipums .org:* np.

74. Hewlett, S. A. & Rashid, R. 2010. The battle for female talent in emerging markets. *Harvard Business Review,* 88(5): 101–107.

75. This section, including the six potential benefits of a diverse workforce, draws on Cox, T. H. & Blake, S. 1991. Managing cultural diversity: Implications for organizational competitiveness. *Academy of Management Executive,* 5(3): 45–56.

76. *www.pwcglobal.com/us/eng/careers/ diversity/index.html.*

77. Hewlett, S. A., Marshall, M., & Sherbin, L. 2013. How diversity can drive innovation. *Harvard Business Review,* 91(12): 30.

78. This discussion draws on Dess, G. G. & Lumpkin, G. T. 2001. Emerging issues in strategy process research. In Hitt, M. A., Freeman, R. E., & Harrison, J. S. (Eds.), *Handbook of strategic management:* 3–34. Malden, MA: Blackwell.

79. Wong, S.-S. & Boh, W. F. 2010. Leveraging the ties of others to build a reputation for trustworthiness among peers. *Academy of Management Journal,* 53(1): 129–148.

80. Adler, P. S. & Kwon, S. W. 2002. Social capital: Prospects for a new concept. *Academy of Management Review,* 27(1): 17–40.

81. Capelli, P. 2000. A market-driven approach to retaining talent. *Harvard Business Review,* 78(1): 103–113.

82. This hypothetical example draws on Peteraf, M. 1993. The cornerstones of competitive advantage. *Strategic Management Journal,* 14: 179–191.

83. Wernerfelt, B. 1984. A resource-based view of the firm. *Strategic Management Journal,* 5: 171–180.

84. Wysocki, B., Jr. 2000. Yet another hazard of the new economy: The Pied Piper effect. *The Wall Street Journal,* March 20: A1–A16.

85. Ideas on how managers can more effectively use their social network are addressed in McGrath, C. & Zell, D. 2009. Profiles of trust: Who to turn to, and for what. *MIT Sloan Management Review,* 50(2): 75–80.

86. Ibid.

87. Buckman, R. C. 2000. Tech defectors from Microsoft resettle together. *The Wall Street Journal,* October: B1–B6.

88. A study of the relationship between social networks and performance in China is found in Li, J. J., Poppo, L., & Zhou, K. Z. 2008. Do managerial ties in China always produce value? Competition, uncertainty, and domestic vs. foreign firms. *Strategic Management Journal,* 29(4): 383–400.

89. Aime, F., Johnson, S., Ridge, J. W., & Hill, A. D. 2010. The routine may be stable but the advantage is not: Competitive implications of key employee mobility. *Strategic Management Journal,* 31(1): 75–87.

90. Ibarra, H. & Hansen, M. T. 2011. Are you a collaborative leader? *Harvard Business Review,* 89(7/8): 68–74.

91. Battilana, J. & Casciaro, T. 2013. The network secrets of great change agents. *Harvard Business Review,* 91(7/8): 62–68.

92. There has been a tremendous amount of theory building and empirical research in recent years in the area of social network analysis. Unquestionably, two of the major contributors to this domain have been Ronald Burt and J. S. Coleman. For excellent background discussions, refer to Burt, R. S. 1992. *Structural holes: The social structure of competition.* Cambridge, MA: Harvard University Press; Coleman, J. S. 1990. *Foundations of social theory.* Cambridge, MA: Harvard University Press; and Coleman, J. S. 1988. Social capital in the creation of human capital. *American Journal of Sociology,* 94: S95–S120. For a more recent review

and integration of current thought on social network theory, consider Burt, R. S. 2005. *Brokerage & closure: An introduction to social capital.* New York: Oxford Press.

93. Our discussion draws on the concepts developed by Burt, 1992, op. cit.; Coleman, 1990, op. cit.; Coleman, 1988, op. cit.; and Oh, H., Chung, M., & Labianca, G. 2004. Group social capital and group effectiveness: The role of informal socializing ties. *Academy of Management Journal,* 47(6): 860–875. We would like to thank Joe Labianca (University of Kentucky) for his helpful feedback and ideas in our discussion of social networks.

94. Arregle, J. L., Hitt, M. A., Sirmon, D. G., & Very, P. 2007. The development of organizational social capital: Attributes of family firms. *Journal of Management Studies,* 44(1): 73–95.

95. A novel perspective on social networks is in Pentland, A. 2009. How social networks network best. *Harvard Business Review,* 87(2): 37.

96. Oh et al., op. cit.

97. Hoppe, op. cit.

98. This section draws on Hansen, M. T. 2009. *Collaboration: How leaders avoid the traps, create unity, and reap big results.* Boston: Harvard Business Press.

99. Perspectives on how to use and develop decision networks are discussed in Cross, R., Thomas, R. J., & Light, D. A. 2009. How "who you know" affects what you decide. *MIT Sloan Management Review,* 50(2): 35–42.

100. Our discussion of the three advantages of social networks draws on Uzzi, B. & Dunlap. S. 2005. How to build your network. *Harvard Business Review,* 83(12): 53–60. For an excellent review on the research exploring the relationship between social capital and managerial performance, read Moran, P. 2005. Structural vs. relational embeddedness: Social capital and managerial performance. *Strategic Management Journal,* 26(12): 1129–1151.

101. A perspective on personal influence is in Christakis, N. A. 2009. The dynamics of personal influence. *Harvard Business Review,* 87(2): 31.

102. Cross, R. & Thomas, R. 2011. A smarter way to network. *Harvard Business Review,* 89(7/8): 149–153.

103. Prusak, L. & Cohen, D. 2001. How to invest in social capital. *Harvard Business Review,* 79(6): 86–93.

104. Leonard, D. & Straus, S. 1997. Putting your company's whole brain to work. *Harvard Business Review,* 75(4): 110–122.

105. For an excellent discussion of public (i.e., the organization) versus private (i.e., the individual manager) benefits of social capital, refer to Leana, C. R. & Van Buren, H. J. 1999. Organizational social capital and employment practices. *Academy of Management Review,* 24(3): 538–555.

106. The authors would like to thank Joe Labianca, University of Kentucky, and John Lin, University of Texas at Dallas, for their very helpful input in our discussion of social network theory and its practical implications.

107. Goldsmith, M. 2009. How not to lose the top job. *Harvard Business Review,* 87(1): 74.

108. Taylor, W. C. 1999. Whatever happened to globalization? *Fast Company,* December: 228–236.

109. Wilson, H. J., Guinan, P. J., Paris, S., & Weinberg, D. 2011. What's your social media strategy? *Harvard Business Review,* 89(7/8): 23–25.

110. Lei, D., Slocum, J., & Pitts, R. A. 1999. Designing organizations for competitive advantage: The power of unlearning and learning. *Organizational Dynamics,* Winter: 24–38.

111. This section draws upon Zaccaro, S. J. & Bader, P. 2002. E-leadership and the challenges of leading e-teams: Minimizing the bad and maximizing the good. *Organizational Dynamics,* 31(4): 377–387.

112. Kirkman, B. L., Rosen, B., Tesluk, P. E., & Gibson, C. B. 2004. The impact of team empowerment on virtual team performance: The moderating role of face-to-face interaction. *Academy of Management Journal,* 47(2): 175–192.

113. The discussion of the advantages and challenges associated with e-teams draws on Zaccaro & Bader, op. cit.

114. For a study exploring the relationship between team empowerment, face-to-face interaction, and performance in virtual teams, read Kirkman, Rosen, Tesluk, & Gibson, op. cit.

115. For an innovative study on how firms share knowledge with competitors and the performance implications, read Spencer, J. W. 2003. Firms' knowledge sharing strategies in the global innovation system: Empirical evidence from the flat panel display industry. *Strategic Management Journal,* 24(3): 217–235.

116. The examples of Andersen Consulting and Access Health draw upon Hansen, M. T., Nohria, N., & Tierney, T. 1999. What's your strategy for managing knowledge? *Harvard Business Review,* 77(2): 106–118.

117. This discussion draws on Conley, J. G. 2005. *Intellectual capital management.* Kellogg School of Management and Schulich School of Business, York University, Toronto, ON; Conley, J. G. & Szobocsan, J. 2001. Snow White shows the way. *Managing Intellectual Property,* June: 15–25; Greenspan, A. 2004. Intellectual property rights. Federal Reserve Board, Remarks by the chairman, February 27; and

Teece, D. J. 1998. Capturing value from knowledge assets. *California Management Review,* 40(3): 54–79. The authors would like to thank Professor Theo Peridis, York University, for his contribution to this section.

118. Wingfield, N. 2012. As Apple and HTC end lawsuits, smartphone patent battles continue. *New York Times,* www.nytimes.com, November 11: 57–63; and Tyrangiel, J. 2012. Tim Cook's freshman year: The Apple CEO speaks. *Bloomberg Businessweek,* December 6: 62–76.

119. E. Danneels. 2011. Trying to become a different type of company: Dynamic capability at Smith Corona. *Strategic Management Journal,* 32(1): 1–31.

120. A study of the relationship between dynamic capabilities and related diversification is Doving, E. & Gooderham, P. N. 2008. *Strategic Management Journal,* 29(8): 841–858.

121. A perspective on strategy in turbulent markets is in Sull, D. 2009. How to thrive in turbulent markets. *Harvard Business Review,* 87(2): 78–88.

122. Lee, G. K. 2008. Relevance of organizational capabilities and its dynamics: What to learn from entrants' product portfolios about the determinants of entry timing. *Strategic Management Journal,* 29(12): 1257–1280.

123. Eisenhardt, K. M. & Martin, J. E. 2000. Dynamic capabilities: What are they? *Strategic Management Journal,* 21: 1105–1121.

photo credits

Business-Level Strategy
Creating and Sustaining Competitive Advantages

After reading this chapter, you should have a good understanding of the following learning objectives:

LO5.1 The central role of competitive advantage in the study of strategic management and the three generic strategies: overall cost leadership, differentiation, and focus.

LO5.2 How the successful attainment of generic strategies can improve a firm's relative power vis-à-vis the five forces that determine an industry's average profitability.

LO5.3 The pitfalls managers must avoid in striving to attain generic strategies.

LO5.4 How firms can effectively combine the generic strategies of overall cost leadership and differentiation.

LO5.5 What factors determine the sustainability of a firm's competitive advantage.

LO5.6 The importance of considering the industry life cycle to determine a firm's business-level strategy and its relative emphasis on functional area strategies and value-creating activities.

LO5.7 The need for turnaround strategies that enable a firm to reposition its competitive position in an industry.

Learning from Mistakes

Crumbs Bake Shop rode the gourmet cupcake boom to great heights. The company was founded in 2003 in the Upper West Side of New York City by Jason Bauer, who designed and baked giant, high-quality cupcakes with decadent flavors, such as cookie dough, caramel macchiato, and red velvet. The cupcakes came with a hefty calorie count of 600 calories and a premium price of $3.50 to $4.50 each. Crumbs grew quickly from a single bakery in 2003 to nearly 80 bakeries in 10 states by 2013 and hoped to grow to 200 stores by 2014. The firm was honored by *Inc.* magazine as a "breakout company" in 2010. It went public in 2011 and saw its stock price rise to $13 per share. However, as fast as the company rose, it fell even more quickly. The firm lost $18.2 million on $47 million in sales in 2013 and saw its cash reserves dwindle from $6.3 million to $893,000. The chain closed nine stores in late 2013 and six more in early 2014 as managers tried to save the company. However, it all came crashing down in July 2014 when Crumbs was delisted by the NASDAQ Stock Exchange after its stock dropped to 30 cents a share. The firm then filed for bankruptcy and closed all of its remaining 48 stores.[1] What went wrong?

Crumbs experienced two of the pitfalls differentiators can fall into. First, the rapid growth of the company strained its ability to sustain the high quality of its products. As it moved from an entrepreneurial firm in which the entire baking process was overseen by the founder to a publicly traded company in which the baking was done by low-wage workers, customers started to question whether their cupcakes were worth $4.50 each. As one customer, Ari Stern, commented, "It's impossible to control quality when you're worrying about your shareholders instead of your product." Second, customer tastes can be fickle. As a result, a highly desirable differentiated product can fall out of favor before firms can react. Crumbs differentiated itself from other bakeries by offering large, 4-inch cupcakes with rich flavors. While demand for these types of cupcakes took off after they were featured in *Sex in the City,* demand quickly slackened as people became more concerned about the calorie count in them and the gluten-free craze took hold.

Crumbs may not be done yet. The firm emerged from bankruptcy in August 2014 with a new ownership team led by self-styled turnaround guru Marcus Lemonis. The new owners planned to reopen about two dozen Crumbs locations in major cities, such as New York, Los Angeles, Chicago, and Boston.

Discussion Questions

1. What lessons can we take from Crumbs Bake Shop's experience?
2. What actions can Crumbs take to increase its chances of survival in a market that no longer puts as high a premium on high-end cupcakes?

In order to create and sustain a competitive advantage, companies such as Crumbs need to stay focused on their customers' evolving wants and needs and not sacrifice their strategic position as they grow. By becoming too growth-oriented and not focusing on customer needs, Crumbs and many other firms have seen their performance drop and even their existence challenged.

business-level strategy
a strategy designed for a firm or a division of a firm that competes within a single business.

Types of Competitive Advantage and Sustainability

Michael Porter presented three **generic strategies** that a firm can use to overcome the five forces and achieve competitive advantage.[2] Each of Porter's generic strategies has the potential to allow a firm to outperform rivals in their industry. The first, *overall cost leadership,* is based on creating a low-cost position. Here, a firm must manage the relationships throughout the value chain and lower costs throughout the entire chain. Second, *differentiation* requires a firm to create products and/or services that are unique and valued. Here, the primary emphasis is on "nonprice" attributes for which customers will gladly pay a premium.[3] Third, a *focus* strategy directs attention (or "focus") toward narrow product lines, buyer segments, or targeted geographic markets, and they must attain advantages through either differentiation or cost leadership.[4] Whereas the overall cost leadership and differentiation strategies strive to attain advantages industrywide, focusers have a narrow target market in mind. Exhibit 5.1 illustrates these three strategies on two dimensions: competitive advantage and markets served.

Both casual observation and research support the notion that firms that identify with one or more of the forms of competitive advantage outperform those that do not.[5] There has been a rich history of strategic management research addressing this topic. One study analyzed 1,789 strategic business units and found that businesses combining multiple forms of competitive advantage (differentiation and overall cost leadership) outperformed businesses that used only a single form. The lowest performers were those that did not identify with any type of advantage. They were classified as "stuck in the middle." Results of this study are presented in Exhibit 5.2.[6]

For an example of the dangers of being stuck in the middle, consider the traditional supermarket.[7] The major supermarket chains, such as Kroger, Ralphs, and Albertsons, used to be the main source of groceries for consumers. However, they find themselves in a situation today where affluent customers are going upmarket to get their organic and gourmet foods at retailers like Whole Foods Market and budget-conscious consumers are drifting to discount chains such as Walmart, Aldi, and Dollar General.

Overall Cost Leadership

overall cost leadership

a firm's generic strategy based on appeal to the industrywide market using a competitive advantage based on low cost.

The first generic strategy is **overall cost leadership.** Overall cost leadership requires a tight set of interrelated tactics that include:

- Aggressive construction of efficient-scale facilities.
- Vigorous pursuit of cost reductions from experience.

generic strategies

basic types of business-level strategies based on breadth of target market (industrywide versus narrow market segment) and type of competitive advantage (low cost versus uniqueness).

EXHIBIT 5.1 Three Generic Strategies

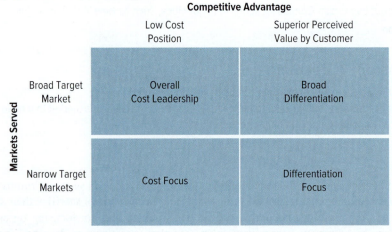

Source: Adapted from *Competitive Strategy: Techniques for Analyzing Industries and Competitors* by Michael E. Porter, 1980, 1998, Free Press.

EXHIBIT 5.2 Competitive Advantage and Business Performance

	Competitive Advantage					
	Differentiation and Cost	Differentiation	Cost	Differentiation and Focus	Cost and Focus	Stuck in the Middle
Performance						
Return on investment (%)	35.5	32.9	30.2	17.0	23.7	17.8
Sales growth (%)	15.1	13.5	13.5	16.4	17.5	12.2
Gain in market share (%)	5.3	5.3	5.5	6.1	6.3	4.4
Sample size	123	160	100	141	86	105

- Tight cost and overhead control.
- Avoidance of marginal customer accounts.
- Cost minimization in all activities in the firm's value chain, such as R&D, service, sales force, and advertising.

Exhibit 5.3 draws on the value-chain concept (see Chapter 3) to provide examples of how a firm can attain an overall cost leadership strategy in its primary and support activities.

One factor often central to an overall cost leadership strategy is the **experience curve,** which refers to how business "learns" to lower costs as it gains experience with production processes. With experience, unit costs of production decline as output increases in most industries. The experience curve, developed by the Boston Consulting Group in 1968, is a way of looking at efficiency gains that come with experience. For a range of products, as cumulative experience doubles, costs and labor hours needed to produce a unit of product decline by 10 to 30 percent. There are a number of reasons why we find this effect. Among the most common factors are workers getting better at what they do, product designs being simplified as the product matures, and production processes being automated and streamlined. However, experience curve gains will be the foundation for a cost advantage only if the firm knows the source of the cost reduction and can keep these gains proprietary.

> **experience curve**
> the decline in unit costs of production as cumulative output increases.

To generate above-average performance, a firm following an overall cost leadership position must attain **competitive parity** on the basis of differentiation relative to competitors.[8] In other words, a firm achieving parity is similar to its competitors, or "on par," with respect to differentiated products.[9] Competitive parity on the basis of differentiation permits a cost leader to translate cost advantages directly into higher profits than competitors. Thus, the cost leader earns above-average returns.[10]

> **competitive parity**
> a firm's achievement of similarity, or being "on par," with competitors with respect to low cost, differentiation, or other strategic product characteristic.

The failure to attain parity on the basis of differentiation can be illustrated with an example from the automobile industry—the ill-fated Yugo. Below is an excerpt from a speech by J. W. Marriott, Jr., chairman of the Marriott Corporation:[11]

> Money is a big thing. But it's not the only thing. In the 1980s, a new automobile reached North America from behind the Iron Curtain. It was called the Yugo, and its main attraction was price. About $3,000 each. But the only way they caught on was as the butt of jokes. Remember the guy who told his mechanic, "I want a gas cap for my Yugo." "OK," the mechanic replied, "that sounds like a fair trade."

Yugo was offering a lousy value proposition. The cars literally fell apart before your eyes. And the lesson was simple. Price is just one component of value. No matter how good the price, the most cost-sensitive consumer won't buy a bad product.

EXHIBIT 5.3

Value-Chain Activities:
Examples of Overall
Cost Leadership

Support Activities

Firm Infrastructure

- Few management layers to reduce overhead costs.
- Standardized accounting practices to minimize personnel required.

Human Resource Management

- Minimize costs associated with employee turnover through effective policies.
- Effective orientation and training programs to maximize employee productivity.

Technology Development

- Effective use of automated technology to reduce scrappage rates.
- Expertise in process engineering to reduce manufacturing costs.

Procurement

- Effective policy guidelines to ensure low-cost raw materials (with acceptable quality levels).
- Shared purchasing operations with other business units.

Primary Activities

Inbound Logistics

- Effective layout of receiving dock operations.

Operations

- Effective use of quality control inspectors to minimize rework.

Outbound Logistics

- Effective utilization of delivery fleets.

Marketing and Sales

- Purchase of media in large blocks.
- Sales-force utilization is maximized by territory management.

Service

- Thorough service repair guidelines to minimize repeat maintenance calls.
- Use of single type of vehicle to minimize repair costs.

Source: Adapted from Porter, M. E. 1985. *Competitive Advantage: Creating and Sustaining Superior Performance.* New York: Free Press.

Gordon Bethune, the former CEO of Continental Airlines, summed up the need to provide good products or services when employing a low-cost strategy this way: "You can make a pizza so cheap, nobody will buy it."[12]

Next, we discuss some examples of how firms enhance a cost leadership position.

Aldi, a discount supermarket retailer, has grown from its German base to the rest of Europe, Australia, and the United States by replicating a simple business format. Aldi limits the number of products (SKUs in the grocery business) in each category to ensure product turn, to ease stocking shelves, and to increase its power over suppliers. It also sells mostly private-label products to minimize cost. It has small, efficient, and simply designed stores. It offers limited services and expects customers to bring their own bags and bag their own groceries. As a result, Aldi can offer its products at prices 40 percent lower than competing supermarkets.[13]

Tesco, Britain's largest grocery retailer, has changed how it views waste in order to become more efficient. To cut its costs, Tesco has begun shipping off food waste to

RENAULT FINDS LOW COST WORKS WELL IN THE NEW EUROPE

The European economic crisis has changed how Renault, a French carmaker, designs and produces cars for European customers. Historically, European car buyers have been sophisticated, demanding well-designed, feature-laden cars from manufacturers. When the economic crisis hit Europe in 2007, automakers saw a dramatic shift in demand. Overall demand dropped, and the customers who did come in to buy became much more cost-conscious.

In these difficult conditions, Renault has been able to carve out a profitable market for itself, selling low-cost, no-frills cars. Renault responded to this shift by creating an entry-level car group that was charged with designing and producing cars for these more cost-conscious consumers. For example, the group took an ultra-cheap car, the Logan, that was originally aimed for emerging markets and redesigned it to meet the new needs of the European market. The boxy sedan, which sells for around $10,000, is now one of Renault's best sellers. Its entry-level cars accounted for 30 percent of the cars sold by Renault in 2011 and generated operating profit margins over twice the profit margins of the higher-priced cars Renault sold.

What is the recipe for success Renault has found to generate high profits on low-priced cars? It uses simple designs that incorporate components from older car designs at Renault and employs a no-discount retail policy. At the center of its design procedure is a "design-to-cost" philosophy. In this process, designers and engineers no longer strive for the cutting edge. Instead, they focus on choosing parts and materials for simplicity, ease of manufacturing, and availability. This often involves using components that were engineered for prior vehicle designs. When needing a new component, Renault begins by assessing how much customers would be willing to pay for certain features, such as air conditioning or power door locks, and then asks suppliers whether they can propose a way to offer this feature at a cost that matches what customers are willing to pay.

As it faces imitation of this strategy by Volkswagen and Toyota, Renault is not sitting idle. As Carlos Ghosn, Renault's CEO, stated, "Our low-cost offering isn't low-cost enough. So we're working on a new platform that will be ultra low-cost."

Sources: Pearson, D. 2012. Renault takes low-cost lead. *wsj.com,* April 16: np; and Ciferri, L. 2013. How Renault's low-cost Dacia has become a "cash cow." *Automotive News Europe,* January 3: np.

---

bioenergy plants to convert the waste onto electricity. This allows Tesco to both avoid landfill taxes of $98 per ton and also save on the cost of its electricity by providing the fuel for the power plant. Tesco is saving $3 million a year alone in landfill taxes by simply sending its used cooking oil and chicken fat to be used to generate bioenergy rather than putting it in a landfill. Overall, Tesco estimates that energy-saving efforts are shaving over $300 million a year from its energy bills.[14]

Zulily, an online retailer, has built its business model around lower-cost operations in order to carve out a unique position relative to Amazon and other online retailers. Zulily keeps very little inventory and typically orders products from vendors only when customers purchase the product. It also has developed a bare-bones distribution system. Together, these actions result in deliveries that take an average of 11.5 days to get to customers and can sometimes stretch out to several weeks. Due to its reduced operational costs, Zulily is able to offer attractive prices to customers who are willing to wait.[15]

A business that strives for a low-cost advantage must attain an absolute cost advantage relative to its rivals.[16] This is typically accomplished by offering a no-frills product or service to a broad target market using standardization to derive the greatest benefits from economies of scale and experience. However, such a strategy may fail if a firm is unable to attain parity on important dimensions of differentiation such as quick responses to customer requests for services or design changes. Strategy Spotlight 5.1 discusses how Renault is leveraging a low-cost strategy to draw in auto buyers in Europe.

Overall Cost Leadership: Improving Competitive Position vis-à-vis the Five Forces An overall low-cost position enables a firm to achieve above-average returns despite strong competition. It protects a firm against rivalry from competitors, because lower costs allow a firm to earn returns even if its competitors eroded their profits through intense rivalry. A low-cost position also protects firms against powerful buyers. Buyers can exert power to drive down prices only to the level of the next most efficient producer. Also, a low-cost position provides more flexibility to cope with demands from powerful suppliers for input cost

LO5.2

How the successful attainment of generic strategies can improve a firm's relative power vis-à-vis the five forces that determine an industry's average profitability.

increases. The factors that lead to a low-cost position also provide a substantial entry barriers position with respect to substitute products introduced by new and existing competitors.[17]

A few examples will illustrate these points. Zulily's close attention to costs helps to protect the company from buyer power and intense rivalry from competitors. Thus, Zulily is able to drive down costs and reduce the bargaining power of its customers. By increasing productivity and lowering unit costs, Renault both lessens the degree of rivalry it faces and increases entry barriers for new entrants. Aldi's extreme focus on minimizing costs across its operations makes it less vulnerable to substitutes, such as discount retailers like Walmart and dollar stores.

LO5.3

The pitfalls managers must avoid in striving to attain generic strategies.

Potential Pitfalls of Overall Cost Leadership Strategies   Potential pitfalls of an overall cost leadership strategy include:

- ***Too much focus on one or a few value-chain activities.*** Would you consider a person to be astute if he canceled his newspaper subscription and quit eating out to save money but then "maxed out" several credit cards, requiring him to pay hundreds of dollars a month in interest charges? Of course not. Similarly, firms need to pay attention to all activities in the value chain.[18] Too often managers make big cuts in operating expenses but don't question year-to-year spending on capital projects. Or managers may decide to cut selling and marketing expenses but ignore manufacturing expenses. Managers should explore *all* value-chain activities, including relationships among them, as candidates for cost reductions.

- ***Increase in the cost of the inputs on which the advantage is based.*** Firms can be vulnerable to price increases in the factors of production. For example, consider manufacturing firms based in China that rely on low labor costs. Due to demographic factors, the supply of workers 16 to 24 years old has peaked and will drop by a third in the next 12 years, thanks to stringent family-planning policies that have sharply reduced China's population growth.[19] This is leading to upward pressure on labor costs in Chinese factories, undercutting the cost advantage of firms producing there.

- ***A strategy that can be imitated too easily.*** One of the common pitfalls of a cost leadership strategy is that a firm's strategy may consist of value-creating activities that are easy to imitate.[20] Such has been the case with online brokers in recent years.[21] As of early 2015, there were over 200 online brokers listed on allstocks.com, hardly symbolic of an industry where imitation is extremely difficult. And according to Henry McVey, financial services analyst at Morgan Stanley, "We think you need five to ten" online brokers.

- ***A lack of parity on differentiation.*** As noted earlier, firms striving to attain cost leadership advantages must obtain a level of parity on differentiation.[22] Firms providing online degree programs may offer low prices. However, they may not be successful unless they can offer instruction that is perceived as comparable to traditional providers. For them, parity can be achieved on differentiation dimensions such as reputation and quality and through signaling mechanisms such as accreditation agencies.

- ***Reduced flexibility.*** Building up a low-cost advantage often requires significant investments in plant and equipment, distribution systems, and large, economically scaled operations. As a result, firms often find that these investments limit their flexibility, leading to great difficulty responding to changes in the environment. For example, Coors Brewing developed a highly efficient, large-scale brewery in Golden, Colorado. Coors was one of the most efficient brewers in the world, but its plant was designed to mass-produce one or two types of beer. When the craft brewing craze started to grow, the plant was not well equipped to produce smaller batches of craft beer, and Coors found it difficult to meet this opportunity. Ultimately, Coors had to buy its way into this movement by acquiring small craft breweries.[23]

- **Obsolescence of the basis of cost advantage.** Ultimately, the foundation of a firm's cost advantage may become obsolete. In such circumstances, other firms develop new ways of cutting costs, leaving the old cost leaders at a significant disadvantage. The older cost leaders are often locked into their way of competing and are unable to respond to the newer, lower-cost means of competing. This is what happened to the U.S. auto industry in the 1970s. Ford, GM, and Chrysler had built up efficient mass-manufacturing auto plants. However, when Toyota and other Japanese manufacturers moved into the North American car market using lean manufacturing, a new and more efficient means of production, the U.S. firms found themselves at a significant cost disadvantage. It took the U.S. firms over 30 years to redesign and retool their plants and restructure the responsibilities of line workers to get to a position where they were on cost parity with the Japanese firms.

Differentiation

As the name implies, a **differentiation strategy** consists of creating differences in the firm's product or service offering by creating something that is perceived *industrywide* as unique and valued by customers.[24] Differentiation can take many forms:

- Prestige or brand image (Hotel Monaco, BMW automobiles).[25]
- Quality (Apple, Ruth's Chris steak houses, Michelin tires).
- Technology (Martin guitars, Marantz stereo components, North Face camping equipment).
- Innovation (Medtronic medical equipment, Apple's iPhones and iPads).
- Features (Cannondale mountain bikes, Honda Goldwing motorcycles).
- Customer service (Nordstrom department stores, USAA financial services).
- Dealer network (Lexus automobiles, Caterpillar earthmoving equipment).

Exhibit 5.4 draws on the concept of the value chain as an example of how firms may differentiate themselves in primary and support activities.

Firms may differentiate themselves along several different dimensions at once.[26] For example, the Cheesecake Factory, an upscale casual restaurant, differentiates itself by offering high-quality food, the widest and deepest menu in its class of restaurants, and premium locations.[27]

Firms achieve and sustain differentiation advantages and attain above-average performance when their price premiums exceed the extra costs incurred in being unique.[28] For example, the Cheesecake Factory must increase consumer prices to offset the higher cost of premium real estate and producing such a wide menu. Thus, a differentiator will always seek out ways of distinguishing itself from similar competitors to justify price premiums greater than the costs incurred by differentiating.[29] Clearly, a differentiator cannot ignore costs. After all, its premium prices would be eroded by a markedly inferior cost position. Therefore, it must attain a level of cost *parity* relative to competitors. Differentiators can do this by reducing costs in all areas that do not affect differentiation. Porsche, for example, invests heavily in engine design—an area in which its customers demand excellence—but it is less concerned and spends fewer resources in the design of the instrument panel or the arrangement of switches on the radio.[30] Although a differentiation firm needs to be mindful of costs, it must also regularly and consistently reinforce the foundations of its differentiation advantage. In doing so, the firm builds a stronger reputation for differentiation, and this reputation can be an enduring source of advantage in its market.[31] As seen

differentiation strategy
a firm's generic strategy based on creating differences in the firm's product or service offering by creating something that is perceived *industrywide* as unique and valued by customers.

EXHIBIT 5.4

Value-Chain Activities:
Examples of
Differentiation

Support Activities

Firm Infrastructure

- Superior MIS—to integrate value-creating activities to improve quality.
- Facilities that promote firm image.
- Widely respected CEO who enhances firm reputation.

Human Resource Management

- Programs to attract talented engineers and scientists.
- Provision of training and incentives to ensure a strong customer service orientation.

Technology Development

- Superior material handling and sorting technology.
- Excellent applications engineering support.

Procurement

- Purchase of high-quality components to enhance product image.
- Use of most-prestigious outlets.

Primary Activities

Inbound Logistics

- Superior material handling operations to minimize damage.
- Quick transfer of inputs to manufacturing process.

Operations

- Flexibility and speed in responding to changes in manufacturing specifications.
- Low defect rates to improve quality.

Outbound Logistics

- Accurate and responsive order processing.
- Effective product replenishment to reduce customer inventory.

Marketing and Sales

- Creative and innovative advertising programs.
- Fostering of personal relationship with key customers.

Service

- Rapid response to customer service requests.
- Complete inventory of replacement parts and supplies.

Source: Adapted from Porter, M. E. 1985. *Competitive Advantage: Creating and Sustaining Superior Performance.*
New York: Free Press.

in Spotlight 5.2, Quiznos is a firm that provided mixed messages to its customers as to how focused the firm was on retaining a differentiated advantage, and this led to declining performance that ultimately resulted in bankruptcy.

Many companies successfully follow a differentiation strategy. For example, Zappos may sell shoes, but it sees the core element of its differentiation advantage as service. Zappos CEO Tony Hsieh puts it this way:[32]

We hope that 10 years from now people won't even realize that we started out selling shoes online, and that when you say "Zappos," they'll think, "Oh, that's the place with the

QUIZNOS LOSES ITS EDGE

Quiznos was once one of the fastest-growing quick-service restaurants in the world. Founded in 1981, the chain had grown to nearly 5,000 restaurants worldwide by 2008. The secret to the chain's success was its subs. It built its reputation for differentiated subs by using a unique toasting technique and offering meatier subs than its competitors. But three factors led to a quick decline in the firm's differentiation and its financial performance. First, when the Great Recession hit in 2008, Quiznos entered into a price competition with Subway. This was damaging to the firm on two levels. It eroded the chain's differentiation image. Additionally, since it had a higher cost structure than Subway, the price war left it financially wounded. Second, Quiznos did not reinforce its differentiation advantage with an adequate marketing campaign, leading to a decline in customer perceptions about the chain. Third, the chain had a very tense relationship with its franchisees. Franchisee groups sued Quiznos, claiming the chain overcharged them for supplies and provided insufficient marketing. Due to their concerns and also the financial distress they faced, franchisees did not heavily invest in their stores, thus reinforcing the perception that Quiznos was no longer a premium, differentiated sub chain. In 2012, Quiznos reversed course and tried to reassert its product differentiation by introducing a new menu that included artisan breads, all-natural chicken, natural cheeses, and raw vegetables. But the damage was done, and Quiznos found it hard to rebuild its reputation with customers.

While Quiznos struggled, competing chains pushed forward with their own differentiation elements. For example, Jimmy John's emphasized its speedy service, and Potbelly Sandwich Shops positioned itself as the chain with better condiments, side elements such as milkshakes, and a restaurant environment that feels more like a coffee shop, even at times including a musician in the corner. Thus, as Quiznos slid in customers' eyes, other firms were willing to step in and take its place. Quiznos now has less than half the stores it once had and filed for bankruptcy in March 2014.

Quiznos serves as a cautionary tale of what happens when a differentiation-oriented firm fails to reinforce its differentiation over time and across all elements of its value chain. By entering into a price war with Subway, Quiznos eroded its own image with customers and the value of its brand. By not building strong, cooperative relationships with its franchisees, Quiznos limited the franchisees' willingness to invest in the restaurants and in the service they provided customers. As Elizabeth Friend, a senior food service analyst at Euromonitor International, states, "It's hard to remain successful and implement new menu items if you can't keep the franchisees happy. It speaks to there being something broken in the basic business model."

Sources: Zillman, C. 2014. Quiznos and Potbelly: A tale of two sandwich chains. *CNNMoney.com*, March 18: np; and Jargon, J. & Glazer, E. 2014. Crisis quickens at Quiznos. *wsj.com*, December 6: np.

absolute best customer service." And that doesn't even have to be limited to being an online experience. We've had customers email us and ask us if we would please start an airline, or run the IRS.

This emphasis on service has led to great success. Growing from an idea to a billion-dollar company in only a dozen years, Zappos is seeing the benefits of providing exemplary service. In Insights from Research, we see that firms are better able to provide excellent customer service when corporate leaders model a service orientation and customer service representatives are given the latitude to react genuinely and creatively with customers.

 INSIGHTS **FROM RESEARCH**

SERVICE REPRESENTATIVES MUST GET REAL WITH CUSTOMERS

Overview

Customer service organizations expect their representatives to act in positive ways toward customers, even if they have to manufacture the positive interactions. Yet standardizing these expectations can create internal psychological conflicts in employees, so companies benefit from experimenting with alternatives.

What the Research Shows

Psychologists have long understood that people have a strong need for genuine self-expression and authentic functioning. In a 2013 study, researchers at the University of Haifa and the Academic College of Tel-Aviv-Yaffo acknowledge that customer service representatives must do a great deal of "acting" to complete positive service encounters with customers.

continued

They used a grounded theory approach in their article, published in the *Academy of Management Journal*. This entailed interviewing 44 employees from 27 organizations providing cellular and Internet services, along with a few employees from travel agencies.

The research reveals that employees were drawn to being sincere with customers if they associated with them personally or if the employees had a strong identification with the company's message or product. In these genuine interactions, the employees spontaneously expressed their natural emotions with authentic behaviors such as being completely honest with customers or performing above and beyond what the company expected. Most of the genuine interactions were positive. However, if the employees' behavior was in conflict with the organization's rules and expectations, the employees felt strong internal conflicts, including a sense of disloyalty to the company.

Why This Matters

To ensure standard and pleasant customer service experiences, executives of many organizations tightly control employee interactions with rules, scripts, and monitoring. For example, in 2009, researchers from the University of Central Oklahoma found that if a complaint letter was sent to American Airlines, an automatic "apology" letter was sent to the customer. Each letter was exactly the same, leaving no opportunity for an authentic reaction to the customer's dissatisfaction, further devaluing the customer's experience. These types of scripted responses tend to drive employees into distancing their real emotions from their encounters with customers and becoming "numb" to their authentic feelings. These coping mechanisms are harmful to the psychological well-being of the employees and often result in behaviors counterproductive to the company's aim.

Business leaders in customer service organizations would be better served by focusing less on controlling the service interaction and more on creating a positive disposition toward customers. Then, in unpredictable situations, employees will behave in genuinely positive ways. Here is a near-perfect real-life example: Jia Jiang is afraid of rejection and decided to beat his fear by going to different shops, restaurants, and so forth, and making outrageous requests that readily deserve a "No, we can't do that" response, all the while secretly videoing all interactions for his You-Tube channel. Jiang experienced an above-and-beyond customer-care moment when he walked into a Krispy Kreme Doughnuts store and requested that a doughnut shaped like an Olympic symbol, featuring accurate frosting colors, be made especially for him—within 15 minutes. Krispy Kreme employee Jackie met Jia Jiang's challenge, apologized for the doughnut not looking as perfect as she wished, and didn't charge him since it didn't meet her own expectations for the company's product. This video went viral, and Krispy Kreme publicists seized the opportunity to make a Twitter shout-out to Jackie, thanking her for her fantastic customer care.

How can you utilize social media to encourage such excellent customer care?

Former Wachovia Corp. CEO Ken Thompson said, "If [a great service culture] is not important to the CEO, it won't be important to others in the company." As a leader, you have the ability to set the example for your employees' interactions with customers. Try rewarding your employees for every positive comment they make about a customer. Additionally, Greg Gianforte, founder and CEO of RightNow Technologies Inc., says product and customer knowledge allow employees to have a personal experience with the customers, focusing on their core needs more quickly.

Key Takeaways

- Requiring employees to obey rules about behaving positively toward customers may cause them to become "numb" to their real feelings or to experience negative inner conflicts.
- Rewarding employees for being positive with customers may cause their behavior to be externally motivated rather than genuine.
- Employees act in genuine ways toward customers when they have a strong personal association with the customer or a strong personal identification with the task.
- When employees act in genuine ways toward customers, they may experience a sense of disloyalty to the company if their actions are in conflict with organizational expectations.
- When employees act in genuine ways toward customers, they may experience social rejection if their actions are in conflict with customers' expectations.
- A positive disposition toward customers must be modeled and rewarded by leaders.

Apply This Today

Superb service begins with leaders. Create a positive response to customers, reward employees who emulate it, and ensure that employees have the knowledge to exceed customers' expectations. To learn more, visit businessminded.com.

Research Reviewed

Walker, H. J., Bauer, T.N., Cole, M.S., Bernerth, J. B., Field, H. S., & Short, J. C. 2013. Is this how I will be treated? Reducing uncertainty through recruitment interactions. *Academy of Management Journal,* 56(5): 1325–1347. We thank Matthew Gilley, Ph.D., of *businessminded.com* for contributing this Research Brief.

CROWDSOURCING FOR DIFFERENTIATION IDEAS: UNILEVER'S EFFORTS TO PROPEL FORWARD ITS SUSTAINABILITY INITIATIVES

Unilever, a global manufacturer of consumer products such as Dove soap, Ben and Jerry's ice cream, Lipton ice tea, Axe deodorants, and many other widely used products, is aiming to lead the market in its ability to run a sustainable business enterprise. As part of this effort, the company published its Sustainable Living Plan in November 2010. Included in this plan were Unilever's ambitious goals to reduce its environmental footprint by 50 percent and source all of its agricultural inputs from sustainable growers by 2020.

Knowing that these goals will be challenging to achieve, Unilever turned to the power of the crowd to develop initiatives to meet these targets. In April 2012, it hosted a 24-hour global crowdsourcing event, called the Sustainable Living Lab, to generate creative ideas on how to improve Unilever's sustainability. Speaking of the challenges facing Unilever as it strives to lead the market in sustainability, Miguel Pestana, VP of Global External Affairs at Unilever, stated, "We can't solve these issues on our own. We need to engage with civil society, companies, government, and other key stakeholders." Unilever designed the lab as an invitation-only event where it would get input from sustainability leaders and experts. The response it received from invited participants was very positive, with over 2,200 individuals, including over 100 Unilever managers, coming together to co-create ideas and solutions to advance Unilever's agenda of increasing the sustainability of its business and product line. Unilever hosted discussion groups on four broad topics that encompassed activities across the company's entire value chain. The topics discussed were sustainable sourcing, sustainable production and distribution, consumer behavior change, and recycling and waste.

The boards generated a large volume of discussion and also triggered a follow-up survey completed by over 400 participants. Unilever then used the discussions as a basis for extending current partnerships and developing new ones with participating firms and organizations to help it achieve its sustainability goals.

Unilever's efforts for sustainability appear to be paying off. According to a GlobalScan survey, Unilever is the corporate leader in sustainability, being ranked the top firm by 33 sustainability experts, nearly four times as frequently as the second-highest-mentioned firm.

Sources: Holme, C. 2012. How Unilever crowdsourced creativity to meet its sustainability goals. *Greenbiz.com,* June 7, np; Peluso, M. 2012. Unilever to crowdsource sustainability. *MarketingWeek,* April 10, np; and Coulter, C. & Guenther, C. 2014. The expert view: Top corporate sustainability leaders of 2014. *Theguardian.com,* May 14: np.

Strategy Spotlight 5.3 discusses how Unilever, a global consumer products firm, uses crowdsourcing to differentiate itself through increased sustainability.

Differentiation: Improving Competitive Position vis-à-vis the Five Forces   Differentiation provides protection against rivalry since brand loyalty lowers customer sensitivity to price and raises customer switching costs.[33] By increasing a firm's margins, differentiation also avoids the need for a low-cost position. Higher entry barriers result because of customer loyalty and the firm's ability to provide uniqueness in its products or services.[34] Differentiation also provides higher margins that enable a firm to deal with supplier power. And it reduces buyer power, because buyers lack comparable alternatives and are therefore less price-sensitive.[35] Supplier power is also decreased because there is a certain amount of prestige associated with being the supplier to a producer of highly differentiated products and services. Last, differentiation enhances customer loyalty, thus reducing the threat from substitutes.[36]

Our examples illustrate these points. Porsche has enjoyed enhanced power over buyers because its strong reputation makes buyers more willing to pay a premium price. This lessens rivalry, since buyers become less price-sensitive. The prestige associated with its brand name also lowers supplier power since margins are high. Suppliers would probably desire to be associated with prestige brands, thus lessening their incentives to drive up prices. Finally, the loyalty and "peace of mind" associated with a service provider such as Zappos makes such firms less vulnerable to rivalry or substitute products and services.

Potential Pitfalls of Differentiation Strategies   Potential pitfalls of a differentiation strategy include:

- *Uniqueness that is not valuable.* A differentiation strategy must provide unique bundles of products and/or services that customers value highly. It's not enough just to be "different." An example is Gibson's Dobro bass guitar. Gibson came up with a unique idea: Design and build an acoustic bass guitar with sufficient sound volume so that amplification wasn't necessary. The problem with other acoustic bass guitars was that they did not project enough volume because of the low-frequency bass notes. By adding a resonator plate on the body of the traditional acoustic bass, Gibson increased the sound volume. Gibson believed this product would serve a particular niche market—bluegrass and folk artists who played in small group "jams" with other acoustic musicians. Unfortunately, Gibson soon discovered that its targeted market was content with the existing options: an upright bass amplified with a microphone or an acoustic electric guitar. Thus, Gibson developed a unique product, but it was not perceived as valuable by its potential customers.[37]

- *Too much differentiation.* Firms may strive for quality or service that is higher than customers desire.[38] Thus, they become vulnerable to competitors that provide an appropriate level of quality at a lower price. For example, consider the expensive Mercedes-Benz S-Class, which ranged in price between $93,650 and $138,000 for the 2011 models.[39] *Consumer Reports* described it as "sumptuous," "quiet and luxurious," and a "delight to drive." The magazine also considered it to be the least reliable sedan available in the United States. According to David Champion, who runs the testing program, the problems are electronic. "The engineers have gone a little wild," he says. "They've put every bell and whistle that they think of, and sometimes they don't have the attention to detail to make these systems work." Some features include a computer-driven suspension that reduces body roll as the vehicle whips around a corner; cruise control that automatically slows the car down if it gets too close to another car; and seats that are adjustable 14 ways and are ventilated by a system that uses eight fans.

- *Too high a price premium.* This pitfall is quite similar to too much differentiation. Customers may desire the product, but they are repelled by the price premium. For example, Duracell recently charged too much for batteries.[40] The firm tried to sell consumers on its superior-quality products, but the mass market wasn't convinced. Why? The price differential was simply too high. At one CVS drugstore, a four-pack of Energizer AA batteries was on sale at $2.99 compared with a Duracell four-pack at $4.59. Duracell's market share dropped 2 percent in a recent two-year period, and its profits declined over 30 percent. Clearly, the price/performance proposition Duracell offered customers was not accepted.

- *Differentiation that is easily imitated.* As we noted in Chapter 3, resources that are easily imitated cannot lead to sustainable advantages. Similarly, firms may strive for, and even attain, a differentiation strategy that is successful for a time. However, the advantages are eroded through imitation. Consider Cereality's innovative differentiation strategy of stores that offer a wide variety of cereals and toppings for around $4.[41] As one would expect, once the idea proved successful, competitors entered the market because much of the initial risk had already been taken. These new competitors included stores with the following names: the Cereal Cabinet, The Cereal Bowl, and Bowls: A Cereal Joint. Says David Roth, one of Cereality's founders: "With any good business idea, you're faced with people who see you've cracked the code and who try to cash in on it."

- *Dilution of brand identification through product-line extensions.* Firms may erode their quality brand image by adding products or services with lower prices and less quality. Although this can increase short-term revenues, it may be detrimental in the long run. Consider Gucci.[42] In the 1980s Gucci wanted to capitalize on its prestigious brand name by launching an aggressive strategy of revenue growth. It added a set of lower-priced canvas goods to its product line. It also pushed goods heavily into department stores and duty-free channels and allowed its name to appear on a host of licensed items such as watches, eyeglasses, and perfumes. In the short term, this strategy worked. Sales soared. However, the strategy carried a high price. Gucci's indiscriminate approach to expanding its products and channels tarnished its sterling brand. Sales of its high-end goods (with higher profit margins) fell, causing profits to decline.

Overall Cost Leadership
• Too much focus on one or a few value-chain activities.
• Increase in the cost of the inputs on which the advantage is based.
• A strategy that can be imitated too easily.
• A lack of parity on differentiation.
• Reduced flexibility.
• Obsolescence of the basis of cost advantage.

Differentiation
• Uniqueness that is not valuable.
• Too much differentiation.
• A price premium that is too high.
• Differentiation that is easily imitated.
• Dilution of brand identification through product-line extensions.
• Perceptions of differentiation that vary between buyers and sellers.

EXHIBIT 5.5
Potential Pitfalls of Overall Cost Leadership and Differentiation Strategies

- *Perceptions of differentiation that vary between buyers and sellers.* The issue here is that "beauty is in the eye of the beholder." Companies must realize that although they may perceive their products and services as differentiated, their customers may view them as commodities. Indeed, in today's marketplace, many products and services have been reduced to commodities.[43] Thus, a firm could overprice its offerings and lose margins altogether if it has to lower prices to reflect market realities.

Exhibit 5.5 summarizes the pitfalls of overall cost leadership and differentiation strategies. In addressing the pitfalls associated with these two generic strategies, there is one common, underlying theme: Managers must be aware of the dangers associated with concentrating so much on one strategy that they fail to attain parity on the other.

Focus

A **focus strategy** is based on the choice of a narrow competitive scope within an industry. A firm following this strategy selects a segment or group of segments and tailors its strategy to serve them. The essence of focus is the exploitation of a particular market niche. As you might expect, narrow focus itself (like merely "being different" as a differentiator) is simply not sufficient for above-average performance.

The focus strategy, as indicated in Exhibit 5.1, has two variants. In a cost focus, a firm strives to create a cost advantage in its target segment. In a differentiation focus, a firm seeks to differentiate in its target market. Both variants of the focus strategy rely on providing better service than broad-based competitors that are trying to serve the focuser's target segment. Cost focus exploits differences in cost behavior in some segments, while differentiation focus exploits the special needs of buyers in other segments.

Let's look at examples of two firms that have successfully implemented focus strategies. LinkedIn has staked out a position as the business social media site of choice. Rather than compete with Facebook head on, LinkedIn created a strategy that focuses on individuals who wish to share their business experience and make connections with individuals with whom they share or could potentially share business ties. In doing so, it has created an extremely strong business model. LinkedIn monetizes its user information in three ways: subscription fees from some users, advertising fees, and recruiter fees. The first two are fairly standard for social media sites, but the advertising fees are higher for LinkedIn since

focus strategy
a firm's generic strategy based on appeal to a narrow market segment within an industry.

LUXURY IN THE E-COMMERCE WORLD

Traditionally, luxury retailers have relied on high levels of personal touch in their stores as well as a sense of exclusivity in order to differentiate themselves from the mass retail markets. As a result, many luxury retailers have looked on the Internet retail market skeptically, thinking it didn't fit their products and the needs of their customers. Rather than offering an indulgent and exclusive retail experience, the Internet promotes accessibility and efficiency. Yoox, an Italian firm, appears to have solved the mystery of how to turn e-commerce into a luxury experience. Yoox designs and manages online stores for nearly 40 luxury brands, including Armani, Diesel, Emilio Pucci, and Brunello Cucinelli. In 2013, the firm booked over 3 million orders for over 1 million customers in 100 countries, generating $563 million in sales and $15.6 million in net income.

How has Yoox translated the luxury retail experience to the online world? Its expertise at creating the right experience cuts across the value chain. First, Yoox views itself as a craftsperson, designing each website specifically to the brand. Second, it focuses on the details. This includes training its 60 photographers to create images for each product that match the specific guidelines of each brand. For one clothing retailer, this included using flamenco dancers in its designer images, rather than fashion models. The attention to detail flows through to the packaging. Packers at Yoox's five fulfillment centers are trained on the specific angle of the ribbons for a box containing an Alexander Wang dress versus one containing a Bottega Veneta bag. Third, Yoox has developed innovative algorithms to predict which products will sell at which times and in which geographic regions, allowing effective stocking to meet the needs of customers and providing guidance to retailers on optimal pricing. Finally, Yoox has insisted on exclusive contracts with luxury brands to ensure that it can control the brands' images in the online retail space. These luxury brands have grown reliant on Yoox. About one-third of Yoox's revenue derives from the creation and management of the luxury brands' websites, while the remainder comes from its order-fulfillment services.

Sources: Fairchild, C. 2014. A luxe look for e-commerce. *Fortune,* June 16: 83–84; and Clark, N. 2014. Success draws competition for luxury e-retailer Yoox. *nytimes. com,* December 6: np.

---

the ads can be more effectively targeted as a result of LinkedIn's focus. The third income source is fairly unique for LinkedIn. Headhunters and human resource departments pay significant user fees, up to $8,200 a year, to have access to LinkedIn's recruiting search engine, which can sift through LinkedIn profiles to identify individuals with desired skills and experiences. The power of this business model can be seen in the difference in user value for LinkedIn when compared to Facebook. For every hour that a user spends on the site, LinkedIn generates $1.30 in income. For Facebook, it is a paltry 6.2 cents.[44]

Marlin Steel Wire Products, a Baltimore-based manufacturing company, has also seen great benefit from developing a niche-differentiator strategy. Marlin, a manufacturer of commodity wire products, faced stiff and ever-increasing competition from rivals based in China and other emerging markets. These rivals had labor-based cost advantages that Marlin found hard to counter. Marlin responded by changing the game it played. Drew Greenblatt, Marlin's president, decided to go upmarket, automating his production and specializing in high-end products. For example, Marlin produces antimicrobial baskets for restaurant kitchens and exports its products globally. Marlin provides products to customers in 36 countries and, in 2012, was listed as the 162nd fastest-growing private manufacturing company in the United States.[45]

Strategy Spotlight 5.4 illustrates how Yoox has carved out a profitable niche in the online retailing world as a luxury goods provider.

Focus: Improving Competitive Position vis-à-vis the Five Forces   Focus requires that a firm have either a low-cost position with its strategic target, high differentiation, or both. As we discussed with regard to cost and differentiation strategies, these positions provide defenses against each competitive force. Focus is also used to select niches that are least vulnerable to substitutes or where competitors are weakest.

Let's look at our examples to illustrate some of these points. First, by providing a platform for a targeted customer group, businesspeople, to share key work information, LinkedIn insulated itself from rivalrous pressure from existing social networks, such as

Facebook. It also felt little threat from new generalist social networks, such as Google +. Similarly, the new focus of Marlin Steel lessened the power of buyers since the company provides specialized products. Also, it is insulated from competitors, which manufacture the commodity products Marlin used to produce.

Potential Pitfalls of Focus Strategies   Potential pitfalls of focus strategies include:

- *Cost advantages may erode within the narrow segment.* The advantages of a cost focus strategy may be fleeting if the cost advantages are eroded over time. For example, early pioneers in online education, such as the University of Phoenix, have faced increasing challenges as traditional universities have entered with their own online programs that allow them to match the cost benefits associated with online delivery systems. Similarly, other firms have seen their profit margins drop as competitors enter their product segment.

- *Even product and service offerings that are highly focused are subject to competition from new entrants and from imitation.* Some firms adopting a focus strategy may enjoy temporary advantages because they select a small niche with few rivals. However, their advantages may be short-lived. A notable example is the multitude of dot-com firms that specialize in very narrow segments such as pet supplies, ethnic foods, and vintage automobile accessories. The entry barriers tend to be low, there is little buyer loyalty, and competition becomes intense. And since the marketing strategies and technologies employed by most rivals are largely nonproprietary, imitation is easy. Over time, revenues fall, profits margins are squeezed, and only the strongest players survive the shakeout.

- *Focusers can become too focused to satisfy buyer needs.* Some firms attempting to attain advantages through a focus strategy may have too narrow a product or service. Consider many retail firms. Hardware chains such as Ace and True Value are losing market share to rivals such as Lowe's and Home Depot that offer a full line of home and garden equipment and accessories. And given the enormous purchasing power of the national chains, it would be difficult for such specialty retailers to attain parity on costs.

Combination Strategies: Integrating Overall Low Cost and Differentiation

LO5.4

How firms can effectively combine the generic strategies of overall cost leadership and differentiation.

Perhaps the primary benefit to firms that integrate low-cost and differentiation strategies is the difficulty for rivals to duplicate or imitate.[46] This strategy enables a firm to provide two types of value to customers: differentiated attributes (e.g., high quality, brand identification, reputation) and lower prices (because of the firm's lower costs in value-creating activities). The goal is thus to provide unique value to customers in an efficient manner.[47] Some firms are able to attain both types of advantages simultaneously.[48] For example, superior quality can lead to lower costs because of less need for rework in manufacturing, fewer warranty claims, a reduced need for customer service personnel to resolve customer complaints, and so forth. Thus, the benefits of combining advantages can be additive, instead of merely involving trade-offs. Next, we consider four approaches to combining overall low cost and differentiation.

combination strategies
firms' integrations of various strategies to provide multiple types of value to customers.

Adopting Automated and Flexible Manufacturing Systems   Given the advances in manufacturing technologies such as CAD/CAM (computer aided design and computer aided manufacturing) as well as information technologies, many firms have been able to manufacture unique products in relatively small quantities at lower costs—a concept known as **mass customization**.[49]

mass customization
a firm's ability to manufacture unique products in small quantities at low cost.

Let's consider Andersen Windows of Bayport, Minnesota—a $2.3 billion manufacturer of windows for the building industry.[50] Until about 20 years ago, Andersen was a mass producer, in small batches, of a variety of standard windows. However, to meet changing customer needs, Andersen kept adding to its product line. The result was catalogs of ever-increasing size and a bewildering set of choices for both homeowners and contractors. Over a six-year period, the number of products tripled, price quotes took several hours, and the error rate increased. This not only damaged the company's reputation but also added to its manufacturing expenses.

To bring about a major change, Andersen developed an interactive computer version of its paper catalogs that it sold to distributors and retailers. Salespersons can now customize each window to meet the customer's needs, check the design for structural soundness, and provide a price quote. The system is virtually error-free, customers get exactly what they want, and the time to develop the design and furnish a quotation has been cut by 75 percent. Each showroom computer is connected to the factory, and customers are assigned a code number that permits them to track the order. The manufacturing system has been developed to use some common finished parts, but it also allows considerable variation in the final products. Despite its huge investment, Andersen has been able to lower costs, enhance quality and variety, and improve its response time to customers.

Using Data Analytics Corporations are increasingly collecting and analyzing data on their customers, including data on customer characteristics, purchasing patterns, employee productivity, and physical asset utilization. These efforts, commonly referred to as "Big Data," have the potential to allow firms to better customize their product and service offerings to customers while more efficiently and fully using the resources of the company. For example, Pepsi used data analytics to develop an algorithm that lowers the rate of inventory out-of-stocks and has shared the algorithm with partners and retailers. Similarly, Kaiser Permanente collects petabytes of data on the health treatment of its 8 million health care members. This has allowed Kaiser to develop insights on the cost, efficacy, and safety of the treatments provided by doctors and procedures in hospitals—leading to more effective and cost-conscious treatment patterns.[51]

profit pool
the total profits in an industry at all points along the industry's value chain.

Exploiting the Profit Pool Concept for Competitive Advantage A **profit pool** is defined as the total profits in an industry at all points along the industry's value chain.[52] Although the concept is relatively straightforward, the structure of the profit pool can be complex.[53] The potential pool of profits will be deeper in some segments of the value chain than in others, and the depths will vary within an individual segment. Segment profitability may vary widely by customer group, product category, geographic market, or distribution channel. Additionally, the pattern of profit concentration in an industry is very often different from the pattern of revenue generation. Strategy Spotlight 5.5 outlines how airlines have expanded the profit pools of their market by adding fees for a variety of services.

Coordinating the "Extended" Value Chain by Way of Information Technology Many firms have achieved success by integrating activities throughout the "extended value chain" by using information technology to link their own value chain with the value chains of their customers and suppliers. As noted in Chapter 3, this approach enables a firm to add value not only through its own value-creating activities but also for its customers and suppliers.

Such a strategy often necessitates redefining the industry's value chain. A number of years ago, Walmart took a close look at its industry's value chain and decided to reframe the competitive challenge. Although its competitors were primarily focused on retailing—merchandising and promotion—Walmart determined that it was not so much in the retailing industry as in the transportation logistics and communications industries.

EXPANDING THE PROFIT POOL IN THE SKY

Commercial airlines find themselves in a very competitive market, facing a number of competitors, having high fixed costs, and experiencing demand that is largely driven by economic conditions. As a result, profits in the airline industry are typically fairly low and often negative. The challenges in this industry are evident in the 23 separate bankruptcies that have occurred in the U.S. airline industry since 2000. However, as anyone who has flown in recent years can attest, airlines have found new sources of profit to augment their income beyond what customers are willing to pay when purchasing a ticket. The fees airlines have added on for ancillary services accounted for $27.1 billion in additional revenue for global airlines in 2012, up from a paltry $2.5 billion in 2008.

The range of revenue sources has expanded in recent years. The most obvious source of service revenue is baggage fees. However, airlines also generate revenue by charging booking fees and by selling premium economy seating, the right to assigned seats, exit-row seating, guarantees that family members can all sit together, earlier boarding of flights, premium meals, pillow and blanket sets, Internet access on board, and the right to hold a reservation before making a purchase commitment. Outside the flight experience itself, airlines are generating revenue by charging fees for credit cards, frequent-flyer programs, and access to airport lounges. The importance of these fees is staggering for some airlines. While Emirates Air relies on these service fees for less than 1 percent of its revenue, 22 percent of Ryanair's revenue and 38 percent of Spirit Airlines' revenue is accounted for by these fees.

By separating the value of the actual flight from the services associated with flying, airlines have greatly expanded the profit pool associated with flying. They have found that flyers may be very price-conscious when purchasing tickets but are willing to shell out more for a range of services. While this does increase their revenue, it may also provide benefits for at least some customers. As Jay Sorensen, CEO of IdeaWorks, notes, "It offers the potential for an airline to better tailor service to the needs of individual customers. They can click and buy the amenities they want rather than the airline deciding what is bundled in the base fare."

Sources: Akasie, J. 2013. With a fee for everything, airlines jet toward a new business model. *minyanville.com*, October 1: np; and Perera, J. 2014. Looking at airline fees in 2008 compared to 2014. *chron.com*, November 25: np.

Here, linkages in the extended value chain became central. That became Walmart's chosen battleground. By redefining the rules of competition that played to its strengths, Walmart has attained competitive advantages and dominates its industry.

Integrated Overall Low-Cost and Differentiation Strategies: Improving Competitive Position vis-à-vis the Five Forces   Firms that successfully integrate both differentiation and cost advantages create an enviable position. For example, Walmart's integration of information systems, logistics, and transportation helps it to drive down costs and provide outstanding product selection. This dominant competitive position serves to erect high entry barriers to potential competitors that have neither the financial nor physical resources to compete head-to-head. Walmart's size—with over $475 billion in sales in 2014—provides the chain with enormous bargaining power over suppliers. Its low pricing and wide selection reduce the power of buyers (its customers), because there are relatively few competitors that can provide a comparable cost/value proposition. This reduces the possibility of intense head-to-head rivalry, such as protracted price wars. Finally, Walmart's overall value proposition makes potential substitute products (e.g., Internet competitors) a less viable threat.

Pitfalls of Integrated Overall Cost Leadership and Differentiation Strategies   The pitfalls of integrated overall cost leadership and differentiation include:

- *Failing to attain both strategies and possibly ending up with neither, leaving the firm "stuck in the middle."* A key issue in strategic management is the creation of competitive advantages that enable a firm to enjoy above-average returns. Some firms may become stuck in the middle if they try to attain both cost and differentiation advantages. As mentioned earlier in this chapter, mainline supermarket chains find themselves stuck in the middle as their cost structure is higher than discount retailers offering groceries and their products and services are not seen by consumers as being as valuable as those of high-end grocery chains, such as Whole Foods.

- *Underestimating the challenges and expenses associated with coordinating value-creating activities in the extended value chain.* Integrating activities across a firm's value chain with the value chain of suppliers and customers involves a significant investment in financial and human resources. Firms must consider the expenses linked to technology investment, managerial time and commitment, and the involvement and investment required by the firm's customers and suppliers. The firm must be confident that it can generate a sufficient scale of operations and revenues to justify all associated expenses.

- *Miscalculating sources of revenue and profit pools in the firm's industry.* Firms may fail to accurately assess sources of revenue and profits in their value chain. This can occur for several reasons. For example, a manager may be biased due to his or her functional area background, work experiences, and educational background. If the manager's background is in engineering, he or she might perceive that proportionately greater revenue and margins were being created in manufacturing, product, and process design than a person whose background is in a "downstream" value-chain activity such as marketing and sales. Or politics could make managers "fudge" the numbers to favor their area of operations. This would make them responsible for a greater proportion of the firm's profits, thus improving their bargaining position.

A related problem is directing an overwhelming amount of managerial time, attention, and resources to value-creating activities that produce the greatest margins—to the detriment of other important, albeit less profitable, activities. For example, a car manufacturer may focus too much on downstream activities, such as warranty fulfillment and financing operations, to the detriment of differentiation and cost of the cars themselves.

LO5.5

What factors determine the sustainability of a firm's competitive advantage.

Can Competitive Strategies Be Sustained? Integrating and Applying Strategic Management Concepts

Thus far this chapter has addressed how firms can attain competitive advantages in the marketplace. We discussed the three generic strategies—overall cost leadership, differentiation, and focus—as well as combination strategies. Next we discussed the importance of linking value-chain activities (both those within the firm and those linkages between the firm's suppliers and customers) to attain such advantages. We also showed how successful competitive strategies enable firms to strengthen their position vis-à-vis the five forces of industry competition as well as how to avoid the pitfalls associated with the strategies.

Competitive advantages are, however, often short-lived. As we discussed in the beginning of Chapter 1, the composition of the firms that constitute the Fortune 500 list has experienced significant turnover in its membership over the years—reflecting the temporary nature of competitive advantages. Consider Dell's fall from grace. Here was a firm whose advantages in the marketplace seemed unassailable in the early 2000s. In fact, it was *Fortune*'s "Most Admired Firm" in 2005. However, cracks began to appear in 2007, and its competitive position has recently been severely eroded both by its traditional competitors and by an onslaught of firms selling tablets and other mobile devices. In short, Dell focused so much on operational efficiency and perfecting its "direct model" that it failed to deliver innovations that an increasingly sophisticated market demanded.[54]

Clearly, "nothing is forever" when it comes to competitive advantages. Rapid changes in technology, globalization, and actions by rivals from within—as well as outside—the industry can quickly erode a firm's advantages. It is becoming increasingly important to recognize that the duration of competitive advantages is declining, especially in technology-intensive industries.[55] Even in industries that are normally viewed as "low tech," the increasing use of technology has suddenly made competitive advantages less sustainable.[56] Amazon's success in book retailing at the cost of Barnes & Noble, the former industry leader, as well as BlackBerry's difficulties in responding to Apple's innovations in the smartphone market, serves to illustrate how difficult it has become for industry leaders to sustain competitive advantages that they once thought would last forever.

In this section, we will discuss some factors that help determine whether a strategy is sustainable over a long period of time. We will draw on some strategic management concepts from the first five chapters. To illustrate our points, we will look at a company, Atlas Door, which created an innovative strategy in its industry and enjoyed superior performance for several years. Our discussion of Atlas Door draws on a *Harvard Business Review* article by George Stalk, Jr.[57] It was published some time ago (1988), which provides us the benefit of hindsight to make our points about the sustainability of competitive advantage. After all, the strategic management concepts we have been addressing in the text are quite timeless in their relevance to practice. A brief summary follows.

Atlas Door: A Case Example

Atlas Door, a U.S.-based company, has enjoyed remarkable success. It has grown at an average annual rate of 15 percent in an industry with an overall annual growth rate of less than 5 percent. Recently, its pretax earnings were 20 percent of sales—about five times the industry average. Atlas is debt-free, and by its 10th year, the company achieved the number-one competitive position in its industry.

Atlas produces industrial doors—a product with almost infinite variety, involving limitless choices of width and height and material. Given the importance of product variety, inventory is almost useless in meeting customer orders. Instead, most doors can be manufactured only after the order has been placed.

How Did Atlas Door Create Its Competitive Advantages in the Marketplace? *First,* Atlas built just-in-time factories. Although simple in concept, they require extra tooling and machinery to reduce changeover times. Further, the manufacturing process must be organized by product and scheduled to start and complete with all of the parts available at the same time.

Second, Atlas reduced the time to receive and process an order. Traditionally, when customers, distributors, or salespeople called a door manufacturer with a request for price and delivery, they would have to wait more than one week for a response. In contrast, Atlas first streamlined and then automated its entire order-entry, engineering, pricing, and scheduling process. Atlas can price and schedule 95 percent of its incoming orders while the callers are still on the telephone. It can quickly engineer new special orders because it has preserved on computer the design and production data of all previous special orders—which drastically reduces the amount of reengineering necessary.

Third, Atlas tightly controlled logistics so that it always shipped only fully complete orders to construction sites. Orders require many components, and gathering all of them at the factory and making sure that they are with the correct order can be a time-consuming task. Of course, it is even more time-consuming to get the correct parts to the job site after the order has been shipped! Atlas developed a system to track the parts in production and the purchased parts for each order. This helped to ensure the arrival of all necessary parts at the shipping dock in time—a just-in-time logistics operation.

The Result? When Atlas began operations, distributors had little interest in its product. The established distributors already carried the door line of a much larger competitor and saw little to no reason to switch suppliers except, perhaps, for a major price concession. But as a start-up, Atlas was too small to compete on price alone. Instead, it positioned itself as the door supplier of last resort—the company people came to if the established supplier could not deliver or missed a key date.

Of course, with an average industry order-fulfillment time of almost four months, some calls inevitably came to Atlas. And when it did get the call, Atlas commanded a higher price because of its faster delivery. Atlas not only got a higher price, but its effective integration of value-creating activities saved time and lowered costs. Thus, it enjoyed the best of both worlds.

In 10 short years, the company replaced the leading door suppliers in 80 percent of the distributors in the United States. With its strategic advantage, the company could be selective—becoming the supplier for only the strongest distributors.

Are Atlas Door's Competitive Advantages Sustainable?

We will now take both the "pro" and "con" positions as to whether or not Atlas Door's competitive advantages will be sustainable for a very long time. It is important, of course, to assume that Atlas Door's strategy is unique in the industry, and the central issue becomes whether or not rivals will be able to easily imitate its strategy or create a viable substitute strategy.

"Pro" Position: The Strategy Is Highly Sustainable   Drawing on Chapter 2, it is quite evident that Atlas Door has attained a very favorable position vis-à-vis the five forces of industry competition. For example, it is able to exert power over its customers (distributors) because of its ability to deliver a quality product in a short period of time. Also, its dominance in the industry creates high entry barriers for new entrants. It is also quite evident that Atlas Door has been able to successfully integrate many value-chain activities within the firm—a fact that is integral to its just-in-time strategy. As noted in Chapter 3, such integration of activities provides a strong basis for sustainability, because rivals would have difficulty in imitating this strategy due to causal ambiguity and path dependency (i.e., it is difficult to build up in a short period of time the resources that Atlas Door has accumulated and developed as well as disentangle the causes of what the valuable resources are or how they can be re-created). Further, as noted in Chapter 4, Atlas Door benefits from the social capital that it has developed with a wide range of key stakeholders (Chapter 1). These would include customers, employees, and managers (a reasonable assumption, given how smoothly the internal operations flow and the company's long-term relationships with distributors). It would be very difficult for a rival to replace Atlas Door as the supplier of last resort—given the reputation that it has earned over time for "coming through in the clutch" on time-sensitive orders. Finally, we can conclude that Atlas Door has created competitive advantages in both overall low cost and differentiation (Chapter 5). Its strong linkages among value-chain activities—a requirement for its just-in-time operations—not only lower costs but enable the company to respond quickly to customer orders. As noted in Exhibit 5.4, many of the value-chain activities associated with a differentiation strategy reflect the element of speed or quick response.

"Con" Position: The Strategy Can Be Easily Imitated or Substituted   An argument could be made that much of Atlas Door's strategy relies on technologies that are rather well known and nonproprietary. Over time, a well-financed rival could imitate its strategy (via trial and error), achieve a tight integration among its value-creating activities, and implement a just-in-time manufacturing process. Because human capital is highly mobile (Chapter 4), a rival could hire away Atlas Door's talent, and these individuals could aid the rival in transferring Atlas Door's best practices. A new rival could also enter the industry with a large resource base, which might enable it to price its doors well under Atlas Door to build market share (but this would likely involve pricing below cost and would be a risky and nonsustainable strategy). Finally, a rival could potentially "leapfrog" the technologies and processes that Atlas Door has employed and achieve competitive superiority. With the benefit of hindsight, it could use the Internet to further speed up the linkages among its value-creating activities and the order-entry processes with its customers and suppliers. (But even this could prove to be a temporary advantage, since rivals could relatively easily do the same thing.)

What Is the Verdict?   Both positions have merit. Over time, it would be rather easy to see how a new rival could achieve parity with Atlas Door—or even create a superior competitive position with new technologies or innovative processes. However, two factors make it extremely difficult for a rival to challenge Atlas Door in the short term: (1) The success that Atlas Door has enjoyed with its just-in-time scheduling and production systems—which involve the successful integration of many value-creating activities—helps the firm not only lower costs but also respond quickly to customer needs, and (2) the strong, positive reputational effects that it has earned with its customers increases their loyalty and would take significant time for rivals to match.

Finally, it is important to also understand that it is Atlas Door's ability to appropriate most of the profits generated by its competitive advantages that make it a highly successful company. As we discussed in Chapter 3, profits generated by resources can be appropriated by a number of stakeholders such as suppliers, customers, employees, or rivals. The structure of the industrial door industry makes such value appropriation difficult: The suppliers provide generic parts, no one buyer is big enough to dictate prices, the tacit nature of the knowledge makes imitation difficult, and individual employees may be easily replaceable. Still, even with the advantages that Atlas Door enjoys, it needs to avoid becoming complacent or will suffer the same fate as the dominant firm it replaced.

Industry Life-Cycle Stages: Strategic Implications

LO5.6

The importance of considering the industry life cycle to determine a firm's business-level strategy and its relative emphasis on functional area strategies and value-creating activities.

The **industry life cycle** refers to the stages of introduction, growth, maturity, and decline that occur over the life of an industry. In considering the industry life cycle, it is useful to think in terms of broad product lines such as personal computers, photocopiers, or long-distance telephone service. Yet the industry life-cycle concept can be explored from several levels, from the life cycle of an entire industry to the life cycle of a single variation or model of a specific product or service.

industry life cycle

the stages of introduction, growth, maturity, and decline that typically occur over the life of an industry.

Why are industry life cycles important?[58] The emphasis on various generic strategies, functional areas, value-creating activities, and overall objectives varies over the course of an industry life cycle. Managers must become even more aware of their firm's strengths and weaknesses in many areas to attain competitive advantages. For example, firms depend on their research and development (R&D) activities in the introductory stage. R&D is the source of new products and features that everyone hopes will appeal to customers. Firms develop products and services to stimulate consumer demand. Later, during the maturity phase, the functions of the product have been defined, more competitors have entered the market, and competition is intense. Managers then place greater emphasis on production efficiencies and process (as opposed to the product) engineering in order to lower manufacturing costs. This helps to protect the firm's market position and to extend the product life cycle because the firm's lower costs can be passed on to consumers in the form of lower prices, and price-sensitive customers will find the product more appealing.

Exhibit 5.6 illustrates the four stages of the industry life cycle and how factors such as generic strategies, market growth rate, intensity of competition, and overall objectives change over time. Managers must strive to emphasize the key functional areas during each of the four stages and to attain a level of parity in all functional areas and value-creating activities. For example, although controlling production costs may be a primary concern

EXHIBIT 5.6 Stages of the Industry Life Cycle

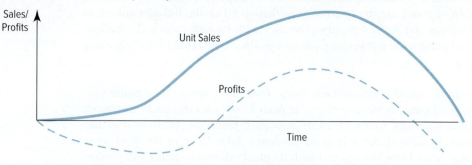

Stage Factor	Introduction	Growth	Maturity	Decline
Generic strategies	Differentiation	Differentiation	Differentiation Overall cost leadership	Overall cost leadership Focus
Market growth rate	Low	Very large	Low to moderate	Negative
Number of segments	Very few	Some	Many	Few
Intensity of competition	Low	Increasing	Very intense	Changing
Emphasis on product design	Very high	High	Low to moderate	Low
Emphasis on process design	Low	Low to moderate	High	Low
Major functional area(s) of concern	Research and development	Sales and marketing	Production	General management and finance
Overall objective	Increase market awareness	Create consumer demand	Defend market share and extend product life cycles	Consolidate, maintain, harvest, or exit

during the maturity stage, managers should not totally ignore other functions such as marketing and R&D. If they do, they can become so focused on lowering costs that they miss market trends or fail to incorporate important product or process designs. Thus, the firm may attain low-cost products that have limited market appeal.

It is important to point out a caveat. While the life-cycle idea is analogous to a living organism (i.e., birth, growth, maturity, and death), the comparison has limitations.[59] Products and services go through many cycles of innovation and renewal. Typically, only fad products have a single life cycle. Maturity stages of an industry can be "transformed" or followed by a stage of rapid growth if consumer tastes change, technological innovations take place, or new developments occur. The cereal industry is a good example. When medical research indicated that oat consumption reduced a person's cholesterol, sales of Quaker Oats increased dramatically.[60]

Strategies in the Introduction Stage

In the **introduction stage,** products are unfamiliar to consumers.[61] Market segments are not well defined, and product features are not clearly specified. The early development of an industry typically involves low sales growth, rapid technological change, operating losses, and the need for strong sources of cash to finance operations. Since there are few players and not much growth, competition tends to be limited.

Success requires an emphasis on research and development and marketing activities to enhance awareness. The challenge becomes one of (1) developing the product and finding a way to get users to try it and (2) generating enough exposure so the product emerges as the "standard" by which all other rivals' products are evaluated.

There's an advantage to being the "first mover" in a market.[62] It led to Coca-Cola's success in becoming the first soft-drink company to build a recognizable global brand and enabled Caterpillar to get a lock on overseas sales channels and service capabilities.

However, there can also be a benefit to being a "late mover." Target carefully considered its decision to delay its Internet strategy. Compared to its competitors Walmart and Kmart, Target was definitely an industry laggard. But things certainly turned out well:[63]

> By waiting, Target gained a late-mover advantage. The store was able to use competitors' mistakes as its own learning curve. This saved money, and customers didn't seem to mind the wait: When Target finally opened its website, it quickly captured market share from both Kmart and Walmart Internet shoppers. Forrester Research Internet analyst Stephen Zrike commented, "There's no question, in our mind, that Target has a far better understanding of how consumers buy online."

Examples of products currently in the introductory stages of the industry life cycle include electric vehicles and space tourism.

Strategies in the Growth Stage

The **growth stage** is characterized by strong increases in sales. Such potential attracts other rivals. In the growth stage, the primary key to success is to build consumer preferences for specific brands. This requires strong brand recognition, differentiated products, and the financial resources to support a variety of value-chain activities such as marketing and sales, and research and development. Whereas marketing and sales initiatives were mainly directed at spurring *aggregate* demand—that is, demand for all such products in the introduction stage—efforts in the growth stage are directed toward stimulating *selective* demand, in which a firm's product offerings are chosen instead of a rival's.

Revenues increase at an accelerating rate because (1) new consumers are trying the product and (2) a growing proportion of satisfied consumers are making repeat purchases.[64] In general, as a product moves through its life cycle, the proportion of repeat buyers to new purchasers increases. Conversely, new products and services often fail if there are relatively few repeat purchases. For example, Alberto-Culver introduced Mr. Culver's Sparklers, which were solid air fresheners that looked like stained glass. Although the product quickly went from the introductory to the growth stage, sales collapsed. Why? Unfortunately, there were few repeat purchasers because buyers treated them as inexpensive window decorations, left them there, and felt little need to purchase new ones. Examples of products currently in the growth stage include cloud computing data storage services and ultra-high-definition television (UHD TV).

Strategies in the Maturity Stage

In the **maturity stage** aggregate industry demand softens. As markets become saturated, there are few new adopters. It's no longer possible to "grow around" the competition, so direct competition becomes predominant.[65] With few attractive prospects, marginal competitors exit the market. At the same time, rivalry among existing rivals intensifies because of fierce price competition at the same time that expenses associated with attracting new buyers are rising. Advantages based on efficient manufacturing operations and process engineering become more important for keeping costs low as customers become more price-sensitive. It also becomes more difficult for firms to differentiate their offerings, because users have a greater understanding of products and services.

An article in *Fortune* magazine that addressed the intensity of rivalry in mature markets was aptly titled "A Game of Inches." It stated, "Battling for market share in a slowing industry can be a mighty dirty business. Just ask laundry soap archrivals Unilever and Procter & Gamble."[66] These two firms have been locked in a battle for market share since 1965. Why is the competition so intense? There is not much territory to gain and industry sales were flat. An analyst noted, "People aren't getting any dirtier." Thus, the only way to win is to take market share from the competition. To increase its share, Procter & Gamble (P&G) spends $100 million a year promoting its Tide brand on television, billboards, buses, magazines, and the Internet. But Unilever isn't standing still. Armed with an $80 million budget, it launched a soap tablet product named Wisk Dual Action Tablets. For example, it delivered samples of this product to 24 million U.S. homes in Sunday newspapers, followed by a series of TV ads. P&G launched a counteroffensive with Tide Rapid Action Tablets ads showed in side-by-side comparisons of the two products dropped into beakers of water. In the promotion, P&G claimed that its product is superior because it dissolves faster than Unilever's product.

Although this is only one example, many product classes and industries, including consumer products such as beer, automobiles, and athletic shoes, are in maturity.

Firms do not need to be "held hostage" to the life-cycle curve. By positioning or repositioning their products in unexpected ways, firms can change how customers mentally categorize them. Thus, firms are able to rescue products floundering in the maturity phase of their life cycles and return them to the growth phase.

Two positioning strategies that managers can use to affect consumers' mental shifts are **reverse positioning,** which strips away "sacred" product attributes while adding new ones, and **breakaway positioning,** which associates the product with a radically different category.[67] We discuss each of these positioning strategies below and then provide an example of each in Strategy Spotlight 5.6.

Reverse Positioning   This strategy assumes that although customers may desire more than the baseline product, they don't necessarily want an endless list of features. With reverse positioning, companies make the creative decision to step off the augmentation treadmill and shed product attributes that the rest of the industry considers sacred. Then, once a product is returned to its baseline state, the stripped-down product adds one or more carefully selected attributes that would usually be found only in a highly augmented product. Such an unconventional combination of attributes allows the product to assume a new competitive position within the category and move backward from maturity into a growth position on the life-cycle curve.

Breakaway Positioning   As noted above, with reverse positioning, a product establishes a unique position in its category but retains a clear category membership. However, with breakaway positioning, a product escapes its category by deliberately associating with a different one. Thus, managers leverage the new category's conventions to change both how products are consumed and with whom they compete. Instead of merely seeing the breakaway product as simply an alternative to others in its category, consumers perceive it as altogether different.

When a breakaway product is successful in leaving its category and joining a new one, it is able to redefine its competition. Similar to reverse positioning, this strategy permits the product to shift backward on the life-cycle curve, moving from the rather dismal maturity phase to a thriving growth opportunity.

reverse positioning
a break in the industry tendency to continuously augment products, characteristic of the product life cycle, by offering products with fewer product attributes and lower prices.

breakaway positioning
a break in the industry tendency to incrementally improve products along specific dimensions, characteristic of the product life cycle, by offering products that are still in the industry but are perceived by customers as being different.

REVERSE AND BREAKAWAY POSITIONING: HOW TO AVOID BEING HELD HOSTAGE TO THE LIFE-CYCLE CURVE

When firms adopt a reverse or breakaway positioning strategy, there is typically no pretense about what they are trying to accomplish. In essence, they subvert convention through unconventional promotions, prices, and attributes. That becomes a large part of their appeal—a cleverly positioned product offering. Next, we discuss Commerce Bank's reverse positioning and Swatch's breakaway positioning.

Commerce Bank

While most banks offer dozens of checking and savings accounts and compete by trying to offer the highest interest rates, Commerce Bank, a regional bank on the East Coast, took a totally different approach. It paid among the lowest rates in its market. Further, it offered a limited product line—just four checking accounts, for example. One would think that such a stingy approach would have scared off customers. However, Commerce Bank was very successful. Between 1999 and 2007, it expanded from 120 to 435 branches. Growing from a single branch in 1973, it was purchased by TD Bank in 2007 for $8.5 billion.

Why was it so successful? It stripped away all of what customers expected—lots of choices and peak interest rates and it *reverse positioned* itself as "the most convenient bank in America." It was open seven days a week, including evenings until 8 p.m. You could get a debit card while you waited. And when it rained, an escort with an umbrella walked you to your car. Further, the bank offered free coffee and newspapers for customers. Not too surprisingly, despite the inferior rates and few choices, customers regularly flocked to the bank, making it an attractive target for a larger bank to buy.

Swatch

Interestingly, the name "Swatch" is often misconstrued as a contraction of the words *Swiss watch.* However, Nicolas Hayek, chairman, affirms that the original contraction was *second watch*—the new watch was introduced as a new concept of watches as casual, fun, and relatively disposable accessories. And therein lies Swatch's *breakaway positioning.*

When Swatch was launched in 1983, Swiss watches were marketed as a form of jewelry. They were serious, expensive, enduring, and discreetly promoted. Once a customer purchased one, it lasted a lifetime. Swatch changed all of that by defining its watches as playful fashion accessories which were showily promoted. They inspired impulse buying—customers would often purchase half a dozen in different designs. Their price—$40 when the brand was introduced—expanded Swatch's reach beyond its default category (watches as high-end jewelry) and moved it into the fashion accessory category, where it has different customers and competitors. Swatch became the official timekeeper of the Summer Olympics in 1996, has continued to support the Olympics since, and has already signed on as a top sponsor of the 2016 Olympic Games in Rio.

Today, The Swatch Group is the largest watch company in the world. It has acquired many brands over the years, including Omega, Longines, Harry Winston, Calvin Klein, and Hamilton. Revenues have grown to $8.5 billion in 2013, and net income has increased to $1.9 billion. These figures represent increases of 65 percent and 153 percent, respectively, since 2009.

Sources: Moon, Y. 2005. Break free from the product life cycle. *Harvard Business Review,* 83(5): 87–94; *www.hoovers.com;* and *http://rio2016.com/en/sponsors/omega.*

Strategies in the Decline Stage

Although all decisions in the phases of an industry life cycle are important, they become particularly difficult in the **decline stage.** Firms must face up to the fundamental strategic choices of either exiting or staying and attempting to consolidate their position in the industry.[68]

The decline stage occurs when industry sales and profits begin to fall. Typically, changes in the business environment are at the root of an industry or product group entering this stage.[69] Changes in consumer tastes or a technological innovation can push a product into decline. Compact discs forced cassette tapes into decline in the prerecorded music industry in the 1980s, and now digital devices have pushed CDs into decline.

Products in the decline stage often consume a large share of management time and financial resources relative to their potential worth. Sales and profits decline. Also, competitors may start drastically cutting their prices to raise cash and remain solvent. The situation is further aggravated by the liquidation of assets, including inventory, of some of the competitors that have failed. This further intensifies price competition.

In the decline stage, a firm's strategic options become dependent on the actions of rivals. If many competitors leave the market, sales and profit opportunities increase. On the other hand, prospects are limited if all competitors remain.[70] If some competitors merge,

decline stage
the fourth stage of the product life cycle, characterized by (1) falling sales and profits, (2) increasing price competition, and (3) industry consolidation.

their increased market power may erode the opportunities for the remaining players. Managers must carefully monitor the actions and intentions of competitors before deciding on a course of action.

Four basic strategies are available in the decline phase: *maintaining, harvesting, exiting,* and *consolidating.*[71]

- ***Maintaining*** refers to keeping a product going without significantly reducing marketing support, technological development, or other investments, in the hope that competitors will eventually exit the market. Many offices, for example, still use typewriters for filling out forms and other purposes that cannot be completed on a PC. In some rural areas, rotary (or dial) telephones persist because of the older technology used in central switching offices. Thus, there may still be the potential for revenues and profits.

- **Harvesting** involves obtaining as much profit as possible and requires that costs be reduced quickly. Managers should consider the firm's value-creating activities and cut associated budgets. Value-chain activities to consider are primary (e.g., operations, sales and marketing) and support (e.g., procurement, technology development). The objective is to wring out as much profit as possible.

- ***Exiting the market*** involves dropping the product from a firm's portfolio. Since a residual core of consumers exist, eliminating it should be carefully considered. If the firm's exit involves product markets that affect important relationships with other product markets in the corporation's overall portfolio, an exit could have repercussions for the whole corporation. For example, it may involve the loss of valuable brand names or human capital with a broad variety of expertise in many value-creating activities such as marketing, technology, and operations.

- **Consolidation** involves one firm acquiring at a reasonable price the best of the surviving firms in an industry. This enables firms to enhance market power and acquire valuable assets. One example of a consolidation strategy took place in the defense industry in the early 1990s. As the cliché suggests, "peace broke out" at the end of the Cold War and overall U.S. defense spending levels plummeted.[72] Many companies that make up the defense industry saw more than 50 percent of their market disappear. Only one-quarter of the 120,000 companies that once supplied the Department of Defense still serve in that capacity; the others have shut down their defense business or dissolved altogether. But one key player, Lockheed Martin, became a dominant rival by pursuing an aggressive strategy of consolidation. During the 1990s, it purchased 17 independent entities, including General Dynamics' tactical aircraft and space systems divisions, GE Aerospace, Goodyear Aerospace, and Honeywell Electro-Optics. These combinations enabled Lockheed Martin to emerge as the top provider to three governmental customers: the Department of Defense, the Department of Energy, and NASA.

Examples of products currently in the decline stage of the industry life cycle include the video-rental business (being replaced by video on demand), hard disk drives (being replaced by solid-state memory and cloud storage), and desktop computers (being replaced by notebook and tablet computers).

The introduction of new technologies and associated products does not always mean that old technologies quickly fade away. Research shows that in a number of cases, old technologies actually enjoy a very profitable "last gasp."[73] Examples include personal computers (versus tablet computers and other mobile devices), coronary artery bypass graft surgery (versus angioplasty), and vinyl records (versus CDs and digital downloads of music). In each case, the advent of new technology prompted predictions of the demise of the older technology, but each of these has proved to be a resilient survivor. What accounts for their continued profitability and survival?

harvesting strategy
a strategy of wringing as much profit as possible out of a business in the short to medium term by reducing costs.

consolidation strategy
a firm's acquiring or merging with other firms in an industry in order to enhance market power and gain valuable assets.

Retreating to more defensible ground is one strategy that firms specializing in technologies threatened with rapid obsolescence have followed. For example, while angioplasty may be appropriate for relatively healthier patients with blocked arteries, sicker, higher-risk patients seem to benefit more from coronary artery bypass graft surgery. This enabled the surgeons to concentrate on the more difficult cases and improve the technology itself. The advent of television unseated the radio as the major source of entertainment from American homes. However, the radio has survived and even thrived in venues where people are also engaged in other activities, such as driving.

Using the new to improve the old is a second approach. Microsoft has integrated elements of mobile technology into the Windows operating system to address the challenge of Google's Android and Apple's iOS.

Improving the price-performance trade-off is a third approach. IBM continues to make money selling mainframes long after their obituary was written. It retooled the technology using low-cost microprocessors and cut their prices drastically. Further, it invested and updated the software, enabling it to offer clients such as banks better performance and lower costs.

Turnaround Strategies

A **turnaround strategy** involves reversing performance decline and reinvigorating growth toward profitability.[74] A need for turnaround may occur at any stage in the life cycle but is more likely to occur during maturity or decline.

turnaround strategy
a strategy that reverses a firm's decline in performance and returns it to growth and profitability.

Most turnarounds require a firm to carefully analyze the external and internal environments.[75] The external analysis leads to identification of market segments or customer groups that may still find the product attractive.[76] Internal analysis results in actions aimed at reduced costs and higher efficiency. A firm needs to undertake a mix of both internally and externally oriented actions to effect a turnaround.[77] In effect, the cliché "You can't shrink yourself to greatness" applies.

A study of 260 mature businesses in need of a turnaround identified three strategies used by successful companies.[78]

LO5.7

The need for turnaround strategies that enable a firm to reposition its competitive position in an industry.

- *Asset and cost surgery.* Very often, mature firms tend to have assets that do not produce any returns. These include real estate, buildings, and so on. Outright sales or sale and leaseback free up considerable cash and improve returns. Investment in new plants and equipment can be deferred. Firms in turnaround situations try to aggressively cut administrative expenses and inventories and speed up collection of receivables. Costs also can be reduced by outsourcing production of various inputs for which market prices may be cheaper than in-house production costs.

- *Selective product and market pruning.* Most mature or declining firms have many product lines that are losing money or are only marginally profitable. One strategy is to discontinue such product lines and focus all resources on a few core profitable areas. For example, in 2014, Procter & Gamble announced that it would sell off or close down up to 100 of its brands, allowing the firm to improve its efficiency and its innovativeness as it focused on its core brands. The remaining 70 to 80 "core" brands accounted for 90 percent of the firm's sales.

- *Piecemeal productivity improvements.* There are many ways in which a firm can eliminate costs and improve productivity. Although individually these are small gains, they cumulate over a period of time to substantial gains. Improving business processes by reengineering them, benchmarking specific activities against industry leaders, encouraging employee input to identify excess costs, increasing capacity utilization, and improving employee productivity lead to a significant overall gain.

Strategy Spotlight 5.7 provides an illustration of a turnaround effort by focusing on the dramatic strategic realignment that Mindy Grossman undertook at HSN (formerly the Home Shopping Network).

HOW MINDY GROSSMAN LED HSN'S REMARKABLE TURNAROUND

Mindy Grossman took over the helm of HSN, formerly known as the Home Shopping Network, in 2008, at a very trying time. The Home Shopping Network was falling behind the times as retailing technology changed rapidly in the digital age and was saddled with the reputation of being the home for C-list celebrities hawking relatively low-grade jewelry, fashion, and health and beauty products to couch potatoes. The firm had experienced significant leadership turmoil, with seven CEOs in the prior 10 years. It was also facing some of the worst economic conditions since the 1930s. Not surprisingly, the firm experienced a multibillion-dollar loss in 2008.

However, things have changed dramatically since those dark days. HSN generated $178 million in profit on $3.4 billion in 2013. The firm's stock price, which traded as low as $1.42 in 2008, was trading at over $70 a share in late 2014.

At the center of HSN's turnaround is Mindy Grossman, the firm's CEO. She came to HSN after working for a number of clothing manufacturers, including Ralph Lauren, Tommy Hilfiger, and, most recently, Nike. Her recipe for the turnaround reflects a mix of hard business acumen combined with an ability to engage stakeholders in the firm to move the turnaround forward. With her changes, she's moved HSN from being a dowdy cable TV channel to a retailer that meets the needs of busy women by providing them a place to shop wherever they are—at home through their TVs or while traveling for work or at their kids' soccer games through their phones or tablets.

What are Grossman's lessons for managing a turnaround? First, she found value in engaging with employees. Her first day at HSN, she chose to go through the same new-employee orientation that all employees go through. She felt this humanized her in the minds of other employees. On her second day, she held a town-hall meeting so that she could directly introduce herself and set the tone that she was accessible and that all employees were valued and could have a future at HSN. She also set up a policy to regularly have breakfasts and lunches with employees and says, "I learn more from those than from reading any report."

Second, she got the lineup of employees right. She categorizes workers into three categories. "Evangelists" are the employees who are truly enthusiastic about the company and try to rally others. The "Interested" are those who are invested in the firm's success but have something of a wait-and-see attitude. The "Blockers" are toxic and work to limit the firm's ability to change. She saw the need to rid the company of toxicity and pushed out the Blockers quickly. This allowed her to develop a management team, which largely stayed intact for several years, that reflected the strong skills and commitment she desired.

She tailored the company's offerings to meet the changing needs of her customer base. In the deep days of the recession in 2008–2009, this meant shifting from offering high-priced jewelry and fashions to providing products and services that helped HSN's customers save time and money. Later, this meant dramatically growing the company's mobile platforms. Today, over half the new customers come to HSN through their mobile phones. One of the new services attracting them is HSN's online arcade, where customers can play games that allow them to win HSN merchandise, which generated over 100 million plays in its first year.

Key to it all is staying focused on what HSN's strategy is and who its customers are. In the words of Grossman, "We're not trying to be Amazon, all things to all people. We have a highly specialized customer and want to give her the best experience somewhere she can trust."

Sources: Goudreau, J. 2012. How Mindy Grossman is transforming HSN. *forbes. com*, August 29: np; Banjo, S. 2013. HSN enjoys a mobile-shopping rebirth in the digital age. *wsj.com*, July 5: np; and Snyder, B. 2014. How Mindy Grossman turned around HSN. *gsb.stanford.edu/insights,* June 5: np.

ISSUE FOR DEBATE

Uncertain Course for Jet Blue

JetBlue appears to be stuck in the middle. The airline has grown rapidly since its founding in 1999 to become the fifth-largest airline in the United States. It has long positioned itself as the "egalitarian" airline, where customers all get the same level of service at largely the same price-point. It structured itself as a low-cost airline but one that provided a higher level of service that included more legroom than competitors, individual TV screens, and Wi-Fi access in its all-coach cabins. In essence, it was the "cheap chic" airline that generated great customer appreciation and commitment.

But JetBlue now faces some challenges. Internally, its costs are rising. After being pressured by its pilots, JetBlue collectively raised pilot pay by $145 million from 2014 through 2017.

But its pilots decided to unionize anyway—which suggests future cost increases. Externally, JetBlue faces increasing pressures on both ends of the strategy spectrum. At the low-cost end, hard-discount airlines, most notably Spirit Airlines, are effectively undercutting JetBlue's prices and stealing the price-conscious consumer. At the differentiation end, the mainline airlines, such as Delta and American, have expanded the services and amenities they provide, especially for higher-fare business travelers. And JetBlue has difficulty matching the global network of routes these airlines can provide business travelers. As a result, JetBlue's sales growth and profitability have lagged its main competitors.

JetBlue has responded by moving to become more like the mainline airlines. The firm ordered new jets that have first-class cabins for use on their flights between the east and west coasts. JetBlue restructured its pricing system to offer different levels of service, with the lowest level requiring that passengers pay to check luggage and providing lower frequent-flyer credit than other fares. JetBlue is also adding seats to its planes by reducing legroom. Airline executives argue JetBlue isn't abandoning its core customers, but others argue the changes will erode the airline's reputation and customer loyalty.

Discussion Questions

1. Is it wise for JetBlue to change its strategy to become more like Delta, American, and United?
2. What are the risks and benefits of this change?
3. What does JetBlue need to do to retain its distinctiveness in customers' eyes?

Sources: Carey, S. 2013. Discount carrier JetBlue goes upmarket. *wsj.com*, August 5: np; Carey, S. 2014. JetBlue CEO in hot seat as airline lags rivals. *wsj.com*, May 13: np; and *finance.yahoo.com*.

Reflecting on Career Implications . . .

◾ **Types of Competitive Advantage:** Are you aware of your organization's business-level strategy? What do you do to help your firm either increase differentiation or lower costs? Can you demonstrate to your superiors how you have contributed to the firm's chosen business-level strategy?

◾ **Types of Competitive Advantage:** What is your own competitive advantage? What opportunities does your current job provide to enhance your competitive advantage? Are you making the best use of your competitive advantage? If not, what organizations might provide you with better opportunities for doing so? Does your résumé clearly reflect your competitive advantage? Or are you "stuck in the middle"?

◾ **Understanding *Your* Differentiation:** When looking for a new job or for advancement in your current firm, be conscious of being able to identify what differentiates you from other applicants. Consider the items in Exhibit 5.4 as you work to identify what distinguishes you from others.

◾ **Industry Life Cycle:** Before you go for a job interview, identify the life-cycle stage of the industry within which your firm is located. You are more likely to have greater opportunities for career advancement in an industry in the growth stage than one in the decline stage.

◾ **Industry Life Cycle:** If you sense that your career is maturing (or in the decline phase!), what actions can you take to restore career growth and momentum (e.g., training, mentoring, professional networking)? Should you actively consider professional opportunities in other industries?

How and why firms outperform each other goes to the heart of strategic management. In this chapter, we identified three generic strategies and discussed how firms are able not only to attain advantages over competitors but also to sustain such advantages over time. Why do some advantages become long-lasting while others are quickly imitated by competitors?

The three generic strategies—overall cost leadership, differentiation, and focus—form the core of this chapter. We began by providing a brief description of each generic strategy (or competitive advantage) and furnished examples of firms that have successfully implemented these strategies. Successful generic strategies invariably enhance a firm's position vis-à-vis the five forces of that industry—a point that we stressed and illustrated with examples. However, as we pointed out, there are pitfalls to each of the generic strategies. Thus, the sustainability of a firm's advantage is always challenged because of imitation or substitution by new or existing rivals. Such competitor moves erode a firm's advantage over time.

We also discussed the viability of combining (or integrating) overall cost leadership and generic differentiation strategies. If successful, such integration can enable a firm to enjoy superior performance and improve its competitive position. However, this is challenging, and managers must be aware of the potential downside risks associated with such an initiative.

We addressed the challenges inherent in determining the sustainability of competitive advantages. Drawing on an example from a manufacturing industry, we discussed both the "pro" and "con" positions as to why competitive advantages are sustainable over a long period of time.

The concept of the industry life cycle is a critical contingency that managers must take into account in striving to create and sustain competitive advantages. We identified the four stages of the industry life cycle—introduction, growth, maturity, and decline—and suggested how these stages can play a role in decisions that managers must make at the business level. These include overall strategies as well as the relative emphasis on functional areas and value-creating activities.

When a firm's performance severely erodes, turnaround strategies are needed to reverse its situation and enhance its competitive position. We have discussed three approaches—asset cost surgery, selective product and market pruning, and piecemeal productivity improvements.

SUMMARY REVIEW QUESTIONS

1. Explain why the concept of competitive advantage is central to the study of strategic management.

2. Briefly describe the three generic strategies—overall cost leadership, differentiation, and focus.

3. Explain the relationship between the three generic strategies and the five forces that determine the average profitability within an industry.

4. What are some of the ways in which a firm can attain a successful turnaround strategy?

5. Describe some of the pitfalls associated with each of the three generic strategies.

6. Can firms combine the generic strategies of overall cost leadership and differentiation? Why or why not?

7. Explain why the industry life-cycle concept is an important factor in determining a firm's business-level strategy.

key terms

business-level strategy 147
generic strategies 148
overall cost leadership 148
experience curve 149
competitive parity 149
differentiation strategy 153
focus strategy 159

combination strategies 161
mass customization 161
profit pool 162
industry life cycle 167
introduction stage 169
growth stage 169
maturity stage 169
reverse positioning 170
breakaway positioning 170
decline stage 171
harvesting strategy 172
consolidation strategy 172
turnaround strategy 173

experiential exercise

What are some examples of primary and support activities that enable Nucor, a $21 billion steel manufacturer, to achieve a low-cost strategy? (Fill in the table below.)

Value-Chain Activity	Yes/No	How Does Nucor Create Value for the Customer?
Primary:		
Inbound logistics		
Operations		
Outbound logistics		
Marketing and sales		
Service		
Support:		
Procurement		
Technology development		
Human resource management		
General administration		

application questions & exercises

1. Go to the Internet and look up *www.walmart.com*. How has this firm been able to combine overall cost leadership and differentiation strategies?

2. Choose a firm with which you are familiar in your local business community. Is the firm successful in following one (or more) generic strategies? Why or why not? What do you think are some of the challenges it faces in implementing these strategies in an effective manner?

3. Think of a firm that has attained a differentiation focus or cost focus strategy. Are its advantages sustainable? Why? Why not? (*Hint:* Consider its position vis-à-vis Porter's five forces.)

4. Think of a firm that successfully achieved a combination overall cost leadership and differentiation strategy. What can be learned from this example? Are the advantages sustainable? Why? Why not? (*Hint:* Consider its competitive position vis-à-vis Porter's five forces.)

ethics questions

1. Can you think of a company that suffered ethical consequences as a result of an overemphasis on a cost leadership strategy? What do you think were the financial and nonfinancial implications?

2. In the introductory stage of the product life cycle, what are some of the unethical practices that managers could engage in to enhance their firm's market position? What could be some of the long-term implications of such actions?

references

1. Randazzo, S. 2014. Sticky time for Crumbs Bake Shop. *wsj.com*, July 8: np; O'Donnell, J. 2014. Here's why the cupcake crumbled at Crumbs. *nydailynews.com*, np; and Randazzo, S. 2014. Crumbs Bake Shop to reopen stores after court approval. *wsj.com*, np.

2. For a perspective by Porter on competitive strategy, refer to Porter, M. E. 1996. What is strategy? *Harvard Business Review*, 74(6): 61–78.

3. For insights into how a start-up is using solar technology, see Gimbel, B. 2009. Plastic power. *Fortune*, February 2: 34.

4. Useful insights on strategy in an economic downturn are in Rhodes, D. & Stelter, D. 2009. Seize advantage in a downturn. *Harvard Business Review*, 87(2): 50–58.

5. Some useful ideas on maintaining competitive advantages can be found in Ma, H. & Karri, R. 2005. Leaders beware: Some sure ways to lose your competitive advantage. *Organizational Dynamics*, 343(1): 63–76.

6. Miller, A. & Dess, G. G. 1993. Assessing Porter's model in terms of its generalizability, accuracy, and simplicity. *Journal of Management Studies*, 30(4): 553–585.

7. Gasparro, A. & Martin, T. 2012. What's wrong with America's supermarkets? *wsj.com*, July 12: np.

8. For insights on how discounting can erode a firm's performance, read Stibel, J. M. & Delgrosso, P. 2008. Discounts can be dangerous. *Harvard Business Review*, 66(12): 31.

9. For a scholarly discussion and analysis of the concept of competitive parity, refer to Powell, T. C. 2003. Varieties of competitive parity. *Strategic Management Journal*, 24(1): 61–86.

10. Rao, A. R., Bergen, M. E., & Davis, S. 2000. How to fight a price war. *Harvard Business Review*, 78(2): 107–120.

11. Marriot, J. W., Jr. Our competitive strength: Human capital. A speech given to the Detroit Economic Club on October 2, 2000.

12. Burrus, D. 2011. *Flash foresight: How to see the invisible and do the impossible*. New York: HarperCollins.

13. Corstjens, M. & Lal, R. 2012. Retail doesn't cross borders. *Harvard Business Review*, April: 104–110.

14. Downing, L. 2012. Finally, a use for sandwich crusts. *Bloomberg Businessweek*, June 18: 18–19.

15. Ng, S. 2014. Zulily customers play the waiting game. *wsj.com*, May 4: np.

16. Interesting insights on Walmart's effective cost leadership strategy are found in Palmeri, C. 2008. Wal-Mart is up for this downturn. *BusinessWeek*, November 6: 34.

17. An interesting perspective on the dangers of price discounting is Mohammed, R. 2011. Ditch the discounts. *Harvard Business Review*, 89(1/2): 23–25.

18. Dholakia, U. M. 2011. Why employees can wreck promotional offers. *Harvard Business Review*, 89(1/2): 28.

19. Jacobs, A. 2010. Workers in China voting with their feet. *International Herald Tribune*, July 13: 1, 14.

20. For a perspective on the sustainability of competitive advantages, refer to Barney, J. 1995. Looking inside for competitive advantage. *Academy of Management Executive*, 9(4): 49–61.

21. Thornton, E. 2001. Why e-brokers are broker and broker. *BusinessWeek*, January 22: 94.

22. Mohammed, R. 2011. Ditch the discounts. *Harvard Business Review*, 89(1/2): 23–25.

23. Wilson, D. 2012. Big Beer dresses up in craft brewers' clothing. *Fortune.com*, November 15: np.

24. For an "ultimate" in differentiated services, consider time-shares in exotic automobiles such as Lamborghinis and Bentleys. Refer to Stead, D. 2008. My Lamborghini— today, anyway. *BusinessWeek*, January 18:17.

25. For an interesting perspective on the value of corporate brands and how they may be leveraged, refer to Aaker, D. A. 2004, *California Management Review*, 46(3): 6–18.

26. A unique perspective on differentiation strategies is Austin, R. D. 2008. High margins and the quest for aesthetic coherence. *Harvard Business Review*, 86(1): 18–19.

27. Eng, D. 2011. Cheesecake Factory's winning formula. *Fortune*, May 2: 19–20.

28. For a discussion on quality in terms of a company's software and information systems, refer to

Prahalad, C. K. & Krishnan, M. S. 1999. The new meaning of quality in the information age. *Harvard Business Review,* 77(5): 109–118.

29. The role of design in achieving differentiation is addressed in Brown, T. 2008. Design thinking. *Harvard Business Review,* 86(6): 84–92.

30. Taylor, A., III. 2001. Can you believe Porsche is putting its badge on this car? *Fortune,* February 19: 168–172.

31. Roberts, P. & Dowling, G. 2008. Corporate reputation and sustained superior financial performance. *Strategic Management Journal,* 23: 1077–1093.

32. Mann, J. 2010. The best service in the world. *Networking Times,* January: np.

33. Bonnabeau, E., Bodick, N., & Armstrong, R. W. 2008. A more rational approach to new-product development. *Harvard Business Review,* 66(3): 96–102.

34. Insights on Google's innovation are in Iyer, B. & Davenport, T. H. 2008. Reverse engineering Google's innovation machine. *Harvard Business Review,* 66(4): 58–68.

35. A discussion of how a firm used technology to create product differentiation is in Mehta, S. N. 2009. Under Armour reboots. *Fortune,* February 2: 29–33 (5).

36. Bertini, M. & Wathieu, L. 2010. How to stop customers from fixating on price. *Harvard Business Review,* 88(5): 84–91.

37. The authors would like to thank Scott Droege, a faculty member at Western Kentucky University, for providing this example.

38. Dixon, M., Freeman, K., & Toman, N. 2010. Stop trying to delight your customers. *Harvard Business Review,* 88(7/8).

39. Flint, J. 2004. Stop the nerds. *Forbes,* July 5: 80; and Fahey, E. 2004. Over-engineering 101. *Forbes,* December 13: 62.

40. Symonds, W. C. 2000. Can Gillette regain its voltage? *BusinessWeek,* October 16: 102–104.

41. Caplan, J. 2006. In a real crunch. *Inside Business,* July: A37–A38.

42. Gadiesh, O. & Gilbert, J. L. 1998. Profit pools: A fresh look at strategy. *Harvard Business Review,* 76(3): 139–158.

43. Colvin, G. 2000. Beware: You could soon be selling soybeans. *Fortune,* November 13: 80.

44. Anders, G. 2012. How LinkedIn has turned your resume into a cash machine. *Forbes.com,* July 16: np.

45. Burrus, D. 2011. *Flash foresight: How to see the invisible and do the impossible.* New York: HarperCollins.

46. Hall, W. K. 1980. Survival strategies in a hostile environment, *Harvard Business Review,* 58: 75–87; on the paint and allied products industry, see Dess, G. G. & Davis, P. S. 1984. Porter's (1980) generic strategies as determinants of strategic group membership and organizational performance. *Academy of Management Journal,* 27: 467–488; for the Korean electronics industry, see Kim, L. & Lim, Y. 1988. Environment, generic strategies, and performance in a rapidly developing country: A taxonomic approach. *Academy of Management Journal,* 31: 802–827; Wright, P., Hotard, D., Kroll, M., Chan, P., & Tanner, J. 1990. Performance and multiple strategies in a firm: Evidence from the apparel industry. In Dean, B. V. & Cassidy, J. C. (Eds.), *Strategic management: Methods and studies:* 93–110. Amsterdam: Elsevier-North Holland; and Wright, P., Kroll, M., Tu, H., & Helms, M. 1991. Generic strategies and business performance: An empirical study of the screw machine products industry. *British Journal of Management,* 2: 1–9.

47. Gilmore, J. H. & Pine, B. J., II. 1997. The four faces of customization. *Harvard Business Review,* 75(1): 91–101.

48. Heracleous, L. & Wirtz, J. 2010. Singapore Airlines' balancing act. *Harvard Business Review,* 88(7/8): 145–149.

49. Gilmore & Pine, op. cit. For interesting insights on mass customization, refer to Cattani, K., Dahan, E., & Schmidt, G. 2005. Offshoring versus "spackling." *MIT Sloan Management Review,* 46(3): 6–7.

50. Goodstein, L. D. & Butz, H. E. 1998. Customer value: The linchpin of organizational change. *Organizational Dynamics,* Summer: 21–34.

51. Kiron, D. 2013. From value to vision: Reimagining the possible with data analytics. *MIT Sloan Management Review Research Report,* Spring: 1–19.

52. Gadiesh & Gilbert, op. cit., pp. 139–158.

53. Insights on the profit pool concept are addressed in Reinartz, W. & Ulaga, W. 2008. How to sell services more profitably. *Harvard Business Review,* 66(5): 90–96.

54. A rigorous and thorough discussion of the threats faced by industries due to the commoditization of products and services and what strategic actions firms should consider is found in D'Aveni, R. A. 2010. *Beating the commodity trap.* Boston: Harvard Business Press.

55. For an insightful, recent discussion on the difficulties and challenges associated with creating advantages that are sustainable for any reasonable period of time and suggested strategies, refer to D'Aveni, R. A., Dagnino, G. B., & Smith, K. G. 2010. The age of temporary advantage. *Strategic Management Journal,* 31(13): 1371–1385. This is the lead article in a special issue of this journal that provides many ideas that are useful to both academics and practicing managers. For an additional examination of declining advantage in technologically intensive industries, see Vaaler, P. M. & McNamara, G. 2010. Are technology-intensive industries more dynamically competitive? No and yes. *Organization Science,* 21: 271–289.

56. Rita McGrath provides some interesting ideas on possible strategies for firms facing highly uncertain competitive environments: McGrath, R. G. 2011. When your business model is in trouble. *Harvard Business Review,* 89(1/2): 96–98.

57. The Atlas Door example draws on Stalk, G., Jr. 1988. Time—the next source of competitive advantage. *Harvard Business Review,* 66(4): 41–51.

58. For an interesting perspective on the influence of the product life cycle and rate of technological change on competitive strategy, refer to Lei, D. & Slocum, J. W., Jr. 2005. Strategic and organizational requirements for competitive advantage. *Academy of Management Executive,* 19(1): 31–45.

59. Dickson, P. R. 1994. *Marketing management:* 293. Fort Worth, TX: Dryden Press; Day, G. S. 1981. The product life cycle: Analysis and application. *Journal of Marketing Research,* 45: 60–67.

60. Bearden, W. O., Ingram, T. N., & LaForge, R. W. 1995. *Marketing principles and practices.* Burr Ridge, IL: Irwin.

61. MacMillan, I. C. 1985. Preemptive strategies. In Guth, W. D. (Ed.), *Handbook of business strategy:* 9-1–9.22. Boston: Warren,

Gorham & Lamont; Pearce, J. A. & Robinson, R. B. 2000. *Strategic management* (7th ed.). New York: McGraw-Hill; and Dickson, op. cit., pp. 295–296.

62. Bartlett, C. A. & Ghoshal, S. 2000. Going global: Lessons for late movers. *Harvard Business Review,* 78(2): 132–142.

63. Neuborne, E. 2000. E-tailers hit the relaunch key. *BusinessWeek,* October 17: 62.

64. Berkowitz, E. N., Kerin, R. A., & Hartley, S. W. 2000. *Marketing* (6th ed.). New York: McGraw-Hill.

65. MacMillan, op. cit.

66. Brooker, K. 2001. A game of inches. *Fortune,* February 5: 98–100.

67. Our discussion of reverse and breakaway positioning draws on Moon, Y. 2005. Break free from the product life cycle. *Harvard Business Review,* 83(5): 87–94. This article also discusses stealth positioning as a means of overcoming consumer resistance and advancing a product from the introduction to the growth phase.

68. MacMillan, op. cit.

69. Berkowitz et al., op. cit.

70. Bearden et al., op. cit.

71. The discussion of these four strategies draws on MacMillan, op. cit.; Berkowitz et al., op. cit.; and Bearden et al., op. cit.

72. Augustine, N. R. 1997. Reshaping an industry: Lockheed Martin's survival story. *Harvard Business Review,* 75(3): 83–94.

73. Snow, D. C. 2008. Beware of old technologies' last gasps. *Harvard Business Review,* January: 17–18; Lohr, S. 2008. Why old technologies are still kicking. *New York Times,* March 23: np; and McGrath, R. G. 2008. Innovation and the last gasps of dying technologies. *ritamcgrath. com,* March 18: np.

74. Coyne, K. P., Coyne, S. T., & Coyne, E. J., Sr. 2010. When you've got to cut costs—now. *Harvard Business Review,* 88(5): 74–83.

75. A study that draws on the resource-based view of the firm to investigate successful turnaround strategies is Morrow, J. S., Sirmon, D. G.,

Hitt, M. A., & Holcomb, T. R. 2007. Creating value in the face of declining performance: Firm strategies and organizational recovery. *Strategic Management Journal,* 28(3): 271–284.

76. For a study investigating the relationship between organizational restructuring and acquisition performance, refer to Barkema, H. G. & Schijven, M. Toward unlocking the full potential of acquisitions: The role of organizational restructuring. *Academy of Management Journal,* 51(4): 696–722.

77. For some useful ideas on effective turnarounds and handling downsizings, refer to Marks, M. S. & De Meuse, K. P. 2005. Resizing the organization: Maximizing the gain while minimizing the pain of layoffs, divestitures and closings. *Organizational Dynamics,* 34(1): 19–36.

78. Hambrick, D. C. & Schecter, S. M. 1983. Turnaround strategies for mature industrial product business units. *Academy of Management Journal,* 26(2): 231–248.

Corporate-Level Strategy

Creating Value through Diversification

chapter 6

chapter 6

After reading this chapter, you should have a good understanding of the following learning objectives:

LO6.1 The reasons for the failure of many diversification efforts.

LO6.2 How managers can create value through diversification initiatives.

LO6.3 How corporations can use related diversification to achieve synergistic benefits through economies of scope and market power.

LO6.4 How corporations can use unrelated diversification to attain synergistic benefits through corporate restructuring, parenting, and portfolio analysis.

LO6.5 The various means of engaging in diversification—mergers and acquisitions, joint ventures/strategic alliances, and internal development.

LO6.6 Managerial behaviors that can erode the creation of value.

Learning from Mistakes

The Flip video camera burst onto the scene in 2007 and took off, selling over 2 million of the simple, small, and easy-to-use cameras in two years. Sensing opportunity in the digital video market, Cisco Systems snapped up Pure Digital Technologies, the parent company of Flip, in 2009 for $590 million.[1] Just two years later, Cisco announced that it was pulling the plug on the Flip video camera and shutting down the Flip division. Why did Cisco, an experienced acquirer, fail with the Flip acquisition?

Cisco, a computer networking giant, has been extremely successful over the last several years, producing over $47 billion in sales and $7.9 billion in net income in 2014. As part of its business model, Cisco regularly undertakes acquisitions to extend its technology base and product portfolio. In the last decade, Cisco acquired over 80 firms as it extended its product portfolio.

Even with this experience with acquisitions, Cisco was unable to avoid failure with Flip for two reasons. First, Cisco's core business operations are in business networking equipment and software. Flip's business was selling video cameras to individual customers. This is a very different business, where Cisco's knowledge and other competencies were of little value. While Cisco has had some success extending into the consumer market, such as with its acquisition of Linksys, this success has come in the home networking business, a market to which Cisco can transfer some of its business networking competencies.

Second, in large, widely diversified firms, decision making can become slow and remote to market conditions. Cisco competes in a wide range of markets and had nearly 60 decision-making groups in its structure, with several layers separating John Chambers, the CEO of Cisco, from the individual markets. In such a large and diversified firm, the decision making in a small division with only $400 million in annual sales, 1 percent of the overall sales of Cisco, was not the top priority of corporate managers. Stephen Baker, an analyst with NPD Group, saw this and commented that "Cisco was never really committed to the product." As a result, Flip was slower and less responsive to market pressures than it was when it was an entrepreneurial firm.

These two factors left Flip unable to respond to the rapid changes occurring in the home market. Flip experienced a meteoric rise from 2007 to 2009, but this simply triggered an onslaught of competing cameras. Flip also faced an increasing threat from video-camera-enabled smartphones and tablets. There was also a shift in how customers used video devices during this period. Users increasingly wanted the ability to share videos in real time and also upload videos easily to YouTube, Flickr, and other social media sites. Cisco failed to see this shift and didn't add wireless transmission technology into the cameras. John Chambers, Cisco's CEO, admitted this failure. "With Flip, we missed the transition. . . . it was about software that goes into the cloud—the way you're going to really deliver information in the future. We should have been developing our software for the cloud as opposed to the device. And we missed the window of opportunity."

In the end, Cisco didn't have the necessary vision to succeed in this market or the ability to respond quickly enough to the dynamic changes in customer desires.

Discussion Questions

1. Would Flip have had a better chance at success as a stand-alone firm than it did as part of Cisco? Why or why not?
2. Cisco didn't have the right market focus or competencies to win with Flip. What firms could have succeeded by acquiring Flip?

LO6.1

The reasons for
the failure of many
diversification efforts.

**corporate-level
strategy**
a strategy that focuses
on gaining long-term
revenue, profits, and
market value through
managing operations in
multiple businesses.

Cisco's experience with Flip is more the rule than the exception. Research shows that a majority of acquisitions of public corporations result in value destruction rather than value creation. Many large multinational firms have also failed to effectively integrate their acquisitions, paid too high a premium for the target's common stock, or were unable to understand how the acquired firm's assets would fit with their own lines of business.[2] And, at times, top executives may not have acted in the best interests of shareholders. That is, the motive for the acquisition may have been to enhance the executives' power and prestige rather than to improve shareholder returns. At times, the only other people who may have benefited were the shareholders of the *acquired* firms—or the investment bankers who advise the acquiring firm, because they collect huge fees up front regardless of what happens afterward![3]

There have been several studies that were conducted over a variety of time periods that show how disappointingly acquisitions have typically turned out. For example:

- A study evaluated the stock market reaction of 600 acquisitions over the period between 1975 and 1991. The results indicated that the acquiring firms suffered an average 4 percent drop in market value (after adjusting for market movements) in the three months following the acquisitions announcement.[4]
- In a study by Salomon Smith Barney of U.S. companies acquired since 1997 in deals for $15 billion or more, the stocks of the acquiring firms have, on average, underperformed the S&P stock index by 14 percentage points and underperformed their peer group by 4 percentage points after the deals were announced.[5]
- A study investigated 270 mergers that took place between 2000 and 2003 in multiple countries and regions. It found that after a merger, sales growth decreased by 6 percent, earnings growth dropped 9.4 percent, and market valuations declined 2.5 percent (figures are adjusted for industry trends and refer to three years pre- or postmerger).[6]
- A study that investigated 86 completed takeover bids that took place between 1993 and 2008 noted a negative return of 2 percent per month in long-term performance for the three-year postacquisition period.[7]

Exhibit 6.1 lists some well-known examples of failed acquisitions and mergers.

EXHIBIT 6.1 Some Well-Known M&A Blunders

Examples of Some Very Expensive Blunders

- Sprint and Nextel merged in 2005. On January 31, 2008, the firm announced a merger-related charge of $31 billion. Its stock had lost 76 percent of its value by late 2012 when it was announced that Sprint Nextel would be purchased by SoftBank, a Japanese telecommunications and Internet firm. SoftBank's stock price dropped 20 percent in the week after announcing it would acquire Sprint.
- AOL paid $114 billion to acquire Time Warner in 2001. Over the next two years, AOL Time Warner lost $150 billion in market valuation.
- Conseco paid $5.8 billion to buy Green Tree, a mobile home mortgage lender, in 1998 though the company's net worth was not even $1 billion. In the next two years, Conseco lost 90 percent of its market value!
- Daimler Benz paid $36 billion to acquire Chrysler in 1998. After years of losses, it sold 80.1 percent of the unit to Cerberus Capital Management for $7.4 billion in 2007. Cerberus didn't do any better, losing its ownership stake when Chrysler went into a government-managed bankruptcy in 2009.
- In 2012, Hewlett-Packard wrote off $9 billion of the $11 billion it paid for Autonomy, a software company that it purchased one year earlier. After the purchase, HP realized that Autonomy's accounting statements were not accurate, resulting in a nearly 80 percent drop in the value of Autonomy once those accounting irregularities were corrected.
- Similarly, in 2012, Microsoft admitted to a major acquisition mistake when it wrote off essentially the entire $6.2 billion it paid for a digital advertising firm, aQuantive, that it purchased in 2007.

Sources: Ante, S. E. 2008. Sprint's wake-up call. *businessweek.com,* February 21: np; Gupta, P. 2008. Daimler may sell remaining Chrysler stake. *www.reuters.com,* September 24: np; Tully, S. 2006. The (second) worst deal ever. *Fortune,* October 16: 102–119; and Wakabayashi, D., Troianovski, A., & Ante, S. 2012. Bravado behind Softbank's Sprint deal. October 16, *wsj.com:* np.

Many acquisitions ultimately result in divestiture—an admission that things didn't work out as planned. In fact, some years ago, a writer for *Fortune* magazine lamented, "Studies show that 33 percent to 50 percent of acquisitions are later divested, giving corporate marriages a divorce rate roughly comparable to that of men and women."[8]

Admittedly, we have been rather pessimistic so far.[9] Clearly, many diversification efforts have worked out very well—whether through mergers and acquisitions, strategic alliances and joint ventures, or internal development. We will discuss many success stories throughout this chapter. Next, we will discuss the primary rationales for diversification.

Making Diversification Work: An Overview

LO6.2

How managers can create value through diversification initiatives.

Clearly, not all **diversification** moves, including those involving mergers and acquisitions, erode performance. For example, acquisitions in the oil industry, such as British Petroleum's purchases of Amoco and Arco, are performing well, as is the Exxon-Mobil merger. MetLife was able to dramatically expand its global footprint by acquiring Alico, a global player in the insurance business, from AIG in 2010 when AIG was in financial distress. Since AIG was desperate to sell assets, MetLife was able to acquire this business at an attractive price. With this acquisition, MetLife expanded its global reach from 17 to 64 countries and increased its non-U.S. revenue from 15 to 40 percent.[10] Many leading high-tech firms such as Google, Apple, and Intel have dramatically enhanced their revenues, profits, and market values through a wide variety of diversification initiatives, including acquisitions, strategic alliances, and joint ventures, as well as internal development.

diversification
the process of firms expanding their operations by entering new businesses.

So the question becomes: Why do some diversification efforts pay off and others produce poor results? This chapter addresses two related issues: (1) What businesses should a corporation compete in? and (2) How should these businesses be managed to jointly create more value than if they were freestanding units?

Diversification initiatives—whether through mergers and acquisitions, strategic alliances and joint ventures, or internal development—must be justified by the creation of value for shareholders.[11] But this is not always the case.[12] Acquiring firms typically pay high premiums when they acquire a target firm. For example, in 2006 Freeport-McMoRan paid a 30 percent premium to acquire Phelps Dodge in order to create the largest metals and mining concern in the U.S. In contrast, you and I, as private investors, can diversify our portfolio of stocks very cheaply. With an intensely competitive online brokerage industry, we can acquire hundreds (or thousands) of shares for a transaction fee of as little as $10 or less—a far cry from the 30 to 40 percent (or higher) premiums that corporations typically must pay to acquire companies.

Given the seemingly high inherent downside risks and uncertainties, one might ask: Why should companies even bother with diversification initiatives? The answer, in a word, is *synergy,* derived from the Greek word *synergos,* which means "working together." This can have two different, but not mutually exclusive, meanings.

First, a firm may diversify into *related* businesses. Here, the primary potential benefits to be derived come from *horizontal relationships,* that is, businesses sharing intangible resources (e.g., core competencies such as marketing) and tangible resources (e.g., production facilities, distribution channels).[13] Firms can also enhance their market power via pooled negotiating power and vertical integration. For example, Procter & Gamble enjoys many synergies from having businesses that share distribution resources.

Second, a corporation may diversify into *unrelated* businesses.[14] Here, the primary potential benefits are derived largely from *hierarchical relationships,* that is, value creation derived from the corporate office. Examples of the latter would include leveraging some of the support activities in the value chain that we discussed in Chapter 3, such as information systems or human resource practices.

EXHIBIT 6.2

Creating Value through
Related and Unrelated
Diversification

Related Diversification: Economies of Scope

Leveraging core competencies
- 3M leverages its competencies in adhesives technologies to many industries, including automotive, construction, and telecommunications.

Sharing activities
- Polaris, a manufacturer of snowmobiles, motorcycles, watercraft, and off-road vehicles, shares manufacturing operations across its businesses. It also has a corporate R&D facility and staff departments that support all of Polaris's operating divisions.

Related Diversification: Market Power

Pooled negotiating power
- ConAgra, a diversified food producer, increases its power over suppliers by centrally purchasing huge quantities of packaging materials for all of its food divisions.

Vertical integration
- Shaw Industries, a giant carpet manufacturer, increases its control over raw materials by producing much of its own polypropylene fiber, a key input to its manufacturing process.

Unrelated Diversification: Parenting, Restructuring, and Financial Synergies

Corporate restructuring and parenting
- The corporate office of Cooper Industries adds value to its acquired businesses by performing such activities as auditing their manufacturing operations, improving their accounting activities, and centralizing union negotiations.

Portfolio management
- Novartis, formerly Ciba-Geigy, uses portfolio management to improve many key activities, including resource allocation and reward and evaluation systems.

Please note that such benefits derived from horizontal (related diversification) and hierarchical (unrelated diversification) relationships are not mutually exclusive. Many firms that diversify into related areas benefit from information technology expertise in the corporate office. Similarly, unrelated diversifiers often benefit from the "best practices" of sister businesses even though their products, markets, and technologies may differ dramatically.

Exhibit 6.2 provides an overview of how we will address the various means by which firms create value through both related and unrelated diversification and also includes a summary of some examples that we will address in this chapter.[15]

Related Diversification: Economies of Scope and Revenue Enhancement

Related diversification enables a firm to benefit from horizontal relationships across different businesses in the diversified corporation by leveraging core competencies and sharing activities (e.g., production and distribution facilities). This enables a corporation to benefit from economies of scope. **Economies of scope** refers to cost savings from leveraging core competencies or sharing related activities among businesses in the corporation. A firm can also enjoy greater revenues if two businesses attain higher levels of sales growth combined than either company could attain independently.

Leveraging Core Competencies

The concept of core competencies can be illustrated by the imagery of the diversified corporation as a tree.[16] The trunk and major limbs represent core products; the smaller branches are business units; and the leaves, flowers, and fruit are end products. The core

---

related diversification
a firm entering a different business in which it can benefit from leveraging core competencies, sharing activities, or building market power.

economies of scope
cost savings from leveraging core competencies or sharing related activities among businesses in a corporation.

LO6.3

How corporations can use related diversification to achieve synergistic benefits through economies of scope and market power.

competencies are represented by the root system, which provides nourishment, sustenance, and stability. Managers often misread the strength of competitors by looking only at their end products, just as we can fail to appreciate the strength of a tree by looking only at its leaves. Core competencies may also be viewed as the "glue" that binds existing businesses together or as the engine that fuels new business growth.

Core competencies reflect the collective learning in organizations—how to coordinate diverse production skills, integrate multiple streams of technologies, and market diverse products and services.[17] Casio, a giant electronic products producer, synthesizes its abilities in miniaturization, microprocessor design, material science, and ultrathin precision castings to produce digital watches. These are the same skills it applies to design and produce its miniature card calculators, digital cameras, pocket electronic dictionaries, and other small electronics.

For a core competence to create value and provide a viable basis for synergy among the businesses in a corporation, it must meet three criteria:[18]

- ***The core competence must enhance competitive advantage(s) by creating superior customer value.*** Every value-chain activity has the potential to provide a viable basis for building on a core competence.[19] At Gillette, for example, scientists have developed a series of successful new razors, including the Sensor, Fusion, Mach 3, and ProGlide, building on a thorough understanding of several phenomena that underlie shaving. These include the physiology of facial hair and skin, the metallurgy of blade strength and sharpness, the dynamics of a cartridge moving across skin, and the physics of a razor blade severing hair. Such innovations are possible only with an understanding of such phenomena and the ability to combine such technologies into innovative products. Customers are willing to pay more for such technologically differentiated products.

- ***Different businesses in the corporation must be similar in at least one important way related to the core competence.*** It is not essential that the products or services themselves be similar. Rather, at least one element in the value chain must require similar skills in creating competitive advantage if the corporation is to capitalize on its core competence. At first glance you might think that computers and health care have little in common. However, Strategy Spotlight 6.1 discusses how IBM is combining its competencies in computing technology with crowdsourced knowledge to provide health care services.

- ***The core competencies must be difficult for competitors to imitate or find substitutes for.*** As we discussed in Chapter 5, competitive advantages will not be sustainable if the competition can easily imitate or substitute them. Similarly, if the skills associated with a firm's core competencies are easily imitated or replicated, they are not a sound basis for sustainable advantages.

Consider Amazon's retailing operations. Amazon developed strong competencies in Internet retailing, website infrastructure, warehousing, and order fulfillment to dominate the online book industry. It used these competencies along with its brand name to expand into a range of online retail businesses. Competitors in these other market areas have had great difficulty imitating Amazon's competencies, and many have simply stopped trying. Instead, they have partnered with Amazon and contracted with Amazon to provide these services for them.[20]

Steve Jobs provided insight on the importance of a firm's core competence. The Apple CEO was considered one of the world's most respected business leaders:[21]

One of our biggest insights (years ago) was that we didn't want to get into any business where we didn't own or control the primary technology, because you'll get your head handed to you. We realized that for almost all future consumer electronics, the primary technology was going to be software. And we were pretty good at software. We could

core competencies
a firm's strategic resources that reflect the collective learning in the organization.

IBM: THE NEW HEALTH CARE EXPERT

Watson, the supercomputer IBM used to win a competition against the best players on the quiz show *Jeopardy!* is now working toward becoming Dr. Watson. Over the decades, IBM has developed strong competencies in raw computing power. With Watson, a computer named after IBM founder Thomas J. Watson, IBM engineers and scientists set out to extend IBM's competencies by building a computing system that can process natural language. Their goal was to build a system that could rival a human's ability to answer questions posed in natural language with speed, accuracy, and confidence. They took four years to develop the system and demonstrated its capabilities in beating two of the greatest champions of *Jeopardy!* in 2011.

Now IBM is aiming to leverage its competencies in the health care arena. In 2013, IBM introduced three applications, one which recommends cancer treatment options and two for reviewing and authorizing treatments and related insurance claims. IBM developed the cancer treatment application with Memorial Sloan-Kettering, one of the world's premier cancer treatment clinics. IBM chose to work on cancer treatment since the volume of research on cancer doubles every five years. As a result, oncologists, the doctors treating cancer, can easily fall behind the cutting edge of research. As Dr. Mark Kris, chief of Memorial Sloan Kettering's Thoracic Oncology Service, stated, "There has been an explosion in medical research, and doctors can't possibly keep up." That is not a problem for Watson. IBM sees this massive volume of research as an opportunity to crowdsource knowledge to develop new, integrated insights. IBM regularly feeds massive amounts of data from medical studies into Watson. In a one-year period, Watson absorbed and analyzed more than 600,000 pieces of medical data and 2 million pages of text from 42 medical journals and clinical trials of cancer treatments. IBM then adds the individual patient's health history and current symptoms to the system. With its natural-language capabilities, Watson can easily process and codify all of the information fed into it. Doctors access the system, using an iPad, enter the patient's symptoms, and within three seconds receive a personalized diagnosis and a prioritized list of recommended tests and treatment options.

While oncology is the first medical specialty for Watson, IBM is looking to take the same approach to providing guidance for the treatment of diabetes, kidney disease, heart disease, and many other areas of medicine. It has enlisted leading health care partners, such as the Cleveland Clinic and Cedars-Sinai Hospital, in its efforts to expand into other treatment areas.

Sources: Frier, S. 2012. IBM wants to put a Watson in your pocket. *Bloomberg Businessweek,* September 17: 41–42; Groenfeldt, T. 2012. IBM's Watson, Cedars-Sinai and WellPoint take on cancer. *forbes.com,* February 1: np; Henschen, D. 2013. IBM's Watson could be healthcare game changer. *informationweek.com,* February 3: np; and *ibm.com.*

do the operating system software. We could write applications like iTunes on the Mac or even PC. And we could write the back-end software that runs on a cloud like iTunes. So we could write all these different kinds of software and tweed it all together and make it work seamlessly. And you ask yourself: What other companies can do that? It's a pretty short list.

Sharing Activities

sharing activities
having activities of two or more businesses' value chains done by one of the businesses.

As we saw above, leveraging core competencies involves transferring accumulated skills and expertise across business units in a corporation. Corporations also can achieve synergy by **sharing activities** across their business units. These include value-creating activities such as common manufacturing facilities, distribution channels, and sales forces. As we will see, sharing activities can potentially provide two primary payoffs: cost savings and revenue enhancements.

Deriving Cost Savings   Typically, this is the most common type of synergy and the easiest to estimate. Peter Shaw, head of mergers and acquisitions at the British chemical and pharmaceutical company ICI, refers to cost savings as "hard synergies" and contends that the level of certainty of their achievement is quite high. Cost savings come from many sources, including from the elimination of jobs, facilities, and related expenses that are no longer needed when functions are consolidated and from economies of scale in purchasing. Cost savings are generally highest when one company acquires another from the same industry in the same country. Shaw Industries, a division of Berkshire Hathaway, is the nation's largest carpet producer. Over the years, it has dominated the competition through a strategy of acquisition that has enabled Shaw, among other things, to consolidate its manufacturing operations in a few, highly efficient plants and to lower costs through higher capacity utilization.

Sharing activities inevitably involve costs that the benefits must outweigh such as the greater coordination required to manage a shared activity. Even more important is the need to compromise on the design or performance of an activity so that it can be shared. For example, a salesperson handling the products of two business units must operate in a way that is usually not what either unit would choose if it were independent. If the compromise erodes the unit's effectiveness, then sharing may reduce rather than enhance competitive advantage.

Enhancing Revenue and Differentiation

Often an acquiring firm and its target may achieve a higher level of sales growth together than either company could on its own. For example, Starbucks has acquired a number of small firms, including La Boulange, a small bakery chain; Teavana, a tea producer; and Evolution Fresh, a juice company. Starbucks can add value to all of these firms by expanding their market exposure as Starbucks offers these products for sale in its national retail chain.[22]

Firms also can enhance the effectiveness of their differentiation strategies by means of sharing activities among business units. A shared order-processing system, for example, may permit new features and services that a buyer will value. As another example, financial service providers strive to provide differentiated bundles of services to customers. By having a single point of contact where customers can manage their checking accounts, investment accounts, insurance policies, bill-payment services, mortgages, and many other services, they create value for their customers.

As a cautionary note, managers must keep in mind that sharing activities among businesses in a corporation can have a negative effect on a given business's differentiation. For example, when Ford owned Jaguar, customers had lower perceived value of Jaguar automobiles when they learned that the entry-level Jaguar shared its basic design with and was manufactured in the same production plant as the Ford Mondeo, a European midsize car. Perhaps it is not too surprising that Jaguar was divested by Ford in 2008.

Related Diversification: Market Power

We now discuss how companies achieve related diversification through **market power.** We also address the two principal means by which firms achieve synergy through market power: *pooled negotiating power* and *vertical integration.* Managers do, however, have limits on their ability to use market power for diversification, because government regulations can sometimes restrict the ability of a business to gain very large shares of a particular market. For example, in 2011 AT&T attempted to acquire T-Mobile, a wireless service provider, but the acquisition was blocked by federal regulators who feared the combined firm would have too much market power in the telecommunications industry.

market power
firms' abilities to profit through restricting or controlling supply to a market or coordinating with other firms to reduce investment.

Pooled Negotiating Power

Similar businesses working together or the affiliation of a business with a strong parent can strengthen an organization's bargaining position relative to suppliers and customers and enhance its position vis-à-vis competitors. Compare, for example, the position of an independent food manufacturer with that of the same business within Nestlé. Being part of Nestlé provides the business with significant clout—greater bargaining power with suppliers and customers—since it is part of a firm that makes large purchases from suppliers and provides a wide variety of products. Access to the parent's deep pockets

pooled negotiating power
the improvement in bargaining position relative to suppliers and customers.

increases the business's strength, and the Nestlé unit enjoys greater protection from substitutes and new entrants. Not only would rivals perceive the unit as a more formidable opponent, but the unit's association with Nestlé would also provide greater visibility and improved image.

When acquiring related businesses, a firm's potential for pooled negotiating power vis-à-vis its customers and suppliers can be very enticing. However, managers must carefully evaluate how the combined businesses may affect relationships with actual and potential customers, suppliers, and competitors. For example, when PepsiCo diversified into the fast-food industry with its acquisitions of Kentucky Fried Chicken, Taco Bell, and Pizza Hut (now part of Yum! Brands), it clearly benefited from its position over these units that served as a captive market for its soft-drink products. However, many competitors, such as McDonald's, refused to consider PepsiCo as a supplier of its own soft-drink needs because of competition with Pepsi's divisions in the fast-food industry. Simply put, McDonald's did not want to subsidize the enemy! Thus, although acquiring related businesses can enhance a corporation's bargaining power, it must be aware of the potential for retaliation.

Vertical Integration

Vertical integration occurs when a firm becomes its own supplier or distributor. That is, it represents an expansion or extension of the firm by integrating preceding or successive production processes.[23] The firm incorporates more processes toward the original source of raw materials (backward integration) or toward the ultimate consumer (forward integration). For example, a car manufacturer might supply its own parts or make its own engines to secure sources of supply or control its own system of dealerships to ensure retail outlets for its products. Similarly, an oil refinery might secure land leases and develop its own drilling capacity to ensure a constant supply of crude oil. Or it could expand into retail operations by owning or licensing gasoline stations to guarantee customers for its petroleum products.

Vertical integration can be a viable strategy for many firms. Strategy Spotlight 6.2 discusses Nutriva, a Canadian dairy firm, that has backward integrated in order to ensure that the inputs it uses in its dairy business support and reinforce the firm's differentiated market position.

Benefits and Risks of Vertical Integration   Vertical integration is a means for an organization to reduce its dependence on suppliers or its channels of distribution to end users. However, the benefits associated with vertical integration—backward or forward—must be carefully weighed against the risks.[24] The primary benefits and risks of vertical integration are listed in Exhibit 6.3.

Winnebago, the leader in the market for drivable recreational vehicles, with a 20.6 percent market share, illustrates some of vertical integration's benefits.[25] The word *Winnebago* means "big RV" to most Americans. And the firm has a sterling reputation for great quality. The firm's huge northern Iowa factories do everything from extruding aluminum for body parts to molding plastics for water and holding tanks to dashboards. Such vertical integration at the factory may appear to be outdated and expensive, but it guarantees excellent quality. The Recreational Vehicle Dealer Association started giving a quality award in 1996, and Winnebago has won it every year.

In making vertical integration decisions, five issues should be considered:[26]

1. *Is the company satisfied with the quality of the value that its present suppliers and distributors are providing?* If the performance of organizations in the vertical chain—both suppliers and distributors—is satisfactory, it may not, in general, be appropriate for a company to perform these activities itself. Nike and

VERTICAL INTEGRATION AT NUTRIVA

After graduating with a master's degree in animal science from Michigan State University, Bill Vanderkooi returned to British Columbia to help run his family's dairy business. He saw the need to break out of the low-margin, commodity nature of the dairy business. His desire was to build a brand that emphasized health consciousness and environmental sustainability. He developed a line of organic dairy products enriched with DHA, an omega-3 fatty acid that is thought to provide several health benefits. To ensure that his dairy products met his desire for healthy differentiation, he backward integrated into a number of businesses that provide high-quality feed designed to result in higher nutrient qualities in the firm's dairy products. First, he started a business that developed seeds that produce nutrient-rich grains to feed his cows without the use of pesticides. He also built a feed business in which samples of grain are analyzed and graded on their nutrient values. He founded an organic-milk trucking company so that he can be sure the milk he receives from supplier farms is not contaminated by being transported in trucks that also carry nonorganic milk. Finally, he built a demonstration dairy farm at which Nutriva can educate consumers on the health attributes of its dairy products and the environmental consciousness of the company's dairy operations. In Vanderkooi's words, all of these efforts allow the firm to have "traceable quality control." His desire is to have transparency so that customers can have confidence in the health attributes of the products they purchase and in the environmental sustainability efforts of the supplier farms and dairy operations.

These efforts appear to be paying off. The firm's sales doubled from 2009 to 2013. Vanderkooi's desire to provide healthy food products and increase consumer demand has led the firm to expand its offerings to other food products, such as vitamin-rich eggs from free-range chickens, and consulting services for other food producers.

Sources: Vanderkooi, B. 2012. Bill Vanderkooi, president of Bakerview Ecodairy and CEO of Nutriva Group. *dairyindustries.com*, August 12: np; Ebner, D. 2012. Farmer rips page from corporate strategy handbook. *theglobeandmail.com*, August 23: np; and *nutrivagroup.com*.

Benefits
• A secure source of raw materials or distribution channels.
• Protection of and control over valuable assets.
• Proprietary access to new technologies developed by the unit.
• Simplified procurement and administrative procedures.

Risks
• Costs and expenses associated with increased overhead and capital expenditures.
• Loss of flexibility resulting from large investments.
• Problems associated with unbalanced capacities along the value chain. (For example, the in-house supplier has to be larger than your needs in order to benefit from economies of scale in that market.)
• Additional administrative costs associated with managing a more complex set of activities.

EXHIBIT 6.3

Benefits and Risks of Vertical Integration

Reebok have outsourced the manufacture of their shoes for years, because they have found the independent suppliers capable of providing low-cost, acceptable-quality shoes.

2. ***Are there activities in the industry value chain presently being outsourced or performed independently by others that are a viable source of future profits?***
   Even if a firm is outsourcing value-chain activities to companies that are doing a credible job, it may be missing out on substantial profit opportunities. Consider Best Buy. When it realized that the profit potential of providing installation and service was substantial, Best Buy forward integrated into this area by acquiring Geek Squad.

3. ***Is there a high level of stability in the demand for the organization's products?***
   High demand or sales volatility is not conducive to vertical integration. With the high level of fixed costs in plant and equipment as well as operating costs that accompany endeavors toward vertical integration, widely fluctuating sales demand

can either strain resources (in times of high demand) or result in unused capacity (in times of low demand). The cycles of "boom and bust" in the automobile industry are a key reason why the manufacturers have increased the amount of outsourced inputs.

4. ***Does the company have the necessary competencies to execute the vertical integration strategies?*** As many companies would attest, successfully executing strategies of vertical integration can be very difficult. For example, Boise Cascade, a lumber firm, once forward integrated into the home-building industry but found that it didn't have the design and marketing competencies needed to compete in this market.

5. ***Will the vertical integration initiative have potential negative impacts on the firm's stakeholders?*** Managers must carefully consider the impact that vertical integration may have on existing and future customers, suppliers, and competitors. After Lockheed Martin, a dominant defense contractor, acquired Loral Corporation, an electronics supplier, for $9.1 billion, it had an unpleasant and unanticipated surprise. Loral, as a subsidiary of Lockheed, was viewed as a rival by many of its previous customers. Thus, while Lockheed Martin may have seen benefits by being able to coordinate operations with Loral as a captive supplier, it also saw a decline in business for Loral with other defense contractors.

transaction cost perspective

a perspective that the choice of a transaction's governance structure, such as vertical integration or market transaction, is influenced by transaction costs, including search, negotiating, contracting, monitoring, and enforcement costs, associated with each choice.

Analyzing Vertical Integration: The Transaction Cost Perspective   Another approach that has proved very useful in understanding vertical integration is the **transaction cost perspective.**[27] According to this perspective, every market transaction involves some *transaction costs.* First, a decision to purchase an input from an outside source leads to *search* costs (i.e., the cost to find where it is available, the level of quality, etc.). Second, there are costs associated with *negotiating.* Third, a *contract* needs to be written spelling out future possible contingencies. Fourth, parties in a contract have to *monitor* each other. Finally, if a party does not comply with the terms of the contract, there are *enforcement* costs. Transaction costs are thus the sum of search costs, negotiation costs, contracting costs, monitoring costs, and enforcement costs. These transaction costs can be avoided by internalizing the activity, in other words, by producing the input in-house.

A related problem with purchasing a specialized input from outside is the issue of *transaction-specific investments.* For example, when an automobile company needs an input specifically designed for a particular car model, the supplier may be unwilling to make the investments in plant and machinery necessary to produce that component for two reasons. First, the investment may take many years to recover but there is no guarantee the automobile company will continue to buy from the supplier after the contract expires, typically in one year. Second, once the investment is made, the supplier has no bargaining power. That is, the buyer knows that the supplier has no option but to supply at ever-lower prices because the investments were so specific that they cannot be used to produce alternative products. In such circumstances, again, vertical integration may be the only option.

Vertical integration, however, gives rise to a different set of costs. These costs are referred to as *administrative costs.* Coordinating different stages of the value chain now internalized within the firm causes administrative costs to go up. Decisions about vertical integration are, therefore, based on a comparison of transaction costs and administrative costs. If transaction costs are lower than administrative costs, it is best to resort to market transactions and avoid vertical integration. For example, McDonald's may be the world's biggest buyer of beef, but it does not raise cattle. The market for beef has low transaction costs and requires no transaction-specific investments. On the other hand, if transaction costs are higher than administrative costs, vertical integration becomes an attractive strategy. Most automobile manufacturers produce their own engines because the market for engines involves high transaction costs and transaction-specific investments.

Unrelated Diversification: Financial Synergies and Parenting

LO6.4

How corporations can use unrelated diversification to attain synergistic benefits through corporate restructuring, parenting, and portfolio analysis.

With **unrelated diversification,** unlike related diversification, few benefits are derived from *horizontal relationships*—that is, the leveraging of core competencies or the sharing of activities across business units within a corporation. Instead, potential benefits can be gained from *vertical (or hierarchical) relationships*—the creation of synergies from the interaction of the corporate office with the individual business units. There are two main sources of such synergies. First, the corporate office can contribute to "parenting" and restructuring of (often acquired) businesses. Second, the corporate office can add value by viewing the entire corporation as a family or "portfolio" of businesses and allocating resources to optimize corporate goals of profitability, cash flow, and growth. Additionally, the corporate office enhances value by establishing appropriate human resource practices and financial controls for each of its business units.

unrelated diversification
a firm entering a different business that has little horizontal interaction with other businesses of a firm.

Corporate Parenting and Restructuring

We have discussed how firms can add value through related diversification by exploring sources of synergy *across* business units. Now, we discuss how value can be created *within* business units as a result of the expertise and support provided by the corporate office.

Parenting   The positive contributions of the corporate office are called the **"parenting advantage."**[28] Many firms have successfully diversified their holdings without strong evidence of the more traditional sources of synergy (i.e., horizontally across business units). Diversified public corporations such as Berkshire Hathaway and Virgin Group and leveraged buyout firms such as KKR and Clayton, Dubilier & Rice are a few examples.[29] These parent companies create value through management expertise. How? They improve plans and budgets and provide especially competent central functions such as legal, financial, human resource management, procurement, and the like. They also help subsidiaries make wise choices in their own acquisitions, divestitures, and new internal development decisions. Such contributions often help business units to substantially increase their revenues and profits. For example, KKR, a private equity firm, has a team of parenting experts, called KKR Capstone, that works with newly acquired firms for 12 to 24 months to enhance the acquired firm's value. The team works to improve a range of operating activities, such as new product development processes, sales force activities, quality improvement, and supply chain management.

parenting advantage
the positive contributions of the corporate office to a new business as a result of expertise and support provided and not as a result of substantial changes in assets, capital structure, or management.

Restructuring   **Restructuring** is another means by which the corporate office can add value to a business.[30] The central idea can be captured in the real estate phrase "Buy low and sell high." Here, the corporate office tries to find either poorly performing firms with unrealized potential or firms in industries on the threshold of significant, positive change. The parent intervenes, often selling off parts of the business; changing the management; reducing payroll and unnecessary sources of expenses; changing strategies; and infusing the company with new technologies, processes, reward systems, and so forth. When the restructuring is complete, the firm can either "sell high" and capture the added value or keep the business and enjoy financial and competitive benefits.[31]

Loews Corporation, a conglomerate with $15 billion in revenues, competes in such industries as oil and gas, tobacco, watches, insurance, and hotels. It provides an exemplary example of how firms can successfully "buy low and sell high" as part of their corporate strategy.[32]

restructuring
the intervention of the corporate office in a new business that substantially changes the assets, capital structure, and/or management, including selling off parts of the business, changing the management, reducing payroll and unnecessary sources of expenses, changing strategies, and infusing the new business with new technologies, processes, and reward systems.

> Energy accounts for 33 percent of Loews' $30 billion in total assets. In the 1980s it bought six oil tankers for only $5 million each during a sharp slide in oil prices. The downside was limited. After all, these huge hulks could easily have been sold as scrap steel. However,

that didn't have to happen. Eight years after Loews purchased the tankers, it sold them for $50 million each.

Loews was also extremely successful with its next energy play—drilling equipment. Although wildcatting for oil is very risky, selling services to wildcatters is not, especially if the assets are bought during a down cycle. Loews did just that. It purchased 10 offshore drilling rigs for $50 million in 1989 and formed Diamond Offshore Drilling. In 1995 Loews received $338 million after taking a 30 percent piece of this operation public!

For the restructuring strategy to work, the corporate management must have the insight to detect undervalued companies (otherwise, the cost of acquisition would be too high) or businesses competing in industries with a high potential for transformation.[33] Additionally, of course, it must have the requisite skills and resources to turn the businesses around, even if they may be in new and unfamiliar industries.

Restructuring can involve changes in assets, capital structure, or management.

- *Asset restructuring* involves the sale of unproductive assets, or even whole lines of businesses, that are peripheral. In some cases, it may even involve acquisitions that strengthen the core business.
- *Capital restructuring* involves changing the debt-equity mix, or the mix between different classes of debt or equity. Although the substitution of equity with debt is more common in buyout situations, occasionally the parent may provide additional equity capital.
- *Management restructuring* typically involves changes in the composition of the top management team, organizational structure, and reporting relationships. Tight financial control, rewards based strictly on meeting short- to medium-term performance goals, and reduction in the number of middle-level managers are common steps in management restructuring. In some cases, parental intervention may even result in changes in strategy as well as infusion of new technologies and processes.

Portfolio Management

portfolio management
a method of (a) assessing the competitive position of a portfolio of businesses within a corporation, (b) suggesting strategic alternatives for each business, and (c) identifying priorities for the allocation of resources across the businesses.

During the 1970s and early 1980s, several leading consulting firms developed the concept of **portfolio management** to achieve a better understanding of the competitive position of an overall portfolio (or family) of businesses, to suggest strategic alternatives for each of the businesses, and to identify priorities for the allocation of resources. Several studies have reported widespread use of these techniques among American firms.[34]

While portfolio management tools have been widely used in corporations, research on their use has offered mixed support. However, recent research has suggested that strategically channeling resources to units with the most promising prospects can lead to corporate advantage. Research suggests that many firms do not adjust their capital allocations in response to changes in the performance of units or the attractiveness of the markets in which units of the corporation compete. Instead, allocations are fairly consistent from year to year. However, firms that assess the attractiveness of markets in which the firm competes and the capabilities of each division and then choose allocations of corporate resources based on these assessments exhibit higher levels of corporate survival, overall corporate performance, stock market performance, and the performance of individual business units within the corporation. These effects have also been shown to be stronger when firms compete in more competitive markets and in times of economic distress.[35] These findings have shown that the ability to effectively allocate financial capital is a key competence of high-performance diversified firms.

Description and Potential Benefits The key purpose of portfolio models is to assist a firm in achieving a balanced portfolio of businesses.[36] This consists of businesses whose profitability, growth, and cash flow characteristics complement each other and adds up to a satisfactory overall corporate performance. Imbalance, for example, could be caused either by excessive cash generation with too few growth opportunities or by insufficient cash generation to fund the growth requirements in the portfolio.

The Boston Consulting Group's (BCG's) growth/share matrix is among the best known of these approaches.[37] In the BCG approach, each of the firm's strategic business units (SBUs) is plotted on a two-dimensional grid in which the axes are relative market share and industry growth rate. The grid is broken into four quadrants. Exhibit 6.4 depicts the BCG matrix. Following are a few clarifications:

1. Each circle represents one of the corporation's business units. The size of the circle represents the relative size of the business unit in terms of revenues.
2. Relative market share, measured by the ratio of the business unit's size to that of its largest competitor, is plotted along the horizontal axis.
3. Market share is central to the BCG matrix. This is because high relative market share leads to unit cost reduction due to experience and learning curve effects and, consequently, superior competitive position.

Each of the four quadrants of the grid has different implications for the SBUs that fall into the category:

- **Stars** are SBUs competing in high-growth industries with relatively high market shares. These firms have long-term growth potential and should continue to receive substantial investment funding.
- **Question marks** are SBUs competing in high-growth industries but having relatively weak market shares. Resources should be invested in them to enhance their competitive positions.
- **Cash cows** are SBUs with high market shares in low-growth industries. These units have limited long-run potential but represent a source of current cash flows to fund investments in "stars" and "question marks."
- **Dogs** are SBUs with weak market shares in low-growth industries. Because they have weak positions and limited potential, most analysts recommend that they be divested.

EXHIBIT 6.4 The Boston Consulting Group (BCG) Portfolio Matrix

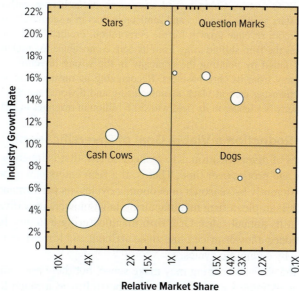

In using portfolio strategy approaches, a corporation tries to create shareholder value in a number of ways.[38] First, portfolio analysis provides a snapshot of the businesses in a corporation's portfolio. Therefore, the corporation is in a better position to allocate resources among the business units according to prescribed criteria (e.g., use cash flows from the cash cows to fund promising stars). Second, the expertise and analytical resources in the corporate office provide guidance in determining what firms may be attractive (or unattractive) acquisitions. Third, the corporate office is able to provide financial resources to the business units on favorable terms that reflect the corporation's overall ability to raise funds. Fourth, the corporate office can provide high-quality review and coaching for the individual businesses. Fifth, portfolio analysis provides a basis for developing strategic goals and reward/evaluation systems for business managers. For example, managers of cash cows would have lower targets for revenue growth than managers of stars, but the former would have higher threshold levels of profit targets on proposed projects than the managers of star businesses. Compensation systems would also reflect such realities. Managers of cash cows understandably would be rewarded more on the basis of cash that their businesses generate than would managers of star businesses. Similarly, managers of star businesses would be held to higher standards for revenue growth than managers of cash cow businesses.

Limitations   Despite the potential benefits of portfolio models, there are also some notable downsides. First, they compare SBUs on only two dimensions, making the implicit but erroneous assumption that (1) those are the only factors that really matter and (2) every unit can be accurately compared on that basis. Second, the approach views each SBU as a stand-alone entity, ignoring common core business practices and value-creating activities that may hold promise for synergies across business units. Third, unless care is exercised, the process becomes largely mechanical, substituting an oversimplified graphical model for the important contributions of the CEO's (and other corporate managers') experience and judgment. Fourth, the reliance on "strict rules" regarding resource allocation across SBUs can be detrimental to a firm's long-term viability. Finally, while colorful and easy to comprehend, the imagery of the BCG matrix can lead to some troublesome and overly simplistic prescriptions. For example, division managers are likely to want to jump ship as soon as their division is labeled a "dog."

To see what can go wrong, consider Cabot Corporation.

> Cabot Corporation supplies carbon black for the rubber, electronics, and plastics industries. Following the BCG matrix, Cabot moved away from its cash cow, carbon black, and diversified into stars such as ceramics and semiconductors in a seemingly overaggressive effort to create more revenue growth for the corporation. Predictably, Cabot's return on assets declined as the firm shifted away from its core competence to unrelated areas. The portfolio model failed by pointing the company in the wrong direction in an effort to spur growth—away from its core business. Recognizing its mistake, Cabot Corporation returned to its mainstay carbon black manufacturing and divested unrelated businesses. Today the company is a leader in its field with $3.6 billion in revenues in 2014.[39]

Caveat: Is Risk Reduction a Viable Goal of Diversification?

One of the purposes of diversification is to reduce the risk that is inherent in a firm's variability in revenues and profits over time. That is, if a firm enters new products or markets that are affected differently by seasonal or economic cycles, its performance over time will be more stable. For example, a firm manufacturing lawn mowers may diversify into snowblowers to even out its annual sales. Or a firm manufacturing a luxury line of household furniture may introduce a lower-priced line since affluent and lower-income customers are affected differently by economic cycles.

At first glance the above reasoning may make sense, but there are some problems with it. First, a firm's stockholders can diversify their portfolios at a much lower cost than a corporation, and they don't have to worry about integrating the acquisition into their portfolio. Second, economic cycles as well as their impact on a given industry (or firm) are difficult to predict with any degree of accuracy.

Notwithstanding the above, some firms have benefited from diversification by lowering the variability (or risk) in their performance over time. Consider GE, a firm that manufactures a wide range of products, including aircraft engines, power-generation equipment, locomotive trains, large appliances, healthcare equipment, lighting, water treatment equipment, oil well drilling equipment, and many other products. Offering such a wide range of products has allowed GE to generate stable earnings and a low-risk profile. Due to its earning stability, GE is able to borrow money at favorable rates which it then uses to invest in its own operations and to extend its portfolio even further by acquiring other manufacturers.

Risk reduction in and of itself is rarely viable as a means to create shareholder value. It must be undertaken with a view of a firm's overall diversification strategy.

The Means to Achieve Diversification

LO6.5

The various means of engaging in diversification—mergers and acquisitions, joint ventures/strategic alliances, and internal development.

We have addressed the types of diversification (e.g., related and unrelated) that a firm may undertake to achieve synergies and create value for its shareholders. Now, we address the means by which a firm can go about achieving these desired benefits.

There are three basic means. First, through acquisitions or mergers, corporations can directly acquire a firm's assets and competencies. Although the terms *mergers* and *acquisitions* are used quite interchangeably, there are some key differences. With **acquisitions,** one firm buys another through a stock purchase, cash, or the issuance of debt.[40] **Mergers,** on the other hand, entail a combination or consolidation of two firms to form a new legal entity. Mergers are relatively rare and entail a transaction among two firms on a relatively equal basis. Despite such differences, we consider both mergers and acquisitions to be quite similar in terms of their implications for a firm's corporate-level strategy.[41]

acquisitions
the incorporation of one firm into another through purchase.

Second, corporations may agree to pool the resources of other companies with their resource base, commonly known as a joint venture or strategic alliance. Although these two forms of partnerships are similar in many ways, there is an important difference. Joint ventures involve the formation of a third-party legal entity where by the two (or more) firms each contribute equity, whereas strategic alliances do not.

mergers
the combining of two or more firms into one new legal entity.

Third, corporations may diversify into new products, markets, and technologies through internal development. Called corporate entrepreneurship, it involves the leveraging and combining of a firm's own resources and competencies to create synergies and enhance shareholder value. We address this subject in greater length in Chapter 12.

Mergers and Acquisitions

The most visible and often costly means to diversify is through acquisitions. Over the past several years, several large acquisitions were announced. These include:[42]

- InBev's acquisition of Anheuser-Busch for $52 billion.
- Pfizer's acquisition of Wyeth for $68 billion.
- AT&T's acquisition of DirecTV for $67 billion.
- Boston Scientific's $27 billion acquisition of medical device maker Guidant.
- Facebook's acquisition of WhatsApp for $19.4 billion.
- Duke Energy's acquisition of Progress Energy for $25.5 billion.
- Softbank's acquisition of Sprint for $20 billion.

Exhibit 6.5 illustrates the volatility in worldwide M&A activity over the last several years. Several factors influence M&A activity. Julia Coronado, the chief economist at the investment bank BNP Paribas, highlights two of the key determinants, stating, "When mergers and acquisitions pick up, that's a good sign that businesses are feeling confident

EXHIBIT 6.5 Global Value of Mergers and Acquisitions ($ trillions)

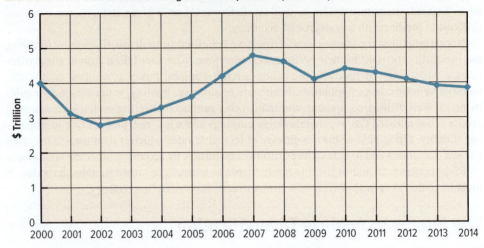

Source: Thomson Financial, Institute of Mergers, Acquisitions, and Alliances (IMAA) analysis.

enough about the future that they're willing to become aggressive, look for deals, look for ways to grow and expand their operations. And it's also an indication that markets are willing to finance these transactions. So it's optimism from the markets and from the businesses themselves."[43] Thus, the general economic conditions and level of optimism about the future influence managers' willingness to take on the risk of acquisitions. Additionally, the availability of financing can influence acquisition activity. During boom periods, financing is typically widely available. In contrast, during recessionary periods, potential acquirers typically find it difficult to borrow money to finance acquisitions.

Governmental policies such as regulatory actions and tax policies can also make the M&A environment more or less favorable. For example, increased antitrust enforcement will decrease the ability of firms to acquire their competitors or possibly firms in closely related markets. In contrast, increased regulatory pressures for good corporate governance may leave boards of directors more open to acquisition offers.

Finally, currency fluctuations can influence the rate of cross-border acquisitions, with firms in countries with stronger currencies being in a stronger position to acquire. For example, the U.S. dollar has increased in value from just over 75 to nearly 120 Japanese Yen from 2012 to the mid-2015, making it relatively cheaper for U.S. firms to acquire Japanese firms.

Motives and Benefits Growth through mergers and acquisitions has played a critical role in the success of many corporations in a wide variety of high-technology and knowledge-intensive industries. Here, market and technology changes can occur very quickly and unpredictably.[44] Speed—speed to market, speed to positioning, and speed to becoming a viable company—is critical in such industries. For example, in 2010, Apple acquired Siri Inc. so that it could quickly fully integrate Siri's natural-language voice recognition software into iOS, Apple's operating system.

Mergers and acquisitions also can be a means of *obtaining valuable resources that can help an organization expand its product offerings and services.* As noted earlier in the chapter, Cisco Systems, a computer networking firm, has undertaken over 80 acquisitions in the last decade. Cisco uses these acquisitions to quickly add new technology to its product offerings to meet changing customer needs. Then it uses its excellent sales force to market the new technology to its corporate customers. Cisco also provides strong incentives to the staff of acquired companies to stay on. To realize the greatest value from its acquisitions, Cisco also has learned to integrate acquired companies efficiently and effectively.[45]

Acquiring firms often use acquisitions to acquire critical human capital. These acquisitions have been referred to as acq-hires. In an acq-hire, the acquiring firm believes it needs the specific technical knowledge or the social network contacts of individuals in the target firm. This is especially important in settings where the technology or consumer preferences are highly dynamic. For example, in 2014, Apple purchased Beats Electronics for $3 billion. While Apple valued the product portfolio of Beats, its primary aim was to pull the founders of Beats, Jimmy Iovine and Dr. Dre (aka Andrew Young), into the Apple family. With Apple's iTunes business having hit a wall in growth, experiencing a 1 percent decline in 2013, Apple wanted to acquire new management talent to turn this business around. In addition to their experience at Beats, Iovine and Dr. Dre both have over 20 years of experience in the music industry, with Iovine founding and heading InterScope Records and Dr. Dre being a hip-hop pioneer and music producer. With this acquisition, Apple believes it brought in a wealth of knowledge about the music business, the ability to identify music trends, up-and-coming talent, and industry contacts needed to rejuvenate Apple's music business.[46]

Mergers and acquisitions also can *provide the opportunity for firms to attain the three bases of synergy—leveraging core competencies, sharing activities, and building market power.* Consider some of eBay's acquisitions. eBay has purchased a range of businesses in related product markets, such as GSI Commerce, a company that designs and runs online shopping sites for brick-and-mortar retailers, and StubHub, an online ticket broker. Additionally, it has purchased Korean online auction company Gmarket to expand its geographic scope. Finally, it has purchased firms providing related services, such as Shutl, a rapid-order-fulfillment service provider.

These acquisitions offer the opportunity to leverage eBay's competencies.[47] For example, with the acquisition of GSI, eBay saw opportunities to leverage its core competencies in online systems as well as its reputation to strengthen GSI while also expanding eBay's ability to work with medium to large merchants and brands. eBay can also benefit from these acquisitions by sharing activities. In acquiring firms in related product markets and in new geographic markets, eBay has built a set of businesses that can share in the development of e-commerce and mobile commerce systems. Finally, by expanding into new geographic markets and offering a wider range of services, eBay can build market power as one of the few online retailer systems that provide a full set of services on a global platform.

Merger and acquisition activity also can *lead to consolidation within an industry and can force other players to merge.*[48] The airline industry has seen a great deal of consolidation in the last several years. With a number of large-scale acquisitions, including Delta's acquisition of Northwest Airlines in 2008, United's acquisition of Continental in 2010, and American's purchase of US Airways in 2013, the U.S. airlines industry has been left with only four major players. In combining, these airlines are both seeking greater efficiencies by combining their networks and hoping that consolidation will dampen the rivalry in the industry.[49]

Corporations can also *enter new market segments by way of acquisitions.* As mentioned above, eBay, a firm that specialized in providing services to individuals and small businesses, moved into providing online retail systems for large merchants with its acquisition of GSI Commerce. Similarly, one of the reasons Fiat acquired Chrysler was to gain access to the U.S. auto market. Exhibit 6.6 summarizes the benefits of mergers and acquisitions.

- Obtain valuable resources, such as critical human capital, that can help an organization expand its product offerings.
- Provide the opportunity for firms to attain three bases of synergy: leveraging core competencies, sharing activities, and building market power.
- Lead to consolidation within an industry and force other players to merge.
- Enter new market segments.

EXHIBIT 6.6

Benefits of Mergers and Acquisitions

Potential Limitations   As noted in the previous section, mergers and acquisitions provide a firm with many potential benefits. However, at the same time, there are many potential drawbacks or limitations to such corporate activity.[50]

First, *the takeover premium that is paid for an acquisition typically is very high.* Two times out of three, the stock price of the acquiring company falls once the deal is made public. Since the acquiring firm often pays a 30 percent or higher premium for the target company, the acquirer must create synergies and scale economies that result in sales and market gains exceeding the premium price. Firms paying higher premiums set the performance hurdle even higher. For example, Household International paid an 82 percent premium to buy Beneficial, and Conseco paid an 83 percent premium to acquire Green Tree Financial. Historically, paying a high premium over the stock price has been a poor strategy.

Second, *competing firms often can imitate any advantages realized or copy synergies that result from the M&A.*[51] Thus, a firm can often see its advantages quickly erode. Unless the advantages are sustainable and difficult to copy, investors will not be willing to pay a high premium for the stock. Similarly, the time value of money must be factored into the stock price. M&A costs are paid up front. Conversely, firms pay for R&D, ongoing marketing, and capacity expansion over time. This stretches out the payments needed to gain new competencies. The M&A argument is that a large initial investment is worthwhile because it creates long-term advantages. However, stock analysts want to see immediate results from such a large cash outlay. If the acquired firm does not produce results quickly, investors often divest the stock, driving the price down.

Third, *managers' credibility and ego can sometimes get in the way of sound business decisions.* If the M&A does not perform as planned, managers who pushed for the deal find their reputation tarnished. This can lead them to protect their credibility by funneling more money, or escalating their commitment, into an inevitably doomed operation. Further, when a merger fails and a firm tries to unload the acquisition, the firm often must sell at a huge discount. These problems further compound the costs and erode the stock price.

Fourth, *there can be many cultural issues that may doom the intended benefits from M&A endeavors.* Consider the insights of Joanne Lawrence, who played an important role in the merger between SmithKline and the Beecham Group.[52]

> The key to a strategic merger is to create a new culture. This was a mammoth challenge during the SmithKline Beecham merger. We were working at so many different cultural levels, it was dizzying. We had two national cultures to blend—American and British—that compounded the challenge of selling the merger in two different markets with two different shareholder bases. There were also two different business cultures: One was very strong, scientific, and academic; the other was much more commercially oriented. And then we had to consider within both companies the individual businesses, each of which has its own little culture.

Exhibit 6.7 summarizes the limitations of mergers and acquisitions.

Strategy Spotlight 6.3 discusses the characteristics of acquisitions that lead investors to see greater value in the combinations. In Insights from Executives, Archie Jones, a senior executive at IBM, offers further insight on the factors that impact the likelihood of the success of an acquisition.

EXHIBIT 6.7

Limitations of Mergers and Acquisitions

- Takeover premiums paid for acquisitions are typically very high.
- Competing firms often can imitate any advantages or copy synergies that result from the merger or acquisition.
- Managers' egos sometimes get in the way of sound business decisions.
- Cultural issues may doom the intended benefits from M&A endeavors.

THE WISDOM OF CROWDS: WHEN DO INVESTORS SEE VALUE IN ACQUISITIONS?

By some estimates, 70 to 90 percent of acquisitions destroy share-holder value. But investors do see value in some acquisitions. The question is, When does the wisdom of the investment crowd indicate there is value with acquisitions? Recent research suggests it rests in both the characteristics of the deal and the motivation of the acquiring firm.

The Characteristics of the Deal

Research has identified several deal characteristics that lead to positive investor reactions. Not surprisingly, investors see greater value in acquisitions when the acquiring and the acquired (target) firm are in the same or closely related industries. This is consistent with there being greater potential for synergies when the firms are in similar markets. Second, investors see greater value potential when acquiring managers are seen as responding quickly to new opportunities, such as those provided by the emergence of new technologies or market deregulation. Third, investors have a more positive reaction when the acquiring firm used cash to buy the target, as opposed to giving the target shareholders stock in the combined firm. Acquiring firms often use stock to finance acquisitions when they think their own stock is overvalued. Thus, the use of cash signals that the acquiring firm's managers have confidence in the value of the deal. Fourth, the less the acquiring firm relies on outside advisers, such as investment banks, the more investors see value in the deal. As with the use of cash, managers who rely primarily on their own knowledge

and abilities to manage deals are seen as more confident. Finally, when the target firm tries to avoid the acquisition, investors see less value potential. Defense actions by targets are seen as signals that the target firm will not be open to easy integration with the acquiring firm. Thus, it may be difficult to leverage synergies.

The Motivation of the Acquirer

How much value investors see in the deal is also affected by the motivation of the acquirer. Interestingly, if the acquiring firm is highly profitable, investors see less value in the acquisition. The concern here is that strong performance likely leads managers to become overconfident and more likely to undertake "empire building" acquisitions as opposed to acquisitions that generate shareholder value. Second, if the acquiring firm is highly leveraged, having a high debt-equity ratio, investors see more value in the acquisition. Since the acquiring firm is at a higher risk of bankruptcy, managers of highly leveraged firms are likely to undertake acquisitions only if they are low risk and likely to generate synergistic benefits.

In total, the stock investors look to logical clues about the potential value of the deal and the motives of the acquiring firm managers to assess the value they see. Thus, there appears to be simple but logical wisdom in the crowd.

Sources: McNamara, G., Haleblian, J., & Dykes, B. 2008. Performance implications of participating in an acquisition wave: Early mover advantages, bandwagon effects, and the moderating influence of industry characteristics and acquirer tactics. *Academy of Management Journal*, 51: 113–130; and Schijven, M. & Hitt, M. 2012. The vicarious wisdom of crowds: Toward a behavioral perspective on investor reactions to acquisition announcements. *Strategic Management Journal*, 33: 1247–1268.

6.1 INSIGHTS **FROM EXECUTIVES**

ARCHIE L. JONES, VICE PRESIDENT OF BUSINESS DEVELOPMENT AT KENEXA, A SUBSIDIARY OF IBM

BIOSKETCH

Archie L. Jones is the vice president of business development at Kenexa, a subsidiary of IBM that provides workforce management and recruitment service solutions to a wide range of corporations. Kenexa has grown from a start-up firm in 1987 to a company with over 2,600 employees providing services to clients in over 20 countries. Jones began his career in private equity in 1993 after graduating from Morehouse College. After completing his MBA at Harvard Business School, Jones invested in Kenexa and served on its board of directors. He brought his expertise in strategic planning and M&A management inside Kenexa in 2005 and has helped guide Kenexa to expand into new product and geographic markets through organic growth, strategic alliances, and acquisitions.

1. *The value of acquisitions is often easy to see in capital-intensive industries, where acquisitions allow for the development of market power and economies of scale and scope. The value can be more difficult to see in service industries, such as in talent management consulting. How has Kenexa used acquisitions to build and extend its competencies, and how has this helped you better serve your customers?*

As our strategy calls for us to have a comprehensive suite of solutions, we use acquisitions to broaden and strengthen our suite of offerings. Most of our customers are looking to buy from fewer suppliers to simplify their supply chain. By offering our clients the broadest suite of solutions in our market, we are able to better serve our clients and differentiate from the competition.

We also use M&A to expand Kenexa's global footprint. We have purchased seven companies outside the

continued

continued

U.S., including in Canada, Europe, and Asia Pacific, and formed a joint venture in China. By acquiring local market knowledge and delivery capabilities in key international markets, we are able to serve the world's largest employers in their home market and abroad, creating another level of differentiation.

The most valuable asset in most of our acquisitions is the human capital that is acquired. A growing talent pool is our greatest source of growth, innovation, and thought leadership. The core of the Kenexa Leadership Institute, a recognized center for human capital research, was acquired as part of an M&A transaction.

2. *Differences in the cultures of acquiring and target firms can make integrating firms challenging. What have you found to be the most critical steps to take to ensure that these cultural differences don't derail acquisitions and destroy their value-creating potential?*

Understanding the human capital of the firm we are considering acquiring is key to our success. Therefore, assessing talent and its fit is integral in our due diligence. If you plan to retain and engage key employees, you have to meet them early in the acquisition process. At Kenexa, we routinely use leadership assessments of the key managers of the target company to better understand their strengths and motivations. In our experience, CEOs have a low survival rate postclosing. Quite simply, most CEO/founders find it difficult to have a boss again. Thus, we don't make acquisitions that are heavily dependent on the target CEO/founder. We have found it critical to get to know the senior team beyond the C-suite. Also, we openly share our company's values and culture up front and are prepared for some of the target company employees to self-select out. We have found that the sooner we figure out who will stay and assimilate well, the better the acquisition will go.

3. *What do you see as the most important drivers of acquisition success, and what are the steps you take to make sure you maximize the opportunities for success with an acquisition?*

The acquisition has to be tightly aligned with the firm's overall strategy. Your board or investment committee should be "presold" on the type of businesses you are targeting because it is explicitly called for in your strategy. The M&A team must work closely with the business unit leaders to understand their strategic needs and how M&A can play a role. This also allows you to identify and engage targets directly and proactively.

You have to get the price right. Establish minimum guidelines regarding how quickly an acquisition has to contribute to the growth in the firm's sales and earnings as well as the length of the payback period. Don't pay the seller for your synergies. Develop a downside case, a realistic/likely case, and an upside case. You should still be able to hit your minimum guidelines in the downside case.

Conduct a full due diligence to avoid later surprises. Start with a well-developed and comprehensive investment logic. Clearly outline the rationale for and expected benefits of the purchase and then test that rationale in due diligence. This is where you have to be brutally honest with yourself. Did the majority of the reasons for the acquisition survive diligence? If not, adjust the price or exit the process.

Undertake early integration planning. Integration starts during due diligence. Business unit managers and key functional leaders should develop the financial and strategic postclose plan and understand that these postclose numbers will be a part of their future targets and compensation plans.

Divestment: The Other Side of the "M&A Coin"   When firms acquire other businesses, it typically generates quite a bit of "press" in business publications such as *The Wall Street Journal, Bloomberg Businessweek,* and *Fortune.* It makes for exciting news, and one thing is for sure—large acquiring firms automatically improve their standing in the Fortune 500 rankings (since it is based solely on total revenues). However, managers must also carefully consider the strategic implications of exiting businesses.

divestment
the exit of a business from a firm's portfolio.

Divestments, the exit of a business from a firm's portfolio, are quite common. One study found that large, prestigious U.S. companies divested more acquisitions than they kept.[53]

Divesting a business can accomplish many different objectives.* It can be used to help a firm reverse an earlier acquisition that didn't work out as planned. Often, this is simply to

---

*Firms can divest their businesses in a number of ways. Sell-offs, spin-offs, equity carve-outs, asset sales/dissolution, and split-ups are some such modes of divestment. In a sell-off, the divesting firm privately negotiates with a third party to divest a unit/subsidiary for cash/stock. In a spin-off, a parent company distributes shares of the unit/subsidiary being divested pro rata to its existing shareholders and a new company is formed. Equity carve-outs are similar to spin-offs except that shares in the unit/subsidiary being divested are offered to new shareholders. Dissolution involves sale of redundant assets, not necessarily as an entire unit/subsidiary as in sell-offs but a few bits at a time. A split-up, on the other hand, is an instance of divestiture where by the parent company is split into two or more new companies and the parent ceases to exist. Shares in the parent company are exchanged for shares in new companies, and the exact distribution varies case by case.

SLIMMING DOWN BRISTOL-MYERS SQUIBB

From 2011 to 2014, Bristol-Myers Squibb saw its sales decline from $21 billion to $16 billion. For most firms, a 22 percent decline in sales would be seen as a disaster and a call for action. For Bristol-Myers Squibb, a global pharmaceutical firm, this was the successful implementation of its corporate strategy.

Rather than striving to be a pharmaceutical firm that provides solutions for a wide range of medical conditions and diseases, Bristol-Myers Squibb divested a number of its businesses, including selling its diabetes division, which provided over 10 percent of the corporation's sales, to a rival firm, AstraZeneca, as it focused on a few treatment areas where it could truly excel. The slimming of Bristol allowed it to reduce its costs by $2.5 billion, lower its workforce size by one-third, and close over half of its manufacturing operations. The sale of some of the firm's assets also generated resources that it used to invest in its remaining areas of business focus. For example, while the firm shrunk in size, its investment in R&D increased from 2011 to 2014. Also, while closing numerous plants, Bristol-Myers Squibb simultaneously committed to invest $900 million in a new biologics plant in Ireland to provide a more global manufacturing footprint in this growing medical treatment segment.

Bristol-Myers Squibb decided to focus on pharmaceutical segments that met three conditions. First, it invested in segments where it would face a limited number of competitors. Second, it focused on areas where it could find partners to share the development costs. Third, the firm emphasized product segments where it had expertise. The firm has settled on immune system treatments for chronic diseases (such as Crohn's disease and arthritis), virology (including treatments for HIV and hepatitis), and oncology (cancer treatments). Bristol-Myers Squibb's former chairman, Jim Cornelius, referred to the remaining businesses as the firm's "string of pearls." Recently, the firm has leveraged its expertise in immunology and oncology to develop potentially revolutionary immune system–based treatments for cancer.

One industry analyst, Jami Rubin, commented that the transformation at Bristol has been "really quite startling. It's a completely different company today than it was back in 2007. They've gone from a big, diversified drug company to a highly focused biopharma firm." The stock market appears to like the change. The firm's stock price doubled from early 2012 to the end of 2014.

Sources: Fry, E. 2014. Big pharma's small wonder. *Fortune,* June 16: 178-186; Calia, M. 2014. Bristol-Myers Squibb to build biologics plant in Ireland. *wsj.com,* November 14: np; and *finance.yahoo.com.*

help "cut their losses." Other objectives include (1) enabling managers to focus their efforts more directly on the firm's core businesses,[54] (2) providing the firm with more resources to spend on more attractive alternatives, and (3) raising cash to help fund existing businesses. Strategy Spotlight 6.4 discusses how Bristol-Myers Squibb has experienced these benefits of divestment.

Divesting can enhance a firm's competitive position only to the extent that it reduces its tangible (e.g., maintenance, investments, etc.) or intangible (e.g., opportunity costs, managerial attention) costs without sacrificing a current competitive advantage or the seeds of future advantages.[55] To be effective, divesting requires a thorough understanding of a business unit's current ability and future potential to contribute to a firm's value creation. However, since such decisions involve a great deal of uncertainty, it is very difficult to make such evaluations. In addition, because of managerial self-interests and organizational inertia, firms often delay divestments of underperforming businesses.

The Boston Consulting Group has identified seven principles for successful divestiture.[56]

1. ***Remove the emotion from the decision.*** Managers need to consider objectively the prospects for each unit in the firm and how this unit fits with the firm's overall strategy. Issues related to personal relationships with the managers of the unit, the length of time the unit has been part of the company, and other emotional elements should not be considered in the decision.[57]

2. ***Know the value of the business you are selling.*** Divesting firms can generate greater interest in and higher bids for units they are divesting if they can clearly articulate the strategic value of the unit.

3. ***Time the deal right.*** This involves both internal timing, where by the firm regularly evaluates all its units so that it can divest units when they are no longer highly valued in the firm but will still be of value to the outside market, and external timing, being ready to sell when the market conditions are right.

4. ***Maintain a sizable pool of potential buyers.*** Divesting firms should not focus on a single potential buyer. Instead, they should discuss possible deals with several hand-picked potential bidders.

5. ***Tell a story about the deal.*** For each potential bidder it talks with, the divesting firm should develop a narrative about how the unit it is interested in selling will create value for that buyer.

6. ***Run divestitures systematically through a project office.*** Firms should look at developing the ability to divest units as a distinct form of corporate competencies. While many firms have acquisition units, they often don't have divesting units even though there is significant potential value in divestitures.

7. ***Communicate clearly and frequently.*** Corporate managers need to clearly communicate to internal stakeholders, such as employees, and external stakeholders, such as customers and stockholders, what their goals are with divestment activity, how it will create value, and how the firm is moving forward strategically with these decisions.

Strategic Alliances and Joint Ventures

| **strategic alliance** |
| a cooperative relationship between two or more firms. |

A **strategic alliance** is a cooperative relationship between two (or more) firms.[58] Alliances may be either informal or formal—that is, involving a written contract. **Joint ventures** represent a special case of alliances, wherein two (or more) firms contribute equity to form a new legal entity.

Strategic alliances and joint ventures are assuming an increasingly prominent role in the strategy of leading firms, both large and small.[59] Such cooperative relationships have many potential advantages.[60] Among these are entering new markets, reducing manufacturing (or other) costs in the value chain, and developing and diffusing new technologies.[61]

| **joint ventures** |
| new entities formed within a strategic alliance in which two or more firms, the parents, contribute equity to form the new legal entity. |

Entering New Markets Often a company that has a successful product or service wants to introduce it into a new market. However, it may not have the financial resources or the requisite marketing expertise because it does not understand customer needs, know how to promote the product, or have access to the proper distribution channels.[62]

Zara, a Spanish clothing company, operates stores in over 70 countries. Still, when entering markets very distant from its home markets, Zara often uses local alliance partners to help it negotiate the different cultural and regulatory environments. For example, when Zara expanded into India in 2010, it did it in cooperation with Tata, an Indian conglomerate.[63]

Strategy Spotlight 6.5 discusses how a strategic alliance between Lionsgate and Alibaba provides Lionsgate with a strong partner to expand its business in China.

Reducing Manufacturing (or Other) Costs in the Value Chain Strategic alliances (or joint ventures) often enable firms to pool capital, value-creating activities, or facilities in order to reduce costs. For example, SABMiller and Molson Coors, the number-two and number-three brewers in the United States, created a joint venture to combine their U.S. brewing operations in 2007. In combining brewery and distribution operations, they would benefit from economies of scale and better utilization of their facilities. The two firms projected $500 million in annual cost savings as a result of the integration of their operations.[64]

Developing and Diffusing New Technologies Strategic alliances also may be used to build jointly on the technological expertise of two or more companies. This may enable them to develop products technologically beyond the capability of the companies acting independently.[65] IBM's alliances with Memorial Sloan Kettering, the Cleveland Clinic, and Cedars-Sinai, which were discussed in Strategic Spotlight 6.1, provide IBM with expert medical knowledge necessary for the computing giant to be able to leverage its technological skills in order to develop new medical insights.

LIONSGATE'S ALLIANCE WITH ALIBABA OFFERS ACCESS TO THE CHINESE MARKET

Lionsgate has been one of the most successful Hollywood studios over the last several years, with movie and TV hits such as the *Twilight* films, *The Hunger Games,* and *Mad Men.* Still, it faced challenges expanding its footprint on a global scale. To gain better access in the world's largest market, Lionsgate has allied with Alibaba, the Chinese Internet giant. Through this alliance, Alibaba gains exclusive rights in the Chinese market to stream Lionsgate's shows and movies through Alibaba's set-top boxes. Viewers will get to see not only Lionsgate's television shows and movies but also behind-the-scenes footage, as well as related merchandise and invitations to private screenings. This alliance allows Lionsgate to overcome a number of challenges in entering the Chinese market. By using Internet streaming of movies, it overcomes China's quota system for theatrical release. It also lessens

the likelihood of having a movie blocked by Chinese censors, as occurred with both *Django Unchained* and *Noah.* Finally, having a strong local partner also lessens concerns about intellectual property rights protection in China.

The alliance also brings benefits to Alibaba. The Internet retailing firm is expanding into media content in order to increase demand for and traffic on its set-top boxes. In addition to the alliance with Lionsgate, Alibaba has acquired a controlling stake in ChinaVision Media Group, has developed an online gaming business, and has ties with Wasu, an online video business. The Lionsgate alliance fits into its efforts to expand beyond retailing into a range of digital content.

Sources: McNary, D. 2014. Lionsgate, Alibaba teaming on streaming service for China. *variety.com,* July 14: np; Miller, D., Faughnder, R., & Chang, A. 2014. Alibaba could give Hollywood studios new pipeline into China. *latimes.com,* October 24: np; and Chen, L. & Palazzo, A. 2014. Alibaba joins Lionsgate for video service in China. *bloomberg.com,* July 15: np.

Potential Downsides Despite their promise, many alliances and joint ventures fail to meet expectations for a variety of reasons.[66] First, without the proper partner, a firm should never consider undertaking an alliance, even for the best of reasons.[67] Each partner should bring the desired complementary strengths to the partnership. Ideally, the strengths contributed by the partners are unique; thus synergies created can be more easily sustained and defended over the longer term. The goal must be to develop synergies between the contributions of the partners, resulting in a win–win situation. Moreover, the partners must be compatible and willing to trust each other.[68] Unfortunately, often little attention is given to nurturing the close working relationships and interpersonal connections that bring together the partnering organizations.[69]

Internal Development

Firms can also diversify by means of corporate entrepreneurship and new venture development. **In today's economy, internal development is such an important means by which companies expand their businesses that we have devoted a whole chapter to it (see Chapter 12).** Sony and the Minnesota Mining & Manufacturing Co. (3M), for example, are known for their dedication to innovation, R&D, and cutting-edge technologies. For example, 3M has developed its entire corporate culture to support its ongoing policy of generating at least 25 percent of total sales from products created within the most recent four-year period. While 3M exceeded this goal for decades, a push for improved efficiency that began in the early 2000s resulted in a drop to generating only 21 percent of sales from newer products in 2005. By refocusing on innovation, 3M raised that value back up to 30 percent in 2011.

Biocon, the largest Indian biotechnology firm, shows the power of internal development. Kiran Mazumdar-Shaw, the firm's founder, took the knowledge she learned while studying malting and brewing in college to start a small firm that produced enzymes for the beer industry in her Bangalore garage in 1978. The firm first expanded into providing enzymes for other food and textile industries. From there, Biocon expanded on to producing generic drugs and is now the largest producer of insulin in Asia.[70]

Compared to mergers and acquisitions, firms that engage in internal development capture the value created by their own innovative activities without having to "share the wealth" with alliance partners or face the difficulties associated with combining activities across the value chains of several firms or merging corporate cultures.[71] Also, firms can

> **internal development**
> entering a new business through investment in new facilities, often called corporate entrepreneurship and new venture development.

often develop new products or services at a relatively lower cost and thus rely on their own resources rather than turning to external funding.[72]

There are also potential disadvantages. It may be time-consuming; thus, firms may forfeit the benefits of speed that growth through mergers or acquisitions can provide. This may be especially important among high-tech or knowledge-based organizations in fast-paced environments where being an early mover is critical. Thus, firms that choose to diversify through internal development must develop capabilities that allow them to move quickly from initial opportunity recognition to market introduction.

LO6.6

Managerial behaviors that can erode the creation of value.

How Managerial Motives Can Erode Value Creation

Thus far in the chapter, we have implicitly assumed that CEOs and top executives are "rational beings"; that is, they act in the best interests of shareholders to maximize long-term shareholder value. In the real world, however, they may often act in their own self-interest. We now address some **managerial motives** that can serve to erode, rather than enhance, value creation. These include "growth for growth's sake," excessive egotism, and the creation of a wide variety of antitakeover tactics.

managerial motives
managers acting in their own self-interest rather than to maximize long-term shareholder value.

Growth for Growth's Sake

growth for growth's sake
managers' actions to grow the size of their firms not to increase long-term profitability but to serve managerial self-interest.

There are huge incentives for executives to increase the size of their firm. And these are not consistent with increasing shareholder wealth. Top managers, including the CEO, of larger firms typically enjoy more prestige, higher rankings for their firms on the Fortune 500 list (based on revenues, *not* profits), greater incomes, more job security, and so on. There is also the excitement and associated recognition of making a major acquisition. As noted by Harvard's Michael Porter, "There's a tremendous allure to mergers and acquisitions. It's the big play, the dramatic gesture. With one stroke of the pen you can add billions to size, get a front-page story, and create excitement in markets."[73]

In recent years many high-tech firms have suffered from the negative impact of their uncontrolled growth. Consider, for example, Priceline.com's ill-fated venture into an online service to offer groceries and gasoline.[74] A myriad of problems—perhaps most importantly, a lack of participation by manufacturers—caused the firm to lose more than $5 million a *week* prior to abandoning these ventures. Such initiatives are often little more than desperate moves by top managers to satisfy investor demands for accelerating revenues. Unfortunately, the increased revenues often fail to materialize into a corresponding hike in earnings.

At times, executives' overemphasis on growth can result in a plethora of ethical lapses, which can have disastrous outcomes for their companies. A good example (of bad practice) is Joseph Berardino's leadership at Andersen Worldwide. Berardino had a chance early on to take a hard line on ethics and quality in the wake of earlier scandals at clients such as Waste Management and Sunbeam. Instead, according to former executives, he put too much emphasis on revenue growth. Consequently, the firm's reputation quickly eroded when it audited and signed off on the highly flawed financial statements of such infamous firms as Enron, Global Crossing, and WorldCom. Berardino ultimately resigned in disgrace in March 2002, and his firm was dissolved later that year.[75]

Egotism

egotism
managers' actions to shape their firms' strategies to serve their selfish interests rather than to maximize long-term shareholder value.

A healthy ego helps make a leader confident, clearheaded, and able to cope with change. CEOs, by their very nature, are intensely competitive people in the office as well as on the tennis court or golf course. But sometimes when pride is at stake, individuals will go to great lengths to win.

Egos can get in the way of a "synergistic" corporate marriage. Few executives (or lower-level managers) are exempt from the potential downside of excessive egos. Consider, for example, the reflections of General Electric's former CEO Jack Welch, considered by many to be the world's most admired executive. He admitted to a regrettable decision: "My hubris got in the way in the Kidder Peabody deal. [He was referring to GE's buyout of the soon-to-be-troubled Wall Street firm.] I got wise advice from Walter Wriston and other directors who said, 'Jack, don't do this.' But I was bully enough and on a run to do it. And I got whacked right in the head."[76] In addition to poor financial results, Kidder Peabody was wracked by a widely publicized trading scandal that tarnished the reputations of both GE and Kidder Peabody. Welch ended up selling Kidder.

The business press has included many stories of how egotism and greed have infiltrated organizations.[77] Some incidents are considered rather astonishing, such as Tyco's former (and now convicted) CEO Dennis Kozlowski's purchase of a $6,000 shower curtain and vodka-spewing, full-size replica of Michelangelo's *David*.[78] Other well-known examples of power grabs and extraordinary consumption of compensation and perks include executives at Enron, the Rigas family who were convicted of defrauding Adelphia of roughly $1 billion, former CEO Bernie Ebbers's $408 million loan from WorldCom, and so on.

A more recent example of excess and greed was exhibited by John Thain.[79] On January 22, 2009, he was ousted as head of Merrill Lynch by Bank of America's CEO, Ken Lewis:

> Thain embarrassingly doled out $4 billion in discretionary year-end bonuses to favored employees just before Bank of America's rescue purchase of failing Merrill. The bonuses amounted to about 10 percent of Merrill's 2008 losses.
>
> Obviously, John Thain believed that he was entitled. When he took over ailing Merrill in early 2008, he began planning major cuts, but he also ordered that his office be redecorated. He spent $1.22 million of company funds to make it "livable," which, in part, included $87,000 for a rug, $87,000 for a pair of guest chairs, $68,000 for a 19th-century credenza, and (what really got the attention of the press) $35,000 for a "commode with legs."
>
> He later agreed to repay the decorating costs. However, one might still ask: What kind of person treats other people's money like this? And who needs a commode that costs as much as a new Lexus? Finally, a comment by Bob O'Brien, stock editor at Barrons.com, clearly applies: "The sense of entitlement that's been engendered in this group of people has clearly not been beaten out of them by the brutal performance of the financial sector over the course of the last year."

Antitakeover Tactics

Unfriendly or hostile takeovers can occur when a company's stock becomes undervalued. A competing organization can buy the outstanding stock of a takeover candidate in sufficient quantity to become a large shareholder. Then it makes a tender offer to gain full control of the company. If the shareholders accept the offer, the hostile firm buys the target company and either fires the target firm's management team or strips the team members of their power. Thus, **antitakeover tactics** are common, including greenmail, golden parachutes, and poison pills.[80]

The first, **greenmail,** is an effort by the target firm to prevent an impending takeover. When a hostile firm buys a large block of outstanding target company stock and the target firm's management feels that a tender offer is impending, it offers to buy the stock back from the hostile company at a higher price than the unfriendly company paid for it. Although this often prevents a hostile takeover, the same price is not offered to preexisting shareholders. However, it protects the jobs of the target firm's management.

Second, a **golden parachute** is a prearranged contract with managers specifying that, in the event of a hostile takeover, the target firm's managers will be paid a significant severance package. Although top managers lose their jobs, the golden parachute provisions protect their income.

Third, **poison pills** are used by a company to give shareholders certain rights in the event of a takeover by another firm. They are also known as shareholder rights plans.

Clearly, antitakeover tactics can often raise some interesting ethical—and legal—issues. Strategy Spotlight 6.6 addresses how antitakeover measures can benefit multiple stakeholders—not just management.

antitakeover tactics
managers' actions to avoid losing wealth or power as a result of a hostile takeover.

greenmail
a payment by a firm to a hostile party for the firm's stock at a premium, made when the firm's management feels that the hostile party is about to make a tender offer.

golden parachute
a prearranged contract with managers specifying that, in the event of a hostile takeover, the target firm's managers will be paid a significant severance package.

poison pill
used by a company to give shareholders certain rights in the event of takeover by another firm.

HOW ANTITAKEOVER MEASURES MAY BENEFIT MULTIPLE STAKEHOLDERS, NOT JUST MANAGEMENT

Antitakeover defenses represent a gray area, because management can often legitimately argue that such actions are not there solely to benefit themselves. Rather, they can benefit other stakeholders, such as employees, customers, and the community.

In the late 1980s, takeovers were very popular. The Dayton Hudson Corporation (now Target) even appealed to the Minnesota legislature to pass an antitakeover bill to help Dayton Hudson in its struggle with Hafts—the former owners of Dart, a drugstore chain on the east coast. History had shown that the Dayton Hudson management in place at the time was much better able to manage Dayton Hudson in the long run. In addition to Minnesota, many states now have laws that allow firms to take the interests of all stakeholders into account when considering a takeover bid.

In the summer of 2003, Oracle launched a hostile bid for PeopleSoft. Many analysts charged that the tactics of Oracle CEO Larry Ellison had been unfair, and many of PeopleSoft's customers took its side, indicating that Oracle ownership would not be of benefit to them. PeopleSoft was concerned that Oracle was merely seeking to buy PeopleSoft for its lucrative base of application software and was not interested in supporting the company's products. Oracle, on the other hand, sued PeopleSoft in an attempt to have the latter's so-called poison pill takeover defense removed.

In December 2004, Oracle struck a deal to buy PeopleSoft—ending a bitter 18-month hostile takeover battle. Oracle's $10.3 billion acquisition valued the firm at $26.50 a share—an increase of 66 percent over its initial offer of $16 a share. Noted analyst John DiFucci: "This is a financial acquisition primarily. Oracle is buying PeopleSoft for its maintenance stream." And, worth noting, PeopleSoft executives, including CEO and company founder David Duffield, did not join Oracle during the conference call announcing the acquisition. Oracle dropped its suit against PeopleSoft in which the former charged that PeopleSoft's "poison pill" takeover defense should be dismissed.

On moral grounds, some antitakeover defenses are not undertaken to entrench and protect management, but often they are. When such defenses are used simply to keep management in power, they are wrong. However, when they are used to defend the long-term financial health of the company and to protect broader stakeholder interests, they will be morally permissible.

Sources: Bowie, N. E. & Werhane, P. H. 2005. *Management ethics*. Malden, MA: Blackwell; and La Monica, P. R. 2004. Finally, Oracle to buy PeopleSoft. *CNNMoney.com*, December 13: np.

ISSUE FOR DEBATE

Starbucks Moves Far Outside the Coffeehouse

When you say Starbucks, most people instantly think of coffee, specifically coffee prepared by a barista just the way you want it—once you get the Starbucks lingo down. Starbucks is available in over 20,000 coffeehouses in more than 60 countries. Starbucks has experienced amazing growth over the last 30 years as it moved from a small chain of coffeehouses in Seattle to the global powerhouse that it is now. However, the firm faces more limited prospects for growth in its coffee business from this point forward. The coffee market is fairly mature, and Starbucks sees a limited number of new markets in which to expand.

In recent years, Starbucks has diversified into a number of new products and distribution channels to stoke up its growth potential. This has included diversifying into new products to sell through its cafes. Starbucks purchased La Boulange Bakery and now produces baked goods to sell in its cafes. Similarly, it purchased Teavana and is adding tea bars to its cafes. It also purchased Evolution Fresh juice company and now supplies the juices it sells in Starbucks coffeehouses. It is also test marketing additional new products in its cafes—beer and wine in Starbucks Evening concept stores and carbonated beverages in several markets. Starbucks is also making a major push in the grocery aisle. The firm has developed a "signature aisle" which features wood shelving that reflects the appearance of a Starbucks Café. The aisle's desirable end cap (the high-traffic shelf area at the end of an aisle) attracts shoppers' attention to products such as Starbucks' bagged coffee, its single-serve K-cups, and its Via brand instant coffee. But selling coffee in grocery stores is just the first step. Starbucks aims to also distribute its La Boulange bakery products, Teavana teas, and Evolution Fresh juices in grocery stores. It has even been looking further afield as it developed Evolution Harvest snack bars for the grocery aisle and also crafted an alliance with Danone to produce and sell Evolution Fresh yogurt products in grocery stores. The grocery aisle business now accounts for about 7 percent of Starbucks' business, but CEO Howard Schultz envisions the grocery aisle business producing half of the company's sales.

While the growth potential is enticing, there are some potential pitfalls associated with Starbucks' push into new arenas. The perceived differentiation of its coffee products could erode as they become a grocery aisle staple. Also, the growth of grocery sales could cannibalize the sales at cafes as people simply brew their K-cup coffee at home rather than swinging through the Starbucks drive-through on the way to work. In moving into noncoffee products, the question becomes whether or not Starbucks has the competencies to manage other businesses well. While Starbucks has mastered the management of the coffee supply chain and developed a distinctive product, it is not clear that the company has the competencies to produce bakery products, juice, tea, beer, and wine better than outside suppliers. Finally, managing all of these new businesses may distract Starbucks from its core coffee cafe business. The challenge for Starbucks is to know what its core competencies are and to focus on markets that allow it to best exploit those competencies.

Discussion Questions

1. What are Starbucks' core competencies? Do the new businesses allow Starbucks to leverage those competencies?
2. Do Starbucks' diversification efforts appear to be primarily about increasing growth or increasing shareholder value by sharing activities, building market power, and/or leveraging core competencies?
3. Where do you think Starbucks should draw boundaries on what businesses to compete in? Should it keep the new products in the corporate family? Should it continue to move into the grocery retailing space?

Sources: Levine-Weinberg, A. 2014. Starbucks has decades of growth ahead. *money.cnn.com*, November 19: np; Kowitt, B. 2013. Starbucks' grocery gambit. *Fortune,* December 23: np; Strom, S. 2013. Starbucks aims to move beyond beans. *nytimes.com*, October 8: np; and *starbucks.com*.

Reflecting on Career Implications . . .

- **Corporate-Level Strategy:** Is your current employer a single business firm or a diversified firm? If it is diversified, does it pursue related or unrelated diversification? Does its diversification provide you with career opportunities, especially lateral moves? What organizational policies are in place to either encourage or discourage you from moving from one business unit to another?

- **Core Competencies:** What do you see as your core competencies? How can you leverage them within your business unit as well as across other business units?

- **Sharing Infrastructures:** Identify what infrastructure activities and resources (e.g., information systems, legal) are available in the corporate office that are shared by various business units in the firm. How often do you take advantage of these shared resources? Identify ways in which you can enhance your performance by taking advantage of these shared infrastructure resources.

- **Diversification:** From your career perspective, what actions can you take to diversify your employment risk (e.g., doing coursework at a local university, obtaining professional certification such as a CPA, networking through professional affiliation, etc.)? In periods of retrenchment, such actions will provide you with a greater number of career options.

summary

A key challenge for today's managers is to create "synergy" when engaging in diversification activities. As we discussed in this chapter, corporate managers do not, in general, have a very good track record in creating value in such endeavors when it comes to mergers and acquisitions. Among the factors that serve to erode shareholder values are paying an excessive premium for the target firm, failing to integrate the activities of the newly acquired businesses into the corporate family, and undertaking diversification initiatives that are too easily imitated by the competition.

We addressed two major types of corporate-level strategy: related and unrelated diversification. With *related diversification* the corporation strives to enter into areas in which key resources and capabilities of the corporation can be shared or leveraged. Synergies come from horizontal relationships between business units. Cost savings and enhanced revenues can be derived from two major sources. First, economies of scope can be achieved from the leveraging of core competencies and the sharing of activities. Second, market power can be attained from greater, or pooled, negotiating power and from vertical integration.

When firms undergo *unrelated diversification,* they enter product markets that are dissimilar to their present businesses. Thus, there is generally little opportunity to either leverage core competencies or share activities across business units. Here, synergies are created from vertical relationships between the corporate office and the individual business units. With unrelated diversification, the primary ways to create value are corporate restructuring and parenting, as well as the use of portfolio analysis techniques.

Corporations have three primary means of diversifying their product markets—mergers and acquisitions, joint ventures/strategic alliances, and internal development. There are key trade-offs associated with each of these. For example, mergers and acquisitions are typically the quickest means to enter new markets and provide the corporation with a high level of control over the acquired business. However, with the expensive premiums that often need to be paid to the shareholders of the target firm and the challenges associated with integrating acquisitions, they can also be quite expensive. Not surprisingly, many poorly performing acquisitions are subsequently divested. At times, however, divestitures can help firms refocus their efforts and generate resources. Strategic alliances and joint ventures between two or more firms, on the other hand, may be a means of reducing risk since they involve the sharing and combining of resources. But such joint initiatives also provide a firm with less control (than it would have with an acquisition) since governance is shared between two independent entities. Also, there is a limit to the potential upside for each partner because returns must be shared as well. Finally, with internal development, a firm is able to capture all of the value from its initiatives (as opposed to sharing it with a merger or alliance partner). However, diversification by means of internal development can be very time-consuming—a disadvantage that becomes even more important in fast-paced competitive environments.

Finally, some managerial behaviors may serve to erode shareholder returns. Among these are "growth for growth's sake," egotism, and antitakeover tactics. As we discussed, some of these issues—particularly antitakeover tactics—raise ethical considerations because the managers of the firm are not acting in the best interests of the shareholders.

SUMMARY REVIEW QUESTIONS

1. Discuss how managers can create value for their firm through diversification efforts.
2. What are some of the reasons that many diversification efforts fail to achieve desired outcomes?
3. How can companies benefit from related diversification? Unrelated diversification? What are some of the key concepts that can explain such success?
4. What are some of the important ways in which a firm can restructure a business?
5. Discuss some of the various means that firms can use to diversify. What are the pros and cons associated with each of these?
6. Discuss some of the actions that managers may engage in to erode shareholder value.

key terms

corporate-level
  strategy 182
diversification 183
related diversification 184
economies of scope 184
core competencies 185
sharing activities 186
market power 187
pooled negotiating
  power 187
vertical integration 188
transaction cost
  perspective 190

unrelated diversification 191
parenting advantage 191
restructuring 191
portfolio management 192
acquisitions 195
mergers 195
divestment 200
strategic alliance 202
joint ventures 202
internal development 203
managerial motives 204
growth for growth's
  sake 204
egotism 204
antitakeover tactics 205
greenmail 205
golden parachute 205
poison pill 205

application questions & exercises

1. What were some of the largest mergers and acquisitions over the last two years? What was the rationale for these actions? Do you think they will be successful? Explain.
2. Discuss some examples from business practice in which an executive's actions appear to be in his or her self-interest rather than the corporation's well-being.
3. Discuss some of the challenges that managers must overcome in making strategic alliances successful. What are some strategic alliances with which you are familiar? Were they successful or not? Explain.
4. Use the Internet and select a company that has recently undertaken diversification into new product markets. What do you feel were some of the reasons for this diversification (e.g., leveraging core competencies, sharing infrastructures)?

experiential exercise

Time Warner (formerly AOL Time Warner) is a firm that follows a strategy of related diversification. Evaluate its success (or lack thereof) with regard to how well it has (1) built on core competencies, (2) shared infrastructures, and (3) increased market power. (Fill answers in table below.)

ethics questions

1. In recent years there has been a rash of corporate downsizing and layoffs. Do you feel that such actions raise ethical considerations? Why or why not?

2. What are some of the ethical issues that arise when managers act in a manner that is counter to their firm's best interests? What are the long-term implications for both the firms and the managers themselves?

Rationale for Related Diversification	Successful/Unsuccessful?	Why?
1. Build on core competencies		
2. Share infrastructures		
3. Increase market power		

references

1. Grobart, S. & Rusli, E. 2011. For Flip video camera, four years from hot start-up to obsolete. *NYTimes.com,* April 4: np; Chen, B. 2011. Why Cisco's Flip flopped in the camera business. *Wired.com,* April 11: np; Rose, C. 2012. Charlie Rose talks to Cisco's John Chambers. *Bloomberg Businessweek,* April 24: 41; and www.cisco.com.

2. Insights on measuring M&A performance are addressed in Zollo, M. & Meier, D. 2008. What is M&A performance? *BusinessWeek,* 22(3): 55–77.

3. Insights on how and why firms may overpay for acquisitions are addressed in Malhotra, D., Ku, G., & Murnighan, J. K. 2008. When winning is everything. *Harvard Business Review,* 66(5): 78–86.

4. Dr. G. William Schwert, University of Rochester study cited in Pare, T. P. 1994. The new merger boom. *Fortune,* November 28: 96.

5. Lipin, S. & Deogun, N. 2000. Big mergers of the 1990's prove disappointing to shareholders. *The Wall Street Journal,* October 30: C1.

6. Rothenbuecher, J. & Schrottke, J. 2008. To get value from a merger, grow sales. *Harvard Business Review,* 86(5): 24–25; and Rothenbuecher, J. 2008. Personal communication, October 1.

7. Kyriazis, D. 2010. The long-term post acquisition performance of Greek acquiring firms. *International Research Journal of Finance and Economics,* 43: 69–79.

8. Pare, T. P. 1994. The new merger boom. *Fortune,* November 28: 96.

9. A discussion of the effects of director experience and acquisition performance is in McDonald, M. L. & Westphal, J. D. 2008. What do they know? The effects of outside director acquisition experience on firm acquisition performance. *Strategic Management Journal,* 29(11): 1155–1177.

10. Finance and economics: Snoopy sniffs an opportunity; MetLife buys Alico. 2010. *Economist.com,* March 13: np.

11. For a study that investigates several predictors of corporate diversification, read Wiersema, M. F. & Bowen, H. P. 2008. Corporate diversification: The impact of foreign competition, industry globalization, and product diversification. *Strategic Management Journal,* 29(2): 114–132.

12. Kumar, M. V. S. 2011. Are joint ventures positive sum games? The relative effects of cooperative and non-cooperative behavior. *Strategic Management Journal,* 32(1): 32–54.

13. Makri, M., Hitt, M. A., & Lane, P. J. 2010. Complementary technologies, knowledge relatedness, and invention outcomes in high technology mergers and acquisitions. *Strategic Management Journal,* 31(6): 602–628.

14. A discussion of Tyco's unrelated diversification strategy is in Hindo, B. 2008. Solving Tyco's identity crisis. *BusinessWeek,* February 18: 62.

15. Our framework draws upon a variety of sources, including Goold, M. & Campbell, A. 1998. Desperately seeking synergy. *Harvard Business Review,* 76(5): 131–143; Porter, M. E. 1987. From advantage to corporate strategy. *Harvard Business Review,* 65(3): 43–59; and Hitt, M. A., Ireland, R. D., & Hoskisson, R. E. 2001. *Strategic management: Competitiveness and globalization* (4th ed.). Cincinnati, OH: South-Western.

16. This imagery of the corporation as a tree and related discussion draws on Prahalad, C. K. & Hamel, G. 1990. The core competence of the corporation. *Harvard Business Review,* 68(3): 79–91. Parts of this section also draw on Picken, J. C. & Dess, G. G. 1997. *Mission critical:* chap. 5. Burr Ridge, IL: Irwin Professional.

17. Graebner, M. E., Eisenhardt, K. M., & Roundy, P. T. 2010. Success and failure in technology acquisitions: Lessons for buyers and sellers. *Academy of Management Perspectives,* 24(3): 73–92.

18. This section draws on Prahalad & Hamel, op. cit.; and Porter, op. cit.

19. A study that investigates the relationship between a firm's technology resources, diversification, and performance can be found in Miller, D. J. 2004. Firms' technological resources and the performance effects of diversification. A longitudinal study. *Strategic Management Journal,* 25: 1097–1119.

20. Chesbrough, H. 2011. Bringing open innovation to services. *MIT Sloan Management Review,* 52(2): 85–90.

21. Fisher, A. 2008. America's most admired companies. *Fortune,* March 17: 74.

22. Levine-Weinberg, A. 2014. Starbucks has decades of growth ahead. *money.cnn.com,* November 19: np.

23. This section draws on Hrebiniak, L. G. & Joyce, W. F. 1984. *Implementing strategy.* New York: Macmillan; and Oster, S. M. 1994. *Modern competitive analysis.* New York: Oxford University Press.

24. The discussion of the benefits and costs of vertical integration draws on Hax, A. C. & Majluf, N. S. 1991. *The strategy concept and process: A pragmatic approach:* 139. Englewood Cliffs, NJ: Prentice Hall.

25. Fahey, J. 2005. Gray winds. *Forbes,* January 10: 143.

26. This discussion draws on Oster, op. cit.; and Harrigan, K. 1986. Matching vertical integration strategies to competitive conditions. *Strategic Management Journal,* 7(6): 535–556.

27. For a scholarly explanation on how transaction costs determine the boundaries of a firm, see Oliver E. Williamson's pioneering books *Markets and hierarchies: Analysis and antitrust implications* (New York: Free Press, 1975) and *The economic institutions of capitalism* (New York: Free Press, 1985).

28. Campbell, A., Goold, M., & Alexander, M. 1995. Corporate strategy: The quest for parenting advantage. *Harvard Business Review,* 73(2): 120–132; and Picken & Dess, op. cit.

29. Anslinger, P. A. & Copeland, T. E. 1996. Growth through acquisition: A fresh look. *Harvard Business Review,* 74(1): 126–135.

30. This section draws on Porter, op. cit.; and Hambrick, D. C. 1985. Turnaround strategies. In Guth, W. D. (Ed.), *Handbook of business strategy:* 10-1–10-32. Boston: Warren, Gorham & Lamont.

31. There is an important delineation between companies that are operated for a long-term profit and those that are bought and sold for short-term gains. The latter are sometimes referred to as "holding companies" and are generally more concerned about financial issues than strategic issues.

32. Lenzner, R. 2007. High on Loews. *Forbes,* February 26: 98–102.

33. Casico, W. F. 2002. Strategies for responsible restructuring. *Academy of Management Executive,* 16(3): 80–91; and Singh, H. 1993. Challenges in researching corporate restructuring. *Journal of Management Studies,* 30(1): 147–172.

34. Hax & Majluf, op. cit. By 1979, 45 percent of Fortune 500 companies employed some form of portfolio analysis, according to Haspelagh, P. 1982. Portfolio planning: Uses and limits. *Harvard Business Review,* 60: 58–73. A later study conducted in 1993 found that over 40 percent of the respondents used portfolio analysis techniques, but the level of usage was expected to increase to more than 60 percent in the near future: Rigby, D. K. 1994. Managing the management tools. *Planning Review,* September–October: 20–24.

35. Fruk, M., Hall, S., & Mittal, D. 2013. Never let a good crisis go to waste. *mckinsey.com,* October: np; and Arrfelt, M., Wiseman, R., McNamara, G., & Hult, T., 2015. Examining a key corporate role: The influence of capital allocation competency on business unit performance. *Strategic Management Journal,* in press.

36. Goold, M. & Luchs, K. 1993. Why diversify? Four decades of management thinking. *Academy of Management Executive,* 7(3): 7–25.

37. Other approaches include the industry attractiveness–business strength matrix developed jointly by General Electric and McKinsey and Company, the life-cycle matrix developed by Arthur D. Little, and the profitability matrix proposed by Marakon. For an extensive review, refer to Hax & Majluf, op. cit.: 182–194.

38. Porter, op. cit.: 49–52.

39. Picken & Dess, op. cit.; Cabot Corporation. 2001. 10-Q filing, Securities and Exchange Commission, May 14.

40. Insights on the performance of serial acquirers is found in Laamanen, T. & Keil, T. 2008. Performance of serial acquirers: Toward an acquisition program perspective. *Strategic Management Journal,* 29(6): 663–672.

41. Some insights from Lazard's CEO on mergers and acquisitions are addressed in Stewart, T. A. & Morse, G. 2008. Giving great advice. *Harvard Business Review,* 66(1): 106–113.

42. Coy, P., Thornton, E., Arndt, M., & Grow, B. 2005. Shake, rattle, and merge. *BusinessWeek,* January 10: 32–35; and Anonymous. 2005. Love is in the air. *The Economist,* February 5: 9.

43. Hill, A. 2011. Mergers indicate market optimism. *www.marketplace.org,* March 21: np.

44. For an interesting study of the relationship between mergers and a firm's product-market strategies, refer to Krishnan, R. A., Joshi, S., & Krishnan, H. 2004. The influence of mergers on firms' product-mix strategies. *Strategic Management Journal,* 25: 587–611.

45. Like many high-tech firms during the economic slump that began in mid-2000, Cisco Systems experienced declining performance. On April 16, 2001, it announced that its revenues for the quarter closing April 30 would drop 5 percent from a year earlier—and a stunning 30 percent from the previous three months—to about $4.7 billion. Furthermore, Cisco announced that it would lay off 8,500 employees and take an enormous $2.5 billion charge to write down inventory. By late October 2002, its stock was trading at around $10, down significantly from its 52-week high of $70. Elstrom, op. cit.: 39.

46. Sisario, B. 2014. Jimmy Iovine, a master of Beats, lends Apple a skilled ear. *nytimes.com,* May 28: np; and Dickey, M. 2014. Meet the executives Apple is paying $3 billion to get. *businessinsider.com,* May 28: np.

47. Ignatius, A. 2011. How eBay developed a culture of experimentation. *Harvard Business Review,* 89(3): 92–97.

48. For a discussion of the trend toward consolidation of the steel industry and how Lakshmi Mittal is becoming a dominant player, read Reed, S. & Arndt, M. 2004. The raja of steel. *BusinessWeek,* December 20: 50–52.

49. Colvin, G. 2011. Airline king. *Fortune,* May 2: 50–57.

50. This discussion draws upon Rappaport, A. & Sirower, M. L. 1999. Stock or cash? The trade-offs for buyers and sellers in mergers and acquisitions. *Harvard Business Review,* 77(6): 147–158; and Lipin, S. & Deogun, N. 2000. Big mergers of 90s prove disappointing to shareholders. *The Wall Street Journal,* October 30: C1.

51. The downside of mergers in the airline industry is found in Gimbel, B. 2008. Why airline mergers don't fly. *BusinessWeek,* March 17: 26.

52. Mouio, A. (Ed.). 1998. Unit of one. *Fast Company,* September: 82.

53. Porter, M. E. 1987. From competitive advantage to corporate strategy. *Harvard Business Review,* 65(3): 43.

54. The divestiture of a business that is undertaken in order to enable managers to better focus on its core business has been termed "downscoping." Refer to Hitt, M. A., Harrison, J. S., & Ireland, R. D. 2001. *Mergers and acquisitions: A guide to creating value for stakeholders.* New York: Oxford University Press.

55. Sirmon, D. G., Hitt, M. A., & Ireland, R. D. 2007. Managing firm resources in dynamic environments to create value: Looking inside the black box. *Academy of Management Review,* 32(1): 273–292.

56. Kengelbach, J., Klemmer, D., & Roos, A. 2012. Plant and prune: How M&A can grow portfolio value. *BCG Report,* September: 1–38.

57. Berry, J., Brigham, B., Bynum, A., Leu, C., & McLaughlin, R. 2012. Creating value through divestitures— Deans Foods: Theory in practice. *Unpublished manuscript.*

58. A study that investigates alliance performance is Lunnan, R. & Haugland, S. A. 2008. Predicting and measuring alliance performance: A multidimensional analysis. *Strategic Management Journal,* 29(5): 545–556.

59. For scholarly perspectives on the role of learning in creating value in strategic alliances, refer to Anard, B. N. & Khanna, T. 2000. Do firms learn to create value? *Strategic Management Journal,* 12(3): 295–317; and Vermeulen, F. & Barkema, H. P. 2001. Learning through acquisitions. *Academy of Management Journal,* 44(3): 457–476.

60. For a detailed discussion of transaction cost economics in strategic alliances, read Reuer, J. J. & Arno, A. 2007. Strategic alliance contracts: Dimensions and determinants of contractual complexity. *Strategic Management Journal,* 28(3): 313–330.

61. This section draws on Hutt, M. D., Stafford, E. R., Walker, B. A., & Reingen, P. H. 2000. Case study: Defining the strategic alliance. *Sloan Management Review,* 41(2): 51–62; and Walters, B. A., Peters, S., & Dess, G. G. 1994. Strategic alliances and joint ventures: Making them work. *Business Horizons,* 4: 5–10.

62. A study that investigates strategic alliances and networks is Tiwana, A. 2008. Do bridging ties complement strong ties? An empirical examination of alliance ambidexterity. *Strategic Management Journal,* 29(3): 251–272.

63. Fashion chain Zara opens its first Indian store. 2010. *bbc.co.uk/news/,* May 31: np.

64. Martin, A. 2007. Merger for SABMiller and Molson Coors. *nytimes.com,* October 10: np.

65. Phelps, C. 2010. A longitudinal study of the influence of alliance network structure and composition on firm exploratory innovation. *Academy of Management Journal,* 53(4): 890–913.

66. For an institutional theory perspective on strategic alliances, read Dacin, M. T., Oliver, C., & Roy, J. P. 2007. The legitimacy of strategic alliances: An institutional perspective. *Strategic Management Journal,* 28(2): 169–187.

67. A study investigating factors that determine partner selection in strategic alliances is found in Shah, R. H. & Swaminathan, V. 2008. *Strategic Management Journal,* 29(5): 471–494.

68. Arino, A. & Ring, P. S. 2010. The role of fairness in alliance formation. *Strategic Management Journal,* 31(6): 1054–1087.

69. Greve, H. R., Baum, J. A. C., Mitsuhashi, H. & Rowley, T. J. 2010. Built to last but falling apart: Cohesion, friction, and withdrawal from interfirm alliances. *Academy of Management Journal,* 53(4): 302–322.

70. Narayan, A. 2011. From brewing, an Indian biotech is born. *Bloomberg Businessweek,* February 28: 19–20.

71. For an insightful perspective on how to manage conflict between innovation and ongoing operations in an organization, read Govindarajan, V. & Trimble, C. 2010. *The other side of innovation: Solving the execution challenge.* Boston: Harvard Business School Press.

72. Dunlap-Hinkler, D., Kotabe, M., & Mudambi, R. 2010. A story of breakthrough versus incremental innovation: Corporate entrepreneurship in the global pharmaceutical industry. *Strategic Entrepreneurship Journal,* 4(2): 106–127.

73. Porter, op. cit.: 43–59.

74. Angwin, J. S. & Wingfield, N. 2000. How Jay Walker built WebHouse on a theory that he couldn't prove. *The Wall Street Journal,* October 16: A1, A8.

75. The fallen. 2003. *BusinessWeek,* January 13: 80–82.

76. The Jack Welch example draws upon Sellers, P. 2001. Get over yourself. *Fortune,* April 30: 76–88.

77. Li, J. & Tang, Y. 2010. CEO hubris and firm risk taking in China: The moderating role of managerial discretion. *Academy of Management Journal,* 53(1): 45–68.

78. Polek, D. 2002. The rise and fall of Dennis Kozlowski. *BusinessWeek,* December 23: 64–77.

79. John Thain and his golden commode. 2009. Editorial. *Dallasnews.com,* January 26: np; Task, A. 2009. Wall Street's $18.4B bonus: The sense of entitlement has not been beaten out. *finance.yahoo.com,* January 29: np; and Exit Thain. 2009. *Newsfinancialcareers.com,* January 22: np.

80. This section draws on Weston, J. F., Besley, S., & Brigham, E. F. 1996. *Essentials of managerial finance* (11th ed.): 18–20. Fort Worth, TX: Dryden Press, Harcourt Brace.

International Strategy
Creating Value in Global Markets

After reading this chapter, you should have a good understanding of the following learning objectives:

LO7.1 The importance of international expansion as a viable diversification strategy.

LO7.2 The sources of national advantage; that is, why an industry in a given country is more (or less) successful than the same industry in another country.

LO7.3 The motivations (or benefits) and the risks associated with international expansion, including the emerging trend for greater offshoring and outsourcing activity.

LO7.4 The two opposing forces—cost reduction and adaptation to local markets—that firms face when entering international markets.

LO7.5 The advantages and disadvantages associated with each of the four basic strategies: international, global, multidomestic, and transnational.

LO7.6 The difference between regional companies and truly global companies.

LO7.7 The four basic types of entry strategies and the relative benefits and risks associated with each of them.

Learning from Mistakes

SAIC, a major Chinese automaker, wanted to grow outside its home market. As a step to achieve this aim, it acquired a controlling interest in SsangYong, a struggling Korean automaker, in 2004.[1] However, this investment didn't turn out as SAIC had hoped. After five tumultuous years and $618 million in investment, SAIC decided to stop any further investments in SsangYong and saw its ownership stake erode when SsangYong went into bankruptcy in 2009. Why did SAIC's takeover of SsangYong turn out so badly?

SAIC, formerly known as Shanghai Automotive Industry Corporation, grew from a small firm in the 1970s to the largest Chinese-based automaker by 2010. It has leveraged relationships with major global automakers, including Volkswagen and GM, to develop its resources to design and build world-class cars. Building off its success at home, SAIC wanted to grow its global footprint.

As a first step in this effort, SAIC undertook its first acquisition of a non-Chinese firm. In 2004, SAIC paid $500 million to acquire 49 percent of SsangYong, the number-four auto manufacturer in South Korea. SsangYong had a 10 percent share of the Korean car market and was especially strong in the small SUV market. In addition to its Korean sales base, it was building its export business.

Analysts saw the acquisition as one with strong promise. SAIC would gain access to its first foreign markets and also access to SsangYong's advanced technologies. Of great potential value was SsangYong's hybrid engine technology. SsangYong, which was burdened by heavy debt, would be recapitalized by SAIC. Additionally, SAIC, which had very efficient plant operations, could help improve SsangYong's production efficiency.

Even with all of the potential, problems quickly arose. Cultural differences between Chinese and Korean managers hampered their ability to agree on how to restructure SsangYong. SAIC had even greater difficulties negotiating with SsangYong's unions. South Korea has a heritage of strong unions and difficult management–labor relations, something that was entirely new to SAIC.

These differences were exacerbated by a steep drop in demand for SsangYong's vehicles. When gasoline prices spiked in 2006, SUV sales dropped dramatically. Further, when the global recession hit in late 2007, global auto sales tanked. SsangYong's sales were cut in half by the end of 2008.

SAIC proposed a dramatic overhaul at SsangYong, with major changes in shop-floor practices to improve efficiency and a 36 percent reduction in SsangYong's workforce. SsangYong's unions rebelled and charged that SAIC was illegally transferring technology designs and technology to China. Without any further cash infusion from SAIC, SsangYong filed for bankruptcy in January 2009. The unions went on strike and barricaded themselves in SsangYong's plants for 77 days. SAIC wrote off its investments in SsangYong and blamed the experience for its 26 percent drop in profits in the first half of 2009.

Discussion Questions

1. What lessons should SAIC learn from its acquisition of SsangYong?
2. When buying a firm in another country, what issues should the acquiring firm think about to limit the risks it will face with the acquisition?
3. How can a firm bridge cultural differences between its home market and a country it is moving into?

In this chapter we discuss how firms create value and achieve competitive advantage in the global marketplace. Multinational firms are constantly faced with the dilemma of choosing between local adaptation—in product offerings, locations, advertising, and pricing—and global integration. We discuss how firms can avoid pitfalls such as those experienced by SAIC, a major Chinese automaker. In addition, we address factors that can influence a nation's success in a particular industry. In our view, this is an important context in determining how well firms might eventually do when they compete beyond their nation's boundaries.

The Global Economy: A Brief Overview

LO7.1

The importance of international expansion as a viable diversification strategy.

Managers face many opportunities and risks when they diversify abroad.[2] The trade among nations has increased dramatically in recent years, and it is estimated that by 2015 the trade *across* nations will exceed the trade within nations. In a variety of industries such as semiconductors, automobiles, commercial aircraft, telecommunications, computers, and consumer electronics, it is almost impossible to survive unless firms scan the world for competitors, customers, human resources, suppliers, and technology.[3]

GE's wind energy business benefits by tapping into talent around the world. The firm has built research centers in China, Germany, India, and the U.S. "We did it," says CEO Jeffrey Immelt, "to access the best brains everywhere in the world." All four centers have played a key role in GE's development of huge 92-ton turbines:[4]

- Chinese researchers in Shanghai designed the microprocessors that control the pitch of the blade.
- Mechanical engineers from India (Bangalore) devised mathematical models to maximize the efficiency of materials in the turbine.
- Power-systems experts in the U.S. (Niskayuna, New York), which has researchers from 55 countries, do the design work.
- Technicians in Munich, Germany, have created a "smart" turbine that can calculate wind speeds and signal sensors in other turbines to produce maximum electricity.

globalization

a term that has two meanings: (1) the increase in international exchange, including trade in goods and services as well as exchange of money, ideas, and information; (2) the growing similarity of laws, rules, norms, values, and ideas across countries.

The rise of **globalization**—meaning the rise of market capitalism around the world—has undeniably created tremendous business opportunities for multinational corporations. For example, while smartphone sales declined in Western Europe in the third quarter of 2014, they grew at a 50 percent rate in Eastern Europe, the Middle East, and Africa.[5]

This rapid rise in global capitalism has had dramatic effects on the growth in different economic zones. As shown in Exhibit 7.1, the growth experienced by developed economies in the first decade of the 2000s was anemic, while the growth in developing economies was robust.[6] This has resulted in a dramatic shift in the structure of the global economy. Over half the world's output now comes from emerging markets. This is leading to a convergence of living standards across the globe and is changing the face of business. One example of this is the shift in the global automobile market. China supplanted the United States as the largest market for automobiles in 2009.

One of the challenges with globalization is determining how to meet the needs of customers at very different income levels. In many developing economies, distributions of income remain much wider than they do in the developed world, leaving many impoverished even as the economies grow. The challenge for multinational firms is to tailor their products and services to meet the needs of the "bottom of the pyramid." Global corporations are increasingly changing their product offerings to meet the needs of the nearly 5 billion poor people in the world who inhabit developing countries. Collectively, this represents a very large market with $14 trillion in purchasing power.

Next, we will address in more detail the question of why some nations and their industries are more competitive.[7] This establishes an important context or setting for the

EXHIBIT 7.1 Rate of Growth in GDP per Person, 2001–2011, by Region

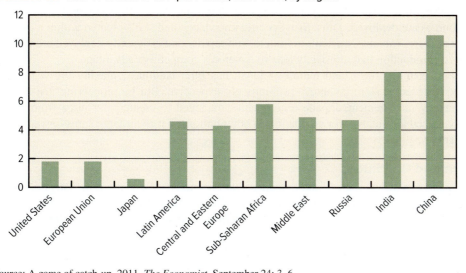

Source: A game of catch-up. 2011. *The Economist,* September 24: 3–6.

remainder of the chapter. After we discuss why some *nations and their industries* outper-form others, we will be better able to address the various strategies that *firms* can take to create competitive advantage when they expand internationally.

Factors Affecting a Nation's Competitiveness

Michael Porter of Harvard University conducted a four-year study in which he and a team of 30 researchers looked at the patterns of competitive success in 10 leading trading nations. He concluded that there are four broad attributes of nations that individually, and as a system, constitute what is termed the **diamond of national advantage.** In effect, these attributes jointly determine the playing field that each nation establishes and operates for its industries. These factors are:

- *Factor endowments.* The nation's position in factors of production, such as skilled labor or infrastructure, necessary to compete in a given industry.
- *Demand conditions.* The nature of home-market demand for the industry's product or service.
- *Related and supporting industries.* The presence or absence in the nation of supplier industries and other related industries that are internationally competitive.
- *Firm strategy, structure, and rivalry.* The conditions in the nation governing how companies are created, organized, and managed, as well as the nature of domestic rivalry.

Factor Endowments[8,9]

Classical economics suggests that factors of production such as land, labor, and capital are the building blocks that create usable consumer goods and services.[10] However, companies in advanced nations seeking competitive advantage over firms in other nations *create* many of the factors of production. For example, a country or industry dependent on scientific innovation must have a skilled human resource pool to draw upon. This resource pool is not inherited; it is created through investment in industry-specific knowledge and talent. The supporting infrastructure of a country—that is, its transportation and communication systems as well as its banking system—is also critical.

diamond of national advantage
a framework for explaining why countries foster successful multinational corporations; consists of four factors—factor endowments; demand conditions; related and supporting industries; and firm strategy, structure, and rivalry.

factor endowments (national advantage)
a nation's position in factors of production.

LO7.2

The sources of national advantage; that is, why an industry in a given country is more (or less) successful than the same industry in another country.

Factors of production must be developed that are industry- and firm-specific. In addition, the pool of resources is less important than the speed and efficiency with which these resources are deployed. Thus, firm-specific knowledge and skills created within a country that are rare, valuable, difficult to imitate, and rapidly and efficiently deployed are the factors of production that ultimately lead to a nation's competitive advantage.

For example, the island nation of Japan has little landmass, making the warehouse space needed to store inventory prohibitively expensive. But by pioneering just-in-time inventory management, Japanese companies managed to create a resource from which they gained advantage over companies in other nations that spent large sums to warehouse inventory.

Demand Conditions

demand conditions (national advantage) the nature of home-market demand for the industry's product or service.

Demand conditions refer to the demands that consumers place on an industry for goods and services. Consumers who demand highly specific, sophisticated products and services force firms to create innovative, advanced products and services to meet the demand. This consumer pressure presents challenges to a country's industries. But in response to these challenges, improvements to existing goods and services often result, creating conditions necessary for competitive advantage over firms in other countries.

Countries with demanding consumers drive firms in that country to meet high standards, upgrade existing products and services, and create innovative products and services. The conditions of consumer demand influence how firms view a market. This, in turn, helps a nation's industries to better anticipate future global demand conditions and proactively respond to product and service requirements.

Denmark, for instance, is known for its environmental awareness. Demand from consumers for environmentally safe products has spurred Danish manufacturers to become leaders in water pollution control equipment—products it successfully exported.

Related and Supporting Industries

related and supporting industries (national advantage) the presence, absence, and quality in the nation of supplier industries and other related industries that supply services, support, or technology to firms in the industry value chain.

Related and supporting industries enable firms to manage inputs more effectively. For example, countries with a strong supplier base benefit by adding efficiency to downstream activities. A competitive supplier base helps a firm obtain inputs using cost-effective, timely methods, thus reducing manufacturing costs. Also, close working relationships with suppliers provide the potential to develop competitive advantages through joint research and development and the ongoing exchange of knowledge.

Related industries offer similar opportunities through joint efforts among firms. In addition, related industries create the probability that new companies will enter the market, increasing competition and forcing existing firms to become more competitive through efforts such as cost control, product innovation, and novel approaches to distribution. Combined, these give the home country's industries a source of competitive advantage.

In the Italian footwear industry the supporting industries enhance national competitive advantage. In Italy, shoe manufacturers are geographically located near their suppliers. The manufacturers have ongoing interactions with leather suppliers and learn about new textures, colors, and manufacturing techniques while a shoe is still in the prototype stage. The manufacturers are able to project future demand and gear their factories for new products long before companies in other nations become aware of the new styles.

Firm Strategy, Structure, and Rivalry

firm strategy, structure, and rivalry (national advantage) the conditions in the nation governing how companies are created, organized, and managed, as well as the nature of domestic rivalry.

Rivalry is particularly intense in nations with conditions of strong consumer demand, strong supplier bases, and high new-entrant potential from related industries. This competitive rivalry in turn increases the efficiency with which firms develop, market, and distribute products and services within the home country. Domestic rivalry thus provides a strong impetus for firms to innovate and find new sources of competitive advantage.

This intense rivalry forces firms to look outside their national boundaries for new markets, setting up the conditions necessary for global competitiveness. Among all the points on Porter's diamond of national advantage, domestic rivalry is perhaps the strongest indicator of global competitive success. Firms that have experienced intense domestic competition are more likely to have designed strategies and structures that allow them to successfully compete in world markets.

In the European grocery retail industry, intense rivalry has led firms such as Aldi and Tesco to tighten their supply chains and improve store efficiency. Thus, it is no surprise that these firms are also strong global players.

The Indian software industry offers a clear example of how the attributes in Porter's "diamond" interact to lead to the conditions for a strong industry to grow. Exhibit 7.2 illustrates India's "software diamond," and Strategy Spotlight 7.1 further discusses the mutually reinforcing elements at work in this market.

STRATEGY SPOTLIGHT

7.1

INDIA AND THE DIAMOND OF NATIONAL ADVANTAGE

The Indian software industry has become one of the leading global markets for software. The industry has grown to over $60 billion, and Indian IT firms provide software and services to over half the Fortune 500 firms. What are the factors driving this success? Porter's diamond of national advantage helps clarify this question. See Exhibit 7.2.

First, *factor endowments* are conducive to the rise of India's software industry. Through investment in human resource development with a focus on industry-specific knowledge, India's universities and software firms have literally created this essential factor of production. For example, India produces the second-largest annual output of scientists and engineers in the world, behind only the United States. In a knowledge-intensive industry such as software, development of human resources is fundamental to both domestic and global success.

EXHIBIT 7.2 India's Software Diamond

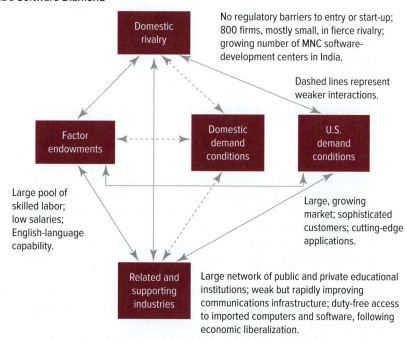

Source: From Kampur D. and Ramamurti R., "India's Emerging Competition Advantage in Services," *Academy of Management Executive: The Thinking Manager's Source.* Copyright © 2001 by Academy of Management.

continued

Second, *demand conditions* require that software firms stay on the cutting edge of technological innovation. India has already moved toward globalization of its software industry; consumer demand conditions in developed nations such as Germany, Denmark, parts of Southeast Asia, and the United States created the consumer demand necessary to propel India's software makers toward sophisticated software solutions.*

Third, India has the *supplier base as well as the related industries* needed to drive competitive rivalry and enhance competitiveness. In particular, information technology (IT) hardware prices declined rapidly in the 1990s. Furthermore, rapid technological change in IT hardware meant that latecomers like India were not locked into older-generation technologies. Thus, both the IT hardware and software industries could "leapfrog" older technologies. In addition, relationships among knowledge workers in these IT hardware and software industries offer the social structure for ongoing knowledge exchange, promoting further enhancement of existing products. Further infrastructure improvements are occurring rapidly.

*Although India's success cannot be explained in terms of its home-market demand (according to Porter's model), the nature of the industry enables software to be transferred among different locations simultaneously by way of communications links. Thus, competitiveness of markets outside India can be enhanced without a physical presence in those markets.

Fourth, with over 800 firms in the software services industry in India, *intense rivalry forces firms to develop competitive strategies and structures.* Although firms like TCS, Infosys, and Wipro have become large, they still face strong competition from dozens of small and midsize companies aspiring to catch them. This intense rivalry is one of the primary factors driving Indian software firms to develop overseas distribution channels, as predicted by Porter's diamond of national advantage.

It is interesting to note that the cost advantage of Indian firms has eroded. For example, TCS's engineers' compensation soared 13 percent in 2010. Further, IBM and Accenture are aggressively building up their Indian operations, hiring tens of thousands of sought-after Indians by paying them more, thereby lowering their costs while raising those of TCS. Finally, many low-labor-cost countries, such as China, the Philippines, and Vietnam, are emerging as threats to the Indian competitors.

Sources: Sachitanand, R. 2010. The new face of IT. *Business Today,* 19: 62; Anonymous. 2010. Training to lead. *www.Dqindia.com,* October 5: np; Nagaraju, B. 2011. India's software exports seen up 16–18 pct. in Fy12. *www.reuters.com,* February 2: np; Ghemawat, P. & Hout, T. 2008. Tomorrow's global giants. *Harvard Business Review,* 86(11): 80–88; Mathur, S. K. 2007. Indian IT industry: A performance analysis and a model for possible adoption. *ideas.repec.org,* January 1: np; Kripalani, M. 2002. Calling Bangalore: Multinationals are making it a hub for high-tech research *BusinessWeek,* November 25: 52–54; Kapur, D. & Ramamurti, R. 2001. India's emerging competitive advantage in services. 2001. *Academy of Management Executive,* 15(2): 20–33; World Bank. 2001 *World Development Report:* 6. New York: Oxford University Press; and Reuters. 2001. Oracle in India push, taps software talent. *Washington Post Online,* July 3.

Concluding Comment on Factors Affecting a Nation's Competitiveness

Porter drew his conclusions based on case histories of firms in more than 100 industries. Despite the differences in strategies employed by successful global competitors, a common theme emerged: Firms that succeeded in global markets had first succeeded in intensely competitive home markets. We can conclude that competitive advantage for global firms typically grows out of relentless, continuing improvement, and innovation.[11]

LO7.3

The motivations (or benefits) and the risks associated with international expansion, including the emerging trend for greater offshoring and outsourcing activity.

multinational firms
firms that manage operations in more than one country.

International Expansion: A Company's Motivations and Risks

Motivations for International Expansion

Increase Market Size   There are many motivations for a company to pursue international expansion. The most obvious one is to *increase the size of potential markets* for a firm's products and services.[12] The world's population approached 7.5 billion in early 2015, with the U.S. representing less than 5 percent.

Many **multinational firms** are intensifying their efforts to market their products and services to countries such as India and China as the ranks of their middle class have increased over the past decade. The potential is great. An OECD study predicts that consumption by middle-class consumers in Asian markets will grow from $4.9 trillion in 2009 to over $30 trillion by 2020. At that point, Asia will make up 60 percent of global middle-class consumption, up from 20 percent in 2009.[13]

Expanding a firm's global presence also automatically increases its scale of operations, providing it with a larger revenue and asset base.[14] As we noted in Chapter 5 in discussing overall cost leadership strategies, such an increase in revenues and asset base potentially enables a firm to *attain economies of scale.* This provides multiple benefits. One advantage is the spreading of fixed costs such as R&D over a larger volume of production. Examples include the sale of Boeing's commercial aircraft and Microsoft's operating systems in many foreign countries.

Filmmaking is another industry in which international sales can help amortize huge developmental costs.[15] For example, 77 percent of the $1.1 billion box-office take for *Transformers: Age of Extinction* came from overseas moviegoers. Similarly, the market for kids' movies is largely outside the U.S., with 70 percent of *Frozen's* $1.3 billion in box-office take coming from overseas.

Take Advantage of Arbitrage   *Taking advantage of* **arbitrage opportunities** is a second advantage of international expansion. In its simplest form, arbitrage involves buying something where it is cheap and selling it where it commands a higher price. A big part of Walmart's success can be attributed to the company's expertise in arbitrage. The possibilities for arbitrage are not necessarily confined to simple trading opportunities. It can be applied to virtually any factor of production and every stage of the value chain. For example, a firm may locate its call centers in India, its manufacturing plants in China, and its R&D in Europe, where the specific types of talented personnel may be available at the lowest possible cost. In today's integrated global financial markets, a firm can borrow anywhere in the world where capital is cheap and use it to fund a project in a country where capital is expensive. Such arbitrage opportunities are even more attractive to global corporations because their larger size enables them to buy in huge volume, thus increasing their bargaining power with suppliers.

Enhancing a Product's Growth Potential   *Enhancing the growth rate of a product* that is in its maturity stage in a firm's home country but that has greater demand potential elsewhere is another benefit of international expansion. As we noted in Chapter 5, products (and industries) generally go through a four-stage life cycle of introduction, growth, maturity, and decline. In recent decades, U.S. soft-drink producers such as Coca-Cola and PepsiCo have aggressively pursued international markets to attain levels of growth that simply would not be available in the United States. The differences in market growth potential have even led some firms to restructure their operations. For example, Procter & Gamble relocated its global skin, cosmetics, and personal care unit headquarters from Cincinnati to Singapore to be closer to the fast-growing Asian market.[16]

Optimize the Location of Value-Chain Activities   *Optimizing the physical location for every activity in the firm's value chain* is another benefit. Recall from our discussions in Chapters 3 and 5 that the value chain represents the various activities in which all firms must engage to produce products and services. It includes primary activities, such as inbound logistics, operations, and marketing, as well as support activities, such as procurement, R&D, and human resource management. All firms have to make critical decisions as to where each activity will take place.[17] Optimizing the location for every activity in the value chain can yield one or more of three strategic advantages: performance enhancement, cost reduction, and risk reduction. We will now discuss each of these.

Performance Enhancement   Microsoft's decision to establish a corporate research laboratory in Cambridge, England, is an example of a location decision that was guided mainly by the goal of building and sustaining world-class excellence in selected value-creating activities.[18] This strategic decision provided Microsoft with access to outstanding technical and professional talent. Location decisions can affect the quality with which any activity is performed in terms of the availability of needed talent, speed of learning, and the quality of external and internal coordination.

Cost Reduction Two location decisions founded largely on cost-reduction considerations are (1) Nike's decision to source the manufacture of athletic shoes from Asian countries such as China, Vietnam, and Indonesia and (2) the decision of Volkswagen to locate a new auto production plant in Chattanooga, Tennessee, to leverage the relatively low labor costs in the area as well as low shipping costs due to Chattanooga's close proximity to both rail and river transportation. Such location decisions can affect the cost structure in terms of local manpower and other resources, transportation and logistics, and government incentives and the local tax structure.

Performance enhancement and cost-reduction benefits parallel the business-level strategies (discussed in Chapter 5) of differentiation and overall cost leadership. They can at times be attained simultaneously. Consider our example in the previous section on the Indian software industry. When Oracle set up a development operation in that country, the company benefited both from lower labor costs and operational expenses and from performance enhancements realized through the hiring of superbly talented professionals.

Risk Reduction Given the erratic swings in the exchange ratios between the U.S. dollar and the Japanese yen (in relation to each other and to other major currencies), an important basis for cost competition between Ford and Toyota has been their relative ingenuity at managing currency risks. One way for such rivals to manage currency risks has been to spread the high-cost elements of their manufacturing operations across a few select and carefully chosen locations around the world. Location decisions such as these can affect the overall risk profile of the firm with respect to currency, economic, and political risks.[19]

Learning Opportunities By expanding into new markets, corporations expose themselves to differing market demands, R&D capabilities, functional skills, organizational processes, and managerial practices. This provides opportunities for managers to transfer the knowledge that results from these exposures back to their home office and to other divisions in the firm. Thus, expansion into new markets provides a range of learning opportunities. For example, when L'Oréal, a French personal care product manufacturer, acquired two U.S. firms that developed and sold hair care products to African-American customers, L'Oréal gained knowledge on what is referred to in the industry as "ethnic hair care." It then took this knowledge and built a new ethnic hair care division in Europe and later began making inroads in African markets. More generally, research suggests that overseas expansion leads to valuable learning at home. One study found that, rather than distracting the firm in its efforts in its home market, overseas acquisitions led to substantial performance improvements, an average of a 12 percent increase, in home markets.[20]

reverse innovation
new products developed by developed-country multinational firms for emerging markets that have adequate functionality at a low cost.

Explore Reverse Innovation Finally, *exploring possibilities for* **reverse innovation** has become a major motivation for international expansion. Many leading companies are discovering that developing products specifically for emerging markets can pay off in a big way. In the past, multinational companies typically developed products for their rich home markets and then tried to sell them in developing countries with minor adaptations. However, as growth slows in rich nations and demand grows rapidly in developing countries such as India and China, this approach becomes increasingly inadequate. Instead, companies like GE have committed significant resources to developing products that meet the needs of developing nations, products that deliver adequate functionality at a fraction of the cost. Interestingly, these products have subsequently found considerable success in value segments in wealthy countries as well. Hence, this process is referred to as reverse innovation, a new motivation for international expansion.

REVERSE INNOVATION: HOW DEVELOPING COUNTRIES ARE BECOMING HOTBEDS OF INNOVATION

A number of firms have seen the need to develop technologies and products that are appropriate to developing markets, only to find that these innovations are valuable in their home markets as well. Here are a few examples of firms that have leveraged or are striving to leverage "reverse innovation."

- GE Healthcare developed a portable, inexpensive ultrasound device, called the Vscan, in China. This device cost one-tenth what a full-scale ultrasound device would cost in the United States. The product is a hit in China as well as in other developing markets. GE also sees tremendous potential for the product in developed markets. The main unit of the device is small enough and cheap enough to put one in the pocket of every physician, paramedic, and emergency room nurse. GE's vision is to have the Vscan become as indispensable as the stethoscope as a diagnostic tool.

- Moline, Illinois–based Deere & Co. opened a center in Pune, India, almost a decade ago with the intention to penetrate the Indian market. Deere, a firm known for its heavy-duty farm equipment and big construction gear, used the Pune facility to design four no-frills models. Though lacking first-world features like GPS and air conditioning, they were sturdy enough to handle the rigors of commercial farming. The tractors cost as little as $7,000, compared to over $300,000 for a fully loaded 8360R tractor in the United States. Subsequently, Deere targeted a segment of the home market that it had previously largely ignored— hobbyists as well as bargain hunters. These buyers do not care for advanced features but covet the same qualities as Indian farmers: affordability and maneuverability. Today, half of the no-frills models that Deere produces in India are exported to other countries.

- The potential even exists in service industries. Walmart developed "small mart stores" to meet the needs of customers in Argentina, Brazil, and Mexico but is now transferring this idea back to the United States to compete in areas, such as urban markets, where a full-size Walmart is not workable.

- PepsiCo is now seeing potential with this model. It built a global innovation center in India in 2010 and hopes to develop products and packaging that will meet the needs of the Indian market and other markets as well.

Sources: Frugal ideas are spreading from East to West. 2012. *The Economist,* March 24: 68; and Singh, S. & Nagarajan, G. 2011. Small is beautiful for John Deere. *Bloomberg Businessweek,* September 26: 33–34.

As $3,000 cars, $300 computers, and $30 mobile phones bring what were previously considered as luxuries within the reach of the middle class of emerging markets, it is important to understand the motivations and implications of reverse innovation. *First,* it is impossible to sell first-world versions of products with minor adaptations in countries where the average annual income per person is between $1,000 and $4,000, as is the case in most developing countries. To sell in these markets, entirely new products must be designed and developed by local technical talent and manufactured with local components. *Second,* although these countries are relatively poor, they are growing rapidly. *Third,* if the innovation does not come from first-world multinationals, there are any number of local firms that are ready to grab the market with low-cost products. *Fourth,* as the consumers and governments of many first-world countries are rediscovering the virtues of frugality and are trying to cut down expenses, these products and services originally developed for the first world may gain significant market shares in developing countries as well.

Strategy Spotlight 7.2 describes some examples of reverse innovation.

Potential Risks of International Expansion

When a company expands its international operations, it does so to increase its profits or revenues. As with any other investment, however, there are also potential risks.[21] To help companies assess the risk of entering foreign markets, rating systems have been developed to evaluate political and economic, as well as financial and credit, risks.[22] *Euromoney* magazine publishes a semiannual "Country Risk Rating" that evaluates political, economic, and other risks that entrants potentially face.[23] Exhibit 7.3 presents a sample of country risk ratings, published by AM Best. Note that the overall ratings range from 1 to 5, with higher risk receiving the higher score.

EXHIBIT 7.3 A Sample of Country Risk Ratings, August 2014

Country Score	Overall Country Rating	Economic Risk	Political Risk	Financial System Risk
Norway	1	1	1	1
Canada	1	1	1	1
United States	1	1	1	1
Singapore	1	2	1	1
Hong Kong	2	2	1	1
South Korea	2	1	2	2
South Africa	3	3	3	2
China	3	2	3	3
Bahrain	3	3	4	3
Kazakhstan	4	3	4	4
Colombia	4	3	4	4
Russia	4	3	4	4
Argentina	5	4	4	5
Libya	5	5	5	5

Source: A.M. Best Company - Used by permission.

Next we will discuss the four main types of risk: political risk, economic risk, currency risk, and management risk.

Political and Economic Risk Generally speaking, the business climate in the United States is very favorable. However, some countries around the globe may be hazardous to the health of corporate initiatives because of **political risk.**[24] Forces such as social unrest, military turmoil, demonstrations, and even violent conflict and terrorism can pose serious threats.[25] Consider, for example, the ongoing tension and violence in the Middle East associated with the revolutions and civil wars in Egypt, Libya, Syria, and other countries. Such conditions increase the likelihood of destruction of property and disruption of operations as well as nonpayment for goods and services. Thus, countries that are viewed as high risk are less attractive for most types of business.[26]

Another source of political risk in many countries is the absence of the **rule of law.** The absence of rules or the lack of uniform enforcement of existing rules leads to what might often seem to be arbitrary and inconsistent decisions by government officials. This can make it difficult for foreign firms to conduct business.

For example, consider Renault's experience in Russia. Renault paid $1 billion to acquire a 25 percent ownership stake in the Russian automaker AvtoVAZ in 2008. Just one year later, Russian Prime Minister Vladimir Putin threatened to dilute Renault's ownership stake unless it contributed more money to prop up AvtoVAZ, which was then experiencing a significant slide in sales. Renault realized its ownership claim may not have held up in the corrupt Russian court system. Therefore, it was forced to negotiate and eventually agreed to transfer over $300 million in technology and expertise to the Russian firm to ensure its ownership stake would stay at 25 percent.[27]

Interestingly, while corporations have historically been concerned about rule-of-law issues in developing markets, such issues have also become a significant concern in developed markets, most critically in the United States. In a 2012 World Economic Forum Global Competitive Report that examined the quality of governmental institutions and the rule of law, the United

political risk

potential threat to a firm's operations in a country due to ineffectiveness of the domestic political system.

rule of law

a characteristic of legal systems where by behavior is governed by rules that are uniformly enforced.

States fared poorly. Starkly, the United States was ranked among the top 20 countries on only 1 of the 22 measures of institutional quality the survey included. In line with these findings, the International Finance Corporation (IFC) found that governmental hurdles businesses face have become a greater challenge in the U.S. in recent years. The IFC compiles data annually on the burdens of doing business that are put in place by governments and found that the U.S. is one of only a few countries surveyed in which doing business has become more burdensome. In nearly 90 percent of countries, governmental burdens have eased since 2006, but the U.S. has bucked that trend and become a more difficult location in which to operate. As institutions deteriorate, the U.S. loses its luster as a place to base operations. This sentiment was reflected in a survey of business executives who are alumni of the Harvard Business School. When asked whether they had recently favored basing new operations in the U.S. or in a foreign location, an overwhelming majority, 84 percent, responded that they had chosen the foreign location. Thus, advanced economies, such as the U.S., risk losing out to other countries if they fail to reinforce and strengthen their legal and political institutions.[28]

The laws, and the enforcement of laws, associated with the protection of intellectual property rights can be a major potential **economic risk** in entering new countries.[29] Microsoft, for example, has lost billions of dollars in potential revenue through piracy of its software products in many countries, including China. Other areas of the globe, such as the former Soviet Union and some eastern European nations, have piracy problems as well.[30] Firms rich in intellectual property have encountered financial losses as imitations of their products have grown due to a lack of law enforcement of intellectual property rights.[31]

Counterfeiting, a direct form of theft of intellectual property rights, is a significant and growing problem. The International Chamber of Commerce estimated that the value of counterfeit goods will exceed $1.7 trillion in 2015. "The whole business has just exploded," said Jeffrey Hardy, head of the anticounterfeiting program at ICC. "And it goes way beyond music and Gucci bags." Counterfeiting has moved well beyond handbags and shoes to include chemicals, pharmaceuticals, and aircraft parts. According to a University of Florida study, 25 percent of the pesticide market in some parts of Europe is estimated to be counterfeit. This is especially troubling since these chemicals are often toxic.[32] In Strategy Spotlight 7.3, we discuss the challenge of fighting counterfeiting in the pharmaceutical business and how Pfizer is attempting to fight this threat to its business.

Currency Risks   Currency fluctuations can pose substantial risks. A company with operations in several countries must constantly monitor the exchange rate between its own currency and that of the host country to minimize **currency risks.** Even a small change in the exchange rate can result in a significant difference in the cost of production or net profit when doing business overseas. When the U.S. dollar appreciates against other currencies, for example, U.S. goods can be more expensive to consumers in foreign countries. At the same time, however, appreciation of the U.S. dollar can have negative implications for American companies that have branch operations overseas. The reason for this is that profits from abroad must be exchanged for dollars at a more expensive rate of exchange, reducing the amount of profit when measured in dollars. For example, consider an American firm doing business in Italy. If this firm had a 20 percent profit in euros at its Italian center of operations, this profit would be totally wiped out when converted into U.S. dollars if the euro had depreciated 20 percent against the U.S. dollar. (U.S. multinationals typically engage in sophisticated "hedging strategies" to minimize currency risk. The discussion of this is beyond the scope of this section.)

Below, we discuss how Israel's strong currency—the shekel—forced a firm to reevaluate its strategy.

> For years O.R.T. Technologies resisted moving any operations outside Israel. However, when faced with a sharp rise in the value of the shekel, the maker of specialized software for managing gas stations froze all local hiring and decided to transfer some

economic risk
potential threat to a firm's operations in a country due to economic policies and conditions, including property rights laws and enforcement of those laws.

counterfeiting
selling of trademarked goods without the consent of the trademark holder.

currency risk
potential threat to a firm's operations in a country due to fluctuations in the local currency's exchange rate.

COUNTERFEIT DRUGS: A DANGEROUS AND GROWING PROBLEM

Brian Donnelly has an interesting background. He's both a cop and a pharmacist. He worked as a special agent for the FBI for 21 years, but he also has a PhD in pharmacology. Now he's on the front lines of an important fight: keeping counterfeit drugs from the market. He works as an investigator for Pfizer, one of the world's largest pharmaceutical companies, putting both his pharmacology and law enforcement skills at work to blunt the growing flow of counterfeit drugs. He is one of a small army of former law enforcement officers employed by the pharmaceutical companies working for the same aim.

This is an important fight for two reasons. First, it is of economic consequence for the pharmaceutical companies. Counterfeit drugs are big business. In the United States alone, counterfeit drugs generated around $75 billion in revenue in 2010. They are enticing to customers. For example, while Pfizer's erectile dysfunction pill, Viagra, sells for $15 per tablet, fake versions sold online can be gotten for as little as $1 a pill. The sales of counterfeit drugs cut into the sales and profits of Pfizer and the other pharmaceutical firms. Second and more importantly, these fake drugs are potentially dangerous. The danger comes from both what they contain and what they don't contain. Fake pills have been found to contain chalk, brick dust, paint, and even pesticides. Thus, they may be toxic, and ingesting them may cause significant health problems. On the other side, they may not contain the correct dose or even any of the active ingredients they are supposed to have. This may lead to severe health consequences. For example, fake Zithromax,

an antibiotic, may contain none of the necessary chemical components, leaving the patient unable to fight the infection. According to one estimate, counterfeit drugs contribute to the death of upward of 100,000 people a year globally.

The pharmaceutical firms are fighting back with Donnelly and his colleagues. They use a common law enforcement technique. The fake drugs are sold by local dealers in the United States, who typically sell through websites, such as hardtofindrx.com and even Craigslist. These local dealers, called drop dealers, are the easiest to catch. From there, the investigators try to gain information on the major dealers from whom the drop dealers order. If they can get to these folks, they try to take it back to the kingpins manufacturing the drugs. This typically takes them through multiple law enforcement agencies in multiple countries, often back to manufacturing plants in China and India. To find the source, the pharmaceutical companies also use advanced technology. They determine the chemical composition of fake drugs they seize to search for common chemical signatures that point to the possible sourcing plant.

Pfizer is also fighting the fight from another angle. It is now tagging every bottle of Viagra and many other pharmaceuticals with radio-frequency identification (RFID) tags. Pharmacies can read these tags and input the data into Pfizer's system to confirm that these bottles are legitimate Pfizer drugs. This won't stop shady websites from delivering counterfeit drugs, but it will help keep the counterfeits out of legitimate pharmacies.

Sources: O'Connor, M. 2006. Pfizer using RFID to fight fake Viagra. *RFIDjournal .com,* January 6: np; and Gillette, F. 2013. Inside Pfizer's fight against counterfeit drugs. *Bloomberg Businessweek,* January 17: np.

---

developmental work to Eastern Europe. Laments CEO Alex Milner, "I never thought I'd see the day when we would have to move R&D outside of Israel, but the strong shekel has forced us to do so."[33]

management risk
potential threat to a firm's operations in a country due to the problems that managers have making decisions in the context of foreign markets.

Management Risks   **Management risks** may be considered the challenges and risks that managers face when they must respond to the inevitable differences that they encounter in foreign markets. These take a variety of forms: culture, customs, language, income levels, customer preferences, distribution systems, and so on.[34] As we will note later in the chapter, even in the case of apparently standard products, some degree of local adaptation will become necessary.[35]

Differences in cultures across countries can also pose unique challenges for managers.[36] Cultural symbols can evoke deep feelings.[37] For example, in a series of advertisements aimed at Italian vacationers, Coca-Cola executives turned the Eiffel Tower, Empire State Building, and Tower of Pisa into the familiar Coke bottle. So far, so good. However, when the white marble columns of the Parthenon that crowns the Acropolis in Athens were turned into Coke bottles, the Greeks became outraged. Why? Greeks refer to the Acropolis as the "holy rock," and a government official said the Parthenon is an "international symbol of excellence" and that "whoever insults the Parthenon insults international culture." Coca-Cola apologized. Below are some cultural tips for conducting business in HongKong:

- Handshakes when greeting and before leaving are customary.
- After the initial handshake, business cards are presented with both hands on the card. Carefully read the card before putting it away.

- In Hong Kong, Chinese people should be addressed by their professional title (or Mr., Mrs., Miss) followed by their surname.
- Appointments should be made as far in advance as possible.
- Punctuality is very important and demonstrates respect.
- Negotiations in Hong Kong are normally very slow, with much attention to detail. The same negotiating team should be kept throughout the proceedings.
- Tea will be served during the negotiations. Always accept and wait for the host to begin drinking before you partake.
- Be aware that "yes" may just be an indication that the person heard you rather than indicating agreement. A Hong Kong Chinese businessperson will have a difficult time saying "no" directly.

Below, we discuss a rather humorous example of how a local custom can affect operations at a manufacturing plant in Singapore.

> Larry Henderson, plant manager, and John Lichtental, manager of human resources, were faced with a rather unique problem. They were assigned by Celanese Chemical Corp. to build a plant in Singapore, and the plant was completed in July. However, according to local custom, a plant should be christened only on "lucky" days. Unfortunately, the next lucky day was not until September 3.
>
> The managers had to convince executives at Celanese's Dallas headquarters to delay the plant opening. As one might expect, it wasn't easy. But after many heated telephone conversations and flaming emails, the president agreed to open the new plant on a lucky day—September 3.[38]

In the nearby Insights from Executives box, Terrie Campbell, a senior executive at Ricoh Americas, offers further thoughts on the opportunities and risks for multinational firms.

Global Dispersion of Value Chains: Outsourcing and Offshoring

A major recent trend has been the dispersion of the value chains of multinational corporations across different countries; that is, the various activities that constitute the value chain of a firm are now spread across several countries and continents. Such dispersion of value occurs mainly through increasing offshoring and outsourcing.

A report issued by the World Trade Organization described the production of a particular U.S. car as follows: "30 percent of the car's value goes to Korea for assembly, 17.5 percent to Japan for components and advanced technology, 7.5 percent to Germany for design, 4 percent to Taiwan and Singapore for minor parts, 2.5 percent to U.K. for advertising and marketing services, and 1.5 percent to Ireland and Barbados for data processing. This means that only 37 percent of the production value is generated in the U.S."[39] In today's economy, we are increasingly witnessing two interrelated trends: outsourcing and offshoring.

Outsourcing occurs when a firm decides to utilize other firms to perform value-creating activities that were previously performed in-house.[40] It may be a new activity that the firm is perfectly capable of doing but chooses to have someone else perform for cost or quality reasons. Outsourcing can be to either a domestic or foreign firm.

Offshoring takes place when a firm decides to shift an activity that it was performing in a domestic location to a foreign location.[41] For example, both Microsoft and Intel now have R&D facilities in India, employing a large number of Indian scientists and engineers. Often, offshoring and outsourcing go together; that is, a firm may outsource an activity to a foreign supplier, thereby causing the work to be offshored as well.[42]

The recent explosion in the volume of outsourcing and offshoring is due to a variety of factors. Up until the 1960s, for most companies, the entire value chain was in one location. Further, the production took place close to where the customers were in order to keep transportation costs under control. In the case of service industries, it was generally believed that offshoring was not possible because the producer and consumer had to be

outsourcing
using other firms to perform value-creating activities that were previously performed in-house.

offshoring
shifting a value-creating activity from a domestic location to a foreign location.

TERRIE CAMPBELL, VICE PRESIDENT OF STRATEGIC MARKETING AT RICOH AMERICAS CORPORATION

BIOSKETCH

Terrie Campbell serves as vice president of strategic marketing for Ricoh Americas Corporation. In this role, she is responsible for the strategy, direction, and execution of Ricoh's Managed Document Services approach, as well as key vertical marketing strategies and programs, for both direct and dealer channels. Campbell is also the global lead for the development of tools and processes to ensure consistent execution of Ricoh Managed Document Services around the world. Prior to this appointment, Campbell served as vice president of Managed Document Services for Ricoh USA.

1. Ricoh has significant international operations. What do you see as some of the primary opportunities and threats in global expansion?

Opportunities are primarily found in the area of being able to leverage our global footprint and support customers that want a level of consistency from region to region. We also find that by having such a significant number of locations and customers, we are very well positioned to understand the best practices, benchmarks, and trends that help us continue to innovate and find new ways to solve our customer problems. With such a large network of resources, there are very few issues or challenges in our space that we have not addressed somewhere in our organization before.

The challenges include regional culture differences and time-zone management when trying to collaborate via conference calls or video. There are also limitations on what our systems are allowed to pass from region to region due to legislation and regional regulations. There is also the dynamic that as an organization, a significant portion of our growth came through acquisitions, which may create headwind from assimilation issues. For our model to work, we have also embraced a distributor model in some of our noncore markets. This brings us a high degree of flexibility to meet our customer needs, but it also adds a new level of oversight to ensure consistency in the delivery of services and support. The biggest challenge is around the ability of systems to speak to one another when translation and currency conversions are needed. The reality is that it requires a lot of heavy lifting to get a global view of business when you take these issues into consideration.

2. What are some of the challenges associated with adapting your marketing strategies to local tastes and cultures?

Different words have different meanings from region to region. It is critical to define the vision first for the organization and then allow the resources that best understand the regional connotation to edit for final copy. The risk, when this happens, is that the message may lose some of the nuance that brings "punch" to the story. Getting everyone to understand the intent of the message must be the first order of business. You will often find that an entirely different approach is needed in a region, but given flexibility, it will achieve even stronger alignment and customer engagement.

Another challenge that is fairly typical is that the "not invented here" mentality may set in when one region proposes an idea across the globe. There is no question that the passion for an idea is typically going to lie with the originator; as a result, it may be difficult for that person to understand or accept resistance from another region when that region does not feel the same passion for the idea or concept. It may turn into a long, emotional battle of wills if the other region believes it has a superior idea, concept, or current way of operating. This is often a surprise to a person new to global marketing or communications. The key to success is to ensure that the key stakeholders have a voice in the process early and can see their "fingerprints" on the finished idea. The time invested in the up-front collaboration and engagement is well worth your effort to ensure adoption and success.

3. How does Ricoh facilitate the transmission of knowledge and learning from one market to another?

Facilitation of learning across markets begins with a strong best-practice collection and development process. Additionally, tools to enable the organization to share wins and learning that may be part of an innovation process ensure that new ideas and successes are formalized and shared. Once an idea is defined as a repeatable solution or process, then leveraging field deployment teams and training tools will instill knowledge, manage testing, and report certifications. These tools will include online, self-paced courses, classroom courses, and facilitator-led, manager-led, or virtual-classroom options. There is also the need to proliferate casual or "tribal" knowledge, which can be facilitated through social platforms or knowledge libraries that provide access to the appropriate employees.

4. What are some of the human resource management challenges and opportunities with regard to Ricoh's different international operations?

As a global company, it would be ideal to have all employees in common job descriptions, with common pay grades, incentives, and so on. The idea is great, but the fact is that with local competition for talent present at the same place at the same time. After all, a haircut could not be performed if the barber and the client were separated!

For manufacturing industries, the rapid decline in transportation and coordination costs has enabled firms to disperse their value chains over different locations. For example, Nike's R&D takes place in the U.S., raw materials are procured from a multitude of countries, actual manufacturing takes place in China, Indonesia, or Vietnam, advertising is produced in the U.S., and sales and service take place in practically all the countries. Each value-creating activity is performed in the location where the cost is the lowest or the quality is the best. Without finding optimal locations for each activity, Nike could not have attained its position as the world's largest shoe company.

The experience of the manufacturing sector was also repeated in the service sector by the mid-1990s. A trend that began with the outsourcing of low-level programming and data entry work to countries such as India and Ireland suddenly grew manyfold, encompassing a variety of white-collar and professional activities ranging from call centers to R&D.

Bangalore, India, in recent years, has emerged as a location where more and more U.S. tax returns are prepared. In India, U.S.-trained and licensed radiologists interpret chest X-rays and CT scans from U.S. hospitals for half the cost. The advantages from offshoring go beyond mere cost savings today. In many specialized occupations in science and engineering, there is a shortage of qualified professionals in developed countries, whereas countries like India, China, and Singapore have what seems like an inexhaustible supply.[43]

While offshoring offers the potential to cut costs in corporations across a wide range of industries, many firms are finding the benefits of offshoring to be more elusive and the costs greater than they anticipated.[44] A study by AMR Research found that 56 percent of companies moving production offshore experienced an increase in total costs, contrary to their expectations of cost savings. In a more focused study, 70 percent of managers said sourcing in China is more costly than they initially estimated.

The cause of this contrary outcome is actually not all that surprising. Common savings from offshoring, such as lower wages, benefits, energy costs, regulatory costs, and taxes, are all easily visible and immediate. In contrast, there are a host of hidden costs that arise over time and often overwhelm the cost savings of offshoring. These hidden costs include:

- *Total wage costs.* Labor cost per hour may be significantly lower in developing markets, but this may not translate into lower overall costs. If workers in these markets are less productive or less skilled, firms end up with a higher number of hours needed to produce the same quantity of product. This necessitates hiring more workers and having employees work longer hours.
- *Indirect costs.* In addition to higher labor costs, there are also a number of indirect costs that pop up. If there are problems with the skill level of workers, the firm will find the need for more training and supervision of workers, more raw material and greater scrap due to the lower skill level, and greater rework to fix quality problems. The firm may also experience greater need for security staff in its facilities.
- *Increased inventory.* Due to the longer delivery times, firms often need to tie up more capital in work in progress and inventory.

RESHORING OPERATIONS: OTIS STRUGGLES TO LIFT ITS U.S. MANUFACTURING OFF THE GROUND

United Technologies Corporation has found that reshoring manufacturing to the United States is a very challenging experience. In late 2012, the firm announced with great fanfare that it would relocate an Otis elevator plant from Mexico to South Carolina. The relocation was seen both as a boon to the community, since it would generate nearly 400 good-paying jobs, and as another signal of the renaissance of American manufacturing. For Otis, the move promised to save the firm money, streamline operations, and speed up order fulfillment by bringing manufacturing closer to customers and locating manufacturing right next to the engineering staff. The firm anticipated seeing a 17 percent reduction in freight and logistics costs and a 20 percent efficiency gain by co-locating all staff involved in elevator design and manufacturing.

However, it has proved to be a challenging transition. Due to production delays as Otis ramped up U.S. production, a large backlog in orders arose. Some customers canceled their orders after waiting months for delivery. Otis was forced to keep its Nogales, Mexico, plant open six months longer than it had anticipated due to delays in ramping up the manufacturing unit in South Carolina. All totaled, the problems led to a $60 million hit to Otis's bottom line in 2013 and continued to weigh on earnings through the first half of 2014.

The key challenge Otis faced was constructing the skilled labor pool it needed. Although the firm transferred some workers from operations in Arizona and Indiana, it had difficulty finding skilled manufacturing workers in South Carolina. Florence, South Carolina, the town Otis moved to, had a long history of being a manufacturing town but saw its manufacturing base decline rapidly in the 1980s and 1990s. It is a geographically attractive location, with available manufacturing sites and easy access to rail and port locations. As a result, Otis was able to move into an empty facility that used to house a Maytag plant. However, Otis found that the current manufacturing systems required higher technology-based skills than those in the past and that the skill set of the region's workers was not up to the demands of the job.

In the words of Robert McDonough, COO of the business unit that includes Otis, "I think we failed on both the planning and the execution side." To address these issues, Otis brought in new leadership for its North American operations. At the plant level, Otis brought in additional workers and invested in greater training than it had anticipated. Otis is still committed to the Florence plant and has brought the backlog down, but its experience does highlight some of the challenges firms face as they bring manufacturing operations back to the U.S.

Sources: Mann, T. 2014. Otis finds reshoring manufacturing is not easy. *wsj.com*, May 2: np; and Anonymous. 2014. Supply chain news: When it comes to reshoring, detailed planning and expectation setting is key, Otis elevators learns the hard way. *scdigest.com*, May 5: np.

- *Reduced market responsiveness.* The long supply lines from low-cost countries may leave firms less responsive to shifts in customer demands. This may damage their brand image and also increase product obsolescence costs, as they may have to scrap or sell at a steep discount products that fail to meet quickly changing technology standards or customer tastes.
- *Coordination costs.* Coordinating product development and manufacturing can be difficult with operations undertaking different tasks in different countries. This may hamper innovation. It may also trigger unexpected costs, such as paying overtime in some markets so that staff across multiple time zones can meet to coordinate their activities.
- *Intellectual property rights.* Firms operating in countries with weak IP protection can wind up losing their trade secrets or taking costly measures to protect these secrets.
- *Wage inflation.* In moving overseas, firms often assume some level of wage stability, but wages in developing markets can be volatile and spike dramatically. For example, minimum wages set by provinces in China increased at an average of 18 percent per year in the 2010–2014 period.[45] As Roger Meiners, chairman of the Department of Economics at the University of Texas at Arlington, stated, "The U.S. is more competitive on a wage basis because average wages have come down, especially for entry-level workers, and wages in China have been increasing."

Firms need to take into account all of these costs in determining whether or not to move their operations offshore. Strategy Spotlight 7.4 discusses the experience Otis, the elevator manufacturer, had when it decided to "reshore" its manufacturing.

Achieving Competitive Advantage in Global Markets

LO7.4

The two opposing forces—cost reduction and adaptation to local markets—that firms face when entering international markets.

We now discuss the two opposing forces that firms face when they expand into global markets: cost reduction and adaptation to local markets. Then we address the four basic types of international strategies that they may pursue: international, global, multidomestic, and transnational. The selection of one of these four types of strategies is largely dependent on a firm's relative pressure to address each of the two forces.

Two Opposing Pressures: Reducing Costs and Adapting to Local Markets

Many years ago, the famed marketing strategist Theodore Levitt advocated strategies that favored global products and brands. He suggested that firms should standardize all of their products and services for all of their worldwide markets. Such an approach would help a firm lower its overall costs by spreading its investments over as large a market as possible. Levitt's approach rested on three key assumptions:

1. Customer needs and interests are becoming increasingly homogeneous worldwide.
2. People around the world are willing to sacrifice preferences in product features, functions, design, and the like for lower prices at high quality.
3. Substantial economies of scale in production and marketing can be achieved through supplying global markets.[46]

However, there is ample evidence to refute these assumptions.[47] Regarding the first assumption—the increasing worldwide homogeneity of customer needs and interests—consider the number of product markets, ranging from watches and handbags to soft drinks and fast foods. Companies have identified global customer segments and developed global products and brands targeted to those segments. Also, many other companies adapt lines to idiosyncratic country preferences and develop local brands targeted to local market segments. For example, Nestlé's line of pizzas marketed in the United Kingdom includes cheese with ham and pineapple topping on a French bread crust. Similarly, Coca-Cola in Japan markets Georgia (a tonic drink) as well as Classic Coke and Hi-C.

Consider the second assumption—the sacrifice of product attributes for lower prices. While there is invariably a price-sensitive segment in many product markets, there is no indication that this is increasing. In contrast, in many product and service markets—ranging from watches, personal computers, and household appliances to banking and insurance—there is a growing interest in multiple product features, product quality, and service.

Finally, the third assumption is that significant economies of scale in production and marketing could be achieved for global products and services. Although standardization may lower manufacturing costs, such a perspective does not consider three critical and interrelated points. First, as we discussed in Chapter 5, technological developments in flexible factory automation enable economies of scale to be attained at lower levels of output and do not require production of a single standardized product. Second, the cost of production is only one component, and often not the critical one, in determining the total cost of a product. Third, a firm's strategy should not be product-driven. It should also consider other activities in the firm's value chain, such as marketing, sales, and distribution.

Based on the above, we would have a hard time arguing that it is wise to develop the same product or service for all markets throughout the world. While there are some exceptions, such as Boeing airplanes and some of Coca-Cola's soft-drink products, managers

EXHIBIT 7.4 Opposing Pressures and Four Strategies

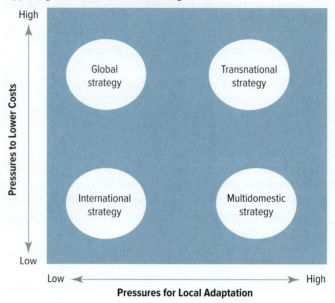

must also strive to tailor their products to the culture of the country in which they are attempting to do business. Few would argue that "one size fits all" generally applies.

The opposing pressures that managers face place conflicting demands on firms as they strive to be competitive.[48] On the one hand, competitive pressures require that firms do what they can to *lower unit costs* so that consumers will not perceive their product and service offerings as too expensive. This may lead them to consider locating manufacturing facilities where labor costs are low and developing products that are highly standardized across multiple countries.

In addition to responding to pressures to lower costs, managers must strive to be *responsive to local pressures* in order to tailor their products to the demand of the local market in which they do business. This requires differentiating their offerings and strategies from country to country to reflect consumer tastes and preferences and making changes to reflect differences in distribution channels, human resource practices, and governmental regulations. However, since the strategies and tactics to differentiate products and services to local markets can involve additional expenses, a firm's costs will tend to rise.

The two opposing pressures result in four different basic strategies that companies can use to compete in the global marketplace: international, global, multidomestic, and transnational. The strategy that a firm selects depends on the degree of pressure that it is facing for cost reductions and the importance of adapting to local markets. Exhibit 7.4 shows the conditions under which each of these strategies would be most appropriate.

It is important to note that we consider these four strategies to be "basic" or "pure"; that is, in practice, all firms will tend to have some elements of each strategy.

International Strategy

LO7.5

The advantages and disadvantages associated with each of the four basic strategies: international, global, multidomestic, and transnational.

There are a small number of industries in which pressures for both local adaptation and lowering costs are rather low. An extreme example of such an industry is the "orphan" drug industry. These are medicines for diseases that are severe but affect only a small number of people. Diseases such as Gaucher disease and Fabry disease fit into this category. Companies such as Genzyme and Oxford GlycoSciences are active in this segment of the drug industry. There is virtually no need to adapt their products to the local markets. And the pressures to reduce costs are low; even though only a few thousand patients are affected, the revenues and margins are significant, because patients are charged up to $100,000 per year.

An **international strategy** is based on diffusion and adaptation of the parent company's knowledge and expertise to foreign markets. Country units are allowed to make some minor adaptations to products and ideas coming from the head office, but they have far less independence and autonomy compared to multidomestic companies. The primary goal of the strategy is worldwide exploitation of the parent firm's knowledge and capabilities. All sources of core competencies are centralized.

The majority of large U.S. multinationals pursued the international strategy in the decades following World War II. These companies centralized R&D and product development but established manufacturing facilities as well as marketing organizations abroad. Companies such as McDonald's and Kellogg are examples of firms following such a strategy. Although these companies do make some local adaptations, they are of a very limited nature. With increasing pressures to reduce costs due to global competition, especially from low-cost countries, opportunities to successfully employ an international strategy are becoming more limited. This strategy is most suitable in situations where a firm has distinctive competencies that local companies in foreign markets lack.

Risks and Challenges   Below are some of the risks and challenges associated with an international strategy.

- Different activities in the value chain typically have different optimal locations. That is, R&D may be optimally located in a country with an abundant supply of scientists and engineers, whereas assembly may be better conducted in a low-cost location. Nike, for example, designs its shoes in the United States, but all the manufacturing is done in countries like China or Thailand. The international strategy, with its tendency to concentrate most of its activities in one location, fails to take advantage of the benefits of an optimally distributed value chain.
- The lack of local responsiveness may result in the alienation of local customers. Worse still, the firm's inability to be receptive to new ideas and innovation from its foreign subsidiaries may lead to missed opportunities.

Exhibit 7.5 summarizes the strengths and limitations of international strategies in the global marketplace.

Global Strategy

As indicated in Exhibit 7.4, a firm whose emphasis is on lowering costs tends to follow a **global strategy.** Competitive strategy is centralized and controlled to a large extent by the corporate office. Since the primary emphasis is on controlling costs, the corporate office strives to achieve a strong level of coordination and integration across the various businesses.[49] Firms following a global strategy strive to offer standardized products and services as well as to locate manufacturing, R&D, and marketing activities in only a few locations.[50]

A global strategy emphasizes economies of scale due to the standardization of products and services and the centralization of operations in a few locations. As such, one advantage may be that innovations that come about through efforts of either a business unit or the

international strategy
a strategy based on firms' diffusion and adaptation of the parent companies' knowledge and expertise to foreign markets; used in industries where the pressures for both local adaptation and lowering costs are low.

global strategy
a strategy based on firms' centralization and control by the corporate office, with the primary emphasis on controlling costs; used in industries where the pressure for local adaptation is low and the pressure for lowering costs is high.

EXHIBIT 7.5 Strengths and Limitations of International Strategies in the Global Marketplace

Strengths	Limitations
• Leverage and diffusion of a parent firm's knowledge and core competencies. • Lower costs because of less need to tailor products and services.	• Limited ability to adapt to local markets. • Inability to take advantage of new ideas and innovations occurring in local markets.

corporate office can be transferred more easily to other locations. Although costs may be lower, the firm following a global strategy may, in general, have to forgo opportunities for revenue growth since it does not invest extensive resources in adapting product offerings from one market to another.

A global strategy is most appropriate when there are strong pressures for reducing costs and comparatively weak pressures for adaptation to local markets. Economies of scale become an important consideration.[51] Advantages to increased volume may come from larger production plants or runs as well as from more efficient logistics and distribution networks. Worldwide volume is also especially important in supporting high levels of investment in research and development. As we would expect, many industries requiring high levels of R&D, such as pharmaceuticals, semiconductors, and jet aircraft, follow global strategies.

Another advantage of a global strategy is that it can enable a firm to create a standard level of quality throughout the world. Let's look at what Tom Siebel, former chairman of Siebel Systems (now part of Oracle), the $2 billion developer of e-business application software, said about global standardization:

> Our customers—global companies like IBM, Zurich Financial Services, and Citicorp—expect the same high level of service and quality, and the same licensing policies, no matter where we do business with them around the world. Our human resources and legal departments help us create policies that respect local cultures and requirements worldwide, while at the same time maintaining the highest standards. We have one brand, one image, one set of corporate colors, and one set of messages, across every place on the planet. An organization needs central quality control to avoid surprises.[52]

Risks and Challenges   There are, of course, some risks associated with a global strategy:[53]

- A firm can enjoy scale economies only by concentrating scale-sensitive resources and activities in one or few locations. Such concentration, however, becomes a "double-edged sword." For example, if a firm has only one manufacturing facility, it must export its output (e.g., components, subsystems, or finished products) to other markets, some of which may be a great distance from the operation. Thus, decisions about locating facilities must weigh the potential benefits from concentrating operations in a single location against the higher transportation and tariff costs that result from such concentration.

- The geographic concentration of any activity may also tend to isolate that activity from the targeted markets. Such isolation may be risky since it may hamper the facility's ability to quickly respond to changes in market conditions and needs.

- Concentrating an activity in a single location also makes the rest of the firm dependent on that location. Such dependency implies that, unless the location has world-class competencies, the firm's competitive position can be eroded if problems arise. A European Ford executive, reflecting on the firm's concentration of activities during a global integration program in the mid-1990s, lamented, "Now if you misjudge the market, you are wrong in 15 countries rather than only one."

Exhibit 7.6 summarizes the strengths and limitations of global strategies.

EXHIBIT 7.6 Strengths and Limitations of Global Strategies

Strengths	Limitations
• Strong integration occurs across various businesses.	• Limited ability exists to adapt to local markets.
• Standardization leads to higher economies of scale, which lower costs.	• Concentration of activities may increase dependence on a single facility.
• Creation of uniform standards of quality throughout the world is facilitated.	• Single locations may lead to higher tariffs and transportation costs.

Multidomestic Strategy

According to Exhibit 7.4, a firm whose emphasis is on differentiating its product and service offerings to adapt to local markets follows a **multidomestic strategy**.[54] Decisions evolving from a multidomestic strategy tend to be decentralized to permit the firm to tailor its products and respond rapidly to changes in demand. This enables a firm to expand its market and to charge different prices in different markets. For firms following this strategy, differences in language, culture, income levels, customer preferences, and distribution systems are only a few of the many factors that must be considered. Even in the case of relatively standardized products, at least some level of local adaptation is often necessary.

Consider, for example, the Oreo cookie.[55] Kraft has tailored the iconic cookie to better meet the tastes and preferences in different markets. For example, Kraft has created green tea Oreos in China, chocolate and peanut butter Oreos for Indonesia, and banana and dulce de leche Oreos for Argentina. Kraft has also lowered the sweetness of the cookie for China and reduced the bitterness of the cookie for India. The shape is also on the table for change. Kraft has even created wafer-stick-style Oreos.

Kraft has tailored other products to meet local market needs. For example, with its Tang drink product, it developed local flavors, such as a lime and cinnamon flavor for Mexico and mango Tang for the Philippines. It also looked to the nutritional needs in different countries. True to the heritage of the brand, Kraft has kept the theme that Tang is a good source of vitamin C. But in Brazil, where children often have iron deficiencies, it added iron as well as other vitamins and minerals. The local-focus strategy has worked well, with Tang's sales almost doubling in five years.

To meet the needs of local markets, companies need to go beyond just product designs. One of the simple ways firms have worked to meet market needs is by finding appropriate names for their products. For example, in China, the names of products imbue them with strong meanings and can be significant drivers of their success. As a result, firms have been careful with how they translate their brands. For example, Reebok became *Rui bu,* which means "quick steps." Lay's snack foods became *Le shi,* which means "happy things." And Coca-Cola's Chinese name, *Ke Kou Ke Le,* translates to "tasty fun."

Strategy Spotlight 7.5 discusses how Honda experienced challenges in moving fully to multidomestic operations and how it responded.

Risks and Challenges   As you might expect, there are some risks associated with a multidomestic strategy. Among these are the following:

- Typically, local adaptation of products and services will increase a company's cost structure. In many industries, competition is so intense that most firms can ill afford any competitive disadvantages on the dimension of cost. A key challenge of managers is to determine the trade-off between local adaptation and its cost structure. For example, cost considerations led Procter & Gamble to standardize its diaper design across all European markets. This was done despite research data indicating that Italian mothers, unlike those in other countries, preferred diapers that covered the baby's navel. Later, however, P&G recognized that this feature was critical to these mothers, so the company decided to incorporate this feature for the Italian market despite its adverse cost implications.

- At times, local adaptations, even when well intentioned, may backfire. When the American restaurant chain TGI Fridays entered the South Korean market, it purposely incorporated many local dishes, such as kimchi (hot, spicy cabbage), in its menu. This responsiveness, however, was not well received. Company analysis of the weak market acceptance indicated that Korean customers anticipated a visit

multidomestic strategy
a strategy based on firms' differentiating their products and services to adapt to local markets; used in industries where the pressure for local adaptation is high and the pressure for lowering costs is low.

HONDA ACTS TO IMPROVE ITS MARKET RESPONSIVENESS

Two attributes have set Honda apart in the automobile industry. First, it has always had outstanding engineering skills. Second, it has built an organization oriented to design and build cars that meet the needs of the markets in which it operates. Honda expanded its R&D and engineering staff globally and was the first automaker to create new models in the markets it served. For several decades, this had provided a basis for continued success in the market. But Honda's position took a downturn with the Great Recession of 2008. Honda saw its U.S. market share peak in 2009 at 11.1 percent and then fall to 9 percent by 2011. In the words of Ian Fletcher, senior analyst with HIS automotive, "Honda's management has lost its way somewhat. Over the past decade, they've lost track of what the fundamental basis of their business is and what appeal they hold on the market."

What led to this crisis? With its engineering-centered organizational culture, Honda had developed local engineering staffs but had never developed fully integrated operations in the North American market. Some R&D and engineering issues were initially handled solely with R&D staffs in the local market and then reviewed and approved in corporate headquarters in Japan before the decisions were communicated to the manufacturing and marketing staffs. This worked well until Honda faced market turbulence associated with the Great Recession and was unable to effectively coordinate engineering, manufacturing, and marketing

to launch new models that met the evolving customer demands in a timely way.

Honda's answer was to change the organization's structure to better coordinate the functions in each region and to bring in new talent to raise the profile of the marketing staff in the company. First, the company created a seven-member North American regional operating board that includes key members from all of the major functional areas. The board was tasked with overseeing and coordinating the design process for new models to speed decision making and shorten time to market. At lower levels in the organization, instead of having engineering drive the initial stages of new product development, sales, manufacturing, engineering, and purchasing, associates now work as an integrated team and make decisions on their own. Second, Honda went outside and hired a new chief marketing officer for North American operations, tapping Mike Accavitti, a marketing executive from Chrysler. Honda signaled the importance of having a marketing perspective driving the design process by promoting him to senior vice president of automobile operations in North America.

The goal of all of these changes is to develop a more integrated operation in North America to allow Honda to be more responsive to local market needs and to be swifter in meeting ever-evolving market needs.

Sources: Reed, J. & Simon, B. 2012. Honda faces challenges in the U.S. market. *ft.com*, January 5: np; and Taylor, A. 2013. Honda gets its mojo back. *Fortune*, August 12: 68–72.

---

to TGI Fridays as a visit to America. Thus, finding Korean dishes was inconsistent with their expectations.

- The optimal degree of local adaptation evolves over time. In many industry segments, a variety of factors, such as the influence of global media, greater international travel, and declining income disparities across countries, may lead to increasing global standardization. On the other hand, in other industry segments, especially where the product or service can be delivered over the Internet (such as music), the need for even greater customization and local adaptation may increase over time. Firms must recalibrate the need for local adaptation on an ongoing basis; excessive adaptation extracts a price as surely as underadaptation.

Exhibit 7.7 summarizes the strengths and limitations of multidomestic strategies.

EXHIBIT 7.7 Strengths and Limitations of Multidomestic Strategies

Strengths	Limitations
• Ability to adapt products and services to local market conditions.	• Decreased ability to realize cost savings through scale economies.
• Ability to detect potential opportunities for attractive niches in a given market, enhancing revenue.	• Greater difficulty in transferring knowledge across countries.
	• Possibility of leading to "overadaptation" as conditions change.

Transnational Strategy

A **transnational strategy** strives to optimize the trade-offs associated with efficiency, local adaptation, and learning.[56] It seeks efficiency not for its own sake but as a means to achieve global competitiveness.[57] It recognizes the importance of local responsiveness as a tool for flexibility in international operations.[58] Innovations are regarded as an outcome of a larger process of organizational learning that includes the contributions of everyone in the firm.[59] Also, a core tenet of the transnational model is that a firm's assets and capabilities are dispersed according to the most beneficial location for each activity. Thus, managers avoid the tendency to either concentrate activities in a central location (a global strategy) or disperse them across many locations to enhance adaptation (a multidomestic strategy). Peter Brabeck, chairman of Nestlé, the giant food company, provides such a perspective:

transnational strategy
a strategy based on firms' optimizing the trade-offs associated with efficiency, local adaptation, and learning; used in industries where the pressures for both local adaptation and lowering costs are high.

> We believe strongly that there isn't a so-called global consumer, at least not when it comes to food and beverages. People have local tastes based on their unique cultures and traditions—a good candy bar in Brazil is not the same as a good candy bar in China. Therefore, decision making needs to be pushed down as low as possible in the organization, out close to the markets. Otherwise, how can you make good brand decisions? That said, decentralization has its limits. If you are too decentralized, you can become too complicated—you get too much complexity in your production system. The closer we come to the consumer, in branding, pricing, communication, and product adaptation, the more we decentralize. The more we are dealing with production, logistics, and supply-chain management, the more centralized decision making becomes. After all, we want to leverage Nestlé's size, not be hampered by it.[60]

The Nestlé example illustrates a common approach in determining whether or not to centralize or decentralize a value-chain activity. Typically, primary activities that are "downstream" (e.g., marketing and sales, and service), or closer to the customer, tend to require more decentralization in order to adapt to local market conditions. On the other hand, primary activities that are "upstream" (e.g., logistics and operations), or further away from the customer, tend to be centralized. This is because there is less need for adapting these activities to local markets and the firm can benefit from economies of scale. Additionally, many support activities, such as information systems and procurement, tend to be centralized in order to increase the potential for economies of scale.

A central philosophy of the transnational organization is enhanced adaptation to all competitive situations as well as flexibility by capitalizing on communication and knowledge flows throughout the organization.[61] A principal characteristic is the integration of unique contributions of all units into worldwide operations. Thus, a joint innovation by headquarters and by one of the overseas units can lead potentially to the development of relatively standardized and yet flexible products and services that are suitable for multiple markets. Strategy Spotlight 7.6 discusses how Panasonic benefited from moving from a global to a transnational strategy.

Risks and Challenges   As with the other strategies, there are some unique risks and challenges associated with a transnational strategy:

- **The choice of a seemingly optimal location cannot guarantee that the quality and cost of factor inputs (i.e., labor, materials) will be optimal.** Managers must ensure that the relative advantage of a location is actually realized, not squandered because of weaknesses in productivity and the quality of internal operations. Ford Motor Co., for example, has benefited from having some of its manufacturing operations in Mexico. While some have argued that the benefits of lower wage rates will be partly offset by lower productivity, this does not always have to be the case. Since unemployment in Mexico is higher than in the United States, Ford

PANASONIC'S CHINA EXPERIENCE SHOWS THE BENEFITS OF BEING A TRANSNATIONAL

Panasonic moved into China in the late 1980s, seeing it as a low-cost region in which to manufacture its products. Traditionally, Panasonic had used a global strategy in its operations. It designed standardized products in Japan, manufactured them in low-cost markets, and sold its products primarily in developed markets. China simply served as a manufacturing location.

This worked well until the Chinese economy started to grow and mature. As the Chinese middle class began to emerge, local competitors, such as Haier, quickly jumped in with products designed for the Chinese market and outcompeted Panasonic in the growing market. This led Panasonic to radically change its way of competing in the global market.

Panasonic embraced the need to balance global integration with local adaptation. It set up a Lifestyle Research Center in China. In this center, marketing and product development staff compiled and interpreted data on customer wants and needs. Their charge was to uncover hidden needs in the Chinese market and design products to meet those needs. At the same time, country managers emphasized the need for the center staff to design products that benefited from global integration. For example, staff members were told to regularly work with engineers in Japan to ensure that product designs used standard global parts in the Panasonic system and also leveraged technologies being developed in Japan. Over time, this built trust with the Japanese engineers, who began to discuss how to draw on their knowledge to help design products that could be sold in other markets. Thus, knowledge flowed in both directions: from Japan to China and from China to Japan and, by extension, the rest of the world. The system has worked so well in China that Panasonic has expanded its policies and built lifestyle research centers in Europe and India.

There are five key elements of Panasonic's transnational initiatives. Each allows Panasonic to manage the tension for global integration and local adaptation.

- **Establish a dedicated unit.** One organization should be devoted to embracing the tension. The aim of Panasonic's China Lifestyle Research Center was to both understand Chinese consumers and draw on Panasonic Japan's R&D capabilities.

- **Create an on-the-ground mission.** The unit's mission should state explicitly how local adaptation and cross-border integration support company strategy. The lifestyle center's mission was "data interpretation," not just data collection, to ensure that insights led to viable product proposals that leveraged Panasonic's technology assets.

- **Develop core local staff.** The unit should develop local staff who can engage in both localization and integration activities. At the lifestyle center, each staff member spent a year getting training and extensive coaching in fieldwork and proposal writing for products that leverage Panasonic's technology to meet local needs.

- **Extend the reach.** The unit must constantly push to expand its influence. The lifestyle center's leader ratcheted up communication and interaction between the center and engineers at Panasonic's headquarters to broaden the organization's scope and influence.

- **Strengthen local authority.** Sufficient authority should be given to overseas subsidiaries to enhance their autonomy while ensuring sound global integration. Seeing the early successes of the lifestyle center, Panasonic gave increasing authority to its Chinese operations for deeper local adaptation while also maintaining integrated working relationships between Japan and China.

Sources: Wakayama, T., Shintaku, J., & Amano, T. 2012. What Panasonic learned in China. *Harvard Business Review,* December: 109–113; and Osawa, J. 2012. Panasonic pins hopes on home appliances. *wsj.com,* March 25: np.

can be more selective in its hiring practices for its Mexican operations. And, given the lower turnover among its Mexican employees, Ford can justify a high level of investment in training and development. Thus, the net result can be not only lower wage rates but also higher productivity than in the United States.

- **Although knowledge transfer can be a key source of competitive advantage, it does not take place "automatically."** For knowledge transfer to take place from one subsidiary to another, it is important for the source of the knowledge, the target units, and the corporate headquarters to recognize the potential value of such unique know-how. Given that there can be significant geographic, linguistic, and cultural distances that typically separate subsidiaries, the potential for knowledge transfer can become very difficult to realize. Firms must create mechanisms to systematically and routinely uncover the opportunities for knowledge transfer.

Exhibit 7.8 summarizes the relative advantages and disadvantages of transnational strategies.

EXHIBIT 7.8 Strengths and Limitations of Transnational Strategies

Strengths	Limitations
• Ability to attain economies of scale. • Ability to adapt to local markets. • Ability to locate activities in optimal locations. • Ability to increase knowledge flows and learning.	• Unique challenges in determining optimal locations of activities to ensure cost and quality. • Unique managerial challenges in fostering knowledge transfer.

Global or Regional? A Second Look at Globalization

LO7.6

The difference between regional companies and truly global companies.

Thus far, we have suggested four possible strategies from which a firm must choose once it has decided to compete in the global marketplace. In recent years, many writers have asserted that the process of globalization has caused national borders to become increasingly irrelevant.[62] However, some scholars have questioned this perspective, and they have argued that it is unwise for companies to rush into full-scale globalization.[63]

Before answering questions about the extent of firms' globalization, let's try to clarify what "globalization" means. Traditionally, a firm's globalization is measured in terms of its foreign sales as a percentage of total sales. However, this measure can be misleading. For example, consider a U.S. firm that has expanded its activities into Canada. Clearly, this initiative is qualitatively different from achieving the same sales volume in a distant country such as China. Similarly, if a Malaysian firm expands into Singapore or a German firm starts selling its products in Austria, this would represent an expansion into a geographically adjacent country. Such nearby countries would often share many common characteristics in terms of language, culture, infrastructure, and customer preferences. In other words, this is more a case of regionalization than globalization.

Extensive analysis of the distribution data of sales across different countries and regions led Alan Rugman and Alain Verbeke to conclude that there is a stronger case to be made in favor of **regionalization** than globalization. According to their study, a company would have to have at least 20 percent of its sales in each of the three major economic regions—North America, Europe, and Asia—to be considered a global firm. However, they found that only 9 of the world's 500 largest firms met this standard! Even when they relaxed the criterion to 20 percent of sales each in at least two of the three regions, the number only increased to 25. *Thus, most companies are regional or, at best, biregional—not global—even today.*

In a world of instant communication, rapid transportation, and governments that are increasingly willing to open up their markets to trade and investment, why are so few firms "global"? The most obvious answer is that distance still matters. After all, it is easier to do business in a neighboring country than in a faraway country, all else being equal. Distance, in the final analysis, may be viewed as a concept with many dimensions, not just a measure of geographic distance. For example, both Canada and Mexico are the same distance from the U.S. However, U.S. companies find it easier to expand operations into Canada than into Mexico. Why? Canada and the U.S. share many commonalities in terms of language, culture, economic development, legal and political systems, and infrastructure development. Thus, if we view distance as having many dimensions, the U.S. and Canada are very close, whereas there is greater distance between the U.S. and Mexico. Similarly, when we look at what we might call the "true" distance between the U.S. and China, the effects of geographic distance are multiplied by distance in terms of culture, language, religion, and legal and political systems between the two countries. On the other hand, although U.S. and Australia are geographically distant, the "true" distance is somewhat less when one considers distance along the other dimensions.

regionalization increasing international exchange of goods, services, money, people, ideas, and information; and the increasing similarity of culture, laws, rules, and norms within a region such as Europe, North America, or Asia.

Another reason for regional expansion is the rise of **trading blocs** and free trade zones. A number of regional agreements have been created that facilitate the growth of business within these regions by easing trade restrictions and taxes and tariffs. These have included the European Union (EU), North American Free Trade Agreement (NAFTA), Association of Southeast Asian Nations (ASEAN), and MERCOSUR (a South American trading block).

Regional economic integration has progressed at a faster pace than global economic integration, and the trade and investment patterns of the largest companies reflect this reality. After all, regions represent the outcomes of centuries of political and cultural history that results in not only commonalities but also mutual affinity. For example, stretching from Algeria and Morocco in the West to Oman and Yemen in the East, more than 30 countries share the Arabic language and the Muslim religion, making these countries a natural regional bloc. Similarly, the countries of South and Central America share the Spanish language (except Brazil), the Catholic religion, and a history of Spanish colonialism. No wonder firms find it easier and less risky to expand within their region than to other regions.

Entry Modes of International Expansion

A firm has many options available to it when it decides to expand into international markets. Given the challenges associated with such entry, many firms first start on a small scale and then increase their level of investment and risk as they gain greater experience with the overseas market in question.[64]

Exhibit 7.9 illustrates a wide variety of modes of foreign entry, including exporting, licensing, franchising, joint ventures, strategic alliances, and wholly owned subsidiaries.[65] As the exhibit indicates, the various types of entry form a continuum ranging from exporting (low investment and risk, low control) to a wholly owned subsidiary (high investment and risk, high control).[66]

There can be frustrations and setbacks as a firm evolves its international entry strategy from exporting to more expensive types, including wholly owned subsidiaries. For example, according to the CEO of a large U.S. specialty chemical company:

> In the end, we always do a better job with our own subsidiaries; sales improve, and we have greater control over the business. But we still need local distributors for entry, and we are still searching for strategies to get us through the transitions without battles over control and performance.[67]

EXHIBIT 7.9 Entry Modes for International Expansion

Exporting

Exporting consists of producing goods in one country to sell in another.[68] This entry strategy enables a firm to invest the least amount of resources in terms of its product, its organization, and its overall corporate strategy. Many host countries dislike this entry strategy because it provides less local employment than other modes of entry.[69]

Multinationals often stumble onto a stepwise strategy for penetrating markets, beginning with the exporting of products. This often results in a series of unplanned actions to increase sales revenues. As the pattern recurs with entries into subsequent markets, this approach, named a "beachhead strategy," often becomes official policy.[70]

Benefits   Such an approach definitely has its advantages. After all, firms start from scratch in sales and distribution when they enter new markets. Because many foreign markets are nationally regulated and dominated by networks of local intermediaries, firms need to partner with local distributors to benefit from their valuable expertise and knowledge of their own markets. Multinationals, after all, recognize that they cannot master local business practices, meet regulatory requirements, hire and manage local personnel, or gain access to potential customers without some form of local partnership.

Multinationals also want to minimize their own risk. They do this by hiring local distributors and investing very little in the undertaking. In essence, the firm gives up control of strategic marketing decisions to the local partners—much more control than they would be willing to give up in their home market.

Risks and Limitations   Exporting is a relatively inexpensive way to enter foreign markets. However, it can still have significant downsides. Most centrally, the ability to tailor the firm's products to meet local market needs is typically very limited. In a study of 250 instances in which multinational firms used local distributors to implement their exporting entry strategy, the results were dismal. In the vast majority of the cases, the distributors were bought (to increase control) by the multinational firm or were fired. In contrast, successful distributors shared two common characteristics:

- They carried product lines that complemented, rather than competed with, the multinational's products.
- They behaved as if they were business partners with the multinationals. They shared market information with the corporations, they initiated projects with distributors in neighboring countries, and they suggested initiatives in their own or nearby markets. Additionally, these distributors took on risk themselves by investing in areas such as training, information systems, and advertising and promotion in order to increase the business of their multinational partners.

The key point is the importance of developing collaborative, win–win relationships.

To ensure more control over operations without incurring significant risks, many firms have used licensing and franchising as a mode of entry. Let's now discuss these and their relative advantages and disadvantages.

Licensing and Franchising

Licensing and franchising are both forms of contractual arrangements. **Licensing** enables a company to receive a royalty or fee in exchange for the right to use its trademark, patent, trade secret, or other valuable item of intellectual property.[71]

Franchising contracts generally include a broader range of factors in an operation and have a longer time period during which the agreement is in effect. Franchising remains a primary form of American business. According to a survey, more than 400 U.S. franchisers have international exposure.[72] This is greater than the combined totals of the next four largest franchiser home countries—France, the United Kingdom, Mexico, and Austria.

exporting
producing goods in one country to sell to residents of another country.

licensing
a contractual arrangement in which a company receives a royalty or fee in exchange for the right to use its trademark, patent, trade secret, or other valuable intellectual property.

franchising
a contractual arrangement in which a company receives a royalty or fee in exchange for the right to use its intellectual property; franchising usually involves a longer time period than licensing and includes other factors, such as monitoring of operations, training, and advertising.

Benefits   In international markets, an advantage of licensing is that the firm granting a license incurs little risk, since it does not have to invest any significant resources into the country itself. In turn, the licensee (the firm receiving the license) gains access to the trademark, patent, and so on, and is able to potentially create competitive advantages. In many cases, the country also benefits from the product being manufactured locally. For example, Yoplait yogurt is licensed by General Mills from Sodima, a French cooperative, for sale in the United States. The logos of college and professional athletic teams in the United States are another source of trademarks that generate significant royalty income domestically and internationally.

Franchising has the advantage of limiting the risk exposure that a firm has in overseas markets. At the same time, the firm is able to expand the revenue base of the company.

Risks and Limitations   The licensor gives up control of its product and forgoes potential revenues and profits. Furthermore, the licensee may eventually become so familiar with the patent and trade secrets that it may become a competitor; that is, the licensee may make some modifications to the product and manufacture and sell it independently of the licensor without having to pay a royalty fee. This potential situation is aggravated in countries that have relatively weak laws to protect intellectual property. Additionally, if the licensee selected by the multinational firm turns out to be a poor choice, the brand name and reputation of the product may be tarnished.[73]

With franchising, the multinational firm receives only a portion of the revenues, in the form of franchise fees. Had the firm set up the operation itself (e.g., a restaurant through direct investment), it would have had the entire revenue to itself.

Companies often desire a closer collaboration with other firms in order to increase revenue, reduce costs, and enhance their learning—often through the diffusion of technology. To achieve such objectives, they enter into strategic alliances or joint ventures, two entry modes we will discuss next.

Strategic Alliances and Joint Ventures

Joint ventures and strategic alliances have recently become increasingly popular.[74] These two forms of partnership differ in that joint ventures entail the creation of a third-party legal entity, whereas strategic alliances do not. In addition, strategic alliances generally focus on initiatives that are smaller in scope than joint ventures.[75]

Benefits   As we discussed in Chapter 6, these strategies have been effective in helping firms increase revenues and reduce costs as well as enhance learning and diffuse technologies.[76] These partnerships enable firms to share the risks as well as the potential revenues and profits. Also, by gaining exposure to new sources of knowledge and technologies, such partnerships can help firms develop core competencies that can lead to competitive advantages in the marketplace.[77] Finally, entering into partnerships with host-country firms can provide very useful information on local market tastes, competitive conditions, legal matters, and cultural nuances.[78]

Risks and Limitations   Managers must be aware of the risks associated with strategic alliances and joint ventures and how they can be minimized.[79] First, there needs to be a clearly defined strategy that is strongly supported by the organizations that are party to the partnership. Otherwise, the firms may work at cross-purposes and not achieve any of their goals. Second, and closely allied to the first issue, there must be a clear understanding of capabilities and resources that will be central to the partnership. Without such clarification, there will be fewer opportunities for learning and developing competencies that could lead to competitive advantages. Third, trust is a vital element. Phasing in the relationship between alliance partners permits them to get to know each other better and develop trust. Without trust, one party may take advantage of the other by, for example, withholding its fair share of resources and gaining access to privileged information through unethical (or illegal) means.

Fourth, cultural issues that can potentially lead to conflict and dysfunctional behaviors need to be addressed. An organization's culture is the set of values, beliefs, and attitudes that influence the behavior and goals of its employees.[80] Thus, recognizing cultural differences, as well as striving to develop elements of a "common culture" for the partnership, is vital. Without a unifying culture, it will become difficult to combine and leverage resources that are increasingly important in knowledge-intensive organizations (discussed in Chapter 4).[81]

Finally, the success of a firm's alliance should not be left to chance.[82] To improve their odds of success, many companies have carefully documented alliance-management knowledge by creating guidelines and manuals to help them manage specific aspects of the entire alliance life cycle (e.g., partner selection and alliance negotiation and contracting). For example, Hewlett-Packard developed 60 different tools and templates, which it placed in a 300-page manual for guiding decision making. The manual included such tools as a template for making the business case for an alliance, a partner evaluation form, a negotiation template outlining the roles and responsibilities of different departments, a list of the ways to measure alliance performance, and an alliance termination checklist.

When a firm desires the highest level of control, it develops wholly owned subsidiaries. Although wholly owned subsidiaries can generate the greatest returns, they also have the highest levels of investment and risk. We will now discuss them.

Wholly Owned Subsidiaries

A **wholly owned subsidiary** is a business in which a multinational company owns 100 percent of the stock. Two ways a firm can establish a wholly owned subsidiary are to (1) acquire an existing company in the home country or (2) develop a totally new operation (often referred to as a "greenfield venture").

wholly owned subsidiary
a business in which a multinational company owns 100 percent of the stock.

Benefits Establishing a wholly owned subsidiary is the most expensive and risky of the various entry modes. However, it can also yield the highest returns. In addition, it provides the multinational company with the greatest degree of control of all activities, including manufacturing, marketing, distribution, and technology development.[83]

Wholly owned subsidiaries are most appropriate where a firm already has the appropriate knowledge and capabilities that it can leverage rather easily through multiple locations. Examples range from restaurants to semiconductor manufacturers. To lower costs, for example, Intel Corporation builds semiconductor plants throughout the world—all of which use virtually the same blueprint. Knowledge can be further leveraged by hiring managers and professionals from the firm's home country, often through hiring talent from competitors.

Risks and Limitations As noted, wholly owned subsidiaries are typically the most expensive and risky entry mode. With franchising, joint ventures, or strategic alliances, the risk is shared with the firm's partners. With wholly owned subsidiaries, the entire risk is assumed by the parent company. The risks associated with doing business in a new country (e.g., political, cultural, and legal) can be lessened by hiring local talent.

For example, Wendy's avoided committing two blunders in Germany by hiring locals to its advertising staff.[84] In one case, the firm wanted to promote its "old-fashioned" qualities. However, a literal translation would have resulted in the company promoting itself as "outdated." In another situation, Wendy's wanted to emphasize that its hamburgers could be prepared 256 ways. The problem? The German word that Wendy's wanted to use for "ways" usually meant "highways" or "roads." Although such errors may sometimes be entertaining to the public, it is certainly preferable to catch these mistakes before they confuse the consumer or embarrass the company.

We have addressed entry strategies as a progression from exporting to the creation of wholly owned subsidiaries. However, we must point out that many firms do not follow such an evolutionary approach.

ISSUE FOR DEBATE

The Ethicality of Tax Inversions

In June 2014, Medtronic, a Minneapolis-based medical device manufacturer, announced that it would join the tax-inversion acquisition parade. A tax-inversion acquisition occurs when a corporation acquires a target firm based in a lower-tax country and, as part of the transaction, moves its legal headquarters to the target firm's nation. After making this move, the combined corporation's taxes are based on the lower rate of its new home country. This move is perfectly legal according to U.S. law as long as the target firm's shareholders own at least 20 percent of the combined firm. About 50 U.S. corporations have undertaken tax inversions over the last 10 years, but the rate of occurrence appears to be increasing.

Medtronic's plan is to acquire Covidien, an Irish-based medical equipment manufacturer, for $43 billion and move its legal home to Ireland. Not much else will change. Medtronic will keep its corporate headquarters in Minneapolis. But Medtronic benefits from the move in two primary ways. First, while the tax rate on profits of U.S. corporations is 35 percent, the tax rate on Ireland-based corporate profits is only 12.5 percent. Additionally, the U.S. is one of only six developed economies that tax the global profits of corporations. If a multinational corporation makes profits in a foreign country, the firm pays taxes on those profits to the foreign government at the rate the foreign country charges. For corporations based in most countries, that is the end of their tax obligations. However, if a U.S.-based firm wants to bring those profits back to its home country either to invest in new facilities or to distribute dividends to its stockholders, it has to pay income tax on the profits earned in foreign markets. The rate the firm pays is the difference in the tax rate in the foreign country and the U.S. rate. For example, if Medtronic earned income in Ireland and then repatriated the profits to the U.S., it would face a 22.5 percent additional tax rate, the difference between the U.S. and Irish corporate tax rates. Since Medtronic has accumulated $13 billion in earned profits abroad, it could face $3.5 billion to $4 billion in taxes if it brought those profits home. Thus, corporations, such as Medtronic, undertake tax inversions to save on taxes and, by extension, benefit their shareholders by being able to invest more in the firm to help it grow and/or return higher levels of dividends to shareholders.

Critics, however, point out that these firms are choosing not to pay taxes at the U.S. rates even though they have benefited and will continue to benefit from being American corporations. While inverters change their legal residence, they typically keep their corporate headquarters in the U.S. and stay listed on a U.S. stock exchange. As a result, they benefit from America's deep financial markets, military might, intellectual property rights and other legal protections, intellectual and physical infrastructure, substantial human capital base, and national research programs. For example, Medtronic won $484 million in contracts with the U.S. government in recent years and plans to complete these contracts even though it will no longer be an American company; it hires students from top-notch American universities; and it files patents for all of its new technologies in the United States. Critics see the decision to move to a lower-tax country as unethical and unpatriotic. Jack Lew, the U.S. Treasury secretary, echoed this perspective when he stated, "We should prevent companies from effectively renouncing their citizenship to get out of paying taxes. What we need is a new sense of economic patriotism, where we all rise and fall together."

Reflecting on Career Implications . . .

◼ **International Strategy:** Be aware of your organization's international strategy. What percentage of the total firm activity is international? What skills are needed to enhance your company's international efforts? How can you get more involved in your organization's international strategy? For your career, what conditions in your home country might cause you to seek a career abroad?

◼ **Outsourcing and Offshoring:** More and more organizations have resorted to outsourcing and offshoring in recent years. To what extent has your firm engaged in either? What activities in your organization can/should be outsourced or offshored? Be aware that you are competing in the global marketplace for employment and professional advancement. What is the likelihood that your own job may be outsourced or offshored? In what ways can you enhance your talents, skills,

and competencies to reduce the odds that your job may be offshored or outsourced?

◼ **International Career Opportunities:** Taking on overseas assignments in other countries can often provide a career boost. There are a number of ways in which you can improve your odds of being selected for an overseas assignment. Studying abroad for a semester or doing an overseas internship are two obvious strategies. Learning a foreign language can also greatly help. Anticipate how such opportunities will advance your short- and long-term career aspirations.

◼ **Management Risks:** Explore ways in which you can develop cultural sensitivity. Interacting with people from other cultures, foreign travel, reading about foreign countries, watching foreign movies, and similar activities can increase your cultural sensitivity. Identify ways in which your perceptions and behaviors have changed as a result of increased cultural sensitivity.

summary

We live in a highly interconnected global community where many of the best opportunities for growth and profitability lie beyond the boundaries of a company's home country. Along with the opportunities, of course, there are many risks associated with diversification into global markets.

The first section of the chapter addressed the factors that determine a nation's competitiveness in a particular industry. The framework was developed by Professor Michael Porter of Harvard University and was based on a four-year study that explored the competitive success of 10 leading trading nations. The four factors, collectively termed the "diamond of national advantage," were factor endowments, demand conditions, related and supporting industries, and firm strategy, structure, and rivalry.

The discussion of Porter's "diamond" helped, in essence, to set the broader context for exploring competitive advantage

at the firm level. In the second section, we discussed the primary motivations and the potential risks associated with international expansion. The primary motivations included increasing the size of the potential market for the firm's products and services, achieving economies of scale, extending the life cycle of the firm's products, and optimizing the location for every activity in the value chain. On the other hand, the key risks included political and economic risks, currency risks, and management risks. Management risks are the challenges associated with responding to the inevitable differences that exist across countries such as customs, culture, language, customer preferences, and distribution systems. We also addressed some of the managerial challenges and opportunities associated with offshoring and outsourcing.

Next, we addressed how firms can go about attaining competitive advantage in global markets. We began by discussing the two opposing forces—cost reduction and adaptation to local markets—that managers must contend with when entering global markets. The relative importance of these two factors plays a major part in determining which of the four basic types of strategies to select: international, global, multidomestic, or transnational. The chapter covered the benefits and risks associated with each type of strategy.

The final section discussed the four types of entry strategies that managers may undertake when entering international markets. The key trade-off in each of these strategies is the level of investment or risk versus the level of control. In order of their progressively greater investment/risk and control, the strategies range from exporting to licensing and franchising, to strategic alliances and joint ventures, to wholly owned subsidiaries. The relative benefits and risks associated with each of these strategies were addressed.

SUMMARY REVIEW QUESTIONS

1. What are some of the advantages and disadvantages associated with a firm's expansion into international markets?

2. What are the four factors described in Porter's diamond of national advantage? How do the four factors explain why some industries in a given country are more successful than others?

3. Explain the two opposing forces—cost reduction and adaptation to local markets—that firms must deal with when they go global.

4. There are four basic strategies—international, global, multidomestic, and transnational. What are the advantages and disadvantages associated with each?

5. What is the basis of Alan Rugman's argument that most multinationals are still more regional than global? What factors inhibit firms from becoming truly global?

6. Describe the basic entry strategies that firms have available when they enter international markets. What are the relative advantages and disadvantages of each?

key terms

globalization 214
diamond of national advantage 215
factor endowments (national advantage) 215
demand conditions (national advantage) 216
related and supporting industries (national advantage) 216
firm strategy, structure, and rivalry (national advantage) 216
multinational firms 218
arbitrage opportunities 219
reverse innovation 220
political risk 222
rule of law 222
economic risk 223
counterfeiting 223
currency risk 223
management risk 224
outsourcing 225
offshoring 225
international strategy 231
global strategy 231
multidomestic strategy 233
transnational strategy 235
regionalization 237
trading blocs 238
exporting 239
licensing 239
franchising 239
wholly owned subsidiary 241

experiential exercise

The United States is considered a world leader in the motion picture industry. Using Porter's diamond framework for national competitiveness, explain the success of this industry. (Fill in the chart on page 245.)

application questions & exercises

1. Data on the "competitiveness of nations" can be found at *www.imd.org/research/publications/wcy/index.cfm.* This website provides a ranking on 329 criteria for 59 countries. How might Porter's diamond of national advantage help to explain the rankings for some of these countries for certain industries that interest you?

2. The Internet has lowered the entry barriers for smaller firms that wish to diversify into international markets. Why is this so? Provide an example.

3. Many firms fail when they enter into strategic alliances with firms that link up with companies based in other countries. What are some reasons for this failure? Provide an example.

4. Many large U.S.-based management consulting companies such as McKinsey and Company and the BCG Group have been very successful in the international marketplace. How can Porter's diamond explain their success?

ethics questions

1. Over the past few decades, many American firms have relocated most or all of their operations from the United States to countries such as Mexico and China that pay lower wages. What are some of the ethical issues that such actions may raise?

2. Business practices and customs vary throughout the world. What are some of the ethical issues concerning payments that must be made in a foreign country to obtain business opportunities?

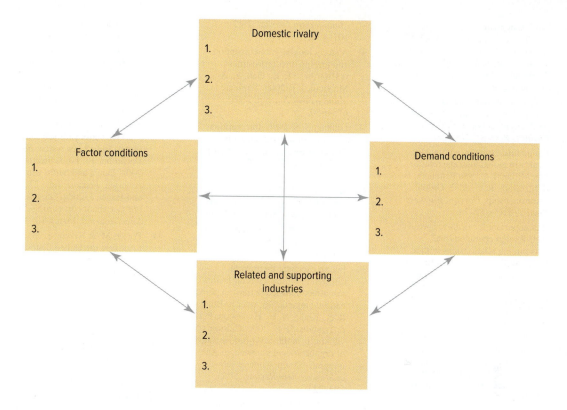

Domestic rivalry

1.

2.

3.

Factor conditions

1.

2.

3.

Demand conditions

1.

2.

3.

Related and supporting
industries

1.

2.

3.

references

1. Williamson, P. & Raman, A. 2011. How China reset its global acquisition agenda. *Harvard Business Review,* April: 109–114; and SAIC under pressure to help save SsangYong. 2009. *nytimes.com,* January 12: np.

2. For a discussion on globalization by one of international business's most respected authors, read Ohmae, K. 2005. *The next global stage: Challenges and opportunities in our borderless world.* Philadelphia: Wharton School.

3. Our discussion of globalization draws upon Engardio, P. & Belton, C. 2000. Global capitalism: Can it be made to work better? *BusinessWeek,* November 6: 72–98.

4. Sellers, P. 2005. Blowing in the wind. *Fortune,* July 25: 63.

5. Rivera, J. 2014. Gartner says sales of smartphones grew 20 percent in third quarter of 2014. *gartner.com,* December 15: np.

6. A game of catch-up. 2011. *The Economist,* September 24: 3–6.

7. Some insights into how winners are evolving in emerging markets are addressed in Ghemawat, P. & Hout,

T. 2008. Tomorrow's global giants: Not the usual suspects. *Harvard Business Review,* 66(11): 80–88.

8. For another interesting discussion on a country perspective, refer to Makino, S. 1999. MITI Minister Kaora Yosano on reviving Japan's competitive advantages. *Academy of Management Executive,* 13(4): 8–28.

9. The following discussion draws heavily upon Porter, M. E. 1990. The competitive advantage of nations. *Harvard Business Review,* March–April: 73–93.

10. Landes, D. S. 1998. *The wealth and poverty of nations.* New York: W. W. Norton.

11. A study that investigates the relationship between international diversification and firm performance is Lu, J. W. & Beamish, P. W. 2004. International diversification and firm performance: The s-curve hypothesis. *Academy of Management Journal,* 47(4): 598–609.

12. Part of our discussion of the motivations and risks of international expansion draws upon Gregg, F. M. 1999. International strategy. In Helms, M. M. (Ed.), *Encyclopedia of*

management: 434–438. Detroit: Gale Group.

13. Anthony, S. 2012. Singapore sessions. *Harvard Business Review,* 90(4): np.

14. Eyring, M. J., Johnson, M. W., & Nair, H. 2011. New business models in emerging markets. *Harvard Business Review,* 89 (1/2): 88–98.

15. Cieply, M. & Barnes, B. 2010. After rants, skepticism over Gibson bankability grows in non-U.S. markets. *International Herald Tribune,* July 23: 1.

16. Glazer, E. 2012. P&G unit bids goodbye to Cincinnati, hello to Asia. *wsj.com,* May 10: np.

17. This discussion draws upon Gupta, A. K. & Govindarajan, V. 2001. Converting global presence into global competitive advantage. *Academy of Management Executive,* 15(2): 45–56.

18. Stross, R. E. 1997. Mr. Gates builds his brain trust. *Fortune,* December 8: 84–98.

19. For a good summary of the benefits and risks of international expansion, refer to Bartlett, C. A. & Ghoshal, S. 1987. Managing across borders:

New strategic responses. *Sloan Management Review,* 28(5): 45–53; and Brown, R. H. 1994. *Competing to win in a global economy.* Washington, DC: U.S. Department of Commerce.

20. Capron, L. & Bertrand, O. 2014. Going abroad in search of higher productivity at home. *Harvard Business Review,* 92(6): 26.

21. For an interesting insight into rivalry in global markets, refer to MacMillan, I. C., van Putten, A. B., & McGrath, R. G. 2003. Global gamesmanship. *Harvard Business Review,* 81(5): 62–73.

22. It is important for firms to spread their foreign operations and outsourcing relationships with a broad, well-balanced mix of regions and countries to reduce risk and increase potential reward. For example, refer to Vestring, T., Rouse, T., & Reinert, U. 2005. Hedge your offshoring bets. *MIT Sloan Management Review,* 46(3): 27–29.

23. An interesting discussion of risks faced by Lukoil, Russia's largest oil firm, is in Gimbel, B. 2009. Russia's king of crude. *Fortune,* February 2: 88–92.

24. For a discussion of some of the challenges associated with government corruption regarding entry strategies in foreign markets, read Rodriguez, P., Uhlenbruck, K., & Eden, L. 2005. Government corruption and entry strategies of multinationals. *Academy of Management Review,* 30(2): 383–396.

25. For a discussion of the political risks in China for United States companies, refer to Garten, J. E. 1998. Opening the doors for business in China. *Harvard Business Review,* 76(3): 167–175.

26. Insights on how forensic economics can be used to investigate crimes and wrongdoing are in Fisman, R. 2009. The rise of forensic economics. *Harvard Business Review,* 87(2): 26.

27. Iosebashvili, I. 2012. Renault-Nissan buy into Russia's aged auto giant. *wsj.com,* May 3: np.

28. Ferguson, N. 2013. Is the business of America still business? *Harvard Business Review,* 91(6): 40.

29. For an interesting perspective on the relationship between diversification and the development of a nation's institutional environment, read Chakrabarti, A., Singh, K., & Mahmood, I. 2007. Diversification and performance: Evidence from East Asian firms. *Strategic Management Journal,* 28(2): 101–120.

30. A study looking into corruption and foreign direct investment is Brouthers, L. E., Gao, Y., & McNicol, J. P. 2008. *Strategic Management Journal,* 29(6): 673–680.

31. Gikkas, N. S. 1996. International licensing of intellectual property: The promise and the peril. *Journal of Technology Law & Policy,* 1(1): 1–26.

32. Hargreaves, S. 2012. Counterfeit goods becoming more dangerous. *cnnmoney.com,* September 27: np.

33. Sandler, N. 2008. Israel: Attack of the super-shekel. *BusinessWeek,* Februrary 25: 38.

34. For an excellent theoretical discussion of how cultural factors can affect knowledge transfer across national boundaries, refer to Bhagat, R. S., Kedia, B. L., Harveston, P. D., & Triandis, H. C. 2002. Cultural variations in the cross-border transfer of organizational knowledge: An integrative framework. *Academy of Management Review,* 27(2): 204–221.

35. An interesting discussion on how local companies compete effectively with large multinationals is in Bhatacharya, A. K. & Michael, D. C. 2008. *Harvard Business Review,* 66(3): 84–95.

36. To gain insights on the role of national and regional cultures on knowledge management models and frameworks, read Pauleen, D. J. & Murphy, P. 2005. In praise of cultural bias. *MIT Sloan Management Review,* 46(2): 21–22.

37. Berkowitz, E. N. 2000. *Marketing* (6th ed.). New York: McGraw-Hill.

38. Harvey, M. & Buckley, M. R. 2002. Assessing the "conventional wisdoms" of management for the 21st century organization. *Organization Dynamics,* 30(4): 368–378.

39. World Trade Organization. *Annual Report 1998.* Geneva: World Trade Organization.

40. Lei, D. 2005. Outsourcing. In Hitt, M. A. & Ireland, R. D. (Eds.), *The Blackwell encyclopedia of management,* Entrepreneurship: 196–199. Malden, MA: Blackwell.

41. Future trends in offshoring are addressed in Manning, S., Massini, S., & Lewin, A. Y. 2008. A dynamic perspective on next-generation offshoring: The global sourcing of science and engineering talent. *Academy of Management Perspectives,* 22(3): 35–54.

42. An interesting perspective on the controversial issue regarding the offshoring of airplane maintenance is in Smith, G. & Bachman, J. 2008. Flying in for a tune-up overseas. *BusinessWeek,* April 21: 26–27.

43. The discussion draws from Colvin, J. 2004. Think your job can't be sent to India? Just watch. *Fortune,* December 13: 80; Schwartz, N. D. 2004. Down and out in white collar America. *Fortune,* June 23: 321–325; and Hagel, J. 2004. Outsourcing is not just about cost cutting. *The Wall Street Journal,* March 18: A3.

44. Porter, M. & Rivkin, J. 2012 Choosing the United States. *Harvard Business Review,* 90(3): 80–93; Bussey, J. 2012. U.S. manufacturing, defying naysayers. *wsj.com,* April 19: np; and Jean, S. & Alcott, K. 2013. Manufacturing jobs have slid steadily as work has moved offshore. *Dallas Morning News,* January 14: 1D.

45. Wong, C. 2014. As China's economy slows, so too does growth in workers' wages. *blogs.wsj.com,* December 17: np.

46. Levitt, T. 1983. The globalization of markets. *Harvard Business Review,* 61(3): 92–102.

47. Our discussion of these assumptions draws upon Douglas, S. P. & Wind, Y. 1987. The myth of globalization. *Columbia Journal of World Business,* Winter: 19–29.

48. Ghoshal, S. 1987. Global strategy: An organizing framework. *Strategic Management Journal,* 8: 425–440.

49. For insights on global branding, refer to Aaker, D. A. & Joachimsthaler, E. 1999. The lure of global branding. *Harvard Business Review,* 77(6): 137–146.

50. Dawar, N. & Frost, T. 1999. Competing with Giants: Survival Strategies for Local Companies in Emerging Markets. *Harvard Business Review,* 77(3): 119–129.

51. Hout, T., Porter, M. E., & Rudden, E. 1982. How global companies win out. *Harvard Business Review,* 60(5): 98–107.

52. Fryer, B. 2001. Tom Siebel of Siebel Systems: High tech the old-fashioned way. *Harvard Business Review,* 79(3): 118–130.

53. The risks that are discussed for the global, multidomestic, and transnational strategies draw upon Gupta & Govindarajan, op. cit.

54. A discussion on how McDonald's adapts its products to overseas markets is in Gumbel, P. 2008. Big

Mac's local flavor. *Fortune,* May 5: 115–121.

55. Einhorn, B. & Winter, C. 2012. Want some milk with your green tea Oreos? *Bloomberg Businessweek,* May 7: 25–26; Khosla, S. & Sawhney, M. 2012. Blank checks: Unleashing the potential of people and business. *Strategy-Business.com,* Autumn: np; and In China, brands more than symbolic. 2012. *Dallas Morning News,* November 27: 3D.

56. Prahalad, C. K. & Doz, Y. L. 1987. *The multinational mission: Balancing local demands and global vision.* New York: Free Press.

57. For an insightful discussion on knowledge flows in multinational corporations, refer to Yang, Q., Mudambi, R., & Meyer, K. E. 2008. Conventional and reverse knowledge flows in multinational corporations. *Journal of Management,* 34(5): 882–902.

58. Kidd, J. B. & Teramoto, Y. 1995. The learning organization: The case of Japanese RHQs in Europe. *Management International Review,* 35 (Special Issue): 39–56.

59. Gupta, A. K. & Govindarajan, V. 2000. Knowledge flows within multinational corporations. *Strategic Management Journal,* 21(4): 473–496.

60. Wetlaufer, S. 2001. The business case against revolution: An interview with Nestlé's Peter Brabeck. *Harvard Business Review,* 79(2): 112–121.

61. Nobel, R. & Birkinshaw, J. 1998. Innovation in multinational corporations: Control and communication patterns in international R&D operations. *Strategic Management Journal,* 19(5): 461–478.

62. Chan, C. M., Makino, S., & Isobe, T. 2010. Does subnational region matter? Foreign affiliate performance in the United States and China. *Strategic Management Journal,* 31(11): 1226–1243.

63. This section draws upon Ghemawat, P. 2005. Regional strategies for global leadership. *Harvard Business Review,* 84(12): 98–108; Ghemawat, P. 2006. Apocalypse now? *Harvard Business Review,* 84(12): 32; Ghemawat, P. 2001. Distance still matters: The hard reality of global expansion. *Harvard Business Review,* 79(8): 137–147; Peng, M. W.

2006. *Global strategy:* 387. Mason, OH: Thomson South-Western; and Rugman, A. M. & Verbeke, A. 2004. A perspective on regional and global strategies of multinational enterprises. *Journal of International Business Studies,* 35: 3–18.

64. For a rigorous analysis of performance implications of entry strategies, refer to Zahra, S. A., Ireland, R. D., & Hitt, M. A. 2000. International expansion by new venture firms: International diversity, modes of entry, technological learning, and performance. *Academy of Management Journal,* 43(6): 925–950.

65. Li, J. T. 1995. Foreign entry and survival: The effects of strategic choices on performance in international markets. *Strategic Management Journal,* 16: 333–351.

66. For a discussion of how home-country environments can affect diversification strategies, refer to Wan, W. P. & Hoskisson, R. E. 2003. Home country environments, corporate diversification strategies, and firm performance. *Academy of Management Journal,* 46(1): 27–45.

67. Arnold, D. 2000. Seven rules of international distribution. *Harvard Business Review,* 78(6): 131–137.

68. Sharma, A. 1998. Mode of entry and ex-post performance. *Strategic Management Journal,* 19(9): 879–900.

69. This section draws upon Arnold, op. cit., pp. 131–137; and Berkowitz, op. cit.

70. Salomon, R. & Jin, B. 2010. Do leading or lagging firms learn more from exporting? *Strategic Management Journal,* 31(6): 1088–1113.

71. Kline, D. 2003. Strategic licensing. *MIT Sloan Management Review,* 44(3): 89–93.

72. Martin, J. 1999. Franchising in the Middle East. *Management Review,* June: 38–42.

73. Arnold, op. cit.; and Berkowitz, op. cit.

74. An in-depth case study of alliance dynamics is found in Faems, D., Janssens, M., Madhok, A., & Van Looy, B. 2008. Toward an integrative perspective on alliance governance: Connecting contract design, trust dynamics, and contract application. *Academy of Management Journal,* 51(6): 1053–1078.

75. Knowledge transfer in international joint ventures is addressed in Inkpen, A. 2008. Knowledge transfer and international joint ventures. *Strategic Management Journal,* 29(4): 447–453.

76. Wen, S. H. & Chuang, C.-M. 2010. To teach or to compete? A strategic dilemma of knowledge owners in international alliances. *Asia Pacific Journal of Management,* 27(4): 697–726.

77. Manufacturer–supplier relationships can be very effective in global industries such as automobile manufacturing. Refer to Kotabe, M., Martin, X., & Domoto, H. 2003. Gaining from vertical partnerships: Knowledge transfer, relationship duration, and supplier performance improvement in the U.S. and Japanese automotive industries. *Strategic Management Journal,* 24(4): 293–316.

78. For a good discussion, refer to Merchant, H. & Schendel, D. 2000. How do international joint ventures create shareholder value? *Strategic Management Journal,* 21(7): 723–738.

79. This discussion draws upon Walters, B. A., Peters, S., & Dess, G. G. 1994. Strategic alliances and joint ventures: Making them work. *Business Horizons,* 37(4): 5–11.

80. Some insights on partnering in the global area are discussed in MacCormack, A. & Forbath, T. 2008. *Harvard Business Review,* 66(1): 24, 26.

81. For a rigorous discussion of the importance of information access in international joint ventures, refer to Reuer, J. J. & Koza, M. P. 2000. Asymmetric information and joint venture performance: Theory and evidence for domestic and international joint ventures. *Strategic Management Journal,* 21(1): 81–88.

82. Dyer, J. H., Kale, P., & Singh, H. 2001. How to make strategic alliances work. *MIT Sloan Management Review,* 42(4): 37–43.

83. For a discussion of some of the challenges in managing subsidiaries, refer to O'Donnell, S. W. 2000. Managing foreign subsidiaries: Agents of headquarters, or an independent network? *Strategic Management Journal,* 21(5): 525–548.

84. Ricks, D. 2006. *Blunders in international business* (4th ed.). Malden, MA: Blackwell.

Entrepreneurial Strategy and Competitive Dynamics

After reading this chapter, you should have a good understanding of the following learning objectives:

LO8.1 The role of opportunities, resources, and entrepreneurs in successfully pursuing new ventures.

LO8.2 Three types of entry strategies—pioneering, imitative, and adaptive—commonly used to launch a new venture.

LO8.3 How the generic strategies of overall cost leadership, differentiation, and focus are used by new ventures and small businesses.

LO8.4 How competitive actions, such as the entry of new competitors into a marketplace, may launch a cycle of actions and reactions among close competitors.

LO8.5 The components of competitive dynamics analysis—new competitive action, threat analysis, motivation and capability to respond, types of competitive actions, and likelihood of competitive reaction.

Learning from Mistakes

Digg was an early social network pioneer. In 2004, its founder, Kevin Rose, had an innovative idea. Rather than allow major news services to decide what the big news stories of the day were, Rose figured that people could make that choice. He founded Digg, a news-sharing site, to give them that choice.[1] Users would post news articles they found interesting. Other users would then vote the story up or down and also post comments about the article. Articles that were voted up moved up in prominence on the site. Those voted down sank and eventually disappeared. The business took off and served as a front-page article in *BusinessWeek* in 2006. Notable venture capitalists like Marc Andreessen, Ron Conway, and Greylock Partners invested $45 million in Digg. It was rumored that Google was interested in buying Digg in 2008 for a reported $200 million.

But the deal never happened, and Digg quickly fell from favor. It struggled due to two major issues—new competition and poor operational decisions. As we'll discuss later in this chapter, innovative business ideas are typically quickly imitated. Digg faced two forms of imitation. First, Reddit and other sites came online to challenge Digg by implementing similar business models. Second, other social network sites, such as Facebook and Twitter, ate away at Digg's business by letting users share news articles they found interesting with their friends and followers. This seemed much more personalized to many, since they would be more interested in what their friends recommended than how the general population voted on Digg.

Digg also suffered by not building the resource set needed to serve its users effectively. The company struggled to handle the volume of traffic on its site, leaving users frustrated when the site kept going down. When Digg finally went to a wholesale upgrade of its systems in 2010, there were a number of technical glitches that drove users away. Digg also didn't make the site as easy to use as it should have or as easy as its competitors' sites. As Rose himself noted, "It took eight steps to post a link on Digg."[2]

What was the cost of Digg's missteps? Even though Digg was still drawing over 7 million visitors a month in early 2012, it was no longer a valued brand or corporation. The firm, which was at one time thought to be worth $200 million, was sold to Betaworks in July 2012 for the whopping sum of $500,000.

Discussion Questions

1. What lessons can we learn from Digg?
2. Can you think of other Internet firms that have failed and recovered? If so, what lessons can Betaworks draw from these experiences to help Digg recover?

By offering a service allowing users to share and vote on news stories, Digg seemed to have identified an attractive opportunity. But the start-up's failure shows what can go wrong when—even though a good opportunity and a skilled entrepreneurial team are brought together—a business opportunity disappears as quickly as it appeared.

The Digg case illustrates how important it is for new entrepreneurial entrants—whether they are start-ups or incumbents—to think and act strategically. Even with a strong initial resource base, entrepreneurs are unlikely to succeed if their business ideas are easily imitated or the execution of the strategy falls short.

In this chapter we address entrepreneurial strategies. The previous three chapters have focused primarily on the business-level, corporate-level, and international strategies of incumbent firms. Here we ask: What about the strategies of those entering into a market or industry for the first time? Whether it's a fast-growing start-up such as Digg or an existing company seeking growth opportunities, new entrants need effective strategies.

Companies wishing to launch new ventures must also be aware that, consistent with the five-forces model in Chapter 2, new entrants are a threat to existing firms in an industry. Entry into a new market arena is intensely competitive from the perspective of incumbents in that arena. Therefore, new entrants can nearly always expect a competitive response from other companies in the industry they are entering. Knowledge of the competitive dynamics that are at work in the business environment is an aspect of entrepreneurial new entry that will be addressed later in this chapter.

Before moving on, it is important to highlight the role that entrepreneurial start-ups and small businesses play in entrepreneurial value creation. Small businesses, those defined as having 500 employees or fewer, create about 65 percent of all new jobs in the United States and also generate 13 times as many new patents per employee as larger firms.[3]

Recognizing Entrepreneurial Opportunities

entrepreneurship
the creation of new value by an existing organization or new venture that involves the assumption of risk.

Defined broadly, **entrepreneurship** refers to new value creation. Even though entrepreneurial activity is usually associated with start-up companies, new value can be created in many different contexts, including:

- Start-up ventures
- Major corporations
- Family-owned businesses
- Nonprofit organizations
- Established institutions

LO8.1

The role of opportunities, resources, and entrepreneurs in successfully pursuing new ventures.

For an entrepreneurial venture to create new value, three factors must be present—an entrepreneurial opportunity, the resources to pursue the opportunity, and an entrepreneur or entrepreneurial team willing and able to undertake the opportunity.[4] The entrepreneurial strategy that an organization uses will depend on these three factors. Thus, beyond merely identifying a venture concept, the opportunity recognition process also involves organizing the key people and resources that are needed to go forward. Exhibit 8.1 depicts the three factors that are needed to successfully proceed—opportunity, resources, and entrepreneur(s). In the sections that follow, we address each of these factors.

Entrepreneurial Opportunities

The starting point for any new venture is the presence of an entrepreneurial opportunity. Where do opportunities come from? For new business start-ups, opportunities come from many sources—current or past work experiences, hobbies that grow into businesses or lead to inventions, suggestions by friends or family, or a chance event that makes an entrepreneur aware of an unmet need. Terry Tietzen, founder and CEO of Edatanetworks, puts it this way, "You get ideas through watching the world and through relationships. You get ideas from looking down the road."[5] For established firms, new business opportunities come from the needs of existing customers, suggestions by suppliers, or technological developments that lead to new advances.[6] For all firms, there is a major, overarching factor behind all viable opportunities that emerge in the business landscape: change. Change creates opportunities. Entrepreneurial firms make the most of changes brought about by new technology, sociocultural trends, and shifts in consumer demand.

How do changes in the external environment lead to new business creation? They spark creative new ideas and innovation. Businesspeople often have ideas for entrepreneurial ventures. However, not all such ideas are good ideas—that is, viable business opportunities. To determine which ideas are strong enough to become new ventures, entrepreneurs

EXHIBIT 8.1 Opportunity Analysis Framework

Sources: Based on Timmons, J. A. & Spinelli, S. 2004. *New Venture Creation* (6th ed.). New York: McGraw-Hill/Irwin; and Bygrave, W. D. 1997. The Entrepreneurial Process. In W. D. Bygrave (Ed.), *The Portable MBA in Entrepreneurship* (2nd ed.). New York: Wiley.

must go through a process of identifying, selecting, and developing potential opportunities. This is the process of **opportunity recognition.**[7]

Opportunity recognition refers to more than just the "Eureka!" feeling that people sometimes experience at the moment they identify a new idea. Although such insights are often very important, the opportunity recognition process involves two phases of activity—discovery and evaluation—that lead to viable new venture opportunities.[8]

The discovery phase refers to the process of becoming aware of a new business concept.[9] Many entrepreneurs report that their idea for a new venture occurred to them in an instant, as a sort of "Aha!" experience—that is, they had some insight or epiphany, often based on their prior knowledge, that gave them an idea for a new business. The discovery of new opportunities is often spontaneous and unexpected. For example, Howard Schultz, CEO of Starbucks, was in Milan, Italy, when he suddenly realized that the coffee-and-conversation cafe model that was common in Europe would work in the U.S. as well. According to Schultz, he didn't need to do research to find out if Americans would pay $3 for a cup of coffee—he just *knew.* Starbucks was just a small business at the time but Schultz began literally shaking with excitement about growing it into a bigger business.[10] Strategy Spotlight 8.1 tells how two brothers took the realization that many people wanted to wear their optimism and turned it into a growing business empire.

Opportunity discovery also may occur as the result of a deliberate search for new venture opportunities or creative solutions to business problems. Viable opportunities often emerge only after a concerted effort. The search process is very similar to a creative process, which may be unstructured and "chaotic" at first but eventually leads to a practical solution or business innovation. To stimulate the discovery of new opportunities, companies often encourage creativity, out-of-the-box thinking, and brainstorming. While a deliberate search can aim to identify truly novel and creative entrepreneurial opportunities, it can also be more focused to look for "obvious" opportunities that others have failed to see. Experienced entrepreneurs discussing ways to look for new entrepreneurial opportunities identify several ways to undertake a structured search for entrepreneurial ideas:[11]

- ***Look at what's bugging you.*** What are the frustrations you have with current products or processes? Search for ideas on how to address these annoyances to identify entrepreneurial opportunities. For example, David Cohen found an idea for an entrepreneurial venture in his frustration with finding news regarding music groups he followed. Normal web search engines and news compilers didn't provide

opportunity recognition
the process of discovering and evaluating changes in the business environment, such as a new technology, sociocultural trends, or shifts in consumer demand, that can be exploited.

SEEING OPPORTUNITY IN THE BRIGHT SIDE

People were craving something positive that focused on the good, instead of what is wrong with the world.

—John Jacobs

That simple inspiration was the insight that has driven the success of Life is Good T-shirts. Beginning in 1989, John Jacobs and his brother, Bert, had been selling T-shirts out of their van, scraping out a living. They used their own artwork on the shirts and found an audience for their funky designs, especially on college campuses. But after five and a half years in the business, they had a whopping $78 in the bank.

Their business turned with a simple conversation. As John explained, "Then in 1994, we talked about how people seemed worn down by the media's constant focus on the negative side of information." They had a keg party at which they asked friends to comment on drawings they were considering for new shirts. The design that received the most buzz was a simple stick figure that smiled. They paired this design with a simple slogan, "Life is Good," to offer a positive message. They printed up 48 shirts with the new design and sold out within an hour at a street fair. Their inspiration seemed correct. People craved a sense of positivity.

They started working with retailers to sell the shirts. The retailers liked the design but also started asking questions, such as, "Does the smiley guy eat ice cream? Does he roller-skate?" Bert and John responded by starting to draw designs that reflected what made life good. In Bert's words, "Our concept was that optimism is powerful." What they found out was that optimism is a powerful sales slogan. Their sales topped $250,000 within two years.

It's been over 20 years since they had the simple but profound insight that people buy into a positive message. Life is Good now generates nearly $150 million in sales and distributes its clothing through more than 4,500 retail stores in over 30 countries. The firm also has strategic alliances with Hallmark and Smucker's that extend its message to additional products, and John and Bert see further opportunities in publishing and filmmaking with their message that life is good. The brothers have also set up a foundation that hosts festivals to benefit kids overcoming poverty, illness, and violence. Their goal is clear. As Bert stated, "We can be a billion dollar company driving positive social change, teaching, and reinforcing the values we think are most important in the world." The message isn't that life is great or life is perfect but that even in hard times, life is good.

Sources: Buchanan, L. 2006. Life lessons. *inc.com,* October 1: np; Eng, D. 2014. Life is good in the T-shirt business. *Fortune,* May 19: 39–42; and *hoovers.com.*

what he wanted. In response, he developed earFeeder, a program that checks computers for music that is stored on the hard drive and feeds listeners news, tour, and ticket information on the bands they like.

- *Talk to the people who know.* These people can include your suppliers, customers, and frontline employees. Interactions can include visits with them, group discussions, and even role playing, such as having senior executives take shifts in frontline jobs or use the firm's online ordering system. These discussions and role-playing exercises can lead to insights on how these stakeholders' needs aren't being met and can also open avenues to hearing from these people regarding what they would like to see in new products and processes. For example, Sam Palmisano, former CEO of IBM, realized there was tremendous potential in providing outsourced services, such as IT and accounting systems, when he had a conversation with the CEO of Procter & Gamble. In this conversation, A. G. Lafley, the CEO of P&G, discussed the possibility of improving firm efficiency by focusing his firm on its core operations and outsourcing a range of services to specialized service firms.

- *Look to other markets.* One of the most powerful ways of finding new ideas is by borrowing ideas from other markets. This could involve looking at other industries or other geographic markets to identify new ideas. For example, in developing the idea for CarMax, the used-car superstore chain, Richard Sharp drew on his experience leading a major consumer electronics retailer to lay out the logic for his "big box" used-car lots, which allowed him to streamline operations and improve the efficiency of the used-car market. In essence, he decided to build the Best Buy or the Home Depot of the used-car market.

- *Get inspired by history.* Sometimes, the best ideas are not actually new ideas. Opportunities in industries can often be discovered by looking to the past to find good ideas that have slipped out of practice but might now be valued by the market again. For example, Sam Calagione, founder of Ancient Ales, developed an innovative line of craft beers by using ancient brewing techniques and ingredients that differ from modern brews.

Opportunity evaluation, which occurs after an opportunity has been identified, involves analyzing an opportunity to determine whether it is viable and strong enough to be developed into a full-fledged new venture. Ideas developed by new product groups or in brainstorming sessions are tested by various methods, including talking to potential target customers and discussing operational requirements with production or logistics managers. A technique known as feasibility analysis is used to evaluate these and other critical success factors. This type of analysis often leads to the decision that a new venture project should be discontinued. If the venture concept continues to seem viable, a more formal business plan may be developed.[12]

Among the most important factors to evaluate is the market potential for the product or service. Established firms tend to operate in established markets. They have to adjust to market trends and to shifts in consumer demand, of course, but they usually have a customer base for which they are already filling a marketplace need. New ventures, in contrast, must first determine whether a market exists for the product or service they are contemplating. Thus, a critical element of opportunity recognition is assessing to what extent the opportunity is viable *in the marketplace.*

For an opportunity to be viable, it needs to have four qualities:[13]

- *Attractive.* The opportunity must be attractive in the marketplace; that is, there must be market demand for the new product or service.
- *Achievable.* The opportunity must be practical and physically possible.
- *Durable.* The opportunity must be attractive long enough for the development and deployment to be successful; that is, the window of opportunity must be open long enough for it to be worthwhile.
- *Value creating.* The opportunity must be potentially profitable; that is, the benefits must surpass the cost of development by a significant margin.

If a new business concept meets these criteria, two other factors must be considered before the opportunity is launched as a business: the resources available to undertake it and the characteristics of the entrepreneur(s) pursuing it. In the next section, we address the issue of entrepreneurial resources; following that, we address the importance of entrepreneurial leaders and teams. But first, consider the opportunities that have been created by the recent surge in interest in environmental sustainability. Strategy Spotlight 8.2 discusses how an entrepreneurial firm is building a strong market position with eco-friendly cleaning products.

Entrepreneurial Resources

As Exhibit 8.1 indicates, resources are an essential component of a successful entrepreneurial launch. For start-ups, the most important resource is usually money because a new firm typically has to expend substantial sums just to start the business. However, financial resources are not the only kind of resource a new venture needs. Human capital and social capital are also important. Many firms also rely on government resources to help them thrive.[14]

Financial Resources Hand-in-hand with the importance of markets (and marketing) to new venture creation, entrepreneurial firms must also have financing. In fact, the level of available financing is often a strong determinant of how the business is launched and its eventual success. Cash finances are, of course, highly important. But access to capital, such as a line of credit or favorable payment terms with a supplier, can also help a new venture succeed.

The types of financial resources that may be needed depend on two factors: the stage of venture development and the scale of the venture.[15] Entrepreneurial firms that are starting from scratch—start-ups—are at the earliest stage of development. Most start-ups also begin on a relatively small scale. The funding available to young and small firms tends to be quite limited. In fact, the majority of new firms are low-budget start-ups launched with

SOAKING IN THE MARKET WITH GREEN CLEANERS

Adam Lowry wanted to put his Stanford University chemical engineering degree to work to help create a more sustainable world. He searched for a consumer product market that was large and established but had not yet responded to the desire of many for a healthier and more sustainable planet. He had an inspiration when he opened a bottle of Snapple Element to drink and wondered, "Why can't Pine-Sol smell like this?" This was the thought that led Lowry and his childhood friend and roommate, Eric Ryan, to start their eco-friendly cleaner products firm, Method Products. They took their personal savings and contributions from family and friends to cobble together $90,000 to launch the firm in 2000. Lowry's logic for the business was clear: "Before us, you got either a toxic product that got the job done or a green product that didn't."

Lowry and Ryan developed their first four products—kitchen, shower, glass, and bathroom cleaners—and tested the products themselves, as well as enlisting friends to try them out. Ryan jokes that this was the time when their apartment "was the cleanest it'd ever been." It took six months before they convinced a single store to carry their products. Mollie Stone's Market in Burlingame, California, first put their products on its shelves in February 2001. By the end of 2002, Method products were in 700 stores and the founders were growing their product line. In addition to their first four products, they added dish soap, laundry detergent, automotive cleaners, air fresheners, and room sprays. Across all of the products, Method aims to use natural ingredients, ensures that no animal testing was used in developing its products, uses a third-party laboratory to test all of its product components for health and environmental safety, and bottles its products in recycled plastic containers. The firm has also worked to reduce its carbon footprint as much as possible.

Method now generates over $100 million in sales per year. The strength of its idea and market position is evident in the reaction of its major competitors. Most of its primary competitors, including S.C. Johnson and Clorox, have launched their own green cleaning-products lines. In spite of the increased competition, Method Products continues to grow at a healthy 10 percent rate.

Sources: Eng, D. 2013. Mopping up with green cleaners. *Fortune,* October 28: 47–50; *methodhome.com;* and *privco.com.*

personal savings and the contributions of family and friends.[16] Among firms included in the *Entrepreneur* list of the 100 fastest-growing new businesses, 61 percent reported that their start-up funds came from personal savings.[17]

Although bank financing, public financing, and venture capital are important sources of small business finance, these types of financial support are typically available only after a company has started to conduct business and generate sales. Even **angel investors**—private individuals who provide equity investments for seed capital during the early stages of a new venture—favor companies that already have a winning business model and dominance in a market niche.[18] According to Cal Simmons, coauthor of *Every Business Needs an Angel,* "I would much rather talk to an entrepreneur who has already put his money and his effort into proving the concept."[19]

Thus, while the press commonly talks about the role of **venture capitalists** and angel investors in start-up firms, the majority of external funding for young and small firms comes from informal sources such as family and friends. Based on a Kauffman Foundation survey

angel investors
private individuals who provide equity investments for seed capital during the early stages of a new venture.

venture capitalists
companies organized to place their investors' funds in lucrative business opportunities.

EXHIBIT 8.2

Sources of Capital for Start-Up Firms

	Capital Invested in Their First Year	Percentage of Capital Invested in Their First Year	Capital Invested in Their Fifth Year	Percentage of Capital Invested in Their Fifth Year
Insider equity	$33,034	41.1	$13,914	17.9
Investor equity	$ 4,108	5.1	$ 3,108	4.0
Personal debt of owners	$23,353	29.1	$21,754	28.0
Business debt	$19,867	24.7	$39,009	50.1
Total average capital invested	$80,362		$77,785	

Source: From Robb, A., Reedy, E. J., Ballou, J., DesRoches, D., Potter, F., & Zhao, A. 2010. An Overview of the Kauffman Firm Survey. Reproduced with permission from the Ewing Marion Kauffman Foundation.

of entrepreneurial firms, Exhibit 8.2 identifies the source of funding used by start-up businesses and by ongoing firms that are five years old. The survey shows that most start-up funding, about 70 percent, comes from either equity investments by the entrepreneur and the entrepreneur's family and friends or personal loans taken out by the entrepreneur.

Once a venture has established itself as a going concern, other sources of financing become readily available. Banks, for example, are more likely to provide later-stage financing to companies with a track record of sales or other cash-generating activity. According to the Kauffman Foundation study, after five years of operation, the largest source of funding is from loans taken out by the business.

At both stages, 5 percent or less of the funding comes from outside investors, such as angel investors or venture capitalists. In fact, few firms ever receive venture capital investments—only 7 of 2,606 firms in the Kauffman study received money from outside investors. But when they do, these firms receive a substantial level of investment—over $1 million on average in the survey—because they tend to be the firms that are the most innovative and have the greatest growth potential. These start-ups typically involve large capital investments or extensive development costs—such as manufacturing or engineering firms trying to commercialize an innovative product—and have high cash requirements soon after they are founded. Since these investments are typically well beyond the capability of the entrepreneur or even a local bank to fund, entrepreneurs running these firms turn to the venture capital market. Other firms turn to venture capitalists when they are on the brink of rapid growth.

Venture capital is a form of private equity financing through which entrepreneurs raise money by selling shares in the new venture. In contrast to angel investors, who invest their own money, venture capital companies are organized to place the funds of private investors into lucrative business opportunities. Venture capitalists nearly always have high performance expectations from the companies they invest in, but they also provide important managerial advice and links to key contacts in an industry.[20]

In recent years, a new source of funding, **crowdfunding,** has emerged as a means for start-ups to amass significant pools of capital.[21] In these peer-to-peer investment systems, individuals striving to grow their business post their business ideas on a crowdfunding website. Potential investors who go to the site evaluate the proposals listed and decide which, if any, to fund. Typically, no individual makes a very sizable funding allotment. Most investors contribute up to a few hundred dollars to any investment, but the power of the crowd is at work. If a few thousand investors sign up for a venture, it can potentially raise over a million dollars.

crowdfunding
funding a venture by pooling small investments from a large number of investors; often raised on the Internet.

The crowdfunding market has taken off since the term was first coined in 2006. The total value of crowdfunding investments passed $5 billion in 2013, and according to a World Bank study, it could reach $90 billion by 2025.[22] Some crowdfunding websites allow investors to own actual equity in the firms they fund. Others, such as Kickstarter, don't offer investors equity. Instead, they get a reward from the entrepreneurial firm. For example, Mystery Brewing Company gave its investors logoed bottle openers, tulip-shaped beer glasses, T-shirts, posters, and home-brew recipes.

While crowdfunding offers a new avenue for corporations to raise funding, there are some potential downsides. First, the crowdfunding sites take a slice of the funds raised—typically 4 to 9 percent. Second, while crowdfunding offers a marketplace in which to raise funds, it also puts additional pressure on entrepreneurs. The social network–savvy investors who fund these ventures are quick to comment on their social media websites if the firm misses deadlines or falls short of its revenue projections. Finally, entrepreneurs can struggle with how much information to share about their business ideas. They want to share enough information without releasing critical information that competitors trolling these sites can benefit from. They also may be concerned about posting their financials, since these statements give their suppliers and customers access to sensitive information about margins and earnings.

There are also some concerns that the loose rules in the regulation of crowdfunding could lead to significant fraud by firms soliciting investment. According to Stephen

EVALUATING CROWDFUNDING OPPORTUNITIES

Because the requirements for firms raising funds through crowd-funding are lax, investors need to do their homework. Here are some simple recommendations to keep from getting burned.

- **Financial statements.** Be sure to closely review the corporate tax returns that firms are required to post. Better yet, have your accountant review them to see if anything looks fishy.

- **Licenses and registrations.** You should check to see if the company has current licenses and registrations needed to operate in its chosen industry. This can often be done through online checks with the secretary of state's office or the state's corporation department. Sometimes, it will take a phone call or two. This provides a simple check to see if the company is legitimate.

- **Litigation.** Check to see if the company has been sued. You can search online at the free site justia.com and the law-oriented information sites Westlaw and Lexis. Be sure to check under current and former names of the firm and its principals (top managers).

- **Better Business Bureau.** Check the firm's BBB report. Does the firm appear to exist? What is the grade the BBB gives it? Is the firm a BBB member? All of this information gives insight into the firm's current operations and its customer relations.

- **Employment and educational history.** This is a bit tricky because of privacy issues, but you can typically contact colleges listed on the filing forms and inquire if the principals of the firm attended and graduated from the schools they list. You can also search employment histories on the websites of the companies the principals used to work at as well as social network sites, such as LinkedIn and Facebook.

- **Required disclosures.** Read all of the documentation carefully. This includes the shareholder rights statement. This statement will provide information on how much of a stake in the firm you get and how this will be diluted by future offerings. Also, read statements on the company's competition and risks it faces.

Sources: Wasik, J. 2012. The brilliance (and madness) of crowdfunding. *Forbes*, June 25: 144–146; and Burke, A. 2012. Crowdfunding set to explode with passage of Entrepreneur Access to Capital Act. *Forbes.com*, February 29: np.

Goodman, an attorney with Pryor Cashman LLP, "The SEC has been extremely skeptical of this [crowdfunding] process." Others have faith in the wisdom of the crowd to catch fraud. They point to the experience with Little Monster Productions, a video game developer. Little Monster was set to raise funds on Kickstarter, but the fund call was closed by Kickstarter when potential investors noticed and commented that Little Monster had stolen some of the images it was using in its game from another game site. Even with potential investors identifying glaring problems with some crowdfunding projects, the likelihood of success with crowdfunded projects is somewhat low. One study found that 75 percent of crowdfunded projects failed to meet their anticipated launch dates.[23] Strategy Spotlight 8.3 provides a checklist for investors considering participating in a crowdfunding effort. Regardless of their source, financial resources are essential for entrepreneurial ventures.[24]

Human Capital   Bankers, venture capitalists, and angel investors agree that the most important asset an entrepreneurial firm can have is strong and skilled management.[25] According to Stephen Gaal, founding member of Walnut Venture Associates, venture investors do not invest in businesses; instead, "We invest in people . . . very smart people with very high integrity." Managers need to have a strong base of experience and extensive domain knowledge, as well as an ability to make rapid decisions and change direction as shifting circumstances may require. In the case of start-ups, more is better. New ventures that are started by teams of three, four, or five entrepreneurs are more likely to succeed in the long run than are ventures launched by "lone wolf" entrepreneurs.[26]

Social Capital   New ventures founded by entrepreneurs who have extensive social contacts are more likely to succeed than are ventures started without the support of a social network.[27] Even though a venture may be new, if the founders have contacts who will vouch for them, they gain exposure and build legitimacy faster.[28] This support can come from several sources: prior jobs, industry organizations, and local business groups such as the chamber of commerce. These contacts can all contribute to a growing network that provides support for the entrepreneurial firm. Janina Pawlowski, cofounder of the online lending company E-Loan, attributes part of her success to the strong advisers she persuaded to serve on her board of directors, including Tim Koogle, former CEO of Yahoo![29]

Strategic alliances represent a type of social capital that can be especially important to young and small firms.[30] Strategic alliances can provide a key avenue for growth by entrepreneurial firms.[31] By partnering with other companies, young or small firms can expand or give the appearance of entering numerous markets or handling a range of operations. According to the National Federation of Independent Business (NFIB), nearly two-thirds of small businesses currently hold or have held some type of alliance. Here are a few types of alliances that have been used to extend or strengthen entrepreneurial firms:

- *Technology alliances.* Tech-savvy entrepreneurial firms often benefit from forming alliances with older incumbents. The alliance allows the larger firm to enhance its technological capabilities and expands the revenue and reach of the smaller firm.
- *Manufacturing alliances.* The use of outsourcing and other manufacturing alliances by small firms has grown dramatically in recent years. Internet-enabled capabilities such as collaborating online about delivery and design specifications have greatly simplified doing business, even with foreign manufacturers.
- *Retail alliances.* Licensing agreements allow one company to sell the products and services of another in different markets, including overseas. Specialty products—the types sometimes made by entrepreneurial firms—often seem more exotic when sold in another country.

Although such alliances often sound good, there are also potential pitfalls. Lack of oversight and control is one danger of partnering with foreign firms. Problems with product quality, timely delivery, and receiving payments can also sour an alliance relationship if it is not carefully managed. With technology alliances, there is a risk that big firms may take advantage of the technological know-how of their entrepreneurial partners. However, even with these potential problems, strategic alliances provide a good means for entrepreneurial firms to develop and grow.

Government Resources   In the U.S., the federal government provides support for entrepreneurial firms in two key arenas—financing and government contracting. The Small Business Administration (SBA) has several loan guarantee programs designed to support the growth and development of entrepreneurial firms. The government itself does not typically lend money but underwrites loans made by banks to small businesses, thus reducing the risk associated with lending to firms with unproven records. The SBA also offers training, counseling, and support services through its local offices and Small Business Development Centers.[32] State and local governments also have hundreds of programs to provide funding, contracts, and other support for new ventures and small businesses. These programs are often designed to grow the economy of a region.

Another key area of support is government contracting. Programs sponsored by the SBA and other government agencies ensure that small businesses have the opportunity to bid on contracts to provide goods and services to the government. Although working with the government sometimes has its drawbacks in terms of issues of regulation and time-consuming decision making, programs to support small businesses and entrepreneurial activity constitute an important resource for entrepreneurial firms.

Entrepreneurial Leadership

Whether a venture is launched by an individual entrepreneur or an entrepreneurial team, effective leadership is needed. Launching a new venture requires a special kind of

entrepreneurial leadership
leadership appropriate for new ventures that requires courage, belief in one's convictions, and the energy to work hard even in difficult circumstances and that embodies vision, dedication and drive, and commitment to excellence.

leadership. Research indicates that entrepreneurs tend to have characteristics that distinguish them from corporate managers. Differences include:

- **Higher core self-evaluation.** Successful entrepreneurs evidence higher levels of self-confidence and a higher assessment of the degree to which an individual controls his or her own destiny.[33]
- **Higher conscientiousness.** Entrepreneurs tend to have a higher degree of organization, persistence, hard work, and pursuit of goal accomplishment.
- **Higher openness to experience.** Entrepreneurs also tend to score higher on openness to experience, a personality trait associated with intellectual curiosity and a desire to explore novel ideas.
- **Higher emotional stability.** Entrepreneurs exhibit a higher ability to handle ambiguity and maintain even emotions during stressful periods, and they are less likely to be overcome by anxieties.
- **Lower agreeableness.** Finally, entrepreneurs tend to score lower on agreeableness. This suggests they typically look out primarily for their own self-interest and also are willing to influence or manipulate others for their own advantage.[34]

These personality traits are embodied in the behavioral attributes necessary for successful entrepreneurial leadership—vision, dedication and drive, and commitment to excellence:

- **Vision.** This may be an entrepreneur's most important asset. Entrepreneurs envision realities that do not yet exist. But without a vision, most entrepreneurs would never even get their venture off the ground. With vision, entrepreneurs are able to exercise a kind of transformational leadership that creates something new and, in some way, changes the world. Just having a vision, however, is not enough. To develop support, get financial backing, and attract employees, entrepreneurial leaders must share their vision with others.
- **Dedication and drive.** Dedication and drive are reflected in hard work. Drive involves internal motivation; dedication calls for an intellectual commitment that keeps an entrepreneur going even in the face of bad news or poor luck. They both require patience, stamina, and a willingness to work long hours. However, a business built on the heroic efforts of one person may suffer in the long run. That's why the dedicated entrepreneur's enthusiasm is also important—like a magnet, it attracts others to the business to help with the work.[35]
- **Commitment to excellence.** Excellence requires entrepreneurs to commit to knowing the customer, providing quality goods and services, paying attention to details, and continuously learning. Entrepreneurs who achieve excellence are sensitive to how these factors work together. However, entrepreneurs may flounder if they think they are the only ones who can create excellent results. The most successful, by contrast, often report that they owe their success to hiring people smarter than themselves.

In his book *Good to Great,* Jim Collins makes another important point about entrepreneurial leadership: Ventures built on the charisma of a single person may have trouble growing "from good to great" once that person leaves.[36] Thus, the leadership that is needed to build a great organization is usually exercised by a team of dedicated people working together rather than a single leader. Another aspect of this team approach is attracting team members who fit with the company's culture, goals, and work ethic. Thus, for a venture's leadership to be a valuable resource and not a liability, it must be cohesive in its vision, drive and dedication, and commitment to excellence.

David Drews is a senior executive at the entrepreneurial marketing firm Project: World-Wide. In the Insights from Executives box, he provides additional thoughts on both identifying entrepreneurial opportunities and leading entrepreneurial firms.

DAVID DREWS, EXECUTIVE VICE PRESIDENT AND CFO OF PROJECT: WORLDWIDE

BIOSKETCH

David Drews has been executive vice president and CFO of Project: WorldWide for over 20 years. Project: WorldWide is an independent, global network of complementary, wholly owned marketing agencies that has grown from $30 million in annual revenue in the mid-1980s to nearly $1 billion in revenue today. Drews began his career in public accounting after graduating from Michigan State University in 1982. He received his MBA from the University of Michigan in 1987. He joined the company in 1986, has served on the executive committee since 1993, and has been a board member since 2005. He has helped guide Project: WorldWide's expansion into new product and geographic markets through organic growth, strategic alliances, and acquisitions, as well as completing an employee-led, S corporation ESOP buyout of the company in 2005.

1. *You've been involved with multiple situations in which your firm has identified attractive opportunities for growth. What has been the source of insight that you and your colleagues have drawn on to identify these profitable opportunities?*

   Attractive growth always begins with our clients' needs. Listening carefully to their needs—and anticipating their needs—is the key driver for strategic initiatives. Knowing the competitive landscape and leaning forward, adopting new offerings before they're widely available in the market, creates opportunity for profitable growth. Hiring staff with diverse backgrounds has allowed new thinking to broaden our offering. Hiring talent—world-class talent—leads to winning business from much larger competitors. The key across all opportunities for growth centers on finding the right talent that can bring tremendous value to our clients.

2. *Adequate financial capital is a key resource for growing firms. Firms can access this resource from a variety of sources, including the personal investment of entrepreneurs, bank loans, angel investors, venture capital, crowdfunding, and many other sources. What sources of financing have your firms used? What have you found to be the advantages and disadvantages of each source?*

   Wealth is created with equity. Equity provides the opportunity for tremendous returns for angel investors, private equity, venture capital, and the like. It also provides the most upside for entrepreneurs. Inasmuch as salary, short-term incentives, and long-term incentives are important, real wealth comes from owning the business. Before sharing equity with others, entrepreneurs should very carefully evaluate the alternatives. If the business can be financed another way, through debt and the entrepreneur's own

capital, for instance, that should be a much more attractive alternative—unless other capital sources multiply earnings growth. Project: WorldWide has used past earnings and debt to finance growth. This creates the most upside for our employee-owners. In the end, the owner of equity will be rewarded for the risk taken by achieving a multiple of EBITDA when the business is sold. Be slow to give up equity. It is the crown jewel of finance for entrepreneurs.

3. *By some estimates, up to 90 percent of new ventures fail. What do you see as the most common drivers of venture failure? What steps as an entrepreneur did you take to enhance your chances of success?*

   As the saying goes, "Failure to plan means you are planning to fail." That said, only so much analysis can be done before launching a new venture. Analyzing the market demand is critical. Coming up short on revenue is the number-one reason for failure. Having enough—but not too much—top-end talent is critical. Revenue must be able to support the staff load. As a result, staff need to be able to wear multiple "hats." The "burn rate" needs to be determined to see how long the business can sustain itself before the next injection of capital—or when revenue is adequate to achieve break-even. Knowing your business model and key success factors is critical. Entrepreneurs who lead, inspire, and recruit outstanding people greatly enhance the chance of success.

4. *How have ventures you've been involved in drawn on ties in social networks to create competitive advantages? This could include informal ties, such as personal ties of the firm's founders with potential customers, investors, or government officials, or more formal social capital, such as strategic alliances with suppliers, customers, or technology partners.*

   Social networks can provide excellent background information on people your business is looking to do business with. However, nothing replaces a personal relationship. Strong personal relationships lead to opportunities which lead to sustainable revenue. In a service-based business, these relationships are key. Becoming a trusted adviser means solving real business problems for clients, addressing their current needs, and anticipating their future needs. Social networks aid in cataloging contacts, but they don't create the foundation for long-term success with clients. This must be done personally, with great work earning trust over an extended period of time. The same can be said for suppliers and technology partners. Finding partners, through social networks or diligent research, that fulfill the outsourced portion of your product offering is key to sustained success. A common thread of successful entrepreneurs is the ability to develop truly trusted relationships across the entire spectrum of clients, suppliers, employees, and other business contracts.

Once an opportunity has been recognized, and an entrepreneurial team and resources have been assembled, a new venture must craft a strategy. Prior chapters have addressed the strategies of incumbent firms. In the next section, we highlight the types of strategies and strategic considerations faced by new entrants.

Entrepreneurial Strategy

Successfully creating new ventures requires several ingredients. As indicated in Exhibit 8.1, three factors are necessary—a viable opportunity, sufficient resources, and a skilled and dedicated entrepreneur or entrepreneurial team. Once these elements are in place, the new venture needs a strategy. In this section, we consider several different strategic factors that are unique to new ventures and also how the generic strategies introduced in Chapter 5 can be applied to entrepreneurial firms. We also indicate how combination strategies might benefit entrepreneurial firms and address the potential pitfalls associated with launching new venture strategies.

To be successful, new ventures must evaluate industry conditions, the competitive environment, and market opportunities in order to position themselves strategically. However, a traditional strategic analysis may have to be altered somewhat to fit the entrepreneurial situation. For example, five-forces analysis (as discussed in Chapter 2) is typically used by established firms. It can also be applied to the analysis of new ventures to assess the impact of industry and competitive forces. But you may ask: How does a new entrant evaluate the threat of other new entrants?

First, the new entrant needs to examine barriers to entry. If the barriers are too high, the potential entrant may decide not to enter or to gather more resources before attempting to do so. Compared to an older firm with an established reputation and available resources, the barriers to entry may be insurmountable for an entrepreneurial start-up. Therefore, understanding the force of these barriers is critical in making a decision to launch.

A second factor that may be especially important to a young venture is the threat of retaliation by incumbents. In many cases, entrepreneurial ventures *are* the new entrants that pose a threat to incumbent firms. Therefore, in applying the five-forces model to new ventures, the threat of retaliation by established firms needs to be considered.

Part of any decision about what opportunity to pursue is a consideration of how a new entrant will actually enter a new market. The concept of entry strategies provides a useful means of addressing the types of choices that new ventures have.

Entry Strategies

One of the most challenging aspects of launching a new venture is finding a way to begin doing business that quickly generates cash flow, builds credibility, attracts good employees, and overcomes the liability of newness. The idea of an entry strategy or "entry wedge" describes several approaches that firms may take to get a foothold in a market.[37] Several factors will affect this decision:

- Is the product/service high-tech or low-tech?
- What resources are available for the initial launch?
- What are the industry and competitive conditions?
- What is the overall market potential?
- Does the venture founder prefer to control the business or to grow it?

In some respects, any type of entry into a market for the first time may be considered entrepreneurial. But the entry strategy will vary depending on how risky and innovative the new business concept is.[38] New-entry strategies typically fall into one of three categories—pioneering new entry, imitative new entry, or adaptive new entry.[39]

Pioneering New Entry New entrants with a radical new product or highly innovative service may change the way business is conducted in an industry. This kind of

ROCKET INTERNET FINDS THAT IMITATION IS THE MOST PROFITABLE FORM OF FLATTERY

Since its founding in 2007, Rocket Internet has funded over 100 start-ups in 50 countries that now generate over $4 billion in revenue. What is the secret to Rocket's success? It is blatant imitation. Employees of the firm scour the Internet looking for successful businesses and then create copies of these existing e-commerce sites, typically in underserved European and emerging markets. For example, one of the firm's most successful ventures is Lamoda, a retailing fashion site in Russia that is modeled after Zappos. Similarly, it created Food Panda, a GrubHub-clone food-delivery service in Asia, and Linio, a site that has been called the "Amazon of Latin America." More recently, it launched Helpling, a system to book and rate home cleaning services in Germany that copies the formula of San Francisco–based Homejoy.

While the stereotype of a successful entrepreneur is one who creates bold and novel products and services, Rocket Internet demonstrates that taking a proven idea to new and underserved markets is a very viable form of entrepreneurship. In the words of Jennifer Binder-LePape, a partner in the consulting firm Bain & Company, "The reality is that not everyone can be Elon Musk. Rocket's play is just another form of innovation." Rocket Internet pushes for speed and efficiency in launching its businesses. Rocket's U.K. managing director, Ian Marsh, asserts that the firm can launch a new business in 60 days. Rocket reduces costs and risk by imitating established business models that it tweaks slightly for each market and by hiring seasoned, professional managers to run each site. The success of the business was evident when it listed its stock on the Frankfurt Stock Exchange in October 2014, at a firm market value of $8 billion.

Sources: Cava, M. 2014. Berlin's copycats. *Lansing State Journal,* June 1: 8B; and Williams-Grut, O. 2014. Rocket Internet: Attack of the online clone. *independent .co.uk,* December 18: np.

breakthrough—creating new ways to solve old problems or meeting customers' needs in a unique new way—is referred to as a **pioneering new entry.** If the product or service is unique enough, a pioneering new entrant may actually have little direct competition. The first personal computer was a pioneering product; there had never been anything quite like it, and it revolutionized computing. The first Internet browser provided a type of pioneering service. These breakthroughs created whole new industries and changed the competitive landscape. And breakthrough innovations continue to inspire pioneering entrepreneurial efforts.

> **pioneering new entry**
> a firm's entry into an industry with a radical new product or highly innovative service that changes the way business is conducted.

The pitfalls associated with a pioneering new entry are numerous. For one thing, there is a strong risk that the product or service will not be accepted by consumers. The history of entrepreneurship is littered with new ideas that never got off the launching pad. Take, for example, Smell-O-Vision, an invention designed to pump odors into movie theaters from the projection room at preestablished moments in a film. It was tried only once (for the film *Scent of a Mystery*) before it was declared a major flop. Innovative? Definitely. But hardly a good idea at the time.[40]

A pioneering new entry is disruptive to the status quo of an industry. It is likely based on a technological breakthrough. If it is successful, other competitors will rush in to copy it. This can create issues of sustainability for an entrepreneurial firm, especially if a larger company with greater resources introduces a similar product. For a new entrant to sustain its pioneering advantage, it may be necessary to protect its intellectual property, advertise heavily to build brand recognition, form alliances with businesses that will adopt its products or services, and offer exceptional customer service.

Imitative New Entry   Whereas pioneers are often inventors or tinkerers with new technology, imitators usually have a strong marketing orientation. They look for opportunities to capitalize on proven market successes. An **imitative new entry** strategy is used by entrepreneurs who see products or business concepts that have been successful in one market niche or physical locale and introduce the same basic product or service in another segment of the market. Strategy Spotlight 8.4 discusses how Rocket Internet has built an imitative business empire.

> **imitative new entry**
> a firm's entry into an industry with products or services that capitalize on proven market successes and that usually have a strong marketing orientation.

Sometimes the key to success with an imitative strategy is to fill a market space where the need had previously been filled inadequately. Entrepreneurs are also prompted to be imitators when they realize that they have the resources or skills to do a job better than an existing competitor. This can actually be a serious problem for entrepreneurial start-ups if the imitator is an established company. Consider the example of Square.[41] Founded in 2010, Square provides a means for small businesses to process credit and debit card sales without signing up for a traditional credit card arrangement that typically includes monthly fees and minimum charges. Square provides a small credit card reader that plugs into a smartphone to users who sign up for its service. Users swipe the card and input the charge amount. Square does the rest for a 2.75 percent transaction fee. As of 2014, Square was processing $30 billion in transactions annually. But success triggers imitation. A host of both upstart and established firms have moved into this new segment. While Square has quickly established itself in the market, it now faces strong competition from major competitors, including Apple, Google, and PayPal. With the strong competition it faces and the thin margins in its business, Square is bleeding cash. This has led to persistent rumors that it will look for a larger firm to buy it out.[42]

Adaptive New Entry Most new entrants use a strategy somewhere between "pure" imitation and "pure" pioneering. That is, they offer a product or service that is somewhat new and sufficiently different to create new value for customers and capture market share. Such firms are adaptive in the sense that they are aware of marketplace conditions and conceive entry strategies to capitalize on current trends.

According to business creativity coach Tom Monahan, "Every new idea is merely a spin of an old idea. [Knowing that] takes the pressure off from thinking [you] have to be totally creative. You don't. Sometimes it's one slight twist to an old idea that makes all the difference."[43] An **adaptive new entry** approach does not involve "reinventing the wheel," nor is it merely imitative either. It involves taking an existing idea and adapting it to a particular situation. Exhibit 8.3 presents examples of four young companies that successfully modified or adapted existing products to create new value.

There are several pitfalls that might limit the success of an adaptive new entrant. First, the value proposition must be perceived as unique. Unless potential customers believe a

> **adaptive new entry**
> a firm's entry into an industry by offering a product or service that is somewhat new and sufficiently different to create value for customers by capitalizing on current market trends.

EXHIBIT 8.3 Examples of Adaptive New Entrants

Company Name	Product	Adaptation	Result
Under Armour, Inc. Founded in 1995	Undershirts and other athletic gear	Used moisture-wicking fabric to create better gear for sweaty sports.	Under Armour generated nearly $3 billion in 2014 and is now the number-two athletic-clothing firm in the U.S. after Nike.
Mint.com Founded in 2005	Comprehensive online money management	Created software that tells users what they are spending by aggregating financial information from online bank and credit card accounts.	Mint has over 10 million users and is helping them manage over $1 billion in assets.
Plum Organics Founded in 2005	Organic baby food and snack foods for children	Made convenient line of baby food using organic ingredients.	Plum now has over 20 products and is ranked number 19 on Forbes's "Most Promising Companies" list.
Spanx Founded in 2000	Footless pantyhose and other undergarments for women	Combined nylon and Lycra to create a new type of undergarment that is comfortable and eliminates panty lines.	Spanx now produces over 200 products generating over $250 million in sales annually.

Sources: Bryan, M. 2007. Spanx Me, Baby! *www.observer.com,* December 10, np.; Carey, J. 2006. Perspiration Inspiration. *BusinessWeek,* June 5: 64; Palanjian, A. 2008. A Planner Plumbs for a Niche. *www.wsj.com,* September 30, np.; Worrell, D. 2008. Making Mint. *Entrepreneur,* September: 55; *www.mint.com; www.spanx.com; www.underarmour.com;* Buss, D. 2010. The Mothers of Invention. *Wall Street Journal,* February 8: R7; Crook, J. 2012. Mint.com Tops 10 Million Registered Users, 70% Use Mobile. *techcrunch.com,* August 29: np; *plumorganics.com; forbes.com/companies/plum-organics/;* and Germano, S. 2015. Under Armour Overtakes Adidas in U.S. Sportswear Market. *wsj.com,* January 8: np.

new product or service does a superior job of meeting their needs, they will have little motivation to try it. Second, there is nothing to prevent a close competitor from mimicking the new firm's adaptation as a way to hold on to its customers. Third, once an adaptive entrant achieves initial success, the challenge is to keep the idea fresh. If the attractive features of the new business are copied, the entrepreneurial firm must find ways to adapt and improve the product or service offering.

Considering these choices, an entrepreneur or entrepreneurial team might ask, Which new entry strategy is best? The choice depends on many competitive, financial, and marketplace considerations. Nevertheless, research indicates that the greatest opportunities may stem from being willing to enter new markets rather than seeking growth only in existing markets. One study found that companies that ventured into arenas that were new to the world or new to the company earned total profits of 61 percent. In contrast, companies that made only incremental improvements, such as extending an existing product line, grew total profits by only 39 percent.[44]

However, whether to be pioneering, imitative, or adaptive when entering markets is only one question the entrepreneur faces. A new entrant must also decide what type of strategic positioning will work best as the business goes forward. The strategic choices can be informed by the guidelines suggested for the generic strategies. We turn to that subject next.

Generic Strategies

Typically, a new entrant begins with a single business model that is equivalent in scope to a business-level strategy (Chapter 5). In this section we address how overall low cost, differentiation, and focus strategies can be used to achieve competitive advantages.

Overall Cost Leadership One of the ways entrepreneurial firms achieve success is by doing more with less. By holding down costs or making more efficient use of resources than larger competitors, new ventures are often able to offer lower prices and still be profitable. Thus, under the right circumstances, a low-cost leader strategy is a viable alternative for some new ventures. The way most companies achieve low-cost leadership, however, is typically different for young or small firms.

Recall from Chapter 5 that three of the features of a low-cost approach include operating at a large-enough scale to spread costs over many units of production (economies of scale), making substantial capital investments in order to increase scale economies, and using knowledge gained from experience to make cost-saving improvements. These elements of a cost-leadership strategy may be unavailable to new ventures. Because new ventures are typically small, they usually don't have high economies of scale relative to competitors. Because they are usually cash strapped, they can't make large capital investments to increase their scale advantages. And because many are young, they often don't have a wealth of accumulated experience to draw on to achieve cost reductions.

Given these constraints, how can new ventures successfully deploy cost-leader strategies? Compared to large firms, new ventures often have simple organizational structures that make decision making both easier and faster. The smaller size also helps young firms change more quickly when upgrades in technology or feedback from the marketplace indicate that improvements are needed. They are also able to make decisions at the time they are founded that help them deal with the issue of controlling costs. For example, they may source materials from a supplier that provides them more cheaply or set up manufacturing facilities in another country where labor costs are especially low. Thus, new firms have several avenues for achieving low-cost leadership.

Strategy Spotlight 8.5 highlights the success of Tuft and Needle, a growing mattress manufacturer with an overall cost leadership strategy. Whatever methods young firms use to achieve a low-cost advantage, this has always been a way that entrepreneurial firms take business away from incumbents—by offering a comparable product or service at a lower price.

LO8.3

How the generic strategies of overall cost leadership, differentiation, and focus are used by new ventures and small businesses.

TUFT AND NEEDLE CONSTRUCTS A LOW-COST MATTRESS

J. T. Marino had to buy a new mattress. He researched the options online and was overwhelmed by the competing claims and marketing lingo. He visited mattress stores and found even more confusion. He saw dozens of competing mattresses and couldn't figure out why two models that appeared identical could have prices that varied by several hundred dollars. "Honestly, it was a lot like the Taco Bell menu," Marino quips. "It's all these same ingredients mixed around with different formats, like a different mix of fabric, springs and thicknesses." In the end, he laid down $3,200 to buy a memory-foam mattress that he realized he didn't find comfortable once he started using it. Marino concluded, "It was a terrible experience."

This experience led Marino and a college buddy, Daehee Park, on the path to launching a low-cost mattress manufacturer. They researched the industry, discussed mattress manufacturing with component suppliers, and dissected mattresses they bought. What they realized was that the expensive mattress Marino purchased cost only about $300 to manufacture, including materials and labor. Considering all of the markups across the supply chain, they realized big-brand mattresses are priced up to 1,000 percent of their actual cost.

Their response was to build a cheaper mattress. Their company, Tuft and Needle, sells mattresses through its own website and on Amazon for a fraction of the cost of a brand-name mattress at a furniture store. Tuft and Needle reduces cost by removing the retailer and salespeople's commissions, having a limited marketing campaign, offering a narrow range of models built with standardized components, and cutting back on some of the plush extras on store mattresses that do little to add to the comfort or durability of the mattress. The company also sucks all of the air out of the foam in a mattress and vacuum seal it so that it can be shipped cheaply in small boxes. Its mattresses are priced from $200 to $600, less than one-third of the price of a typical foam mattress at retailers.

So far, the company is having great success. Launched in 2012, Tuft and Needle surpassed $1 million in sales in 2013 and was expected to gross $5 million in sales in 2014. Customers also seem to appreciate both the service Tuft and Needle provides and the quality of its products. Its mattresses are the top-rated mattresses on Amazon. What is left to be seen is when and how the major players in the industry will respond to Tuft and Needle.

Sources: Helft, M. 2014. Meet the Warby Parker of mattresses. *cnnmoney.com*, January 22: np; and Daley, J. 2014. How Tuft & Needle disrupted a tired mattress marketplace. *entrepreneur.com*, October 20: np.

Differentiation　Both pioneering and adaptive entry strategies involve some degree of differentiation. That is, the new entry is based on being able to offer a differentiated value proposition. In the case of pioneers, the new venture is attempting to do something strikingly different, either by using a new technology or by deploying resources in a way that radically alters the way business is conducted. Often, entrepreneurs do both.

Amazon founder Jeff Bezos set out to use Internet technology to revolutionize the way books are sold. He garnered the ire of other booksellers and the attention of the public by making bold claims about being the "earth's largest bookseller." As a bookseller, Bezos was not doing anything that had not been done before. But two key differentiating features—doing it on the Internet and offering extraordinary customer service—made Amazon a differentiated success.

There are several factors that make it more difficult for new ventures to be successful as differentiators. For one thing, the strategy is generally thought to be expensive to enact. Differentiation is often associated with strong brand identity, and establishing a brand is usually considered to be expensive because of the cost of advertising and promotion, paid endorsements, exceptional customer service, and so on. Differentiation successes are sometimes built on superior innovation or use of technology. These are also factors that might make it challenging for young firms to excel relative to established competitors.

Nevertheless, all of these areas—innovation, technology, customer service, distinctive branding—are also arenas where new ventures have sometimes made a name for themselves even though they must operate with limited resources and experience. To be successful, according to Garry Ridge, CEO of the WD-40 Company, "You need to have a great product, make the end user aware of it, and make it easy to buy."[45] It sounds simple, but it is a difficult challenge for new ventures with differentiation strategies.

Focus　Focus strategies are often associated with small businesses because there is a natural fit between the narrow scope of the strategy and the small size of the firm. A focus strategy may include elements of differentiation and overall cost leadership, as well as combinations of these approaches. But to be successful within a market niche, the key strategic requirement is to stay focused. Let's consider why that is so.

Despite all the attention given to fast-growing new industries, most start-ups enter industries that are mature.[46] In mature industries, growth in demand tends to be slow and there are often many competitors. Therefore, if a start-up wants to get a piece of the action, it often has to take business away from an existing competitor. If a start-up enters a market with a broad or aggressive strategy, it is likely to evoke retaliation from a more powerful competitor. Young firms can often succeed best by finding a market niche where they can get a foothold and make small advances that erode the position of existing competitors.[47] From this position, they can build a name for themselves and grow.

Consider, for example, the "Miniature Editions" line of books launched by Running Press, a small Philadelphia publisher. The books are palm-size minibooks positioned at bookstore cash registers as point-of-sale impulse items costing about $4.95. Beginning with just 10 titles in 1993, Running Press grew rapidly and within 10 years had sold over 20 million copies. Even though these books represent just a tiny fraction of total sales in the $23 billion publishing industry, they have been a mainstay for Running Press.[48] As the Running Press example indicates, many new ventures are successful even though their share of the market is quite small.

Combination Strategies

One of the best ways for young and small businesses to achieve success is by pursuing combination strategies. By combining the best features of low-cost, differentiation, and focus strategies, new ventures can often achieve something truly distinctive.

Entrepreneurial firms are often in a strong position to offer a combination strategy because they have the flexibility to approach situations uniquely. For example, holding down expenses can be difficult for big firms because each layer of bureaucracy adds to the cost of doing business across the boundaries of a large organization.[49]

A similar argument could be made about entrepreneurial firms that differentiate. Large firms often find it difficult to offer highly specialized products or superior customer services. Entrepreneurial firms, by contrast, can often create high-value products and services through their unique differentiating efforts.

For nearly all new entrants, one of the major dangers is that a large firm with more resources will copy what they are doing. Well-established incumbents that observe the success of a new entrant's product or service will copy it and use their market power to overwhelm the smaller firm. The threat may be lessened for firms that use combination strategies. Because of the flexibility of entrepreneurial firms, they can often enact combination strategies in ways that the large firms cannot copy. This makes the new entrant's strategies much more sustainable.

Perhaps more threatening than large competitors are close competitors, because they have similar structural features that help them adjust quickly and be flexible in decision making. Here again, a carefully crafted and executed combination strategy may be the best way for an entrepreneurial firm to thrive in a competitive environment. Nevertheless, competition among rivals is a key determinant of new venture success. To address this, we turn next to the topic of competitive dynamics.

Competitive Dynamics

New entry into markets, whether by start-ups or by incumbent firms, nearly always threatens existing competitors. This is true in part because, except in very new markets, nearly every market need is already being met, either directly or indirectly, by existing firms. As a result, the competitive actions of a new entrant are very likely to provoke a competitive response from companies that feel threatened. This, in turn, is likely to evoke a reaction to

LO8.4

How competitive actions, such as the entry of new competitors into a marketplace, may launch a cycle of actions and reactions among close competitors.

the response. As a result, a competitive dynamic—action and response—begins among the firms competing for the same customers in a given marketplace.

Competitive dynamics—intense rivalry among similar competitors—has the potential to alter a company's strategy. New entrants may be forced to change their strategies or develop new ones to survive competitive challenges by incumbent rivals. New entry is among the most common reasons why a cycle of competitive actions and reactions gets started. It might also occur because of threatening actions among existing competitors, such as aggressive cost cutting. Thus, studying competitive dynamics helps explain why strategies evolve and reveals how, why, and when to respond to the actions of close competitors. Exhibit 8.4 identifies the factors that competitors need to consider when determining how to respond to a competitive act.

New Competitive Action

Entry into a market by a new competitor is a good starting point to begin describing the cycle of actions and responses characteristic of a competitive dynamic process.[50] However, new entry is only one type of competitive action. Price cutting, imitating successful products, and expanding production capacity are other examples of competitive acts that might provoke competitors to react.

Why do companies launch new competitive actions? There are several reasons:

- Improve market position
- Capitalize on growing demand
- Expand production capacity
- Provide an innovative new solution
- Obtain first-mover advantages

Underlying all of these reasons is a desire to strengthen financial outcomes, capture some of the extraordinary profits that industry leaders enjoy, and grow the business. Some companies are also motivated to launch competitive challenges because they want to build their reputation for innovativeness or efficiency. For example, Toyota's success with the Prius signaled to its competitors the potential value of high-fuel-economy cars, and these firms have responded with their own hybrids, electric cars, high-efficiency diesel engines, and even more fuel-efficient traditional gasoline engines. This is indicative of the competitive dynamic cycle. As former Intel chairman Andy Grove stated, "Business success contains the seeds of its own destruction. The more successful you are, the more people want a chunk of your business and then another chunk and then another until there is nothing left."[51]

competitive dynamics

intense rivalry, involving actions and responses, among similar competitors vying for the same customers in a marketplace.

LO8.5

The components of competitive dynamic analysis—new competitive action, threat analysis, motivation and capability to respond, types of competitive actions, and likelihood of competitive reaction.

new competitive action

acts that might provoke competitors to react, such as new market entry, price cutting, imitating successful products, and expanding production capacity.

EXHIBIT 8.4 Model of Competitive Dynamics

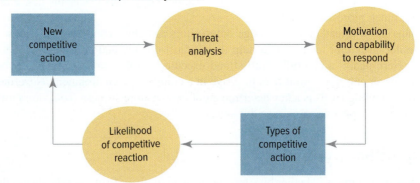

Sources: Adapted from Chen, M. J. 1996. Competitor Analysis and Interfirm Rivalry: Toward a Theoretical Integration. *Academy of Management Review,* 21(1): 100–134; Ketchen, D. J., Snow, C. C., & Hoover, V. L. 2004. Research on Competitive Dynamics: Recent Accomplishments and Future Challenges. *Journal of Management,* 30(6): 779–804; and Smith, K. G., Ferrier, W. J., & Grimm, C. M. 2001. King of the Hill: Dethroning the Industry Leader. *Academy of Management Executive,* 15(2): 59–70.

When a company enters into a market for the first time, it is an attack on existing competitors. As indicated earlier in the chapter, any of the entry strategies can be used to take competitive action. But competitive attacks come from many sources besides new entrants. Some of the most intense competition is among incumbent rivals intent on gaining strategic advantages. "Winners in business play rough and don't apologize for it," according to Boston Consulting Group authors George Stalk, Jr., and Rob Lachenauer in their book *Hardball: Are You Playing to Play or Playing to Win?*[52] Exhibit 8.5 outlines their five strategies.

The likelihood that a competitor will launch an attack depends on many factors.[53] In the remaining sections, we discuss factors such as competitor analysis, market conditions, types of strategic actions, and the resource endowments and capabilities companies need to take competitive action.

EXHIBIT 8.5 Five "Hardball" Strategies

Strategy	Description	Examples
Devastate rivals' profit sanctuaries	Not all business segments generate the same level of profits for a company. Through focused attacks on a rival's most profitable segments, a company can generate maximum leverage with relatively smaller-scale attacks. Recognize, however, that companies closely guard the information needed to determine just what their profit sanctuaries are.	In 2005, Walmart began offering low-priced extended warranties on home electronics after learning that its rivals such as Best Buy derived most of their profits from extended warranties.
Plagiarize with pride	Just because a close competitor comes up with an idea first does not mean it cannot be successfully imitated. Second movers, in fact, can see how customers respond, make improvements, and launch a better version without all the market development costs. Successful imitation is harder than it may appear and requires the imitating firm to keep its ego in check.	In designing its smartphones, Samsung copied the look, feel, and technological attributes of Apple's IPhone. Samsung lost a patent infringement lawsuit to Apple, but by copying Apple, Samsung was able to improve its market position.
Deceive the competition	A good gambit sends the competition off in the wrong direction. This may cause the rivals to miss strategic shifts, spend money pursuing dead ends, or slow their responses. Any of these outcomes support the deceiving firms' competitive advantage. Companies must be sure not to cross ethical lines during these actions.	Max Muir knew that Australian farmers liked to buy from family-firm suppliers but also wanted efficient suppliers. To meet both needs, he quietly bought a number of small firms to build economies of scale but didn't consolidate brands or his sales force so that, to his customers and rivals, they still looked like independent family firms.
Unleash massive and overwhelming force	While many hardball strategies are subtle and indirect, this one is not. This is a full-frontal attack where by a firm commits significant resources to a major campaign to weaken rivals' positions in certain markets. Firms must be sure they have the mass and stamina required to win before they declare war against a rival.	Unilever has taken a dominant position, with 65 percent market share, in the Vietnamese laundry detergent market by employing a massive investment and marketing campaign. In doing so, it decimated the market position of the local, incumbent competitors.
Raise competitors' costs	If a company has superior insight into the complex cost and profit structure of the industry, it can compete in a way that steers its rivals into relatively higher cost/lower profit arenas. This strategy uses deception to make the rivals think they are winning, when in fact they are not. Again, companies using this strategy must be confident that they understand the industry better than their rivals.	Ecolab, a company that sells cleaning supplies to businesses, encouraged a leading competitor, Diversity, to adopt a strategy to go after the low-volume, high-margin customers. What Ecolab knew that Diversity didn't is that the high servicing costs involved with this segment make the segment unprofitable—a situation Ecolab ensured by bidding high enough to lose the contracts to Diversity but low enough to ensure the business lost money for Diversity.

Sources: Berner, R. 2005. Watch Out, Best Buy and Circuit City. *BusinessWeek,* November 10; Stalk, G., Jr. 2006. Curveball Strategies to Fool the Competition. *Harvard Business Review,* 84(9): 114–121; and Stalk, G., Jr., & Lachenauer, R. 2004. *Hardball: Are You Playing to Play or Playing to Win?* Cambridge, MA: Harvard Business School Press. Reprinted by permission of Harvard Business School Press from G. Stalk, Jr., and R. Lachenauer. Copyright 2004 by the Harvard Business School Publishing Corporation; all rights reserved; Lam, Y. 2013. FDI Companies Dominate Vietnam's Detergent Market. *www.saigon-gpdaily.com.vn,* January 22: np; Vascellaro, J. 2012. Apple Wins Big in Patent Case. *www.wsj.com,* August 25: np; and Pech, R. & Stamboulidis, G. 2010. How Strategies of Deception Facilitate Business Growth. *Journal of Business Strategy,* 31(6): 37–45.

Threat Analysis

Prior to actually observing a competitive action, companies may need to become aware of potential competitive threats. That is, companies need to have a keen sense of who their closest competitors are and the kinds of competitive actions they might be planning.[54] This may require some environmental scanning and monitoring of the sort described in Chapter 2. Awareness of the threats posed by industry rivals allows a firm to understand what type of competitive response, if any, may be necessary.

Being aware of competitors and cognizant of whatever threats they might pose is the first step in assessing the level of competitive threat. Once a new competitive action becomes apparent, companies must determine how threatening it is to their business. Competitive dynamics are likely to be most intense among companies that are competing for the same customers or that have highly similar sets of resources.[55] Two factors are used to assess whether or not companies are close competitors:

- *Market commonality.* Whether or not competitors are vying for the same customers and how many markets they share in common. For example, aircraft manufacturers Boeing and Airbus have a high degree of market commonality because they make very similar products and have many buyers in common.

- *Resource similarity.* The degree to which rivals draw on the same types of resources to compete. For example, the home pages of Google and Yahoo! may look very different, but behind the scenes, they both rely on the talent pool of high-caliber software engineers to create the cutting-edge innovations that help them compete.

When any two firms have both a high degree of market commonality and highly similar resource bases, a stronger competitive threat is present. Such a threat, however, may not lead to competitive action. On the one hand, a market rival may be hesitant to attack a company that it shares a high degree of market commonality with because it could lead to an intense battle. On the other hand, once attacked, rivals with high market commonality will be much more motivated to launch a competitive response. This is especially true in cases where the shared market is an important part of a company's overall business.

How strong a response an attacked rival can mount will be determined by its strategic resource endowments. In general, the same set of conditions holds true with regard to resource similarity. Companies that have highly similar resource bases will be hesitant to launch an initial attack but pose a serious threat if required to mount a competitive response.[56] Greater strategic resources increase a firm's capability to respond.

Motivation and Capability to Respond

Once attacked, competitors are faced with deciding how to respond. Before deciding, however, they need to evaluate not only how they will respond but also their reasons for responding and their capability to respond. Companies need to be clear about what problems a competitive response is expected to address and what types of problems it might create.[57] There are several factors to consider.

First, how serious is the impact of the competitive attack to which they are responding? For example, a large company with a strong reputation that is challenged by a small or unknown company may elect to simply keep an eye on the new competitor rather than quickly react or overreact. Part of the story of online retailer Amazon's early success is attributed to Barnes & Noble's overreaction to Amazon's claim that it was "earth's biggest bookstore." Because Barnes & Noble was already using the phrase "world's largest bookstore," it sued Amazon, but lost. The confrontation made it to the front pages of *The Wall Street Journal,* and Amazon was on its way to becoming a household name.[58]

Companies planning to respond to a competitive challenge must also understand their motivation for responding. What is the intent of the competitive response? Is it merely to blunt the attack of the competitor, or is it an opportunity to enhance its competitive position? Sometimes the most a company can hope for is to minimize the damage caused by a competitive action.

A company that seeks to improve its competitive advantage may be motivated to launch an attack rather than merely respond to one. For example, a few years ago, the *Wall Street Journal (WSJ)* attacked the *New York Times* by adding a local news section to the New York edition of the *WSJ*. Its aim was to become a more direct competitor of the *Times*. The publishers of the *WSJ* undertook this attack when they realized the *Times* was in a weakened financial condition and would be unable to respond to the attack.[59] A company must also assess its capability to respond. What strategic resources can be deployed to fend off a competitive attack? Does the company have an array of internal strengths it can draw on, or is it operating from a position of weakness?

Consider the role of firm age and size in calculating a company's ability to respond. Most entrepreneurial new ventures start out small. The smaller size makes them more nimble compared to large firms so they can respond quickly to competitive attacks. Because they are not well-known, start-ups also have the advantage of the element of surprise in how and when they attack. Innovative uses of technology, for example, allow small firms to deploy resources in unique ways.

Because they are young, however, start-ups may not have the financial resources needed to follow through with a competitive response.[60] In contrast, older and larger firms may have more resources and a repertoire of competitive techniques they can use in a counterattack. Large firms, however, tend to be slower to respond. Older firms tend to be predictable in their responses because they often lose touch with the competitive environment and rely on strategies and actions that have worked in the past.

Other resources may also play a role in whether a company is equipped to retaliate. For example, one avenue of counterattack may be launching product enhancements or new product/service innovations. For that approach to be successful, it requires a company to have both the intellectual capital to put forward viable innovations and the teamwork skills to prepare a new product or service and get it to market. Resources such as cross-functional teams and the social capital that makes teamwork production effective and efficient represent the type of human capital resources that enhance a company's capability to respond.

Types of Competitive Actions

Once an organization determines whether it is willing and able to launch a competitive action, it must determine what type of action is appropriate. The actions taken will be determined by both its resource capabilities and its motivation for responding. There are also marketplace considerations. What types of actions are likely to be most effective given a company's internal strengths and weaknesses as well as market conditions?

Two broadly defined types of competitive action include strategic actions and tactical actions. **Strategic actions** represent major commitments of distinctive and specific resources. Examples include launching a breakthrough innovation, building a new production facility, or merging with another company. Such actions require significant planning and resources and, once initiated, are difficult to reverse.

Tactical actions include refinements or extensions of strategies. Examples of tactical actions include cutting prices, improving gaps in service, or strengthening marketing efforts. Such actions typically draw on general resources and can be implemented quickly. Exhibit 8.6 identifies several types of strategic and tactical competitive actions that illustrate the range of actions that can occur in a rivalrous relationship.

Some competitive actions take the form of frontal assaults, that is, actions aimed directly at taking business from another company or capitalizing on industry weaknesses. This can be especially effective when firms use a low-cost strategy. The airline industry provides a good example of this head-on approach. When Southwest Airlines began its no-frills, no-meals strategy in the late-1960s, it represented a direct assault on the major carriers of the

strategic actions
major commitments of distinctive and specific resources to strategic initiatives.

tactical actions
refinements or extensions of strategies usually involving minor resource commitments.

EXHIBIT 8.6 Strategic and Tactical Competitive Actions

	Actions	Examples
Strategic Actions	• Entering new markets	• Make geographical expansions • Expand into neglected markets • Target rivals' markets • Target new demographics
	• New product introductions	• Imitate rivals' products • Address gaps in quality • Leverage new technologies • Leverage brand name with related products • Protect innovation with patents
	• Changing production capacity	• Create overcapacity • Tie up raw materials sources • Tie up preferred suppliers and distributors • Stimulate demand by limiting capacity
	• Mergers/Alliances	• Acquire/partner with competitors to reduce competition • Tie up key suppliers through alliances • Obtain new technology/intellectual property • Facilitate new market entry
Tactical Actions	• Price cutting (or increases)	• Maintain low-price dominance • Offer discounts and rebates • Offer incentives (e.g., frequent flyer miles) • Enhance offering to move upscale
	• Product/service enhancements	• Address gaps in service • Expand warranties • Make incremetal product improvements
	• Increased marketing efforts	• Use guerilla marketing • Conduct selective attacks • Change product packaging • Use new marketing channels
	• New distribution channels	• Access suppliers directly • Access customers directly • Develop multiple points of contact with customers • Expand Internet presence

Sources: Chen, M. J. & Hambrick, D. 1995. Speed, Stealth, and Selective Attack: How Small Firms Differ from Large Firms in Competitive Behavior. *Academy of Management Journal,* 38: 453–482; Davies, M. 1992. Sales Promotions as a Competitive Strategy. *Management Decision,* 30(7): 5–10; Ferrier, W., Smith, K., & Grimm, C. 1999. The Role of Competitive Action in Market Share Erosion and Industry Dethronement: A Study of Industry Leaders and Challengers. *Academy of Management Journal,* 42(4): 372–388; and Garda, R. A. 1991. Use Tactical Pricing to Uncover Hidden Profits. *Journal of Business Strategy,* 12(5): 17–23.

day. In Europe, Ryanair has similarly directly challenged the traditional carriers with an overall cost leadership strategy.

Guerilla offensives and selective attacks provide an alternative for firms with fewer resources.[61] These draw attention to products or services by creating buzz or generating enough shock value to get some free publicity. TOMS Shoes has found a way to generate interest in its products without a large advertising budget to match Nike. Its policy of donating one pair of shoes to those in need for every pair of shoes purchased by customers has generated a lot of buzz on the Internet.[62] Over 3 million people have given a "like" rating on TOMS's Facebook page. The policy has a real impact as well, with over 35 million shoes donated as of January 2015.[63]

Some companies limit their competitive response to defensive actions. Such actions rarely improve a company's competitive advantage, but a credible defensive action can lower the risk of being attacked and deter new entry.

Several of the factors discussed earlier in the chapter, such as types of entry strategies and the use of cost leadership versus differentiation strategies, can guide the decision about what types of competitive actions to take. Before launching a given strategy, however, assessing the likely response of competitors is a vital step.[64]

Likelihood of Competitive Reaction

The final step before initiating a competitive response is to evaluate what a competitor's reaction is likely to be. The logic of competitive dynamics suggests that once competitive actions are initiated, it is likely they will be met with competitive responses.[65] The last step before mounting an attack is to evaluate how competitors are likely to respond. Evaluating potential competitive reactions helps companies plan for future counterattacks. It may also lead to a decision to hold off—that is, not to take any competitive action at all because of the possibility that a misguided or poorly planned response will generate a devastating competitive reaction.

How a competitor is likely to respond will depend on three factors: market dependence, competitor's resources, and the reputation of the firm that initiates the action (actor's reputation). The implications of each of these are described briefly in the following sections.

Market Dependence   If a company has a high concentration of its business in a particular industry, it has more at stake because it must depend on that industry's market for its sales. Single-industry businesses or those where one industry dominates are more likely to mount a competitive response. Young and small firms with a high degree of **market dependence** may be limited in how they respond due to resource constraints.

market dependence
degree of concentration of a firm's business in a particular industry.

Competitor's Resources   Previously, we examined the internal resource endowments that a company must evaluate when assessing its capability to respond. Here, it is the competitor's resources that need to be considered. For example, a small firm may be unable to mount a serious attack due to lack of resources. As a result, it is more likely to react to tactical actions such as incentive pricing or enhanced service offerings because they are less costly to attack than large-scale strategic actions. In contrast, a firm with financial "deep pockets" may be able to mount and sustain a costly counterattack.

Actor's Reputation   Whether a company should respond to a competitive challenge will also depend on who launched the attack against it. Compared to relatively smaller firms with less market power, competitors are more likely to respond to competitive moves by market leaders. Another consideration is how successful prior attacks have been. For example, price cutting by the big automakers usually has the desired result—increased sales to price-sensitive buyers—at least in the short run. Given that history, when GM offers discounts or incentives, rivals Ford and Chrysler cannot afford to ignore the challenge and quickly follow suit.

Choosing Not to React: Forbearance and Co-opetition

The above discussion suggests that there may be many circumstances in which the best reaction is no reaction at all. This is known as **forbearance**—refraining from reacting at

forbearance
a firm's choice of not reacting to a rival's new competitive action.

CLEANING UP IN THE SOAP BUSINESS

Consumer product companies Colgate-Palmolive, Unilever, Procter & Gamble (P&G), and Henkel compete with each other globally in the soap business. But as regulators found after a long investigation, this wasn't true in France. The firms in this market had colluded to fix prices for nearly a decade. In the words of a Henkel executive, the detergent makers wanted "to limit the intensity of competition between them and clean up the market." The Autorité de la Concurrance, the French antitrust watchdog, hit these four firms with fines totaling $484 million after completing its investigation.

The firms started sharing pricing information in the 1980s, but by the 1990s their cooperation got bolder, morphing into behavior that sounds like something out of a spy novel. In 1996, four brand directors secretly met in a restaurant in a suburb of Paris and agreed to coordinate the pricing of their soap products. They agreed to prearranged prices at which they would sell to retailers and agreed to notify each other of any planned special offers. They gave each firm a secret alias: Pierre for Procter &

Gamble, Laurence for Unilever, Hugues for Henkel, and Christian for Colgate-Palmolive. From that point forward, they allegedly scheduled clandestine meetings four times a year. The meetings, which they called "store checks" in their schedules to limit any questioning they may have received, often lasted an entire afternoon. They would set complex pricing schemes. For example, P&G sold its Ariel brand as an upscale product and coordinated with Unilever to keep Ariel at a 3 percent markup over Unilever's Skip brand. At these meetings, they would also hash out any complaints about whether and how any of the participants had been bending the rules.

The collusion lasted for almost 10 years until it broke down in 2004. Unilever was the first to defect, offering a 10 percent "D-Day" price cut without negotiating it with the three other firms. Other competitors quickly responded with actions that violated the pricing norms they had set.

Sources: Colchester, M. & Passariello, C. 2011. Dirty secrets in soap prices. *wsj .com*, December 9: np; and Smith, H. & White, A. 2011. P&G, Colgate fined by France in $484 million detergent cartel. *Bloomberg.com*, December 11: np.

all as well as holding back from initiating an attack. The decision of whether a firm should respond or show forbearance is not always clear.

co-opetition
a firm's strategy of both cooperating and competing with rival firms.

Related to forbearance is the concept of **co-opetition.** This is a term that was coined by network software company Novell's founder and former CEO Raymond Noorda to suggest that companies often benefit most from a combination of competing and cooperating.[66] Close competitors that differentiate themselves in the eyes of consumers may work together behind the scenes to achieve industrywide efficiencies.[67] For example, breweries in Sweden cooperate in recycling used bottles but still compete for customers on the basis of taste and variety. Similarly, several competing Hollywood studios came together and agreed to cooperate on buying movie film. They negotiated promises to buy certain quantities of film to keep Kodak from closing down its film manufacturing business.[68] As long as the benefits of cooperating are enjoyed by all participants in a co-opetition system, the practice can aid companies in avoiding intense and damaging competition.[69]

Despite the potential benefits of co-opetition, companies need to guard against cooperating to such a great extent that their actions are perceived as collusion, a practice that has legal ramifications in the United States. In Strategy Spotlight 8.6, we see an example of crossing the line into illegal cooperation.

Once a company has evaluated a competitor's likelihood of responding to a competitive challenge, it can decide what type of action is most appropriate. Competitive actions can take many forms: the entry of a start-up into a market for the first time, an attack by a lower-ranked incumbent on an industry leader, or the launch of a breakthrough innovation that disrupts the industry structure. Such actions forever change the competitive dynamics of a marketplace. Thus, the cycle of actions and reactions that occur in business every day is a vital aspect of entrepreneurial strategy that leads to continual new value creation and the ongoing advancement of economic well-being.

Where Have the Entrepreneurs Gone?

The United States has long been seen as the home of a vibrant entrepreneurial economy, but the statistics call this into question. From 1977 to 2011, the number of new start-up firms in the U.S. declined by 28 percent. More dramatically, relative to the size of the working population, the number of new start-ups has fallen by half. Even Silicon Valley has seen the rate of new business start-ups decline by 50 percent over the last three decades. Entrepreneurial actions have fallen most sharply among younger adults. People age 20 to 34 created only 22.7 percent of all new companies in 2013, down from 34.8 percent in 1996. This is an ironic change given that enrollment in college entrepreneurship programs has been growing.

This declining rate of entrepreneurship is setting off warning bells for many. It leads to less innovation in the economy and slower job opportunity growth. Over the long run, it would lead to lower living standards and stagnant economic growth.

Concerns on this issue have led to a discussion of the underlying causes of this change. The causes of this decline may be emotional or institutional. On the emotional level, it may be that the aftereffects of the Great Recession have tilted society toward risk aversion. Additionally, many would-be entrepreneurs are saddled with significant student loan debt, leaving them less willing to take on the risk of entrepreneurship. Consistent with this view, Audrey Baxter, a woman who won a business proposal award as a student at UCLA, opted to take a corporate job when she graduated rather than pushing her small business forward. "Having a secure job with a really good salary was something to be considered carefully," Baxter said.

It may also be that institutional factors are reducing people's willingness or ability to start a business. Weakened antitrust enforcement may be playing a role. Firms have been able to grow and combine in a range of markets, leading to extremely large competitors that dominate markets, increasing the entry barriers for entrepreneurs. Also, lax antitrust enforcement has made it easier for large incumbent firms to respond very aggressively to newcomers, increasing the risk for entrepreneurs. Government red tape is another institutional barrier to entrepreneurs. For example, Celeste Kelly opened a business offering horse massage but had to shut down the business when the Arizona State Veterinary Medical Examining Board ordered her to "cease and desist" because it ruled she was practicing veterinary medicine without a license—even though no veterinarians in the area offered horse massage as a treatment. This may seem like an obscure example, but many businesses, including barbers, bartenders, cosmetologists, and even tour guides, are required to obtain licenses. Less than 5 percent of workers required licenses in the 1950s. That number is now 35 percent. According to economists Morris Kleiner and Alan Krueger, licenses increase the wage costs for a business by 18 percent.

Discussion Questions

1. How concerned are you about the drop in the rate of entrepreneurship?
2. What do you think are the primary causes of the decline?
3. What actions should be taken to increase the rate of new business start-ups? How effective will these actions be?
4. What factors influence your desire to work in an entrepreneurial firm versus an established firm?

Sources: Hamilton, W. 2014. A drop-off in start-ups: Where are all the entrepreneurs? *latimes.com*, September 7: np; Anonymous. 2014. Red tape blues: The best and worst states for small business. *The Economist*, July 5: 23–24; and Anonymous. 2014. Unshackle the entrepreneurs; America's license raj. *The Economist*, July 5: 14.

Reflecting on Career Implications . . .

- **Opportunity Recognition:** What ideas for new business activities are actively discussed in your work environment? Could you apply the four characteristics of an opportunity to determine whether they are viable opportunities? If no one in your organization is excited about or even considering new opportunities, you may want to ask yourself if you want to continue with your current firm.

- **Entrepreneurial New Entry:** Are there opportunities to launch new products or services that might add value to the organization? What are the best ways for you to bring these opportunities to the attention of key managers? Or might this provide an opportunity for you to launch your own entrepreneurial venture?

- **Entrepreneurial Resources:** Evaluate your resources in terms of financial resources, human capital, and social capital. Are these enough to launch your own venture? If you are deficient in one area, are there ways to compensate for it? Even if you are not interested in starting a new venture, can you use your entrepreneurial resources to advance your career within your firm?

- **Competitive Dynamics:** There is always internal competition within organizations: among business units and sometimes even individuals within the same unit. What types of strategic and tactical actions are employed in these internal rivalries? What steps have you taken to strengthen your own position given the "competitive dynamics" within your organization?

summary

New ventures and entrepreneurial firms that capitalize on marketplace opportunities make an important contribution to the U.S. economy. They are leaders in terms of implementing new technologies and introducing innovative products and services. Yet entrepreneurial firms face unique challenges if they are going to survive and grow.

To successfully launch new ventures or implement new technologies, three factors must be present: an entrepreneurial opportunity, the resources to pursue the opportunity, and an entrepreneur or entrepreneurial team willing and able to undertake the venture. Firms must develop a strong ability to recognize viable opportunities. Opportunity recognition is a process of determining which venture ideas are, in fact, promising business opportunities.

In addition to strong opportunities, entrepreneurial firms need resources and entrepreneurial leadership to thrive. The resources that start-ups need include financial resources as well as human and social capital. Many firms also benefit from government programs that support new venture development and growth. New ventures thrive best when they are led by founders or owners who have vision, drive and dedication, and a commitment to excellence.

Once the necessary opportunities, resources, and entrepreneur skills are in place, new ventures still face numerous strategic challenges. Decisions about the strategic positioning of new entrants can benefit from conducting strategic analyses and evaluating the requirements of niche markets. Entry strategies used by new ventures take several forms, including pioneering new entry, imitative new entry, and adaptive new entry. Entrepreneurial firms can benefit from using overall low cost, differentiation, and focus strategies although each of these approaches has pitfalls that are unique to young and small firms. Entrepreneurial firms are also in a strong position to benefit from combination strategies.

The entry of a new company into a competitive arena is like a competitive attack on incumbents in that arena. Such actions often provoke a competitive response, which may, in turn, trigger a reaction to the response. As a result, a competitive dynamic—action and response—begins among close competitors. In deciding whether to attack or counterattack, companies must analyze the seriousness of the competitive threat, their ability to mount a competitive response, and the type of action—strategic or tactical—that the situation requires. At times, competitors find it is better not to respond at all or to find avenues to cooperate with, rather than challenge, close competitors.

SUMMARY REVIEW QUESTIONS

1. Explain how the combination of opportunities, resources, and entrepreneurs helps determine the character and strategic direction of an entrepreneurial firm.

2. What is the difference between discovery and evaluation in the process of opportunity recognition? Give an example of each.

3. Describe the three characteristics of entrepreneurial leadership: vision, dedication and drive, and commitment to excellence.

4. Briefly describe the three types of entrepreneurial entry strategies: pioneering, imitative, and adaptive.

5. Explain why entrepreneurial firms are often in a strong position to use combination strategies.

6. What does the term *competitive dynamics* mean?

7. Explain the difference between strategic actions and tactical actions and provide examples of each.

application questions & exercises

1. E-Loan and Lending Tree are two entrepreneurial firms that offer lending services over the Internet. Evaluate the features of these two companies. (Fill in the table below.)

   a. Evaluate their characteristics and assess the extent to which they are comparable in terms of market commonality and resource similarity.

   b. Based on your analysis, what strategic and/or tactical actions might these companies take to improve their competitive position? Could E-Loan and Lending Tree improve their performance more through co-opetition than competition? Explain your rationale.

2. Using the Internet, research the Small Business Administration's website (*www.sba.gov*). What different types of financing are available to small firms? Besides financing, what other programs are available to support the growth and development of small businesses?

3. Think of an entrepreneurial firm that has been successfully launched in the last 10 years. What kind of entry strategy did it use—pioneering, imitative, or adaptive? Since the firm's initial entry, how has it used or combined overall low-cost, differentiation, and/or focus strategies?

4. Select an entrepreneurial firm you are familiar with in your local community. Research the company and discuss how it has positioned itself relative to its close competitors. Does it have a unique strategic advantage? Disadvantage? Explain.

ethics questions

1. Imitation strategies are based on the idea of copying another firm's idea and using it for your own purposes. Is this unethical or simply a smart business practice? Discuss the ethical implications of this practice (if any).

2. Intense competition such as price wars are an accepted practice in the United States, but cooperation between companies has legal ramifications because of antitrust laws. Should price wars that drive small businesses or new entrants out of business be illegal? What ethical considerations are raised (if any)?

Company	Market Commonality	Resource Similarity
E-Loan		
Lending Tree		

Company	Strategic Actions	Tactical Actions
E-Loan		
Lending Tree		

references

1. Pepitone, J. 2012. Digg sold to Betaworks for pocket change. *cnnmoney.com,* July 12: np.

2. Ante, S. & Walker, J. 2012. Digg admits missteps. *wsj.com,* July 16: np.

3. *http://web.sba.gov.*

4. Timmons, J. A. & Spinelli, S. 2004. *New venture creation* (6th ed.). New York: McGraw-Hill/Irwin; and Bygrave, W. D. 1997. The entrepreneurial process. In W. D. Bygrave (Ed.), *The portable MBA in entrepreneurship* (2nd ed.). New York: Wiley.

5. Bryant, A. 2012. Want to innovate? Feed a cookie to the monster. *nytimes.com,* March 24: np.

6. Fromartz, S. 1998. How to get your first great idea. *Inc. Magazine,* April 1: 91–94; and Vesper, K. H. 1990. *New venture strategies* (2nd ed.). Englewood Cliffs, NJ: Prentice Hall.

7. For an interesting perspective on the nature of the opportunity recognition process, see Baron, R. A. 2006. Opportunity recognition as pattern recognition: How entrepreneurs "connect the dots" to identify new business opportunities. *Academy of*

Management Perspectives, February: 104–119.

8. Gaglio, C. M. 1997. Opportunity identification: Review, critique and suggested research directions. In Katz, J. A. (Ed.), *Advances in entrepreneurship, firm emergence and growth,* vol. 3. Greenwich, CT: JAI Press: 139–202; Lumpkin, G. T., Hills, G. E., & Shrader, R. C. 2004. Opportunity recognition. In Welsch, H. L. (Ed.), *Entrepreneurship: The road ahead:* 73–90. London: Routledge; and Long, W. & McMullan, W. E. 1984. Mapping the new venture opportunity identification process. *Frontiers of entrepreneurship research, 1984:* 567–590. Wellesley, MA: Babson College.

9. For an interesting discussion of different aspects of opportunity discovery, see Shepherd, D. A. & De Tienne, D. R. 2005. Prior knowledge, potential financial reward, and opportunity identification. *Entrepreneurship Theory & Practice,* 29(1): 91–112; and Gaglio, C. M. 2004. The role of mental simulations and counterfactual thinking in the opportunity identification process. *Entrepreneurship Theory & Practice,* 28(6): 533–552.

10. Stewart, T. A. 2002. How to think with your gut. *Business 2.0,* November: 99–104.

11. Anonymous. 2013. How entrepreneurs come up with great ideas. *wsj.com,* April 29: np.

12. For more on the opportunity recognition process, see Smith, B. R., Matthews, C. H., & Schenkel, M. T. 2009. Differences in entrepreneurial opportunities: The role of tacitness and codification in opportunity identification. *Journal of Small Business Management,* 47(1): 38–57.

13. Timmons, J. A. 1997. Opportunity recognition. In Bygrave, W. D. (Ed.), *The portable MBA in entrepreneurship* (2nd ed.): 26–54. New York: Wiley.

14. Social networking is also proving to be an increasingly important type of entrepreneurial resource. For an interesting discussion, see Aldrich, H. E. & Kim, P. H. 2007. Small worlds, infinite possibilities? How social networks affect entrepreneurial team formation and search. *Strategic Entrepreneurship Journal,* 1(1): 147–166.

15. Bhide, A. V. 2000. *The origin and evolution of new businesses.* New York: Oxford University Press.

16. Small business 2001: Where are we now? 2001. *Inc.,* May 29: 18–19; and

Zacharakis, A. L., Bygrave, W. D., & Shepherd, D. A. 2000. *Global entrepreneurship monitor—National entrepreneurship assessment: United States of America 2000 Executive Report.* Kansas City, MO: Kauffman Center for Entrepreneurial Leadership.

17. Cooper, S. 2003. Cash cows. *Entrepreneur,* June: 36.

18. Seglin, J. L. 1998. What angels want. *Inc.,* 20(7): 43–44.

19. Torres, N. L. 2002. Playing an angel. *Entrepreneur,* May: 130–138.

20. For an interesting discussion of how venture capital practices vary across different sectors of the economy, see Gaba, V. & Meyer, A. D. 2008. Crossing the organizational species barrier: How venture capital practices infiltrated the information technology sector. *Academy of Management Journal,* 51(5): 391–412.

21. Our discussion of crowdfunding draws on Wasik, J. 2012. The brilliance (and madness) of crowdfunding. *Forbes,* June 25: 144–146; Anonymous. 2012. Why crowdfunding may not be path to riches. *Finance.yahoo.com,* October 23: np; and Espinoza, J. 2012. Doing equity crowd funding right. *The Wall Street Journal,* May 21: R3.

22. Noyes, K. 2014. Why investors are pouring millions into crowdfunding. *fortune.com,* April 17. np.

23. Shchetko, N. 2014. There's no refunding in crowdfunding. *The Wall Street Journal,* November 26: B1, B4.

24. For more on how different forms of organizing entrepreneurial firms as well as different stages of new firm growth and development affect financing, see Cassar, G. 2004. The financing of business start-ups. *Journal of Business Venturing,* 19(2): 261–283.

25. Kroll, M., Walters, B., & Wright, P. 2010. The impact of insider control and environment on post-IPO performance. *Academy of Management Journal,* 53: 693–725.

26. Eisenhardt, K. M. & Schoonhoven, C. B. 1990. Organizational growth: Linking founding team, strategy, environment, and growth among U.S. semiconductor ventures, 1978–1988. *Administrative Science Quarterly,* 35: 504–529.

27. Dubini, P. & Aldrich, H. 1991. Personal and extended networks are central to the entrepreneurship process. *Journal of Business Venturing,* 6(5): 305–333.

28. For more on the role of social contacts in helping young firms

build legitimacy, see Chrisman, J. J. & McMullan, W. E. 2004. Outside assistance as a knowledge resource for new venture survival. *Journal of Small Business Management,* 42(3): 229–244.

29. Vogel, C. 2000. Janina Pawlowski. *Working Woman,* June: 70.

30. For a recent perspective on entrepreneurship and strategic alliances, see Rothaermel, F. T. & Deeds, D. L. 2006. Alliance types, alliance experience and alliance management capability in high-technology ventures. *Journal of Business Venturing,* 21(4): 429–460; and Lu, J. W. & Beamish, P. W. 2006. Partnering strategies and performance of SMEs' international joint ventures. *Journal of Business Venturing,* 21(4): 461–486.

31. Monahan, J. 2005. All systems grow. *Entrepreneur,* March: 78–82; Weaver, K. M. & Dickson, P. 2004. Strategic alliances. In Dennis, W. J., Jr. (Ed.), *NFIB national small business poll.* Washington, DC: National Federation of Independent Business; and Copeland, M. V. & Tilin, A. 2005. Get someone to build it. *Business 2.0,* 6(5): 88.

32. For more information, go to the Small Business Administration website at *www.sba.gov.*

33. Simsek, Z., Heavey, C., & Veiga, J. 2009. The impact of CEO core self-evaluation on entrepreneurial orientation. *Strategic Management Journal,* 31: 110–119.

34. Zhao, H. & Seibert, S. 2006. The big five personality dimensions and entrepreneurial status: A meta-analytic review. *Journal of Applied Psychology,* 91: 259–271.

35. For an interesting study of the role of passion in entrepreneurial success, see Chen, X-P., Yao, X., & Kotha, S. 2009. Entrepreneur passion and preparedness in business plan presentations: A persuasion analysis of venture capitalists' funding decisions. *Academy of Management Journal,* 52(1): 101–120.

36. Collins, J. 2001. *Good to great.* New York: HarperCollins.

37. The idea of entry wedges was discussed by Vesper, K. 1990. *New venture strategies* (2nd ed.). Englewood Cliffs, NJ: Prentice Hall; and Drucker, P. F. 1985. *Innovation and entrepreneurship.* New York: HarperBusiness.

38. See Dowell, G. & Swaminathan, A. 2006. Entry timing, exploration, and firm survival in the early U.S. bicycle industry. *Strategic Management Journal,* 27:

1159–1182, for a recent study of the timing of entrepreneurial new entry.

39. Dunlap-Hinkler, D., Kotabe, M., & Mudambi, R. 2010. A story of breakthrough vs. incremental innovation: Corporate entrepreneurship in the global pharmaceutical industry. *Strategic Entrepreneurship Journal*, 4: 106–127.

40. Maiello, M. 2002. They almost changed the world. *Forbes,* December 22: 217–220.

41. Pogue, D. 2012. Pay by app: No cash or card needed. *International Herald Tribune,* July 19: 18.

42. Helft, M. 2014. Square's status? It's complicated. *fortune.com,* May 14: np.

43. Williams, G. 2002. Looks like rain. *Entrepreneur,* September: 104–111.

44. Pedroza, G. M. 2002. Tech tutors. *Entrepreneur,* September: 120.

45. Romanelli, E. 1989. Environments and strategies of organization start-up: Effects on early survival. *Administrative Science Quarterly,* 34(3): 369–387.

46. Wallace, B. 2000. Brothers. *Philadelphia Magazine,* April: 66–75.

47. Buchanan, L. 2003. The innovation factor: A field guide to innovation. *www.forbes.com,* April 21.

48. Kim, W. C. & Mauborgne, R. 2005. *Blue ocean strategy.* Boston: Harvard Business School Press.

49. For more on how unique organizational combinations can contribute to competitive advantages of entrepreneurial firms, see Steffens, P., Davidsson, P., & Fitzsimmons, J. Performance configurations over time: Implications for growth- and profit-oriented strategies. *Entrepreneurship Theory & Practice,* 33(1): 125–148.

50. Smith, K. G., Ferrier, W. J., & Grimm, C. M. 2001. King of the hill: Dethroning the industry leader. *Academy of Management Executive,* 15(2): 59–70.

51. Grove, A. 1999. *Only the paranoid survive: How to exploit the crisis points that challenge every company.* New York: Random House.

52. Stalk, G., Jr., & Lachenauer, R. 2004. *Hardball: Are you playing to play or playing to win?* Cambridge, MA: Harvard Business School Press.

53. Chen, M. J., Lin, H. C., & Michel, J. G. 2010. Navigating in a hypercompetitive environment: The roles of action aggressiveness and TMT integration. *Strategic Management Journal,* 31: 1410–1430.

54. Peteraf, M. A. & Bergen, M. A. 2003. Scanning competitive landscapes: A market-based and resource-based framework. *Strategic Management Journal,* 24: 1027–1045.

55. Chen, M. J. 1996. Competitor analysis and interfirm rivalry: Toward a theoretical integration. *Academy of Management Review,* 21(1): 100–134.

56. Chen, 1996, op.cit.

57. Chen, M. J., Su, K. H, & Tsai, W. 2007. Competitive tension: The awareness-motivation-capability perspective. *Academy of Management Journal,* 50(1): 101–118.

58. St. John, W. 1999. Barnes & Noble's epiphany. *www.wired.com,* June.

59. Anonymous. 2010. Is the *Times* ready for a newspaper war? *Bloomberg Businessweek,* April 26: 30–31.

60. Souder, D. & Shaver, J. M. 2010. Constraints and incentives for making long horizon corporate investments. *Strategic Management Journal,* 31: 1316–1336.

61. Chen, M. J. & Hambrick, D. 1995. Speed, stealth, and selective attack: How small firms differ from large firms in competitive behavior. *Academy of Management Journal,* 38: 453–482.

62. Fenner, L. 2009. TOMS Shoes donates one pair of shoes for every pair purchased. *America.gov,* October 19: np.

63. *www.facebook.com/tomsshoes.*

64. For a discussion of how the strategic actions of Apple Computer contribute to changes in the competitive dynamics in both the cellular phone and music industries, see Burgelman, R. A. & Grove, A. S. 2008. Cross-boundary disruptors: Powerful interindustry entrepreneurial change agents. *Strategic Entrepreneurship Journal,* 1(1): 315–327.

65. Smith, K. G., Ferrier, W. J., & Ndofor, H. 2001. Competitive dynamics research: Critique and future directions. In Hitt, M. A., Freeman, R. E., & Harrison, J. S. (Eds.), *The Blackwell handbook of strategic management:* 315–361. Oxford, UK: Blackwell.

66. Gee, P. 2000. Co-opetition: The new market milieu. *Journal of Healthcare Management,* 45: 359–363.

67. Ketchen, D. J., Snow, C. C., & Hoover, V. L. 2004. Research on competitive dynamics: Recent accomplishments and future challenges. *Journal of Management,* 30(6): 779–804.

68. Fritz, B. 2014. Movie film, at death's door, gets a reprieve. *wsj.com,* July 29: np.

69. Khanna, T., Gulati, R., & Nohria, N. 2000. The economic modeling of strategy process: Clean models and dirty hands. *Strategic Management Journal,* 21: 781–790.

Strategic Control and Corporate Governance

After reading this chapter, you should have a good understanding of the following learning objectives:

LO9.1 The value of effective strategic control systems in strategy implementation.

LO9.2 The key difference between "traditional" and "contemporary" control systems.

LO9.3 The imperative for contemporary control systems in today's complex and rapidly changing competitive and general environments.

LO9.4 The benefits of having the proper balance among the three levers of behavioral control: culture, rewards and incentives, and boundaries.

LO9.5 The three key participants in corporate governance: shareholders, management (led by the CEO), and the board of directors.

LO9.6 The role of corporate governance mechanisms in ensuring that the interests of managers are aligned with those of shareholders from both the United States and international perspectives.

Learning from Mistakes

Just a few years ago, Tesco was a high-flying global retailer. Throughout the 1990s and early 2000s, Tesco grew to dominate the U.K. retailing market, attaining a 33 percent market share, and successfully expanded into new geographic markets. However, over the last several years, Tesco has faced increasing pressures at home and large struggles outside the U.K. This included a failed entry into the U.S. market and increasing pressure at home from hard-discounting competitors, most notably Lidl and Aldi. In recent years, Tesco has seen its stock price drop by nearly 40 percent, major investors including Warren Buffett bail out, and pressures from investors that forced the ousting of the firm's CEO.

In September 2014, the situation for Tesco got much worse.[1] After an employee alerted the firm's general counsel of accounting irregularities, a full-blown accounting scandal erupted. Senior managers in the U.K. food business had been booking income early and delaying the booking of costs to shore up the financial performance of the firm. The firm was forced to restate its earnings for the first half of 2014, initially to the tune of $408 million, which was later increased to $431 million as the scope of the problem increased. The scandal led to the suspension or dismissal of eight senior executives at Tesco, the suspension of retirement packages for the firm's prior CEO and CFO, and the eventual resignation of the chairman of the board of Tesco. It also triggered an investigation by the U.K.'s accounting watchdog, the Financial Reporting Council, into Tesco's accounting practices for the years 2012, 2013, and 2014.

The scandal has triggered commentators to reassert some long-standing concerns about Tesco's governance and also led them to point out some new concerns. Industry analysts have long been critical of Tesco's board of directors, especially noting that the board lacks retail experience. This likely played a role in the scandal, since the board would have had limited ability to notice the arcane, retail-related accounting practices at the center of the accounting deception. Interestingly, four months before the scandal arose, Tesco's auditor, PricewaterhouseCoopers, warned of the "risk of manipulation" in the accounting of promotional events, the areas that were manipulated, but the board appeared to take no action in its following meeting. The accounting irregularities also arose at a time of limited oversight within the firm. Laurie McIlwee, the firm's chief financial officer, stepped down in April 2014, but her replacement didn't take up the CFO position until December 2014. During that time, Tesco's finances were managed by the CEO's office. Thus, the firm did not have a senior executive whose primary task was to ensure the validity of the firm's financial reporting. Finally, the most senior leadership of the firm was distracted by other tasks. The firm's prior CEO was dismissed in July, and the new CEO took the reins in August 2014. Thus, Dave Lewis, the new CEO, was focusing on learning the business and the firm's operations just as the scandal broke.

The scandal has been quite damaging to the firm, with Tesco's already battered stock price plunging an additional 28 percent during the period the scandal unfolded.

Discussion Questions

1. What changes should Tesco make to avoid future similar scandals?
2. To what degree do you think the scandal at Tesco was related to how the firm had been performing?

We first explore two central aspects of **strategic control:**[2] (1) *informational control,* which is the ability to respond effectively to environmental change, and (2) *behavioral control,* which is the appropriate balance and alignment among a firm's culture, rewards, and boundaries. In the final section of this chapter, we focus on strategic control from a much broader perspective—what is referred to as *corporate governance.*[3] Here, we direct our attention to the need for a firm's shareholders (the owners) and their elected representatives (the board of directors) to ensure that the firm's executives (the management team) strive to fulfill their fiduciary duty of maximizing long-term shareholder value. As we just saw in the Tesco example, poor governance and control can lead to damaging scandals in firms.

Ensuring Informational Control: Responding Effectively to Environmental Change

We discuss two broad types of control systems: "traditional" and "contemporary." As both general and competitive environments become more unpredictable and complex, the need for contemporary systems increases.

A Traditional Approach to Strategic Control

The **traditional approach to strategic control** is sequential: (1) strategies are formulated and top management sets goals, (2) strategies are implemented, and (3) performance is measured against the predetermined goal set, as illustrated in Exhibit 9.1.

Control is based on a feedback loop from performance measurement to strategy formulation. This process typically involves lengthy time lags, often tied to a firm's annual planning cycle. Such traditional control systems, termed "single-loop" learning by Harvard's Chris Argyris, simply compare actual performance to a predetermined goal.[4] They are most appropriate when the environment is stable and relatively simple, goals and objectives can be measured with a high level of certainty, and there is little need for complex measures of performance. Sales quotas, operating budgets, production schedules, and similar quantitative control mechanisms are typical. The appropriateness of the business strategy or standards of performance is seldom questioned.[5]

James Brian Quinn of Dartmouth College has argued that grand designs with precise and carefully integrated plans seldom work.[6] Rather, most strategic change proceeds incrementally—one step at a time. Leaders should introduce some sense of direction, some logic in incremental steps.[7] Similarly, McGill University's Henry Mintzberg has written about leaders "crafting" a strategy.[8] Drawing on the parallel between the potter at her wheel and the strategist, Mintzberg pointed out that the potter begins work with some general idea of the artifact she wishes to create, but the details of design—even possibilities for a different design—emerge as the work progresses. For businesses facing complex and turbulent business environments, the craftsperson's method helps us deal with the uncertainty about how a design will work out in practice and allows for a creative element.

Mintzberg's argument, like Quinn's, questions the value of rigid planning and goal-setting processes. Fixed strategic goals also become dysfunctional for firms competing in highly unpredictable competitive environments. Strategies need to change frequently and opportunistically. An inflexible commitment to predetermined goals and milestones can prevent the very adaptability that is required of a good strategy.

EXHIBIT 9.1 Traditional Approach to Strategic Control

A Contemporary Approach to Strategic Control

Adapting to and anticipating both internal and external environmental change is an integral part of strategic control. The relationships between strategy formulation, implementation, and control are highly interactive, as suggested by Exhibit 9.2. The exhibit also illustrates two different types of strategic control: informational control and behavioral control. **Informational control** is primarily concerned with whether or not the organization is "doing the right things." **Behavioral control,** on the other hand, asks if the organization is "doing things right" in the implementation of its strategy. Both the informational and behavioral components of strategic control are necessary, but not sufficient, conditions for success. What good is a well-conceived strategy that cannot be implemented? Or what use is an energetic and committed workforce if it is focused on the wrong strategic target?

John Weston is the former CEO of ADP Corporation, the largest payroll and tax-filing processor in the world. He captures the essence of contemporary control systems:

> At ADP, 39 plus 1 adds up to more than 40 plus 0. The 40-plus-0 employee is the harried worker who at 40 hours a week just tries to keep up with what's in the "in" basket. . . . Because he works with his head down, he takes zero hours to think about what he's doing, why he's doing it, and how he's doing it. . . . On the other hand, the 39-plus-1 employee takes at least 1 of those 40 hours to think about what he's doing and why he's doing it. That's why the other 39 hours are far more productive.[9]

Informational control deals with the internal environment as well as the external strategic context. It addresses the assumptions and premises that provide the foundation for an organization's strategy. Do the organization's goals and strategies still "fit" within the context of the current strategic environment? Depending on the type of business, such assumptions may relate to changes in technology, customer tastes, government regulation, and industry competition.

This involves two key issues. First, managers must scan and monitor the external environment, as we discussed in Chapter 2. Also, conditions can change in the internal environment of the firm, as we discussed in Chapter 3, requiring changes in the strategic direction of the firm. These may include, for example, the resignation of key executives or delays in the completion of major production facilities.

In the contemporary approach, information control is part of an ongoing process of organizational learning that continuously updates and challenges the assumptions that underlie the organization's strategy. In such double-loop learning, the organization's assumptions, premises, goals, and strategies are continuously monitored, tested, and reviewed. The benefits of continuous monitoring are evident—time lags are dramatically shortened, changes in the competitive environment are detected earlier, and the organization's ability to respond with speed and flexibility is enhanced.

Contemporary control systems must have four characteristics to be effective:[10]

1. The focus is on constantly changing information that has potential strategic importance.
2. The information is important enough to demand frequent and regular attention from all levels of the organization.

informational control
a method of organizational control in which a firm gathers and analyzes information from the internal and external environment in order to obtain the best fit between the organization's goals and strategies and the strategic environment.

behavioral control
a method of organizational control in which a firm influences the actions of employees through culture, rewards, and boundaries.

EXHIBIT 9.2 Contemporary Approach to Strategic Control

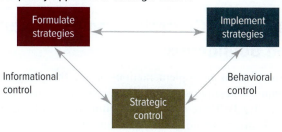

9.1

HOW DO MANAGERS AND EMPLOYEES VIEW THEIR FIRM'S CONTROL SYSTEM?

Top executives of organizations often assert that they are pushing for more contemporary control systems. The centralized, periodic setting of objectives and rules with top-down implementation processes is ineffective for organizations facing heterogeneous and dynamic environments. For example, Walmart has, in recent years, realized its top-down, rule-based leadership system was too rigid for a firm emphasizing globalization and technological change. Like many other firms, Walmart is moving to a more decentralized, values-based leadership system where lower-level managers make key decisions, keeping the values of the firm in mind as they do so.

Managers of firms see the need to make this transition, but do lower-level managers and workers see a change in the control systems at their organizations? To get at this question, the Boston Research Group conducted a study of 36,000 managers and employees to get their views on their firm's control systems. Their findings are enlightening. Only 3 percent of employees saw their firm's culture as "self-governing," in which decision making is driven by a "set of core principles and values." In contrast, 43 percent of employees saw their firm as operating using a top-down, command-and-control decision process, what the authors of the study labeled as the "blind-obedience" model; and 53 percent of employees saw their firm following an "informed-acquiescence" model, in which the overall style is top-down but with skilled management that used a mix of rewards and rules to get the desired behavior. In total, 97 percent of employees saw their firm's culture and decision style as being top-down.

Interestingly, managers had a different view. The survey found that 24 percent of managers believed their organizations used the values-driven, decentralized "self-governing" model. Thus, managers were eight times more likely than employees to see the firm employing a contemporary, values-driven control system. Similarly, while 41 percent of managers said that their firm rewarded performance based on values and not just financial outcomes, only 14 percent of employees saw this.

The cynicism employees expressed regarding the control systems in their firms had important consequences for the firm. Almost half of the employees who had described their firms as blind-obedience firms had witnessed unethical behavior in the firm within the last year. Only one in four employees in firms with the other two control types said they had witnessed unethical behavior. Additionally, only one-fourth of the employees in blind-obedience firms would blow the whistle on unethical behavior, but this rate went up to nine in ten if the firm relied on self-governance. Finally, the impressions of employees influence the ability of the firm to be responsive and innovative. Among those surveyed, 90 percent of employees in self-governing and 67 percent of employees in informed-acquiescence firms agreed with the statement that "good ideas are readily adopted by my company." Less than 20 percent of employees in blind-obedience firms agreed with the same statement.

These findings indicate that managers need to be aware of how the actions they take to improve the control systems in their firms are being received by employees. If the employees see the pronouncements of management regarding moving toward a decentralized, culture-centered control system as simply propaganda, the firm is unlikely to experience the positive changes it desires.

Sources: Anonymous. 2011. The view from the top and bottom. *The Economist,* September 24: 76; and Levit, A. 2012. Your employees aren't wearing your rose colored glasses. *openforum.com,* November 12: np.

3. The data and information generated are best interpreted and discussed in face-to-face meetings.
4. The control system is a key catalyst for an ongoing debate about underlying data, assumptions, and action plans.

An executive's decision to use the control system interactively—in other words, to invest the time and attention to review and evaluate new information—sends a clear signal to the organization about what is important. The dialogue and debate that emerge from such an interactive process can often lead to new strategies and innovations. Strategy Spotlight 9.1 discusses how managers and employees each see the control systems at work in their companies and identifies some of the consequences of those impressions.

LO9.4

The benefits of having the proper balance among the three levers of behavioral control: culture, rewards and incentives, and boundaries.

Attaining Behavioral Control: Balancing Culture, Rewards, and Boundaries

Behavioral control is focused on implementation—doing things right. Effectively implementing strategy requires manipulating three key control "levers": culture, rewards, and boundaries (see Exhibit 9.3). There are two compelling reasons for an increased emphasis on culture and rewards in a system of behavioral controls.[11]

282 PART 3 :: STRATEGIC IMPLEMENTATION

EXHIBIT 9.3 Essential Elements of Behavioral Control

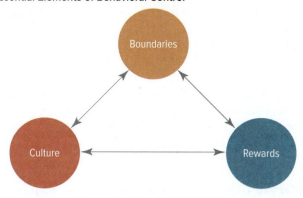

First, the competitive environment is increasingly complex and unpredictable, demanding both flexibility and quick response to its challenges. As firms simultaneously downsize and face the need for increased coordination across organizational boundaries, a control system based primarily on rigid strategies, rules, and regulations is dysfunctional. The use of rewards and culture to align individual and organizational goals becomes increasingly important.

Second, the implicit long-term contract between the organization and its key employees has been eroded.[12] Today's younger managers have been conditioned to see themselves as "free agents" and view a career as a series of opportunistic challenges. As managers are advised to "specialize, market yourself, and have work, if not a job," the importance of culture and rewards in building organizational loyalty claims greater importance.

Each of the three levers—culture, rewards, and boundaries—must work in a balanced and consistent manner. Let's consider the role of each.

Building a Strong and Effective Culture

Organizational culture is a system of shared values (what is important) and beliefs (how things work) that shape a company's people, organizational structures, and control systems to produce behavioral norms (the way we do things around here).[13] How important is culture? Very. Over the years, numerous best sellers, such as *Theory Z, Corporate Cultures, In Search of Excellence,* and *Good to Great,*[14] have emphasized the powerful influence of culture on what goes on within organizations and how they perform.

Collins and Porras argued in *Built to Last* that the key factor in sustained exceptional performance is a cultlike culture.[15] You can't touch it or write it down, but it's there in every organization; its influence is pervasive; it can work for you or against you.[16] Effective leaders understand its importance and strive to shape and use it as one of their important levers of strategic control.[17]

The Role of Culture Culture wears many different hats, each woven from the fabric of those values that sustain the organization's primary source of competitive advantage. Some examples are:

- FedEx and Amazon focus on customer service.
- Lexus (a division of Toyota) and Apple emphasize product quality.
- Google and 3M place a high value on innovation.
- Nucor (steel) and Walmart are concerned, above all, with operational efficiency.

Culture sets implicit boundaries—unwritten standards of acceptable behavior—in dress, ethical matters, and the way an organization conducts its business.[18] By creating a

organizational culture

a system of shared values and beliefs that shape a company's people, organizational structures, and control systems to produce behavioral norms.

framework of shared values, culture encourages individual identification with the organization and its objectives. Culture acts as a means of reducing monitoring costs.[19]

Strong culture can lead to greater employee engagement and provide a common purpose and identity. Firms have typically relied on economic incentives for workers, using a combination of rewards (carrots) and rules and threats (sticks) to get employees to act in desired ways. But these systems rely on the assumption that individuals are fundamentally self-interested and selfish. However, research suggests that this assumption is overstated.[20] When given a chance to act selfishly or cooperatively with others, over half of employees choose to cooperate, while only 30 percent consistently choose to act selfishly. Thus, cultural systems that build engagement, communication, and a sense of common purpose and identity would allow firms to leverage these collaborative workers.

Sustaining an Effective Culture   Powerful organizational cultures just don't happen overnight, and they don't remain in place without a strong commitment—in terms of both words and deeds—by leaders throughout the organization.[21] A viable and productive organizational culture can be strengthened and sustained. However, it cannot be "built" or "assembled"; instead, it must be cultivated, encouraged, and "fertilized."[22]

Storytelling is one way effective cultures are maintained. 3M is a company that uses powerful stories to reinforce the culture of the firm. One of those is the story of Francis G. Okie.[23] In 1922 Okie came up with the idea of selling sandpaper to men as a replacement for razor blades. The idea obviously didn't pan out, but Okie was allowed to remain at 3M. Interestingly, the technology developed by Okie led 3M to develop its first blockbuster product: a waterproof sandpaper that became a staple of the automobile industry. Such stories foster the importance of risk taking, experimentation, freedom to fail, and innovation—all vital elements of 3M's culture. Strategy Spotlight 9.2 discusses the power of pictures and stories in building a customer-centric culture.

Rallies or "pep talks" by top executives also serve to reinforce a firm's culture. The late Sam Walton was known for his pep rallies at local Walmart stores. Four times a year, the founders of Home Depot—Bernard Marcus and Arthur Blank—used to don orange aprons and stage Breakfast with Bernie and Arthur, a 6:30 a.m. pep rally, broadcast live over the firm's closed-circuit TV network to most of its 45,000 employees.[24]

Southwest Airlines' "Culture Committee" is a unique vehicle designed to perpetuate the company's highly successful culture. The following excerpt from an internal company publication describes its objectives:

> The goal of the Committee is simple—to ensure that our unique Corporate Culture stays alive. . . . Culture Committee members represent all regions and departments across our system and they are selected based upon their exemplary display of the "Positively Outrageous Service" that won us the first-ever Triple Crown; their continual exhibition of the "Southwest Spirit" to our Customers and to their fellow workers; and their high energy level, boundless enthusiasm, unique creativity, and constant demonstration of teamwork and love for their fellow workers.[25]

Motivating with Rewards and Incentives

Reward and incentive systems represent a powerful means of influencing an organization's culture, focusing efforts on high-priority tasks, and motivating individual and collective task performance.[26] Just as culture deals with influencing beliefs, behaviors, and attitudes of people within an organization, the **reward system**—by specifying who gets rewarded and why—is an effective motivator and control mechanism.[27] The managers at Not Your Average Joe's, a Massachusetts-based restaurant chain, changed their staffing procedures both to let their servers better understand their performance and to better motivate them.[28] The chain uses sophisticated software to track server performance—in both per customer sales and customer satisfaction as seen in tips. Highly rated servers are given more tables

reward system
policies that specify who gets rewarded and why.

USING PICTURES AND STORIES TO BUILD A CUSTOMER-ORIENTED CULTURE

Most firms tout that customers are their most important stakeholders. In firms that have value statements, these statements typically list the firms' responsibilities to their customers first. But it is hard to build and maintain a customer-centric culture. Using visual imagery and stories can help firms put customers at the center of their culture.

The old saying is that "a picture is worth a thousand words." This is certainly true when building a culture. A simple snapshot of a customer or end user can be a powerful motivating tool for workers to care about that customer. For example, radiologists rarely see patients. They look at X-rays from the files of patients, but these patients are typically faceless and anonymous to them. However, when pictures of the patients were added to their files, one study found that radiologists increased the length of their reports on the patients' X-rays by 29 percent and improved the accuracy of their diagnoses by 46 percent. Other firms have found the same effect. Microfinance provider Kiva includes pictures of the entrepreneurs whom it is trying to fund, believing that potential donors feel more of a connection with an entrepreneur when they have seen a picture of him or her.

Stories can also help build a customer-centric culture. Inside the firm, the stories that employees share with each other become imprinted on the organizational mind. Thus, as employees share their positive stories of experiences with customers, they not only provide encouragement for other employees to better meet the needs of customers but also reinforce the storytelling employee's desire to work hard to serve customers. For example, at Ritz-Carlton hotels, employees meet each day for 15 minutes to share stories about how they went the extra yard to meet customers' needs. These stories can even be more significant for new employees, helping them learn about the values of the firm. With outside stories, firms can draw on the accounts of customers to reinvigorate their employees. These can be based on personal statements from customers or even from news stories. To test these effects, one researcher gave lifeguards a few short news stories about swimmers who were saved by lifeguards on other beaches. The lifeguards who heard these stories reported that they found their job more meaningful, volunteered to work more hours, and were rated by their supervisors as being more vigilant in their work one month later.

Managers can help ensure that the stories told support the firm's customer-centric culture by taking the following steps:

- Tell positive stories about employees' interactions with customers.
- Share positive customer feedback with employees.
- Tie employee recognition to positive employee actions.
- Weave stories into the employee handbook and new employee orientation.
- Make sure that mentors in the firm know about the importance of using stories in their mentoring efforts.

The "short story" here is that firms can help build and reinforce a customer-centric culture if they just keep the customer in the center of the stories they tell and make the customer personally relevant to workers.

Sources: Grant, A. 2011. How customers rally your troops. *Harvard Business Review,* 89(6): 96–103; and Heathfield, S. 2014. How stories strengthen your work culture—or not. *humanresources.about.com,* December 29: np.

and preferred schedules. In shifting more work and better schedules to the best workers, the chain hopes to improve profitability and motivate all workers.

The Potential Downside While they can be powerful motivators, reward and incentive policies can also result in undesirable outcomes in organizations. At the individual level, incentives can go wrong for multiple reasons. First, if individual workers don't see how their actions relate to how they are compensated, incentives can be demotivating. For example, if the rewards are related to the firm's stock price, workers may feel that their efforts have little if any impact and won't perceive any benefit from working harder. On the other hand, if the incentives are too closely tied to their individual work, they may lead to dysfunctional outcomes. For example, if a sales representative is rewarded for sales volume, she will be incentivized to sell at all costs. This may lead her to accept unprofitable sales or push sales through distribution channels the firm would rather avoid. Thus, the collective sum of individual behaviors of an organization's employees does not always result in what is best for the organization; individual rationality is no guarantee of organizational rationality.

Reward and incentive systems can also cause problems across organizational units. As corporations grow and evolve, they often develop different business units with multiple reward systems. These systems may differ based on industry contexts, business situations, stage of product life cycles, and so on. Subcultures within organizations may reflect differences among functional areas, products, services, and divisions. To the extent that reward systems reinforce such behavioral norms, attitudes, and belief systems, cohesiveness is reduced; important information is hoarded rather than shared, individuals begin working at cross-purposes, and they lose sight of overall goals.

Such conflicts are commonplace in many organizations. For example, sales and marketing personnel promise unrealistically quick delivery times to bring in business, much to the dismay of operations and logistics; overengineering by R&D creates headaches for manufacturing; and so on. Conflicts also arise across divisions when divisional profits become a key compensation criterion. As ill will and anger escalate, personal relationships and performance may suffer.

Creating Effective Reward and Incentive Programs   To be effective, incentive and reward systems need to reinforce basic core values, enhance cohesion and commitment to goals and objectives, and meet with the organization's overall mission and purpose.[29]

At General Mills, to ensure a manager's interest in the overall performance of his or her unit, half of a manager's annual bonus is linked to business unit results and half to individual performance.[30] For example, if a manager simply matches a rival manufacturer's performance, his or her salary is roughly 5 percent lower. However, if a manager's product ranks in the industry's top 10 percent in earnings growth and return on capital, the manager's total pay can rise to nearly 30 percent beyond the industry norm.

Effective reward and incentive systems share a number of common characteristics[31] (see Exhibit 9.4). The perception that a plan is "fair and equitable" is critically important. The firm must have the flexibility to respond to changing requirements as its direction and objectives change. In recent years many companies have begun to place more emphasis on growth. To ensure that managers focus on growth, a number of firms have changed their compensation systems to move from a bottom-line focus to one that emphasizes growth, new products, acquisitions, and international expansion.

However, incentive and reward systems don't have to be all about money. Employees respond not only to monetary compensation but also to softer forms of incentives and rewards. In fact, a number of studies have found that for employees who are satisfied with their base salary, nonfinancial motivators are more effective than cash incentives in building long-term employee motivation.[32] Three key reward systems appear to provide the greatest incentives. First, employees respond to managerial praise. This can include formal recognition policies and events. For example, at Mars Central Europe, the company holds an event twice a year at which they celebrate innovative ideas generated by employees. Recognition at the Mars "Make a Difference" event is designed to motivate the winners and also other employees who want to receive the same recognition. Employees also respond well to informal recognition rewards, such as personal praise, written praise, and public praise. This is especially effective when it includes small perks, such as a gift certificate for dinner, some scheduling flexibility, or even an extra day off. Positive words and actions are especially powerful since almost two-thirds of employees in one study said management was much more likely to criticize them for poor performance than praise them for good work. Second, employees feel rewarded when they receive attention from

EXHIBIT 9.4

Characteristics of Effective Reward and Incentive Systems

- Objectives are clear, well understood, and broadly accepted.
- Rewards are clearly linked to performance and desired behaviors.
- Performance measures are clear and highly visible.
- Feedback is prompt, clear, and unambiguous.
- The compensation "system" is perceived as fair and equitable.
- The structure is flexible; it can adapt to changing circumstances.

INSPIRE PASSION—MOTIVATE TOP PERFORMANCE

Overview

Often, managers approach and strive to motivate employees with extrinsic rewards. These produce some results; however, employees tend to perform best when their intrinsic needs are met. Think of ways to highlight the purpose of your employees' work. Allow employees to work on projects that ignite their passions.

What the Research Shows

Employees who are passionate about their jobs are more engaged in their jobs. And employees who are more engaged in their jobs perform them better, according to investigators from the University of Richmond, Nanyang Technological University, and Keppel Offshore and Marine Ltd. in Singapore. Their 2011 research, published in the *Journal of Management Studies,* utilized the performance appraisals of 509 headquarters employees of a large insurance company. The employees were given a survey to identify their attitudes toward their jobs. Using structural equations modeling, the researchers found a relationship between the employees' passion for their jobs and their performance of their jobs. However, the effect was significant only when mediated by the employees' absorption in their jobs.

Employees who had job passion identified with their jobs intrinsically and believed their work was meaningful. Therefore, they were able to feel passionate about their jobs while balancing that passion with other aspects of their lives that were also important to them. This resulted in an intensity of focus on and deep immersion in their tasks while they were working. When they were deeply engrossed in work, the employees were not distracted by other activities or roles in their lives. In turn, this job absorption resulted in superior performance on the job.

Why This Matters

While many managers attempt to tap into their employees' passions to motivate them to perform their jobs, external incentives are not the best way to engender internal identification with work. Even positive feedback can become an external incentive if employees work toward receiving that recognition rather than working simply because they identify with and enjoy their jobs. A better way to nurture employees' identification with their work is to provide them with a sense of ownership of their work and, more importantly, to help them see how meaningful their jobs are. For example, to help their employees see the impact of their work on others, Cancer Treatment Centers of America in the Tulsa, Oklahoma, area recruits spouses of employees to form and run a nonprofit organization to raise money for cancer patients' nonmedical expenses.

Kevin Cleary, CEO of Clif Bar and Co., says success is contingent upon an "engaged, inspired and outrageously committed team." He breaks this down into these steps:

1. Engage your employees with the company's mission and vision. If you don't have a mission and vision statement, get employees' contributions to create one you believe in.

2. Once people understand the mission and vision, trust your employees to work. Do not micromanage or assume they need a held hand.

3. Have a business model in which people come first, second, and third.

Cleary says exceptional talent is valuable only when employees believe in the organization's mission.

Key Takeaways

- Employees who are passionate about their jobs will be more engaged and absorbed in them and will perform better.

- When employees like their jobs and view them as important, they will be more passionate about their work.

- Employees whose jobs are significant to their personal identities—relative to the other roles they play in their lives—will be more passionate about their jobs.

- When employees are passionate about their jobs, they become deeply engrossed in their job tasks and aren't easily distracted by other activities.

- Although job passion must be voluntary and driven by employees' internal identities, managers can encourage it by helping employees see the significance of their work.

Apply This Today

Managers can fuel employees' intrinsic motivation by helping them see the meaning in their tasks, the company, and its mission. If employees can find personal meaning and passion in their jobs, the company will be rewarded with significant improvements in performance. To learn more about motivating your employees, visit *businessminded.com.*

Research Reviewed

Ho, V. T., Wong, S. S., & Lee, C. H. 2011. A tale of passion: Linking job passion and cognitive engagement to employee work performance. *Journal of Management Studies,* 48(1): 26–47.

leaders and, as a result, feel valued and involved. One survey found that the number-one factor employees valued was "managerial support and involvement"—having their managers ask for their opinions, involve them in decisions, and give them authority to complete tasks. Third, managers can reward employees by giving them opportunities to lead projects or task forces. In sum, incentives and rewards can go well beyond simple pay to include formal recognition, praise, and the self-esteem that comes from feeling valued.

The Insights from Research box provides further evidence that employees are motivated more when they feel a sense of purpose in their work and feel valued by their employers than when they are only monetarily rewarded for their work.

Setting Boundaries and Constraints

In an ideal world, a strong culture and effective rewards should be sufficient to ensure that all individuals and subunits work toward the common goals and objectives of the whole organization.[33] However, this is not usually the case. Counterproductive behavior can arise because of motivated self-interest, lack of a clear understanding of goals and objectives, or outright malfeasance. **Boundaries and constraints** can serve many useful purposes for organizations, including:

- Focusing individual efforts on strategic priorities.
- Providing short-term objectives and action plans to channel efforts.
- Improving efficiency and effectiveness.
- Minimizing improper and unethical conduct.

Focusing Efforts on Strategic Priorities Boundaries and constraints play a valuable role in focusing a company's strategic priorities. For example, in 2015, GE sold off its financial services businesses in order to refocus on its manufacturing businesses. Similarly, Pfizer sold its infant formula business as it refocused its attention on core pharmaceutical products.[34] This concentration of effort and resources provides the firm with greater strategic focus and the potential for stronger competitive advantages in the remaining areas.

Steve Jobs would use whiteboards to set priorities and focus attention at Apple. For example, he would take his "top 100" people on a retreat each year. One year, he asked the group what 10 things Apple should do next. The group identified ideas. Ideas went up on the board and then got erased or revised; new ones were added, revised, and erased. The group argued about it for a while and finally identified their list of top 10 initiatives. Jobs proceeded to slash the bottom seven, stating, "We can only do three."[35]

Boundaries also have a place in the nonprofit sector. For example, a British relief organization uses a system to monitor strategic boundaries by maintaining a list of companies whose contributions it will neither solicit nor accept. Such boundaries are essential for maintaining legitimacy with existing and potential benefactors.

Providing Short-Term Objectives and Action Plans In Chapter 1 we discussed the importance of a firm having a vision, mission, and strategic objectives that are internally consistent and that provide strategic direction. In addition, short-term objectives and action plans provide similar benefits. That is, they represent boundaries that help to allocate resources in an optimal manner and to channel the efforts of employees at all levels throughout the organization.[36] To be effective, short-term objectives must have several attributes. They should:

- Be specific and measurable.
- Include a specific time horizon for their attainment.
- Be achievable, yet challenging enough to motivate managers who must strive to accomplish them.

Research has found that performance is enhanced when individuals are encouraged to attain specific, difficult, yet achievable, goals (as opposed to vague "do your best" goals).[37]

BREAKING DOWN SUSTAINABILITY INTO MEASURABLE GOALS

Marks and Spencer (M&S) laid out an ambitious goal in early 2010 to become "the world's most sustainable retailer" by 2015. To meet this goal, M&S needed to substantially change how it undertook nearly all of its business operations. To make this process more tractable and to provide opportunities to identify a range of actions managers could take, M&S developed an overarching plan for its sustainability efforts, dubbed Plan A. They called it Plan A because, as M&S managers put it, when it comes to building environmental sustainability, there is no Plan B. Everyone in the firm needed to be committed to the one vision. In this plan, M&S identified three broad themes:

- Aim for all M&S products to have at least one Plan A quality.
- Help our customers make a difference to the social and environmental causes that matter to them.
- Help our customers live a more sustainable life.

Thus, M&S aimed not only to improve its own operations but also to change the lives of its customers and the operations of its suppliers and other partners. Marc Bolland, M&S's CEO, fleshed out the general Plan A goal with 180 environmental commitments. These commitments all had time targets associated with them, some short term and some longer term. For example, one commitment was to make the company carbon-neutral, a goal it achieved in 2014. To meet its goal, M&S estimated it needed to achieve a 25 percent reduction in energy use in its stores by 2012 and extended it to 35 percent by 2015. This provided clear targets for store managers to work toward. Similarly, M&S set a goal to improve its water use efficiency in stores by 25 percent by the year 2015. Additionally, M&S set out to design new stores that used 35 percent less water than current stores. These targets provided clear metrics for store managers as well as architects and designers working on new stores.

In working with its suppliers, M&S similarly rolled out a series of time-based commitments. For example, it conducted a review with all suppliers on the Plan A initiatives in the first year of the plan. M&S required all suppliers of fresh meat, dairy, produce, and flowers to engage in a sustainable agriculture program by 2012. All clothing suppliers were required to install energy-efficient lighting and improved insulation by 2015 to attain a 10 percent reduction in energy usage. These types of efforts spanned across the firm and its supply chain. As of 2014, 85 of M&S's top 100 suppliers had introduced energy-efficient best practices.

With its Plan A, M&S broke down a huge initiative into clear targets that were actionable by managers across the firm and in its partner firms. Interestingly, while this initiative was hatched as a means to achieve environmental sustainability gains, it has also turned out to be an economic win for M&S. In the first year of the plan, the firm experienced an $80 million profit on the actions it undertook. The surplus has resulted from gains in energy efficiency, lower packaging costs, lower waste bills, and profit from a sustainable energy business it set up that relies on burning biowaste to generate electricity.

Sources: Felsted, A. 2011. Marks and Spencer's green blueprint. *ft.com,* March 17: np; Anonymous. 2012. Marks & Spencer's ambitious sustainability goals. *sustainablebusiness.com,* March 3: np; and *planareport.marksandspencer.com.*

Short-term objectives must provide proper direction and also provide enough flexibility for the firm to keep pace with and anticipate changes in the external environment, new government regulations, a competitor introducing a substitute product, or changes in consumer taste. Unexpected events within a firm may require a firm to make important adjustments in both strategic and short-term objectives. The emergence of new industries can have a drastic effect on the demand for products and services in more traditional industries.

Action plans are critical to the implementation of chosen strategies. Unless action plans are specific, there may be little assurance that managers have thought through all of the resource requirements for implementing their strategies. In addition, unless plans are specific, managers may not understand what needs to be implemented or have a clear time frame for completion. This is essential for the scheduling of key activities that must be implemented. Finally, individual managers must be held accountable for the implementation. This helps to provide the necessary motivation and "sense of ownership" to implement action plans on a timely basis. Strategy Spotlight 9.3 illustrates how Marks and Spencer puts its sustainability mission into action by creating clear, measurable goals.

Improving Operational Efficiency and Effectiveness Rule-based controls are most appropriate in organizations with the following characteristics:

- Environments are stable and predictable.
- Employees are largely unskilled and interchangeable.

- Consistency in product and service is critical.
- The risk of malfeasance is extremely high (e.g., in banking or casino operations).[38]

McDonald's Corp. has extensive rules and regulations that regulate the operation of its franchises.[39] Its policy manual from a number of years ago stated, "Cooks must turn, never flip, hamburgers. If they haven't been purchased, Big Macs must be discarded in 10 minutes after being cooked and French fries in 7 minutes. Cashiers must make eye contact with and smile at every customer."

Guidelines can also be effective in setting spending limits and the range of discretion for employees and managers, such as the $2,500 limit that hotelier Ritz-Carlton uses to empower employees to placate dissatisfied customers.

Minimizing Improper and Unethical Conduct   Guidelines can be useful in specifying proper relationships with a company's customers and suppliers.[40] Many companies have explicit rules regarding commercial practices, including the prohibition of any form of payment, bribe, or kickback. For example, Singapore Airlines has a 17-page policy outlining its anticorruption and antibribery policies.[41]

Regulations backed up with strong sanctions can also help an organization avoid conducting business in an unethical manner. Since the passing of the Sarbanes-Oxley Act (which provides for stiffer penalties for financial reporting misdeeds) in 2002, many chief financial officers (CFOs) have taken steps to ensure ethical behavior in the preparation of financial statements. For example, Home Depot's CFO, Carol B. Tomé, strengthened the firm's code of ethics and developed stricter guidelines. Now all 25 of her subordinates must sign personal statements that all of their financial statements are correct—just as she and her CEO have to do.[42]

Behavioral Control in Organizations: Situational Factors

Here, the focus is on ensuring that the behavior of individuals at all levels of an organization is directed toward achieving organizational goals and objectives. The three fundamental types of control are culture, rewards and incentives, and boundaries and constraints. An organization may pursue one or a combination of them on the basis of a variety of internal and external factors.

Not all organizations place the same emphasis on each type of control.[43] In high-technology firms engaged in basic research, members may work under high levels of autonomy. An individual's performance is generally quite difficult to measure accurately because of the long lead times involved in R&D activities. Thus, internalized norms and values become very important.

When the measurement of an individual's output or performance is quite straightforward, control depends primarily on granting or withholding rewards. Frequently, a sales manager's compensation is in the form of a commission and bonus tied directly to his or her sales volume, which is relatively easy to determine. Here, behavior is influenced more strongly by the attractiveness of the compensation than by the norms and values implicit in the organization's culture. The measurability of output precludes the need for an elaborate system of rules to control behavior.[44]

Control in bureaucratic organizations is dependent on members following a highly formalized set of rules and regulations. Most activities are routine, and the desired behavior can be specified in a detailed manner because there is generally little need for innovative or creative activity. Managing an assembly plant requires strict adherence to many rules as well as exacting sequences of assembly operations. In the public sector, the Department of Motor Vehicles in most states must follow clearly prescribed procedures when issuing or renewing driver licenses. Strategy Spotlight 9.4 highlights how Digital Reasoning is using data analytics to strengthen control in major financial firms.

Exhibit 9.5 provides alternative approaches to behavioral control and some of the situational factors associated with them.

USING DATA ANALYTICS TO ENHANCE ORGANIZATIONAL CONTROL

Tim Estes's goal was to develop cognitive computing as a useful business tool. Cognitive computing strives to integrate raw computing power with natural-language processing and pattern recognition to build powerful computer systems that mimic human problem solving and learning. He first found a ready home for his vision in national security. The U.S. Army's Ground Intelligence Center contracted with Digital Reasoning to develop systems to identify potential terrorists on the basis of analyses of large volumes of different sources of data, including emails, travel information, and other data.

More recently, Digital Reasoning has taken its expertise to the financial services industry and, in doing so, is providing a new type of control system to catch potential rogue traders and market manipulators within the firms. Digital Reasoning provides systems Estes refers to as "proactive compliance" to a number of major financial services providers, including Credit Suisse and Goldman Sachs. Digital Reasoning has developed software that looks for information in and patterns across billions of emails, instant messages, media reports, and memos that suggest an employee's intention to engage in illegal or prohibited behavior before the employee crosses the line. Rather than looking for evidence of actions already taken, Digital Reasoning's software looks into ongoing patterns of correspondence to search for evolving personal relationships within the company, putting up red flags when it sees unexpected patterns, such as people in different units of the firm suddenly communicating with unusual frequency or a heightened level of discussion on topics that may be tied to unethical or illegal behavior. Any unusual patterns are then investigated by analysts in each of the financial services' firms. The goal for the firms is to both control employee behavior to stay on the right side of the law and also to send signals to customers and regulators that they are taking steps to stay on the right side of legal and ethical boundaries.

Sources: McGee, J. 2014. When crisis strikes, Digital Reasoning takes action. *tennessean.com,* October 9: np; McGee, J. 2014. Digital reasoning gains $24M from Goldman, Credit Suisse. *tennessean.com,* October 9: np; and Dillow, C. 2014. Nothing to hide, everything to fear. *Fortune,* September 1: 45–48.

Evolving from Boundaries to Rewards and Culture

In most environments, organizations should strive to provide a system of rewards and incentives, coupled with a culture strong enough that boundaries become internalized. This reduces the need for external controls such as rules and regulations.

First, hire the right people—individuals who already identify with the organization's dominant values and have attributes consistent with them. Kroger, a supermarket chain, uses a preemployment test to assess the degree to which potential employees will be friendly and communicate well with customers.[45] Microsoft's David Pritchard is well aware of the consequences of failing to hire properly:

> If I hire a bunch of bozos, it will hurt us, because it takes time to get rid of them. They start infiltrating the organization and then they themselves start hiring people of lower quality. At Microsoft, we are always looking for people who are better than we are.

Second, training plays a key role. For example, in elite military units such as the Green Berets and Navy SEALs, the training regimen so thoroughly internalizes the culture that

EXHIBIT 9.5 Organizational Control: Alternative Approaches

Approach	Some Situational Factors
Culture: A system of unwritten rules that forms an internalized influence over behavior.	• Often found in professional organizations. • Associated with high autonomy. • Norms are the basis for behavior.
Rules: Written and explicit guidelines that provide external constraints on behavior.	• Associated with standardized output. • Most appropriate when tasks are generally repetitive and routine. • Little need for innovation or creative activity.
Rewards: The use of performance-based incentive systems to motivate.	• Measurement of output and performance is rather straightforward. • Most appropriate in organizations pursuing unrelated diversification strategies. • Rewards may be used to reinforce other means of control.

individuals, in effect, lose their identity. The group becomes the overriding concern and focal point of their energies. At firms such as FedEx, training not only builds skills but also plays a significant role in building a strong culture on the foundation of each organization's dominant values.

Third, managerial role models are vital. Andy Grove, former CEO and cofounder of Intel, didn't need (or want) a large number of bureaucratic rules to determine who is responsible for what, who is supposed to talk to whom, and who gets to fly first class (no one does). He encouraged openness by not having many of the trappings of success—he worked in a cubicle like all the other professionals. Can you imagine any new manager asking whether or not he can fly first class? Grove's personal example eliminated such a need.

Fourth, reward systems must be clearly aligned with the organizational goals and objectives. For example, as part of its efforts to drive sustainability efforts down through its suppliers, Marks and Spencer pushes the suppliers to develop employee reward systems that support a living wage and team collaboration.

The Role of Corporate Governance

We now address the issue of strategic control in a broader perspective, typically referred to as "corporate governance." Here we focus on the need for both shareholders (the owners of the corporation) and their elected representatives, the board of directors, to actively ensure that management fulfills its overriding purpose of increasing long-term shareholder value.[46]

Robert Monks and Nell Minow, two leading scholars in **corporate governance,** define it as "the relationship among various participants in determining the direction and performance of corporations. The primary participants are (1) the shareholders, (2) the management (led by the CEO), and (3) the board of directors."* Our discussion will center on how corporations can succeed (or fail) in aligning managerial motives with the interests of the shareholders and their elected representatives, the board of directors.[47] As you will recall from Chapter 1, we discussed the important role of boards of directors and provided some examples of effective and ineffective boards.[48]

Good corporate governance plays an important role in the investment decisions of major institutions, and a premium is often reflected in the price of securities of companies that practice it. The corporate governance premium is larger for firms in countries with sound corporate governance practices compared to countries with weaker corporate governance standards.[49]

Sound governance practices often lead to superior financial performance. However, this is not always the case. For example, practices such as independent directors (directors who are not part of the firm's management) and stock options are generally assumed to result in better performance. But in many cases, independent directors may not have the necessary expertise or involvement, and the granting of stock options to the CEO may lead to decisions and actions calculated to prop up share price only in the short term.

At the same time, few topics in the business press are generating as much interest (and disdain!) as corporate governance.

Some recent notable examples of flawed corporate governance include:[50]

- In 2014, three senior executives at Walmart resigned from the firm in the wake of accusations of bribery of government officials in Mexico. In response, Walmart changed both the leadership in this region and its compliance structure.[51]

*Management cannot ignore the demands of other important firm stakeholders such as creditors, suppliers, customers, employees, and government regulators. At times of financial duress, powerful creditors can exert strong and legitimate pressures on managerial decisions. In general, however, the attention to stakeholders other than the owners of the corporation must be addressed in a manner that is still consistent with maximizing long-term shareholder returns. For a seminal discussion on stakeholder management, refer to Freeman, R. E. 1984. *Strategic Management: A Stakeholder Approach.* Boston: Pitman.

- In 2012 Japanese camera and medical equipment maker Olympus Corporation and three of its former executives pleaded guilty to charges that they falsified accounting records over a five-year period to inflate the financial performance of the firm. The total value of the accounting irregularities came to $1.7 billion.[52]
- In October 2010, Angelo Mozilo, the cofounder of Countrywide Financial, agreed to pay $67.5 million to the Securities and Exchange Commission (SEC) to settle fraud charges. He was charged with deceiving the home loan company's investors while reaping a personal windfall. He was accused of hiding risks about Countrywide's loan portfolio as the real estate market soured. Former Countrywide president David Sambol and former chief financial officer Eric Sieracki were also charged with fraud, as they failed to disclose the true state of Countrywide's deteriorating mortgage portfolio. The SEC accused Mozilo of insider trading, alleging that he sold millions of dollars worth of Countrywide stock after he knew the company was doomed.

Because of the many lapses in corporate governance, we can see the benefits associated with effective practices.[53] However, corporate managers may behave in their own self-interest, often to the detriment of shareholders. Next we address the implications of the separation of ownership and management in the modern corporation, and some mechanisms that can be used to ensure consistency (or alignment) between the interests of shareholders and those of the managers to minimize potential conflicts.

The Modern Corporation: The Separation of Owners (Shareholders) and Management

Some of the proposed definitions for a *corporation* include:

- "The business corporation is an instrument through which capital is assembled for the activities of producing and distributing goods and services and making investments. Accordingly, a basic premise of corporation law is that a business corporation should have as its objective the conduct of such activities with a view to enhancing the corporation's profit and the gains of the corporation's owners, that is, the shareholders." (Melvin Aron Eisenberg, *The Structure of Corporation Law*)
- "A body of persons granted a charter legally recognizing them as a separate entity having its own rights, privileges, and liabilities distinct from those of its members." (*American Heritage Dictionary*)
- "An ingenious device for obtaining individual profit without individual responsibility." (Ambrose Bierce, *The Devil's Dictionary*)[54]

All of these definitions have some validity and each one reflects a key feature of the corporate form of business organization—its ability to draw resources from a variety of groups and establish and maintain its own persona that is separate from all of them. As Henry Ford once said, "A great business is really too big to be human."

Simply put, a **corporation** is a mechanism created to allow different parties to contribute capital, expertise, and labor for the maximum benefit of each party.[55] The shareholders (investors) are able to participate in the profits of the enterprise without taking direct responsibility for the operations. The management can run the company without the responsibility of personally providing the funds. The shareholders have limited liability as well as rather limited involvement in the company's affairs. However, they reserve the right to elect directors who have the fiduciary obligation to protect their interests.

Over 80 years ago, Columbia University professors Adolf Berle and Gardiner C. Means addressed the divergence of the interests of the owners of the corporation from the professional managers who are hired to run it. They warned that widely dispersed ownership "released management from the overriding requirement that it serve stockholders." The separation of

corporation
a mechanism created to allow different parties to contribute capital, expertise, and labor for the maximum benefit of each party.

ownership from management has given rise to a set of ideas called "agency theory." Central to agency theory is the relationship between two primary players—the *principals,* who are the owners of the firm (stockholders), and the *agents,* who are the people paid by principals to perform a job on their behalf (management). The stockholders elect and are represented by a board of directors that has a fiduciary responsibility to ensure that management acts in the best interests of stockholders to ensure long-term financial returns for the firm.

agency theory
a theory of the relationship between principals and their agents, with emphasis on two problems: (1) the conflicting goals of principals and agents, along with the difficulty of principals to monitor the agents, and (2) the different attitudes and preferences toward risk of principals and agents.

Agency theory is concerned with resolving two problems that can occur in agency relationships.[56] *The first is the agency problem that arises (1) when the goals of the principals and agents conflict and (2) when it is difficult or expensive for the principal to verify what the agent is actually doing.*[57] The board of directors would be unable to confirm that the managers were actually acting in the shareholders' interests because managers are "insiders" with regard to the businesses they operate and thus are better informed than the principals. Thus, managers may act "opportunistically" in pursuing their own interests—to the detriment of the corporation.[58] Managers may spend corporate funds on expensive perquisites (e.g., company jets and expensive art), devote time and resources to pet projects (initiatives in which they have a personal interest but that have limited market potential), engage in power struggles (where they may fight over resources for their own betterment and to the detriment of the firm), and negate (or sabotage) attractive merger offers because they may result in increased employment risk.[59]

The second issue is the problem of risk sharing. This arises when the principal and the agent have different attitudes and preferences toward risk. The executives in a firm may favor additional diversification initiatives because, by their very nature, they increase the size of the firm and thus the level of executive compensation.[60] At the same time, such diversification initiatives may erode shareholder value because they fail to achieve some synergies that we discussed in Chapter 6 (e.g., building on core competencies, sharing activities, or enhancing market power). Agents (executives) may have a stronger preference toward diversification than shareholders because it reduces their personal level of risk from potential loss of employment. Executives who have large holdings of stock in their firms were more likely to have diversification strategies that were more consistent with shareholder interests—increasing long-term returns.[61]

At times, top-level managers engage in actions that reflect their self-interest rather than the interests of shareholders. We provide two examples below:

- Steve Wynn, the CEO of Wynn Resorts, had a great year in 2011, even though his stockholders barely broke even. He received a starting salary of $3.9 million. On top of that, he received two bonuses, one worth $2 million and another for $9 million. In addition to cash compensation, he received over $900,000 worth of personal flying time on the corporate jet and over $500,000 worth of use of the company's villa.[62]
- John Sperling retired as chairman emeritus of Apollo Group in early 2013. He founded Apollo, the for-profit education company best known for its University of Phoenix unit, in 1973. Even though he already owned stock in Apollo worth in excess of $200 million, the board of directors, which includes his son as a member, granted him a "special retirement bonus" of $5 million, gave him two cars, and awarded him a lifetime annuity of $71,000 a month. He received all of these benefits even though Apollo's stock at the time of his retirement was worth one-fourth of its value in early 2009.[63]

LO9.6

The role of corporate governance mechanisms in ensuring that the interests of managers are aligned with those of shareholders from both the United States and international perspectives.

Governance Mechanisms: Aligning the Interests of Owners and Managers

As noted above, a key characteristic of the modern corporation is the separation of ownership from control. To minimize the potential for managers to act in their own self-interest, or "opportunistically," the owners can implement some governance mechanisms.[64] First, there are two primary means of monitoring the behavior of managers. These include (1) a committed and involved *board of directors* that acts in the best interests of the shareholders to create long-term value and (2) *shareholder activism,* wherein the owners view themselves as share*owners* instead of share*holders* and become actively engaged in the governance of the corporation. Finally, there are managerial incentives, sometimes called "contract-based outcomes," which consist of *reward and compensation agreements.* Here the goal is to carefully craft managerial incentive packages to align the interests of management with those of the stockholders.[65]

We close this section with a brief discussion of one of the most controversial issues in corporate governance—duality. Here, the question becomes: Should the CEO also be chairman of the board of directors? In many Fortune 500 firms, the same individual serves in both roles. However, in recent years, we have seen a trend toward separating these two positions. The key issue is what implications CEO duality has for firm governance and performance.

A Committed and Involved Board of Directors   The **board of directors** acts as a fulcrum between the owners and controllers of a corporation. The directors are the intermediaries who provide a balance between a small group of key managers in the firm based at the corporate headquarters and a sometimes vast group of shareholders.[66] In the United States, the law imposes on the board a strict and absolute fiduciary duty to ensure that a company is run consistent with the long-term interests of the owners—the shareholders. The reality, as we have seen, is somewhat more ambiguous.[67]

The Business Roundtable, representing the largest U.S. corporations, describes the duties of the board as follows:

> **board of directors**
> a group that has a fiduciary duty to ensure that the company is run consistently with the long-term interests of the owners, or shareholders, of a corporation and that acts as an intermediary between the shareholders and management.

1. Making decisions regarding the selection, compensation and evaluation of a well-qualified and ethical CEO. The board also appoints or approves other members of the senior management team.
2. Directors monitor management on behalf of the corporation's shareholders. Exercise vigorous and diligent oversight of the corporation's affairs. This includes the following activities.
   a. Plan for senior management development and succession.
   b. Review, understand and monitor the implementation of the corporation's strategic plans.
   c. Review and understand the corporation's risk assessment and oversee the corporation's risk management processes.
   d. Review, understand and oversee annual operating plans and budgets.
   e. Ensure the integrity and clarity of the corporation's financial statements and financial reporting.
   f. Advise management on significant issues facing the corporation.
   g. Review and approve significant corporate actions.
   h. Nominate directors and committee members and oversee effective corporate governance.
   i. Oversee legal and ethical compliance.
3. Represent the interests of all shareholders.[68]

While the roles of the board are fairly clear, following these guidelines does not guarantee that the board will be effective. To be effective, the board needs to allocate its scarce time to the most critical issues to which its members can add value. A survey of several hundred corporate board members revealed dramatic differences in how the most and least effective boards allocated their time. Boards that were seen as being ineffective, meaning they had limited impact on the direction and success of the firm, spent almost all of their time on the basic requirements of ensuring compliance, reviewing financial reports,

MOVING THE BOARD FROM AUDITOR TO ADVISER

Boards of directors are given the formal role of representing shareholders of a corporation and overseeing corporate managers to make sure managers act to enhance shareholder value. However, for decades, boards were often little more than cozy clubs, populated by the friends of the CEO who would meet every few months to rubber-stamp the CEO's plans for the firm. Financial scandals and corporate failures in the late 1990s and early 2000s changed this. New regulations came about, pushing for stronger oversight by the board, more independent directors, and greater penalties for boards that failed to fulfill their duties. This has resulted in stronger boards that more diligently oversee and discipline firm management. But it doesn't mean that the firm is leveraging all of the talent on the board, unless the firm finds a way to effectively draw on the experiences and expertise of its board.

Ram Charan, Dennis Carey, and Michael Useem argue in their book *Boards That Lead* that boards need to change, and are dramatically changing, their role, moving away from being auditors that check on the performance of managers and, instead, becoming strategic partners with firm management. The key change is that rather than reviewing and ratifying managers' decisions, the board can serve as a panel of strategic advisers to the firm, aiding in the formulation of the firm's strategy and not simply reviewing the firm's strategy. To do so, board members work to build strong relationships with the firm's CEO, actively mentor the CEO by providing advice from the wealth of their experience, and serve as talent scouts to help identify new executives for the firm. For example, the board of Ford Motor Company was instrumental in the firm's turnaround by convincing the firm's CEO, Bill Ford, of the need for new leadership, recruiting Alan Mulally from Boeing to be Ford's new CEO, and working with and advising Ford management as it worked to reorient the firm. More generally, research on a broad range of companies has found that boards that have the skills and knowledge to advise CEOs on potential key strategic initiatives are able to add more value to the firm.

The potential benefits of a leading board are clear, but so are the risks of this change. Can boards that work with and advise the CEO also serve as effective overseers of firm management, or will they end up in the cozy relationships seen in the past? Will the CEO be comfortable sharing power with the board, or will there be a power struggle as the board weighs in with advice? Finding the right balance will require not only negotiations between the board and the CEO to define the roles effectively but also the efforts of institutional investors and regulators to ensure the board doesn't get too friendly with the CEO.

Sources: McDonald, M., Westphal, J., & Graebner, M. 2008. What do they know? The effects of outside director acquisition experience on firm acquisition performance. *Strategic Management Journal,* 29: 1155–1177; Haynes, K. & Hillman, A. 2010. The effect of board capital and CEO power on strategic change. *Strategic Management Journal,* 31: 1145–1163; and Anonymous. 2013. From cuckolds to captains. *The Economist,* December 7: 72.

assessing corporate diversification, and evaluating current performance metrics. Effective boards examined these issues but also expanded the range of issues they discussed to include more forward-looking strategic issues. Effective boards discussed potential performance synergies and the value of strategic alternatives open to the firm, assessed the firm's value drivers, and evaluated potential resource reallocation options. In the end, effective and ineffective boards spent about the same time on their basic board roles, but effective boards spent additional time together to discuss more forward-looking, strategic issues. As a result, board members of effective boards spent twice as many days, about 40 per year, in their role as a board member compared to only about 19 days per year for members of ineffective boards.[69]

Strategy Spotlight 9.5 extends our discussion of the growing role of the effective boards as strategic advisers to firm management.

Although boards in the past were often dismissed as CEOs' rubber stamps, increasingly they are playing a more active role by forcing out CEOs who cannot deliver on performance.[70] Not only are they dismissing CEOs, but boards are more willing to make strong public statements about CEOs they dismissed. In the past, firms would often announce that a CEO was leaving the position to spend more time with family or pursue new opportunities. More frequently, boards are unambiguously labeling the action a dismissal to signal that they are active and engaged boards. For example, when Symantec's board removed the firm's CEO in March 2014, the board announced it was bringing in an interim CEO following "the termination of Steve Bennett." Sanofi, a French pharmaceutical firm, went even further when it fired CEO Christopher Viehbacher. In a conference call with stock analysts, the firm's board chairman discussed how a "lack of trust" between the board and Viehbacher led to his dismissal. Sometimes even the CEO clarifies the situation. When Andrew Mason was ousted as head of Groupon, he released a humorous statement saying, "After four and a half intense and wonderful years as CEO of Groupon, I've decided to spend more time with my family. Just kidding—I was fired today."[71]

Another key component of top-ranked boards is director independence.[72] Governance experts believe that a majority of directors should be free of all ties to either the CEO or the company.[73] This means that a minimum of "insiders" (past or present members of the management team) should serve on the board and that directors and their firms should be barred from doing consulting, legal, or other work for the company.[74] Interlocking directorships—in which CEOs and other top managers serve on each other's boards—are not desirable. But perhaps the best guarantee that directors act in the best interests of shareholders is the simplest: Most good companies now insist that directors own significant stock in the company they oversee.[75]

Taking it one step further, research and simple observations of boards indicate that simple prescriptions, such as having a majority of outside directors, are insufficient to lead to effective board operations. Firms need to cultivate engaged and committed boards. There are several actions that can have a positive influence on board dynamics as the board works to both oversee and advise management.[76]

1. ***Build in the right expertise on the board.*** Outside directors can bring in experience that the management team is missing. For example, corporations that are considering expanding into a new region of the globe may want to add a board member who brings expertise on and connections in that region. Similarly, research suggests that firms that are focusing on improving their operational efficiency benefit from having an external board member whose full-time position is as a chief operating officer, a position that typically focuses on operational activities.

2. ***Keep your board size manageable.*** Small, focused boards, generally with 5 to 11 members, are preferable to larger ones. As boards grow in size, the ability for them to function as a team declines. The members of the board feel less connected with each other, and decision making can become unwieldy.

3. ***Choose directors who can participate fully.*** The time demands on directors have increased as their responsibilities have grown to include overseeing management, verifying the firm's financial statements, setting executive compensation, and advising on the strategic direction of the firm. As a result, the average number of hours per year spent on board duties has increased to over 350 hours for directors of large firms. Directors have to dedicate significant time to their roles—not just for scheduled meetings but also to review materials between meetings and to respond to time-sensitive challenges. Thus, firms should strive to include directors who are not currently overburdened by their core occupation or involvement on other boards.

4. ***Balance the need to focus on the past, the present, and the future.*** Boards have a three-tiered role. They need to focus on the recent performance of the firm, how the firm is meeting current milestones and operational targets, and what the strategic direction of the firm will be moving forward. Under current regulations, boards are required to spend a great amount of time on the past as they vet the firm's financials. However, effective boards balance this time and ensure that they give adequate consideration to the present and the future.

5. ***Consider management talent development.*** As part of their future-oriented focus, effective boards develop succession plans for the CEO but also focus on talent development at other upper echelons of the organization. In a range of industries,

human capital is an increasingly important driver of firm success, and boards should be involved in evaluating and developing the top management core.

6. ***Get a broad view.*** In order to better understand the firm and make contact with key managers, the meetings of the board should rotate to different operating units and sites of the firm.

7. ***Maintain norms of transparency and trust.*** Highly functioning boards maintain open, team-oriented dialogue wherein information flows freely and questions are asked openly. Directors respect each other and trust that they are all working in the best interests of the corporation.

Because of financial crises and corporate scandals, regulators and investors have pushed for significant changes in the structure and actions of boards. Exhibit 9.6 highlights some of the changes seen among firms in the S&P 500.

Shareholder Activism As a practical matter, there are so many owners of the largest American corporations that it makes little sense to refer to them as "owners" in the sense of

EXHIBIT 9.6

The Changing Face of the Board of Firms in the S&P 500

Issue	Then and Now		Explanation
	1987	**2011**	
Percentage of boards that have an average age of 64 or older	3	37	Fewer sitting CEOs are willing to serve on the boards of other firms. As a result, companies are raising the retirement age for directors and pulling in retired executives to their boards.
Average pay for directors	$36,667	$95,262	Board work has taken greater time and commitment. Additionally, the personal liability directors face has increased. As a result, compensation has increased to attract and retain board members.
Percentage of board members who are female	9	16.2	While the number of boards with women and minorities has increased, these groups are still underrepresented. Still, companies have emphasized including female directors in key roles. For example, over half the audit and compensation committees of S&P 500 firms have at least one female member.
Percentage of boards with 12 or fewer members	22	83	As the strategic role and the legal requirements of the board have increased, firms have opted for smaller boards since these smaller boards better operate as true decision-making groups.
Percentage of the directors who are independent	68	84	The Sarbanes-Oxley Act and pressure from investors have led to an increase in the number of independent directors. In fact, over half the S&P 500 firms now have no insiders other than the CEO on the board.

Sources: Anonymous. 2011. Corporate boards: Now and then. *Harvard Business Review,* 89(11): 38–39; and Dalton, D. & Dalton, C. 2010. Women and corporate boards of directors: The promise of increased, and substantive, participation in the post Sarbanes-Oxley era. *Business Horizons,* 53: 257–268.

individuals becoming informed and involved in corporate affairs.[77] However, even an individual shareholder has several rights, including (1) the right to sell the stock, (2) the right to vote the proxy (which includes the election of board members), (3) the right to bring suit for damages if the corporation's directors or managers fail to meet their obligations, (4) the right to certain information from the company, and (5) certain residual rights following the company's liquidation (or its filing for reorganization under bankruptcy laws), once creditors and other claimants are paid off.[78]

Collectively, shareholders have the power to direct the course of corporations.[79] This may involve acts such as being party to shareholder action suits and demanding that key issues be brought up for proxy votes at annual board meetings.[80] The power of shareholders has intensified in recent years because of the increasing influence of large institutional investors such as mutual funds (e.g., T. Rowe Price and Fidelity Investments) and retirement systems such as TIAA-CREF (for university faculty members and school administrative staff).[81] Institutional investors hold over 50 percent of all listed corporate stock in the United States.[82]

Shareholder activism refers to actions by large shareholders, both institutions and individuals, to protect their interests when they feel that managerial actions diverge from shareholder value maximization.

Many institutional investors are aggressive in protecting and enhancing their investments. They are shifting from traders to owners. They are assuming the role of permanent shareholders and rigorously analyzing issues of corporate governance. In the process they are reinventing systems of corporate monitoring and accountability.[83]

Consider the proactive behavior of CalPERS, the California Public Employees' Retirement System, which manages nearly $300 billion in assets and is the third-largest pension fund in the world.[84] Every year CalPERS reviews the performance of the 1,000 firms in which it retains a sizable investment.[85] It reviews each firm's short- and long-term performance, governance characteristics, and financial status, as well as market expectations for the firm. CalPERS then meets with selected companies to better understand their governance and business strategy. If needed, CalPERS requests changes in the firm's governance structure and works to ensure shareholders' rights. If CalPERS does not believe that the firm is responsive to its concerns, it considers filing proxy actions at the firm's next shareholders meeting and possibly even court actions. CalPERS's research suggests that these actions lead to superior performance. The portfolio of firms it has included in its review program produced a cumulative return that was 11.59 percent higher than a respective set of benchmark firms over a three-year period. Thus, CalPERS has seen a real benefit of acting as an interested owner, rather than as a passive investor.

Strategy Spotlight 9.6 discusses how institutional investors have moved beyond only filing proxy actions designed to create shareholder value. In addition to pushing for changes in executive pay and increasing stock buyback initiatives, institutional investors are now pushing social initiatives.

Managerial Rewards and Incentives   As we discussed earlier in the chapter, incentive systems must be designed to help a company achieve its goals.[86] From the perspective of governance, one of the most critical roles of the board of directors is to create incentives that align the interests of the CEO and top executives with the interests of owners of the corporation—long-term shareholder returns.[87] Shareholders rely on CEOs to adopt policies and strategies that maximize the value of their shares.[88] A combination of three basic policies may create the right monetary incentives for CEOs to maximize the value of their companies:[89]

1. Boards can require that the CEOs become substantial owners of company stock.
2. Salaries, bonuses, and stock options can be structured so as to provide rewards for superior performance and penalties for poor performance.
3. Dismissal for poor performance should be a realistic threat.

shareholder activism
actions by large shareholders to protect their interests when they feel that managerial actions of a corporation diverge from shareholder value maximization.

INSTITUTIONAL INVESTORS PUSH SOCIAL CONCERNS

Traditionally, activist investors have been very bottom-line-focused. They've pushed firms to unlock more value for shareholders. This led firms to take actions such as appointing a nonexecutive chairman of the board, altering compensation for top managers, divesting business units, increasing dividends, adding activist representatives to the board of directors, changing CEOs, and undertaking stock buyback programs. However, activist investors are now pushing a broader range of issues with managers, most notably pushing social initiatives. In the first quarter of 2014, 56 percent of shareholder proposals related to environmental and social issues. These proposals have resulted in shareholders voting on issues related to greenhouse gas emissions, political spending, and labor rights.

These initiatives rarely find strong support from shareholders, with environmental and social resolutions garnering only 21 percent support from shareholders when they get to an actual vote. About 30 percent of these proposals never get to a vote. Instead, corporate leaders and the activist investors negotiate an agreement on the issue. Corporations are often open to finding a negotiated solution to avoid unnecessary negative press coverage of the firm. For example, after being pressured by the $160 billion New York State Common Retirement Fund, Safeway, a major grocery retailer, agreed to buy only palm oil produced in ways that don't harm rainforests. Similarly, after being pressured by Greenpeace and associated activist investors, Lego agreed to not renew a contract with Royal Dutch Shell that had allowed Lego to sell kits with the Shell logo on trucks and gas pumps. The activists were concerned that Shell was not developing Arctic drilling areas in an environmentally responsible way and pressured Lego to disassociate itself from Shell. The effects of such activist investors can be seen more broadly as well. For example, 53 percent of firms in the S&P 500 now publish sustainability reports, and 80 percent publish data on their political giving—both of which are common concerns of social-oriented activist investors.

These pressures also put managers in a difficult position as they potentially face competing pressures. One class of activist investors may be pushing the firm to take aggressive, profitability-oriented actions, while other activist investors may be pushing competing initiatives for the firm to take social or environmental actions.

Sources: Studzinski, J. 2014. Shareholder activists up their game. *Fortune,* April 28: 20; Chasan, E. 2014. More companies bow to investors with a social cause. *wsj.com,* March 31: np; and Hansegard, J. 2014. Lego to stop making Shell play sets after Greenpeace campaign. *wsj.com,* October 9: np.

In recent years the granting of stock options has enabled top executives of publicly held corporations to earn enormous levels of compensation. In 2013, the average CEO in the Standard & Poor's 500 stock index took home 330 times the pay of the average worker—up from 40 times the average in 1980.[90] The counterargument, that the ratio is down from the 514 multiple in 2000, doesn't get much traction.[91]

Many boards have awarded huge option grants despite poor executive performance, and others have made performance goals easier to reach. However, stock options can be a valuable governance mechanism to align the CEO's interests with those of the shareholders. The extraordinarily high level of compensation can, at times, be grounded in sound governance principles.[92] Research by Steven Kaplan at the University of Chicago found that firms with CEOs in the top quintile of pay generated stock returns 60 percent higher than their direct competitors, while firms with CEOs in the bottom quintile of pay saw their stock underperform their rivals by almost 20 percent.[93] For example, Robert Kotik, CEO of video game firm Activision Blizzard, made $64.9 million in 2013, but the firm's stock price rose by over 60 percent that year, producing a strong return for stockholders as well.

That doesn't mean that executive compensation systems can't or shouldn't be improved. Exhibit 9.7 outlines a number of ways to build effective compensation packages for executives.[94]

CEO Duality: Is It Good or Bad?

CEO duality is one of the most controversial issues in corporate governance. It refers to the dual-leadership structure wherein the CEO acts simultaneously as the chair of the board of directors.[95] Scholars, consultants, and executives who are interested in determining the best way to manage a corporation are divided on the issue of the roles and responsibilities of a CEO. Two schools of thought represent the alternative positions.

Boards need to be diligent in building executive compensation packages that will incentivize executives to build long-term shareholder value and to address the concerns that regulators and the public have about excessive compensation. The key is to have open, fair, and consistent pay plans. Here are six policies to achieve that.

1. **Increase transparency.** Principles and pay policies should be consistent over time and fully disclosed in company documents. For example, Novartis has emphasized making its compensation policies fully transparent and not altering the targets used for incentive compensation in midstream.

2. **Build long-term performance with long-term pay.** The timing of compensation can be structured to force executives to think about the long-term success of the organization. For example, ExxonMobil times two-thirds of its senior executives' incentive compensation so that they don't receive it until they retire or for 10 years, whichever is longer. Similarly, in 2009, Goldman Sachs replaced its annual bonuses for its top managers with restricted stock grants that executives could sell in three to five years.

3. **Reward executives for performance, not simply for changes in the company's stock price.** To keep them from focusing only on stock price, Target includes a component in its executives' compensation plan for same-store sales performance over time.

4. **Have executives put some "skin in the game."** Firms should create some downside risk for managers. Relying more on restricted stock, rather than stock options, can achieve this. But some experts suggest that top executives should purchase sizable blocks of the firm's stock with their own money.

5. **Avoid overreliance on simple metrics.** Rather than rewarding for short-term financial performance metrics, firms should include future-oriented qualitative measures to incentivize managers to build for the future. Companies could include criteria such as customer retention rates, innovation and new product launch milestones, and leadership development criteria. For example, IBM added bonuses for executives who evidenced actions fostering global cooperation.

6. **Increase equity between workers and executives.** Top executives, with their greater responsibilities, should and will continue to make more than frontline employees, but firms can signal equity by dropping special perks, plans, and benefits for top managers. Additionally, companies can give employees the opportunity to share in the success of the firm by establishing employee stock ownership plans.

Sources: George, B. 2010. Executive pay: Rebuilding trust in an era of rage. *Bloomberg Businessweek,* September 13: 56; and Barton, D. 2011. Capitalism for the long term. *Harvard Business Review,* 89(3): 85.

Unity of Command Advocates of the unity-of-command perspective believe that when one person holds both roles, he or she is able to act more efficiently and effectively. CEO duality provides firms with a clear focus on both objectives and operations as well as eliminates confusion and conflict between the CEO and the chairman. Thus, it enables smoother, more effective strategic decision making. Holding dual roles as CEO/chairman creates unity across a company's managers and board of directors and ultimately allows the CEO to serve the shareholders even better. Having leadership focused in a single individual also enhances a firm's responsiveness and ability to secure critical resources. This perspective maintains that separating the two jobs—that of a CEO and that of the chairperson of the board of directors—may produce all types of undesirable consequences. CEOs may find it harder to make quick decisions. Ego-driven chief executives and chairmen may squabble over who is ultimately in charge. The shortage of first-class business talent may mean that bosses find themselves second-guessed by people who know little about the business.[96] Companies like Coca-Cola, JPMorgan, and Time Warner have refused to divide the CEO's and chairman's jobs and support this duality structure.

Agency Theory Supporters of agency theory argue that the positions of CEO and chairman should be separate. The case for separation is based on the simple principle of the separation of power. How can a board discharge its basic duty—monitoring the boss—if the boss is chairing its meetings and setting its agenda? How can a board act as a safeguard against corruption or incompetence when the possible source of that corruption and incompetence is sitting at the head of the table? CEO duality can create a conflict of interest that could negatively affect the interests of the shareholders.

Duality also complicates the issue of CEO succession. In some cases, a CEO/chairman may choose to retire as CEO but keep his or her role as the chairman. Although this splits up the roles, which appeases an agency perspective, it nonetheless puts the new CEO in a difficult position. The chairman is bound to question some of the new changes put in place, and the board as a whole might take sides with the chairman they trust and with whom they have a history. This conflict of interest would make it difficult for the new CEO to institute any changes, as the power and influence would still remain with the former CEO.[97]

Duality also serves to reinforce popular doubts about the legitimacy of the system as a whole and evokes images of bosses writing their own performance reviews and setting their own salaries. A number of the largest corporations, including Ford Motor Company, General Motors, Citigroup, Oracle, Apple, and Microsoft, have divided the roles between the CEO and chairman and eliminated duality. Finally, more than 90 percent of S&P 500 companies with CEOs who also serve as chairman of the board have appointed "lead" or "presiding" directors to act as a counterweight to a combined chairman and chief executive.

Research suggests that the effects of going from having a joint CEO/chairman to separating the two positions is contingent on how the firm is doing. When the positions are broken apart, there is a clear shift in the firm's performance. If the firm has been performing well, its performance declines after the separation. If the firm has been doing poorly, it experiences improvement after separating the two roles. This research suggests that there is no one correct answer on duality, but that firms should consider its current position and performance trends when deciding whether to keep the CEO and chairman positions in the hands of one person.[98]

External Governance Control Mechanisms

Thus far, we've discussed internal governance mechanisms. Internal controls, however, are not always enough to ensure good governance. The separation of ownership and control that we discussed earlier requires multiple control mechanisms, some internal and some external, to ensure that managerial actions lead to shareholder value maximization. Further, society-at-large wants some assurance that this goal is met without harming other stakeholder groups. Now we discuss several **external governance control mechanisms** that have developed in most modern economies. These include the market for corporate control, auditors, banks and analysts, governmental regulatory bodies, media, and public activists.

The Market for Corporate Control Let us assume for a moment that internal control mechanisms in a company are failing. This means that the board is ineffective in monitoring managers and is not exercising the oversight required of it and that shareholders are passive and are not taking any actions to monitor or discipline managers. Under these circumstances managers may behave opportunistically.[99] Opportunistic behavior can take many forms. First, managers can *shirk* their responsibilities. Shirking means that managers fail to exert themselves fully, as is required of them. Second, they can engage in *on-the-job consumption.* Examples of on-the-job consumption include private jets, club memberships, expensive artwork in the offices, and so on. Each of these represents consumption by managers that does not in any way increase shareholder value. Instead, they actually diminish shareholder value. Third, managers may engage in *excessive product-market diversification.*[100] As we discussed in Chapter 6, such diversification serves to reduce only the employment risk of the managers rather than the financial risk of the shareholders, who can more cheaply diversify their risk by owning a portfolio of investments. Is there any external mechanism to stop managers from shirking, consumption on the job, and excessive diversification?

The **market for corporate control** is one external mechanism that provides at least some partial solution to the problems described. If internal control mechanisms fail and the management is behaving opportunistically, the likely response of most shareholders will be to sell their stock rather than engage in activism.[101] As more stockholders vote with their feet, the value of the stock begins to decline. As the decline continues, at some point the market value of the firm becomes less than the book value. A corporate raider can take over the company

external governance control mechanisms
methods that ensure that managerial actions lead to shareholder value maximization and do not harm other stakeholder groups that are outside the control of the corporate governance system.

market for corporate control
an external control mechanism in which shareholders dissatisfied with a firm's management sell their shares.

for a price less than the book value of the assets of the company. The first thing that the raider may do on assuming control over the company is fire the underperforming management. The risk of being acquired by a hostile raider is often referred to as the **takeover constraint.** The takeover constraint deters management from engaging in opportunistic behavior.[102]

takeover constraint
the risk to management of the firm being acquired by a hostile raider.

Although in theory the takeover constraint is supposed to limit managerial opportunism, in recent years its effectiveness has become diluted as a result of a number of defense tactics adopted by incumbent management (see Chapter 6). Foremost among them are poison pills, greenmail, and golden parachutes. Poison pills are provisions adopted by the company to reduce its worth to the acquirer. An example would be payment of a huge one-time dividend, typically financed by debt. Greenmail involves buying back the stock from the acquirer, usually at an attractive premium. Golden parachutes are employment contracts that cause the company to pay lucrative severance packages to top managers fired as a result of a takeover, often running to several million dollars.

Auditors   Even when there are stringent disclosure requirements, there is no guarantee that the information disclosed will be accurate. Managers may deliberately disclose false information or withhold negative financial information as well as use accounting methods that distort results based on highly subjective interpretations. Therefore, all accounting statements are required to be audited and certified to be accurate by external auditors. These auditing firms are independent organizations staffed by certified professionals who verify the firm's books of accounts. Audits can unearth financial irregularities and ensure that financial reporting by the firm conforms to standard accounting practices.

However, these audits often fail to catch accounting irregularities. In the past, auditing failures played an important part in the failures of firms such as Enron and WorldCom. A recent study by the Public Company Accounting Oversight Board (PCAOB) found that audits conducted by the Big 4 accounting firms were often deficient. For example, 20 percent of the Ernst & Young audits examined by the PCAOB failed. And this was the best of the Big 4! The PCAOB found fault with 45 percent of the Deloitte audits it examined. Why do these reputable firms fail to find all of the issues in audits they conduct? First, auditors are appointed by the firm being audited. The desire to continue that business relationship sometimes makes them overlook financial irregularities. Second, most auditing firms also do consulting work and often have lucrative consulting contracts with the firms that they audit. Understandably, some of them tend not to ask too many difficult questions, because they fear jeopardizing the consulting business, which is often more profitable than the auditing work.

Banks and Analysts   Commercial and investment banks have lent money to corporations and therefore have to ensure that the borrowing firm's finances are in order and that the loan covenants are being followed. Stock analysts conduct ongoing in-depth studies of the firms that they follow and make recommendations to their clients to buy, hold, or sell. Their rewards and reputation depend on the quality of these recommendations. Their access to information, their knowledge of the industry and the firm, and the insights they gain from interactions with the management of the company enable them to alert the investing community of both positive and negative developments relating to a company.

It is generally observed that analyst recommendations are often more optimistic than warranted by facts. "Sell" recommendations tend to be exceptions rather than the norm. Many analysts failed to grasp the gravity of the problems surrounding failed companies such as Lehman Brothers and Countrywide till the very end. Part of the explanation may lie in the fact that most analysts work for firms that also have investment banking relationships with the companies they follow. Negative recommendations by analysts can displease the management, who may decide to take their investment banking business to a rival firm. Otherwise independent and competent analysts may be pressured to overlook negative information or tone down their criticism.

Governmental Regulatory Bodies   The extent of government regulation is often a function of the type of industry. Banks, utilities, and pharmaceuticals are subject to more regulatory oversight because of their importance to society. Public corporations are subject to more regulatory requirements than private corporations.[103]

All public corporations are required to disclose a substantial amount of financial information by bodies such as the Securities and Exchange Commission. These include quarterly and annual filings of financial performance, stock trading by insiders, and details of executive compensation packages. There are two primary reasons behind such requirements. First, markets can operate efficiently only when the investing public has faith in the market system. In the absence of disclosure requirements, the average investor suffers from a lack of reliable information and therefore may completely stay away from the capital market. This will negatively impact an economy's ability to grow. Second, disclosure of information such as insider trading protects the small investor to some extent from the negative consequences of information asymmetry. The insiders and large investors typically have more information than the small investor and can therefore use that information to buy or sell before the information becomes public knowledge.

The failure of a variety of external control mechanisms led the U.S. Congress to pass the Sarbanes-Oxley Act in 2002. This act calls for many stringent measures that would ensure better governance of U.S. corporations. Some of these measures include:[104]

- *Auditors* are barred from certain types of nonaudit work. They are not allowed to destroy records for five years. Lead partners auditing a client should be changed at least every five years.
- *CEOs* and *CFOs* must fully reveal off-balance-sheet finances and vouch for the accuracy of the information revealed.
- *Executives* must promptly reveal the sale of shares in firms they manage and are not allowed to sell when other employees cannot.
- *Corporate lawyers* must report to senior managers any violations of securities law lower down.

Media and Public Activists   The press is not usually recognized as an external control mechanism in the literature on corporate governance. There is no denying that in all developed capitalist economies, the financial press and media play an important indirect role in monitoring the management of public corporations. In the United States, business magazines such as *Bloomberg Businessweek* and *Fortune,* financial newspapers such as *The Wall Street Journal* and *Investor's Business Daily,* as well as television networks like Fox Business Network and CNBC are constantly reporting on companies. Public perceptions about a company's financial prospects and the quality of its management are greatly influenced by the media. Food Lion's reputation was sullied when ABC's *Prime Time Live* in 1992 charged the company with employee exploitation, false package dating, and unsanitary meat-handling practices. Bethany McLean of *Fortune* magazine is often credited as the first to have raised questions about Enron's long-term financial viability.[105]

Similarly, consumer groups and activist individuals often take a crusading role in exposing corporate malfeasance.[106] Well-known examples include Ralph Nader and Erin Brockovich, who played important roles in bringing to light the safety issues related to GM's Corvair and environmental pollution issues concerning Pacific Gas and Electric Company, respectively. Ralph Nader has created over 30 watchdog groups, including:[107]

- *Aviation Consumer Action Project.* Works to propose new rules to prevent flight delays, impose penalties for deceiving passengers about problems, and push for higher compensation for lost luggage.

- **Center for Auto Safety.** Helps consumers find plaintiff lawyers and agitate for vehicle recalls, increased highway safety standards, and lemon laws.
- **Center for Study of Responsive Law.** This is Nader's headquarters. Home of a consumer project on technology, this group sponsored seminars on Microsoft remedies and pushed for tougher Internet privacy rules. It also took on the drug industry over costs.
- **Pension Rights Center.** This center helped employees of IBM, General Electric, and other companies to organize themselves against cash-balance pension plans.

Corporate Governance: An International Perspective

The topic of corporate governance has long been dominated by agency theory and based on the explicit assumption of the separation of ownership and control.[108] The central conflicts are principal–agent conflicts between shareholders and management. However, such an underlying assumption seldom applies outside the United States and the United Kingdom. This is particularly true in emerging economies and continental Europe. Here, there is often concentrated ownership, along with extensive family ownership and control, business group structures, and weak legal protection for minority shareholders. Serious conflicts tend to exist between two classes of principals: controlling shareholders and minority shareholders. Such conflicts can be called **principal–principal (PP) conflicts,** as opposed to *principal–agent* conflicts (see Exhibits 9.8 and 9.9).

Strong family control is one of the leading indicators of concentrated ownership. In East Asia (excluding China), approximately 57 percent of the corporations have board chairmen and CEOs from the controlling families. In continental Europe, this number is 68 percent. A very common practice is the appointment of family members as board chairmen, CEOs, and other top executives. This happens because the families are controlling (not necessarily majority) shareholders. In 2003, 30-year-old James Murdoch was appointed CEO of British Sky Broadcasting (BSkyB), Europe's largest satellite broadcaster. There was very vocal resistance by minority shareholders. Why was he appointed in the first place? James's father just happened to be Rupert Murdoch, who controlled 35 percent of BSkyB and chaired the board. Clearly, this is a case of a PP conflict.

principal–principal conflicts
conflicts between two classes of principals—controlling shareholders and minority shareholders—within the context of a corporate governance system.

EXHIBIT 9.8 Traditional Principal–Agent Conflicts versus Principal–Principal Conflicts: How They Differ along Dimensions

	Principal–Agent Conflicts	Principal–Principal Conflicts
Goal incongruence	Between shareholders and professional managers who own a relatively small portion of the firm's equity.	Between controlling shareholders and minority shareholders.
Ownership pattern	Dispersed—5%–20% is considered "concentrated ownership."	Concentrated—often greater than 50% of equity is controlled by controlling shareholders.
Manifestations	Strategies that benefit entrenched managers at the expense of shareholders in general (e.g., shirking, pet projects, excessive compensation, and empire building).	Strategies that benefit controlling shareholders at the expense of minority shareholders (e.g., minority shareholder expropriation, nepotism, and cronyism).
Institutional protection of minority shareholders	Formal constraints (e.g., judicial reviews and courts) set an upper boundary on potential expropriation by majority shareholders. Informal norms generally adhere to shareholder wealth maximization.	Formal institutional protection is often lacking, corrupted, or unenforced. Informal norms are typically in favor of the interests of controlling shareholders ahead of those of minority investors.

Source: Adapted from Young, M., Peng, M. W., Ahlstrom, D., & Bruton, G. 2002. Governing the Corporation in Emerging Economies: A Principal–Principal Perspective. *Academy of Management Best Papers Proceedings,* Denver.

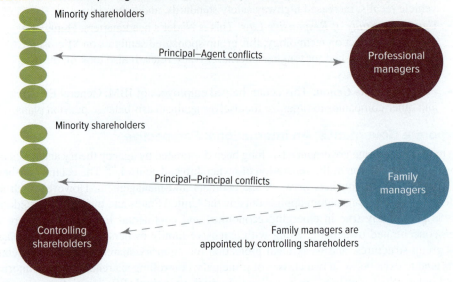

Source: Young, M. N., Peng, M. W., Ahlstrom, D., Bruton, G. D., & Jiang, 2008. Principal–Principal Conflicts in Corporate Governance. *Journal of Management Studies,* 45(1): 196–220; and Peng, M. V. 2006. *Global Strategy.* Cincinnati: Thomson South-Western. We are very appreciative of the helpful comments of Mike Young of Hong Kong Baptist University and Mike Peng of the University of Texas at Dallas.

In general, three conditions must be met for PP conflicts to occur:

- A dominant owner or group of owners who have interests that are distinct from minority shareholders.
- Motivation for the controlling shareholders to exercise their dominant positions to their advantage.
- Few formal (such as legislation or regulatory bodies) or informal constraints that would discourage or prevent the controlling shareholders from exploiting their advantageous positions.

expropriation of minority shareholders activities that enrich the controlling shareholders at the expense of the minority shareholders.

The result is often that family managers, who represent (or actually are) the controlling shareholders, engage in **expropriation of minority shareholders,** which is defined as activities that enrich the controlling shareholders at the expense of minority shareholders. What is their motive? After all, controlling shareholders have incentives to maintain firm value. But controlling shareholders may take actions that decrease aggregate firm performance if their personal gains from expropriation exceed their personal losses from their firm's lowered performance.

Another ubiquitous feature of corporate life outside the United States and United Kingdom is *business groups* such as the keiretsus of Japan and the chaebols of South Korea. This is particularly dominant in emerging economies. A **business group** is "a set of firms that, though legally independent, are bound together by a constellation of formal and informal ties and are accustomed to taking coordinated action."[109] Business groups are especially common in emerging economies, and they differ from other organizational forms in that they are communities of firms without clear boundaries.

business groups a set of firms that, though legally independent, are bound together by a constellation of formal and informal ties and are accustomed to taking coordinated action.

Business groups have many advantages that can enhance the value of a firm. They often facilitate technology transfer or intergroup capital allocation that otherwise might be impossible because of inadequate institutional infrastructure such as excellent financial services firms. On the other hand, informal ties—such as cross-holdings, board interlocks, and coordinated actions—can often result in intragroup activities and transactions, often at very favorable terms to member firms. Expropriation can be legally done through *related transactions,* which can occur when controlling owners sell firm assets to another firm they own at below-market prices or spin off the most profitable part of a public firm and merge it with another of their private firms.

ISSUE FOR DEBATE

CEO Pay: Appropriate Incentives or Always Dealing the CEO a Winning Hand

Alpha Natural Resources had its worst ever financial performance in 2011. The firm shut six mines, laid off over 1,500 workers, and saw its stock price drop by 66 percent. Still, the board of directors granted the firm's CEO a $528,000 bonus on top of his over $6 million pay package, noting his "tremendous efforts" to improve worker safety. Stories like these leave commentators questioning if the game is stacked to ensure that CEOs receive high pay regardless of their firm's performance.

Most large firms structure the pay packages of their top executives so that the CEO and other senior executives' pay is tied to firm performance. A large part of their pay is stock-based. The value of the stock options they receive goes up and down with the price of the firm's stock. Their annual bonuses are conditional on meeting preset performance targets. However, boards often change the rules if the firm performs poorly. If the stock price drops, leaving the options held by the CEO "underwater" and worthless, they often reprice the options the CEO holds to a lower price, making them potentially much more valuable to the CEO if the stock price bounces back. As noted above, boards also often find reasons to grant bonuses to CEOs even if the firm underperforms.

At first blush, this suggests the boards of directors are ineffective and serve to meet the desires of the CEO. But there is a logical reason why boards reprice options and grant bonuses when firms perform poorly. Boards may reprice options or change the goals that justify bonuses as a means to protect CEOs from being harmed by events out of their control. For example, if a spike in fuel prices hurts the performance of an airline or a major hurricane results in a loss for an insurance firm, the boards of these firms may argue that underperformance isn't the fault of the CEO and shouldn't result in less pay.

However, critics of this practice argue that it's wrong to protect CEOs from bad luck but not withhold benefits if the firm benefits from good luck. Boards rarely, if ever, raise the standards on CEO pay when the firm benefits from an unanticipated event. A study by researchers at Claremont Graduate University and Washington University found that executives lost less pay when their firms experienced bad luck than they gained when the firm experienced good luck. Additionally, critics point out that most workers, such as the 1,500 who were laid off by Alpha, don't receive the same protection from adverse events that the CEO does.

Discussion Questions

1. Is it appropriate for firms to insulate their CEOs' pay from bad luck?
2. How can firms restructure pay to ensure that the CEOs also don't benefit from good luck?

Sources: Mider, Z. & Green, J. 2012. Heads or tails, some CEOs win the pay game. *Bloomberg Businessweek,* October 8: 23; and Devers, C., McNamara, G., Wiseman, R., & Arrfelt, M. 2008. Moving closer to the action: Examining compensation design effects on firm risk. *Organization Science,* 19: 548–566.

Reflecting on Career Implications . . .

- ■ **Behavioral Control:** What types of behavioral control does your organization employ? Do you find these behavioral controls helping or hindering you from doing a good job? Some individuals are comfortable with and even desire rules and procedures for everything. Others find that they inhibit creativity and stifle initiative. Evaluate your own level of comfort with the level of behavioral control and then assess the match between your own optimum level of control and the level and type of control used by your organization. If the gap is significant, you might want to consider other career opportunities.

- ■ **Setting Boundaries and Constraints:** Your career success depends to a great extent on you monitoring and regulating your own behavior. Setting boundaries and constraints on yourself can help you focus on strategic priorities, generate short-term objectives and action plans, improve efficiency and effectiveness, and minimize improper conduct. Identify

the boundaries and constraints you have placed on yourself and evaluate how each of those contributes to your personal growth and career development. If you do not have boundaries and constraints, consider developing them.

- ■ **Rewards and Incentives:** Is your organization's reward structure fair and equitable? On what criteria do you base your conclusions? How does the firm define outstanding performance and reward it? Are these financial or nonfinancial rewards? The absence of rewards that are seen as fair and equitable can result in the long-term erosion of morale, which may have long-term adverse career implications for you.

- ■ **Culture:** Given your career goals, what type of organizational culture would provide the best work environment? How does your organization's culture deviate from this concept? Does your organization have a strong and effective culture? In the long run, how likely are you to internalize the culture of your organization? If you believe that there is a strong misfit between your values and the organization's culture, you may want to reconsider your relationship with the organization.

summary

For firms to be successful, they must practice effective strategic control and corporate governance. Without such controls, the firm will not be able to achieve competitive advantages and outperform rivals in the marketplace.

We began the chapter with the key role of informational control. We contrasted two types of control systems: what we termed "traditional" and "contemporary" information control systems. Whereas traditional control systems may have their place in placid, simple competitive environments, there are fewer of those in today's economy. Instead, we advocated the contemporary approach wherein the internal and external environment are constantly monitored so that when surprises emerge, the firm can modify its strategies, goals, and objectives.

Behavioral controls are also a vital part of effective control systems. We argued that firms must develop the proper balance between culture, rewards and incentives, and boundaries and constraints. Where there are strong and positive cultures and rewards, employees tend to internalize the organization's strategies and objectives. This permits a firm to spend fewer resources on monitoring behavior, and assures the firm that the efforts and initiatives of employees are more consistent with the overall objectives of the organization.

In the final section of this chapter, we addressed corporate governance, which can be defined as the relationship between various participants in determining the direction and performance of the corporation. The primary participants include shareholders, management (led by the chief executive officer), and the board of directors. We reviewed studies that indicated a consistent relationship between effective corporate governance and financial performance. There

are also several internal and external control mechanisms that can serve to align managerial interests and shareholder interests. The internal mechanisms include a committed and involved board of directors, shareholder activism, and effective managerial incentives and rewards. The external mechanisms include the market for corporate control, banks and analysts, regulators, the media, and public activists. We also addressed corporate governance from both a United States and an international perspective.

SUMMARY REVIEW QUESTIONS

1. Why are effective strategic control systems so important in today's economy?
2. What are the main advantages of contemporary control systems over traditional control systems? What are the main differences between these two systems?
3. Why is it important to have a balance between the three elements of behavioral control—culture, rewards and incentives, and boundaries?
4. Discuss the relationship between types of organizations and their primary means of behavioral control.
5. Boundaries become less important as a firm develops a strong culture and reward system. Explain.
6. Why is it important to avoid a "one best way" mentality concerning control systems? What are the consequences of applying the same type of control system to all types of environments?
7. What is the role of effective corporate governance in improving a firm's performance? What are some of the key governance mechanisms that are used to ensure that managerial and shareholder interests are aligned?
8. Define principal–principal (PP) conflicts. What are the implications for corporate governance?

monitor the environment and make necessary changes in their strategy and objectives. What companies are you familiar with that responded appropriately (or inappropriately) to environmental change?

2. How can a strong, positive culture enhance a firm's competitive advantage? How can a weak, negative culture erode competitive advantages? Explain and provide examples.

3. Use the Internet to research a firm that has an excellent culture and/or reward and incentive system. What are this firm's main financial and nonfinancial benefits?

4. Using the Internet, go to the website of a large, publicly held corporation in which you are interested. What evidence do you see of effective (or ineffective) corporate governance?

experiential exercise

McDonald's Corporation, the world's largest fast-food restaurant chain, with 2014 revenues of $27 billion, but the firm has stumbled recently. Sales in 2014 dropped by 2%, and its shareholder value declined by 4% from May 2014 to May 2015. Using the Internet, evaluate the quality of the corporation in terms of management, the board of directors, and shareholder activism. (Fill in the chart below.) Are the issues you list favorable or unfavorable for sound corporate governance?

application questions & exercises

1. The problems of many firms may be attributed to a traditional control system that failed to continuously

ethics questions

1. Strong cultures can have powerful effects on employee behavior. How does this create inadvertent control mechanisms? That is, are strong cultures an ethical way to control behavior?

2. Rules and regulations can help reduce unethical behavior in organizations. To be effective, however, what other systems, mechanisms, and processes are necessary?

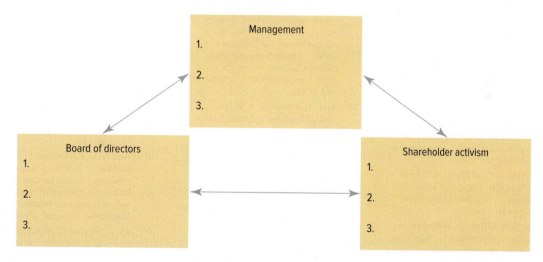

references

1. Anonymous. 2014. Not so funny. e*conomist.com,* September 27: np; Evans, P. & Fleisher, L. 2014. Tesco investigates accounting error. w*sj.com,* September 23: np; Rosenblum, P. 2014. Tesco's accounting irregularities are mind

   blowing. *forbes.com,* September 22: np; and Davey, J. 2014. UK watchdog to investigate Tesco accounts and auditor PwC. *reuters.com,* December 22: np.

2. This chapter draws upon Picken, J. C. & Dess, G. G. 1997. *Mission critical.* Burr Ridge, IL: Irwin Professional.

3. For a unique perspective on governance, refer to Carmeli, A. & Markman, G. D. 2011. Capture, governance, and resilience: Strategy implications from the history of Rome. *Strategic Management Journal,* 32(3): 332–341.

4. Argyris, C. 1977. Double-loop learning in organizations. *Harvard Business Review*, 55: 115–125.

5. Simons, R. 1995. Control in an age of empowerment. *Harvard Business Review*, 73: 80–88. This chapter draws on this source in the discussion of informational control.

6. Goold, M. & Quinn, J. B. 1990. The paradox of strategic controls. *Strategic Management Journal*, 11: 43–57.

7. Quinn, J. B. 1980. *Strategies for change*. Homewood, IL: Irwin.

8. Mintzberg, H. 1987. Crafting strategy. *Harvard Business Review*, 65: 66–75.

9. Weston, J. S. 1992. Soft stuff matters. *Financial Executive*, July–August: 52–53.

10. This discussion of control systems draws upon Simons, op. cit.

11. Ryan, M. K., Haslam, S. A., & Renneboog, L. D. R. 2011. Who gets the carrot and who gets the stick? Evidence of gender discrimination in executive remuneration. *Strategic Management Journal*, 32(3): 301–321.

12. For an interesting perspective on this issue and how a downturn in the economy can reduce the tendency toward "free agency" by managers and professionals, refer to Morris, B. 2001. White collar blues. *Fortune*, July 23: 98–110.

13. For a colorful example of behavioral control in an organization, see Beller, P. C. 2009. Activision's unlikely hero. *Forbes*, February 2: 52–58.

14. Ouchi, W. 1981. *Theory Z*. Reading, MA: Addison-Wesley; Deal, T. E. & Kennedy, A. A. 1982. *Corporate cultures*. Reading, MA: Addison-Wesley; Peters, T. J. & Waterman, R. H. 1982. *In search of excellence*. New York: Random House; and Collins, J. 2001. *Good to great*. New York: HarperCollins.

15. Collins, J. C. & Porras, J. I. 1994. *Built to last: Successful habits of visionary companies*. New York: Harper Business.

16. Lee, J. & Miller, D. 1999. People matter: Commitment to employees, strategy, and performance in Korean firms. *Strategic Management Journal*, 6: 579–594.

17. For an insightful discussion of IKEA's unique culture, see Kling, K. & Goteman, I. 2003. IKEA CEO Anders Dahlvig on international growth and IKEA's unique corporate culture and brand identity. *Academy of Management Executive*, 17(1): 31–37.

18. For a discussion of how professionals inculcate values, refer to Uhl-Bien, M. & Graen, G. B. 1998. Individual self-management: Analysis of professionals' self-managing activities in functional and cross-functional work teams. *Academy of Management Journal*, 41(3): 340–350.

19. A perspective on how antisocial behavior can erode a firm's culture can be found in Robinson, S. L. & O'Leary-Kelly, A. M. 1998. Monkey see, monkey do: The influence of work groups on the antisocial behavior of employees. *Academy of Management Journal*, 41(6): 658–672.

20. Benkler, Y. 2011. The unselfish gene. *Harvard Business Review*, 89(7): 76–85.

21. An interesting perspective on organizational culture is in Mehta, S. N. 2009. Under Armour reboots. *Fortune*, February 2: 29–33.

22. For insights on social pressure as a means for control, refer to Goldstein, N. J. 2009. Harnessing social pressure. *Harvard Business Review*, 87(2): 25.

23. Mitchell, R. 1989. Masters of innovation. *BusinessWeek*, April 10: 58–63.

24. Sellers, P. 1993. Companies that serve you best. *Fortune*, May 31: 88.

25. Southwest Airlines Culture Committee. 1993. *Luv Lines* (company publication), March–April: 17–18; for an interesting perspective on the "downside" of strong "cultlike" organizational cultures, refer to Arnott, D. A. 2000. *Corporate cults*. New York: AMACOM.

26. Kerr, J. & Slocum, J. W., Jr. 1987. Managing corporate culture through reward systems. *Academy of Management Executive*, 1(2): 99–107.

27. For a unique perspective on leader challenges in managing wealthy professionals, refer to Wetlaufer, S. 2000. Who wants to manage a millionaire? *Harvard Business Review*, 78(4): 53–60.

28. Netessine, S. & Yakubovich, V. 2012. The Darwinian workplace. *Harvard Business Review*, 90(5): 25–28.

29. For a discussion of the benefits of stock options as executive compensation, refer to Hall, B. J. 2000. What you need to know about stock options. *Harvard Business Review*, 78(2): 121–129.

30. Tully, S. 1993. Your paycheck gets exciting. *Fortune*, November 13: 89.

31. Carter, N. M. & Silva, C. 2010. Why men still get more promotions than women. *Harvard Business Review*, 88(9): 80–86.

32. Sirota, D., Mischkind, L. & Meltzer, I. 2008. Stop demotivating your employees! *Harvard Management Update*, July: 3–5; Nelson, B. 2003. Five questions about employee recognition and reward. *Harvard Management Update*; Birkinshaw, J., Bouquet, C., & Barsaoux, J. 2011. The 5 myths of innovation. *MIT Sloan Management Review*. Winter, 43–50; and Dewhurst, M. Guthridge, M., & Mohr, E. 2009. Motivating people: Getting beyond money. *mckinsey.com*. November: np.

33. This section draws on Picken & Dess, op. cit., chap. 5.

34. Anonymous. 2012. Nestle set to buy Pfizer unit. *Dallas Morning News*, April 19: 10D.

35. Isaacson, W. 2012. The real leadership lessons of Steve Jobs. *Harvard Business Review*, 90(4): 93–101.

36. This section draws upon Dess, G. G. & Miller, A. 1993. *Strategic management*. New York: McGraw-Hill.

37. For a good review of the goal-setting literature, refer to Locke, E. A. & Latham, G. P. 1990. *A theory of goal setting and task performance*. Englewood Cliffs, NJ: Prentice Hall.

38. For an interesting perspective on the use of rules and regulations that is counter to this industry's (software) norms, refer to Fryer, B. 2001. Tom Siebel of Siebel Systems: High tech the old fashioned way. *Harvard Business Review*, 79(3): 118–130.

39. Thompson, A. A., Jr., & Strickland, A. J., III. 1998. *Strategic management: Concepts and cases* (10th ed.): 313. New York: McGraw-Hill.

40. Weaver, G. R., Trevino, L. K., & Cochran, P. L. 1999. Corporate ethics programs as control systems: Influences of executive commitment and environmental factors. *Academy of Management Journal*, 42(1): 41–57.

41. www.singaporeair.com/pdf/media-centre/anti-corruption-policy-procedures.pdf.

42. Weber, J. 2003. CFOs on the hot seat. *BusinessWeek*, March 17: 66–70.

43. William Ouchi has written extensively about the use of clan control (which is viewed as an alternative to bureaucratic or market control). Here, a powerful culture results in people aligning their individual interests with those of the firm. Refer to Ouchi, op. cit.

This section also draws on Hall, R. H. 2002. *Organizations: Structures, processes, and outcomes* (8th ed.). Upper Saddle River, NJ: Prentice Hall.

44. Poundstone, W. 2003. *How would you move Mount Fuji?* New York: Little, Brown: 59.

45. Abby, E. 2012. Woman sues over personality test job rejection. *abcnews.go.com,* October 1: np.

46. Interesting insights on corporate governance are in Kroll, M., Walters, B. A., & Wright, P. 2008. Board vigilance, director experience, and corporate outcomes. *Strategic Management Journal,* 29(4): 363–382.

47. For a brief review of some central issues in corporate governance research, see Hambrick, D. C., Werder, A. V., & Zajac, E. J. 2008. New directions in corporate governance research. *Organization Science,* 19(3): 381–385.

48. Monks, R. & Minow, N. 2001. *Corporate governance* (2nd ed.). Malden, MA: Blackwell.

49. Pound, J. 1995. The promise of the governed corporation. *Harvard Business Review,* 73(2): 89–98.

50. Maurer, H. & Linblad, C. 2009. Scandal at Satyam. *BusinessWeek,* January 19: 8; Scheck, J. & Stecklow, S. 2008. Brocade ex-CEO gets 21 months in prison. *The Wall Street Journal,* January 17: A3; Levine, D. & Graybow, M. 2010. Mozilo to pay millions in Countrywide settlement. *finance. yahoo.com,* October 15: np; Ellis, B. 2010. Countrywide's Mozilo to pay $67.5 million settlement. *cnnmoney .com,* October 15: np; Frank, R., Efrati, A., Lucchetti, A., & Bray, C. 2009. Madoff jailed after admitting epic scam. *The Wall Street Journal,* March 13: A1; and Henriques, D. B. 2009. Madoff is sentenced to 150 years for Ponzi scheme. *www. nytimes.com,* June 29: np.

51. Harris, E. 2014. After bribery scandal, high-level departures at Walmart. *nytimes.com,* June 4: np.

52. Anonymous. 2012. Olympus and ex-executives plead guilty in accounting fraud. *nytimes.com,* September 25: np.

53. Corporate governance and social networks are discussed in McDonald, M. L., Khanna, P., & Westphal, J. D. 2008. *Academy of Management Journal,* 51(3): 453–475.

54. This discussion draws upon Monks & Minow, op. cit.

55. For an interesting perspective on the politicization of the corporation, read Palazzo, G. & Scherer, A. G.

2008. Corporate social responsibility, democracy, and the politicization of the corporation. *Academy of Management Review,* 33(3): 773–774.

56. Eisenhardt, K. M. 1989. Agency theory: An assessment and review. *Academy of Management Review,* 14(1): 57–74. Some of the seminal contributions to agency theory include Jensen, M. & Meckling, W. 1976. Theory of the firm: Managerial behavior, agency costs, and ownership structure. *Journal of Financial Economics,* 3: 305–360; Fama, E. & Jensen, M. 1983. Separation of ownership and control. *Journal of Law and Economics,* 26: 301, 325; and Fama, E. 1980. Agency problems and the theory of the firm. *Journal of Political Economy,* 88: 288–307.

57. Nyberg, A. J., Fulmer, I. S., Gerhart, B., & Carpenter, M. 2010. Agency theory revisited: CEO return and shareholder interest alignment. *Academy of Management Journal,* 53(5): 1029–1049.

58. Managers may also engage in "shirking"—that is, reducing or withholding their efforts. See, for example, Kidwell, R. E., Jr. & Bennett, N. 1993. Employee propensity to withhold effort: A conceptual model to intersect three avenues of research. *Academy of Management Review,* 18(3): 429–456.

59. For an interesting perspective on agency and clarification of many related concepts and terms, visit *www.encycogov.com.*

60. The relationship between corporate ownership structure and export intensity in Chinese firms is discussed in Filatotchev, I., Stephan, J., & Jindra, B. 2008. Ownership structure, strategic controls and export intensity of foreign-invested firms in transition economies. *Journal of International Business,* 39(7): 1133–1148.

61. Argawal, A. & Mandelker, G. 1987. Managerial incentives and corporate investment and financing decisions. *Journal of Finance,* 42: 823–837.

62. Gross, D. 2012. Outrageous CEO compensation: Wynn, Adelson, Dell and Abercrombie shockers. *finance. yahoo.com,* June 7: np.

63. Anonymous. 2013. Too early for the worst footnote of 2013? *footnoted. com,* January 18: np.

64. For an insightful, recent discussion of the academic research on corporate governance, and in particular the role of boards of directors, refer to Chatterjee, S. & Harrison, J. S. 2001. Corporate

governance. In Hitt, M. A., Freeman, R. E., & Harrison, J. S. (Eds.), *Handbook of strategic management:* 543–563. Malden, MA: Blackwell.

65. For an interesting theoretical discussion on corporate governance in Russia, see McCarthy, D. J. & Puffer, S. M. 2008. Interpreting the ethicality of corporate governance decisions in Russia: Utilizing integrative social contracts theory to evaluate the relevance of agency theory norms. *Academy of Management Review,* 33(1): 11–31.

66. Haynes, K. T. & Hillman, A. 2010. The effect of board capital and CEO power on strategic change. *Strategic Management Journal,* 31(110): 1145–1163.

67. This opening discussion draws on Monks & Minow, op. cit. pp. 164, 169; see also Pound, op. cit.

68. Business Roundtable. 2012. Principles of corporate governance.

69. Bhagat, C. & Kehoe, C. 2014. High performing boards: What's on their agenda? *mckinsey.com,* April: np.

70. The role of outside directors is discussed in Lester, R. H., Hillman, A., Zardkoohi, A., & Cannella, A. A., Jr. 2008. Former government officials as outside directors: The role of human and social capital. *Academy of Management Journal,* 51(5): 999–1013.

71. Feintzeig, R. 2014. You're fired! And we really mean it. *The Wall Street Journal,* November 5: B1, B6.

72. For an analysis of the effects of outside directors' compensation on acquisition decisions, refer to Deutsch, T., Keil, T., & Laamanen, T. 2007. Decision making in acquisitions: The effect of outside directors' compensation on acquisition patterns. *Journal of Management,* 33(1): 30–56.

73. Director interlocks are addressed in Kang, E. 2008. Director interlocks and spillover effects of reputational penalties from financial reporting fraud. *Academy of Management Journal,* 51(3): 537–556.

74. There are benefits, of course, to having some insiders on the board of directors. Inside directors would be more aware of the firm's strategies. Additionally, outsiders may rely too often on financial performance indicators because of information asymmetries. For an interesting discussion, see Baysinger, B. D. & Hoskisson, R. E. 1990. The composition of boards of directors and strategic control: Effects on

corporate strategy. *Academy of Management Review,* 15: 72–87.

75. Hambrick, D. C. & Jackson, E. M. 2000. Outside directors with a stake: The linchpin in improving governance. *California Management Review,* 42(4): 108–127.

76. Corsi, C., Dale, G., Daum, J., Mumm, J., & Schoppen, W. 2010. 5 things board directors should be thinking about. *spencerstuart.com,* December: np; Evans, B. 2007. Six steps to building an effective board. *inc.com:* np; Beatty, D. 2009. New challenges for corporate governance. *Rotman Magazine,* Fall: 58–63; and Krause, R., Semadeni, M., & Cannella, A. 2013. External COO/presidents as expert directors: A new look at the service role of boards. *Strategic Management Journal,* 34(13): 1628–1641.

77. A discussion on the shareholder approval process in executive compensation is presented in Brandes, P., Goranova, M., & Hall, S. 2008. Navigating shareholder influence: Compensation plans and the shareholder approval process. *Academy of Management Perspectives,* 22(1): 41–57.

78. Monks and Minow, op. cit., p. 93.

79. A discussion of the factors that lead to shareholder activism is found in Ryan, L. V. & Schneider, M. 2002. The antecedents of institutional investor activism. *Academy of Management Review,* 27(4): 554–573.

80. For an insightful discussion of investor activism, refer to David, P., Bloom, M., & Hillman, A. 2007. Investor activism, managerial responsiveness, and corporate social performance. *Strategic Management Journal,* 28(1): 91–100.

81. There is strong research support for the idea that the presence of large-block shareholders is associated with value-maximizing decisions. For example, refer to Johnson, R. A., Hoskisson, R. E., & Hitt, M. A. 1993. Board of director involvement in restructuring: The effects of board versus managerial controls and characteristics. *Strategic Management Journal,* 14: 33–50.

82. Anonymous. 2011. Institutional ownership nears all-time highs. Good or bad for alpha-seekers? *allaboutalpha.com,* February 2: np.

83. For an interesting perspective on the impact of institutional ownership on a firm's innovation strategies, see Hoskisson, R. E., Hitt, M. A., Johnson, R. A., & Grossman, W. 2002. *Academy of Management Journal,* 45(4): 697–716.

84. calpers.ca.gov.

85. www.calpers-governance.org.

86. For a study of the relationship between ownership and diversification, refer to Goranova, M., Alessandri, T. M., Brandes, P., & Dharwadkar, R. 2007. Managerial ownership and corporate diversification: A longitudinal view. *Strategic Management Journal,* 28(3): 211–226.

87. Jensen, M. C. & Murphy, K. J. 1990. CEO incentives—It's not how much you pay, but how. *Harvard Business Review,* 68(3): 138–149.

88. For a perspective on the relative advantages and disadvantages of "duality"—that is, one individual serving as both chief executive office and chairman of the board, see Lorsch, J. W. & Zelleke, A. 2005. Should the CEO be the chairman? *MIT Sloan Management Review,* 46(2): 71–74.

89. A discussion of knowledge sharing is addressed in Fey, C. F. & Furu, P. 2008. Top management incentive compensation and knowledge sharing in multinational corporations. *Strategic Management Journal,* 29(12): 1301–1324.

90. Dill, K. 2014. Report: CEOs earn 331 times as much as average workers, 774 times as much as minimum wage earners. *forbes.com,* April 15: np.

91. Sasseen, J. 2007. A better look at the boss's pay. *BusinessWeek,* February 26: 44–45; and Weinberg, N., Maiello, M., & Randall, D. 2008. Paying for failure. *Forbes,* May 19: 114, 116.

92. Research has found that executive compensation is more closely aligned with firm performance in companies with compensation committees and boards dominated by outside directors. See, for example, Conyon, M. J. & Peck, S. I. 1998. Board control, remuneration committees, and top management compensation. *Academy of Management Journal,* 41: 146–157.

93. Anonymous. 2012. American chief executives are not overpaid. *The Economist,* September 8: 67.

94. George, B. 2010. Executive pay: Rebuilding trust in an era of rage. *Bloomberg Businessweek,* September 13: 56.

95. Chahine, S. & Tohme, N. S. 2009. Is CEO duality always negative? An exploration of CEO duality and ownership structure in the Arab IPO context. *Corporate Governance: An International Review,* 17(2): 123–141; and McGrath, J. 2009.

How CEOs work. *HowStuffWorks. com.* January 28: np.

96. Anonymous. 2009. Someone to watch over them. *The Economist,* October 17: 78; Anonymous. 2004. Splitting up the roles of CEO and chairman: Reform or red herring? *Knowledge@Wharton,* June 2: np; and Kim, J. 2010. Shareholders reject split of CEO and chairman jobs at JPMorgan. *FierceFinance. com,* May 18: np.

97. Tuggle, C. S., Sirmon, D. G., Reutzel, C. R., & Bierman, L. 2010. Commanding board of director attention: Investigating how organizational performance and CEO duality affect board members' attention to monitoring. *Strategic Management Journal,* 31: 946–968; Weinberg, N. 2010. No more lapdogs. *Forbes,* May 10: 34–36; and Anonymous. 2010. Corporate constitutions. *The Economist,* October 30: 74.

98. Semadeni, M. & Krause, R. 2012. Splitting the CEO and chairman roles: It's complicated . . . *businessweek.com,* November 1: np.

99. Such opportunistic behavior is common in all principal–agent relationships. For a description of agency problems, especially in the context of the relationship between shareholders and managers, see Jensen, M. C. & Meckling, W. H. 1976. Theory of the firm: Managerial behavior, agency costs, and ownership structure. *Journal of Financial Economics,* 3: 305–360.

100. Hoskisson, R. E. & Turk, T. A. 1990. Corporate restructuring: Governance and control limits of the internal market. *Academy of Management Review,* 15: 459–477.

101. For an insightful perspective on the market for corporate control and how it is influenced by knowledge intensity, see Coff, R. 2003. Bidding wars over R&D-intensive firms: Knowledge, opportunism, and the market for corporate control. *Academy of Management Journal,* 46(1): 74–85.

102. Walsh, J. P. & Kosnik, R. D. 1993. Corporate raiders and their disciplinary role in the market for corporate control. *Academy of Management Journal,* 36: 671–700.

103. The role of regulatory bodies in the banking industry is addressed in Bhide, A. 2009. Why bankers got so reckless. *BusinessWeek,* February 9: 30–31.

104. Wishy-washy: The SEC pulls its punches on corporate-governance rules. 2003. *The Economist,* February 1: 60.

105. McLean, B. 2001. Is Enron overpriced? *Fortune,* March 5: 122–125.

106. Swartz, J. 2010. Timberland's CEO on standing up to 65,000 angry activists. *Harvard Business Review,* 88(9): 39–43.

107. Bernstein, A. 2000. Too much corporate power. *BusinessWeek,* September 11: 35–37.

108. This section draws upon Young, M. N., Peng, M. W., Ahlstrom, D., Bruton, G. D., & Jiang, Y. 2005. Principal–principal conflicts in corporate governance (unpublished manuscript); and, Peng, M. W. 2006. *Global Strategy.* Cincinnati: Thomson South-Western. We appreciate the helpful comments of Mike Young of Hong Kong Baptist University and Mike Peng of the University of Texas at Dallas.

109. Khanna, T. & Rivkin, J. 2001. Estimating the performance effects of business groups in emerging markets. *Strategic Management Journal,* 22: 45–74.

Creating Effective Organizational Designs

After reading this chapter, you should have a good understanding of the following learning objectives:

LO10.1 The growth patterns of major corporations and the relationship between a firm's strategy and its structure.

LO10.2 Each of the traditional types of organizational structure: simple, functional, divisional, and matrix.

LO10.3 The implications of a firm's international operations for organizational structure.

LO10.4 The different types of boundaryless organizations—barrier-free, modular, and virtual—and their relative advantages and disadvantages.

LO10.5 The need for creating ambidextrous organizational designs that enable firms to explore new opportunities and effectively integrate existing operations.

Learning from Mistakes

The Boeing 787 Dreamliner is a game changer in the aircraft market.[1] It is the first commercial airliner that doesn't have an aluminum skin. Instead, Boeing designed it to have a composite exterior, which provides a weight savings that allows the plane to use 20 percent less fuel than the 767, the plane it is designed to replace. The increased fuel efficiency and other design advancements made the 787 very popular with airlines. Boeing received orders for over 900 Dreamliners before the first 787 ever took flight.

It was also a game changer for Boeing. In 2003, when Boeing announced the development of the new plane, it also decided to design and manufacture the 787 in a way that was different from what it had ever done before. In the past, Boeing had internally designed and engineered the major components of its planes. Boeing would then provide detailed engineering designs and specifications to its key suppliers. The suppliers would then build the components to Boeing's specifications. To limit the up-front investment it would need to make with the 787, Boeing moved to a modular structure and outsourced much of the engineering of the components to suppliers. Boeing provided them with basic specifications and left it to the suppliers to undertake the detailed design, engineering, and manufacturing of components and subsystems. Boeing's operations in Seattle were then responsible for assembling the pieces into a completed aircraft.

Working with about 50 suppliers on four continents, Boeing found the coordination and integration of the work of suppliers to be very challenging. Some of the contracted suppliers didn't have the engineering expertise needed to do the work and outsourced the engineering to subcontractors. This made it especially difficult to monitor the engineering work for the plane. Jim Albaugh, Boeing's commercial aviation chief, identified a core issue with this change in responsibility and stated, "We gave work to people that had never really done this kind of technology before, and we didn't provide the oversight that was necessary." With the geographic stretch of the supplier set, Boeing also had difficulty monitoring the progress of the supplying firms. Boeing even ended up buying some of the suppliers once it became apparent they couldn't deliver the designs and products on schedule. For example, Boeing spent about $1 billion to acquire the Vought Aircraft Industries unit responsible for the plane's fuselage. When the suppliers finally delivered the parts, Boeing sometimes found they had difficulty assembling or combining the components. With its first 787, it found that the nose section and the fuselage didn't initially fit together, leaving a sizable gap between the two sections. To address these issues, Boeing was forced to co-locate many of its major suppliers together for six months to smooth out design and integration issues.

In the end, the decision to outsource cost Boeing dearly. The plane was three years behind schedule when the first 787 was delivered to a customer. The entire process took billions of dollars more than originally projected and also more than what it would have cost Boeing to design in-house. In early 2013, all 49 of the 787s that had been delivered to customers were grounded because of concerns about onboard fires in the lithium ion batteries used to power the plane—parts that were not designed by Boeing. The efforts Boeing had to make to fix the supply problems were still being felt in 2014, when it was still losing an estimated $45 million on each 787 it delivered. As Boeing CEO Jim McNerney concluded, "In retrospect, our 787 game plan may have been overly ambitious, incorporating too many firsts all at once—in the application of new technologies, in revolutionary design and build processes, and in increased global sourcing of engineering and manufacturing content."

Discussion Questions

1. A number of firms benefit from outsourcing design and manufacturing. What is different with Boeing that makes it so much harder to be successful?

2. What lessons does its experience with the 787 offer Boeing for its next plane development effort?

One of the central concepts in this chapter is the importance of boundaryless organizations. Successful organizations create permeable boundaries among the internal activities as well as between the organization and its external customers, suppliers, and alliance partners. We introduced this idea in Chapter 3 in our discussion of the value-chain concept, which consisted of several primary (e.g., inbound logistics, marketing and sales) and support activities (e.g., procurement, human resource management). There are a number of possible benefits to outsourcing activities as part of becoming an effective boundaryless organization. However, outsourcing can also create challenges. As in the case of Boeing, the firm lost a large amount of control by using independent suppliers to design and manufacture key subsystems of the 787.

Today's managers are faced with two ongoing and vital activities in structuring and designing their organizations.[2] First, they must decide on the most appropriate type of organizational structure. Second, they need to assess what mechanisms, processes, and techniques are most helpful in enhancing the permeability of both internal and external boundaries.

Traditional Forms of Organizational Structure

organizational structure
the formalized patterns of interactions that link a firm's tasks, technologies, and people.

Organizational structure refers to the formalized patterns of interactions that link a firm's tasks, technologies, and people.[3] Structures help to ensure that resources are used effectively in accomplishing an organization's mission. Structure provides a means of balancing two conflicting forces: a need for the division of tasks into meaningful groupings and the need to integrate such groupings in order to ensure efficiency and effectiveness.[4] Structure identifies the executive, managerial, and administrative organization of a firm and indicates responsibilities and hierarchical relationships. It also influences the flow of information as well as the context and nature of human interactions.[5]

Most organizations begin very small and either die or remain small. Those that survive and prosper embark on strategies designed to increase the overall scope of operations and enable them to enter new product-market domains. Such growth places additional pressure on executives to control and coordinate the firm's increasing size and diversity. The most appropriate type of structure depends on the nature and magnitude of growth.

LO10.1

The growth patterns of major corporations and the relationship between a firm's strategy and its structure.

Patterns of Growth of Large Corporations: Strategy-Structure Relationships

A firm's strategy and structure change as it increases in size, diversifies into new product markets, and expands its geographic scope.[6] Exhibit 10.1 illustrates common growth patterns of firms.

A new firm with a *simple structure* typically increases its sales revenue and volume of outputs over time. It may also engage in some vertical integration to secure sources of supply (backward integration) as well as channels of distribution (forward integration). The simple-structure firm then implements a *functional structure* to concentrate efforts on both increasing

EXHIBIT 10.1 Dominant Growth Patterns of Large Corporations

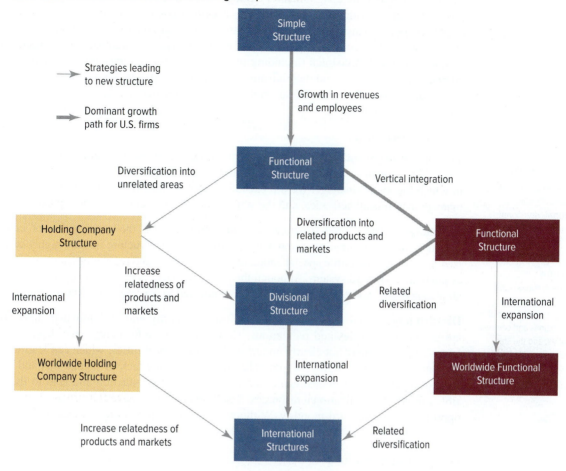

Source: Adapted from J.R. Galbraith and R.K. Kazanjian, *Strategy Implementation: Structure, Systems and Process* 2nd ed., 1986, St. Paul, MN: West Publishing Company.

efficiency and enhancing its operations and products. This structure enables the firm to group its operations into functions, departments, or geographic areas. As its initial markets mature, a firm looks beyond its present products and markets for possible expansion.

A strategy of related diversification requires a need to reorganize around product lines or geographic markets. This leads to a *divisional structure.* As the business expands in terms of sales revenues, and domestic growth opportunities become somewhat limited, a firm may seek opportunities in international markets. A firm has a wide variety of structures to choose from. These include *international division, geographic area, worldwide product division, worldwide functional,* and *worldwide matrix.* Deciding upon the most appropriate structure when a firm has international operations depends on three primary factors: the extent of international expansion, type of strategy (global, multidomestic, or transnational), and degree of product diversity.[7]

Some firms may find it advantageous to diversify into several product lines rather than focus their efforts on strengthening distributor and supplier relationships through vertical integration. They would organize themselves according to product lines by implementing a divisional structure. Also, some firms may choose to move into unrelated product areas, typically by acquiring existing businesses. Frequently, their rationale is that acquiring assets and competencies is more economical or expedient than developing them internally.

Such an unrelated, or conglomerate, strategy requires relatively little integration across businesses and sharing of resources. Thus, a *holding company structure* becomes appropriate. There are many other growth patterns, but these are the most common.*

Now we will discuss some of the most common types of organizational structures—simple, functional, divisional (including two variants: *strategic business unit* and *holding company*), and matrix—and their advantages and disadvantages. We will close the section with a discussion of the structural implications when a firm expands its operations into international markets.[8]

Simple Structure

The **simple organizational structure** is the oldest, and most common, organizational form. Most organizations are very small and have a single or very narrow product line in which the owner-manager (or top executive) makes most of the decisions. The owner-manager controls all activities, and the staff serves as an extension of the top executive.

Advantages   The simple structure is highly informal, and the coordination of tasks is accomplished by direct supervision. Characteristics of this structure include highly centralized decision making, little specialization of tasks, few rules and regulations, and an informal evaluation and reward system. Although the owner-manager is intimately involved in almost all phases of the business, a manager is often employed to oversee day-to-day operations.

Disadvantages   A simple structure may foster creativity and individualism since there are generally few rules and regulations. However, such "informality" may lead to problems. Employees may not clearly understand their responsibilities, which can lead to conflict and confusion. Employees may take advantage of the lack of regulations and act in their own self-interest, which can erode motivation and satisfaction and lead to the possible misuse of organizational resources. Small organizations have flat structures that limit opportunities for upward mobility. Without the potential for future advancement, recruiting and retaining talent may become very difficult.

Functional Structure

When an organization is small (15 or fewer employees), it is not necessary to have a variety of formal arrangements and groupings of activities. However, as firms grow, excessive demands may be placed on the owner-manager in order to obtain and process all of the information necessary to run the business. Chances are the owner will not be skilled in all specialties (e.g., accounting, engineering, production, marketing). Thus, he or she will need to hire specialists in the various functional areas. Such growth in the overall scope and complexity of the business necessitates a **functional organizational structure** wherein the major functions of the firm are grouped internally. The coordination and integration of the functional areas becomes one of the most important responsibilities of the chief executive of the firm (see Exhibit 10.2).

Functional structures are generally found in organizations in which there is a single or closely related product or service, high production volume, and some vertical integration. Initially, firms tend to expand the overall scope of their operations by penetrating existing markets, introducing similar products in additional markets, or increasing the level of vertical integration. Such expansion activities clearly increase the scope and complexity of the

---

*The lowering of transaction costs and globalization have led to some changes in the common historical patterns that we have discussed. Some firms are, in effect, bypassing the vertical integration stage. Instead, they focus on core competencies and outsource other value-creation activities. Also, even relatively young firms are going global early in their history because of lower communication and transportation costs. For an interesting perspective on global start-ups, see McDougall, P. P. & Oviatt, B. M. 1996. New Venture Internationalization, Strategic Change and Performance: A Follow-Up Study. *Journal of Business Venturing*, 11: 23–40; and McDougall, P. P. & Oviatt, B. M. (Eds.). 2000. The Special Research Forum on International Entrepreneurship. *Academy of Management Journal*, October: 902–1003.

EXHIBIT 10.2 Functional Organizational Structure

Lower-level managers, specialists, and operating personnel

operations. The functional structure provides for a high level of centralization that helps to ensure integration and control over the related product-market activities or multiple primary activities (from inbound logistics to operations to marketing, sales, and service) in the value chain (addressed in Chapters 3 and 4).

Advantages By bringing together specialists into functional departments, a firm is able to enhance its coordination and control within each of the functional areas. Decision making in the firm will be centralized at the top of the organization. This enhances the organizational-level (as opposed to functional area) perspective across the various functions in the organization. In addition, the functional structure provides for a more efficient use of managerial and technical talent since functional area expertise is pooled in a single department (e.g., marketing) instead of being spread across a variety of product-market areas. Finally, career paths and professional development in specialized areas are facilitated.

Disadvantages The differences in values and orientations among functional areas may impede communication and coordination. Edgar Schein of MIT has argued that shared assumptions, often based on similar backgrounds and experiences of members, form around functional units in an organization. This leads to what are often called "stove pipes" or "silos," in which departments view themselves as isolated, self-contained units with little need for interaction and coordination with other departments. This erodes communication because functional groups may have not only different goals but also differing meanings of words and concepts. According to Schein:

> The word "marketing" will mean product development to the engineer, studying customers through market research to the product manager, merchandising to the salesperson, and constant change in design to the manufacturing manager. When they try to work together, they will often attribute disagreements to personalities and fail to notice the deeper, shared assumptions that color how each function thinks.[9]

Such narrow functional orientations also may lead to short-term thinking based largely upon what is best for the functional area, not the entire organization. In a manufacturing firm, sales may want to offer a wide range of customized products to appeal to the firm's customers; R&D may overdesign products and components to achieve technical elegance; and manufacturing may favor no-frills products that can be produced at low cost by means of long production runs. Functional structures may overburden the top executives in the firm because conflicts have a tendency to be "pushed up" to the top of the organization since there are no managers who are responsible for the specific product lines. Functional structures make it difficult to establish uniform performance standards across the entire organization. It may be relatively easy to evaluate production managers on the basis of production volume and cost control, but establishing performance measures for engineering, R&D, and accounting becomes more problematic.

Divisional Structure

divisional organizational structure

an organizational form in which products, projects, or product markets are grouped internally.

The **divisional organizational structure** (sometimes called the multidivisional structure or M-Form) is organized around products, projects, or markets. Each of the divisions, in turn, includes its own functional specialists who are typically organized into departments.[10] A divisional structure encompasses a set of relatively autonomous units governed by a central corporate office. The operating divisions are relatively independent and consist of products and services that are different from those of the other divisions.[11] Operational decision making in a large business places excessive demands on the firm's top management. In order to attend to broader, longer-term organizational issues, top-level managers must delegate decision making to lower-level managers. Divisional executives play a key role: They help to determine the product-market and financial objectives for the division as well as their division's contribution to overall corporate performance.[12] The rewards are based largely on measures of financial performance such as net income and revenue. Exhibit 10.3 illustrates a divisional structure.

General Motors was among the earliest firms to adopt the divisional organizational structure.[13] In the 1920s the company formed five major product divisions (Cadillac, Buick, Oldsmobile, Pontiac, and Chevrolet) as well as several industrial divisions. Since then, many firms have discovered that as they diversified into new product-market activities, functional structures—with their emphasis on single functional departments—were unable to manage the increased complexity of the entire business.

Advantages By creating separate divisions to manage individual product markets, there is a separation of strategic and operating control. Divisional managers can focus their efforts on improving operations in the product markets for which they are responsible, and corporate officers can devote their time to overall strategic issues for the entire corporation. The focus on a division's products and markets—by the divisional executives—provides the corporation with an enhanced ability to respond quickly to important changes. Since there are functional departments within each division of the corporation, the problems associated with sharing resources across functional departments are minimized. Because there are multiple levels of general managers (executives responsible for integrating and coordinating all functional areas), the development of general management talent is enhanced.

EXHIBIT 10.3 Divisional Organizational Structure

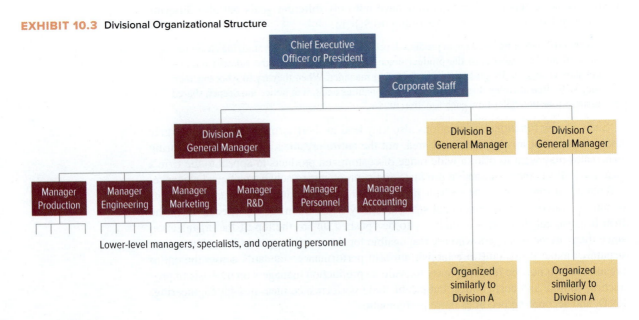

BREAKING DOWN DIVISIONAL BOUNDARIES: LEARNING FROM YOUR TWIN

On the edge of Lake Michigan in Burns Harbor, Indiana, sits a 50-year-old steel mill that produces steel for the automotive, appliance, and other industries with midwestern production plants. The steel mill struggled through the 1980s and 1990s and went bankrupt in 2002. It was bought out of bankruptcy and has been owned by ArcelorMittal, the world's largest steel producer, since 2005. However, the plant faced another crisis in 2007 when it was threatened with closure unless it became more productive and efficient.

Today, this plant requires 1.32 man-hours per ton of steel produced, which is 34 percent more efficient than the average in U.S. steel mills. Further, in 2011, the plant was 19 percent more efficient than it was in 2007 and produced twice the quantity of steel it produced in 2009. Its future as a productive steel plant is now secure.

How did ArcelorMittal achieve these gains and rejuvenate an old steel mill? It did it by breaking down the barriers between organization units to facilitate knowledge transfer and learning. One of the disadvantages of a divisional structure is that the divisions often perceive themselves as being in competition with each other and are therefore unwilling to share information to help other divisions improve. ArcelorMittal has overcome this by "twinning" different steel mills, one efficient and one struggling, and challenging the efficient plant to help out its twin. The Burns Harbor mill was paired with a mill in Ghent, Belgium. Over 100 engineers and managers from Burns Harbor traveled to Belgium to tour the Ghent plant and learn from their colleagues there how to improve operations. They copied routines from that plant, implemented an advanced computer control system used in the Belgian mill, and employed automated machines similar to the ones used in Belgium. ArcelorMittal also provided $150 million in capital investments to upgrade the operations to bring the facilities up to par with the Ghent plant. These changes resulted in dramatic improvements in the efficiency of the Burns Harbor mill. The Belgians take pride in the improvements in Burns Harbor and now find themselves striving to improve their own operations to stay ahead of the Americans. The Ghent plant now produces 950 tons of steel per employee each year, only 50 tons per employee more than Burns Harbor, but the Ghent managers boast they will soon increase productivity to 1,100 tons per employee. Thus, Ghent cooperates and is willing to help Burns Harbor, but the managers and employees at Ghent have a competitive streak as well.

The experience of ArcelorMittal demonstrates how firms can act to overcome the typical disadvantages of their divisional structure.

Source: Miller, J. 2012. Indiana steel mill revived with lessons from abroad. *wsj.com,* May 21: np; *www.nishp.org/bh-history.htm;* and Markovich, S. 2012. Morning brief: Foreign investment revives Indiana steel mill. *blogs.cfr.org,* May 21: np.

Disadvantages   It can be very expensive; there can be increased costs due to the duplication of personnel, operations, and investment since each division must staff multiple functional departments. There also can be dysfunctional competition among divisions since each division tends to become concerned solely about its own operations. Divisional managers are often evaluated on common measures such as return on assets and sales growth. If goals are conflicting, there can be a sense of a "zero-sum" game that would discourage sharing ideas and resources among the divisions for the common good of the corporation. Ghoshal and Bartlett, two leading strategy scholars, note:

> As their label clearly warns, divisions divide. The divisional model fragmented companies' resources; it created vertical communication channels that insulated business units and prevented them from sharing their strengths with one another. Consequently, the whole of the corporation was often less than the sum of its parts.[14]

With many divisions providing different products and services, there is the chance that differences in image and quality may occur across divisions. One division may offer no-frills products of lower quality that may erode the brand reputation of another division that has top-quality, highly differentiated offerings. Since each division is evaluated in terms of financial measures such as return on investment and revenue growth, there is often an urge to focus on short-term performance. If corporate management uses quarterly profits as the key performance indicator, divisional management may tend to put significant emphasis on "making the numbers" and minimizing activities, such as advertising, maintenance, and capital investments, which would detract from short-term performance measures. Strategy Spotlight 10.1 discusses how ArcelorMittal works to overcome some of the disadvantages of the divisional structure by "twinning" its plants.

CARGILL TAILORS ITS SBU STRUCTURE TO BREAK DOWN BOUNDARIES

Cargill is a $130 billion family-owned agribusiness behemoth with over 70 business units. It sells to a range of customer groups, including food, beverage, industrial, pharmaceutical, and personal care product makers, as well as farmers and food service providers. It strives for both efficiency and responsiveness to market opportunities. Greg Page, the firm's chairman and former CEO, strives to find the balance between corporate financial discipline and synergistic opportunities across the business units. He's created a novel SBU structure to help find that balance.

At the top is the company's senior corporate governing body, the Cargill Leadership Team (CLT). This group has only six people. The CLT's role is to set the broad strategy of the firm, set growth goals and directions, and allocate human and financial capital. The next layer is the Corporate Center, which includes CLT members and about 25 others who head up the firm's SBUs. The non-CLT

Corporate Center members are "tagged," using Cargill's terminology, to a CLT member to ensure that administrative matters and lines of responsibility are aligned and clear. Members of the Corporate Center, along with some division heads and next-level functional leaders, populate 12 committees, including the Food Risk Committee, Technology Committee, Strategy and Capital Committee, and the Cargill Brand Reputation Committee. These committees work to leverage economies of scope, to transfer competencies between units, and to maintain consistency across the SBUs.

Page asserts that "by keeping the CLT too small to conduct the day-to-day affairs of the company, it forces that accountability and ownership down the line. With it comes a lot of engagement and shared, or collective, leadership."

Sources: Neilson, G. L. & Wulf, J. 2012. How many direct reports? *Harvard Business Review*, 90(4): 113–118; Anonymous. 2014. Cargill announces additions to board, leadership team. *world-grain.com*, December 9: np; and *yahoo.finance.com*.

We'll discuss two variations of the divisional form: the strategic business unit (SBU) and holding company structures.

Strategic Business Unit (SBU) Structure   Highly diversified corporations such as ConAgra, a $13 billion food producer, may consist of dozens of different divisions.[15] If ConAgra were to use a purely divisional structure, it would be nearly impossible for the corporate office to plan and coordinate activities, because the span of control would be too large. To attain synergies, ConAgra has put its diverse businesses into three primary SBUs: food service (restaurants), retail (grocery stores), and agricultural products.

strategic business unit (SBU) structure an organizational form in which products, projects, or product-market divisions are grouped into homogeneous units.

With an **SBU structure,** divisions with similar products, markets, and/or technologies are grouped into homogeneous units to achieve some synergies. These include those discussed in Chapter 6 for related diversification, such as leveraging core competencies, sharing infrastructures, and market power. Generally the more related businesses are within a corporation, the fewer SBUs will be required. Each of the SBUs in the corporation operates as a profit center. Strategy Spotlight 10.2 discusses how Cargill has built an SBU structure that fosters consistency across units but also learning and collaboration across unit boundaries.

Advantages   The SBU structure makes the task of planning and control by the corporate office more manageable. Also, with greater decentralization of authority, individual businesses can react more quickly to important changes in the environment than if all divisions had to report directly to the corporate office.

Disadvantages   Since the divisions are grouped into SBUs, it may become difficult to achieve synergies across SBUs. If divisions in different SBUs have potential sources of synergy, it may become difficult for them to be realized. The additional level of management increases the number of personnel and overhead expenses, while the additional hierarchical level removes the corporate office further from the individual divisions. The corporate office may become unaware of key developments that could have a major impact on the corporation.

Holding Company Structure The **holding company structure** (sometimes referred to as a *conglomerate*) is also a variation of the divisional structure. Whereas the SBU structure is often used when similarities exist between the individual businesses (or divisions), the holding company structure is appropriate when the businesses in a corporation's portfolio do not have much in common. Thus, the potential for synergies is limited.

Holding company structures are most appropriate for firms with a strategy of unrelated diversification. Companies such as Berkshire Hathaway and Loews use a holding company structure to implement their unrelated diversification strategies. Since there are few similarities across the businesses, the corporate offices in these companies provide a great deal of autonomy to operating divisions and rely on financial controls and incentive programs to obtain high levels of performance from the individual businesses. Corporate staffs at these firms tend to be small because of their limited involvement in the overall operation of their various businesses.[16]

Advantages The holding company structure has the cost savings associated with fewer personnel and the lower overhead resulting from a small corporate office and fewer hierarchical levels. The autonomy of the holding company structure increases the motivational level of divisional executives and enables them to respond quickly to market opportunities and threats.

Disadvantages There is an inherent lack of control and dependence that corporate-level executives have on divisional executives. Major problems could arise if key divisional executives leave the firm, because the corporate office has very little "bench strength"—additional managerial talent ready to quickly fill key positions. If problems arise in a division, it may become very difficult to turn around individual businesses because of limited staff support in the corporate office.

Matrix Structure

One approach that tries to overcome the inadequacies inherent in the other structures is the **matrix organizational structure.** It is a combination of the functional and divisional structures. Most commonly, functional departments are combined with product groups on a project basis. For example, a product group may want to develop a new addition to its line; for this project, it obtains personnel from functional departments such as marketing, production, and engineering. These personnel work under the manager of the product group for the duration of the project, which can vary from a few weeks to an open-ended period of time. The individuals who work in a matrix organization become responsible to two managers: the project manager and the manager of their functional area. Exhibit 10.4 illustrates a matrix structure.

Some large multinational corporations rely on a matrix structure to combine product groups and geographic units. Product managers have global responsibility for the development, manufacturing, and distribution of their own line, while managers of geographic regions have responsibility for the profitability of the businesses in their regions. Vodafone, the wireless service provider, utilizes this type of structure.

Other organizations, such as Cisco, use a matrix structure to try to maintain flexibility. In these firms, individual workers have a permanent functional home but also are assigned to and work within temporary project teams.[17]

Advantages The matrix structure facilitates the use of specialized personnel, equipment, and facilities. Instead of duplicating functions, as would be the case in a divisional structure based on products, the resources are shared. Individuals with high expertise can divide their time among multiple projects. Such resource sharing and collaboration enable a firm to use resources more efficiently and to respond more quickly and effectively to changes in

holding company structure
an organizational form that is a variation of the divisional organizational structure in which the divisions have a high degree of autonomy both from other divisions and from corporate headquarters.

matrix organizational structure
an organizational form in which there are multiple lines of authority and some individuals report to at least two managers.

EXHIBIT 10.4 Matrix Organizational Structure

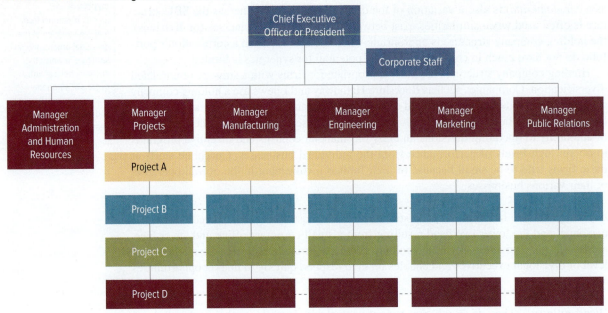

the competitive environment. The flexibility inherent in a matrix structure provides professionals with a broader range of responsibility. Such experience enables them to develop their skills and competencies.

Disadvantages   The dual-reporting structures can result in uncertainty and lead to intense power struggles and conflict over the allocation of personnel and other resources. Working relationships become more complicated. This may result in excessive reliance on group processes and teamwork, along with a diffusion of responsibility, which in turn may erode timely decision making.

Let's look at Procter & Gamble (P&G) to see some of the disadvantages associated with a matrix structure:

> After 50 years with a divisional structure, P&G went to a matrix structure in 1987. In this structure, it had product categories, such as soaps and detergents, on one dimension and functional managers on the other dimension. Within each product category, country managers reported to regional managers who then reported to product managers. The structure became complex to manage, with 13 layers of management and significant power struggles as the functional managers developed their own strategic agendas that often were at odds with the product managers' agendas. After seeing its growth rate decline from 8.5 percent in the 1980s to 2.6 percent in the late 1990s, P&G scrapped the matrix structure to go to a global product structure with three major product categories to offer unity in direction and more responsive decision making.[18]

Exhibit 10.5 briefly summarizes the advantages and disadvantages of the functional, divisional, and matrix organizational structures.

LO10.3

The implications of a firm's international operations for organizational structure.

International Operations: Implications for Organizational Structure

Today's managers must maintain an international outlook on their firm's businesses and competitive strategies. In the global marketplace, managers must ensure consistency between their strategies (at the business, corporate, and international levels) and the structure of their organization. As firms expand into foreign markets, they generally follow a pattern of change

Functional Structure	
Advantages	**Disadvantages**
• Pooling of specialists enhances coordination and control.	• Differences in functional area orientation impede communication and coordination.
• Centralized decision making enhances an organizational perspective across functions.	• Tendency for specialists to develop short-term perspective and narrow functional orientation.
• Efficient use of managerial and technical talent.	• Functional area conflicts may overburden top-level decision makers.
• Facilitates career paths and professional development in specialized areas.	• Difficult to establish uniform performance standards.
Divisional Structure	
Advantages	**Disadvantages**
• Increases strategic and operational control, permitting corporate-level executives to address strategic issues.	• Increased costs incurred through duplication of personnel, operations, and investment.
• Quick response to environmental changes.	• Dysfunctional competition among divisions may detract from overall corporate performance.
• Increases focus on products and markets.	• Difficult to maintain uniform corporate image.
• Minimizes problems associated with sharing resources across functional areas.	• Overemphasis on short-term performance.
• Facilitates development of general managers.	
Matrix Structure	
Advantages	**Disadvantages**
• Increases market responsiveness through collaboration and synergies among professional colleagues.	• Dual-reporting relationships can result in uncertainty regarding accountability.
• Allows more efficient utilization of resources.	• Intense power struggles may lead to increased levels of conflict.
• Improves flexibility, coordination, and communication.	• Working relationships may be more complicated and human resources duplicated.
• Increases professional development through a broader range of responsibility.	• Excessive reliance on group processes and teamwork may impede timely decision making.

in structure that parallels the changes in their strategies.[19] Three major contingencies that influence the chosen structure are (1) the type of strategy that is driving a firm's foreign operations, (2) product diversity, and (3) the extent to which a firm is dependent on foreign sales.[20]

As international operations become an important part of a firm's overall operations, managers must make changes that are consistent with their firm's structure. The primary types of structures used to manage a firm's international operations are:[21]

- International division
- Geographic-area division
- Worldwide functional
- Worldwide product division
- Worldwide matrix

Multidomestic strategies are driven by political and cultural imperatives requiring managers within each country to respond to local conditions. The structures consistent with such a strategic orientation are the **international division** and **geographic-area division structures.** Here, local managers are provided with a high level of autonomy to manage their operations within the constraints and demands of their geographic market. As a firm's foreign sales increase as a percentage of its total sales, it will likely change from an international division to a geographic-area division structure. And, as a firm's product and/or market diversity becomes large, it is likely to benefit from a **worldwide matrix structure.**

Global strategies are driven by economic pressures that require managers to view operations in different geographic areas to be managed for overall efficiency. The structures consistent with the efficiency perspective are the **worldwide functional** and **worldwide product division structures.** Here, division managers view the marketplace as homogeneous and devote relatively little attention to local market, political, and economic factors. The choice between these two types of structures is guided largely by the extent of product diversity. Firms with relatively low levels of product diversity may opt for a worldwide product division structure. However, if significant product-market diversity results from highly unrelated international acquisitions, a worldwide holding company structure should be implemented. Such firms have very little commonality among products, markets, or technologies and have little need for integration.

Global Start-Ups: A Recent Phenomenon

International expansion occurs rather late for most corporations, typically after possibilities of domestic growth are exhausted. Increasingly, we are seeing two interrelated phenomena. First, many firms now expand internationally relatively early in their history. Second, some firms are "born global"—that is, from the very beginning, many start-ups are global in their activities. For example, Logitech International, a leading producer of personal computer accessories, was global from day one. Founded in 1982 by a Swiss national and two Italians, the company was headquartered in both California and Switzerland. R&D and manufacturing were also conducted in both locations and, subsequently, in Taiwan and Ireland.[22]

The success of companies such as Logitech challenges the conventional wisdom that a company must first build up assets, internal processes, and experience before venturing into faraway lands. It also raises a number of questions: What exactly is a global start-up? Under what conditions should a company start out as a global start-up? What does it take to succeed as a global start-up?

A **global start-up** has been defined as a business organization that, from inception, seeks to derive significant competitive advantage from the use of resources and the sale of outputs in multiple countries. Right from the beginning, it uses inputs from around the world and sells its products and services to customers around the world. Geographic boundaries of nation-states are irrelevant for a global start-up.

There is no reason for every start-up to be global. Being global necessarily involves higher communication, coordination, and transportation costs. Therefore, it is important to identify the circumstances under which going global from the beginning is advantageous.[23] First, if the required human resources are globally dispersed, going global may be the best way to access those resources. For example, Italians are masters in fine leather and Europeans in ergonomics. Second, in many cases foreign financing may be easier to obtain and more suitable. Traditionally, U.S. venture capitalists have shown greater willingness to bear risk, but they have shorter time horizons in their expectations for return. If a U.S. start-up is looking for patient capital, it may be better off looking overseas. Third, the target customers in many specialized industries are located in other parts of the world. Fourth, in many industries a gradual move from domestic markets to foreign markets is no longer possible because, if a product is successful, foreign competitors may immediately imitate it. Therefore, preemptive entry into foreign markets may be the only option. Finally, because of high up-front development costs, a global market is often necessary to recover the costs. This is particularly true for start-ups from smaller nations that do not have access to large domestic markets.

GLOBAL START-UP, BRCK, WORKS TO BRING RELIABLE INTERNET CONNECTIVITY TO THE WORLD

BRCK is a notable technology pioneer. It's bringing a novel and potentially very valuable product to market, and it is doing so as a truly global start-up. BRCK's first product is a surge-resistant, battery-powered router to provide Internet service, which the firm is simply calling the BRCK. In many parts of the world, power systems are unreliable and offer only intermittent service. Additionally, they are prone to generate power surges that can fry many electronic products, including Internet routers. For example, in 2013, a single power-surge event in Nairobi, Kenya, blew out more than 3,000 routers. BRCK has developed a product to address these issues. Its router has a built-in battery that charges up whenever the power grid is operating and that runs off the battery for up to eight hours when the power grid goes down. It can also handle power surges up to 400 volts. The BRCK is also flexible as to how it connects to the Internet. It can connect directly to an ethernet line, can link up with a Wi-Fi network in its area, and can connect via a wireless phone connection. BRCK is aiming to sell its product to small and medium-size businesses, schools,

and medical facilities. Its routers allow up to 20 users to simultaneously connect to the Internet. The technologies it uses are not cutting-edge, but the end product itself is innovative and meets a market need.

What really sets BRCK apart is that it is a global start-up that turns the table on typical global structures. Most tech-oriented global firms design their products in a technology center in the developed world and manufacture the products in a developing country. BRCK has flipped this model. BRCK designs its products in a developing country and manufactures in a developed country. Its corporate headquarters are in Nairobi, Kenya, at a technology center that houses a small group of entrepreneurs. The firm employs a dozen engineers to design its products in its corporate headquarters, and while its offices look a bit like those in Silicon Valley, the building has backup power for times when the Kenyan power grid inevitably goes down. The firm sources most of the components for its routers from Asia and manufactures its products in Austin, Texas. Even its sales are also going global right from the start. As of mid-2014, the firm had sold 700 BRCKs to customers in 45 countries.

Sources: Cary, J. 2014. Made in Kenya, assembled in America: This Internet-anywhere company innovates from silicon savannah. *fastcoexist.com*, September 4: np; and Vogt, H. 2014. Made in Africa: A gadget startup. *wsj.com*, July 10: np.

Successful management of a global start-up presents many challenges. Communication and coordination across time zones and cultures are always problematic. Since most global start-ups have far less resources than well-established corporations, one key for success is to internalize few activities and outsource the rest. Managers of such firms must have considerable prior international experience so that they can successfully handle the inevitable communication problems and cultural conflicts. Another key for success is to keep the communication and coordination costs low. The only way to achieve this is by creating less costly administrative mechanisms. The boundaryless organizational designs that we discuss in the next section are particularly suitable for global start-ups because of their flexibility and low cost.

Strategy Spotlight 10.3 discusses a Kenyan technology start-up with a global vision and scope of operations.

How an Organization's Structure Can Influence Strategy Formulation

Discussions of the relationship between strategy and structure usually strongly imply that structure follows strategy. The strategy that a firm chooses (e.g., related diversification) dictates such structural elements as the division of tasks, the need for integration of activities, and authority relationships within the organization. However, an existing structure can influence strategy formulation. Once a firm's structure is in place, it is very difficult and expensive to change.[24] Executives may not be able to modify their duties and responsibilities greatly or may not welcome the disruption associated with a transfer to a new location. There are costs associated with hiring, training, and replacing executive, managerial, and operating personnel. Strategy cannot be formulated without considering structural elements.

An organization's structure can also have an important influence on how it competes in the marketplace. It can also strongly influence a firm's strategy, day-to-day operations, and performance.[25]

BOUNDARY TYPES

There are primarily four types of boundaries that place limits on organizations. In today's dynamic business environment, different types of boundaries are needed to foster high degrees of interaction with outside influences and varying levels of permeability.

1. **Vertical boundaries between levels in the organization's hierarchy.** SmithKline Beecham asks employees at different hierarchical levels to brainstorm ideas for managing clinical trial data. The ideas are incorporated into action plans that significantly cut the new product approval time of its pharmaceuticals. This would not have been possible if the barriers between levels of individuals in the organization had been too high.

2. **Horizontal boundaries between functional areas.** Fidelity Investments makes the functional barriers more porous and flexible among divisions, such as marketing, operations, and customer service, in order to offer customers a more integrated experience when conducting business with the company. Customers can take their questions to one person, reducing the chance that customers will "get the run-around" from employees who feel customer service is not their responsibility. At Fidelity, customer service is everyone's business, regardless of functional area.

3. **External boundaries between the firm and its customers, suppliers, and regulators.** GE Lighting, by working closely with retailers, functions throughout the value chain as a single operation. This allows GE to track point-of-sale purchases, giving it better control over inventory management.

4. **Geographic boundaries between locations, cultures, and markets.** The global nature of today's business environment spurred PricewaterhouseCoopers to use a global groupware system. This allows the company to instantly connect to its 26 worldwide offices.

Source: Ashkenas, R. 1997. The organization's new clothes. In Hesselbein, F., Goldsmith, M., and Beckhard, R. (Eds.), *The organization of the future:* 104–106. San Francisco: Jossey-Bass.

LO10.4

The different types of boundaryless organizations—barrier-free, modular, and virtual—and their relative advantages and disadvantages.

boundaryless organizational designs

organizations in which the boundaries, including vertical, horizontal, external, and geographic boundaries, are permeable.

Boundaryless Organizational Designs

The term *boundaryless* may bring to mind a chaotic organizational reality in which "anything goes." This is not the case. As Jack Welch, GE's former CEO, has suggested, boundaryless does not imply that all internal and external boundaries vanish completely, but that they become more open and permeable.[26] Strategy Spotlight 10.4 discusses four types of boundaries.

We are not suggesting that **boundaryless organizational designs** replace the traditional forms of organizational structure, but they should complement them. Strategy Spotlight 10.5 discusses how Dr. Tracy Gaudet is working to integrate different units in the Veterans Administration to more effectively provide holistic medical services to veterans.

We will discuss three approaches to making boundaries more permeable that help to facilitate the widespread sharing of knowledge and information across both the internal and external boundaries of the organization. The *barrier-free* type involves making all organizational boundaries—internal and external—more permeable. Teams are a central building block for implementing the boundaryless organization. The *modular* and *virtual* types of organizations focus on the need to create seamless relationships with external organizations such as customers or suppliers. While the modular type emphasizes the outsourcing of noncore activities, the virtual (or network) organization focuses on alliances among independent entities formed to exploit specific market opportunities.

The Barrier-Free Organization

The "boundary" mind-set is ingrained deeply into bureaucracies. It is evidenced by such clichés as "That's not my job" and "I'm here from corporate to help" or by endless battles over transfer pricing. In the traditional company, boundaries are clearly delineated in the design of an organization's structure. Their basic advantage is that the roles of managers and employees are simple, clear, well defined, and long-lived. A major shortcoming was pointed out to the authors during an interview with a high-tech executive: "Structure tends to be divisive; it leads to territorial fights."

BREAKING BARRIERS TO BETTER SERVE VETERANS

The Veterans Administration (VA) is the largest health care service provider in the United States, with over 280,000 employees and a budget of more than $150 billion. But it has struggled mightily to meet the growing needs of veterans. This includes the traditional medical care needs of the aging veterans of World War II, the Korean War, and the Vietnam War, and it also includes the complex needs of veterans from Iraq and Afghanistan, who may have both physical and psychological challenges.

Medical care has historically been oriented around reacting to the diseases or injuries of patients. When health problems arise, doctors and other health care providers offer focused treatment to address the current challenge. To provide expertise in each medical area, most medical systems, including the VA, have traditionally been structured functionally along medical specialty lines, such as cardiology, dermatology, and orthopedics. Thus, medical systems in the United States have typically offered effective disease treatment but not effective holistic care for patients. This limitation is especially acute for the VA since veterans often need a more holistic treatment because their physical scars and maladies may be tied into the psychological scars they carry from their time at war.

Dr. Tracy Gaudet has taken on this challenge in her role as the director of the Office of Patient-Centered Care and Cultural Transformation at the VA. Dr. Gaudet is a proponent of integrative medicine, a field that works to treat the whole person and not just a diseased or broken body part. To provide better service, she is pushing for transformation at the VA that will break down traditional medical discipline boundaries in the organization to provide integrative health services to veterans. This includes traditional medical fields but also related supporting services and nontraditional medical disciplines. To pilot test how to do this, the VA has created nine centers of innovation. These centers work to integrate a range of physical and psychological medical services along with health maintenance and lifestyle services. Some centers have nutritionists on staff, along with vegetable gardens; while others offer yoga instruction, massage therapy, acupuncture, and mindfulness instruction. Thus, they strive to meet not only the traditional medical needs but also the lifestyle and emotional needs of veterans to better battle PTSD, substance-abuse problems, sleep disorders, and pain management. The leaders of these centers of innovation will then serve as consultants to facilitate cultural and organizational change in other VA facilities.

The challenge is huge, but the issue is personal for Dr. Gaudet. She recalls her father as a loving man, but also a man who carried pain from his experiences fighting in World War II that led to a long battle with alcoholism. Thus she sees it as a personal challenge, one about which she says, "We need to and can do better" to meet the needs of veterans.

Sources: Kowitt, B. 2013. Can caring cure? *Fortune,* October 28: 22–26; and Whited, R. 2011. VA office developing innovative patient-centered model of care for veterans. *examiner.com,* January 21: np.

Such structures are being replaced by fluid, ambiguous, and deliberately ill-defined tasks and roles. Just because work roles are no longer clearly defined, however, does not mean that differences in skills, authority, and talent disappear. A **barrier-free organization** enables a firm to bridge real differences in culture, function, and goals to find common ground that facilitates information sharing and other forms of cooperative behavior. Eliminating the multiple boundaries that stifle productivity and innovation can enhance the potential of the entire organization.

> **barrier-free organization**
> an organizational design in which firms bridge real differences in culture, function, and goals to find common ground that facilitates information sharing and other forms of cooperative behavior.

Creating Permeable Internal Boundaries For barrier-free organizations to work effectively, the level of trust and shared interests among all parts of the organization must be raised.[27] The organization needs to develop among its employees the skill level needed to work in a more democratic organization. Barrier-free organizations also require a shift in the organization's philosophy from executive to organizational development and from investments in high-potential individuals to investments in leveraging the talents of all individuals.

Teams can be an important aspect of barrier-free structures.[28] Jeffrey Pfeffer, author of several insightful books, including *The Human Equation,* suggests that teams have three primary advantages.[29] First, teams substitute peer-based control for hierarchical control of work activities. Employees control themselves, reducing the time and energy management needs to devote to control. Second, teams frequently develop more creative solutions to problems because they encourage the sharing of the tacit knowledge held by individuals.[30] Brainstorming, or group problem solving, involves the pooling of ideas and expertise to enhance the chances that at least one group member will think of a way to solve the problems at hand. Third, by substituting peer control for hierarchical control, teams permit the removal of layers of hierarchy and absorption of administrative tasks previously performed by specialists. This avoids the costs of having people whose sole job is to watch the people who watch other people do the work. Novartis, the Swiss pharmaceutical giant, is leveraging the power of teams by consolidating its R&D activities in four locations. Novartis believes that grouping together and teaming up researchers from different disciplines into self-managed work teams will foster creativity and cooperation.[31]

Some have argued for the need to move more radically to discard formal hierarchical structures and work toward a more democratic team organizational structure.[32] One version of such systems is called a "holacracy." In a holacracy, there is no formal organizational structure in the traditional sense. Instead, employees self-identify into roles, undertaking the types of tasks that they are highly skilled at and interested in. Most employees will have multiple roles. Employees then group together into self-organized teams—or, in the terminology of holacracy, circles—in which they work together to complete tasks, such as circles for service delivery or product development. Since individual employees have multiple roles, they typically belong to multiple circles. This overlapping membership facilitates communication and coordination between circles. The circles within a firm change over time to meet the evolving situation of the firm. Each circle elects a lead, called a "lead link." This lead link guides meetings and sets the general agenda for the circle, although the members of the circle decide democratically on how the circle will complete tasks. The lead link also serves as a member of a higher-level circle. Overseeing it all is the general company circle, a collection of lead links who serve as the leadership team for the firm.

Most firms that have moved to a holacracy way of organizing are small technology firms. These firms see little need for hierarchical authority, and they are attracted to the promises of improved agility and creativity, as well as higher employee morale, with this flexible, autonomous type of structure. However, in 2014, Zappos decided to transition its entire 1,500 employees to a holacracy structure. The new structure initially consisted of 250 circles, and it may grow to 400 circles as the new system gets fully implemented. Tony Hsieh, who was Zappos' CEO and is now lead link of the Experiential SWAT Team, says he wants "Zappos to function more like a city and less like a top-down bureaucratic organization." In making this change, Zappos is serving as a natural experiment to see if a larger firm can operate as a holacracy.

Developing Effective Relationships with External Constituencies In barrier-free organizations, managers must also create flexible, porous organizational boundaries and establish communication flows and mutually beneficial relationships with internal (e.g., employees) and external (e.g., customers) constituencies.[33] IBM has worked to develop a long-standing cooperative relationship with the Mayo Clinic. The clinic is a customer but more importantly a research partner. IBM has placed staff at the Mayo Clinic, and the two organizations have worked together on technology for the early identification of aneurysms, the mining of data in electronic health records to develop customized treatment plans for patients, and other medical issues.[34]

Barrier-free organizations create successful relationships between both internal and external constituencies, but there is one additional constituency—competitors—with whom some organizations have benefited as they developed cooperative relationships. For example, Coca-Cola and PepsiCo, often argued to be the most intense rivals in business, work together to develop new, environmentally conscious refrigerants for use in their vending machines.[35]

By joining and actively participating in the Business Roundtable—an organization consisting of CEOs of leading U.S. corporations—Walmart has been able to learn about cutting-edge sustainable initiatives of other major firms. This free flow of information has enabled Walmart to undertake a number of steps that increased the energy efficiency of its operations. These are described in Strategy Spotlight 10.6.

THE BUSINESS ROUNDTABLE: A FORUM FOR SHARING BEST ENVIRONMENTAL SUSTAINABILITY PRACTICES

The Business Roundtable is a group of chief executive officers of major U.S. corporations that was created to promote probusiness public policy. It was formed in 1972 through the merger of three existing organizations: The March Group, the Construction Users Anti-Inflation Roundtable, and the Labor Law Study Committee. The group has been called President Obama's "closest ally in the business community."

The Business Roundtable became the first broad-based business group to agree on the need to address climate change through collective action, and it remains committed to limiting greenhouse gas emissions and setting the United States on a more sustainable path. The organization considers that threats to water quality and quantity, rising greenhouse gas emissions, and the risk of climate change—along with increasing energy prices and growing demand—are of great concern.

Its recent report "Create, Grow, Sustain" provides best practices and metrics from Business Roundtable member companies that represent nearly all sectors of the economy with $6 trillion in annual revenues. CEOs from Walmart, FedEx, PepsiCo, Whirlpool, and Verizon are among the 126 executives from leading U.S. companies that shared some of their best sustainability initiatives in this report. These companies are committed to reducing emissions, increasing energy efficiency, and developing more sustainable business practices.

Let's look, for example, at some of Walmart's initiatives. The firm's CEO, Mike Duke, says it is working with suppliers, partners, and consumers to drive its sustainability program. It has helped establish the Sustainability Consortium to drive metrics for measuring the environmental effects of consumer products across their life cycle. The retailer also helped lead the creation of a Sustainable Product Index to provide product information to consumers about the environmental impact of the products they purchase.

As part of its sustainability efforts, Walmart either had initiated or was in the process of developing over 180 renewable energy projects. Combined, these efforts resulted in more than 1 billion kilowatt-hours of renewable energy production each year, enough power to provide the electrical needs of 78,000 homes.

Walmart's renewable energy efforts have focused on three general initiatives:

- It has invested in developing distributed electrical generation systems on its property. As part of this effort, Walmart has installed rooftop solar panels on 127 locations in seven countries. It also has 26 fuel cell installations, 11 micro-wind projects, and 7 solar thermal projects.

- Expanding its contracts with suppliers for renewable energy has also been a focus of Walmart. Thus, Walmart bypasses the local utility to go directly to renewable energy suppliers to sign long-term contracts for renewable energy. With long-term contracts, Walmart has found that providers will give it more favorable terms. Walmart also believes that the long-term contracts give suppliers the incentive to invest in their generation systems, increasing the availability of renewable power for other users.

- In regions where going directly to renewable energy suppliers is difficult or impossible, Walmart has engaged the local utilities to increase their investment in renewable energy.

Sources: Anonymous. 2010. Leading CEOs share best sustainability practices. *www.environmentalleader.com*, April 26: np; Hopkins, M. No date. Sustainable growth. *www.businessroundtable*, np; Anonymous. 2012. Create, grow, sustain. *www.businessroundtable.org*, April 18: 120; and Business Roundtable. *www.en.wikipedia.org*.

Risks, Challenges, and Potential Downsides   Many firms find that creating and managing a barrier-free organization can be frustrating.[36] Puritan-Bennett Corporation, a manufacturer of respiratory equipment, found that its product development time more than doubled after it adopted team management. Roger J. Dolida, director of R&D, attributed this failure to a lack of top management commitment, high turnover among team members, and infrequent meetings. Often, managers trained in rigid hierarchies find it difficult to make the transition to the more democratic, participative style that teamwork requires.

The pros and cons of barrier-free structures are summarized in Exhibit 10.6.

The Modular Organization

As Charles Handy, author of *The Age of Unreason,* has noted:

> While it may be convenient to have everyone around all the time, having all of your workforce's time at your command is an extravagant way of marshaling the necessary resources. It is cheaper to keep them outside the organization . . . and to buy their services when you need them.[37]

EXHIBIT 10.6 Pros and Cons of Barrier-Free Structures

Pros	Cons
• Leverages the talents of all employees. • Enhances cooperation, coordination, and information sharing among functions, divisions, SBUs, and external constituencies. • Enables a quicker response to market changes through a single-goal focus. • Can lead to coordinated win–win initiatives with key suppliers, customers, and alliance partners.	• Difficult to overcome political and authority boundaries inside and outside the organization. • Lacks strong leadership and common vision, which can lead to coordination problems. • Time-consuming and difficult-to-manage democratic processes. • Lacks high levels of trust, which can impede performance.

modular organization
an organization in which nonvital functions are outsourced, using the knowledge and expertise of outside suppliers while retaining strategic control.

The **modular organization** outsources nonvital functions, tapping into the knowledge and expertise of "best in class" suppliers, but retains strategic control. Outsiders may be used to manufacture parts, handle logistics, or perform accounting activities.[38] The value chain can be used to identify the key primary and support activities performed by a firm to create value: Which activities do we keep in-house and which activities do we outsource to suppliers?[39] The organization becomes a central hub surrounded by networks of outside suppliers and specialists, and parts can be added or taken away. Both manufacturing and service units may be modular.[40]

Apparel is an industry in which the modular type has been widely adopted. Nike and Reebok, for example, concentrate on their strengths: designing and marketing high-tech, fashionable footwear. Nike has few production facilities and Reebok owns no plants. These two companies contract virtually all their footwear production to suppliers in China, Vietnam, and other countries with low-cost labor. Avoiding large investments in fixed assets helps them derive large profits on minor sales increases. Nike and Reebok can keep pace with changing tastes in the marketplace because their suppliers have become expert at rapidly retooling to produce new products.[41]

In a modular company, outsourcing the noncore functions offers three advantages:

1. A firm can decrease overall costs, stimulate new product development by hiring suppliers with talent superior to that of in-house personnel, avoid idle capacity, reduce inventories, and avoid being locked into a particular technology.
2. A company can focus scarce resources on the areas where it holds a competitive advantage. These benefits can translate into more funding for R&D to hire the best engineers and for sales and service to provide continuous training for staff.
3. An organization can tap into the knowledge and expertise of its specialized supply chain partners, adding critical skills and accelerating organizational learning.[42]

The modular type enables a company to leverage relatively small amounts of capital and a small management team to achieve seemingly unattainable strategic objectives.[43] Certain preconditions are necessary before the modular approach can be successful. First, the company must work closely with suppliers to ensure that the interests of each party are being fulfilled. Companies need to find loyal, reliable vendors who can be trusted with trade secrets. They also need assurances that suppliers will dedicate their financial, physical, and human resources to satisfy strategic objectives such as lowering costs or being first to market.

Second, the modular company must be sure that it selects the proper competencies to keep in-house. For Nike and Reebok, the core competencies are design and marketing, not shoe manufacturing; for Honda, the core competence is engine technology. An organization must avoid outsourcing components that may compromise its long-term competitive advantages.

Strategic Risks of Outsourcing   The main strategic concerns are (1) loss of critical skills or developing the wrong skills, (2) loss of cross-functional skills, and (3) loss of control over a supplier.[44]

Too much outsourcing can result in a firm "giving away" too much skill and control.[45] Outsourcing relieves companies of the requirement to maintain skill levels needed to manufacture essential components.[46] At one time, semiconductor chips seemed like a simple technology to outsource, but they have now become a critical component of a wide variety of products. Companies that have outsourced the manufacture of these chips run the risk of losing the ability to manufacture them as the technology escalates. They become more dependent upon their suppliers.

Cross-functional skills refer to the skills acquired through the interaction of individuals in various departments within a company.[47] Such interaction assists a department in solving problems as employees interface with others across functional units. However, if a firm outsources key functional responsibilities, such as manufacturing, communication across departments can become more difficult. A firm and its employees must now integrate their activities with a new, outside supplier.

The outsourced products may give suppliers too much power over the manufacturer. Suppliers that are key to a manufacturer's success can, in essence, hold the manufacturer "hostage." Nike manages this potential problem by sending full-time "product expatriates" to work at the plants of its suppliers. Also, Nike often brings top members of supplier management and technical teams to its headquarters. This way, Nike keeps close tabs on the pulse of new developments, builds rapport and trust with suppliers, and develops long-term relationships with suppliers to prevent hostage situations.

Exhibit 10.7 summarizes the pros and cons of modular structures.[48]

The Virtual Organization

In contrast to the "self-reliant" thinking that guided traditional organizational designs, the strategic challenge today has become doing more with less and looking outside the firm for opportunities and solutions to problems. The virtual organization provides a new means of leveraging resources and exploiting opportunities.[49]

The **virtual organization** can be viewed as a continually evolving network of independent companies—suppliers, customers, even competitors—linked together to share skills, costs, and access to one another's markets.[50] The members of a virtual organization, by pooling and sharing the knowledge and expertise of each of the component organizations, simultaneously "know" more and can "do" more than any one member of the group could do alone. By working closely together, each gains in the long run from individual and organizational learning.[51] The term *virtual,* meaning "being in effect but not actually so,"

> **virtual organization** a continually evolving network of independent companies that are linked together to share skills, costs, and access to one another's markets.

EXHIBIT 10.7   Pros and Cons of Modular Structures

Pros	Cons
• Directs a firm's managerial and technical talent to the most critical activities.	• Inhibits common vision through reliance on outsiders.
• Maintains full strategic control over most critical activities—core competencies.	• Diminishes future competitive advantages if critical technologies or other competencies are outsourced.
• Achieves "best in class" performance at each link in the value chain.	• Increases the difficulty of bringing back into the firm activities that now add value due to market shifts.
• Leverages core competencies by outsourcing with smaller capital commitment.	• Leads to an erosion of cross-functional skills.
• Encourages information sharing and accelerates organizational learning.	• Decreases operational control and potential loss of control over a supplier.

is commonly used in the computer industry. A computer's ability to appear to have more storage capacity than it really possesses is called virtual memory. Similarly, by assembling resources from a variety of entities, a virtual organization may seem to have more capabilities than it really possesses.[52]

Virtual organizations need not be permanent, and participating firms may be involved in multiple alliances. Virtual organizations may involve different firms performing complementary value activities or different firms involved jointly in the same value activities, such as production, R&D, and distribution. The percentage of activities that are jointly performed with partners may vary significantly from alliance to alliance.[53]

How does the virtual type of structure differ from the modular type? Unlike the modular type, in which the focal firm maintains full strategic control, the virtual organization is characterized by participating firms that give up part of their control and accept interdependent destinies. Participating firms pursue a collective strategy that enables them to cope with uncertainty through cooperative efforts. The benefit is that, just as virtual memory increases storage capacity, the virtual organizations enhance the capacity or competitive advantage of participating firms.

Each company that links up with others to create a virtual organization contributes only what it considers its core competencies. It will mix and match what it does best with the best of other firms by identifying its critical capabilities and the necessary links to other capabilities.[54]

In addition to linking a set of organizations in a virtual organization, firms can create internal virtual organizations, in which individuals who are not located together and may not even be in the same traditional organizational unit are joined together in virtual teams. These teams may be permanent but often are flexible, with changing membership as business needs evolve. The Insights from Research box offers evidence on how to effectively manage these virtual teams.

Challenges and Risks   The virtual organization demands that managers build relationships both within the firm and with other companies, negotiate win–win deals for all parties, find the right partners with compatible goals and values, and provide the right balance of freedom and control. Information systems must be designed and integrated to facilitate communication with current and potential partners.

Managers must be clear about the strategic objectives while forming alliances. Some objectives are time-bound, and those alliances need to be dissolved once the objective is fulfilled. Some alliances may have relatively long-term objectives and will need to be clearly monitored and nurtured to produce mutual commitment and avoid bitter fights for control. The highly dynamic personal computer industry is characterized by multiple temporary alliances among hardware, operating system, and software producers.[55] But alliances in the more stable automobile industry have long-term objectives and tend to be relatively stable.

The virtual organization is a logical culmination of joint venture strategies of the past. Shared risks, costs, and rewards are the facts of life in a virtual organization.[56] When virtual organizations are formed, they involve tremendous challenges for strategic planning. As with the modular corporation, it is essential to identify core competencies. However, for virtual structures to be successful, a strategic plan is also needed to determine the effectiveness of combining core competencies.

The strategic plan must address the diminished operational control and overwhelming need for trust and common vision among the partners. This new structure may be appropriate for firms whose strategies require merging technologies (e.g., computing and communication) or for firms exploiting shrinking product life cycles that require simultaneous entry into multiple geographic markets. It may be effective for firms that desire to be quick to the market with a new product or service. The recent profusion of alliances

HOW TO LEAD VIRTUAL TEAMS

Overview

Because team members in different locations work together virtually, traditional leadership styles are less effective. What works instead? Emphasize fair rewards, and make sure information sharing and communication are managed well. Empower your team members to serve as substitute leaders for each other, and ensure that everyone has access to functional technology.

What the Research Shows

Researchers from Michigan State University investigated the effectiveness of virtual teams in a 2012 article published in the *Journal of Applied Psychology*. Using structural equation modeling, they studied 101 research and development teams made up of 565 team members from global manufacturing industries. Team members worked across geographic distances, time zones, and cultures using electronic communication. Some teams were more virtual than others in terms of geographic dispersion, electronic versus face-to-face communication, and number of nationalities per team. The study's authors wanted to determine what happens as teams become more virtual. In other words, do changes in leadership behaviors, structures, and communication help teams produce a sufficient quality of work within budget and on schedule?

First, the researchers found that teams performed better under shared leadership, regardless of whether or not they were virtual. This means team members sought feedback to improve their performance, supported one another, and understood their teammates' problems and needs.

Additionally, the researchers determined that hierarchical leaders lost effectiveness as teams became more virtual. Without face-to-face meetings, formal leaders in headquarters lacked opportunities for personal influence or mentoring. On the other hand, structural supports became more important for team performance. For example, the following structural supports facilitated better employee performance:

- A "fair" performance appraisal system.
- Clear information about task completion.
- Details about rewards.

Why This Matters

Virtual teams, virtual meetings, and virtual offices are a reality in many companies today. Reducing travel and overhead expenses seems like a great idea, but what do virtual offices mean for managers? This study shows that leaders must evolve their management techniques to keep up with the technological and organizational changes created by virtual environments.

If you manage a virtual team, you should ease up on traditional leadership methods. For instance, resist the temptation to exert authority via a Lone Ranger approach. A single leader isn't in a position to exert face-to-face influence and may lack the information to effectively monitor behaviors. Instead, you should focus on providing effective structural supports. Make sure your appraisal system is fair and transparent, team members have as much information as they need, and the link between specific efforts and rewards is clear. Team members should hold one another accountable for results and for making sure all employees have the resources they need.

Consultant Jessica Lipnack, chief executive officer of NetAge Inc., says virtual team members should feel they're contributing to meaningful goals. She once worked with a team of rocket scientists who never met face-to-face yet came up with a new rocket design in a fraction of the typical time—at one-tenth of the normal budget. The team reduced the parts used from hundreds to a few and brought the project in ahead of schedule.

Lipnack says the following have become essential supports for virtual teams: good communication, an online "team room," regular meetings, consulting teleconferences, and a clear plan for what to accomplish. Technology remains critical, especially video, but videoconferences can lose effectiveness if the number of participants rises above 15.

Key Takeaways

- Members of virtual teams work together from different locations using electronic communication. Organizations across the globe are using virtual teams more often.
- These arrangements pose a challenge to formal, hierarchical leadership. Teams with far-flung members find substitute leaders help them perform better.
- As hierarchical leaders become less effective, the management of rewards becomes more important. Communication and information sharing become critical.
- Shared leadership among team members helps performance, regardless of how virtual the group is.
- As your teams rely more on electronic communication to bridge distance and cultures, technological acumen grows more valuable. Remain flexible about exercising traditional management behaviors, but be sure your employees have the leadership they need.

Apply This Today

Leaders need to keep up with the times. When it comes to virtual teams, leaders should empower others to manage through rewards and provide information where most needed. Take action based on these research findings, and you could be the most skilled leader at the virtual table.

Research Reviewed

Hoch, J. E. & Kozlowski, S. W. 2012. Leading virtual teams: Hierarchical leadership, structural supports, and shared team leadership. *Journal of Applied Psychology,* doi: 10.1037/a0030264.

EXHIBIT 10.8 Pros and Cons of Virtual Structures

Pros	Cons
• Enables the sharing of costs and skills. • Enhances access to global markets. • Increases market responsiveness. • Creates a "best of everything" organization since each partner brings core competencies to the alliance. • Encourages both individual and organizational knowledge sharing and accelerates organizational learning.	• Harder to determine where one company ends and another begins, due to close interdependencies among players. • Leads to potential loss of operational control among partners. • Results in loss of strategic control over emerging technology. • Requires new and difficult-to-acquire managerial skills.

Source: Miles, R. E., & Snow, C. C. 1986. Organizations: New Concepts for New Forms. *California Management Review,* Spring: 62–73; Miles & Snow. 1999. Causes of Failure in Network Organizations. *California Management Review,* Summer: 53–72; and Bahrami, H. 1991. The Emerging Flexible Organization: Perspectives from Silicon Valley. *California Management Review,* Summer: 33–52.

among airlines was primarily motivated by the need to provide seamless travel demanded by the full-fare-paying business traveler. Exhibit 10.8 summarizes the pros and cons of virtual structures.

Boundaryless Organizations: Making Them Work

Designing an organization that simultaneously supports the requirements of an organization's strategy, is consistent with the demands of the environment, and can be effectively implemented by the people around the manager is a tall order for any manager.[57] The most effective solution is usually a combination of organizational types. That is, a firm may outsource many parts of its value chain to reduce costs and increase quality, engage simultaneously in multiple alliances to take advantage of technological developments or penetrate new markets, and break down barriers within the organization to enhance flexibility.

When an organization faces external pressures, resource scarcity, and declining performance, it tends to become more internally focused, rather than directing its efforts toward managing and enhancing relationships with existing and potential external stakeholders. This may be the most opportune time for managers to carefully analyze their value-chain activities and evaluate the potential for adopting elements of modular, virtual, and barrier-free organizational types.

In this section, we will address two issues managers need to be aware of as they work to design an effective boundaryless organization. First, managers need to develop mechanisms to ensure effective coordination and integration. Second, managers need to be aware of the benefits and costs of developing strong and long-term relationships with both internal and external stakeholders.

Facilitating Coordination and Integration   Achieving the coordination and integration necessary to maximize the potential of an organization's human capital involves much more than just creating a new structure. Techniques and processes to ensure the coordination and integration of an organization's key value-chain activities are critical. Teams are key building blocks of the new organizational forms, and teamwork requires new and flexible approaches to coordination and integration.

Managers trained in rigid hierarchies may find it difficult to make the transition to the more democratic, participative style that teamwork requires. As Douglas K. Smith, co-author of *The Wisdom of Teams,* pointed out, "A completely diverse group must agree on a goal, put the notion of individual accountability aside and figure out how to work with each other. Most of all, they must learn that if the team fails, it's everyone's fault."[58] Within the framework of an appropriate organizational design, managers must select a mix and balance of tools and techniques to facilitate the effective coordination and integration of key activities. Some of the factors that must be considered include:

- Common culture and shared values.
- Horizontal organizational structures.
- Horizontal systems and processes.
- Communications and information technologies.
- Human resource practices.

Common Culture and Shared Values   Shared goals, mutual objectives, and a high degree of trust are essential to the success of boundaryless organizations. In the fluid and flexible environments of the new organizational architectures, common cultures, shared values, and carefully aligned incentives are often less expensive to implement and are often a more effective means of strategic control than rules, boundaries, and formal procedures. Tony Hsieh, the founder of Zappos, echoes this need for a shared culture and values when he describes his role this way: "I think of myself less as a leader and more of being an architect of an environment that enables employees to come up with their own ideas."[59]

Horizontal Organizational Structures   These structures, which group similar or related business units under common management control, facilitate sharing resources and infrastructures to exploit synergies among operating units and help to create a sense of common purpose. Consistency in training and the development of similar structures across business units facilitates job rotation and cross-training and enhances understanding of common problems and opportunities. Cross-functional teams and interdivisional committees and task groups represent important opportunities to improve understanding and foster cooperation among operating units.

> **horizontal organizational structures**
> organizational forms that group similar or related business units under common management control and facilitate sharing resources and infrastructures to exploit synergies among operating units and help to create a sense of common purpose.

Horizontal Systems and Processes   Organizational systems, policies, and procedures are the traditional mechanisms for achieving integration among functional units. Existing policies and procedures often do little more than institutionalize the barriers that exist from years of managing within the framework of the traditional model. Beginning with an understanding of basic business processes in the context of "a collection of activities that takes one or more kinds of input and creates an output that is of value to the customer," Michael Hammer and James Champy's 1993 best-selling *Reengineering the Corporation* outlined a methodology for redesigning internal systems and procedures that has been embraced by many organizations.[60] Successful reengineering lowers costs, reduces inventories and cycle times, improves quality, speeds response times, and enhances organizational flexibility. Others advocate similar benefits through the reduction of cycle times, total quality management, and the like.

Communications and Information Technology (IT)   The effective use of IT can play an important role in bridging gaps and breaking down barriers between organizations. Email and videoconferencing can improve lateral communications across long distances and multiple time zones and circumvent many of the barriers of the traditional model. Information technology can be a powerful ally in the redesign and streamlining of internal business processes and in improving coordination and integration between suppliers and customers. Internet technologies have eliminated the paperwork in many buyer–supplier relationships, enabling cooperating organizations to reduce inventories, shorten delivery cycles, and reduce operating costs. Information technology must be viewed more as a prime component of an organization's overall strategy than simply in terms of administrative support.

Human Resource Practices   Change always involves and affects the human dimension of organizations. The attraction, development, and retention of human capital are vital to value creation. As boundaryless structures are implemented, processes are reengineered, and organizations become increasingly dependent on sophisticated ITs, the skills of workers and managers alike must be upgraded to realize the full benefits.

The Benefits and Costs of Developing Lasting Internal and External Relationships
Successful boundaryless organizations rely heavily on the relational aspects of organizations. Rather than relying on strict hierarchical and bureaucratic systems, these firms are flexible and coordinate action by leveraging shared social norms and strong social relationships between both internal and external stakeholders.[61] At the same time, it is important to acknowledge that relying on relationships can have both positive and negative effects. To successfully move to a more boundaryless organization, managers need to acknowledge and attend to both the costs and benefits of relying on relationships and social norms to guide behavior.

There are three primary benefits that organizations accrue when relying on relationships:

- *Agency costs within the firm can be dramatically cut through the use of relational systems.* Managers and employees in relationship-oriented firms are guided by social norms and relationships they have with other managers and employees. As a result, the firm can reduce the degree to which it relies on monitoring, rules and regulations, and financial incentives to ensure that workers put in a strong effort and work in the firm's interests. A relational view leads managers and employees to act in a supportive manner and makes them more willing to step out of their formal roles when needed to accomplish tasks for others and for the organization. They are also less likely to shirk their responsibilities.

- *There is also likely to be a reduction in the transaction costs between a firm and its suppliers and customers.* If firms have built strong relationships with partnering firms, they are more likely to work cooperatively with these firms and build trust that their partners will work in the best interests of the alliance. This will reduce the need for the firms to write detailed contracts and set up strict bureaucratic rules to outline the responsibilities and define the behavior of each firm. Additionally, partnering firms with strong relationships are more likely to invest in assets that specifically support the partnership. Finally, they will have much less fear that their partner will try to take advantage of them or seize the bulk of the benefits from the partnership.

- *Since they feel a sense of shared ownership and goals, individuals within the firm as well as partnering firms will be more likely to search for win–win rather than win–lose solutions.* When taking a relational view, individuals are less likely to look out solely for their personal best interests. They will also be considerate of the benefits and costs to other individuals in the firm and to the overall firm. The same is true at the organizational level. Firms with strong relationships with their partners are going to look for solutions that not only benefit themselves but also provide equitable benefits and limited downside for the partnering firms. Such a situation was evident with a number of German firms during the economic crisis of 2008–2010. The German government, corporations, and unions worked together to find the fairest way to respond to the crisis. The firms agreed not to lay off workers. The unions agreed to reduce workweeks. The government kicked in a subsidy to make up for some of the lost wages. In other words, they negotiated a shared sacrifice to address the challenge. This positioned the German firms to bounce back quickly once the crisis passed.

While there are a number of benefits with using a relational view, there can also be some substantial costs:

- *As the relationships between individuals and firms strengthen, they are also more likely to fall prey to suboptimal lock-in effects.* The problem here is that as decisions become driven by concerns about relationships, economic factors become less important. As a result, firms become less likely to make decisions that could benefit the firm since those decisions may harm employees or partnering firms. For example, firms may see the economic logic in exiting a market, but the ties they feel with employees that work in that division and partnering firms in that market may reduce their willingness to make the hard decision to exit the market. This can be debilitating to firms in rapidly changing markets where successful firms add, reorganize, and sometimes exit operations and relationships regularly.

- *Since there are no formal guidelines, conflicts between individuals and units within firms, as well as between partnering firms, are typically resolved through ad hoc negotiations and processes.* In these circumstances, there are no legal means or bureaucratic rules to guide decision making. Thus, when firms face a difficult decision where there are differences of opinion about the best course of action, the ultimate choices made are often driven by the inherent power of the individuals or firms involved. This power use may be unintentional and subconscious, but it can result in outcomes that are deemed unfair by one or more of the parties.

- *The social capital of individuals and firms can drive their opportunities.* Thus, rather than identifying the best person to put in a leadership role or the optimal supplier to contract with, these choices are more strongly driven by the level of social connection the person or supplier has. This also increases the entry barriers for potential new suppliers or employees with whom a firm can contract since new firms likely don't have the social connections needed to be chosen as a worthy partner with whom to contract. This also may limit the likelihood that new innovative ideas will enter into the conversations at the firm.

As mentioned earlier in the chapter, the solution may be to effectively integrate elements of formal structure and reward systems with stronger relationships. This may influence specific relationships so that a manager will want employees to build relationships while still maintaining some managerial oversight and reward systems that motivate the desired behavior. This may also result in different emphases with different relationships. For example, there may be some units, such as accounting, where a stronger role for traditional structures and forms of evaluation may be optimal. However, in new product development units, a greater emphasis on relational systems may be more appropriate.

Creating Ambidextrous Organizational Designs

In Chapter 1, we introduced the concept of "ambidexterity," which incorporates two contradictory challenges faced by today's managers.[62] First, managers must explore new opportunities and adjust to volatile markets in order to avoid complacency. They must ensure that they maintain **adaptability** and remain proactive in expanding and/or modifying their product-market scope to anticipate and satisfy market conditions. Such competencies are especially challenging when change is rapid and unpredictable.

Second, managers must also effectively exploit the value of their existing assets and competencies. They need to have **alignment,** which is a clear sense of how value is being created in the short term and how activities are integrated and properly coordinated. Firms that achieve both adaptability and alignment are considered *ambidextrous organizations*— aligned and efficient in how they manage today's business but flexible enough to changes in the environment so that they will prosper tomorrow.

Handling such opposing demands is difficult because there will always be some degree of conflict. Firms often suffer when they place too strong a priority on either adaptability

LO10.5

The need for creating ambidextrous organizational designs that enable firms to explore new opportunities and effectively integrate existing operations.

adaptibility
managers' exploration of new opportunities and adjustment to volatile markets in order to avoid complacency.

alignment
managers' clear sense of how value is being created in the short term and how activities are integrated and properly coordinated.

or alignment. If it places too much focus on adaptability, the firm will suffer low profitability in the short term. If managers direct their efforts primarily at alignment, they will likely miss out on promising business opportunities.

Ambidextrous Organizations: Key Design Attributes

ambidextrous organizational designs
organizational designs that attempt to simultaneously pursue modest, incremental innovations as well as more dramatic, breakthrough innovations.

A study by Charles O'Reilly and Michael Tushman[63] provides some insights into how some firms were able to create successful **ambidextrous organizational designs.** They investigated companies that attempted to simultaneously pursue modest, incremental innovations as well as more dramatic, breakthrough innovations. The team investigated 35 attempts to launch breakthrough innovations undertaken by 15 business units in nine different industries. They studied the organizational designs and the processes, systems, and cultures associated with the breakthrough projects as well as their impact on the operations and performance of the traditional businesses.

Companies structured their breakthrough projects in one of four primary ways:

- Seven were carried out within existing *functional organizational structures.* The projects were completely integrated into the regular organizational and management structure.
- Nine were organized as *cross-functional teams.* The groups operated within the established organization but outside the existing management structure.
- Four were organized as *unsupported teams.* Here, they became independent units set up outside the established organization and management hierarchy.
- Fifteen were conducted within *ambidextrous organizations.* Here, the breakthrough efforts were organized within structurally independent units, each having its own processes, structures, and cultures. However, they were integrated into the existing senior management structure.

The performance results of the 35 initiatives were tracked along two dimensions:

- Their success in creating desired innovations was measured by either the actual commercial results of the new product or the application of practical market or technical learning.
- The performance of the existing business was evaluated.

The study found that the organizational structure and management practices employed had a direct and significant impact on the performance of both the breakthrough initiative and the traditional business. The ambidextrous organizational designs were more effective than the other three designs on both dimensions: launching breakthrough products or services (i.e., adaptation) and improving the performance of the existing business (i.e., alignment).

Why Was the Ambidextrous Organization the Most Effective Structure?

The study found that there were many factors. A clear and compelling vision, consistently communicated by the company's senior management team, was critical in building the ambidextrous designs. The structure enabled cross-fertilization while avoiding cross-contamination. The tight coordination and integration at the managerial levels enabled the newer units to share important resources from the traditional units, such as cash, talent, and expertise. Such sharing was encouraged and facilitated by effective reward systems that emphasized overall company goals. The organizational separation ensured that the new units' distinctive processes, structures, and cultures were not overwhelmed by the forces of "business as usual." The established units were shielded from the distractions of launching new businesses, and they continued to focus all of their attention and energy on refining their operations, enhancing their products, and serving their customers.

McDonald's New Structure

Growing from a single restaurant in 1955 to over 14,000 restaurants in the United States in 2014, McDonald's has experienced nearly continuous growth and success. With over $35 billion in sales in the U.S., McDonald's generates nearly three times the revenue of its closest competitor, Subway. But that doesn't mean that McDonald's is immune to struggles. In 2014, it faced a real challenge to remain relevant as an attractive option for customers and saw its U.S. sales drop by 4.1 percent compared to sales in 2013. This negative turn in the firm's performance is likely related to the surprise retirement of McDonald's CEO, Don Thompson, in February 2015.

To consumers, McDonald's menu appears stale and unhealthy. As a result, customers are flocking to competing restaurants, such as Chipotle and Panera, that are seen as offering healthier food and having fresher ingredients and more interesting menu items. As McDonald's U.S.A. president, Mike Andres, stated, "What has worked for McDonald's for the past decade is not sufficient to propel the business forward in the future."

McDonald's believes that one of the causes of its struggles is the structure of the firm. McDonald's has long aimed for consistency across its units. To maintain this consistency, McDonald's has used a central testing kitchen to develop new products that could be rolled out across the firm. The firm has also relied on a regional structure, with Eastern, Central, and Western divisions. When a new initiative or product was rolled out, the firm would introduce it in each region, moving from north to south. Thus, customers in Minnesota and Louisiana would have the same menu, but new products would first be introduced in Minnesota and later in Louisiana. But this structure is hampering the firm since it is unable to be very responsive to regional taste differences and is very slow in responding to changing customer tastes and preferences. As a result, within McDonald's, "there are too many layers, redundancies in planning and communication, competing priorities, barriers to efficient decision making, and too much talking to ourselves instead of to and about our customers," according to Andres. Thus, the firm has been burdened by organizational boundaries that slow communication and the ability to talk to and respond to customers and other stakeholders.

To shake things up, McDonald's announced it would eliminate layers of management and create a new organizational structure in October 2014. The aim of the changes is to allow the firm to be more responsive to local tastes and to changes in customer demands. At the top level, the chain is moving to four regional divisions: Northeast, South, Central, and West. In McDonald's assessment, this new structure more effectively clusters together customers with similar tastes and preferences. At a lower level, McDonald's is giving leaders in 22 regional groups greater autonomy in making local menu and marketing decisions. In Andres's words, "We need to be more sophisticated in how we use local intelligence to address specific consumer needs . . . and to put decision making closer to our customers." As part of this effort, McDonald's is looking to the regions to learn about emerging customer preferences, and it created a learning lab on the west coast to better understand what consumers in that region want.

The open question is whether or not these structural changes will allow McDonald's to refresh its image and pull in more customers.

Discussion Questions

1. Is this structural change likely to be beneficial to McDonald's as it aims to stop sliding sales?
2. What are the potential costs and benefits of increasing regional autonomy?

continued

continued

3. New initiatives or menu changes in one region may be valuable in another region. What actions can McDonald's take to break through regional boundaries to facilitate learning?

4. What other actions does McDonald's need to take to turn around its sales?

Sources: Lorenzetti, L. 2014. McDonald's struggling to stay relevant with millennials. *fortune.com,* August 25: np; Anonymous. 2014. McDonald's profit, sales decline amid ongoing struggles around the world. *foxbusiness.com,* October 21: np; Jargon, J. 2014. McDonald's plans to change U.S. structure. *wsj.com,* October 30: np; and Jargon, J. & Prior, A. 2014. McDonald's expects further challenges. *wsj.com,* July 22: np.

Reflecting on Career Implications . . .

☒ **Boundaryless Organizational Designs:** Does your firm have structural mechanisms (e.g., culture, human resource practices) that facilitate sharing information across boundaries? Regardless of the level of boundarylessness of your organization, a key issue for your career is the extent to which you are able to cut across boundaries within your organization. Such boundaryless behavior on your part will enable you to enhance and leverage your human capital. Evaluate how boundaryless you are within your organizational context. What actions can you take to become even more boundaryless?

☒ **Horizontal Systems and Processes:** One of the approaches suggested in the chapter to improve boundarylessness

within organizations is *reengineering*. Analyze the work you are currently doing and think of ways in which it can be reengineered to improve quality, accelerate response time, and lower cost. Consider presenting the results of your analysis to your immediate superiors. Do you think they will be receptive to your suggestions?

☒ **Ambidextrous Organizations:** Firms that achieve *adaptability* and *alignment* are considered ambidextrous. As an individual, you can also strive to be ambidextrous. Evaluate your own ambidexterity by assessing your adaptability (your ability to change in response to changes around you) and alignment (how good you are at exploiting your existing competencies). What steps can you take to improve your ambidexterity?

summary

Successful organizations must ensure that they have the proper type of organizational structure. Furthermore, they must ensure that their firms incorporate the necessary integration and processes so that the internal and external boundaries of their firms are flexible and permeable. Such a need is increasingly important as the environments of firms become more complex, changing rapidly and unpredictably.

In the first section of the chapter, we discussed the growth patterns of large corporations. Although most organizations remain small or die, some firms continue to grow in terms of revenues, vertical integration, and diversity of products and services. In addition, their geographic scope may increase to include international operations. We traced the dominant pattern of growth, which evolves from a simple structure to a functional structure as a firm grows in terms of size and increases its level of vertical integration. After a firm expands into related products and services, its structure changes from a functional to a divisional form of organization. Finally, when the firm enters international markets, its

structure again changes to accommodate the change in strategy.

We also addressed the different types of organizational structure—simple, functional, divisional (including two variations: strategic business unit and holding company), and matrix—as well as their relative advantages and disadvantages. We closed the section with a discussion of the implications for structure that arise when a firm enters international markets. The three primary factors to take into account when determining the appropriate structure are type of international strategy, product diversity, and the extent to which a firm is dependent on foreign sales.

The second section of the chapter introduced the concept of the boundaryless organization. We did not suggest that the concept of the boundaryless organization replaces the traditional forms of organizational structure. Rather, it should complement them. This is necessary to cope with the increasing complexity and change in the competitive environment. We addressed three types of boundaryless organizations. The barrier-free type focuses on the need for the internal and external boundaries of a firm to be more flexible and permeable. The modular type emphasizes the strategic outsourcing of noncore activities. The virtual type centers on the strategic benefits of alliances and the forming of network organizations. We discussed both the advantages and disadvantages of each type of boundaryless organization, and we suggested some techniques and processes that are necessary to successfully implement each type. These are common culture and values, horizontal organizational structures, horizontal systems and processes, communications and information technologies, and human resource practices.

The final section addressed the need for managers to develop ambidextrous organizations. In today's rapidly changing global environment, managers must be responsive and proactive in order to take advantage of new opportunities. At the same time, they must effectively integrate and coordinate existing operations. Such requirements call for organizational designs that establish project teams that are structurally independent units, with each having its own processes, structures, and cultures. But, at the same time, each unit needs to be effectively integrated into the existing management hierarchy.

SUMMARY REVIEW QUESTIONS

1. Why is it important for managers to carefully consider the type of organizational structure that they use to implement their strategies?

2. Briefly trace the dominant growth pattern of major corporations from simple structure to functional structure to divisional structure. Discuss the relationship between a firm's strategy and its structure.

3. What are the relative advantages and disadvantages of the types of organizational structure—simple, functional, divisional, matrix—discussed in the chapter?

4. When a firm expands its operations into foreign markets, what are the three most important factors to take into account in deciding what type of structure is most appropriate? What are the types of international structures discussed in the text, and what are the relationships between strategy and structure?

5. Briefly describe the three different types of boundaryless organizations: barrier-free, modular, and virtual.

6. What are some of the key attributes of effective groups? Ineffective groups?

7. What are the advantages and disadvantages of the three types of boundaryless organizations: barrier-free, modular, and virtual?

8. When are ambidextrous organizational designs necessary? What are some of their key attributes?

key terms

organizational structure 316
simple organizational
   structure 318
functional organizational
   structure 318
divisional organizational
   structure 320
strategic business unit (SBU)
   structure 322
holding company
   structure 323
matrix organizational
   structure 323
international division
   structure 326

geographic-area division
   structure 326
worldwide matrix
   structure 326
worldwide functional
   structure 326
worldwide product division
   structure 326
global start-up 326
boundaryless organizational
   designs 328
barrier-free organization 329
modular organization 332
virtual organization 333
horizontal organizational
   structures 337
adaptability 339
alignment 339
ambidextrous organizational
   designs 340

experiential exercise

Many firms have recently moved toward a modular structure. For example, they have increasingly outsourced many of their information technology (IT) activities. Identify three such organizations. Using secondary sources, evaluate (1) the firm's rationale for IT outsourcing and (2) the implications for performance.

Firm	Rationale	Implication(s) for Performance
1.		
2.		
3.		

application questions & exercises

1. Select an organization that competes in an industry in which you are particularly interested. Go on the Internet and determine what type of organizational structure this organization has. In your view, is it consistent with the strategy that it has chosen to implement? Why? Why not?

2. Choose an article from *Bloomberg Businessweek, Fortune, Forbes, Fast Company,* or any other well-known publication that deals with a corporation that has undergone a significant change in its strategic direction. What are the implications for the structure of this organization?

3. Go on the Internet and look up some of the public statements or speeches of an executive in a major corporation about a significant initiative such as entering into a joint venture or launching a new product line. What do you feel are the implications for making the internal and external barriers of the firm more flexible and permeable? Does the executive discuss processes, procedures, integrating mechanisms, or cultural issues that should serve this purpose? Or are other issues discussed that enable a firm to become more boundaryless?

4. Look up a recent article in the publications listed in question 2 that addresses a firm's involvement in outsourcing (modular organization) or in strategic alliance or network organizations (virtual organization). Was the firm successful or unsuccessful in this endeavor? Why? Why not?

ethics questions

1. If a firm has a divisional structure and places extreme pressures on its divisional executives to meet short-term profitability goals (e.g., quarterly income), could this raise some ethical considerations? Why? Why not?

2. If a firm enters into a strategic alliance but does not exercise appropriate behavioral control of its employees (in terms of culture, rewards and incentives, and boundaries—as discussed in Chapter 9) who are involved in the alliance, what ethical issues could arise? What could be the potential long-term and short-term downside for the firm?

references

1. Wilson, K. & Doz, Y. 2012. 10 rules for managing global innovation. *Harvard Business Review,* 90(10): 84–92; Wallace, J. 2007. Update on problems joining 787 fuselage sections. *Seattlepi.com,* June 7: np; Peterson, K. 2011. Special report: A wing and a prayer: Outsourcing at Boeing. *Reuters.com,* January 20: np; Hiltzik, M. 2011. 787 Dreamliner teaches Boeing costly lesson on outsourcing. *Latimes.com,* February 15: np; Gates, D. 2013. Boeing 787's problems blamed on outsourcing, lack of oversight. *Seattletimes.com,* February 2: np; and Ostrower, J. 2014. Boeing's Key Mission: Cut Dreamliner cost. *wsj.com.* January 7: np.

2. For a unique perspective on organization design, see Rao, R. 2010. What 17th century pirates can teach us about job design. *Harvard Business Review,* 88(10): 44.

3. This introductory discussion draws upon Hall, R. H. 2002. *Organizations: Structures, processes, and outcomes* (8th ed.). Upper Saddle River, NJ: Prentice Hall; and Duncan, R. E. 1979. What is the right organization structure? Decision-tree analysis provides the right answer. *Organizational Dynamics,* 7(3): 59–80. For an insightful discussion of strategy-structure relationships in the organization theory and strategic management literatures, refer to Keats, B. & O'Neill, H. M. 2001. Organization structure: Looking through a strategy lens. In Hitt, M. A., Freeman, R. E., & Harrison, J. S. 2001. *The Blackwell handbook of strategic management:* 520–542. Malden, MA: Blackwell.

4. Gratton, L. 2011. The end of the middle manager. *Harvard Business Review,* 89(1/2): 36.

5. An interesting discussion on the role of organizational design in strategy execution is in Neilson, G. L., Martin, K. L., & Powers, E. 2009. The secrets to successful strategy execution. *Harvard Business Review,* 87(2): 60–70.

6. This discussion draws upon Chandler, A. D. 1962. *Strategy and structure.* Cambridge, MA: MIT Press; Galbraith J. R. & Kazanjian, R. K. 1986. *Strategy implementation: The role of structure and process.* St. Paul, MN: West; and Scott, B. R. 1971. Stages of corporate development. Intercollegiate Case Clearing House, 9-371-294, BP 998. Harvard Business School.

7. Our discussion of the different types of organizational structures draws on a variety of sources, including Galbraith & Kazanjian, op. cit.; Hrebiniak, L. G. & Joyce, W. F. 1984. *Implementing strategy.* New York: Macmillan; Distelzweig, H. 2000. Organizational structure. In Helms, M. M. (Ed.), *Encyclopedia of management:* 692–699. Farmington Hills, MI: Gale; and Dess, G. G. & Miller, A. 1993. *Strategic management.* New York: McGraw-Hill.

8. A discussion of an innovative organizational design is in Garvin, D. A. & Levesque, L. C. 2009. The multiunit enterprise. *Harvard Business Review,* 87(2): 106–117.

9. Schein, E. H. 1996. Three cultures of management: The key to organizational learning. *Sloan Management Review,* 38(1): 9–20.

10. Insights on governance implications for multidivisional forms are in Verbeke, A. & Kenworthy, T. P. 2008. Multidivisional vs. metanational governance. *Journal of International Business,* 39(6): 940–956.

11. Martin, J. A. & Eisenhardt, K. 2010. Rewiring: Cross-business-unit collaborations in multibusiness organizations. *Academy of Management Journal,* 53(2): 265–301.

12. For a discussion of performance implications, refer to Hoskisson, R. E. 1987. Multidivisional structure and performance: The contingency of diversification strategy. *Academy*

of Management Journal, 29: 625–644.

13. For a thorough and seminal discussion of the evolution toward the divisional form of organizational structure in the United States, refer to Chandler, op. cit. A rigorous empirical study of the strategy and structure relationship is found in Rumelt, R. P. 1974. *Strategy, structure, and economic performance.* Cambridge, MA: Harvard Business School Press.

14. Ghoshal S. & Bartlett, C. A. 1995. Changing the role of management: Beyond structure to processes. *Harvard Business Review,* 73(1): 88.

15. Koppel, B. 2000. Synergy in ketchup? *Forbes,* February 7: 68–69; and Hitt, M. A., Ireland, R. D., & Hoskisson, R. E. 2001. *Strategic management: Competitiveness and globalization* (4th ed.). Cincinnati, OH: South-Western.

16. Pitts, R. A. 1977. Strategies and structures for diversification. *Academy of Management Journal,* 20(2): 197–208.

17. Silvestri, L. 2012. The evolution of organizational structure. *footnote1 .com,* June 6: np.

18. Andersen, M. M., Froholdt, M., & Poulfelt, F. 2010. *Return on strategy: How to achieve it.* New York: Routledge.

19. Haas, M. R. 2010. The double-edged swords of autonomy and external knowledge: Analyzing team effectiveness in a multinational organization. *Academy of Management Journal,* 53(5): 989–1008.

20. Daniels, J. D., Pitts, R. A., & Tretter, M. J. 1984. Strategy and structure of U.S. multinationals: An exploratory study. *Academy of Management Journal,* 27(2): 292–307.

21. Habib, M. M. & Victor, B. 1991. Strategy, structure, and performance of U.S. manufacturing and service MNCs: A comparative analysis. *Strategic Management Journal,* 12(8): 589–606.

22. Our discussion of global start-ups draws from Oviatt, B. M. & McDougall, P. P. 2005. The internationalization of entrepreneurship. *Journal of International Business Studies,* 36(1): 2–8; Oviatt, B. M. & McDougall, P. P. 1994. Toward a theory of international new ventures. *Journal of International Business Studies,* 25(1): 45–64; and Oviatt, B. M. & McDougall, P. P. 1995. Global start-ups: Entrepreneurs

on a worldwide stage. *Academy of Management Executive,* 9(2): 30–43.

23. Some useful guidelines for global start-ups are provided in Kuemmerle, W. 2005. The entrepreneur's path for global expansion. *MIT Sloan Management Review,* 46(2): 42–50.

24. See, for example, Miller, D. & Friesen, P. H. 1980. Momentum and revolution in organizational structure. *Administrative Science Quarterly,* 13: 65–91.

25. Many authors have argued that a firm's structure can influence its strategy and performance. These include Amburgey, T. L. & Dacin, T. 1995. As the left foot follows the right? The dynamics of strategic and structural change. *Academy of Management Journal,* 37: 1427–1452; Dawn, K. & Amburgey, T. L. 1991. Organizational inertia and momentum: A dynamic model of strategic change. *Academy of Management Journal,* 34: 591–612; Fredrickson, J. W. 1986. The strategic decision process and organization structure. *Academy of Management Review,* 11: 280–297; Hall, D. J. & Saias, M. A. 1980. Strategy follows structure! *Strategic Management Journal,* 1: 149–164; and Burgelman, R. A. 1983. A model of the interaction of strategic behavior, corporate context, and the concept of strategy. *Academy of Management Review,* 8: 61–70.

26. An interesting discussion on how the Internet has affected the boundaries of firms can be found in Afuah, A. 2003. Redefining firm boundaries in the face of the Internet: Are firms really shrinking? *Academy of Management Review,* 28(1): 34–53.

27. Govindarajan, V. G. & Trimble, C. 2010. Stop the innovation wars. *Harvard Business Review,* 88(7/8): 76–83.

28. For a discussion of the role of coaching on developing high-performance teams, refer to Kets de Vries, M. F. R. 2005. Leadership group coaching in action: The zen of creating high performance teams. *Academy of Management Executive,* 19(1): 77–89.

29. Pfeffer, J. 1998. *The human equation: Building profits by putting people first.* Cambridge, MA: Harvard Business School Press.

30. For a discussion on how functional area diversity affects performance, see Bunderson, J. S. & Sutcliffe, K. M. 2002. Comparing alternative conceptualizations of functional diversity in management teams: Process and performance effects.

Academy of Management Journal, 45(5): 875–893.

31. Falconi, M. 2014. Novartis chairman stresses need for R&D investment. *wsj.com,* March 24: np.

32. Groth, A. 2015. Holacracy at Zappos: It's either the future of management or a social experiment gone awry. *qz.com,* January 14: np; Anonymous. 2014. The holes in holacracy. *economist.com,* July 5: np; and Van De Kamp, P. 2014. Holacracy—A radical approach to organizational design. *medium.com,* August 2: np.

33. Public-private partnerships are addressed in Engardio, P. 2009. State capitalism. *BusinessWeek,* February 9: 38–43.

34. Aller, R., Weiner, H., & Weilart, M. 2005. IBM and Mayo collaborating to customize patient treatment plans. *cap.org,* January: np; and McGee, M. 2010. IBM, Mayo partner on aneurysm diagnostics. *informationweek.com,* January 25: np.

35. Winston, A. 2014: *The big pivot.* Boston: Harvard Business Review Press.

36. Dess, G. G., Rasheed, A. M. A., McLaughlin, K. J., & Priem, R. 1995. The new corporate architecture. *Academy of Management Executive,* 9(3): 7–20.

37. Handy, C. 1989. The age of unreason. Boston: Harvard Business School Press; Ramstead, E. 1997. APC maker's low-tech formula: Start with the box. *The Wall Street Journal,* December 29: B1; Mussberg, W. 1997. Thin screen PCs are looking good but still fall flat. *The Wall Street Journal,* January 2: 9; Brown, E. 1997. Monorail: Low cost PCs. *Fortune,* July 7: 106–108; and Young, M. 1996. Ex-Compaq executives start new company. *Computer Reseller News,* November 11: 181.

38. An original discussion on how open sourcing could help the Big 3 automobile companies is in Jarvis, J. 2009. How the Google model could help Detroit. *BusinessWeek,* February 9: 32–36.

39. For a discussion of some of the downsides of outsourcing, refer to Rossetti, C. & Choi, T. Y. 2005. On the dark side of strategic sourcing: Experiences from the aerospace industry. *Academy of Management Executive,* 19(1): 46–60.

40. Tully, S. 1993. The modular corporation. *Fortune,* February 8: 196.

41. Offshoring in manufacturing firms is addressed in Coucke, K. & Sleuwaegen, L. 2008. Offshoring as a survival strategy: Evidence from manufacturing firms in Belgium. *Journal of International Business Studies,* 39(8): 1261–1277.

42. Quinn, J. B. 1992. *Intelligent enterprise: A knowledge and service based paradigm for industry.* New York: Free Press.

43. For an insightful perspective on outsourcing and its role in developing capabilities, read Gottfredson, M., Puryear, R., & Phillips, C. 2005. Strategic sourcing: From periphery to the core. *Harvard Business Review,* 83(4): 132–139.

44. This discussion draws upon Quinn, J. B. & Hilmer, F. C. 1994. Strategic outsourcing. *Sloan Management Review,* 35(4): 43–55.

45. Reitzig, M. & Wagner, S. 2010. The hidden costs of outsourcing: Evidence from patent data. *Strategic Management Journal,* 31(11): 1183–1201.

46. Insights on outsourcing and private branding can be found in Cehn, S-F. S. 2009. A transaction cost rationale for private branding and its implications for the choice of domestic vs. offshore outsourcing. *Journal of International Business Strategy,* 40(1): 156–175.

47. For an insightful perspective on the use of outsourcing for decision analysis, read Davenport, T. H. & Iyer, B. 2009. Should you outsource your brain? *Harvard Business Review,* 87(2): 38.

48. See also Stuckey, J. & White, D. 1993. When and when not to vertically integrate. *Sloan Management Review,* Spring: 71–81; Harrar, G. 1993. Outsource tales. *Forbes ASAP,* June 7: 37–39, 42; and Davis, E. W. 1992. Global outsourcing: Have U.S. managers thrown the baby out with the bath water? *Business Horizons,* July–August: 58–64.

49. For a discussion of knowledge creation through alliances, refer to Inkpen, A. C. 1996. Creating knowledge through collaboration. *California Management Review,* 39(1): 123–140; and Mowery, D. C., Oxley, J. E., & Silverman, B. S. 1996. Strategic alliances and interfirm knowledge transfer. *Strategic Management Journal,* 17 (Special Issue, Winter): 77–92.

50. Doz, Y. & Hamel, G. 1998. *Alliance advantage: The art of creating value through partnering.* Boston: Harvard Business School Press.

51. DeSanctis, G., Glass, J. T., & Ensing, I. M. 2002. Organizational designs for R&D. *Academy of Management Executive,* 16(3): 55–66.

52. Barringer, B. R. & Harrison, J. S. 2000. Walking a tightrope: Creating value through interorganizational alliances. *Journal of Management,* 26: 367–403.

53. One contemporary example of virtual organizations is R&D consortia. For an insightful discussion, refer to Sakaibara, M. 2002. Formation of R&D consortia: Industry and company effects. *Strategic Management Journal,* 23(11): 1033–1050.

54. Bartness, A. & Cerny, K. 1993. Building competitive advantage through a global network of capabilities. *California Management Review,* Winter: 78–103. For an insightful historical discussion of the usefulness of alliances in the computer industry, see Moore, J. F. 1993. Predators and prey: A new ecology of competition. *Harvard Business Review,* 71(3): 75–86.

55. See Lorange, P. & Roos, J. 1991. Why some strategic alliances succeed and others fail. *Journal of Business Strategy,* January–February: 25–30; and Slowinski, G. 1992. The human touch in strategic alliances. *Mergers and Acquisitions,* July–August: 44–47. A compelling argument for strategic alliances is provided by Ohmae, K. 1989. The global logic of strategic alliances. *Harvard Business Review,* 67(2): 143–154.

56. Some of the downsides of alliances are discussed in Das, T. K. & Teng, B. S. 2000. Instabilities of strategic alliances: An internal tensions perspective. *Organization Science,* 11: 77–106.

57. This section draws upon Dess, G. G. & Picken, J. C. 1997. *Mission critical.* Burr Ridge, IL: Irwin Professional.

58. Katzenbach, J. R. & Smith, D. K. 1994. *The wisdom of teams: Creating the high performance organization.* New York: HarperBusiness.

59. Bryant, A. 2011. *The corner office:* 230. New York: St. Martin's Griffin.

60. Hammer, M. & Champy, J. 1993. *Reengineering the corporation: A manifesto for business revolution.* New York: HarperCollins.

61. Gupta, A. 2011. The relational perspective and east meets west. *Academy of Management Perspectives,* 25(3): 19–27.

62. This section draws on Birkinshaw, J. & Gibson, C. 2004. Building ambidexterity into an organization. *MIT Sloan Management Review,* 45(4): 47–55; and Gibson, C. B. & Birkinshaw, J. 2004. The antecedents, consequences, and mediating role of organizational ambidexterity. *Academy of Management Journal,* 47(2): 209–226. Robert Duncan is generally credited with being the first to coin the term "ambidextrous organizations" in his article entitled: Designing dual structures for innovation. In Kilmann, R. H., Pondy, L. R., & Slevin, D. (Eds.). 1976. *The management of organizations,* vol. 1: 167–188. For a seminal academic discussion of the concept of exploration and exploitation, which parallels adaptation and alignment, refer to March, J. G. 1991. Exploration and exploitation in organizational learning. *Organization Science,* 2: 71–86.

63. This section is based on O'Reilly, C. A. & Tushman, M. L. 2004. The ambidextrous organization. *Harvard Business Review,* 82(4): 74–81.

Strategic Leadership

Creating a Learning Organization and an Ethical Organization

chapter

11

LO11.1 The three key interdependent activities in which all successful leaders must be continually engaged.

LO11.2 Two elements of effective leadership: overcoming barriers to change and using power effectively.

LO11.3 The crucial role of emotional intelligence (EI) in successful leadership, as well as its potential drawbacks.

LO11.4 The importance of creating a learning organization.

LO11.5 The leader's role in establishing an ethical organization.

LO11.6 The difference between integrity-based and compliance-based approaches to organizational ethics.

LO11.7 Several key elements that organizations must have to become ethical organizations.

Learning from Mistakes

It took four generations to build Stroh's Brewing into a major player in the beer industry and just one generation to tear it down. Stroh's was founded in Detroit by Bernard Stroh, who had emigrated from Germany in 1850. Bernard took the $150 he had and a cherished family beer recipe and began selling beer door to door. By 1890, his sons, Julius and Bernard, had grown the family business and were shipping beer around the Great Lakes region. The family business survived prohibition by making ice cream and maple syrup. After World War II ended, the business grew along with the industrial Midwest, seeing its sales surge from 500,000 barrels of beer in 1950 to 2.7 million barrels in 1956. The firm succeeded by following a simple business recipe: catering to the needs of working-class tastes by brewing a simple, drinkable, and affordable beer and treating its employees well. Following this business blueprint, the company found success and growth, resulting in a business that was worth an estimated $700 million in the mid-1980s. A little over a decade later, the firm was out of business.[1]

Its rapid descent from a successful and growing firm to failure is tied to a series of disastrous decisions made by Peter Stroh, representing the fifth generation of the family to lead the firm, who took on the role of CEO in 1980. Rather than stick to the tried-and-true business plan of catering to the needs of the Midwest working class, Peter stepped out to build a larger, national beer empire. He purchased F&M Schaefer, a New York–based brewer, in 1981. He followed this up in 1982 by purchasing Joseph Schlitz Brewing, a firm that was much bigger than Stroh's. To undertake this acquisition, Stroh's borrowed $500 million, five times the value of Stroh's itself. Peter's acquisitions hampered the firm in two key ways. First, working to combine the firms distracted Stroh's from seeing the evolving needs of customers. Most notably, it completely missed the most significant shift in customer tastes in a generation—the emergence of light beer. Also, the heavy debt load taken on to finance the acquisitions left the firm with little money to launch the national advertising campaigns needed to support a company that was now the third-largest brewer in the United States. In the words of Greg Stroh, a cousin of Peter and an employee of the firm, "We made the decision to go national without having the budget. It was like going to a gunfight with a knife. We didn't have a chance."

Stroh's tried various tactics to improve its situation. It tried undercutting the price of its major rivals, Anheuser-Busch and Miller, by offering 15 cans of beer for the price of 12. It laid off hundreds of employees to save on cost. It then changed course, raising prices and nixing the 15-pack containers. Customers rebelled, pushing sales down 40 percent in a single year. The firm was left with 6 million barrels of excess brewing capacity. Finally, the firm took on one last, disastrous acquisition. Stroh's purchased another struggling brewer, G. Heileman, for $300 million, saddling itself with even more debt. While the firm struggled in its core beer business, Peter tried to diversify Stroh's into biotechnology and real estate investing. The almost inevitable end came in 1999 when Stroh's assets were purchased by Pabst Brewing for $350 million—$250 million of which went to the debtholders of the firm.

Discussion Questions

1. Why were the acquisitions so debilitating for Stroh's?
2. What would have been the likely outcome for Stroh's if it hadn't purchased other brands?

Under Peter Stroh's leadership, Stroh's Brewing went from being a successful and growing family business to a failed firm. He took the firm away from its traditional strategy and also missed seeing key shifts in the beer industry. This led him to change the firm's strategy in ways that undercut the value of its brand and its culture, ultimately leading to Stroh's demise and the loss of the family's legacy. In contrast to Peter's ineffective leadership, effective leaders set a clear direction for the firm, create and reinforce valuable strategies, and strengthen firm values and culture.

This chapter provides insights into the role of strategic leadership in managing, adapting, and coping in the face of increased environmental complexity and uncertainty. First, we define leadership and its three interdependent activities—setting a direction, designing the organization, and nurturing a culture dedicated to excellence and ethical behavior. Then, we identify two elements of leadership that contribute to success—overcoming barriers to change and using power effectively. The third section focuses on emotional intelligence, a trait that is increasingly acknowledged to be critical to successful leadership. Next, we emphasize the importance of leaders developing competency companions and creating a learning organization. Here, we focus on empowerment wherein employees and managers throughout an organization develop a sense of self-determination, competence, meaning, and impact that is centrally important to learning. Finally, we address the leader's role in building an ethical organization and the elements of an ethical culture that contribute to firm effectiveness.

Leadership: Three Interdependent Activities

In today's chaotic world, few would argue against the need for leadership, but how do we go about encouraging it? Is it enough to merely keep an organization afloat, or is it essential to make steady progress toward some well-defined objective? We believe custodial management is not leadership. Leadership is proactive, goal-oriented, and focused on the creation and implementation of a creative vision. **Leadership** is the process of transforming organizations from what they are to what the leader would have them become. This definition implies a lot: *dissatisfaction* with the status quo, a *vision* of what should be, and a *process* for bringing about change. An insurance company executive shared the following insight: "I lead by the Noah Principle: It's all right to know when it's going to rain, but, by God, you had better build the ark."

| leadership
| the process of transforming organizations from what they are to what the leader would have them become.

Doing the right thing is becoming increasingly important. Many industries are declining; the global village is becoming increasingly complex, interconnected, and unpredictable; and product and market life cycles are becoming increasingly compressed. When asked to describe the life cycle of his company's products, the CEO of a supplier of computer components replied, "Seven months from cradle to grave—and that includes three months to design the product and get it into production!" Richard D'Aveni, author of *Hypercompetition,* argued that in a world where all dimensions of competition appear to be compressed in time and heightened in complexity, *sustainable* competitive advantages are no longer possible.

Despite the importance of doing the "right thing," leaders must also be concerned about "doing things right." Charan and Colvin strongly believe that execution, that is, the implementation of strategy, is also essential to success:

> Mastering execution turns out to be the odds-on best way for a CEO to keep his job. So what's the right way to think about that sexier obsession, strategy? It's vitally important—obviously. The problem is that our age's fascination feeds the mistaken belief that developing exactly the right strategy will enable a company to rocket past competitors. In reality, that's less than half the battle.[2]

LO11.1

The three key interdependent activities in which all successful leaders must be continually engaged.

Thus, leaders are change agents whose success is measured by how effectively they formulate *and* implement a strategic vision and mission.[3]

EXHIBIT 11.1 Three Interdependent Leadership Activities

Many authors contend that successful leaders must recognize three interdependent activities that must be continually reassessed for organizations to succeed. As shown in Exhibit 11.1, these are (1) setting a direction, (2) designing the organization, and (3) nurturing a culture dedicated to excellence and ethical behavior.[4]

The interdependent nature of these three activities is self-evident. Consider an organization with a great mission and a superb organizational structure but a culture that implicitly encourages shirking and unethical behavior. Or one with a sound direction and strong culture but counterproductive teams and a "zero-sum" reward system that leads to the dysfunctional situation in which one party's gain is viewed as another party's loss and collaboration and sharing are severely hampered. Clearly, such combinations would be ineffective.

Often, failure of today's organizations can be attributed to a lack of equal consideration of these three activities. The imagery of a three-legged stool is instructive: The stool will collapse if one leg is missing or broken. Let's briefly look at each of these activities as well as the value of an ambicultural approach to leadership.

Setting a Direction

A holistic understanding of an organization's stakeholders requires an ability to scan the environment to develop a knowledge of all of the company's stakeholders and other salient environmental trends and events. Managers must integrate this knowledge into a vision of what the organization could become.[5] This necessitates the capacity to solve increasingly complex problems, become proactive in approach, and develop viable strategic options. A strategic vision provides many benefits: a clear future direction; a framework for the organization's mission and goals; and enhanced employee communication, participation, and commitment.

Strategy Spotlight 11.1 discusses how Alan Mulally exhibited the three key leadership activities as he brought Ford Motor Company back from the brink.

Designing the Organization

At times, almost all leaders have difficulty implementing their vision and strategies.[6] Such problems may stem from a variety of sources:

- Lack of understanding of responsibility and accountability among managers.
- Reward systems that do not motivate individuals (or collectives such as groups and divisions) toward desired organizational goals.
- Inadequate or inappropriate budgeting and control systems.
- Insufficient mechanisms to integrate activities across the organization.

Successful leaders are actively involved in building structures, teams, systems, and organizational processes that facilitate the implementation of their vision and strategies. Without

setting a direction
a strategic leadership activity of strategy analysis and strategy formulation.

designing the organization
a strategic leadership activity of building structures, teams, systems, and organizational processes that facilitate the implementation of the leader's vision and strategies.

ALAN MULALLY'S LEADERSHIP OF FORD

When Alan Mulally took over Ford Motor Company in 2006, there were a lot of questions about whether he was the right man for the job. He was taking over an automotive firm that had a proud heritage but was struggling mightily, losing money and market share. Yet he had no experience in the automobile industry. He had been successful as the head of Boeing's aircraft division but hadn't impressed Boeing's board of directors enough to be seen as CEO material and had been passed over in the search for Boeing's CEO the year before.

But as he retired from Ford in June 2014, the imprint of his leadership was easy to see. Ford had made more money under his leadership than it had in the history of the firm—$42 billion in profits over the prior five years. The value of the firm had risen from $15 billion to $63 billion under his tenure. More importantly for the long run, he had built a much more driven, focused, and collaborative Ford Motor Company.

The three interdependent activities of a successful leader were easily seen with Mulally. First, he set a clear direction for Ford. Starting with a simple motto, "One Ford," he set the firm on a trajectory to create a unified global firm built around the Blue Oval—Ford's logo. Mulally's One Ford platform included four main points: (1) He emphasized bringing all Ford employees together as a global team. (2) He wanted to globally leverage Ford's unique automotive knowledge and assets. (3) He emphasized building cars and trucks that people wanted and valued, focusing on new technology, safety, and fuel economy as key differentiators. (4) He arranged the financing necessary for the plan to succeed. To make it work, he met with employees and other stakeholders to explain and sell the new direction.

Second, he designed an organization to move Ford forward. Part of this included shedding parts of the organization that didn't fit the new Ford. He shut down the Mercury division and sold off the Volvo, Land Rover, Aston Martin, and Jaguar brands. The new, streamlined structure kept the Ford brand at the center. In the past, different geographic divisions developed completely distinct products for each market. He changed that by developing global-platform teams that designed products that could sell on a global basis. These changes allowed Ford to become much more efficient in developing and maintaining its product portfolio, which now includes 20 different car models, down from 97 when he first took over as CEO.

Third, he nurtured the culture of Ford. Prior to his arrival, Ford had a reputation as a cutthroat place to work. Managers would look for and openly discuss the weaknesses and failures of their peers, practicing self-preservation over collaboration. Mulally set out to change that. He instituted weekly meetings at which managers would openly discuss the status of programs they were managing, using a series of green-, yellow-, and red-light ratings of different aspects of the projects. Early on, when one senior manager, Mark Fields, noted areas of concern—red lights—on a project in his unit, Mulally applauded him and turned to the rest of the team for suggestions to address the problems. This quickly became the norm in the firm—open discussion with collaborative problem solving, making executive meetings a safe environment where data could be shared without blame, improving collaboration, and setting the stage for innovation success.

Through his leadership, Ford moved from being a firm that, in Mulally's own words, had "been going out of business for 40 years" to being a highly profitable and growing firm. Jeff Carlson, a Ford dealership owner, put it this way: "He came with one plan and stayed with one plan, and that continuity of leadership allowed him to manage the company out of dire straits."

Sources: Boudette, N., Rogers, C., & Lublin, J. 2014. Mulally's legacy: Setting Ford on a stronger course. *wsj.com,* April 21: np; and Caldicott, S. 2014. Why Ford's Alan Mulally is an innovation CEO for the record books. *forbes.com,* June 25: np.

appropriately structuring organizational activities, a firm would generally be unable to attain an overall low-cost advantage by closely monitoring its costs through detailed and formalized cost and financial control procedures. With regard to corporate-level strategy, a related diversification strategy would necessitate reward systems that emphasize behavioral measures because interdependence among business units tends to be very important. In contrast, reward systems associated with an unrelated diversification strategy should rely more on financial indicators of performance because business units are relatively autonomous.

These examples illustrate the important role of leadership in creating systems and structures to achieve desired ends. As Jim Collins says about the importance of designing the organization, "Along with figuring out what the company stands for and pushing it to understand what it's really good at, building mechanisms is the CEO's role—the leader as architect."[7]

excellent and ethical organizational culture
an organizational culture focused on core competencies and high ethical standards.

Nurturing a Culture Committed to Excellence and Ethical Behavior

Organizational culture can be an effective means of organizational control.[8] Leaders play a key role in changing, developing, and sustaining an organization's culture. Brian Chesky, cofounder and CEO of Airbnb, clearly understands the role of the leader in building and maintaining an organization's culture. In October 2013, as Airbnb was growing rapidly,

INSTILLING ETHICS AND A FIRM'S VALUES: WALKING THE TALK

Firms often draft elaborate value statements and codes of conduct, yet many firms do not live up to their own standards—or, in other words, fail to "walk the talk." Take the positive example of N. R. Narayana Murthy, chairman and one of the founders of Infosys (a giant Indian technology company). In February 1984, shortly after the firm was founded, Infosys decided to import a super minicomputer so that it could start developing software for overseas clients. When the machine landed at Bangalore Airport, the local customs official refused to clear it unless the company "took care of him"—the Indian euphemism for demanding a bribe. A delay at customs could have threatened the project. Yet, instead of caving in to the unethical customs

official's demands, Murthy kept true to his values and took the more expensive formal route of paying a customs duty of 135 percent with dim chances of successfully appealing the duty and receiving a refund.

Reflecting on these events, Murthy reasons, "We didn't have enough money to pay the duty and had to borrow it. However, because we had decided to do business ethically, we didn't have a choice. We would not pay bribes. We effectively paid twice for the machine and had only a slim chance of recovering our money. But a clear conscience is the softest pillow on which you can lay your head down at night. . . . It took a few years for corrupt officials to stop approaching us for favors."

Source: Raman, A. P. 2011. "Why don't we try to be India's most respected company?" *Harvard Business Review,* 89(11): 82.

Chesky sent out an email to his leadership team imploring the team members to be very conscious to maintain the culture of the firm.[9] He stated, "The culture is what creates the foundation for all future innovation. If you break the culture, you break the machine that creates your products." He then went on to comment that they needed to uphold the firm's values in all they do: who they hire, how they work on a project, how they treat other employees in the hallway, and what they write in emails. Chesky then laid out the power of firm culture in the following words:

> The stronger the culture, the less corporate process a company needs. When the culture is strong, you can trust everyone to do the right thing. People can be independent and autonomous. They can be entrepreneurial. And if we have a company that is entrepreneurial in spirit, we will be able to take our next "(wo)man on the moon" leap. . . . In organizations (or even in a society) where the culture is weak, you need an abundance of heavy, precise rules, and processes.

In sharp contrast, leaders can also have a very detrimental effect on a firm's culture and ethics. Imagine the negative impact that Todd Berman's illegal activities have had on a firm that he cofounded—New York's private equity firm Chartwell Investments.[10] He stole more than $3.6 million from the firm and its investors. Berman pleaded guilty to fraud charges brought by the Justice Department. For 18 months he misled Chartwell's investors concerning the financial condition of one of the firm's portfolio companies by falsely claiming it needed to borrow funds to meet operating expenses. Instead, Berman transferred the money to his personal bank account, along with fees paid by portfolio companies.

Clearly, a leader's behavior and values can make a strong impact on an organization—for good or for bad. Strategy Spotlight 11.2 provides a positive example. It discusses how the chairman of Infosys created an ethical culture by "walking the talk."

Managers and top executives must accept personal responsibility for developing and strengthening ethical behavior throughout the organization. They must consistently demonstrate that such behavior is central to the vision and mission of the organization. Several elements must be present and reinforced for a firm to become highly ethical, including role models, corporate credos and codes of conduct, reward and evaluation systems, and policies and procedures. Given the importance of these elements, we address them in detail in the last section of this chapter.

Michael Williams, a former senior executive at Biggby Coffee, offers further insight on the attributes of effective leaders in Insights from Executives.

MICHAEL WILLIAMS, FORMER CHIEF FINANCIAL OFFICER FOR BIGGBY COFFEE

BIOSKETCH

Michael Williams is the director of Entrepreneurship Activities and the director of the Business and Entrepreneurship Clinic at the University of Wisconsin–Madison School of Business. Prior to working in higher education, Williams was the chief financial officer for Biggby Coffee, a coffee shop franchising company. Prior to Biggby, Williams owned Kismetic Enterprises East, LLC, a consulting business that provided interim-CFO duties, prepared business and financial plans, and strategically prepared small to midsize companies to raise capital. Prior to Kismetic, Williams held various C-level positions with Voyager.net, an entrepreneurial Internet company that experienced explosive growth and went public in 1999.

1. *One of the key roles of a leader is to set the direction for an organization. In your experience, what do effective leaders do to formulate and communicate a vision or direction for the firm?*

   In my experience, the best leaders surround themselves with exceptional people who are not afraid to disagree and give good, constructive feedback. Formulating and executing the vision is always an iterative and fluid process with the top management team and also with the employee base. The vision of a company can change, and the best leaders are not afraid of modifying it, but not whimsically so.

   The best leaders are always fantastic communicators who are trusted by their employees. This is an earned trust because the leaders hold themselves accountable to the goals, mission, and vision of the company. The most effective leaders are not afraid to admit they made mistakes and change course, if needed. This shows the employees that the leaders are honest and have the best interests of the firm and its employees at heart.

   I also had experience with some bad leaders. It was quickly apparent to me these ineffectual leaders were out for themselves and didn't care about the employees or the long-term fate of the company. The most glaring difference between these types of leaders and the best leaders was that the bad leaders held everyone accountable except themselves. These leaders never garnered the trust of the employees, and every facet of the company suffered because of it.

2. *Leaders must also design an organization to achieve the direction they've laid out for the business. What* have you found to be the key elements in designing an effective organization?

   The highest priority of a company trying to design an effective organization is to create *core values* that are simple, clear, and direct. Core values are those values that guide the way employees interact with each other, and the rest of the world, and they also guide the way the company interacts with the most important "person" of all: *the customer.*

   Two other key elements in designing an effective organization are transparency and accountability. I have found that when employees believe they are working in a "fair" environment, they will buy in to the company's vision and mission and work extremely hard to make sure the company succeeds. Their loyalty to the company will be unwavering.

3. *Most successful organizations have a culture that is committed to excellence and ethical behaviors. How can leaders help build, support, and reinforce such a culture in their organizations?*

   This is actually very simple. The leaders must do as they say. They must walk the talk. If they hold themselves to a different standard, then the firm culture will quickly erode. If the company has a strict policy that it will not pay for liquor at a business dinner, then the CEO needs to reach into his or her own pocket to pay for that bottle of wine. It doesn't matter that the CEO is entertaining the biggest client the company has ever entertained. A good CEO walks the talk every single day.

4. *Competitive environments are not static. As a result, even when firms are doing well, they need to change to respond to market dynamics and other changes in their environment. What are the types of actions leaders can take to improve their firm's openness to change?*

   It could be argued that the competitive environment in most industries has never been as fierce as it is now. In an environment where a bad experience could reach millions at the touch of a "Tweet" that goes viral, the ability to change and move has never been more important. But change can be difficult and scary for many people. If something happens in a firm, the first thing most people will think is "How will this affect me?"

   A leader can create an environment that is ready for change by being completely honest and open. Most of the anxiety surrounding change comes from the unknown, which stems from lack of information. The more information that a leader can share with his or her employees, the better. I have found that it is best to have "buy-in" from employees on changes that need to occur. Buy-in comes from the employees feeling like they are engaged and their concerns are heard and taken into consideration. Even if their suggestions are not used, they should still feel like they are part of the process and they will be more accepting of the needed change. Creating an employee feedback loop for difficult situations can build trust and also minimize the unproductive anxiety that gut-wrenching change can create.

5. *Emotional intelligence is a key managerial attribute. Think of a strong leader you have had an opportunity to work with and observe. Discuss which of these traits you saw in that leader and how these traits helped him or her effectively lead his or her organization.*

I have had the pleasure to work with many strong leaders over the years. One of the strongest is Michael McFall, cofounder and president of Biggby Coffee. When we first met in fall 1999, Biggby had just opened its first franchised coffee shop. Now, it is nearing 200 open stores with 50 more under contract to be opened in the next 12 to 18 months. Michael's strengths come from self-awareness, empathy, and a strong motivation to do what is right. He runs the company with honesty, transparency, simplicity, and swift action.

He and his cofounder, Robert Fish, have split responsibilities based on what each one does extremely well (self-awareness), and this has had a huge positive effect on the company's productivity, employee satisfaction and retention, customer loyalty, and, ultimately, on profitability. Michael is a wizard at understanding the economics and financials of a growing company. He designed reports and metrics that the company uses on a daily basis to understand where it may have issues. If it does have issues, Michael requests honest feedback from the employees and takes that into consideration while creating a swift action plan. Michael and Robert have created a culture of "Fun but Serious," and this enabled Biggby to be honored as one of the fastest-growing franchises in the United States in 2012.

Getting Things Done: Overcoming Barriers and Using Power

LO11.2

Two elements of effective leadership: overcoming barriers to change and using power effectively.

The demands on leaders in today's business environment require them to perform a variety of functions. The success of their organizations often depends on how they as individuals meet challenges and deliver on promises. What practices and skills are needed to get the job done effectively? In this section, we focus on two capabilities that are marks of successful leadership—overcoming barriers to change and using power effectively. Then, in the next section, we will examine an important human trait that helps leaders be more effective—emotional intelligence.

Overcoming Barriers to Change

What are the **barriers to change** that leaders often encounter, and how can leaders best bring about organizational change?[11] After all, people generally have some level of choice about how strongly they support or resist a leader's change initiatives. Why is there often so much resistance? Organizations at all levels are prone to inertia and are slow to learn, adapt, and change because:

1. Many people have **vested interests in the status quo.** People tend to be risk-averse and resistant to change. There is a broad stream of research on "escalation," wherein certain individuals continue to throw "good money at bad decisions" despite negative performance feedback.[12]

2. There are **systemic barriers.** The design of the organization's structure, information processing, reporting relationships, and so forth impedes the proper flow and evaluation of information. A bureaucratic structure with multiple layers, onerous requirements for documentation, and rigid rules and procedures will often "inoculate" the organization against change. Lou Gerstner, the former

barriers to change characteristics of individuals and organizations that prevent a leader from transforming an organization.

vested interest in the status quo a barrier to change that stems from people's risk aversion.

systemic barriers barriers to change that stem from an organizational design that impedes the proper flow and evaluation of information.

CEO of IBM, described the challenge of systemic barriers in successful firms the following way:

> Rather than changing, they find it easier to just keep doing the same things that brought them success. They codify why they're successful. They write guidebooks. They create teaching manuals.[13]

behavioral barriers
barriers to change associated with the tendency for managers to look at issues from a biased or limited perspective based on their prior education and experience.

3. **Behavioral barriers** cause managers to look at issues from a biased or limited perspective due to their education, training, work experiences, and so forth. Consider an incident shared by David Lieberman, marketing director at GVO, an innovation consulting firm:

> A company's creative type had come up with a great idea for a new product. Nearly everybody loved it. However, it was shot down by a high-ranking manufacturing representative who exploded: "A new color? Do you have any idea of the spare-parts problem that it will create?" This was not a dimwit exasperated at having to build a few storage racks at the warehouse. He'd been hearing for years about cost cutting, lean inventories, and "focus." Lieberman's comment: "Good concepts, but not always good for innovation."

political barriers
barriers to change related to conflicts arising from power relationships.

4. **Political barriers** refer to conflicts arising from power relationships. This can be the outcome of a myriad of symptoms such as vested interests, refusal to share information, conflicts over resources, conflicts between departments and divisions, and petty interpersonal differences.

personal time constraints
a barrier to change that stems from people's not having sufficient time for strategic thinking and reflection.

5. **Personal time constraints** bring to mind the old saying about "not having enough time to drain the swamp when you are up to your neck in alligators." Gresham's law of planning states that operational decisions will drive out the time necessary for strategic thinking and reflection. This tendency is accentuated in organizations experiencing severe price competition or retrenchment wherein managers and employees are spread rather thin.

Strategy Spotlight 11.3 discusses the challenges Mary Barra faces as she works to change the culture and values of General Motors.

Leaders must draw on a range of personal skills as well as organizational mechanisms to move their organizations forward in the face of such barriers. Two factors mentioned earlier—building a learning organization and building an ethical organization—provide the kind of climate within which a leader can advance the organization's aims and make progress toward its goals.

One of the most important tools a leader has for overcoming barriers to change is his or her personal and organizational power. On the one hand, good leaders must be on guard not to abuse power. On the other hand, successful leadership requires the measured exercise of power. We turn to that topic next.

Using Power Effectively

Successful leadership requires the effective use of power in overcoming barriers to change.[14] As humorously noted by Mark Twain, "I'm all for progress. It's change I object to." **Power** refers to a leader's ability to get things done in a way he or she wants them to be done. It is the ability to influence other people's behavior, to persuade them to do things that they otherwise would not do, and to overcome resistance and opposition. Effective exercise of power is essential for successful leadership.[15]

power
a leader's ability to get things done in a way he or she wants them to be done.

A leader derives his or her power from several sources or bases. The simplest way to understand the bases of power is by classifying them as organizational and personal, as shown in Exhibit 11.2.

organizational bases of power
a formal management position that is the basis of a leader's power.

Organizational bases of power refer to the power that a person wields because of her formal management position.[16] These include legitimate, reward, coercive, and information

MARY BARRA AND THE NEED FOR CHANGE AT GENERAL MOTORS

Mary Barra took over as CEO of General Motors in January 2014 and soon found herself facing an unanticipated crisis that reinforced the widely held view that GM is a company in need of major change. The question is whether or not Barra is up to the task.

GM has struggled for a number of decades, seeing its share of the U.S. market decline from 40 percent in 1985 to 18 percent in 2013. More recently, GM was rocked by the financial crisis of 2008 and only survived due to a government bailout. Just after Barra was appointed CEO, a new crisis arose—a problem with faulty ignition switches in GM cars. While the problem came to light in 2014, engineers at GM knew as early as 2001 that an ignition switch used across a wide range of GM cars could fail and cause crashes, but the firm didn't recall the cars to fix their switches. According to the attorney managing claims for GM, crashes caused by the faulty switches have cost at least 50 lives. Critics say the death toll is much higher.

The problems at GM run deep. Analysts have long criticized the firm for having plodding decision making, with rival departments refusing to share information and being more focused on shifting blame for failures than on working together to solve problems. Further, an internal report on GM's decision making noted that GM was hampered by a "proliferation of committees" whose conclusions were "reported to yet further committees." Analysts also accuse the company of being more cost-conscious than customer-focused.

The near death of GM in 2008 could have provided the setting for major changes to the firm, but leadership turmoil has limited the degree of change. Over the five years prior to Barra's appointment, GM had five different CEOs. None appeared to have the drive or power necessary to undertake major changes in GM's culture and operations. The prior CEO and chairman, Dan Akerson, who had no experience in the auto industry before becoming GM's leader, managed to repay the government for bailing out GM but left abruptly without undertaking a major reorganization effort at the company. He was replaced as CEO by Barra and as chairman of the board by Tim Solso.

Is Barra the right person to bring about the necessary change? Some argue she is too much of a GM insider. She is a second-generation GM lifetime employee. Her father was a die maker who worked at the company for 39 years. Barra has worked at GM for 33 years. She began her career while still a student, worked her way up the ladder in the engineering function at GM, and served as a plant manager, VP of Global Manufacturing, and VP of Global Human Resources before becoming CEO. Yet she may not have the positional power necessary, since she doesn't also carry the role of chairman of the board. Others argue she is the perfect candidate to take on the task. She can act quickly and decisively since she knows the organization inside and out. Her career has taken her through various units of the firm, and she has relationships with people throughout the firm who trust her judgment. Also, at only 52 years of age, she is likely to be at the helm for a while, making it difficult for managers to resist her change efforts and try to wait her out.

So far, Barra is taking some actions that are bold for the GM culture. She fired 15 employees associated with the ignition-failure debacle. She also moved out seven high-level GM managers in her first few months as CEO. While these may seem like minor actions for such a large firm, they are quite bold for the conservative GM culture. She's also championing the use of external measures to assess the success of GM's products and financials. Up to now, GM has almost exclusively used internal measures, such as whether projects are meeting scheduling milestones and whether new-model sales are meeting internal benchmarks. Barra wants the firm to compare itself to its competitors and be much more aggressive and competitive. "I accept no excuses for why we can't be the best," Barra says.

Commentators suggest a major restructuring and turnaround at GM is a monumental task and could take 5 to 10 years. What is unclear at this point is whether or not Barra can be the leader to finally change GM.

Sources: Levin, D. 2014. New GM: Same as it ever was? *Fortune*, April 10: 64–67; Colvin, G. 2014. Mary Barra's (unexpected) opportunity. *Fortune*, October 6: 102–108; and Anonymous. 2009. A giant falls. *economist.com*, June 9: np.

power. *Legitimate power* is derived from organizationally conferred decision-making authority and is exercised by virtue of a manager's position in the organization. *Reward power* depends on the ability of the leader or manager to confer rewards for positive behaviors or outcomes. *Coercive power* is the power a manager exercises over employees using fear of punishment for errors of omission or commission. *Information power* arises from a manager's access, control, and distribution of information that is not freely available to everyone in an organization.

A leader might also be able to influence subordinates because of his or her personality characteristics and behavior. These would be considered the **personal bases of power,** including referent power and expert power. The source of *referent power* is a subordinate's

personal bases of power
a leader's personality characteristics and behavior that are the basis of the leader's power.

EXHIBIT 11.2 A Leader's Bases of Power

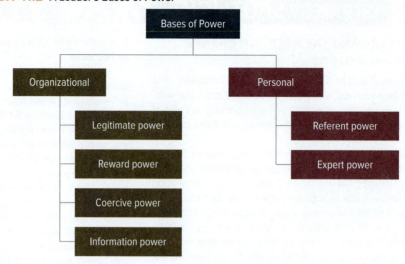

identification with the leader. A leader's personal attributes or charisma might influence subordinates and make them devoted to that leader. The source of *expert power* is the leader's expertise and knowledge. The leader is the expert on whom subordinates depend for information that they need to do their jobs successfully.

Successful leaders use the different bases of power, and often a combination of them, as appropriate to meet the demands of a situation, such as the nature of the task, the personality characteristics of the subordinates, and the urgency of the issue.[17] Persuasion and developing consensus are often essential, but so is pressing for action. At some point stragglers must be prodded into line.[18] Peter Georgescu, former CEO of Young & Rubicam (an advertising and media subsidiary of the U.K.-based WPP Group), summarized a leader's dilemma brilliantly (and humorously), "I have knee pads and a .45. I get down and beg a lot, but I shoot people too."[19]

Strategy Spotlight 11.4 addresses some of the subtleties of power. Here, the CEO of Siemens successfully brought about organizational change by the effective use of peer pressure.

Emotional Intelligence: A Key Leadership Trait

LO11.3

The crucial role of emotional intelligence (EI) in successful leadership, as well as its potential drawbacks.

In the previous sections, we discussed skills and activities of strategic leadership. The focus was on "what leaders do and how they do it." Now the issue becomes "who leaders *are,*" that is, what leadership traits are the most important. Clearly, these two issues are related, because successful leaders possess the valuable traits that enable them to perform effectively in order to create value for their organization.[20]

There has been a vast amount of literature on the successful traits of leaders.[21] These traits include integrity, maturity, energy, judgment, motivation, intelligence, expertise, and so on. For simplicity, these traits may be grouped into three broad sets of capabilities:

emotional intelligence (EI)
an individual's capacity for recognizing his or her own emotions and those of others, including the five components of self-awareness, self-regulation, motivation, empathy, and social skills.

- Purely technical skills (like accounting or operations research).
- Cognitive abilities (like analytical reasoning or quantitative analysis).
- Emotional intelligence (like self-management and managing relationships).

Emotional intelligence (EI) has been defined as the capacity for recognizing one's own emotions and those of others.[22]

THE USE OF "SOFT" POWER AT SIEMENS

Until 1999, not only was paying bribes in international markets legally allowed in Germany, but German corporations could also deduct bribes from taxable income. However, once those laws changed, German industrial powerhouse Siemens found it hard to break its bribing habit in its sprawling global operations. Eventually a major scandal forced many top executives out of the firm, including CEO Klaus Kleinfeld. As the successor to Kleinfeld, Peter Löscher became the first outside CEO in the more than 160-year history of Siemens in 2007. As an outsider Löscher found it challenging to establish himself as a strong leader inside the bureaucratic Siemens organization. However, he eventually found a way to successfully transition into his new position.

Naturally, in the early stage of his tenure, he lacked internal connections and the bases of power associated with inside knowledge of people and processes. Yet Siemens faced tremendous challenges, such as a lack of customer orientation, and required a strong leader with the ability to change the status quo. Absent a more formal power base, he turned to more informal means to accomplish his mandate of organizational change and increasing customer orientation.

Once a year, all 700 of Siemens top managers come together for a leadership conference in Berlin. Given the historical lack of customer focus, Löscher used peer pressure as an informal (or soft) form of power in order to challenge and eventually change the lack of customer orientation. As he recalls from his first leadership conference as CEO, "I collected the Outlook calendars for the previous year from all my division CEOs and board members. Then I mapped how much time they had spent with customers and I ranked them. There was a big debate in my inner circle over whether I should use names. Some felt we would embarrass people, but I decided to put the names on the screen anyway."

The results of this exercise were quite remarkable: Löscher spent around 50 percent of his time with customers, more than any other top executive. Clearly, the people who were running the business divisions should rank higher on customer interaction than the CEO. This confirmed the lack of customer orientation in the organization. This ranking has been repeated at every Siemens leadership conference since Löscher took office. Over time, customer orientation has improved because nobody wants to fall short on this metric and endure potential ridicule. Löscher's leadership style and use of soft power during his early time in office seemed to have paid off, as the Siemens board extended his contract as CEO of the German industry icon a year early.

Source: Löscher, P. 2012. The CEO of Siemens on using a scandal to drive change. *Harvard Business Review,* 90(11): 42; and Anonymous. 2011. Löscher soll vorstandschef bleiben. *www.manager-magazin.de,* July 25: np.

Research suggests that effective leaders at all levels of organizations have high levels of EI.[23] After controlling for cognitive abilities and manager personality attributes, EI leads to stronger job performance across a wide range of professions, with stronger effects for professions that require a great deal of human interaction. Interestingly, there is only partial support for the catchy phrase "IQ gets you hired, but EQ (emotional quotient) gets you promoted." Evidence indicates that high levels of EI increase the likelihood of being promoted up to the middle-manager level. However, managers at high levels of the corporate hierarchy tend to evidence lower levels of EI, with the CEOs having, on average, lower levels of EI than managers at any other level. This is troubling given that firms led by CEOs high in EI outperform firms led by CEOs lower in EI. High-EI CEOs excel in managing relationships, influencing people, and forging alliances both inside and outside the firm. These CEOs can also benefit the firm since their ability to connect with and relate to outside stakeholders helps build the firm's reputation. Thus, firms would benefit from considering more than cognitive ability and easily measured performance metrics when choosing corporate leaders. Including EI as an element to consider would help firms choose superior corporate leaders.

Exhibit 11.3 identifies the five components of EI: self-awareness, self-regulation, motivation, empathy, and social skill.

Self-Awareness

Self-awareness is the first component of EI and brings to mind that Delphic oracle who gave the advice "Know thyself" thousands of years ago. Self-awareness involves a person having a deep understanding of his or her emotions, strengths, weaknesses, and drives.

EXHIBIT 11.3 The Five Components of Emotional Intelligence at Work

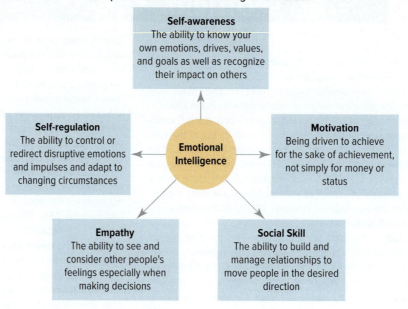

People with strong self-awareness are neither overly critical nor unrealistically optimistic. Instead, they are honest with themselves and others.

People generally admire and respect candor. Leaders are constantly required to make judgment calls that require a candid assessment of capabilities—their own and those of others. People who assess themselves honestly (i.e., self-aware people) are well suited to do the same for the organizations they run.[24]

Self-Regulation

Biological impulses drive our emotions. Although we cannot do away with them, we can strive to manage them. Self-regulation, which is akin to an ongoing inner conversation, frees us from being prisoners of our feelings.[25] People engaged in such conversation feel bad moods and emotional impulses just as everyone else does. However, they find ways to control them and even channel them in useful ways.

Self-regulated people are able to create an environment of trust and fairness where political behavior and infighting are sharply reduced and productivity tends to be high. People who have mastered their emotions are better able to bring about and implement change in an organization. When a new initiative is announced, they are less likely to panic; they are able to suspend judgment, seek out information, and listen to executives explain the new program.

Motivation

Successful executives are driven to achieve beyond expectations—their own and everyone else's. Although many people are driven by external factors, such as money and prestige, those with leadership potential are driven by a deeply embedded desire to achieve for the sake of achievement.

Motivated people show a passion for the work itself, such as seeking out creative challenges, a love of learning, and taking pride in a job well done. They also have a high level of energy to do things better as well as a restlessness with the status quo. They are eager to explore new approaches to their work.

Empathy

Empathy is probably the most easily recognized component of EI. Empathy means thoughtfully considering an employee's feelings, along with other factors, in the process of making intelligent decisions. Empathy is particularly important in today's business environment for at least three reasons: the increasing use of teams, the rapid pace of globalization, and the growing need to retain talent.[26]

When leading a team, a manager is often charged with arriving at a consensus—often in the face of a high level of emotions. Empathy enables a manager to sense and understand the viewpoints of everyone around the table.

Globalization typically involves cross-cultural dialogue that can easily lead to miscues. Empathetic people are attuned to the subtleties of body language; they can hear the message beneath the words being spoken. They have a deep understanding of the existence and importance of cultural and ethnic differences.

Empathy also plays a key role in retaining talent. Human capital is particularly important to a firm in the knowledge economy when it comes to creating advantages that are sustainable. Leaders need empathy to develop and keep top talent, because when high performers leave, they take their tacit knowledge with them.

Social Skill

While the first three components of EI are all self-management skills, the last two—empathy and social skill—concern a person's ability to manage relationships with others. Social skill may be viewed as friendliness with a purpose: moving people in the direction you desire, whether that's agreement on a new marketing strategy or enthusiasm about a new product.

Socially skilled people tend to have a wide circle of acquaintances as well as a knack for finding common ground and building rapport. They recognize that nothing gets done alone, and they have a network in place when the time for action comes.

Social skill can be viewed as the culmination of the other dimensions of EI. People will be effective at managing relationships when they can understand and control their own emotions and empathize with others' feelings. Motivation also contributes to social skill. People who are driven to achieve tend to be optimistic, even when confronted with setbacks. And when people are upbeat, their "glow" is cast upon conversations and other social encounters. They are popular, and for good reason.

A key to developing social skill is to become a good listener—a skill that many executives find to be quite challenging. Teresa Taylor, chief operating officer at Qwest Communications, says:[27]

> Over the years, something I really try to focus on is truly listening. When I say that, I mean sometimes people act like they're listening but they're really formulating their own thoughts in their heads. I'm trying to put myself into someone else's shoes, trying to figure out what's motivating them, and why they are in the spot they are in.

Emotional Intelligence: Some Potential Drawbacks and Cautionary Notes

Many great leaders have great reserves of empathy, interpersonal astuteness, awareness of their own feelings, and an awareness of their impact on others.[28] More importantly, they know how to apply these capabilities judiciously as best benefits the situation. Having some minimum level of EI will help a person be effective as a leader as long as it is channeled appropriately. However, if a person has a high level of these capabilities it may become "too much of a good thing" if he or she is allowed to drive inappropriate behaviors. Some additional potential drawbacks of EI can be gleaned by considering the flip side of its benefits.

Effective Leaders Have Empathy for Others However, they also must be able to make the "tough decisions." Leaders must be able to appeal to logic and reason and acknowledge others' feelings so that people feel the decisions are correct. However, it is easy to overidentify with others or confuse empathy with sympathy. This can make it more difficult to make the tough decisions.

Effective Leaders Are Astute Judges of People A danger is that leaders may become judgmental and overly critical about the shortcomings they perceive in others. They are likely to dismiss other people's insights, making them feel undervalued.

Effective Leaders Are Passionate about What They Do, and They Show It This doesn't mean that they are always cheerleaders. Rather, they may express their passion as persistence in pursuing an objective or a relentless focus on a valued principle. However, there is a fine line between being excited about something and letting your passion close your mind to other possibilities or cause you to ignore realities that others may see.

Effective Leaders Create Personal Connections with Their People Most effective leaders take time to engage employees individually and in groups, listening to their ideas, suggestions, and concerns and responding in ways that make people feel that their ideas are respected and appreciated. However, if the leader makes too many unannounced visits, it may create a culture of fear and micromanagement. Clearly, striking a correct balance is essential.

From a moral standpoint, emotional leadership is neither good nor bad. On the one hand, emotional leaders can be altruistic, focused on the general welfare of the company and its employees, and highly principled. On the other hand, they can be manipulative, selfish, and dishonest. For example, if a person is using leadership solely to gain power, that is not leadership at all.[29] Rather, that person is using his or her EI to grasp what people want and pander to those desires in order to gain authority and influence. After all, easy answers sell.

Creating a Learning Organization

LO11.4

The importance of creating a learning organization.

To enhance the long-term viability of organizations, leaders also need to build a learning organization. Such an organization is capable of adapting to change, fostering creativity, and succeeding in highly competitive markets.

Successful, innovative organizations recognize the importance of having everyone involved in the process of actively learning and adapting. As noted by today's leading expert on learning organizations, MIT's Peter Senge, the days when Henry Ford, Alfred Sloan, and Tom Watson *"learned for the organization"* are gone:

> In an increasingly dynamic, interdependent, and unpredictable world, it is simply no longer possible for anyone to "figure it all out at the top." The old model, "the top thinks and the local acts," must now give way to integrating thinking and acting at all levels. While the challenge is great, so is the potential payoff. "The person who figures out how to harness the collective genius of the people in his or her organization," according to former Citibank CEO Walter Wriston, "is going to blow the competition away."[30]

Learning and change typically involve the ongoing questioning of an organization's status quo or method of procedure. This means that all individuals throughout the organization must be reflective.[31] Many organizations get so caught up in carrying out their day-to-day work that they rarely, if ever, stop to think objectively about themselves and their businesses. They often fail to ask the probing questions that might lead them to call into question their basic assumptions, to refresh their strategies, or to reengineer their work

EXHIBIT 11.4
Key Elements of a
Learning Organization

These are the six key elements of a learning organization. Each of these items should be viewed as *necessary, but not sufficient.* That is, successful learning organizations need all six elements.

1. Inspiring and motivating people with a mission or purpose.
2. Developing leaders.
3. Empowering employees at all levels.
4. Accumulating and sharing internal knowledge.
5. Gathering and integrating external information.
6. Challenging the status quo and enabling creativity.

processes. According to Michael Hammer and Steven Stanton, the pioneer consultants who touched off the reengineering movement:

> Reflection entails awareness of self, of competitors, of customers. It means thinking without preconception. It means questioning cherished assumptions and replacing them with new approaches. It is the only way in which a winning company can maintain its leadership position, by which a company with great assets can ensure that they continue to be well deployed.[32]

To adapt to change, foster creativity, and remain competitive, leaders must build learning organizations. Exhibit 11.4 lists the six key elements of a learning organization.

Inspiring and Motivating People with a Mission or Purpose

Successful **learning organizations** create a proactive, creative approach to the unknown, actively solicit the involvement of employees at all levels, and enable all employees to use their intelligence and apply their imagination. Higher-level skills are required of everyone, not just those at the top.[33] A learning environment involves organizationwide commitment to change, an action orientation, and applicable tools and methods.[34] It must be viewed by everyone as a guiding philosophy and not simply as another change program.

A critical requirement of all learning organizations is that everyone feels and supports a compelling purpose. In the words of William O'Brien, CEO of Hanover Insurance, "Before there can be meaningful participation, people must share certain values and pictures about where we are trying to go. We discovered that people have a real need to feel that they're part of an enabling mission."[35] Such a perspective is consistent with an intensive study by Kouzes and Posner, authors of *The Leadership Challenge*.[36] They analyzed data from nearly 1 million respondents who were leaders at various levels in many organizations throughout the world. A major finding was that what leaders struggle with most is communicating an image of the future that draws others in—that is, it speaks to what others see and feel. To illustrate:

> Buddy Blanton, a principal program manager at Rockwell Collins, learned this lesson firsthand. He asked his team for feedback on his leadership, and the vast majority of it was positive. However, he got some strong advice from his team about how he could be more effective in inspiring a shared vision. "You would benefit by helping us, as a team, to understand how you go to your vision. We want to walk with you while you create the goals and vision, so we all get to the end of the vision together."[37]

Inspiring and motivating people with a mission or purpose is a necessary but not sufficient condition for developing an organization that can learn and adapt to a rapidly changing, complex, and interconnected environment.

Developing Leaders

Leadership development programs aid in the building of a learning organization in two different ways. First, programs help the participants learn new skills that help them be more capable in their current roles and more able to take on additional responsibility.

learning organizations
organizations that create a proactive, creative approach to the unknown; characterized by (1) inspiring and motivating people with a mission and purpose, (2) developing leaders, (3) empowering employees at all levels, (4) accumulating and sharing internal knowledge, (5) gathering and integrating external information, and (6) challenging the status quo and enabling creativity.

In short, this helps enhance individual learning and, thus, increases the human capital of the firm. Second, these development programs can also train employees to be more effective at learning over time by giving them the skills to incorporate new information and better learn from their experiences.

Not all leadership development programs are equally effective. Research suggests that successful development programs share four common traits.[38] First, the programs are designed to fit the firm's overall strategy. For example, if a firm emphasizes organic growth, its leadership development program should emphasize building the skills to see opportunities in the firm's industry and related markets and developing internal talent. This will channel the learning capabilities of its leaders. Second, effective leadership development programs combine real-world experiences with classroom learning to build the desired skills. In line with this concept, one major engineering and construction firm emphasized developing skills in interacting with customers to build additional business. Participants were tasked to identify new business opportunities in their home units. One participant committed his team to develop a new order with a customer that spanned more than one of the group's business lines. Third, leader development programs need to have hard conversations to identify and overcome organizational biases that keep the firm from learning and being more flexible. One European industrial firm included frameworks for driving capital allocation decisions lower in the organization, but the entrenched culture of the firm left managers reluctant to relinquish control. Once the trainers took this issue head-on, enlisting open-minded managers to take the leap first and report back to the team and also emphasizing the learning opportunity for lower-level managers, participants more widely implemented the decentralization program. Fourth, top managers and trainers need to assess the impact of the training by following up with participants several months after the training to assess how effectively they have implemented the training, overcome the barriers to marking it work, and learned from the process.

Empowering Employees at All Levels

"The great leader is a great servant," asserted Ken Melrose, former CEO and chairman of Toro Company and author of *Making the Grass Greener on Your Side*.[39] A manager's role becomes one of creating an environment where employees can achieve their potential as they help move the organization toward its goals. Instead of viewing themselves as resource controllers and power brokers, leaders must envision themselves as flexible resources willing to assume numerous roles as coaches, information providers, teachers, decision makers, facilitators, supporters, or listeners, depending on the needs of their employees.[40]

The central key to empowerment is effective leadership. Empowerment can't occur in a leadership vacuum. According to Melrose, "You best lead by serving the needs of your people. You don't do their jobs for them; you enable them to learn and progress on the job."

Leading-edge organizations recognize the need for trust, cultural control, and expertise at all levels instead of the extensive and cumbersome rules and regulations inherent in hierarchical control.[41] Some commentators have argued that too often organizations fall prey to the "heroes-and-drones syndrome," wherein the value of those in powerful positions is exalted and the value of those who fail to achieve top rank is diminished. Such an attitude is implicit in phrases such as "Lead, follow, or get out of the way" or, even less appealing, "Unless you're the lead horse, the view never changes." Few will ever reach the top hierarchical positions in organizations, but in the information economy, the strongest organizations are those that effectively use the talents of all the players on the team.

Empowering individuals by soliciting their input helps an organization to enjoy better employee morale. It also helps create a culture in which middle- and lower-level employees feel that their ideas and initiatives will be valued and enhance firm performance, as explained in Strategy Spotlight 11.5.

USING THE WISDOM OF YOUR EMPLOYEES TO MAKE BETTER DECISIONS

CEOs are often surrounded by an aura of unfailing business acumen. Yet few CEOs live up to these high expectations over the long run, suggesting that even the most able CEOs have limited abilities. Ironically, shattering the image of the almighty CEO by realizing and identifying cognitive limitations may help us to improve organizational decision making. Consider WBG Construction, a small home builder west of Boston. When important decisions need to be made, Greg Burrill, the president, asks all employees with relevant knowledge or a stake in the outcome for their thoughts. This collaborative approach recently led to a decision that not only sold a house but also inspired a new floor plan that appealed to a whole new segment of buyers.

As another example, EMC, the data storage giant, enables participation by a social media platform called EMC One. When the recession hit and cost cutting became imperative, EMC used this social media platform to do something most companies would leave to top management: decide where to cut costs. Several thousand employees participated and identified cost savings that were largely unknown to top management. The resulting cuts were less painful because employees had a say in the cost reduction. Empowering employees in this manner utilizes the day-to-day insights of lower-level employees and benefits both the firm and the workforce.

In some other cases, bad decisions not only cost money but also can lead to heartbreaking accidents. NASA can look back at some 50 years of pioneering success, but also tragic accidents caused by bad judgment. In February 2009, the flight of space shuttle *Discovery* was overshadowed by uncertainties about whether an issue with the fuel system should delay the launch. Prior space shuttle launch decisions were made by a small group of individuals supported by a culture of complacency born of many prior successes and communication breakdowns. But NASA finally implemented a much-needed change of culture that now values input from all group members. As Mike Ryschkewitsch, NASA's chief engineer, observed, "One of the things that NASA strongly emphasizes now is that any individual who works here, if they see something that doesn't look right, they have a responsibility to raise it, and they can raise it." By utilizing the insights of individuals in their organizations, leaders hope to improve organizational decision making and secure the long-term success of their businesses.

Sources: Davenport, T. H. 2012. The wisdom of your in-house crowd. *Harvard Business Review*, 90(10): 40; and Davenport, T. H., & Manville, B. 2012. *Judgment calls: Twelve stories of big decisions and the teams that got them right:* 25–38. Boston: Harvard Business Review Press.

Accumulating and Sharing Internal Knowledge

Effective organizations must also *redistribute information, knowledge* (skills to act on the information), and *rewards*.[42] A company might give frontline employees the power to act as "customer advocates," doing whatever is necessary to satisfy customers. The company needs to disseminate information by sharing customer expectations and feedback as well as financial information. The employees must know about the goals of the business as well as how key value-creating activities in the organization are related to each other. Finally, organizations should allocate rewards on how effectively employees use information, knowledge, and power to improve customer service quality and the company's overall performance.[43]

Let's take a look at Whole Foods Market, Inc., the largest natural-foods grocer in the United States.[44] An important benefit of the sharing of internal information at Whole Foods becomes the active process of *internal benchmarking*. Competition is intense at Whole Foods. Teams compete against their own goals for sales, growth, and productivity; they compete against different teams in their stores; and they compete against similar teams at different stores and regions. There is an elaborate system of peer reviews through which teams benchmark each other. The "Store Tour" is the most intense. On a periodic schedule, each Whole Foods store is toured by a group of as many as 40 visitors from another region. Lateral learning—discovering what your colleagues are doing right and carrying those practices into your organization—has become a driving force at Whole Foods.

In addition to enhancing the sharing of company information both up and down as well as across the organization, leaders also have to develop means to tap into some of the more informal sources of internal information. In a survey of presidents, CEOs, board members, and top executives in a variety of nonprofit organizations, respondents were asked what differentiated the successful candidates for promotion. The consensus: The executive was seen as a person who listens. According to Peter Meyer, the author of the study, "The value of listening is clear: You cannot succeed in running a company if you do not hear what your people, customers, and suppliers are telling you. . . . Listening and understanding well are key to making good decisions."[45]

Gathering and Integrating External Information

Recognizing opportunities, as well as threats, in the external environment is vital to a firm's success. As organizations *and* environments become more complex and evolve rapidly, it is far more critical for employees and managers to become more aware of environmental trends and events—both general and industry-specific—and more knowledgeable about their firm's competitors and customers. Next, we will discuss some ideas on how to do it.

First, company employees at all levels can use a variety of sources to acquire external information. Much can be gleaned by reading trade and professional journals, books, and popular business magazines. Other venues for gathering external information include membership in professional or trade organizations, attendance at meetings and conventions, and networking among colleagues inside and outside your industry. Online social networks, such as LinkedIn, can also provide access to contacts to learn about changes in the external environment. To gain up-to-date information on particular rivals, firms can monitor the direct communications from rival firms and their executives, such as press releases and quarterly-earnings calls. These communications can provide insight on the rival's actions and intended actions. It may also be valuable to follow rival-firm employees' online postings, on Twitter and other platforms, to gain insights on rivals' investments and actions.

Second, **benchmarking** *can be a useful means of employing external information.* Here managers seek out the best examples of a particular practice as part of an ongoing effort to improve the corresponding practice in their own organization.[46] There are two primary types of benchmarking. **Competitive benchmarking** restricts the search for best practices to competitors, while **functional benchmarking** endeavors to determine best practices regardless of industry. Industry-specific standards (e.g., response times required to repair power outages in the electric utility industry) are typically best handled through competitive benchmarking, whereas more generic processes (e.g., answering 1-800 calls) lend themselves to functional benchmarking because the function is essentially the same in any industry.

Ford Motor Company works with its suppliers on benchmarking its competitors' products during product redesigns. At the launch of the redesign, Ford and its suppliers identify a few key components they want to focus on improving. They then do a "tear down" of Ford's components as well as matching components from three or four rivals. The idea is to get early input from suppliers so that Ford can design components that are best in class—lighter, cheaper, and more reliable.[47]

Third, focus directly on customers for information. For example, William McKnight, head of 3M's Chicago sales office, required that salesmen of abrasives products talk directly to the workers in the shop to find out what they needed, instead of calling on only front-office executives.[48] This was very innovative at the time—1909! But it illustrates the need to get to the end user of a product or service. (McKnight went on to become 3M's president from 1929 to 1949 and chairman from 1949 to 1969.)

Challenging the Status Quo and Enabling Creativity

Earlier in this chapter we discussed some of the barriers that leaders face when trying to bring about change in an organization: vested interests in the status quo, systemic barriers, behavioral barriers, political barriers, and personal time constraints. For a firm to become a learning organization, it must overcome such barriers in order to foster creativity and

benchmarking
managers seeking out best examples of a particular practice as part of an ongoing effort to improve the corresponding practice in their own organization.

competitive benchmarking
benchmarking in which the examples are drawn from competitors in the industry.

functional benchmarking
benchmarking in which the examples are drawn from any organization, even those outside the industry.

enable it to permeate the firm. This becomes quite a challenge if the firm is entrenched in a status quo mentality.

Perhaps the best way to challenge the status quo is for the leader to forcefully create a sense of urgency. For example, when Tom Kasten was vice president of Levi Strauss, he had a direct approach to initiating change:

> You create a compelling picture of the risks of *not* changing. We let our people hear directly from customers. We videotaped interviews with customers and played excerpts. One big customer said, "We trust many of your competitors implicitly. We sample their deliveries. We open *all* Levi's deliveries." Another said, "Your lead times are the worst. If you weren't Levi's, you'd be gone." It was powerful. I wish we had done more of it.[49]

Such initiative, if sincere and credible, establishes a shared mission and the need for major transformations. It can channel energies to bring about both change and creative endeavors.

Establishing a "culture of dissent" can be another effective means of questioning the status quo and serving as a spur toward creativity. Here norms are established whereby dissenters can openly question a superior's perspective without fear of retaliation or retribution.

Closely related to the culture of dissent is the fostering of a culture that encourages risk taking. "If you're not making mistakes, you're not taking risks, and that means you're not going anywhere," claimed John Holt, coauthor of *Celebrate Your Mistakes*.[50] "The key is to make errors faster than the competition, so you have more chances to learn and win."

Companies that cultivate cultures of experimentation and curiosity make sure that *failure* is not, in essence, an obscene word. They encourage mistakes as a key part of their competitive advantage. It has been said that innovation has a great paradox: Success—that is, true breakthroughs—usually come through failure. Below are some approaches to encourage risk taking and learning from mistakes in an organization:[51]

- *Formalize forums for failure.* To keep failures and the important lessons that they offer from getting swept under the rug, carve out time for reflection. GE formalized the sharing of lessons from failure by bringing together managers whose "Imagination Breakthrough" efforts were put on the shelf.
- *Move the goalposts.* Innovation requires flexibility in meeting goals, since early predictions are often little more than educated guesses. Intuit's Scott Cook even goes so far as to suggest that teams developing new products ignore forecasts in the early days. "For every one of our failures, we had spreadsheets that looked awesome," he claims.
- *Bring in outsiders.* Outsiders can help neutralize the emotions and biases that prop up a flop. Customers can be the most valuable. After its DNA chip failed, Corning brought pharmaceutical companies in early to test its new drug-discovery technology, Epic.
- *Prove yourself wrong, not right.* Development teams tend to look for supporting, rather than countervailing, evidence. "You have to reframe what you're seeking in the early days," says Innosight's Scott Anthony. "You're not really seeking proof that you have the right answer. It's more about testing to prove yourself wrong."

Finally, failure can play an important and positive role in one's professional development. John Donahue, eBay's CEO, draws on the sport of baseball in recalling the insight (and inspiration!) one of his former bosses shared with him:[52]

> The best hitters in Major League Baseball, world class, they can strike out six times out of ten and still be the greatest hitters of all time. That's my philosophy—the key is to get up in that batter's box and take a swing. And all you have to do is hit one single, a couple of doubles, and an occasional home run out of every ten at-bats, and you're going to be the best hitter or the best business leader around. You can't play in the major leagues without having a lot of failures.

Creating an Ethical Organization

ethics
a system of right and wrong that assists individuals in deciding when an act is moral or immoral and/or socially desirable or not.

organizational ethics
the values, attitudes, and behavioral patterns that define an organization's operating culture and that determine what an organization holds as acceptable behavior.

ethical orientation
the practices that firms use to promote an ethical business culture, including ethical role models, corporate credos and codes of conduct, ethically based reward and evaluation systems, and consistently enforced ethical policies and procedures.

Ethics may be defined as a system of right and wrong.[53] Ethics assists individuals in deciding when an act is moral or immoral, socially desirable or not. The sources for an individual's ethics include religious beliefs, national and ethnic heritage, family practices, community standards, educational experiences, and friends and neighbors. Business ethics is the application of ethical standards to commercial enterprise.

Individual Ethics versus Organizational Ethics

Many leaders think of ethics as a question of personal scruples, a confidential matter between employees and their consciences. Such leaders are quick to describe any wrongdoing as an isolated incident, the work of a rogue employee. They assume the company should not bear any responsibility for individual misdeeds. In their view, ethics has nothing to do with leadership.

Ethics has everything to do with leadership. Seldom does the character flaw of a lone actor completely explain corporate misconduct. Instead, unethical business practices typically involve the tacit, if not explicit, cooperation of others and reflect the values, attitudes, and behavior patterns that define an organization's operating culture. Ethics is as much an organizational as a personal issue. Leaders who fail to provide proper leadership to institute proper systems and controls that facilitate ethical conduct share responsibility with those who conceive, execute, and knowingly benefit from corporate misdeeds.[54]

The **ethical orientation** of a leader is a key factor in promoting ethical behavior. Ethical leaders must take personal, ethical responsibility for their actions and decision making. Leaders who exhibit high ethical standards become role models for others and raise an organization's overall level of ethical behavior. Ethical behavior must start with the leader before the employees can be expected to perform accordingly.

There has been a growing interest in corporate ethical performance. Some reasons for this trend may be the increasing lack of confidence regarding corporate activities, the growing emphasis on quality-of-life issues, and a spate of recent corporate scandals. Without a strong ethical culture, the chance of ethical crises occurring is enhanced. Ethical crises can be very expensive—both in terms of financial costs and in the erosion of human capital and overall firm reputation. Merely adhering to the minimum regulatory standards may not be enough to remain competitive in a world that is becoming more socially conscious. Strategy Spotlight 11.6 highlights potential ethical problems at utility companies that are trying to capitalize on consumers' desire to participate in efforts to curb global warming.

The past two decades have been characterized by numerous examples of unethical and illegal behavior by many top-level corporate executives. These include executives of firms such as Enron, Tyco, WorldCom, Adelphia, and HealthSouth, who were all forced to resign and are facing (or have been convicted of) criminal charges. Perhaps the most glaring example is Bernie Madoff, whose Ponzi scheme, which unraveled in 2008, defrauded investors of $50 billion in assets they had set aside for retirement and charitable donations.

The ethical organization is characterized by a conception of ethical values and integrity as a driving force of the enterprise.[55] Ethical values shape the search for opportunities, the design of organizational systems, and the decision-making process used by individuals and groups. They provide a common frame of reference that serves as a unifying force across different functions, lines of business, and employee groups. Organizational ethics helps to define what a company is and what it stands for.

There are many potential benefits of an ethical organization, but they are often indirect. Research has found somewhat inconsistent results concerning the overall relationship between ethical performance and measures of financial performance.[56] However, positive relationships have generally been found between ethical performance and strong

GREEN ENERGY: REAL OR JUST A MARKETING PLOY?

Many consumers want to "go green" and are looking for opportunities to do so. Utility companies that provide heat and electricity are one of the most obvious places to turn, because they often use fossil fuels that could be saved through energy conservation or replaced by using alternative energy sources. In fact, some consumers are willing to pay a premium to contribute to environmental sustainability efforts if paying a little more will help curb global warming. Knowing this, many power companies in the United States have developed alternative energy programs and appealed to customers to help pay for them.

Unfortunately, many of the power companies that are offering eco-friendly options are falling short on delivering on them. Some utilities have simply gotten off to a slow start or found it difficult to profitably offer alternative power. Others, however, are suspected of committing a new type of fraud—"greenwashing." This refers to companies that make unsubstantiated claims about how environmentally friendly their products or services really are. In the case of many power companies, their claims of "green power" are empty promises. Instead of actually generating additional renewable energy, most of the premiums are going for marketing costs.

"They are preying on people's goodwill," says Stephen Smith, executive director of the Southern Alliance for Clean Energy, an advocacy group in Knoxville, Tennessee.

Consider what two power companies offered and how the money was actually spent:

- Duke Power of Indiana created a program called "GoGreen Power." Customers were told that they could pay a green-energy premium and a specific amount of electricity would be obtained from renewable sources. What actually happened? Less than 18 percent of voluntary customer contributions in a recent year went to renewable energy development.

- Alliant Energy of Iowa established a program dubbed "Second Nature." Customers were told that they would "support the growth of earth-friendly 'green power' created by wind and biomass." What actually happened? More than 56 percent of expenditures went to marketing and administrative costs, not green-energy development.

Sources: Elgin, B. & Holden, D. 2008. Green power: Buyers beware. *BusinessWeek*, September 29: 68–70; *www.cleanenergy.org*; *duke-energy.com*; and *alliantenergy.com*.

---

organizational culture, increased employee efforts, lower turnover, higher organizational commitment, and enhanced social responsibility.

The advantages of a strong ethical orientation can have a positive effect on employee commitment and motivation to excel. This is particularly important in today's knowledge-intensive organizations, where human capital is critical in creating value and competitive advantages. Positive, constructive relationships among individuals (i.e., social capital) are vital in leveraging human capital and other resources in an organization. Drawing on the concept of stakeholder management, an ethically sound organization can also strengthen its bonds among its suppliers, customers, and governmental agencies.

Integrity-Based versus Compliance-Based Approaches to Organizational Ethics

LO11.6

The difference between integrity-based and compliance-based approaches to organizational ethics.

Before discussing the key elements of an ethical organization, one must understand the links between organizational integrity and the personal integrity of an organization's members.[57] There cannot be high-integrity organizations without high-integrity individuals. However, individual integrity is rarely self-sustaining. Even good people can lose their bearings when faced with pressures, temptations, and heightened performance expectations in the absence of organizational support systems and ethical boundaries. Organizational integrity rests on a concept of purpose, responsibility, and ideals for an organization as a whole. An important responsibility of leadership is to create this ethical framework and develop the organizational capabilities to make it operational.[58]

Lynn Paine, an ethics scholar at Harvard, identifies two approaches: the compliance-based approach and the integrity-based approach. (See Exhibit 11.5 for a comparison of

EXHIBIT 11.5 Approaches to Ethics Management

Characteristics	Approach	Actions
Ethos	Compliance-based	Conformity with externally imposed standards
	Integrity-based	Self-governance according to chosen standards
Objective	Compliance-based	Prevent criminal misconduct
	Integrity-based	Enable responsible conduct
Leadership	Compliance-based	Driven by legal office
	Integrity-based	Driven by management, with input from functional staff
Methods	Compliance-based	Reduced discretion, training, controls, audits, and penalties
	Integrity-based	Education, leadership, accountability, decision processes, auditing, and penalties
Behavioral Assumptions	Compliance-based	Individualistic, self-interested actors
	Integrity-based	Social actors, guided by a combination of self-interest, ideals, values, and social expectations

compliance-based ethics programs
programs for building ethical organizations that have the goal of preventing, detecting, and punishing legal violations.

integrity-based ethics programs
programs for building ethical organizations that combine a concern for law with an emphasis on managerial responsibility for ethical behavior, including (1) enabling ethical conduct; (2) examining the organization's and members' core guiding values, thoughts, and actions; and (3) defining the responsibilities and aspirations that constitute an organization's ethical compass.

compliance-based and integrity-based strategies.) Faced with the prospect of litigation, several organizations reactively implement **compliance-based ethics programs.** Such programs are typically designed by a corporate counsel with the goal of preventing, detecting, and punishing legal violations. But being ethical is much more than being legal, and an integrity-based approach addresses the issue of ethics in a more comprehensive manner.

An **integrity-based ethics program** combines a concern for law with an emphasis on managerial responsibility for ethical behavior. It is broader, deeper, and more demanding than a legal compliance initiative. It is broader in that it seeks to enable responsible conduct. It is deeper in that it cuts to the ethos and operating systems of an organization and its members—their core guiding values, thoughts, and actions. It is more demanding because it requires an active effort to define the responsibilities that constitute an organization's ethical compass. Most importantly, organizational ethics is seen as the responsibility of management.

A corporate counsel may play a role in designing and implementing integrity strategies, but it is managers at all levels and across all functions who are involved in the process. Once integrated into the day-to-day operations, such strategies can prevent damaging ethical lapses, while tapping into powerful human impulses for moral thought and action. Ethics becomes the governing ethos of an organization and not burdensome constraints. Here is an example of an organization that goes beyond mere compliance to laws in building an ethical organization:

In teaching ethics to its employees, Texas Instruments, the $12 billion chip and electronics manufacturer, asks them to run an issue through the following steps: Is it legal? Is it consistent with the company's stated values? Will the employee feel bad doing it? What will the public think if the action is reported in the press? Does the employee think it is wrong? If the employees are not sure of the ethicality of the issue, they are encouraged to ask someone until they are clear about it. In the process, employees can approach high-level personnel and even the company's lawyers. At TI, the question of ethics goes much beyond merely being legal. It is no surprise that this company is a benchmark for corporate ethics and has been a recipient of three ethics awards: the David C. Lincoln Award for Ethics and Excellence in Business, American Business Ethics Award, and Bentley College Center for Business Ethics Award.[59]

Compliance-based approaches are externally motivated—that is, based on the fear of punishment for doing something unlawful. On the other hand, integrity-based approaches are driven by a personal and organizational commitment to ethical behavior.

A firm must have several key elements to become a highly ethical organization:

LO11.7

Several key elements that organizations must have to become ethical organizations.

- Role models.
- Corporate credos and codes of conduct.
- Reward and evaluation systems.
- Policies and procedures.

These elements are highly interrelated. Reward structures and policies will be useless if leaders are not sound role models. That is, leaders who implicitly say, "Do as I say, not as I do," will quickly have their credibility eroded and such actions will sabotage other elements that are essential to building an ethical organization.

Role Models

For good or for bad, leaders are role models in their organizations. Perhaps few executives can share an experience that better illustrates this than Linda Hudson, former president of General Dynamics.[60] Right after she was promoted to become the firm's first female president, she went to Nordstrom and bought some new suits to wear to work. A lady at the store showed her how to tie a scarf in a very unique way. The day after she wore it to work, guess what: No fewer than a dozen women in the organization were wearing scarves tied exactly the same way! She reflects:

> And that's when I realized that life was never going to be the way it had been before, that people were watching everything I did. And it wasn't just going to be about how I dressed. It was about my behavior, the example I set, the tone I set, the way I carried myself, and how confident I was—all those kinds of things. . . . As the leader, people are looking at you in a way you could not have imagined in other roles.

Clearly, leaders must "walk the talk"; they must be consistent in their words and deeds. The values as well as the character of leaders become transparent to an organization's employees through their behaviors. When leaders do not believe in the ethical standards that they are trying to inspire, they will not be effective as good role models. Being an effective leader often includes taking responsibility for ethical lapses within the organization—even though the executives themselves are not directly involved. Consider the perspective of Dennis Bakke, former CEO of AES, a $16 billion global electricity company based in Arlington, Virginia:

> There was a major breach (in 1992) of the AES values. Nine members of the water treatment team in Oklahoma lied to the EPA about water quality at the plant. There was no environmental damage, but they lied about the test results. A new, young chemist at the plant discovered it, told a team leader, and we then were notified. Now, you could argue that the people who lied were responsible and were accountable, but the senior management team also took responsibility by taking pay cuts. My reduction was about 30 percent.[61]

Such action enhances the loyalty and commitment of employees throughout the organization. Many would believe that it would have been much easier (and personally less expensive!) for Bakke and his management team to merely take strong punitive action against the nine individuals who were acting contrary to the behavior expected in AES's ethical culture. However, by sharing responsibility for the misdeeds, the top executives—through their highly visible action—made it clear that responsibility and penalties for ethical lapses go well beyond the "guilty" parties. Such courageous behavior by leaders helps to strengthen an organization's ethical environment.

corporate credo
a statement of the beliefs
typically held by managers
in a corporation.

Corporate Credos and Codes of Conduct

Corporate credos and codes of conduct are mechanisms that provide statements of norms and beliefs as well as guidelines for decision making. They provide employees with a clear understanding of the organization's policies and ethical position. Such guidelines also provide the basis for employees to refuse to commit unethical acts and help to make them aware of issues before they are faced with the situation. For such codes to be truly effective, organization members must be aware of them and what behavioral guidelines they contain.[62]

Large corporations are not the only ones to develop and use codes of conduct. Consider the example of Wetherill Associates (WAI), a small, privately held supplier of electrical parts to the automotive market:

> Rather than a conventional code of conduct, WAI has a Quality Assurance Manual—a combination of philosophy text, conduct guide, technical manual, and company profile—that describes the company's commitment to honesty, ethical action, and integrity. WAI doesn't have a corporate ethics officer, because the company's corporate ethics officer is Marie Bothe, WAI's CEO. She sees her main function as keeping the 350-employee company on the path of ethical behavior and looking for opportunities to help the community. She delegates the "technical" aspects of the business—marketing, finance, personnel, and operations—to other members of the organization.[63]

Reward and Evaluation Systems

It is entirely possible for a highly ethical leader to preside over an organization that commits several unethical acts. How? A flaw in the organization's reward structure may inadvertently cause individuals to act in an inappropriate manner if rewards are seen as being distributed on the basis of outcomes rather than the means by which goals and objectives are achieved.[64]

Generally speaking, unethical (or illegal) behaviors are also more likely to take place when competition is intense. Some researchers have called this the "dark side of competition." Consider a couple of examples:[65]

- Competition among educational institutions for the best students is becoming stiffer. A senior admissions officer at Claremont McKenna College resigned after admitting to inflating SAT scores of the incoming classes for six years. The motive, of course, was to boost the school's rankings in the *U.S. News & World Report*'s annual listing of top colleges and universities in the United States. Carmen Nobel, who reported the incident in *Working Knowledge* (a Harvard Business School publication), suggested that the scandal "questions the value of competitive rankings."
- A study of 11,000 New York vehicle emission test facilities found that companies with a greater number of local competitors passed cars with considerably high emission rates and lost customers when they failed to pass the tests. The authors of the study concluded, "In contexts when pricing is restricted, firms use illicit quality as a business strategy."

Many companies have developed reward and evaluation systems that evaluate whether a manager is acting in an ethical manner. For example, Raytheon, a $24 billion defense contractor, incorporated the following items in its "Leadership Assessment Instrument":[66]

- Maintains unequivocal commitment to honesty, truth, and ethics in every facet of behavior.
- Conforms with the letter and intent of company policies while working to affect any necessary policy changes.

- Actions are consistent with words; follows through on commitments; readily admits mistakes.
- Is trusted and inspires others to be trusted.

As noted by Dan Burnham, Raytheon's former CEO: "What do we look for in a leadership candidate with respect to integrity? What we're really looking for are people who have developed an inner gyroscope of ethical principles. We look for people for whom ethical thinking is part of what they do—no different from 'strategic thinking' or 'tactical thinking.'"

Policies and Procedures

Many situations that a firm faces have regular, identifiable patterns. Leaders tend to handle such routine by establishing a policy or procedure to be followed that can be applied uniformly to each occurrence. Such guidelines can be useful in specifying the proper relationships with a firm's customers and suppliers. For example, Levi Strauss has developed stringent global sourcing guidelines, and Chemical Bank (part of JPMorgan Chase Bank) has a policy of forbidding any review that would determine if suppliers are Chemical customers when the bank awards contracts.

Carefully developed policies and procedures guide behavior so that all employees will be encouraged to behave in an ethical manner. However, they must be reinforced with effective communication, enforcement, and monitoring, as well as sound corporate governance practices. In addition, the Sarbanes-Oxley Act of 2002 provides considerable legal protection to employees of publicly traded companies who report unethical or illegal practices. Provisions in the act:[67]

- Make it unlawful to "discharge, demote, suspend, threaten, harass, or in any manner discriminate against 'a whistleblower.'"
- Establish criminal penalties of up to 10 years in jail for executives who retaliate against whistleblowers.
- Require board audit committees to establish procedures for hearing whistleblower complaints.
- Allow the secretary of labor to order a company to rehire a terminated whistleblower with no court hearings whatsoever.
- Give a whistleblower the right to a jury trial, bypassing months or years of cumbersome administrative hearings.

ISSUE FOR DEBATE

JPMorgan Responds to a Request

In June 2012, Jamie Dimon, the CEO of JPMorgan Chase, met with a Chinese insurance regulatory official, Xiang Junbo, at the bank's headquarters in New York. JPMorgan was seeking to win lucrative work from a Chinese insurance company. Xiang would have a say in whether or not JPMorgan would win the business. Also at that meeting was a woman brought by Xiang who served as the interpreter between Dimon and Xiang.

continued

As the meeting drew to a close, Xiang changed the subject of the meeting and focused on his young interpreter, noting that she was the daughter of a close friend and promoting her as a potential employee at JPMorgan. JPMorgan employees in Hong Kong knew that Xiang hoped to see the woman hired by JPMorgan and had brought her to New York to introduce her to Dimon. Following the meeting, a banker in the Hong Kong office sent an email that outlined how Xiang asked Dimon "for a favor to retain her." In discussing the need to maintain good rapport with Xiang, the banker also emphasized "the importance of this relationship" and the need to "find a solution for her quickly." Dimon passed information on the applicant to others in the bank but took no direct action on whether or not to hire her. After conducting a series of interviews and gaining approval from the bank's compliance department, the bank created a special internship for the woman. She later was hired into a full-time position. But she is not alone. In filings with federal regulators, JPMorgan has reported that it has hired several dozen individuals with close ties to Chinese regulators, government officials, and corporate executives.

In the months after the meeting between Dimon and Xiang, JPMorgan worked on deals with at least four insurance companies overseen by Xiang to take the insurers public via an IPO. More recently, five top insurance companies in China became clients of JPMorgan.

Federal regulators have opened investigations of the hiring practices of JPMorgan as well as several other leading Wall Street firms, including Citigroup, Credit Suisse, Deutsche Bank, Goldman Sachs, Morgan Stanley, and UBS. Banks are not prohibited from hiring individuals with ties to Chinese government officials. They would be in violation of the Foreign Corrupt Practices Act only if they can be shown to have explicitly traded job offers for approval of business deals. In the words of the statute, the banks would have had to act with "corrupt intent" to influence a Chinese official.

Officials at JPMorgan defend their hiring of the interpreter. They argue that she was well qualified, having a graduate degree from NYU, and note that she has received very positive evaluations from her supervisors.

JPMorgan has had ongoing discussions over the years about how to respond to requests for preferential treatment of job candidates with close ties to powerful Chinese officials. In July 2006, JPMorgan executives held a meeting in Hong Kong at which they discussed how to stay in compliance with antibribery laws while pursuing recruits with ties to officials. In response to questions from managers in its Chinese offices, the bank developed new guidelines that were included as part of a broader set of anticorruption measures approved by the board in late 2011. In a January 2014 interview on CNBC, Dimon weighed in on the challenge with such hires, stating it has been a "norm of business for years" for banks to hire "sons and daughters of companies, and to give them proper jobs and don't violate, you know, [the] American Foreign Corrupt Practices Act."

Discussion Questions

1. Was JPMorgan ethical in hiring the friend of the Chinese government official?
2. What should the hiring policies of banks be to meet the needs of being ethical while also building their business in China? Should banks strive to follow their legal requirements, or should their standards be higher?
3. How responsible are senior managers of banks for ensuring that hiring done in regional operations is ethical and in line with legal requirements?

Sources: Barboza, D. & Gough, N. 2014. Chinese official made job plea to JPMorgan Chase chief. *nytimes.com,* February 10: np; and Glazer, E., Fitzpatrick, D., & Eaglesham, J. 2014. J.P. Morgan knew of China hiring concerns before probe. *wsj.com,* October 23: np.

- **Strategic Leadership:** The chapter identifies three interdependent activities that are central to strategic leadership; namely, setting direction, designing the organization, and nurturing a culture dedicated to excellence and ethical behavior. Both during your life as a student and in organizations at which you have worked, you have often assumed leadership positions. To what extent have you consciously and successfully engaged in each of these activities? Observe the leaders in your organization and assess to what extent you can learn from them the qualities of strategic leadership that you can use to advance your own career.

- **Power:** Identify the sources of power used by your superior at work. How do this person's primary source of power and the way he or she uses it affect your own creativity, morale, and willingness to stay with the organization? In addition, identify approaches you will use to enhance your power as you move up your career ladder. Explain why you chose these approaches.

- **Emotional Intelligence:** The chapter identifies the five components of emotional intelligence (self-awareness, self-regulation, motivation, empathy, and social skills). How do you rate yourself on each of these components? What steps can you take to improve your emotional intelligence and achieve greater career success?

- **Creating an Ethical Organization:** Identify an ethical dilemma that you personally faced in the course of your work. How did you respond to it? Was your response compliance-based, integrity-based, or even unethical? If your behavior was compliance-based, speculate on how it would have been different if it were integrity-based. What have you learned from your experience that would make you a more ethical leader in the future?

summary

Strategic leadership is vital in ensuring that strategies are formulated and implemented in an effective manner. Leaders must play a central role in performing three critical and interdependent activities: setting the direction, designing the organization, and nurturing a culture committed to excellence and ethical behavior. If leaders ignore or are ineffective at performing any one of the three, the organization will not be very successful. We identified two elements of leadership that contribute to success—overcoming barriers to change and using power effectively.

For leaders to effectively fulfill their activities, emotional intelligence (EI) is very important. Five elements that contribute to EI are self-awareness, self-regulation, motivation, empathy, and social skill. The first three elements pertain to self-management skills, whereas the last two are associated with a person's ability to manage relationships with others. We addressed some of the potential drawbacks from the ineffective use of EI. These include the dysfunctional use of power as well as a tendency to become overly empathetic, which may result in unreasonably lowered performance expectations.

Leaders need to play a central role in creating a learning organization. Gone are the days when the top-level managers "think" and everyone else in the organization "does." With rapidly changing, unpredictable, and complex competitive environments, leaders must engage everyone in the ideas and energies of people throughout the organization. Great ideas can come from anywhere in the organization—from the executive suite to the factory floor. The five elements that we discussed as central to a learning organization are inspiring and motivating people with a mission or purpose, empowering people at all levels throughout the organization, accumulating and sharing internal knowledge, gathering external information, and challenging the status quo to stimulate creativity.

In the final section of the chapter, we addressed a leader's central role in instilling ethical behavior in the organization. We discussed the enormous costs that firms face when ethical crises arise—costs in terms of financial and reputational loss as well as the erosion of human capital and relationships with suppliers, customers, society at large, and governmental agencies. And, as we would expect, the benefits of having a strong ethical organization are also numerous. We contrasted compliance-based and integrity-based approaches to organizational ethics. Compliance-based approaches are largely externally motivated; that is, they are motivated by the fear of punishment for doing something that is unlawful. Integrity-based approaches, on the other hand, are driven by a personal and organizational commitment to ethical behavior. We also addressed the four key elements of an ethical organization: role models, corporate credos and codes of conduct, reward and evaluation systems, and policies and procedures.

SUMMARY REVIEW QUESTIONS

1. Three key activities—setting a direction, designing the organization, and nurturing a culture and ethics—are all part of what effective leaders do on a regular basis. Explain how these three activities are interrelated.

2. Define emotional intelligence (EI). What are the key elements of EI? Why is EI so important to successful strategic leadership? Address potential "downsides."

3. The knowledge a firm possesses can be a source of competitive advantage. Describe ways that a firm can continuously learn to maintain its competitive position.
4. How can the five central elements of "learning organizations" be incorporated into global companies?
5. What are the benefits to firms and their shareholders of conducting business in an ethical manner?
6. Firms that fail to behave in an ethical manner can incur high costs. What are these costs, and what is their source?
7. What are the most important differences between an "integrity organization" and a "compliance organization" in a firm's approach to organizational ethics?
8. What are some of the important mechanisms for promoting ethics in a firm?

key terms

leadership 350
setting a direction 351
designing the organization 351
excellent and ethical organizational culture 352
barriers to change 355
vested interest in the status quo 355
systemic barriers 355
behavioral barriers 356
political barriers 356
personal time constraints 356
power 356

organizational bases of power 356
personal bases of power 357
emotional intelligence (EI) 358
learning organizations 363
benchmarking 366
competitive benchmarking 366
functional benchmarking 366
ethics 368
organizational ethics 368
ethical orientation 368
compliance-based ethics programs 370
integrity-based ethics programs 370
corporate credo 372

experiential exercise

Select two well-known business leaders—one you admire and one you do not. Evaluate each of them on the five characteristics of emotional intelligence in the table at the bottom of the page.

application questions & exercises

1. Identify two CEOs whose leadership you admire. What is it about their skills, attributes, and effective use of power that causes you to admire them?
2. Founders have an important role in developing their organization's culture and values. At times, their influence persists for many years. Identify and describe two organizations in which the cultures and values established by the founder(s) continue to flourish. You may find research on the Internet helpful in answering this question.
3. Some leaders place a great emphasis on developing superior human capital. In what ways does this help a firm to develop and sustain competitive advantages?
4. In this chapter we discussed the five elements of a "learning organization." Select a firm with which you are familiar and discuss whether or not it epitomizes some (or all) of these elements.

ethics questions

1. Sometimes organizations must go outside the firm to hire talent, thus bypassing employees already working for the firm. Are there conditions under which this might raise ethical considerations?
2. Ethical crises can occur in virtually any organization. Describe some of the systems, procedures, and processes that can help to prevent such crises.

Emotional Intelligence Characteristics	Admired Leader	Leader Not Admired
Self-awareness		
Self-regulation		
Motivation		
Empathy		
Social skills		

references

1. Dolan, K. 2014. How to blow $9 billion. *Forbes,* July 21: 74–77; Woo, E. 2002. Peter Stroh, 74, head of brewery, philanthropist. *latimes.com,* September 21: np; and Anonymous. 2014. How to lose $700 million: The rise and fall of Stroh's. *finance.yahoo.com,* July 15: np.

2. Charan, R. & Colvin, G. 1999. Why CEOs fail. *Fortune,* June 21: 68–78.

3. Yukl, G. 2008. How leaders influence organizational effectiveness. *Leadership Quarterly,* 19(6): 708–722.

4. These three activities and our discussion draw from Kotter, J. P. 1990. What leaders really do. *Harvard Business Review,* 68(3): 103–111; Pearson, A. E. 1990. Six basics for general managers. *Harvard Business Review,* 67(4): 94–101; and Covey, S. R. 1996. Three roles of the leader in the new paradigm. In Hesselbein, F., Goldsmith, M., & Beckhard, R. (Eds.), *The leader of the future:* 149–160. San Francisco: Jossey-Bass. Some of the discussion of each of the three leadership activity concepts draws on Dess, G. G. & Miller, A. 1993. *Strategic management:* 320–325. New York: McGraw-Hill.

5. García-Morales, V. J., Lloréns-Montes, F. J., & Verdú-Jover, A. J. 2008. The effects of transformational leadership on organizational performance through knowledge and innovation. *British Journal of Management,* 19(4): 299–319.

6. Martin, R. 2010. The execution trap. *Harvard Business Review,* 88(7/8): 64–71.

7. Collins, J. 1997. What comes next? *Inc.,* October: 34–45.

8. Hsieh, T. 2010. Zappos's CEO on going to extremes for customers. *Harvard Business Review,* 88(7/8): 41–44.

9. Chesky, B. 2014. Don't f*ck up the culture. *linkedin.com,* April 24: np.

10. Anonymous. 2006. Looking out for number one. *BusinessWeek,* October 30: 66.

11. Schaffer, R. H. 2010. Mistakes leaders keep making. *Harvard Business Review,* 88(9): 86–91.

12. For insightful perspectives on escalation, refer to Brockner, J. 1992. The escalation of commitment to a failing course of action. *Academy of Management Review,* 17(1): 39–61; and Staw, B. M. 1976. Knee-deep in the big muddy: A study of commitment to a chosen course of action. *Organizational Behavior and Human Decision Processes,* 16: 27–44. The discussion of systemic, behavioral, and political barriers draws on Lorange, P. & Murphy, D. 1984. Considerations in implementing strategic control. *Journal of Business Strategy,* 5: 27–35. In a similar vein, Noel M. Tichy has addressed three types of resistance to change in the context of General Electric: technical resistance, political resistance, and cultural resistance. See Tichy, N. M. 1993. Revolutionize your company. *Fortune,* December 13: 114–118. Examples draw from O'Reilly, B. 1997. The secrets of America's most admired corporations: New ideas and new products. *Fortune,* March 3: 60–64.

13. Davis, I. 2014. Lou Gerstner on corporate reinvention and values. *mckinsey.com,* September: np.

14. This section draws on Champoux, J. E. 2000. *Organizational behavior: Essential tenets for a new millennium.* London: South-Western; and The mature use of power in organizations. 2003. *RHR International-Executive Insights,* May 29, *12.19.168.197/execinsights/8-3.htm.*

15. An insightful perspective on the role of power and politics in organizations is provided in Ciampa, K. 2005. Almost ready: How leaders move up. *Harvard Business Review,* 83(1): 46–53.

16. Pfeffer, J. 2010. Power play. *Harvard Business Review,* 88(7/8): 84–92.

17. Westphal, J. D., & Graebner, M. E. 2010. A matter of appearances: How corporate leaders manage the impressions of financial analysts about the conduct of their boards. *Academy of Management Journal,* 53(4): 15–44.

18. A discussion of the importance of persuasion in bringing about change can be found in Garvin, D. A. & Roberto, M. A. 2005. Change through persuasion. *Harvard Business Review,* 83(4): 104–113.

19. Lorsch, J. W. & Tierney, T. J. 2002. *Aligning the stars: How to succeed when professionals drive results.* Boston: Harvard Business School Press.

20. Some consider EI to be a "trait," that is, an attribute that is stable over time. However, many authors, including Daniel Goleman, have argued that it can be developed through motivation, extended practice, and feedback. For example, in D. Goleman, 1998, What makes a leader? *Harvard Business Review,* 76(5): 97, Goleman addresses this issue in a sidebar: "Can emotional intelligence be learned?"

21. For a review of this literature, see Daft, R. 1999. *Leadership: Theory and practice.* Fort Worth, TX: Dryden Press.

22. EI has its roots in the concept of "social intelligence" that was first identified by E. L. Thorndike in 1920 (Intelligence and its uses. *Harper's Magazine,* 140: 227–235). Psychologists have been uncovering other intelligences for some time now and have grouped them into such clusters as abstract intelligence (the ability to understand and manipulate verbal and mathematical symbols), concrete intelligence (the ability to understand and manipulate objects), and social intelligence (the ability to understand and relate to people). See Ruisel, I. 1992. Social intelligence: Conception and methodological problems. *Studia Psychologica,* 34(4–5): 281–296. Refer to *trochim.human.cornell.edu/gallery.*

23. Joseph, D. & Newman, D. 2010. Emotional intelligence: An integrative meta-analysis and cascading model. *Journal of Applied Psychology,* 95(1): 54–78; Brusman, M. 2013. Leadership effectiveness through emotional intelligence. *workingresourcesblog.com,* September 18: np; and Bradberry, T. 2015. Why your boss lacks emotional intelligence. *forbes.com,* January 6: np.

24. Tate, B. 2008. A longitudinal study of the relationships among self-monitoring, authentic leadership, and perceptions of leadership. *Journal of Leadership & Organizational Studies,* 15(1): 16–29.

25. Moss, S. A., Dowling, N., & Callanan, J. 2009. Towards an integrated model of leadership and self-regulation. *Leadership Quarterly,* 20(2): 162–176.

26. An insightful perspective on leadership, which involves

discovering, developing, and celebrating what is unique about each individual, is found in Buckingham, M. 2005. What great managers do. *Harvard Business Review,* 83(3): 70–79.

27. Bryant, A. 2011. *The corner office:* 197. New York: St. Martin's Griffin.

28. This section draws upon Klemp. G. 2005. *Emotional intelligence and leadership: What really matters.* Cambria Consulting, Inc., *www.cambriaconsulting.com.*

29. Heifetz, R. 2004. Question authority. *Harvard Business Review,* 82(1): 37.

30. Senge, P. M. 1990. The leader's new work: Building learning organizations. *Sloan Management Review,* 32(1): 7–23.

31. Bernoff, J. & Schandler, T. 2010. Empowered. *Harvard Business Review,* 88(7/8): 94–101.

32. Hammer, M. & Stanton, S. A. 1997. The power of reflection. *Fortune,* November 24: 291–296.

33. Hannah, S. T. & Lester, P. B. 2009. A multilevel approach to building and leading learning organizations. *Leadership Quarterly,* 20(1): 34–48.

34. For some guidance on how to effectively bring about change in organizations, refer to Wall, S. J. 2005. The protean organization: Learning to love change. *Organizational Dynamics,* 34(1): 37–46.

35. Covey, S. R. 1989. *The seven habits of highly effective people: Powerful lessons in personal change.* New York: Simon & Schuster.

36. Kouzes, J. M. & Posner, B. Z. 2009. To lead, create a shared vision. *Harvard Business Review,* 87(1): 20–21.

37. Ibid.

38. Gurdjian, P. & Halbeisen, T. 2014. Why leadership-development programs fail. *mckinsey.com,* January: np.

39. Melrose, K. 1995. *Making the grass greener on your side: A CEO's journey to leading by servicing.* San Francisco: Barrett-Koehler.

40. Tekleab, A. G., Sims, H. P., Jr., Yun, S., Tesluk, P. E., & Cox, J. 2008. Are we on the same page? Effects of self-awareness of empowering and transformational leadership. *Journal of Leadership & Organizational Studies,* 14(3): 185–201.

41. Helgesen, S. 1996. Leading from the grass roots. In Hesselbein et al., The *leader of the future:* 19–24. San Francisco: Jossey-Bass.

42. Bowen, D. E. & Lawler, E. E., III. 1995. Empowering service employees. *Sloan Management Review,* 37: 73–84.

43. Easterby-Smith, M. & Prieto, I. M. 2008. Dynamic capabilities and knowledge management: An integrative role for learning? *British Journal of Management,* 19(3): 235–249.

44. Schafer, S. 1997. Battling a labor shortage? It's all in your imagination. *Inc.,* August: 24.

45. Meyer, P. 1998. So you want the president's job . . . *Business Horizons,* January–February: 2–8.

46. The introductory discussion of benchmarking draws on Miller, A. 1998. *Strategic management:* 142–143. New York: McGraw-Hill.

47. Sedgwick, D. 2014. Ford and suppliers jointly benchmark competitors' vehicles. *automotivenews.com,* October 19: np.

48. Main, J. 1992. How to steal the best ideas around. *Fortune,* October 19: 102–106.

49. Sheff, D. 1996. Levi's changes everything. *Fast Company,* June–July: 65–74.

50. Holt, J. W. 1996. *Celebrate your mistakes.* New York: McGraw-Hill.

51. McGregor, J. 2006. How failure breeds success. *Bloomberg Businessweek,* July 10: 42–52.

52. Bryant, A. 2011. *The corner office:* 34. New York: St. Martin's Griffin.

53. This opening discussion draws upon Conley, J. H. 2000. Ethics in business. In Helms, M. M. (Ed.), *Encyclopedia of management* (4th ed.): 281–285. Farmington Hills, MI: Gale Group; Paine, L. S. 1994. Managing for organizational integrity. *Harvard Business Review,* 72(2): 106–117; and Carlson, D. S. & Perrewe, P. L. 1995. Institutionalization of organizational ethics through transformational leadership. *Journal of Business Ethics,* 14: 829–838.

54. Pinto, J., Leana, C. R., & Pil, F. K. 2008. Corrupt organizations or organizations of corrupt individuals? Two types of organization-level corruption. *Academy of Management Review,* 33(3): 685–709.

55. Soule, E. 2002. Managerial moral strategies—In search of a few good principles. *Academy of Management Review,* 27(1): 114–124.

56. Carlson & Perrewe, op. cit.

57. This discussion is based upon Paine, Managing for organizational integrity; Paine, L. S. 1997. *Cases in leadership, ethics, and organizational integrity: A Strategic approach.* Burr Ridge, IL: Irwin; and Fontrodona, J. 2002. Business ethics across the Atlantic. Business Ethics Direct, *www.ethicsa.org/BED_art_fontrodone.html.*

58. For more on operationalizing capabilities to sustain an ethical framework, see Largay, J. A., III, & Zhang, R. 2008. Do CEOs worry about being fired when making investment decisions? *Academy of Management Perspectives,* 22(1): 60–61.

59. See *www.ti.com/corp/docs/company/citizen/ethics/benchmark.shtml;* and *www.ti.com/corp/docs/company/citizen/ethics/quicktest.shtml.*

60. Bryant, A. 2011. *The corner office:* 91. New York: St. Martin's Griffin.

61. Wetlaufer, S. 1999. Organizing for empowerment: An interview with AES's Roger Sant and Dennis Bakke. *Harvard Business Review,* 77(1): 110–126.

62. For an insightful, academic perspective on the impact of ethics codes on executive decision making, refer to Stevens, J. M., Steensma, H. K., Harrison, D. A., & Cochran, P. S. 2005. Symbolic or substantive document? The influence of ethics code on financial executives' decisions. *Strategic Management Journal,* 26(2): 181–195.

63. Paine, Managing for organizational integrity.

64. For a study on the effects of goal setting on unethical behavior, read Schweitzer, M. E., Ordonez, L., & Douma, B. 2004. Goal setting as a motivator of unethical behavior. *Academy of Management Journal,* 47(3): 422–432.

65. Williams, R. 2012. How competition can encourage unethical business practices. *business.financialpost.com,* July 31: np.

66. Fulmer, R. M. 2004. The challenge of ethical leadership. *Organizational Dynamics,* 33(3): 307–317.

67. *www.sarbanes-oxley.com.*

Managing Innovation and Fostering Corporate Entrepreneurship

After reading this chapter, you should have a good understanding of the following learning objectives:

LO12.1 The importance of implementing strategies and practices that foster innovation.

LO12.2 The challenges and pitfalls of managing corporate innovation processes.

LO12.3 How corporations use new venture teams, business incubators, and product champions to create an internal environment and culture that promote entrepreneurial development.

LO12.4 How corporate entrepreneurship achieves both financial goals and strategic goals.

LO12.5 The benefits and potential drawbacks of real options analysis in making resource deployment decisions in corporate entrepreneurship contexts.

LO12.6 How an entrepreneurial orientation can enhance a firm's efforts to develop promising corporate venture initiatives.

Learning from Mistakes

If you ask a group of students to name a successful company, Google is likely to be one of the first firms mentioned. It dominates online search and advertising, has developed a successful browser, and developed the operating system that powers 85 percent of the smartphones sold in the second quarter of 2014.[1] Its success is evident in its stock price, which rose from about $150 in early 2009 to over $525 a share in early 2015. But that doesn't mean that Google has been successful at all it has tried. One of Google's most notable failures occurred when it tried to venture outside the online and wireless markets. In 2006, Google decided to expand its advertising business to radio advertising. After spending several hundred million dollars on its entrepreneurial effort in the radio advertising market, Google pulled the plug on this business in 2009.

Google saw great potential in applying its business model to the radio advertising industry. In the traditional radio advertising model, companies that wished to advertise their products and services contracted with an advertising agency to develop a set of radio spots (commercials). They then bought blocks of advertising time from radio stations. Advertisers paid based on the number of listeners on each station. Google believed that it could develop a stronger model. Its design was to purchase large blocks of advertising time from stations. It would then sell the time in a competitive auction to companies that wished to advertise. Google believed it could sell ad time to advertisers at a higher rate if it could identify what ads on what stations had the greatest impact for advertisers. Thus, rather than charging based on audience size, Google would follow the model it used on the web and charge based on ad effectiveness. To develop the competency to measure ad effectiveness, Google purchased dMarc, a company that developed technology to manage and measure radio ads, for $102 million.

Google's overall vision was even broader. The company also planned to enter print and TV advertising. It could then provide a "dashboard" to marketing executives at firms that would provide information on the effectiveness of advertising on the web, on TV, in print, and on radio. Google would then sell them a range of advertising space among all four to maximize a firm's ad expenditures.

However, Google found that its attempt to innovate the radio market bumped up against two core challenges. First, the radio advertising model was based much more on relationships than online advertising was. Radio stations, advertising firms, and advertising agencies had long-standing relationships that limited Google's ability to break into the market. In fact, few radio stations were willing to sell advertising time to Google. Also, advertising agencies saw Google as a threat to their business model and were unwilling to buy time from Google. Second, Google found that its ability to measure the effectiveness of radio ads was limited. Unlike the case with online markets, where it could measure whether people clicked on ads, the company found it difficult to measure whether listeners responded to ads. Google tried ads that mentioned specific websites that listeners could go to, but it found few people accessed these sites. In the end, Google was able to sell radio time at only a fraction of what radio stations could get from working their traditional advertising deals. This led stations to abandon Google's radio business.

Google found that it had the initiative to innovate the radio market but didn't have the knowledge, experience, or social connections needed to win in this market.

Discussion Questions

1. Why didn't the lessons Google learned in the online advertising market apply to the radio market?
2. Radio is increasingly moving to satellite and streaming systems. Is this a new opportunity for Google, or should it steer clear of radio altogether?

LO12.1

The importance of implementing strategies and practices that foster innovation.

Managing change is one of the most important functions performed by strategic leaders. There are two major avenues through which companies can expand or improve their business—innovation and corporate entrepreneurship. These two activities go hand-in-hand because they both have similar aims. The first is strategic renewal. Innovations help an organization stay fresh and reinvent itself as conditions in the business environment change. This is why managing innovation is such an important strategic implementation issue. The second is the pursuit of venture opportunities. Innovative breakthroughs, as well as new product concepts, evolving technologies, and shifting demand, create opportunities for corporate venturing. In this chapter we will explore these topics—how change and innovation can stimulate strategic renewal and foster corporate entrepreneurship.

Managing Innovation

innovation
the use of new knowledge to transform organizational processes or create commercially viable products and services.

One of the most important sources of growth opportunities is innovation. **Innovation** involves using new knowledge to transform organizational processes or create commercially viable products and services. The sources of new knowledge may include the latest technology, the results of experiments, creative insights, or competitive information. However it comes about, innovation occurs when new combinations of ideas and information bring about positive change.

The emphasis on newness is a key point. For example, for a patent application to have any chance of success, one of the most important attributes it must possess is novelty. You can't patent an idea that has been copied. This is a central idea. In fact, the root of the word *innovation* is the Latin *novus,* which means "new." Innovation involves introducing or changing to something new.[2]

Among the most important sources of new ideas is new technology. Technology creates new possibilities. Technology provides the raw material that firms use to make innovative products and services. But technology is not the only source of innovations. There can be innovations in human resources, firm infrastructure, marketing, service, or many other value-adding areas that have little to do with anything "high-tech." Strategy Spotlight 12.1 highlights a simple but effective innovation by Dutch Boy paints. As the Dutch Boy example suggests, innovation can take many forms.

Types of Innovation

Although innovations are not always high-tech, changes in technology can be an important source of change and growth. When an innovation is based on a sweeping new technology, it often has a more far-reaching impact. Sometimes even a small innovation can add value and create competitive advantages. Innovation can and should occur throughout an organization—in every department and all aspects of the value chain.

product innovation
efforts to create product designs and applications of technology to develop new products for end users.

One distinction that is often used when discussing innovation is between process innovation and product innovation.[3] **Product innovation** refers to efforts to create product designs and applications of technology to develop new products for end users. Recall from Chapter 5 how generic strategies were typically different depending on the stage of the industry life cycle. Product innovations tend to be more common during the earlier stages of an industry's life cycle. Product innovations are also commonly associated with a differentiation strategy. Firms that differentiate by providing customers with new products or services that offer unique features or quality enhancements often engage in product innovation.

process innovation
efforts to improve the efficiency of organizational processes, especially manufacturing systems and operations.

Process innovation, by contrast, is typically associated with improving the efficiency of an organizational process, especially manufacturing systems and operations. By drawing on new technologies and an organization's accumulated experience (Chapter 5), firms

DUTCH BOY'S SIMPLE PAINT CAN INNOVATION

Sometimes a simple change can make a vast improvement in a product. Any painter knows that getting the paint can open and pouring out paint without drips are two of the challenges of painting. Dutch Boy addressed this issue by developing a twist and pour paint container. The all-plastic container has a large, easy-to-use twist-off top and a handle on the side. The result was a consumer-friendly product that made painting easier and less messy. The handle also reduces the need for a paint stirring stick since you can mix the paint by shaking the container. Even though Dutch Boy's innovation was simple and nontechnological and had nothing to do with the core product, the launch of the new packaging led to articles in 30 national consumer magazines and 60 major newspapers as well as a story on *Good Morning America*. The Twist and Pour can was also named "Product of the Year" by *USA Today, Bloomberg Businessweek,* and *Better Homes & Gardens.* It was also named a winner of the 2011 Good Housekeeping VIP Awards, which commemorate the most innovative products from the past decade.

Sources: 11 innovative products from the past decade. 2011 *The Good Housekeeping Research Institute;* and www.fallscommunications.com.

can often improve materials utilization, shorten cycle time, and increase quality. Process innovations are more likely to occur in the later stages of an industry's life cycle as companies seek ways to remain viable in markets where demand has flattened out and competition is more intense. As a result, process innovations are often associated with overall cost leader strategies, because the aim of many process improvements is to lower the costs of operations.

Another way to view the impact of an innovation is in terms of its degree of innovativeness, which falls somewhere on a continuum that extends from incremental to radical.[4]

- **Radical innovations** produce fundamental changes by evoking major departures from existing practices. These breakthrough innovations usually occur because of technological change. They tend to be highly disruptive and can transform a company or even revolutionize a whole industry. They may lead to products or processes that can be patented, giving a firm a strong competitive advantage. Examples include electricity, the telephone, the transistor, desktop computers, fiber optics, artificial intelligence, and genetically engineered drugs.

- **Incremental innovations** enhance existing practices or make small improvements in products and processes. They may represent evolutionary applications within existing paradigms of earlier, more radical innovations. Because they often sustain a company by extending or expanding its product line or manufacturing skills, incremental innovations can be a source of competitive advantage by providing new capabilities that minimize expenses or speed productivity. Examples include frozen food, sports drinks, steel-belted radial tires, electronic bookkeeping, shatterproof glass, and digital thermometers.

radical innovation
an innovation that fundamentally changes existing practices.

incremental innovation
an innovation that enhances existing practices or makes small improvements in products and processes.

Some innovations are highly radical; others are only slightly incremental. But most innovations fall somewhere between these two extremes (see Exhibit 12.1).

Harvard Business School Professor Clayton M. Christensen identified another useful approach to characterize types of innovations.[5] Christensen draws a distinction between sustaining and disruptive innovations. *Sustaining innovations* are those that extend sales in an existing market, usually by enabling new products or services to be sold at higher margins. Such innovations may include either incremental or radical innovations. For example, the Internet was a breakthrough technology that transformed retail selling. But rather than disrupting the activities of catalog companies such as Lands' End and L.L. Bean, the Internet energized their existing business by extending their reach and making their operations more efficient.

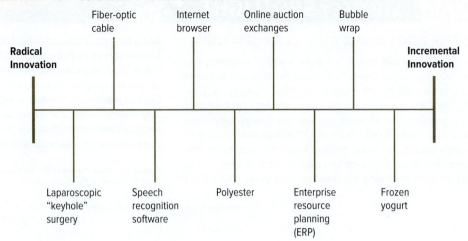

EXHIBIT 12.1 Continuum of Radical and Incremental Innovations

By contrast, *disruptive innovations* are those that overturn markets by providing an altogether new approach to meeting customer needs. The features of a disruptive innovation make it somewhat counterintuitive. Disruptive innovations:

- Are technologically simpler and less sophisticated than currently available products or services.
- Appeal to less demanding customers who are seeking more convenient, less expensive solutions.
- Take time to take effect and only become disruptive once they have taken root in a new market or low-end part of an existing market.

Christensen cites Walmart and Southwest Airlines as two disruptive examples. Walmart started with a single store, Southwest with a few flights. But because they both represented major departures from existing practices and tapped into unmet needs, they steadily grew into ventures that appealed to a new category of customers and eventually overturned the status quo. "Instead of sustaining the trajectory of improvement that has been established in a market," says Christensen, a disruptive innovation "disrupts it and redefines it by bringing to the market something that is simpler."[6]

Spotlight 12.2 discusses how a new technology, graphene, may disrupt the electronics and computer industries.

Innovation is both a force in the external environment (technology, competition) and a factor affecting a firm's internal choices (generic strategy, value-adding activities).[7] Nevertheless, innovation can be quite difficult for some firms to manage, especially those that have become comfortable with the status quo.

Challenges of Innovation

LO12.2

The challenges and pitfalls of managing corporate innovation processes.

Innovation is essential to sustaining competitive advantages. Recall from Chapter 3 that one of the four elements of the balanced scorecard is the innovation and learning perspective. The extent and success of a company's innovation efforts are indicators of its overall performance. As management guru Peter Drucker warned, "An established company which, in an age demanding innovation, is not capable of innovation is doomed to decline and extinction."[8] In today's competitive environment, most firms have only one choice: "Innovate or die."

As with change, however, firms are often resistant to innovation. Only those companies that actively pursue innovation, even though it is often difficult and uncertain, will get a payoff from their innovation efforts. But managing innovation is challenging.[9] As former

WILL GRAPHENE RADICALLY CHANGE THE ELECTRONICS INDUSTRY?

The consumer electronics industry is often thought of as one of the most dynamic industries around, with new product innovations being launched on a regular basis. With this in mind, it is interesting to realize that the base technology standards of the components used to make consumer electronic products have been unchanged for a number of years. For example, the semiconductor chips used in consumer electronics are made from silicon wafers, the same as was the case 30 years ago. The chips have gotten more complex, packed with more and narrower channels in the silicon chip, but the basic technology is the same. Similarly, the screens of devices are primarily LCD panels, which have been widely used in electronic products for over 15 years.

However, a new technology, graphene, may radically change the consumer electronics industry. Graphene, which is produced in a sheet form and is a very thin layer of graphite atoms in a honeycomb lattice, is a product with amazing qualities. In the words of Jeanie Lau, professor of physics at the University of California at Riverside, "Graphene is a wonderful material. It conducts heat 10 times better than copper and electricity, 100 times better than silicon, is transparent like plastic, extremely lightweight, extremely strong, yet flexible and elastic." Additionally, researchers have discovered that they can magnetize graphene. This raises the possibility of building computer systems that use spintronics—that's shorthand for "spin transport electronics." Spintronics involves processing a signal using magnetic spin rather than electric charge. It is still a number of years away, but eventual consumer and business applications for spintronics technology could be faster processors and memory with vastly higher capacities. With such amazing properties, it is not surprising that major players, such as Samsung, have invested heavily in graphene, secured patents related to its use, developed prototypes that use graphene, and plan to produce a number of graphene-based products in the coming years. Its most promising initial use may be as a transparent electrode in monitors, displays, and touch screens. It also has the potential to be used in semiconductor chips in the future, possibly replacing silicon as the primary component of the chip.

As with any radical innovation, it is not yet clear if graphene will live up to its promise. Firms have not yet figured out how to manufacture it on a large scale or at a reasonable cost. It costs around $100 to produce a 1-inch-diameter wafer. There are also questions about whether researchers can figure out how to effectively turn transistors on a graphene chip on and off, an essential element if graphene will ever be used in semiconductor chips. Michael Patterson, CEO of Graphene Frontiers, commented that researchers are "really pushing the edges of technology" with graphene, and it may take 10 years before we know if it will replace current technologies.

Sources: Noyes, K. 2014. The business potential of (amazing, wonderful, futuristic) graphene. *cnnmoney.com*, May 12: np; and Whitwam, R., 2015. Researchers make graphene magnetic, clearing the way for faster everything. *extremetech.com*, January 29: np.

Pfizer former chairman and CEO William Steere puts it: "In some ways, managing innovation is analogous to breaking in a spirited horse. You are never sure of success until you achieve your goal. In the meantime, everyone takes a few lumps."[10]

What is it that makes innovation so difficult? The uncertainty about outcomes is one factor. Companies are often reluctant to invest time and resources in activities with an unknown future. Another factor is that the innovation process involves so many choices. These choices present five dilemmas that companies must wrestle with when pursuing innovation:[11]

- *Seeds versus weeds.* Most companies have an abundance of innovative ideas. They must decide which of these is most likely to bear fruit—the "seeds"—and which should be cast aside—the "weeds." This is complicated by the fact that some innovation projects require a considerable level of investment before a firm can fully evaluate whether they are worth pursuing. Firms need a mechanism with which they can choose among various innovation projects.
- *Experience versus initiative.* Companies must decide who will lead an innovation project. Senior managers may have experience and credibility but tend to be more risk-averse. Midlevel employees, who may be the innovators themselves, may have more enthusiasm because they can see firsthand how an innovation would address specific problems. Firms need to support and reward organizational members who bring new ideas to light.
- *Internal versus external staffing.* Innovation projects need competent staffs to succeed. People drawn from inside the company may have greater social capital

PROCTER & GAMBLE STRIVES TO REMAIN INNOVATIVE

From the development of Ivory Soap in 1879; to Crisco Oil, the first all-vegetable shortening, in 1911; to Crest, the first fluoridated toothpaste in 1955; to the stackable Pringles chips in 1968; to the Swiffer mop in 1998, Procter & Gamble (P&G) has long been known as a successful innovative firm. It led the market with these products and used these innovative products to build up its position as a differentiated consumer products firm. By all measures, P&G is a very successful company and was honored as the Fifth Most Admired Company by *Fortune* magazine in 2012. Still, P&G has found it challenging to remain innovative. The last major innovative blockbuster product P&G launched was Crest Whitestrips, and this product was introduced in 2001. Instead, in recent years, its new products have been extensions of current products, such as adding whitening flecks to Crest toothpaste, or derivatives of current products, such as taking the antihistamine in Nyquil and using it as a sleeping aid, labeled ZzzQuil. With ZzzQuil, P&G is not an innovator in this market, since there were a number of earlier entrants in the sleep market, such as Johnson & Johnson with its Tylenol PM product. One portfolio manager at a mutual fund derided the ZzzQuil product, saying, "It's a sign of what passes for innovation at P&G. It's not enough. It's incremental, derivative."

The factors leading to P&G's struggles to remain innovative should not be surprising. They largely grow out of the success the firm has had. First, with its wide range of products, P&G has a wide range of potential new product extensions and derivatives from which to choose. Though these are unlikely to be blockbusters, they look much safer than truly new innovative ideas. Second, while lower-level managers at P&G may be excited about new, innovative ideas, the division heads of P&G units, who are responsible for developing new products, are likely to shy away from big-bet product launches. These unit heads are also responsible for and rewarded on current division performance, a metric that will be negatively affected by the large costs associated with developing and marketing truly innovative new products. Third, due to its large size, P&G moved R&D responsibilities down to the divisions. While this enhances the divisions' abilities to quickly launch incrementally new products, it doesn't facilitate the collaboration across units often needed to develop boldly new products.

P&G is trying to address these issues by centralizing 20 to 30 percent of its research efforts within a new corporate-level business creation and innovation unit. Having a corporate effort at innovation separates the budget for product development from divisional profit numbers, enhancing the firm's willingness to invest in long-term product development efforts. Also, the corporate unit will be able to foster collaboration between units to develop blockbuster products.

Sources: Coleman-Lochner, L. & Hymowitz, C. 2012. At P&G, the innovation well runs dry. *Bloomberg Businessweek*, September 10: 24–26; and Bussey, J. 2012. The innovator's enigma. *wsj.com*, October 4: np.

and know the organization's culture and routines. But this knowledge may actually inhibit them from thinking outside the box. Staffing innovation projects with external personnel requires that project managers justify the hiring and spend time recruiting, training, and relationship building. Firms need to streamline and support the process of staffing innovation efforts.

- *Building capabilities versus collaborating.* Innovation projects often require new sets of skills. Firms can seek help from other departments and/or partner with other companies that bring resources and experience as well as share costs of development. However, such arrangements can create dependencies and inhibit internal skills development. Further, struggles over who contributed the most or how the benefits of the project are to be allocated may arise. Firms need a mechanism for forging links with outside parties to the innovation process.

- *Incremental versus preemptive launch.* Companies must manage the timing and scale of new innovation projects. An incremental launch is less risky because it requires fewer resources and serves as a market test. But a launch that is too tentative can undermine the project's credibility. It also opens the door for a competitive response. A large-scale launch requires more resources, but it can effectively preempt a competitive response. Firms need to make funding and management arrangements that allow for projects to hit the ground running, and they need to be responsive to market feedback.

These dilemmas highlight why the innovation process can be daunting even for highly successful firms. Strategy Spotlight 12.3 discusses how Procter & Gamble has been struggling with these challenges to improve its innovativeness. Next, we consider five steps that firms can take to improve the innovation process within the firm.[12]

Cultivating Innovation Skills

Some firms, such as Apple, Google, and Amazon, regularly produce innovative products and services, while other firms struggle to generate new, marketable products. What separates these innovative firms from the rest of the pack? Jeff Dyer, Hal Gregersen, and Clayton Christensen argue it is the innovative DNA of the leaders of these firms.[13] The leaders of these firms have exhibited "discovery skills" that allow them to see the potential in innovations and to move the organization forward in leveraging the value of those innovations.[14] These leaders spend 50 percent more time on these discovery activities than the leaders of less innovative firms. To improve their innovative processes, firms need to cultivate the innovation skills of their managers.

The key attribute that firms need to develop in their managers in order to improve their innovative potential is creative intelligence. Creative intelligence is driven by a core skill of associating—the ability to see patterns in data and integrate different questions, information, and insights—and four patterns of action: questioning, observing, experimenting, and networking. As managers practice the four patterns of action, they will begin to develop the skill of association. Dyer and his colleagues offer the following illustration to demonstrate that individuals using these skills are going to develop more creative, higher-potential innovations:

> Imagine that you have an identical twin, endowed with the same brains and natural talents that you have. You're both given one week to come up with a creative new business-venture idea. During that week, you come up with ideas alone in your room. In contrast, your twin (1) talks with 10 people—including an engineer, a musician, a stay-at-home dad, and a designer—about the venture, (2) visits three innovative start-ups to observe what they do, (3) samples five "new to the market" products, (4) shows a prototype he's built to five people, and (5) asks the questions "What if I tried this?" and "Why do you do that?" at least 10 times each day during these networking, observing, and experimenting activities. Who do you bet will come up with the more innovative (and doable) ideas?

The point is that by questioning, observing, experimenting, and networking as part of the innovative process, managers will not only make better innovation decisions now but, more importantly, start to build the innovative DNA needed to be more successful innovators in the future. As they get into the practice of these habits, decision makers will see opportunities and be more creative as they associate information from different parts of their life, different people they come in contact with, and different parts of their organizations. The ability to innovate is not hard-wired into our brains at birth. Research suggests that only one-third of our ability to think creatively is genetic. The other two-thirds is developed over time. Neuroscience research indicates that the brain is "plastic," meaning it changes over time due to experiences. As managers build up the ability to ask creative questions, develop a wealth of experiences from diverse settings, and link together insights from different arenas of their lives, their brains will follow suit and will build the ability to easily see situations creatively and draw upon a wide range of experiences and knowledge to identify creative solutions. The five traits of the effective innovator are described and examples of each trait are presented in Exhibit 12.2.

Defining the Scope of Innovation

Firms must have a means to focus their innovation efforts. By defining the "strategic envelope"—the scope of a firm's innovation efforts—firms ensure that their innovation efforts are not wasted on projects that are outside the firm's domain of interest. Strategic enveloping defines the range of acceptable projects. A **strategic envelope** creates a firm-specific view of innovation that defines how a firm can create new knowledge and learn from an

strategic envelope
a firm-specific view of innovation that defines how a firm can create new knowledge and learn from an innovation initiative even if the project fails.

EXHIBIT 12.2 The Innovator's DNA

Trait	Description	Example
Associating	Innovators have the ability to connect seemingly unrelated questions, problems, and ideas from different fields. This allows them to creatively see opportunities that others miss.	Pierre Omidyar saw the opportunity that led to eBay when he linked three items: (1) a personal fascination with creating more efficient markets, (2) his fiancee's desire to locate hard-to-find collectible Pez dispensers, and (3) the ineffectiveness of local classified ads in locating such items.
Questioning	Innovators constantly ask questions that challenge common wisdom. Rather than accept the status quo, they ask "Why not?" or "What if?" This gets others around them to challenge the assumptions that limit the possible range of actions the firm can take.	After witnessing the emergence of eBay and Amazon, Marc Benioff questioned why computer software was still sold in boxes rather than leased with a subscription and downloaded through the Internet. This was the genesis of Salesforce.com, a firm with over $4.1 billion in sales in 2014.
Observing	Discovery-driven executives produce innovative business ideas by observing regular behavior of individuals, especially customers and potential customers. Such observations often identify challenges customers face and previously unidentified opportunities.	From watching his wife struggle to keep track of the family's finances, Intuit founder Scott Cook identified the need for easy-to-use financial software that provided a single place for managing bills, bank accounts, and investments.
Experimenting	Thomas Edison once said, "I haven't failed. I've simply found 10,000 ways that do not work." Innovators regularly experiment with new possibilities, accepting that many of their ideas will fail. Experimentation can include new jobs, living in different countries, and new ideas for their businesses.	Founders Larry Page and Sergey Brin provide time and resources for Google employees to experiment. Some, such as the Android cell phone platform, have been big winners. Others, such as the Orkut and Buzz social networking systems, have failed. But Google will continue to experiment with new products and services.
Networking	Innovators develop broad personal networks. They use this diverse set of individuals to find and test radical ideas. This can be done by developing a diverse set of friends. It can also be done by attending idea conferences where individuals from a broad set of backgrounds come together to share their perspectives and ideas, such as the Technology, Entertainment, and Design (TED) Conference or the Aspen Ideas Festival.	Michael Lazaridis got the idea for a wireless email device that led him to found Research in Motion, now called BlackBerry, from a conference he attended. At the conference, a speaker was discussing a wireless system Coca-Cola was using that allowed vending machines to send a signal when they needed refilling. Lazaridis saw the opportunity to use the same concept with email communications, and the idea for the BlackBerry was hatched.

Source: Adapted from J.H. Dyer, H.G. Gregerson and C.M. Christensen, "The Innovator's DNA," Harvard Business Review, December 2009, pp. 61–67.

innovation initiative even if the project fails. It also gives direction to a firm's innovation efforts, which helps separate seeds from weeds and builds internal capabilities.

One way to determine which projects to work on is to focus on a common technology. Then innovation efforts across the firm can aim at developing skills and expertise in a given technical area. Another potential focus is on a market theme. Consider how DuPont responded to a growing concern for environmentally sensitive products:

> In the early 1990s, DuPont sought to use its knowledge of plastics to identify products to meet a growing market demand for biodegradable products. It conducted numerous experiments with a biodegradable polyester resin it named Biomax. By trying different applications and formulations demanded by potential customers, the company was finally able to create a product that could be produced economically and had market appeal. DuPont has continued to extend the Biomax brand and now produces a large line of environmentally sensitive plastics.[15]

Companies must be clear about not only the kinds of innovation they are looking for but also the expected results. Each company needs to develop a set of questions to ask itself about its innovation efforts:

- How much will the innovation initiative cost?
- How likely is it to actually become commercially viable?
- How much value will it add; that is, what will it be worth if it works?
- What will be learned if it does not pan out?

However a firm envisions its innovation goals, it needs to develop a systematic approach to evaluating its results and learning from its innovation initiatives. Viewing innovation from this perspective helps firms manage the process.[16]

Managing the Pace of Innovation

Along with clarifying the scope of an innovation by defining a strategic envelope, firms also need to regulate the pace of innovation. How long will it take for an innovation initiative to realistically come to fruition? The project timeline of an incremental innovation may be 6 months to 2 years, whereas a more radical innovation is typically long term—10 years or more.[17] Radical innovations often begin with a long period of exploration in which experimentation makes strict timelines unrealistic. In contrast, firms that are innovating incrementally in order to exploit a window of opportunity may use a milestone approach that is more stringently driven by goals and deadlines. This kind of sensitivity to realistic time frames helps companies separate dilemmas temporally so they are easier to manage.

Time pacing can also be a source of competitive advantage because it helps a company manage transitions and develop an internal rhythm.[18] Time pacing does not mean the company ignores the demands of market timing; instead, companies have a sense of their own internal clock in a way that allows them to thwart competitors by controlling the innovation process. With time pacing, the firm works to develop an internal rhythm that matches the buying practices of customers. For example, for years, Intel worked to develop new microprocessor chips every 18 months. The company would have three chips in process at any point in time—one it was producing and selling, one it was currently developing, and one that was just on the drawing board. This pacing also matched the market, because most corporate customers bought new computers about every three years. Thus, customers were then two generations behind in their computing technology, leading them to feel the need to upgrade at the three-year point. In the post-PC era, Apple has developed a similar but faster internal cycle, allowing it to launch a new generation of the iPhone on an annual basis.

This doesn't mean the aim is always to be faster when innovating. Some projects can't be rushed. Companies that hurry their research efforts or go to market before they are ready can damage their ability to innovate—and their reputation. Thus, managing the pace of innovation can be an important factor in long-term success.

Staffing to Capture Value from Innovation

People are central to the processes of identifying, developing, and commercializing innovations effectively. They need broad sets of skills as well as experience—experience working with teams and experience working on successful innovation projects. To capture value from innovation activities, companies must provide strategic decision makers with staff members who make it possible.

This insight led strategy experts Rita Gunther McGrath and Thomas Keil to research the types of human resource management practices that effective firms use to capture value from their innovation efforts.[19] Four practices are especially important:

- Create innovation teams with experienced players who know what it is like to deal with uncertainty and can help new staff members learn venture management skills.

- Require that employees seeking to advance their career with the organization serve in the new venture group as part of their career climb.
- Once people have experience with the new venture group, transfer them to mainstream management positions where they can use their skills and knowledge to revitalize the company's core business.
- Separate the performance of individuals from the performance of the innovation. Otherwise, strong players may feel stigmatized if the innovation effort they worked on fails.

There are other staffing practices that may sound as if they would benefit a firm's innovation activities but may, in fact, be counterproductive:

- Creating a staff that consists only of strong players whose primary experience is related to the company's core business. This provides too few people to deal with the uncertainty of innovation projects and may cause good ideas to be dismissed because they do not appear to fit with the core business.
- Creating a staff that consists only of volunteers who want to work on projects they find interesting. Such players are often overzealous about new technologies or overly attached to product concepts, which can lead to poor decisions about which projects to pursue or drop.
- Creating a climate where innovation team members are considered second-class citizens. In companies where achievements are rewarded, the brightest and most ambitious players may avoid innovation projects with uncertain outcomes.

Unless an organization can align its key players into effective new venture teams, it is unlikely to create any differentiating advantages from its innovation efforts.[20] An enlightened approach to staffing a company's innovation efforts provides one of the best ways to ensure that the challenges of innovation will be effectively met. The nearby Insights from Research box discusses actions a firm can take to enhance the creativity of its employees in order to increase the innovative potential of the firm.

Collaborating with Innovation Partners

It is rare for any one organization to have all the information it needs to carry an innovation from concept to commercialization. Even a company that is highly competent with its current operations usually needs new capabilities to achieve new results. Innovation partners provide the skills and insights that are needed to make innovation projects succeed.[21]

Innovation partners may come from many sources, including research universities and the federal government. Each year the federal government issues requests for proposals (RFPs) asking private companies for assistance in improving services or finding solutions to public problems. Universities are another type of innovation partner. Chip-maker Intel, for example, has benefited from underwriting substantial amounts of university research. Rather than hand universities a blank check, Intel bargains for rights to patents that emerge from Intel-sponsored research. The university retains ownership of the patent, but Intel gets royalty-free use of it.[22]

Strategic partnering requires firms to identify their strengths and weaknesses and make choices about which capabilities to leverage, which need further development, and which are outside the firm's current or projected scope of operations.

To choose partners, firms need to ask what competencies they are looking for and what the innovation partner will contribute.[23] These might include knowledge of markets, technology expertise, or contacts with key players in an industry. Innovation partnerships also typically need to specify how the rewards of the innovation will be shared and who will own the intellectual property that is developed.[24]

Innovation efforts that involve multiple partners and the speed and ease with which partners can network and collaborate are changing the way innovation is conducted.[25] Strategy

STIMULATING YOUR EMPLOYEES' CREATIVITY: WHAT LEADERS CAN DO

Overview

Business leaders consider creativity a prized characteristic in job candidates. The research suggests that qualities of certain individuals predispose them to produce creative work. How leaders interact with these employees can either promote or hinder employee creativity.

What the Research Shows

Are you wondering how to help your employees boost their creativity? Research conducted by scholars at Monash University and Aston University, as well as ISCTE Business School, provides insights into whom organizations should hire and how to best manage employees to promote creativity. The researchers carried out a questionnaire study of 213 employees and 49 leaders in manufacturing companies in China. This study, published in a 2012 article in the *Journal of Organizational Behavior,* found that employees are generally motivated at work by the achievement of one of two types of goals: Employees driven to achieve positive outcomes such as career advancement and growth were referred to as having a *promotion focus,* and employees whose goals push them to achieve personal security or to fulfill a duty or obligation were referred to as having a *prevention focus.*

Overall, employees with a promotion focus were more creative than employees with a prevention focus. Leaders can improve promotion-focused employees' creativity even further when they allow employees to participate in company decision-making processes and engage employees in intellectually stimulating leadership practices. For instance, they can encourage employees to come up with new ways to complete work tasks.

By hiring the right employees and engaging them through effective management practices, leaders can encourage their employees to flex their creative muscles.

Why This Matters

The results of this research suggest that if you want employees to be innovative, first make sure that you hire people with a promotion focus—those motivated by the achievement of career advancement, growth, and positive outcomes. With that in mind, HR procedures could feature personnel selection processes such as personality diagnostic tests and interview questions to help you, as the hiring manager, understand the promotion or prevention focus of prospective employees. Second, as a leader, you play a key role in helping your employees to produce creative outcomes. By empowering your employees to actively engage in the decision-making processes of the organization and by intellectually stimulating employees with challenges, you can bolster employee creativity.

The e-commerce technology development company iGo-Digital uses employee empowerment and intellectually stimulating leadership practices to inspire employee creativity. The company regularly hosts "Innovation Days." Employees go off-site and participate in idea-generation sessions. During Innovation Days, employees are encouraged to take on new roles in the company to understand how different functional areas work. All iGoDigital employees are treated equally and encouraged to come up with ideas and ways of getting work done, thus promoting a sense of empowerment. Finally, the organization tries to integrate some fun personal growth time into the Innovation Days to allow employees to gain a sense of personal growth and enjoyment. iGoDigital's techniques work, as is evidenced by new product launches including a technology product that helps companies manage email signatures across their businesses.

Key Takeaways

- The factors motivating employees' work efforts, in combination with how leaders interact with workers, can affect employees' creativity on the job.

- Employees are motivated by different outcomes such as achieving career advancement, growth, and personal security and fulfilling obligations. These motivators relate to how creative employees are.

- The researchers say that employees motivated by achieving career advancement and growth have a promotion focus and are more creative than employees motivated by personal security and obligations.

- Leaders can further enhance the creativity of promotion-focused employees by allowing them to participate in decision making and to engage in intellectually stimulating leadership behaviors.

Apply This Today

By hiring employees motivated by the achievement of career advancement and growth and by engaging employees via effective management practices, leaders can support the development of their workers' creativity. To learn more about how iGoDigital and other companies inspire employee creativity, visit BusinessMinded.com.

Research Reviewed

Zhou, Q., Hirst, G., & Shipton, H. (2012). Context matters: Combined influence of participation and intellectual stimulation on the promotion focus–employee creativity relationship. *Journal of Organizational Behavior,* 33(7): 894–909.

12.4 STRATEGY SPOTLIGHT — CROWDSOURCING

NASA WORKS WITH INNOCENTIVE TO ADDRESS CHALLENGES OF SPACE MISSIONS

NASA, the American space agency, regularly faces technological hurdles with space missions it is considering undertaking. Even with a staff of 18,000, its knowledge base is limited and unable to identify all of the innovative ways the agency could overcome the technological hurdles it faces.

One solution NASA has identified is to work with InnoCentive, an open innovation company that specializes in crowdsourcing innovative ideas. InnoCentive draws upon the knowledge and insight of over a quarter of a million "solvers" who have signed up on its site to provide innovative solutions for subscribing firms.

Between 2009 and 2014, NASA ran 13 innovation "challenges" with InnoCentive and awarded prizes up to $20,000 to the "solvers" who came up with the best ideas. Challenges have involved issues ranging from doing laundry in microgravity, to noninvasive ways of measuring intracranial pressure, to systems for better predicting solar events.

In a recent competition, NASA asked InnoCentive to help it identify ways to reduce radiation exposure during extended deep-space exploration missions. Addressing this issue is critical to NASA as it moves forward with plans for manned space missions to Mars and beyond. The challenge resulted in nearly 600 potential solutions, with NASA promising to grant awards of up to $12,000 to at least three of the submitters.

Working with InnoCentive offers NASA a low-cost avenue to crowdsource innovative ideas to address technological challenges the agency faces.

Sources: Anonymous. 2014. NASA joins InnoCentive, seeks ideas from public to reduce radiation exposure. *microfinancemonitor.com*, November 20: np; Hane, P. 2011. Innocentive links problems and problem-solvers. *newsbreaks.infotoday.com*, April 25: np; and *innocentive.com*.

Spotlight 12.4 outlines how NASA is working with an innovation partner, InnoCentive, to crowdsource ideas for overcoming space exploration challenges.

The Value of Unsuccessful Innovation

Companies are often reluctant to pursue innovations due to the high uncertainty associated with innovative efforts. They are torn about whether to invest in emerging technologies, wondering which, if any, will win in the market and offer the best payoff for the firm. Conventional wisdom suggests that firms pay dearly if they bet on the wrong technology or new product direction. However, research by NYU professor J. P. Eggers suggests that betting on a losing technology and then switching to the winner can position a company to come out ahead of competitors that were on the right track all along.[26]

His research shows that firms that initially invest in an unsuccessful innovative effort often end up dominating the market in the long run. The key is that the firm remains open to change and to learning from both its mistakes and the experience of the innovators that initially chose to pursue the winning technology. Eggers offers the following insights for companies competing in a dynamic market where it is uncertain which technology will emerge triumphant:

1. **Avoid overcommitting.** This can be difficult as the firm sees the need to build specific expertise and stake out a decisive position to be seen as a leader in the market. However, managers can become entrenched as confirmation bias leads them to focus only on data that suggest they've made the right choice. Eggers suggests firms consider joint ventures and other alliances to avoid overinvestments they may come to regret.

2. **Don't let shame or despair knock you out of the game.** Shame has been shown to be a particularly destructive reaction to failure. Remember that it is very likely no one could have had complete confidence regarding which technology would win. And try to avoid seeing things as worse than they are. Some companies that bet on the wrong technology decide, unnecessarily, to get out of the market entirely, missing out on any future market opportunities.

3. **Pivot quickly.** Once they realized they made a mistake, firms that were ultimately successful changed course and moved quickly. Studies have shown that the ideal

moment to enter a high-tech industry is just as the dominant design emerges. So missing the target initially doesn't have to mean that a firm is doomed to failure if the firm moves swiftly as the dominant technology becomes clear.

4. ***Transfer knowledge.*** Successful firms use the information they gathered in a losing bet to exploit other market opportunities. For example, when flat-panel computer displays were first emerging, it was unclear if plasma or LCD technology would win. IBM initially invested heavily in plasma displays, a bet that turned out to be wrong when LCD technology won out. But IBM took away valuable knowledge from its plasma investments. For example, the heavy glass required by plasma technology forced IBM to become skilled at glass design, which helped it push glass technology in new directions in products such as the original ThinkPad laptop.

5. ***Be aware that it can be dangerous to be right at the outset.*** Managers in firms that initially select the winning technology have a tendency to interpret their ability to choose the most promising technology as an unconditional endorsement of everything they had been doing. As a result, they fail to recognize the need to rethink some details of their product and the underlying technology. Their complacency can give firms that initially chose the wrong technology the space to catch up and then pull ahead, since the later-moving firms are more open to see the need for improvements and are hungry and aggressive in their actions. The key to who wins typically isn't who is there first. Instead, the winning firm is the one that continuously incrementally innovates on the initial bold innovation to offer the best product at the best price.

Corporate Entrepreneurship

Corporate entrepreneurship (CE) has two primary aims: the pursuit of new venture opportunities and strategic renewal.[27] The innovation process keeps firms alert by exposing them to new technologies, making them aware of marketplace trends, and helping them evaluate new possibilities. Corporate entrepreneurship uses the fruits of the innovation process to help firms build new sources of competitive advantage and renew their value propositions. Just as the innovation process helps firms to make positive improvements, CE helps firms identify opportunities and launch new ventures.

Corporate new venture creation was labeled "intrapreneuring" by Gifford Pinchot because it refers to building entrepreneurial businesses within existing corporations.[28] However, to engage in corporate entrepreneurship that yields above-average returns and contributes to sustainable advantages, it must be done effectively. In this section we will examine the sources of entrepreneurial activity within established firms and the methods large corporations use to stimulate entrepreneurial behavior.

In a typical corporation, what determines how entrepreneurial projects will be pursued? The answer depends on many factors, including:

- Corporate culture.
- Leadership.
- Structural features that guide and constrain action.
- Organizational systems that foster learning and manage rewards.

All of the factors that influence the strategy implementation process will also shape how corporations engage in internal venturing.

Other factors will also affect how entrepreneurial ventures will be pursued:

- The use of teams in strategic decision making.
- Whether the company is product- or service-oriented.
- Whether its innovation efforts are aimed at product or process improvements.
- The extent to which it is high-tech or low-tech.

corporate entrepreneurship (CE)
the creation of new value for a corporation through investments that create either new sources of competitive advantage or renewal of the value proposition.

Because these factors are different in every organization, some companies may be more involved than others in identifying and developing new venture opportunities.[29] These factors will also influence the nature of the CE process.

Successful CE typically requires firms to reach beyond their current operations and markets in the pursuit of new opportunities. It is often the breakthrough opportunities that provide the greatest returns. Such strategies are not without risks, however. In the sections that follow, we will address some of the strategic choice and implementation issues that influence the success or failure of CE activities.

Two distinct approaches to corporate venturing are found among firms that pursue entrepreneurial aims. The first is *focused* corporate venturing, in which CE activities are isolated from a firm's existing operations and worked on by independent work units. The second approach is *dispersed,* in which all parts of the organization and every organization member are engaged in intrapreneurial activities.

LO12.3

How corporations use new venture teams, business incubators, and product champions to create an internal environment and culture that promote entrepreneurial development.

Focused Approaches to Corporate Entrepreneurship

focused approaches to corporate entrepreneurship

corporate entrepreneurship in which the venturing entity is separated from the other ongoing operations of the firm.

Firms using a **focused approach** typically separate the corporate venturing activity from the other ongoing operations of the firm. CE is usually the domain of autonomous work groups that pursue entrepreneurial aims independent of the rest of the firm. The advantage of this approach is that it frees entrepreneurial team members to think and act without the constraints imposed by existing organizational norms and routines. This independence is often necessary for the kind of open-minded creativity that leads to strategic breakthroughs. The disadvantage is that, because of their isolation from the corporate mainstream, the work groups that concentrate on internal ventures may fail to obtain the resources or support needed to carry an entrepreneurial project through to completion. Two forms—new venture groups (NVGs) and business incubators—are among the most common types of focused approaches.

new venture group (NVG)

a group of individuals, or a division within a corporation, that identifies, evaluates, and cultivates venture opportunities.

New Venture Groups   Corporations often form **new venture groups (NVGs)** whose goal is to identify, evaluate, and cultivate venture opportunities. These groups typically function as semiautonomous units with little formal structure. The NVG may simply be a committee that reports to the president on potential new ventures. Or it may be organized as a corporate division with its own staff and budget. The aims of the NVG may be open-ended in terms of what ventures it may consider. Alternatively, some corporations use an NVG to promote concentrated effort on a specific problem. In both cases, NVGs usually have a substantial amount of freedom to take risks and a supply of resources to do it with.[30]

New venture groups usually have a larger mandate than a typical R&D department. Their involvement extends beyond innovation and experimentation to coordinating with other corporate divisions, identifying potential venture partners, gathering resources, and actually launching the venture. Strategy Spotlight 12.5 shows how Taco Bell has used an NVG to improve its CE efforts.

business incubator

a corporate new venture group that supports and nurtures fledgling entrepreneurial ventures until they can thrive on their own as stand-alone businesses.

Business Incubators   The term *incubator* was originally used to describe a device in which eggs are hatched. **Business incubators** are designed to "hatch" new businesses. They are a type of corporate NVG with a somewhat more specialized purpose—to support and nurture fledgling entrepreneurial ventures until they can thrive on their own as stand-alone businesses. Corporations use incubators as a way to grow businesses identified by the NVG. Although they often receive support from many parts of the corporation, they still operate independently until they are strong enough to go it alone. Depending on the type of business, they either are integrated into an existing corporate division or continue to operate as a subsidiary of the parent firm.

STRATEGY SPOTLIGHT

TACO BELL COOKS UP SOME NEW IDEAS

When people think of highly innovative industries, it is unlikely that fast food is going to be one of the first industries that comes to mind. However, that doesn't mean that firms in this market see no need to innovate. One of the most innovative fast-food chains is Taco Bell. Many firms in the fast-food market, such as In-N-Out Burger, are content to deliver a consistent lineup of popular items, but Taco Bell regularly launches new products to keep customers coming back and to try to find the next big-hit product. One example of this occurred, in 2012, when Taco Bell sold over 100 million Doritos Locos Tacos in the first 10 weeks after the product was launched.

The responsibility for coming up with new food ideas falls on Taco Bell's 40-person innovation center team. Their charge, in the words of Greg Creed, CEO of Yum! Brands, the parent corporation of Taco Bell, is to craft the "industry's next big thing." The team tries out new recipes nearly every day and, as a result, is very well fed. Elizabeth Matthews, Taco Bell's chief food and beverage innovation officer, states, "Sometimes, before 10 a.m., I'm sure I've had 3,000 calories." To avoid packing on the Taco Bell 12 (pounds), the innovation center houses a fully equipped gym and offers 20 exercise classes a week for center employees.

To generate new ideas, the center's employees follow social media, consider new ingredients, and track what the firm's rivals are doing. They take field trips to grocery stores to see what new products and flavors are hitting the market. In developing new products, the team must always keep in mind Taco Bell's drive for taste, value, and speed.

A great example of how this works is the process that led to the Waffle Taco. Heather Mottershaw, director of product development, was scrolling through Facebook status updates one morning when a photo a friend posted caught her eye. The photo was of a meal her friend had ordered in a restaurant. The main course looked like a folded-over waffle sandwich stuffed with eggs and avocado. Her reaction was "huh, that's an interesting idea." She ran out to the store and bought a package of waffles and brought them into the office at 7 a.m. on Monday morning. She thawed a waffle out, folded it into a U shape, and flash-fried it in a chalupa basket. She then filled it with eggs, sausage, and cheese. By 9 a.m., executives at Taco Bell were evaluating the idea. The verdict, in Mottershaw's words, was "This is a cool idea, this is a big idea." Even with a "big idea," the development process can be long and arduous. The team first tested the Waffle Taco in the lab and then in test restaurants. The team went through 80 iterations of the new product before it was finalized. But the excitement for it remained, and the Waffle Taco, along with the A.M. Crunchwrap, became the centerpiece menu item in Taco Bell's nationwide breakfast launch in March 2014.

Sources: Rosenfeld, E., 2012. Taco Bell's Doritos Locos Tacos are an insanely huge hit. *time.com,* June 5: np; and Wong, V. 2014. Taco Bell's secret recipe for new products. *bloomberg.com,* May 29: np.

Incubators typically provide some or all of the following five functions:[31]

- *Funding.* This includes capital investments as well as in-kind investments and loans.
- *Physical space.* Incubators in which several start-ups share space often provide fertile ground for new ideas and collaboration.
- *Business services.* Along with office space, young ventures need basic services and infrastructure, which may include anything from phone systems and computer networks to public relations and personnel management.
- *Mentoring.* Senior executives and skilled technical personnel often provide coaching and experience-based advice.
- *Networking.* Contact with other parts of the firm and external resources such as suppliers, industry experts, and potential customers facilitates problem solving and knowledge sharing.

Because Microsoft has struggled to reinvigorate its entrepreneurial capabilities, the company has created a business incubator to enhance corporate entrepreneurship efforts.

To encourage entrepreneurship, corporations sometimes need to do more than create independent work groups or venture incubators to generate new enterprises. In some firms, the entrepreneurial spirit is spread throughout the organization.

Dispersed Approaches to Corporate Entrepreneurship

The second type of CE is dispersed. For some companies, a dedication to the principles and practices of entrepreneurship is spread throughout the organization. One advantage of

dispersed approaches to corporate entrepreneurship

corporate entrepreunership in which a dedication to the principles and policies of entrepreneurship is spread throughout the organization.

this **dispersed approach** is that organizational members don't have to be reminded to think entrepreneurially or be willing to change. The ability to change is considered to be a core capability. This leads to a second advantage: Because of the firm's entrepreneurial reputation, stakeholders such as vendors, customers, or alliance partners can bring new ideas or venture opportunities to anyone in the organization and expect them to be well received. Such opportunities make it possible for the firm to stay ahead of the competition. However, there are disadvantages as well. Firms that are overzealous about CE sometimes feel they must change for the sake of change, causing them to lose vital competencies or spend heavily on R&D and innovation to the detriment of the bottom line. Three related aspects of dispersed entrepreneurship include entrepreneurial cultures that have an overarching commitment to CE activities, resource allotments to support entrepreneurial actions, and the use of product champions in promoting entrepreneurial behaviors.

Entrepreneurial Culture   In some large corporations, the corporate culture embodies the spirit of entrepreneurship. A culture of entrepreneurship is one in which the search for venture opportunities permeates every part of the organization. The key to creating value successfully is viewing every value-chain activity as a source of competitive advantage. The effect of CE on a firm's strategic success is strongest when it animates all parts of an organization. It is found in companies where the strategic leaders and the culture together generate a strong impetus to innovate, take risks, and seek out new venture opportunities.[32]

entrepreneurial culture

corporate culture in which change and renewal are a constant focus of attention.

In companies with an **entrepreneurial culture,** everyone in the organization is attuned to opportunities to help create new businesses. Many such firms use a top-down approach to stimulate entrepreneurial activity. The top leaders of the organization support programs and incentives that foster a climate of entrepreneurship. Many of the best ideas for new corporate ventures, however, come from the bottom up. Catherine Winder, president of Rainmaker Entertainment, discussed how she welcomes any employee to generate and pitch innovative ideas this way:[33]

> We have an open-door policy for anyone in the company to pitch ideas . . . to describe their ideas in 15 to 30 seconds. If we like the core idea, we'll work with them. If you can be concise and come up with your idea in a really clear way, it means you're on to something.

An entrepreneurial culture is one in which change and renewal are on everybody's mind. Amazon, 3M, Intel, and Cisco are among the corporations best known for their corporate venturing activities. Many fast-growing young corporations also attribute much of their success to an entrepreneurial culture. But other successful firms struggle in their efforts to remain entrepreneurial. For example, Microsoft has had great difficulty increasing its innovativeness. One of the challenges has been that the conservatism of the firm's culture has led to a focus on short-term profitability over innovation.[34]

Resource Allotments   Corporate entrepreneurship requires the willingness of the firm to invest in the generation and execution of innovative ideas. On the generation side, employees are much more likely to develop these ideas if they have the time to do so. For decades, 3M allowed its engineers free time, up to 15 percent of their work schedule, to work on developing new products.[35] Intuit follows a similar model, offering employees the opportunity to spend 10 percent of their time on ideas that improve Intuit's processes or on products that address user problems. According to Brad Smith, Intuit's CEO, this time is critical for the future success of Intuit since "innovation is not going to come from me. It's going to come from challenging people to think about new and different ways of solving big, important problems."[36] In addition to time, firms can foster CE by providing monetary investment to fund entrepreneurial ideas. Johnson & Johnson (J&J) uses its Internal Ventures Group to support entrepreneurial ideas developed inside the firm. Entrepreneurs within J&J submit proposals to the group. The review board decides which proposals to fund and then solicits further investments from J&J's operating divisions. Nike's Sustainable Business and Innovation Lab and Google's Ventures Group have a similar charter to review and fund promising corporate entrepreneurship activities. The availability of these time and financing sources can enhance the likelihood of successful entrepreneurial activities within the firm.

Product Champions   Corporate entrepreneurship does not always involve making large investments in start-ups or establishing incubators to spawn new divisions. Often, innovative ideas emerge in the normal course of business and are brought forth and become part of the way of doing business. Entrepreneurial champions are often needed to take charge of internally generated ventures. **Product champions** (or project champions) are those individuals working within a corporation who bring entrepreneurial ideas forward, identify what kind of market exists for the product or service, find resources to support the venture, and promote the venture concept to upper management.[37]

When lower-level employees identify a product idea or novel solution, they will take it to their supervisor or someone in authority. A new idea that is generated in a technology lab may be introduced to others by its inventor. If the idea has merit, it gains support and builds momentum across the organization.[38] Even though the corporation may not be looking for new ideas or have a program for cultivating internal ventures, the independent behaviors of a few organizational members can have important strategic consequences.

No matter how an entrepreneurial idea comes to light, however, a new venture concept must pass through two critical stages or it may never get off the ground:

1. *Project definition.* An opportunity has to be justified in terms of its attractiveness in the marketplace and how well it fits with the corporation's other strategic objectives.
2. *Project impetus.* For a project to gain impetus, its strategic and economic impact must be supported by senior managers who have experience with similar projects. It then becomes an embryonic business with its own organization and budget.

For a project to advance through these stages of definition and impetus, a product champion is often needed to generate support and encouragement. Champions are especially important during the time after a new project has been defined but before it gains momentum. They form a link between the definition and impetus stages of internal development, which they do by procuring resources and stimulating interest for the product among potential customers.[39] Often, they must work quietly and alone. Consider the example of Ken Kutaragi, the Sony engineer who championed the PlayStation.

> Even though Sony had made the processor that powered the first Nintendo video games, no one at Sony in the mid-1980s saw any future in such products. "It was a kind of snobbery," Kutaragi recalled. "For Sony people, the Nintendo product would have been very embarrassing to make because it was only a toy." But Kutaragi was convinced he could make a better product. He began working secretly on a video game. Kutaragi said, "I realized that if it was visible, it would be killed." He quietly began enlisting the support of senior executives, such as the head of R&D. He made a case that Sony could use his project to develop capabilities in digital technologies that would be important in the future. It was not until 1994, after years of "underground" development and quiet building of support, that Sony introduced the PlayStation. By the year 2000, Sony had sold 55 million of them, and Kutaragi became CEO of Sony Computer Entertainment. By 2005, Kutaragi was Sony's chief operating officer, and was supervising efforts to launch PS3, the next generation version of the market-leading PlayStation video game console.[40]

Product champions play an important entrepreneurial role in a corporate setting by encouraging others to take a chance on promising new ideas.[41]

product champion
an individual working within a corporation who brings entrepreneurial ideas forward, identifies what kind of market exists for the product or service, finds resources to support the venture, and promotes the venture concept to upper management.

Measuring the Success of Corporate Entrepreneurship Activities

At this point in the discussion, it is reasonable to ask whether CE is successful. Corporate venturing, like the innovation process, usually requires a tremendous effort. Is it worth it? We consider factors that corporations need to take into consideration when evaluating the success of CE programs. We also examine techniques that companies can use to limit the expense of venturing or to cut their losses when CE initiatives appear doomed.

LO12.4

How corporate entrepreneurship achieves both financial goals and strategic goals.

Comparing Strategic and Financial CE Goals   Not all corporate venturing efforts are financially rewarding. In terms of financial performance, slightly more than 50 percent of corporate venturing efforts reach profitability (measured by ROI) within six years of their launch.[42] If this were the only criterion for success, it would seem to be a rather poor return. On the one hand, these results should be expected, because CE is riskier than other investments such as expanding ongoing operations. On the other hand, corporations expect a higher return from corporate venturing projects than from normal operations. Thus, in terms of the risk–return trade-off, it seems that CE often falls short of expectations.[43]

There are several other important criteria, however, for judging the success of a corporate venture initiative. Most CE programs have strategic goals.[44] The strategic reasons for undertaking a corporate venture include strengthening competitive position, entering into new markets, expanding capabilities by learning and acquiring new knowledge, and building the corporation's base of resources and experience. Three questions should be used to assess the effectiveness of a corporation's venturing initiatives:[45]

1. *Are the products or services offered by the venture accepted in the marketplace?*
   Is the venture considered to be a market success? If so, the financial returns are likely to be satisfactory. The venture may also open doors into other markets and suggest avenues for other venture projects.
2. *Are the contributions of the venture to the corporation's internal competencies and experience valuable?* Does the venture add to the worth of the firm internally? If so, strategic goals such as leveraging existing assets, building new knowledge, and enhancing firm capabilities are likely to be met.[46]
3. *Is the venture able to sustain its basis of competitive advantage?* Does the value proposition offered by the venture insulate it from competitive attack? If so, it is likely to place the corporation in a stronger position relative to competitors and provide a base from which to build other advantages.

These criteria include both strategic and financial goals of CE. Another way to evaluate a corporate venture is in terms of the four criteria from the balanced scorecard (Chapter 3). In a successful venture, not only are financial and market acceptance (customer) goals met but so are the internal business and innovation and learning goals. Thus, when assessing the success of corporate venturing, it is important to look beyond simple financial returns and consider a well-rounded set of criteria.[47]

Exit Champions   Although a culture of championing venture projects is advantageous for stimulating an ongoing stream of entrepreneurial initiatives, many—in fact, most—of the ideas will not work out. At some point in the process, a majority of initiatives will be abandoned. Sometimes, however, companies wait too long to terminate a new venture and do so only after large sums of resources are used up or, worse, result in a marketplace failure. Motorola's costly global satellite telecom project known as Iridium provides a useful illustration. Even though problems with the project existed during the lengthy development process, Motorola refused to pull the plug. Only after investing $5 billion and years of effort was the project abandoned.[48]

One way to avoid these costly and discouraging defeats is to support a key role in the CE process: **exit champions.** In contrast to product champions and other entrepreneurial enthusiasts within the corporation, exit champions are willing to question the viability of

exit champion

an individual working within a corporation who is willing to question the viability of a venture project by demanding hard evidence of venture success and challenging the belief system that carries a venture forward.

a venture project.[49] By demanding hard evidence and challenging the belief system that is carrying an idea forward, exit champions hold the line on ventures that appear shaky.

Both product champions and exit champions must be willing to energetically stand up for what they believe. Both put their reputations on the line. But they also differ in important ways.[50] Product champions deal in uncertainty and ambiguity. Exit champions reduce ambiguity by gathering hard data and developing a strong case for why a project should be killed. Product champions are often thought to be willing to violate procedures and operate outside normal channels. Exit champions often have to reinstate procedures and reassert the decision-making criteria that are supposed to guide venture decisions. Whereas product champions often emerge as heroes, exit champions run the risk of losing status by opposing popular projects.

The role of exit champion may seem unappealing. But it is one that could save a corporation both financially and in terms of its reputation in the marketplace. It is especially important because one measure of the success of a firm's CE efforts is the extent to which it knows when to cut its losses and move on.

Real Options Analysis: A Useful Tool

LO12.5

The benefits and potential drawbacks of real options analysis in making resource deployment decisions in corporate entrepreneurship contexts.

One way firms can minimize failure and avoid losses from pursuing faulty ideas is to apply the logic of real options. **Real options analysis (ROA)** is an investment analysis tool from the field of finance. It has been slowly, but increasingly, adopted by consultants and executives to support strategic decision making in firms. What does ROA consist of and how can it be appropriately applied to the investments required to initiate strategic decisions? To understand *real* options it is first necessary to have a basic understanding of what *options* are.

Options exist when the owner of the option has the right but not the obligation to engage in certain types of transactions. The most common are stock options. A stock option grants the holder the right to buy (call option) or sell (put option) shares of the stock at a fixed price (strike price) at some time in the future.[51] The investment to be made immediately is small, whereas the investment to be made in the future is generally larger. An option to buy a rapidly rising stock currently priced at $50 might cost as little as $.50.[52] Owners of such a stock option have limited their losses to $.50 per share, while the upside potential is unlimited. This aspect of options is attractive, because options offer the prospect of high gains with relatively small up-front investments that represent limited losses.

The phrase "real options" applies to situations where options theory and valuation techniques are applied to real assets or physical things as opposed to financial assets. Applied to entrepreneurship, real options suggest a path that companies can use to manage the uncertainty associated with launching new ventures. Some of the most common applications of real options are with property and insurance. A real estate option grants the holder the right to buy or sell a piece of property at an established price some time in the future. The actual market price of the property may rise above the established (or strike) price—or the market value may sink below the strike price. If the price of the property goes up, the owner of the option is likely to buy it. If the market value of the property drops below the strike price, the option holder is unlikely to execute the purchase. In the latter circumstance, the option holder has limited his or her loss to the cost of the option but during the life of the option retains the right to participate in whatever the upside potential might be.

real options analysis (ROA)

an investment analysis tool that looks at an investment or activity as a series of sequential steps, and for each step the investor has the option of (a) investing additional funds to grow or accelerate, (b) delaying, (c) shrinking the scale of, or (d) abandoning the activity.

Applications of Real Options Analysis to Strategic Decisions

The concept of options can also be applied to strategic decisions where management has flexibility. Situations arise where management must decide whether to invest additional funds to grow or accelerate the activity, perhaps delay in order to learn more, shrink the scale of the activity, or even abandon it. Decisions to invest in new ventures or other business activities such as R&D, motion pictures, exploration and production of oil wells, and the opening and closing of copper mines often have this flexibility.[53] Important issues to note are:

- ROA is appropriate to use when investments can be staged; a smaller investment up front can be followed by subsequent investments. Real options can be applied to an investment decision that gives the company the right, but not the obligation, to make follow-on investments.
- Strategic decision makers have "tollgates," or key points at which they can decide whether to continue, delay, or abandon the project. Executives have flexibility. There are opportunities to make other go or no-go decisions associated with each phase.
- It is expected that there will be increased knowledge about outcomes at the time of the next investment and that additional knowledge will help inform the decision makers about whether to make additional investments (i.e., whether the option is in the money or out of the money).

Many strategic decisions have the characteristic of containing a series of options. The phenomenon is called "embedded options," a series of investments in which at each stage of the investment there is a go/no-go decision. Consider the real options logic that Johnson Controls, a maker of car seats, instrument panels, and interior control systems, uses to advance or eliminate entrepreneurial ideas.[54] Johnson options each new innovative idea by making a small investment in it. To receive additional funding, the idea must continue to prove itself at each stage of development. Here's how Jim Geschke, former vice president and general manager of electronics integration at Johnson, described the process:

> Think of Johnson as an innovation machine. The front end has a robust series of gates that each idea must pass through. Early on, we'll have many ideas and spend a little money on each of them. As they get more fleshed out, the ideas go through a gate where a go or no-go decision is made. A lot of ideas get filtered out, so there are far fewer items, and the spending on each goes up. . . . Several months later each idea will face another gate. If it passes, that means it's a serious idea that we are going to develop. Then the spending goes way up, and the number of ideas goes way down. By the time you reach the final gate, you need to have a credible business case in order to be accepted. At a certain point in the development process, we take our idea to customers and ask them what they think. Sometimes they say, "That's a terrible idea. Forget it." Other times they say, "That's fabulous. I want a million of them."

This process of evaluating ideas by separating winning ideas from losing ones in a way that keeps investments low has helped Johnson Controls grow its revenues to over $43 billion a year. Using real options logic to advance the development process is a key way that firms reduce uncertainty and minimize innovation-related failures.[55] Real options logic can also be used with other types of strategic decisions. Strategy Spotlight 12.6 discusses how Intel uses real options logic in making capacity expansion decisions.

Potential Pitfalls of Real Options Analysis

Despite the many benefits that can be gained from using ROA, managers must be aware of its potential limitations or pitfalls. Below we will address three major issues.[56]

back-solver dilemma problem with investment decisions in which managers scheme to have a project meet investment approval criteria, even though the investment may not enhance firm value.

Agency Theory and the Back-Solver Dilemma Let's assume that companies adopting a real options perspective invest heavily in training and that their people understand how to effectively estimate variance—the amount of dispersion or range that is estimated for potential outcomes. Such training can help them use ROA. However, it does not solve another inherent problem: Managers may have an incentive and the know-how to "game the system." Most electronic spreadsheets permit users to simply back-solve any formula; that is, you can type in the answer you want and ask what values are needed in a formula to get that answer. If managers know that a certain option value must be met in order for the proposal to get approved, they can back-solve the model to find a variance estimate needed to arrive at the answer that upper management desires.

SAVING MILLIONS WITH REAL OPTIONS AT INTEL

The semiconductor business is complex and dynamic. This makes it a difficult one to manage. On the one hand, both the technology in the chips and the consumer demand for chips are highly volatile. This makes it difficult to plan for the future as far as the need for chip designs and production plants is concerned. On the other hand, it is incredibly expensive to build new chip plants, about $5 billion each, and chip manufacturing equipment needs to be ordered well ahead of when it is needed. The lead time for ordering new equipment can be up to three years. This creates a great challenge. Firms have to decide how much and what type of equipment to purchase long before they have a good handle on what the demand for semiconductor chips will be. Guessing wrong leaves the firm with too much or too little capacity.

Intel has figured out a way to limit the risk it faces by using option contracts. Intel pays an up-front fee for the right to purchase key pieces of equipment at a specific future date. At that point, Intel either purchases the equipment or releases the supplier from the contract. In these cases, the supplier is then free to sell the equipment to someone else. This all seems fairly simple. A number of commodities, such as wheat and sugar, have robust option markets. The challenge isn't in setting up the contracts. It is in pricing those contracts. Unlike wheat and sugar, where a large number of suppliers and buyers results in an efficient market that sets the prices of standard commodity products, there are few buyers and suppliers of chip manufacturing equipment. Further,

the equipment is not a standard commodity. As a result, prices for equipment options are the outcome of difficult negotiations.

Karl Kempf, a mathematician with Intel, has figured out how to make this process smoother. Along with a group of mathematicians at Stanford, Kempf has developed a computing logic for calculating the price of options. He and his colleagues create a forecasting model for potential demand. They calculate the likelihood of a range of potential demand levels. They also set up a computer simulation of a production plant. They then use the possible demand levels to predict how many pieces of production equipment they will need in the plant to meet the demand. They run this over and over again, thousands of times, to generate predictions about the likelihood they will need to purchase a specific piece of equipment. They use this information to identify what equipment they definitely need to order. Where there is significant uncertainty about the need for equipment, they use the simulation results to identify the specific equipment for which they need option contracts and the value of those options to Intel. This helps with the pricing.

Intel estimates that in the five years from 2008 to 2012, the use of options in equipment purchases saved the firm in excess of $125 million and provided the firm with at least $2 billion in revenue upside for expansions it could have quickly made using optioned equipment.

Sources: Kempf, K., Erhun, F., Hertzler, E., Rosenberg, T., & Peng, C. 2013. Optimizing capital investment decisions at Intel Corporation. *Interfaces*, 43(1): 62–78; and King, I. 2012. A chipmaker's model mathematician. *Bloomberg Businessweek*, June 4: 35.

Agency problems are typically inherent in investment decisions. They may occur when the managers of a firm are separated from its owners—when managers act as "agents" rather than "principals" (owners). A manager may have something to gain by not acting in the owner's best interests, or the interests of managers and owners are not co-aligned. Agency theory suggests that as managerial and owner interests diverge, managers will follow the path of their own self-interests. Sometimes this is to secure better compensation: Managers who propose projects may believe that if their projects are approved, they stand a much better chance of getting promoted. So while managers have an incentive to propose projects that *should* be successful, they also have an incentive to propose projects that *might* be successful. And because of the subjectivity involved in formally modeling a real option, managers may have an incentive to choose variance values that increase the likelihood of approval.

Managerial Conceit: Overconfidence and the Illusion of Control   Often, poor decisions are the result of such traps as biases, blind spots, and other human frailties. Much of this literature falls under the concept of **managerial conceit.**[57]

First, managerial conceit occurs when decision makers who have made successful choices in the past come to believe that they possess superior expertise for managing uncertainty. They believe that their abilities can reduce the risks inherent in decision making to a much greater extent than they actually can. Such managers are more likely to shift

managerial conceit biases, blind spots, and other human frailties that lead to poor managerial decisions.

away from analysis to trusting their own judgment. In the case of real options, they can simply declare that any given decision is a real option and proceed as before. If asked to formally model their decision, they are more likely to employ variance estimates that support their viewpoint.

Second, employing the real options perspective can encourage decision makers toward a bias for action. Such a bias may lead to carelessness. Managerial conceit is as much a problem (if not more so) for small decisions as for big ones. Why? The cost to write the first stage of an option is much smaller than the cost of full commitment, and managers pay less attention to small decisions than to large ones. Because real options are designed to minimize potential losses while preserving potential gains, any problems that arise are likely to be smaller at first, causing less concern for the manager. Managerial conceit could suggest that managers will assume that those problems are the easiest to solve and control—a concern referred to as the illusion of control. Managers may fail to respond appropriately because they overlook the problem or believe that since it is small, they can easily resolve it. Thus, managers may approach each real option decision with less care and diligence than if they had made a full commitment to a larger investment.

Managerial Conceit: Irrational Escalation of Commitment   A strength of a real options perspective is also one of its Achilles heels. Both real options and decisions involving **escalation of commitment** require specific environments with sequential decisions.[58] As the escalation-of-commitment literature indicates, simply separating a decision into multiple parts does not guarantee that decisions made will turn out well. This condition is potentially present whenever the exercise decision retains some uncertainty, which most still do. The decision to abandon also has strong psychological factors associated with it that affect the ability of managers to make correct exercise decisions.[59]

An option to exit requires reversing an initial decision made by someone in the organization. Organizations typically encourage managers to "own their decisions" in order to motivate them. As managers invest themselves in their decision, it proves harder for them to lose face by reversing course. For managers making the decision, it feels as if they made the wrong decision in the first place, even if it was initially a good decision. The more specific the manager's human capital becomes, the harder it is to transfer it to other organizations. Hence, there is a greater likelihood that managers will stick around and try to make an existing decision work. They are more likely to continue an existing project even if it should perhaps be ended.[60]

Despite the potential pitfalls of a real options approach, many of the strategic decisions that product champions and top managers must make are enhanced when decision makers have an entrepreneurial mind-set.

Entrepreneurial Orientation

Firms that want to engage in successful CE need to have an entrepreneurial orientation (EO).[61] **Entrepreneurial orientation** refers to the strategy-making practices that businesses use in identifying and launching corporate ventures. It represents a frame of mind and a perspective toward entrepreneurship that is reflected in a firm's ongoing processes and corporate culture.[62]

An EO has five dimensions that permeate the decision-making styles and practices of the firm's members: autonomy, innovativeness, proactiveness, competitive aggressiveness, and risk taking. These factors work together to enhance a firm's entrepreneurial performance. But even those firms that are strong in only a few aspects of EO can be very successful.[63] Exhibit 12.3 summarizes the dimensions of entrepreneurial orientation. Below, we discuss the five dimensions of EO and how they have been used to enhance internal venture development.

---

escalation of commitment
the tendency for managers to irrationally stick with an investment, even one that is broken down into a sequential series of decisions, when investment criteria are not being met.

LO12.6

How an entrepreneurial orientation can enhance a firm's efforts to develop promising corporate venture initiatives.

---

entrepreneurial orientation
the practices that businesses use in identifying and launching corporate ventures.

Dimension	Definition
Autonomy	Independent action by an individual or team aimed at bringing forth a business concept or vision and carrying it through to completion.
Innovativeness	A willingness to introduce novelty through experimentation and creative processes aimed at developing new products and services as well as new processes.
Proactiveness	A forward-looking perspective characteristic of a marketplace leader that has the foresight to seize opportunities in anticipation of future demand.
Competitive aggressiveness	An intense effort to outperform industry rivals characterized by a combative posture or an aggressive response aimed at improving position or overcoming a threat in a competitive marketplace.
Risk taking	Making decisions and taking action without certain knowledge of probable outcomes; some undertakings may also involve making substantial resource commitments in the process of venturing forward.

EXHIBIT 12.3

Dimensions of Entrepreneurial Orientation

Sources: Dess, G. G. & Lumpkin, G. T. 2005. The Role of Entrepreneurial Orientation in Stimulating Effective Corporate Entrepreneurship. *Academy of Management Executive,* 19(1): 147–156; Covin, J. G. & Slevin, D. P. 1991. A Conceptual Model of Entrepreneurship as Firm Behavior. *Entrepreneurship Theory & Practice,* Fall: 7–25; Lumpkin, G. T. and Dess, G. G. 1996. Clarifying the Entrepreneurial Orientation Construct and Linking It to Performance. *Academy of Management Review,* 21: 135–172; and Miller, D. 1983. The Correlates of Entrepreneurship in Three Types of Firms. *Management Science,* 29: 770–791.

Autonomy

Autonomy refers to a willingness to act independently in order to carry forward an entrepreneurial vision or opportunity. It applies to both individuals and teams that operate outside an organization's existing norms and strategies. In the context of corporate entrepreneurship, autonomous work units are often used to leverage existing strengths in new arenas, identify opportunities that are beyond the organization's current capabilities, and encourage development of new ventures or improved business practices.[64]

The need for autonomy may apply to either dispersed or focused entrepreneurial efforts. Because of the emphasis on venture projects that are being developed outside the normal flow of business, a focused approach suggests a working environment that is relatively autonomous. But autonomy may also be important in an organization where entrepreneurship is part of the corporate culture. Everything from the methods of group interaction to the firm's reward system must make organizational members feel as if they can think freely about venture opportunities, take time to investigate them, and act without fear of condemnation. This implies a respect for the autonomy of each individual and an openness to the independent thinking that goes into championing a corporate venture idea. Thus, autonomy represents a type of empowerment (see Chapter 11) that is directed at identifying and leveraging entrepreneurial opportunities. Exhibit 12.4 identifies two techniques that organizations often use to promote autonomy.

Creating autonomous work units and encouraging independent action may have pitfalls that can jeopardize their effectiveness. Autonomous teams often lack coordination. Excessive decentralization has a strong potential to create inefficiencies, such as duplicating effort and wasting resources on projects with questionable feasibility. For example, Chris Galvin, former CEO of Motorola, scrapped the skunkworks approach the company had been using to develop new wireless phones. Fifteen teams had created 128 different phones, which led to spiraling costs and overly complex operations.[65]

For autonomous work units and independent projects to be effective, such efforts have to be measured and monitored. This requires a delicate balance: Companies must have the patience and budget to tolerate the explorations of autonomous groups and the strength to cut back efforts that are not bearing fruit. Efforts must be undertaken with a clear sense of purpose—namely, to generate new sources of competitive advantage.

autonomy
independent action by an individual or a team aimed at bringing forth a business concept or vision and carrying it through to completion.

EXHIBIT 12.4 Autonomy Techniques

Autonomy		
Technique	**Description/Purpose**	**Example**
Use skunkworks to foster entrepreneurial thinking.	Skunkworks are independent work units, often physically separate from corporate headquarters. They allow employees to get out from under the pressures of their daily routines to engage in creative problem solving.	Overstock.com created a skunkworks to address the problem of returned merchandise. The solution was a business within a business: Overstock auctions. The unit has grown by selling products returned to Overstock and offers fees 30 percent lower than eBay's auction service.
Design organizational structures that support independent action.	Established companies with traditional structures often need to break out of such old forms to compete more effectively.	Deloitte Consulting, a division of Deloitte Touche Tohmatsu, found it difficult to compete against young agile firms. So it broke the firm into small autonomous units called "chip-aways" that operate with the flexibility of a start-up. In its first year, revenues were $40 million—10 percent higher than its projections.

Sources: Conlin, M. 2006. Square Feet. Oh How Square! *BusinessWeek, www.businessweek.com,* July 3; Cross, K. 2001. Bang the Drum Quickly. *Business 2.0,* May: 28–30; Sweeney, J. 2004. A Firm for All Reasons. *Consulting Magazine, www.consultingmag.com;* and Wagner, M. 2005. Out of the Skunkworks. *Internet Retailer,* January, *www.internetretailer.com.*

Innovativeness

innovativeness

a willingness to introduce novelty through experimentation and creative processes aimed at developing new products and services as well as new processes.

Innovativeness refers to a firm's efforts to find new opportunities and novel solutions. In the beginning of this chapter we discussed innovation; here the focus is on innovativeness—a firm's attitude toward innovation and willingness to innovate. It involves creativity and experimentation that result in new products, new services, or improved technological processes.[66] Innovativeness is one of the major components of an entrepreneurial strategy. As indicated at the beginning of the chapter, however, the job of managing innovativeness can be very challenging.

Innovativeness requires that firms depart from existing technologies and practices and venture beyond the current state of the art. Inventions and new ideas need to be nurtured even when their benefits are unclear. However, in today's climate of rapid change, effectively producing, assimilating, and exploiting innovations can be an important avenue for achieving competitive advantages. Interest in global warming and other ecological concerns has led many corporations to focus their innovativeness efforts on solving environmental problems.

As our earlier discussion of CE indicated, many corporations owe their success to an active program of innovation-based corporate venturing.[67] Exhibit 12.5 highlights two of the methods companies can use to enhance their competitive position through innovativeness.

Innovativeness can be a source of great progress and strong corporate growth, but there are also major pitfalls for firms that invest in innovation. Expenditures on R&D aimed at identifying new products or processes can be a waste of resources if the effort does not yield results. Another danger is related to the competitive climate. Even if a company innovates a new capability or successfully applies a technological breakthrough, another company may develop a similar innovation or find a use for it that is more profitable. Finally R&D and other innovation efforts are among the first to be cut back during an economic downturn.

Even though innovativeness is an important means of internal corporate venturing, it also involves major risks, because investments in innovations may not pay off. For strategic managers of entrepreneurial firms, successfully developing and adopting innovations can generate competitive advantages and provide a major source of growth for the firm.

Proactiveness

proactiveness

a forward-looking perspective characteristic of a marketplace leader that has the foresight to seize opportunities in anticipation of future demand.

Proactiveness refers to a firm's efforts to seize new opportunities. Proactive organizations monitor trends, identify the future needs of existing customers, and anticipate changes in demand or emerging problems that can lead to new venture opportunities. Proactiveness involves not only

EXHIBIT 12.5 Innovativeness Techniques

Innovativeness		
Technique	**Description/Purpose**	**Example**
Foster creativity and experimentation.	Companies that support idea exploration and allow employees to express themselves creatively enhance innovation outcomes.	To tap into its reserves of innovative talent, Royal Dutch Shell created "GameChanger" to help employees develop promising ideas. The process provides funding up to $600,000 for would-be entrepreneurs to pursue innovative projects and conduct experiments.
Invest in new technology, R&D, and continuous improvement.	The latest technologies often provide sources of new competitive advantages. To extract value from a new technology, companies must invest in it.	Dell Computer Corporation's OptiPlex manufacturing system revolutionized the traditional assembly line. Hundreds of custom-built computers can be made in an eight-hour shift using state-of-the-art automation techniques that increased productivity per person by 160 percent.

Sources: Breen, B. 2004. Living in Dell Time. *Fast Company,* November: 88–92: Hammonds, K. H. 2002. Size Is Not a Strategy. *Fast Company,* August: 78–83; Perman, S. 2001. Automate or Die. *eCompanyNow.com,* July; Dell, M. 1999. *Direct from Dell.* New York: HarperBusiness; and Watson, R. 2006. Expand Your Innovation Horizons. *Fast Company, www.fastcompany.com,* May.

recognizing changes but also being willing to act on those insights ahead of the competition.[68] Strategic managers who practice proactiveness have their eye on the future in a search for new possibilities for growth and development. Such a forward-looking perspective is important for companies that seek to be industry leaders. Many proactive firms seek out ways not only to be future-oriented but also to change the very nature of competition in their industry.

Proactiveness puts competitors in the position of having to respond to successful initiatives. The benefit gained by firms that are the first to enter new markets, establish brand identity, implement administrative techniques, or adopt new operating technologies in an industry is called first-mover advantage.[69]

First movers usually have several advantages. First, industry pioneers, especially in new industries, often capture unusually high profits because there are no competitors to drive prices down. Second, first movers that establish brand recognition are usually able to retain their image and hold on to the market share gains they earned by being first. Sometimes these benefits also accrue to other early movers in an industry, but, generally speaking, first movers have an advantage that can be sustained until firms enter the maturity phase of an industry's life cycle.[70]

First movers are not always successful. The customers of companies that introduce novel products or embrace breakthrough technologies may be reluctant to commit to a new way of doing things. In his book *Crossing the Chasm,* Geoffrey A. Moore noted that most firms seek evolution, not revolution, in their operations. This makes it difficult for a first mover to sell promising new technologies.[71]

Even with these caveats, however, companies that are first movers can enhance their competitive position. Exhibit 12.6 illustrates two methods firms can use to act proactively.

Being an industry leader does not always lead to competitive advantages. Some firms that have launched pioneering new products or staked their reputation on new brands have failed to get the hoped-for payoff. Coca-Cola and PepsiCo invested $75 million to launch sodas that would capitalize on the low-carb diet trend. But with half the carbohydrates taken out, neither *C2,* Coke's entry, nor *Pepsi Edge* tasted very good. The two new brands combined never achieved more than 1 percent market share. PepsiCo halted production in 2005 and Coca-Cola followed suit in 2007.[72] Such missteps are indicative of the dangers of trying to proactively anticipate demand. Another danger for opportunity-seeking companies is that they will take their proactiveness efforts too far. For example, Porsche has tried to extend its brand images outside the automotive arena. While some efforts have worked, such as Porsche-designed T-shirts and sunglasses, other efforts have failed, such as the Porsche-branded golf clubs.

EXHIBIT 12.6 Proactiveness Techniques

Proactiveness		
Technique	**Description/Purpose**	**Example**
Introduce new products or technological capabilities ahead of the competition.	Being a first mover provides companies with an ability to shape the playing field and shift competitive advantages in their favor.	Amazon was able to define the online bookselling market by entering the market early and defining the user experience. It further leveraged its position as an early mover when moving into other retailing ventures and later into cloud computing.
Continuously seek out new product or service offerings.	Firms that provide new resources or sources of supply can benefit from a proactive stance.	Costco seized a chance to leverage its success as a warehouse club that sells premium brands when it introduced Costco Home Stores. The home stores are usually located near its warehouse stores, and its rapid inventory turnover gives it a cost advantage of 15 to 25 percent over close competitors such as Bassett Furniture and the Bombay Company.

Sources: Bryce, D. J. & Dyer, J. H. 2007. Strategies to Crack Well-Guarded Markets. *Harvard Business Review,* May: 84–92; Collins, J. C. & Porras, J. I. 1997. *Built to Last.* New York: HarperBusiness; Robinson, D. 2005. Sony Pushes Reliability in Vaio Laptops. *IT Week, www.itweek.co.uk,* October 12; and *www.sony.com.*

Careful monitoring and scanning of the environment, as well as extensive feasibility research, are needed for a proactive strategy to lead to competitive advantages. Firms that do it well usually have substantial growth and internal development to show for it. Many of them have been able to sustain the advantages of proactiveness for years.

Competitive Aggressiveness

competitive aggressiveness
an intense effort to outperform industry rivals; characterized by a combative posture or an aggressive response aimed at improving position or overcoming a threat in a competitive marketplace.

Competitive aggressiveness refers to a firm's efforts to outperform its industry rivals. Companies with an aggressive orientation are willing to "do battle" with competitors. They might slash prices and sacrifice profitability to gain market share or spend aggressively to obtain manufacturing capacity. As an avenue of firm development and growth, competitive aggressiveness may involve being very assertive in leveraging the results of other entrepreneurial activities such as innovativeness or proactiveness.

Competitive aggressiveness is directed toward competitors. The SWOT analysis discussed in Chapters 2 and 3 provides a useful way to distinguish between these different approaches to CE. Proactiveness, as we saw in the previous section, is a response to opportunities—the O in SWOT. Competitive aggressiveness, by contrast, is a response to threats—the T in SWOT. A competitively aggressive posture is important for firms that seek to enter new markets in the face of intense rivalry.

Strategic managers can use competitive aggressiveness to combat industry trends that threaten their survival or market position. Sometimes firms need to be forceful in defending the competitive position that has made them an industry leader. Firms often need to be aggressive to ensure their advantage by capitalizing on new technologies or serving new market needs. Exhibit 12.7 suggests two of the ways competitively aggressive firms enhance their entrepreneurial position.

Another practice companies use to overcome the competition is to make preannouncements of new products or technologies. This type of signaling is aimed not only at potential customers but also at competitors to see how they will react or to discourage them from launching similar initiatives. Sometimes the preannouncements are made just to scare off competitors, an action that has potential ethical implications.

Competitive aggressiveness may not always lead to competitive advantages. Some companies (or their CEOs) have severely damaged their reputations by being overly aggressive. Although Microsoft continues to be a dominant player, its highly aggressive profile makes it the subject of scorn by some businesses and individuals. Efforts to find viable

EXHIBIT 12.7 Competitive Aggressiveness Techniques

Competitive Aggressiveness		
Technique	**Description/Purpose**	**Example**
Enter markets with drastically lower prices.	Narrow operating margins make companies vulnerable to extended price competition.	Using open-source software, California-based Zimbra, Inc. has become a leader in messaging and collaboration software. Its product costs about one-third less than its direct competitor Microsoft Exchange. Zimbra generated $4.3 billion in sales in 2012.
Find successful business models and copy them.	As long as a practice is not protected by intellectual property laws, it's probably OK to imitate it. Finding solutions to existing problems is generally quicker and cheaper than inventing them.	Best Practices LLC is a North Carolina consulting group that seeks out best practices and then repackages and resells them. With annual revenues in excess of $8 million, Best Practices has become a leader in continuous improvement and benchmarking strategies.

Sources: Guth, R. A. 2006. Trolling the Web for Free Labor, Software Upstarts Are New Force. *The Wall Street Journal,* November 12: 1; Mochari, I. 2001. Steal This Strategy. *Inc.,* July: 62–67; *www.best-in-class.com;* and *www.zimbra.com.*

replacements for the Microsoft products have helped fuel interest in alternative options provided by Google, Apple, and the open-source software movement.[73]

Competitive aggressiveness is a strategy that is best used in moderation. Companies that aggressively establish their competitive position and vigorously exploit opportunities to achieve profitability may, over the long run, be better able to sustain their competitive advantages if their goal is to defeat, rather than decimate, their competitors.

Risk Taking

Risk taking refers to a firm's willingness to seize a venture opportunity even though it does not know whether the venture will be successful—to act boldly without knowing the consequences. To be successful through corporate entrepreneurship, firms usually have to take on riskier alternatives, even if it means forgoing the methods or products that have worked in the past. To obtain high financial returns, firms take such risks as assuming high levels of debt, committing large amounts of firm resources, introducing new products into new markets, and investing in unexplored technologies.

All of the approaches to internal development that we have discussed are potentially risky. Whether they are being aggressive, proactive, or innovative, firms on the path of CE must act without knowing how their actions will turn out. Before launching their strategies, corporate entrepreneurs must know their firm's appetite for risk.[74]

Three types of risk that organizations and their executives face are business risk, financial risk, and personal risk:

- *Business risk taking* involves venturing into the unknown without knowing the probability of success. This is the risk associated with entering untested markets or committing to unproven technologies.
- *Financial risk taking* requires that a company borrow heavily or commit a large portion of its resources in order to grow. In this context, risk is used to refer to the risk–return trade-off that is familiar in financial analysis.
- *Personal risk taking* refers to the risks that an executive assumes in taking a stand in favor of a strategic course of action. Executives who take such risks stand to influence the course of their whole company, and their decisions also can have significant implications for their careers.

Even though risk taking involves taking chances, it is not gambling. The best-run companies investigate the consequences of various opportunities and create scenarios of likely outcomes. A key to managing entrepreneurial risks is to evaluate new venture opportunities

risk taking
making decisions and taking action without certain knowledge of probable outcomes. Some undertakings may also involve making substantial resource commitments in the process of venturing forward.

EXHIBIT 12.8 Risk-Taking Techniques

Risk Taking		
Technique	**Description/Purpose**	**Example**
Research and assess risk factors to minimize uncertainty.	Companies that "do their homework"—that is, carefully evaluate the implications of bold actions—reduce the likelihood of failure.	Graybar Electric Co. took a risk when it invested $144 million to revamp its distribution system. It consolidated 231 small centers into 16 supply warehouses and installed the latest communications network. Graybar is now considered a leader in facility redesign, and its sales have increased steadily since the consolidation, topping $5 billion in sales in a recent year.
Use techniques that have worked in other domains.	Risky methods that other companies have tried may provide an avenue for advancing company goals.	Autobytel.com, one of the first companies to sell cars online, decided on an approach that worked well for others—advertising during the Super Bowl. It was the first dot-com ever to do so, and its $1.2 million 30-second ad paid off well by generating weeks of free publicity and favorable business press.

Sources: Anonymous. 2006. Graybar Offers Data Center Redesign Seminars. *Cabling Installation and Maintenance, www.cim.pennnet.com,* September 1; Keenan, F. & Mullaney, T. J. 2001. Clicking at Graybar. *BusinessWeek,* June 18: 132–134; Weintraub, A. 2001. Make or break for Autobytel. *BusinessWeek e.biz,* July 9: EB30–EB32; *www.autobytel.com;* and *www.graybar.com.*

thoroughly enough to reduce the uncertainty surrounding them. Exhibit 12.8 indicates two methods companies can use to strengthen their competitive position through risk taking.

Risk taking, by its nature, involves potential dangers and pitfalls. Only carefully managed risk is likely to lead to competitive advantages. Actions that are taken without sufficient forethought, research, and planning may prove to be very costly. Therefore, strategic managers must always remain mindful of potential risks. In his book *Innovation and Entrepreneurship,* Peter Drucker argued that successful entrepreneurs are typically not risk takers. Instead, they take steps to minimize risks by carefully understanding them. That is how they avoid focusing on risk and remain focused on opportunity.[75] Risk taking is a good place to close this chapter on corporate entrepreneurship. Companies that choose to grow through internal corporate venturing must remember that entrepreneurship always involves embracing what is new and uncertain.

ISSUE FOR DEBATE

The Internet of Things

From activity bracelets that upload metrics of your physical activity to the web, to meat thermometers monitored with a smartphone, to door locks that can be locked and unlocked from a tablet computer anywhere in the world, devices and appliances are increasingly being connected to the Internet. The "Internet of things" is a rapidly growing market space. Cisco estimates that the number of devices connected to the Internet will explode from 10 billion in 2014 to 50 billion by 2020.

Some of the devices are already generating significant interest and sales. For example, over 3 million fitness-tracking devices were sold in the April 2013 to March 2014 period. Additionally, Google saw so much promise with Nest Labs, a company that manufactures Internet-enabled thermostats and smoke detectors, it purchased the firm for $3.2 billion in 2014. Both of these types of devices appear to have significant potential since they benefit from being tied to sociological forces in advanced economies. Fitness-tracking devices tie very directly into desires to lose weight and improve fitness. Similarly, Nest Labs' products are designed to aid in improving the energy efficiency of homes and respond to the desires of many individuals to reduce their carbon footprint. However, the degree of customer demand for such products is still uncertain. In a survey done by Forrester Research in mid-2013, 28 percent of respondents said they were interested in controlling appliances from a smartphone, while 53 percent said they weren't.

Such mixed sentiment isn't stopping other firms from taking the "Internet of things" trend to new classes of products. For example, Procter & Gamble (P&G) introduced a prototype of the world's first web-enabled toothbrush in early 2014. It reports the user's brushing habits to a smartphone. The associated app uses the data to provide mouth-care tips. The toothbrush, which came to market in June 2015, carries a suggested retail price tag of $219. P&G executives believe the toothbrush will be a big hit. "I truly believe that 10 years from now, it's going to be hard to think you didn't have something like it," said Michael Cohen-Dumani, P&G's associate marketing director. Others are skeptical of the market for Internet-enabled products. "We are just at the beginning of seeing a bunch of really ridiculous products that tie pretty much anything to a smartphone," said Stacey Higgenbotham, a writer for the tech website Gigaom.

One overarching concern associated with all Internet-enabled products is privacy. With the devices transmitting information to the web, users' personal data are potentially open for all to see. The default settings on some devices make the data available to the public. For example, some fitness trackers send the data unencrypted, which makes it possible for others to access the fitness data of the users. Additionally, there are fears that devices could be hacked, leaving users vulnerable to thieves. By tracking when users remotely act to control home appliances, thieves could learn information on whether the users are at home.

Thus, while it is a potentially exciting market, there are significant uncertainties about the opportunities and challenges with Internet-enabled products.

Discussion Questions

1. Is the "Internet of things" a market with tremendous growth potential or just a bunch of hype?
2. What types of products are likely to be successful in this market? What characteristics enhance the potential for Internet-enabled products?
3. How much of a concern is the privacy issue with these products?

Sources: Clark, D. 2014. "Internet of Things" in reach. *wsj.com,* January 5: np; Shechner, S. 2014. Web-enabled toothbrushes join the Internet of things. *wsj.com,* March 2: np; and Anonymous. 2015. P&G's smart toothbrush keeps tabs on tooth care. *cnbc.com,* February 20.

Reflecting on Career Implications . . .

▣ **Innovation:** Identify the types of innovations being pursued by your company. Do they tend to be incremental or radical? Product-related or process-related? Are there ways in which you can add value to such innovations, no matter how minor your contributions are?

▣ **Cultivating Innovation Skills:** Exhibit 12.2 describes the five traits of an effective innovator (associating, questioning, observing, experimenting, and networking). Assess yourself on each of these traits. Practice the skills in your work and professional life to build your skills as an innovator. If you are interviewing for a job with an organization that is considered high on innovation, it might be in your interest to highlight these traits.

▣ **Real Options Analysis:** Success in your career often depends on creating and exercising career "options." However, creation of options involves costs as well, such as learning new skills, obtaining additional certifications, and so on. Consider what options you can create for yourself. Evaluate the cost of these options.

▣ **Entrepreneurial Orientation:** Consider the five dimensions of entrepreneurial orientation. Evaluate yourself on each of these dimensions (autonomy, innovativeness, proactiveness, competitive aggressiveness, and risk taking). If you are high on entrepreneurial orientation, you may have a future as an entrepreneur. Consider the ways in which you can use the experience and learning from your current job to become a successful entrepreneur in later years.

summary

To remain competitive in today's economy, established firms must find new avenues for development and growth. This chapter has addressed how innovation and corporate entrepreneurship can be a means of internal venture creation and strategic renewal, and how an entrepreneurial orientation can help corporations enhance their competitive position.

Innovation is one of the primary means by which corporations grow and strengthen their strategic position. Innovations can take several forms, ranging from radical breakthrough innovations to incremental improvement innovations. Innovations are often used to update products and services or to improve organizational processes. Managing the innovation process is often challenging, because it involves a great deal of uncertainty and there are many choices to be made about the extent and type of innovations to pursue. By cultivating innovation skills, defining the scope of innovation, managing the pace of innovation, staffing to capture value from innovation, and collaborating with innovation partners, firms can more effectively manage the innovation process.

We also discussed the role of corporate entrepreneurship in venture development and strategic renewal. Corporations usually take either a focused or dispersed approach to corporate venturing. Firms with a focused approach usually separate the corporate venturing activity from the ongoing operations of the firm in order to foster independent thinking and encourage entrepreneurial team members to think and act without the constraints imposed by the corporation. In corporations where venturing activities are dispersed, a culture of entrepreneurship permeates all parts of the company in order to induce strategic behaviors by all organizational members. In measuring the success of corporate venturing activities, both financial and strategic objectives should be considered. Real options analysis is often used to make better-quality decisions in uncertain entrepreneurial situations. However, a real options approach has potential drawbacks.

Most entrepreneurial firms need to have an entrepreneurial orientation: the methods, practices, and decision-making styles that strategic managers use to act entrepreneurially. Five dimensions of entrepreneurial orientation are found in firms that pursue corporate venture strategies. Autonomy, innovativeness, proactiveness, competitive aggressiveness, and risk taking each make a unique contribution to the pursuit of new opportunities. When deployed effectively, the methods and practices of an entrepreneurial orientation can be used to engage successfully in corporate entrepreneurship and new venture creation. However, strategic managers must remain mindful of the pitfalls associated with each of these approaches.

SUMMARY REVIEW QUESTIONS

1. What is meant by the concept of a continuum of radical and incremental innovations?
2. What are the dilemmas that organizations face when deciding what innovation projects to pursue? What steps can organizations take to effectively manage the innovation process?
3. What is the difference between focused and dispersed approaches to corporate entrepreneurship?
4. How are business incubators used to foster internal corporate venturing?
5. What is the role of the product champion in bringing a new product or service into existence in a corporation? How can companies use product champions to enhance their venture development efforts?
6. Explain the difference between proactiveness and competitive aggressiveness in terms of achieving and sustaining competitive advantage.
7. Describe how the entrepreneurial orientation (EO) dimensions of innovativeness, proactiveness, and risk taking can be combined to create competitive advantages for entrepreneurial firms.

key terms

experiential exercise

Select two different major corporations from two different industries (you might use Fortune 500 companies to make your selection). Compare and contrast these organizations in terms of their entrepreneurial orientation. (Fill in the table below.)

Based on your comparison:

1. How is the corporation's entrepreneurial orientation reflected in its strategy?

2. Which corporation would you say has the stronger entrepreneurial orientation?

3. Is the corporation with the stronger entrepreneurial orientation also stronger in terms of financial performance?

Entrepreneurial Orientation	Company A	Company B
Autonomy		
Innovativeness		
Proactiveness		
Competitive aggressiveness		
Risk taking		

application questions & exercises

1. Select a firm known for its corporate entrepreneurship activities. Research the company and discuss how it has positioned itself relative to its close competitors. Does it have a unique strategic advantage? Disadvantage? Explain.

2. Explain the difference between product innovations and process innovations. Provide examples of firms that have recently introduced each type of innovation. What are the types of innovations related to the strategies of each firm?

3. Using the Internet, select a company that is listed on the NASDAQ or New York Stock Exchange. Research the extent to which the company has an entrepreneurial culture. Does the company use product champions? Does it have a corporate venture capital fund? Do you believe its entrepreneurial efforts are sufficient to generate sustainable advantages?

4. How can an established firm use an entrepreneurial orientation to enhance its overall strategic position? Provide examples.

ethics questions

1. Innovation activities are often aimed at making a discovery or commercializing a technology ahead of the competition. What are some of the unethical practices that companies could engage in during the innovation process? What are the potential long-term consequences of such actions?

2. Discuss the ethical implications of using entrepreneurial policies and practices to pursue corporate social responsibility goals. Are these efforts authentic and genuine or just an attempt to attract more customers?

references

1. Eddy, N. 2014. Android captures 85 percent of smartphone market worldwide. *eweek.com,* August 8: np; Vascellaro, J. 2009. Radio tunes out Google in rare miss for web titan. *wsj.com,* May 12: np; and McGrath, R. 2011. Failing by design. *Harvard Business Review,* 89(4): 76–83.

2. For an interesting discussion, see Johannessen, J. A., Olsen, B., & Lumpkin, G. T. 2001. Innovation as newness: What is new, how new, and new to whom? *European Journal of Innovation Management,* 4(1): 20–31.

3. The discussion of product and process innovation is based on Roberts, E. B. (Ed.). 2002. *Innovation: Driving product, process, and market change.* San Francisco: Jossey-Bass; Hayes, R. & Wheelwright, S. 1985. Competing through manufacturing. *Harvard Business Review,* 63(1): 99–109; and Hayes, R. & Wheelwright, S. 1979. Dynamics of product–process life cycles. *Harvard Business Review,* 57(2): 127–136.

4. The discussion of radical and incremental innovations draws from Leifer, R., McDermott, C. M., Colarelli, G., O'Connor, G. C., Peters, L. S., Rice, M. P., & Veryzer, R. W. 2000. *Radical innovation: How mature companies can outsmart upstarts.* Boston: Harvard Business School Press; Damanpour, F. 1996. Organizational complexity and innovation: Developing and testing multiple contingency models. *Management Science,* 42(5): 693–716; and Hage, J. 1980. *Theories of organizations.* New York: Wiley.

5. Christensen, C. M. & Raynor, M. E. 2003. *The innovator's solution.*

Boston: Harvard Business School
Press.

6. Dressner, H. 2004. The Gartner
Fellows interview: Clayton M.
Christensen. *www.gartner.com*,
April 26.

7. For another perspective on how
different types of innovation affect
organizational choices, see Wolter,
C. & Veloso, F. M. 2008. The effects
of innovation on vertical structure:
Perspectives on transactions
costs and competences. *Academy
of Management Review*, 33(3):
586–605.

8. Drucker, P. F. 1985. *Innovation and
entrepreneurship*. New York: Harper
& Row.

9. Birkinshaw, J., Hamel, G., & Mol,
M. J. 2008. Management innovation.
Academy of Management Review,
33(4): 825–845.

10. Steere, W. C., Jr. & Niblack, J.
1997. Pfizer, Inc. In Kanter, R. M.,
Kao, J., & Wiersema, F. (Eds.),
*Innovation: Breakthrough thinking
at 3M, DuPont, GE, Pfizer, and
Rubbermaid*: 123–145. New York:
HarperCollins.

11. Morrissey, C. A. 2000. Managing
innovation through corporate
venturing. *Graziadio Business
Report*, Spring, *gbr.pepperdine.
edu*; and Sharma, A. 1999. Central
dilemmas of managing innovation in
large firms. *California Management
Review*, 41(3): 147–164.

12. Sharma, op. cit.

13. Dyer, J. H., Gregerson, H. B., &
Christensen, C. M. 2009. The
innovator's DNA. *Harvard Business
Review*, December: 61–67.

14. Eggers, J. P. & Kaplan, S. 2009.
Cognition and renewal: Comparing
CEO and organizational effects on
incumbent adaptation to technical
change. *Organization Science*, 20:
461–477.

15. Biodegradable Products Institute.
2003. "Compostable Logo" of the
Biodegradable Products Institute
gains momentum with approval
of DuPont Biomax resin, *www.
bpiworld.org*, June 12; Leifer et al.,
op. cit.

16. For more on defining the scope of
innovation, see Valikangas, L. &
Gibbert, M. 2005. Boundary-setting
strategies for escaping innovation
traps. *MIT Sloan Management
Review*, 46(3): 58–65.

17. Leifer et al., op. cit.

18. Bhide, A. V. 2000. *The origin and
evolution of new businesses*. New
York: Oxford University Press;
Brown, S. L. & Eisenhardt, K. M.

1998. *Competing on the edge:
Strategy as structured chaos*.
Cambridge, MA: Harvard Business
School Press.

19. McGrath, R. G. & Keil, T. 2007.
The value captor's process: Getting
the most out of your new business
ventures. *Harvard Business Review*,
May: 128–136.

20. For an interesting discussion of how
sharing technology knowledge with
different divisions in an organization
can contribute to innovation
processes, see Miller, D. J., Fern,
M. J., & Cardinal, L. B. 2007. The
use of knowledge for technological
innovation within diversified firms.
Academy of Management Journal,
50(2): 308–326.

21. Ketchen, D. J., Jr., Ireland, R. D.,
& Snow, C. C. 2007 Strategic
entrepreneurship, collaborative
innovation, and wealth creation.
Strategic Entrepreneurship Journal,
1(3–4): 371–385.

22. Chesbrough, H. 2003. *Open
innovation: The new imperative
for creating and profiting from
technology*. Boston: Harvard
Business School Press.

23. For a study of what makes alliance
partnerships successful, see
Sampson, R. C. 2007. R&D alliances
and firm performance: The impact of
technological diversity and alliance
organization on innovation. *Academy
of Management Journal*, 50(2):
364–386.

24. For an interesting perspective on
the role of collaboration among
multinational corporations, see
Hansen, M. T. & Nohria, N.
2004. How to build collaborative
advantage. *MIT Sloan Management
Review*, 46(1): 22–30.

25. Wells, R. M. J. 2008. The
product innovation process: Are
managing information flows and
cross-functional collaboration
key? *Academy of Management
Perspectives*, 22(1): 58–60;
Dougherty, D. & Dunne, D. D. 2011.
Organizing ecologies of complex
innovation. *Organization Science*,
22(5): 1214–1223; and Kim, H. E. &
Pennings, J. M. 2009. Innovation and
strategic renewal in mature markets:
A study of the tennis racket industry.
Organization Science, 20: 368–383.

26. Eggers, J. P. 2014. Get ahead by
betting wrong. *Harvard Business
Review*, 92(7/8): 26; and Lepore, J.
2014. The disruption machine.
newyorker.com, June 23: np.

27. Guth, W. D. & Ginsberg, A.
1990. Guest editor's introduction:
Corporate entrepreneurship.

Strategic Management Journal,
11: 5–15.

28. Pinchot, G. 1985. *Intrapreneuring*.
New York: Harper & Row.

29. For an interesting perspective on
the role of context on the discovery
and creation of opportunities, see
Zahra, S. A. 2008. The virtuous
cycle of discovery and creation
of entrepreneurial opportunities.
Strategic Entrepreneurship Journal,
2(3): 243–257.

30. Birkinshaw, J. 1997. Entrepreneurship
in multinational corporations:
The characteristics of subsidiary
initiatives. *Strategic Management
Journal*, 18(3): 207–229; and
Kanter, R. M. 1985. *The change
masters*. New York: Simon &
Schuster.

31. Hansen, M. T., Chesbrough, H. W.,
Nohria, N., & Sull, D. 2000.
Networked incubators: Hothouses of
the new economy. *Harvard Business
Review*, 78(5): 74–84.

32. For more on the importance of
leadership in fostering a climate
of entrepreneurship, see Ling, Y.,
Simsek, Z., Lubatkin, M. H., &
Veiga, J. F. 2008. Transformational
leadership's role in promoting
corporate entrepreneurship:
Examining the CEO-TMT interface.
Academy of Management Journal,
51(3): 557–576.

33. Bryant, A. 2011. Got an idea? Sell
it to me in 30 seconds. *nytimes.com*,
January 1: np.

34. Ovide, S. 2013. Next CEO's biggest
job: Fixing Microsoft's culture.
wsj.com, August 25: np.

35. Gunther, M. 2010. 3M's innovation
revival. *cnnmoney.com*, September
24: np; Byrne, J. 2012. The 12
greatest entrepreneurs of our
time. *Fortune*, April 9: 76; and
Anonymous. 2007. Johnson &
Johnson turns to internal venturing.
silico.wordpress.com, July 16: np.

36. Colvin, G. 2014. Brad Smith:
Getting rid of friction. *Fortune*,
July 21: 24.

37. For an interesting discussion, see
Davenport, T. H., Prusak, L., &
Wilson, H. J. 2003. Who's bringing
you hot ideas and how are you
responding? *Harvard Business
Review*, 80(1): 58–64.

38. Howell, J. M. 2005. The right stuff.
Identifying and developing effective
champions of innovation. *Academy
of Management Executive*, 19(2):
108–119. See also Greene, P., Brush,
C., & Hart, M. 1999. The corporate
venture champion: A resource-
based approach to role and process.

Entrepreneurship Theory & Practice, 23(3): 103–122; and Markham, S. K. & Aiman-Smith, L. 2001. Product champions: Truths, myths and management. *Research Technology Management,* May–June: 44–50.

39. Burgelman, R. A. 1983. A process model of internal corporate venturing in the diversified major firm. *Administrative Science Quarterly,* 28: 223–244.

40. Hamel, G. 2000. *Leading the revolution.* Boston: Harvard Business School Press.

41. Greene, Brush, & Hart, op. cit.; and Shane, S. 1994. Are champions different from non-champions? *Journal of Business Venturing,* 9(5): 397–421.

42. Block, Z. & MacMillan, I. C. 1993. *Corporate venturing—Creating new businesses with the firm.* Cambridge, MA: Harvard Business School Press.

43. For an interesting discussion of these trade-offs, see Stringer, R. 2000. How to manage radical innovation. *California Management Review,* 42(4): 70–88; and Gompers, P. A. & Lerner, J. 1999. *The venture capital cycle.* Cambridge, MA: MIT Press.

44. Cardinal, L. B., Turner, S. F., Fern, M. J., & Burton, R. M. 2011. Organizing for product development across technological environments: Performance trade-offs and priorities. *Organization Science,* 22: 1000–1025.

45. Albrinck, J., Hornery, J., Kletter, D., & Neilson, G. 2001. Adventures in corporate venturing. *Strategy + Business,* 22: 119–129; and McGrath, R. G. & MacMillan, I. C. 2000. *The entrepreneurial mind-set.* Cambridge, MA: Harvard Business School Press.

46. Kiel, T., McGrath, R. G., & Tukiainen, T. 2009. Gems from the ashes: Capability creation and transforming in internal corporate venturing. *Organization Science,* 20: 601–620.

47. For an interesting discussion of how different outcome goals affect organizational learning and employee motivation, see Seijts, G. H. & Latham, G. P. 2005. Learning versus performance goals: When should each be used? *Academy of Management Executive,* 19(1): 124–131.

48. Crockett, R. O. 2001. Motorola. *BusinessWeek,* July 15: 72–78.

49. The ideas in this section are drawn from Royer, I. 2003. Why bad projects are so hard to kill. *Harvard Business Review,* 80(1): 48–56.

50. For an interesting perspective on the different roles that individuals

play in the entrepreneurial process, see Baron, R. A. 2008. The role of affect in the entrepreneurial process. *Academy of Management Review,* 33(2): 328–340.

51. Hoskin, R. E. 1994. *Financial accounting.* New York: Wiley.

52. We know stock options as derivative assets—that is, "an asset whose value depends on or is derived from the value of another, the underlying asset": Amram, M. & Kulatilaka, N. 1999. *Real options: Managing strategic investment in an uncertain world: 34.* Boston: Harvard Business School Press.

53. For an interesting discussion on why it is difficult to "kill options," refer to Royer, I. 2003. Why bad projects are so hard to kill. *Harvard Business Review,* 81(2): 48–57.

54. Slywotzky, A. & Wise, R. 2003. Double-digit growth in no-growth times. *Fast Company,* April: 66–72; *www.hoovers.com;* and *www.johnsoncontrols.com.*

55. For more on the role of real options in entrepreneurial decision making, see Folta, T. B. & O'Brien, J. P. 2004. Entry in the presence of dueling options. *Strategic Management Journal,* 25: 121–138.

56. This section draws on Janney, J. J. & Dess, G. G. 2004. Can real options analysis improve decision-making? Promises and pitfalls. *Academy of Management Executive,* 18(4): 60–75. For additional insights on pitfalls of real options, consider McGrath, R. G. 1997. A real options logic for initiating technology positioning investment. *Academy of Management Review,* 22(4): 974–994; Coff, R. W. & Laverty, K. J. 2001. Real options on knowledge assets: Panacea or Pandora's box? *Business Horizons,* 73: 79; McGrath, R. G. 1999. Falling forward: Real options reasoning and entrepreneurial failure. *Academy of Management Review,* 24(1): 13–30; and Zardkoohi, A. 2004. Do real options lead to escalation of commitment? *Academy of Management Review,* 29(1): 111–119.

57. For an understanding of the differences between how managers say they approach decisions and how they actually do, March and Shapira's discussion is perhaps the best. March, J. G. & Shapira, Z. 1987. Managerial perspectives on risk and risk-taking. *Management Science,* 33(11): 1404–1418.

58. A discussion of some factors that may lead to escalation in decision

making is included in Choo, C. W. 2005. Information failures and organizational disasters. *MIT Sloan Management Review,* 46(3): 8–10.

59. For an interesting discussion of the use of real options analysis in the application of wireless communications, which helped to lower the potential for escalation, refer to McGrath, R. G., Ferrier, W. J., & Mendelow, A. L. 2004. Real options as engines of choice and heterogeneity. *Academy of Management Review,* 29(1): 86–101.

60. One very useful solution for reducing the effects of managerial conceit is to incorporate an exit champion into the decision process. Exit champions provide arguments for killing off the firm's commitment to a decision. For a very insightful discussion on exit champions, refer to Royer, I. 2003. Why bad projects are so hard to kill. *Harvard Business Review,* 81(2): 49–56.

61. For more on how entrepreneurial orientation influences organizational performance, see Wang, L. 2008. Entrepreneurial orientation, learning orientation, and firm performance. *Entrepreneurship Theory & Practice,* 32(4): 635–657; and Runyan, R., Droge, C., & Swinney, J. 2008. Entrepreneurial orientation versus small business orientation: What are their relationships to firm performance? *Journal of Small Business Management,* 46(4): 567–588.

62. Covin, J. G. & Slevin, D. P. 1991. A conceptual model of entrepreneurship as firm behavior. *Entrepreneurship Theory and Practice,* 16(1): 7–24; Lumpkin, G. T. & Dess, G. G. 1996. Clarifying the entrepreneurial orientation construct and linking it to performance. *Academy of Management Review,* 21(1): 135–172; and McGrath, R. G. & MacMillan, I. C. 2000. *The entrepreneurial mind-set.* Cambridge, MA: Harvard Business School Press.

63. Lumpkin, G. T. & Dess, G. G. 2001. Linking two dimensions of entrepreneurial orientation to firm performance: The moderating role of environment and life cycle. *Journal of Business Venturing,* 16: 429–451.

64. For an interesting discussion, see Day, J. D., Mang, P. Y., Richter, A., & Roberts, J. 2001. The innovative organization: Why new ventures need more than a room of their own. *McKinsey Quarterly,* 2: 21–31.

65. Crockett, R. O. 2001. Chris Galvin shakes things up—again. *BusinessWeek,* May 28: 38–39.

66. For insights into the role of information technology in innovativeness, see Dibrell, C., Davis, P. S., & Craig, J. 2008. Fueling innovation through information technology in SMEs. *Journal of Small Business Management,* 46(2): 203–218.

67. For an interesting discussion of the impact of innovativeness on organizational outcomes, see Cho, H. J. & Pucik, V. 2005. Relationship between innovativeness, quality, growth, profitability, and market value. *Strategic Management Journal,* 26(6): 555–575.

68. Danneels, E. & Sethi, R. 2011. New product exploration under environmental turbulence. *Organization Science,* 22(4): 1026–1039.

69. Lieberman, M. B. & Montgomery, D. B. 1988. First mover advantages. *Strategic Management Journal,* 9 (Special Issue): 41–58.

70. The discussion of first-mover advantages is based on several articles, including Lambkin, M. 1988. Order of entry and performance in new markets. *Strategic Management Journal,* 9: 127–140; Lieberman & Montgomery, op. cit., pp. 41–58; and Miller, A. & Camp, B. 1985. Exploring determinants of success in corporate ventures. *Journal of Business Venturing,* 1(2): 87–105.

71. Moore, G. A. 1999. *Crossing the chasm* (2nd ed.). New York: HarperBusiness.

72. Mallas, S. 2005. PepsiCo loses its Edge. *Motley Fool,* June 1, *www.fool.com.*

73. Lyons, D. 2006. The cheap revolution. *Forbes,* September 18: 102–111.

74. Miller, K. D. 2007. Risk and rationality in entrepreneurial processes. *Strategic Entrepreneurship Journal,* 1(1–2): 57–74.

75. Drucker, op. cit., pp. 109–110.

Analyzing Strategic Management Cases

After reading this chapter, you should have a good understanding of the following learning objectives:

LO13.1 How strategic case analysis is used to simulate real-world experiences.

LO13.2 How analyzing strategic management cases can help develop the ability to differentiate, speculate, and integrate when evaluating complex business problems.

LO13.3 The steps involved in conducting a strategic management case analysis.

LO13.4 How to get the most out of case analysis.

LO13.5 How integrative thinking and conflict-inducing discussion techniques can lead to better decisions.

LO13.6 How to use the strategic insights and material from each of the 12 previous chapters in the text to analyze issues posed by strategic management cases.

Why Analyze Strategic Management Cases?

If you don't ask the right questions, then you're never going to get the right solution. I spent too much of my career feeling like I'd done a really good job answering the wrong question. And that was because I was letting other people give me the question. One of the things that I've tried to do more and more—and I obviously have the opportunity to do as a leader—is to take ownership of the question. And so I'm much more interested these days in having debates about what the questions should be than I necessarily am about the solutions.[1]

—Tim Brown, CEO of IDEO (a leading design consulting firm)

It is often said that the key to finding good answers is to ask good questions. Strategic managers and business leaders are required to evaluate options, make choices, and find solutions to the challenges they face every day. To do so, they must learn to ask the right questions. The study of strategic management poses the same challenge. The process of analyzing, decision making, and implementing strategic actions raises many good questions:

- Why do some firms succeed and others fail?
- Why are some companies higher performers than others?
- What information is needed in the strategic planning process?
- How do competing values and beliefs affect strategic decision making?
- What skills and capabilities are needed to implement a strategy effectively?

How does a student of strategic management answer these questions? By strategic case analysis. **Case analysis** simulates the real-world experience that strategic managers and company leaders face as they try to determine how best to run their companies. It places students in the middle of an actual situation and challenges them to figure out what to do.[2]

case analysis
a method of learning complex strategic management concepts—such as environmental analysis, the process of decision making, and implementing strategic actions—through placing students in the middle of an actual situation and challenging them to figure out what to do.

Asking the right questions is just the beginning of case analysis. In the previous chapters we have discussed issues and challenges that managers face and provided analytical frameworks for understanding the situation. But once the analysis is complete, decisions have to be made. Case analysis forces you to choose among different options and set forth a plan of action based on your choices. But even then the job is not done. Strategic case analysis also requires that you address how you will implement the plan and the implications of choosing one course of action over another.

A strategic management case is a detailed description of a challenging situation faced by an organization.[3] It usually includes a chronology of events and extensive support materials, such as financial statements, product lists, and transcripts of interviews with employees. Although names or locations are sometimes changed to provide anonymity, cases usually report the facts of a situation as authentically as possible.

One of the main reasons to analyze strategic management cases is to develop an ability to evaluate business situations critically. In case analysis, memorizing key terms and conceptual frameworks is not enough. To analyze a case, it is important that you go beyond textbook prescriptions and quick answers. It requires you to look deeply into the information that is provided and root out the essential issues and causes of a company's problems.

The types of skills that are required to prepare an effective strategic case analysis can benefit you in actual business situations. Case analysis adds to the overall learning experience by helping you acquire or improve skills that may not be taught in a typical lecture course.

LO13.2

How analyzing strategic management cases can help develop the ability to differentiate, speculate, and integrate when evaluating complex business problems.

Three capabilities that can be learned by conducting case analysis are especially useful to strategic managers—the ability to differentiate, speculate, and integrate.[4] Here's how case analysis can enhance those skills:

1. *Differentiate.* Effective strategic management requires that many different elements of a situation be evaluated at once. This is also true in case analysis. When analyzing cases, it is important to isolate critical facts, evaluate whether assumptions are useful or faulty, and distinguish between good and bad information. Differentiating between the factors that are influencing the situation presented by a case is necessary for making a good analysis. Strategic management also involves understanding that problems are often complex and multilayered. This applies to case analysis as well. Ask whether the case deals with operational, business-level, or corporate issues. Do the problems stem from weaknesses in the internal value chain or threats in the external environment? Dig deep. Being too quick to accept the easiest or least controversial answer will usually fail to get to the heart of the problem.

2. *Speculate.* Strategic managers need to be able to use their imagination to envision an explanation or solution that might not readily be apparent. The same is true with case analysis. Being able to imagine different scenarios or contemplate the outcome of a decision can aid the analysis. Managers also have to deal with uncertainty since most decisions are made without complete knowledge of the circumstances. This is also true in case analysis. Case materials often seem to be missing data or the information provided is contradictory. The ability to speculate about details that are unknown or the consequences of an action can be helpful.

3. *Integrate.* Strategy involves looking at the big picture and having an organizationwide perspective. Strategic case analysis is no different. Even though the chapters in this textbook divide the material into various topics that may apply to different parts of an organization, all of this information must be integrated into one set of recommendations that will affect the whole company. A strategic manager needs to comprehend how all the factors that influence the organization will interact. This also applies to case analysis. Changes made in one part of the organization affect other parts. Thus, a holistic perspective that integrates the impact of various decisions and environmental influences on all parts of the organization is needed.

In business, these three activities sometimes "compete" with each other for your attention. For example, some decision makers may have a natural ability to differentiate among elements of a problem but are not able to integrate them very well. Others have enough innate creativity to imagine solutions or fill in the blanks when information is missing. But they may have a difficult time when faced with hard numbers or cold facts. Even so, each of these skills is important. The mark of a good strategic manager is the ability to simultaneously make distinctions and envision the whole, and to imagine a future scenario while staying focused on the present. Thus, another reason to conduct case analysis is to help you develop and exercise your ability to differentiate, speculate, and integrate. David C. Novak, the chairman and CEO of Yum! Brands, provides a useful insight on this matter:[5]

> I think what we need in our leaders, the people who ultimately run our companies and run our functions, is whole-brained people—people who can be analytical but also have the creativity, the right-brain side of the equation. There's more and more of a premium on that today than ever before.

Case analysis takes the student through the whole cycle of activity that a manager would face. Beyond the textbook descriptions of concepts and examples, case analysis asks you to "walk a mile in the shoes" of the strategic decision maker and learn to evaluate situations

ANALYSIS, DECISION MAKING, AND CHANGE AT SAPIENT HEALTH NETWORK

Sapient Health Network (SHN) had gotten off to a good start. CEO Jim Kean and his two cofounders had raised $5 million in investor capital to launch their vision: an Internet-based health care information subscription service. The idea was to create an Internet community for people suffering from chronic diseases. It would provide members with expert information, resources, a message board, and chat rooms so that people suffering from the same ailments could provide each other with information and support. "Who would be more voracious consumers of information than people who are faced with life-changing, life-threatening illnesses?" thought Bill Kelly, one of SHN's cofounders. Initial market research and beta tests had supported that view.

During the beta tests, however, the service had been offered for free. The troubles began when SHN tried to convert its trial subscribers into paying ones. Fewer than 5 percent signed on, far less than the 15 percent the company had projected. Sapient hired a vice president of marketing who launched an aggressive promotion, but after three months of campaigning SHN still had only 500 members. SHN was now burning through $400,000 per month, with little revenue to show for it.

At that point, according to SHN board member Susan Clymer, "there was a lot of scrambling around trying to figure out how we could wring value out of what we'd already accomplished." One thing SHN had created was an expert software system which had two components: an "intelligent profile engine" (IPE) and an "intelligent query engine" (IQE). SHN used this system to collect detailed information from its subscribers.

SHN was sure that the expert system was its biggest selling point. But how could the company use it? Then the founders remembered that the original business plan had suggested there might be a market for aggregate data about patient populations gathered from the website. Could they turn the business around by selling patient data? To analyze the possibility, Kean tried out the idea on the market research arm of a huge east coast health care conglomerate. The officials were intrigued. SHN realized that its expert system could become a market research tool.

Once the analysis was completed, the founders made the decision: They would still create Internet communities for chronically ill patients, but the service would be free. And they would transform SHN from a company that processed subscriptions to one that sold market research.

Finally, they enacted the changes. Some of the changes were painful, including laying off 18 employees. However, SHN needed more health care industry expertise. It even hired an interim CEO, Craig Davenport, a 25-year veteran of the industry, to steer the company in its new direction. Finally, SHN had to communicate a new message to its members. It began by reimbursing the $10,000 of subscription fees they had paid.

All of this paid off dramatically in a matter of just two years. Revenues jumped to $1.9 million, and early in the third year SHN was purchased by WebMD. Less than a year after that, WebMD merged with Healtheon. The combined company still operates a thriving office out of SHN's original location in Portland, Oregon.

Sources: Ferguson, S. 2007. Health care gets a better IT prescription. *Baseline,* *www.baselinemag.com,* May 24. Brenneman, K. 2000. Healtheon/WebMD's local office is thriving. *Business Journal of Portland,* June 2; and Raths, D. 1998. Reversal of fortune. *Inc. Technology,* 2: 52–62.

critically. Executives and owners must make decisions every day with limited information and a swirl of business activity going on around them. Consider the example of Sapient Health Network, an Internet start-up that had to undergo some analysis and problem solving just to survive. Strategy Spotlight 13.1 describes how this company transformed itself after a serious self-examination during a time of crisis.

As you can see from the experience of Sapient Health Network, businesses are often faced with immediate challenges that threaten their lives. The Sapient case illustrates how the strategic management process helped it survive. First, the company realistically assessed the environment, evaluated the marketplace, and analyzed its resources. Then it made tough decisions, which included shifting its market focus, hiring and firing, and redeploying its assets. Finally, it took action. The result was not only firm survival but also a quick turnaround leading to rapid success.

How to Conduct a Case Analysis

The process of analyzing strategic management cases involves several steps. In this section we will review the mechanics of preparing a case analysis. Before beginning, there are two things to keep in mind that will clarify your understanding of the process and make the results of the process more meaningful.

LO13.3

The steps involved in conducting a strategic management case analysis.

First, unless you prepare for a case discussion, there is little you can gain from the discussion and even less that you can offer. Effective strategic managers don't enter into problem-solving situations without doing some homework—investigating the situation, analyzing and researching possible solutions, and sometimes gathering the advice of others. Good problem solving often requires that decision makers be immersed in the facts, options, and implications surrounding the problem. In case analysis, this means reading and thoroughly comprehending the case materials before trying to make an analysis.

The second point is related to the first. To get the most out of a case analysis, you must place yourself "inside" the case—that is, think like an actual participant in the case situation. However, there are several positions you can take. These are discussed in the following paragraphs:

- *Strategic decision maker.* This is the position of the senior executive responsible for resolving the situation described in the case. It may be the CEO, the business owner, or a strategic manager in a key executive position.
- *Board of directors.* Since the board of directors represents the owners of a corporation, it has a responsibility to step in when a management crisis threatens the company. As a board member, you may be in a unique position to solve problems.
- *Outside consultant.* Either the board or top management may decide to bring in outsiders. Consultants often have an advantage because they can look at a situation objectively. But they also may be at a disadvantage since they have no power to enforce changes.

Before beginning the analysis, it may be helpful to envision yourself assuming one of these roles. Then, as you study and analyze the case materials, you can make a diagnosis and recommend solutions in a way that is consistent with your position. Try different perspectives. You may find that your view of the situation changes depending on the role you play. As an outside consultant, for example, it may be easy for you to conclude that certain individuals should be replaced in order to solve a problem presented in the case. However, if you take the role of the CEO who knows the individuals and the challenges they have been facing, you may be reluctant to fire them and will seek another solution instead.

The idea of assuming a particular role is similar to the real world in various ways. In your career, you may work in an organization where outside accountants, bankers, lawyers, or other professionals are advising you about how to resolve business situations or improve your practices. Their perspective will be different from yours, but it is useful to understand things from their point of view. Conversely, you may work as a member of the audit team of an accounting firm or the loan committee of a bank. In those situations, it would be helpful if you understood the situation from the perspective of the business leader who must weigh your views against all the other advice that he or she receives. Case analysis can help develop an ability to appreciate such multiple perspectives.

One of the most challenging roles to play in business is as a business founder or owner. For small businesses or entrepreneurial start-ups, the founder may wear all hats at once—key decision maker, primary stockholder, and CEO. Hiring an outside consultant may not be an option. However, the issues faced by young firms and established firms are often not that different, especially when it comes to formulating a plan of action. Business plans that entrepreneurial firms use to raise money or propose a business expansion typically revolve around a few key issues that must be addressed no matter what the size or age of the business. Strategy Spotlight 13.2 reviews business planning issues that are most important to consider when evaluating any case, especially from the perspective of the business founder or owner.

USING A BUSINESS PLAN FRAMEWORK TO ANALYZE STRATEGIC CASES

Established businesses often have to change what they are doing in order to improve their competitive position or sometimes simply to survive. To make the changes effectively, businesses usually need a plan. Business plans are no longer just for entrepreneurs. The kind of market analysis, decision making, and action planning that is considered standard practice among new ventures can also benefit going concerns that want to make changes, seize an opportunity, or head in a new direction.

The best business plans, however, are not those that are loaded with decades of month-by-month financial projections or that depend on rigid adherence to a schedule of events that is impossible to predict. The good ones are focused on four factors that are critical to new venture success. These same factors are important in case analysis as well because they get to the heart of many of the problems found in strategic cases.

1. **The people.** "When I receive a business plan, I always read the résumé section first," says Harvard Professor William Sahlman. The people questions that are critically important to investors include: What are their skills? How much experience do they have? What is their reputation? Have they worked together as a team? These same questions also may be used in case analysis to evaluate the role of individuals in the strategic case.

2. **The opportunity.** Business opportunities come in many forms. They are not limited to new ventures. The chance to enter new markets, introduce new products, or merge with a competitor provides many of the challenges that are found in strategic management cases. What are the consequences of such actions? Will the proposed changes affect the firm's business concept? What factors might stand in the way of success? The same issues are also present in most strategic cases.

3. **The context.** Things happen in contexts that cannot be controlled by a firm's managers. This is particularly true of the general environment, where social trends, economic changes, or events such as the September 11, 2001, terrorist attacks can change business overnight. When evaluating strategic cases, ask: Is the company aware of the impact of context on the business? What will it do if the context changes? Can it influence the context in a way that favors the company?

4. **Risk and reward.** With a new venture, the entrepreneurs and investors take the risks and get the rewards. In strategic cases, the risks and rewards often extend to many other stakeholders, such as employees, customers, and suppliers. When analyzing a case, ask: Are the managers making choices that will pay off in the future? Are the rewards evenly distributed? Will some stakeholders be put at risk if the situation in the case changes? What if the situation remains the same? Could that be even riskier?

Whether a business is growing or shrinking, large or small, industrial or service-oriented, the issues of people, opportunities, context, and risks and rewards will have a large impact on its performance. Therefore, you should always consider these four factors when evaluating strategic management cases.

Sources: Wasserman, E. 2003. A simple plan. *MBA Jungle,* February: 50–55; DeKluyver, C. A. 2000. *Strategic thinking: An executive perspective.* Upper Saddle River, NJ: Prentice Hall; and Sahlman, W. A. 1997. How to write a great business plan. *Harvard Business Review,* 75(4): 98–108.

Next we will review five steps to follow when conducting a strategic management case analysis: becoming familiar with the material, identifying the problems, analyzing the strategic issues using the tools and insights of strategic management, proposing alternative solutions, and making recommendations.[6]

Become Familiar with the Material

Written cases often include a lot of material. They may be complex and include detailed financials or long passages. Even so, to understand a case and its implications, you must become familiar with its content. Sometimes key information is not immediately apparent. It may be contained in the footnotes to an exhibit or in an interview with a lower-level employee. In other cases the important points may be difficult to grasp because the subject matter is so unfamiliar. When you approach a strategic case, try the following technique to enhance comprehension:

- Read quickly through the case one time to get an overall sense of the material.
- Use the initial read-through to assess possible links to strategic concepts.
- Read through the case again, in depth. Make written notes as you read.

- Evaluate how strategic concepts might inform key decisions or suggest alternative solutions.
- After formulating an initial recommendation, thumb through the case again quickly to help assess the consequences of the actions you propose.

Identify Problems

When conducting case analysis, one of your most important tasks is to identify the problem. Earlier we noted that one of the main reasons to conduct case analysis is to find solutions. But you cannot find a solution unless you know the problem. Another saying you may have heard is "A good diagnosis is half the cure." In other words, once you have determined what the problem is, you are well on your way to identifying a reasonable solution.

Some cases have more than one problem. But the problems are usually related. For a hypothetical example, consider the following: Company A was losing customers to a new competitor. Upon analysis, it was determined that the competitor had a 50 percent faster delivery time even though its product was of lower quality. The managers of company A could not understand why customers would settle for an inferior product. It turns out that no one was marketing to company A's customers that its product was superior. A second problem was that falling sales resulted in cuts in company A's sales force. Thus, there were two related problems: inferior delivery technology and insufficient sales effort.

When trying to determine the problem, avoid getting hung up on symptoms. Zero in on the problem. For example, in the company A example above, the symptom was losing customers. But the problems were an underfunded, understaffed sales force combined with an outdated delivery technology. Try to see beyond the immediate symptoms to the more fundamental problems.

Another tip when preparing a case analysis is to articulate the problem.[7] Writing down a problem statement gives you a reference point to turn to as you proceed through the case analysis. This is important because the process of formulating strategies or evaluating implementation methods may lead you away from the initial problem. Make sure your recommendation actually addresses the problems you have identified.

One more thing about identifying problems: Sometimes problems are not apparent until *after* you do the analysis. In some cases the problem will be presented plainly, perhaps in the opening paragraph or on the last page of the case. But in other cases the problem does not emerge until after the issues in the case have been analyzed. We turn next to the subject of strategic case analysis.

Conduct Strategic Analyses

This textbook has presented numerous analytical tools (e.g., five-forces analysis and value-chain analysis), contingency frameworks (e.g., when to use related rather than unrelated diversification strategies), and other techniques that can be used to evaluate strategic situations. The previous 12 chapters have addressed practices that are common in strategic management, but only so much can be learned by studying the practices and concepts. The best way to understand these methods is to apply them by conducting analyses of specific cases.

The first step is to determine which strategic issues are involved. Is there a problem in the company's competitive environment? Or is it an internal problem? If it is internal, does it have to do with organizational structure? Strategic controls? Uses of technology? Or perhaps the company has overworked its employees or underutilized its intellectual capital. Has the company mishandled a merger? Chosen the wrong diversification strategy? Botched a new product introduction? Each of these issues is linked to one or more of the concepts discussed earlier in the text. Determine what strategic issues are associated with the problems you have identified. Remember also that most real-life case situations involve issues that are highly interrelated. Even in cases where there is only one major problem, the strategic processes required to solve it may involve several parts of the organization.

Once you have identified the issues that apply to the case, conduct the analysis. For example, you may need to conduct a five-forces analysis or dissect the company's competitive strategy. Perhaps you need to evaluate whether its resources are rare, valuable, difficult to imitate, or difficult to substitute. Financial analysis may be needed to assess the company's economic prospects. Perhaps the international entry mode needs to be reevaluated because of changing conditions in the host country. Employee empowerment techniques may need to be improved to enhance organizational learning. Whatever the case, all the strategic concepts introduced in the text include insights for assessing their effectiveness. Determining how well a company is doing these things is central to the case analysis process.

Financial ratio analysis is one of the primary tools used to conduct case analysis. Appendix 1 to Chapter 13 includes a discussion and examples of the financial ratios that are often used to evaluate a company's performance and financial well-being. Exhibit 13.1 provides a summary of the financial ratios presented in Appendix 1 to this chapter.

In this part of the overall strategic analysis process, it is also important to test your own assumptions about the case.[8] First, what assumptions are you making about the case materials? It may be that you have interpreted the case content differently than your team

> **financial ratio analysis**
> a method of evaluating a company's performance and financial well-being through ratios of accounting values, including short-term solvency, long-term solvency, asset utilization, profitability, and market value ratios.

EXHIBIT 13.1 Summary of Financial Ratio Analysis Techniques

Ratio	What It Measures
Short-term solvency, or liquidity, ratios:	
Current ratio	Ability to use assets to pay off liabilities.
Quick ratio	Ability to use liquid assets to pay off liabilities quickly.
Cash ratio	Ability to pay off liabilities with cash on hand.
Long-term solvency, or financial leverage, ratios:	
Total debt ratio	How much of a company's total assets are financed by debt.
Debt-equity ratio	Compares how much a company is financed by debt with how much it is financed by equity.
Equity multiplier	How much debt is being used to finance assets.
Times interest earned ratio	How well a company has its interest obligations covered.
Cash coverage ratio	A company's ability to generate cash from operations.
Asset utilization, or turnover, ratios:	
Inventory turnover	How many times each year a company sells its entire inventory.
Days' sales in inventory	How many days on average inventory is on hand before it is sold.
Receivables turnover	How frequently each year a company collects on its credit sales.
Days' sales in receivables	How many days on average it takes to collect on credit sales (average collection period).
Total asset turnover	How much of sales is generated for every dollar in assets.
Capital intensity	The dollar investment in assets needed to generate $1 in sales.
Profitability ratios:	
Profit margin	How much profit is generated by every dollar of sales.
Return on assets (ROA)	How effectively assets are being used to generate a return.
Return on equity (ROE)	How effectively amounts invested in the business by its owners are being used to generate a return.
Market value ratios:	
Price-earnings ratio	How much investors are willing to pay per dollar of current earnings.
Market-to-book ratio	Compares market value of the company's investments to the cost of those investments.

members or classmates. Being clear about these assumptions will be important in determining how to analyze the case. Second, what assumptions have you made about the best way to resolve the problems? Ask yourself why you have chosen one type of analysis over another. This process of assumption checking can also help determine if you have gotten to the heart of the problem or are still just dealing with symptoms.

As mentioned earlier, sometimes the critical diagnosis in a case can be made only after the analysis is conducted. However, by the end of this stage in the process, you should know the problems and have completed a thorough analysis of them. You can now move to the next step: finding solutions.

Propose Alternative Solutions

It is important to remember that in strategic management case analysis, there is rarely one right answer or one best way. Even when members of a class or a team agree on what the problem is, they may not agree upon how to solve the problem. Therefore, it is helpful to consider several different solutions.

After conducting strategic analysis and identifying the problem, develop a list of options. What are the possible solutions? What are the alternatives? First, generate a list of all the options you can think of without prejudging any one of them. Remember that not all cases call for dramatic decisions or sweeping changes. Some companies just need to make small adjustments. In fact, "Do nothing" may be a reasonable alternative in some cases. Although that is rare, it might be useful to consider what will happen if the company does nothing. This point illustrates the purpose of developing alternatives: to evaluate what will happen if a company chooses one solution over another.

Thus, during this step of a case analysis, you will evaluate choices and the implications of those choices. One aspect of any business that is likely to be highlighted in this part of the analysis is strategy implementation. Ask how the choices made will be implemented. It may be that what seems like an obvious choice for solving a problem creates an even bigger problem when implemented. But remember also that no strategy or strategic "fix" is going to work if it cannot be implemented. Once a list of alternatives is generated, ask:

- Can the company afford it? How will it affect the bottom line?
- Is the solution likely to evoke a competitive response?
- Will employees throughout the company accept the changes? What impact will the solution have on morale?
- How will the decision affect other stakeholders? Will customers, suppliers, and others buy into it?
- How does this solution fit with the company's vision, mission, and objectives?
- Will the culture or values of the company be changed by the solution? Is it a positive change?

The point of this step in the case analysis process is to find a solution that both solves the problem and is realistic. A consideration of the implications of various alternative solutions will generally lead you to a final recommendation that is more thoughtful and complete.

Make Recommendations

The basic aim of case analysis is to find solutions. Your analysis is not complete until you have recommended a course of action. In this step the task is to make a set of recommendations that your analysis supports. Describe exactly what needs to be done. Explain why this course of action will solve the problem. The recommendation should also include suggestions for how best to implement the proposed solution because the recommended actions and their implications for the performance and future of the firm are interrelated.

Recall that the solution you propose must solve the problem you identified. This point cannot be overemphasized; too often students make recommendations that treat only symptoms or fail to tackle the central problems in the case. Make a logical argument that shows how the problem led to the analysis and the analysis led to the recommendations you are proposing. Remember, an analysis is not an end in itself; it is useful only if it leads to a solution.

The actions you propose should describe the very next steps that the company needs to take. Don't say, for example, "If the company does more market research, then I would recommend the following course of action. . . ." Instead, make conducting the research part of your recommendation. Taking the example a step further, if you also want to suggest subsequent actions that may be different *depending* on the outcome of the market research, that's OK. But don't make your initial recommendation conditional on actions the company may or may not take.

In summary, case analysis can be a very rewarding process but, as you might imagine, it can also be frustrating and challenging. If you will follow the steps described above, you will address the different elements of a thorough analysis. This approach can give your analysis a solid footing. Then, even if there are differences of opinion about how to interpret the facts, analyze the situation, or solve the problems, you can feel confident that you have not missed any important steps in finding the best course of action.

Students are often asked to prepare oral presentations of the information in a case and their analysis of the best remedies. This is frequently assigned as a group project. Or you may be called upon in class to present your ideas about the circumstances or solutions for a case the class is discussing. Exhibit 13.2 provides some tips for preparing an oral case presentation.

EXHIBIT 13.2 Preparing an Oral Case Presentation

Rule	Description
Organize your thoughts.	Begin by becoming familiar with the material. If you are working with a team, compare notes about the key points of the case and share insights that other team members may have gleaned from tables and exhibits. Then make an outline. This is one of the best ways to organize the flow and content of the presentation.
Emphasize strategic analysis.	The purpose of case analysis is to diagnose problems and find solutions. In the process, you may need to unravel the case material as presented and reconfigure it in a fashion that can be more effectively analyzed. Present the material in a way that lends itself to analysis—don't simply restate what is in the case. This involves three major categories with the following emphasis: Background/Problem Statement 10–20% Strategic Analysis/Options 60–75% Recommendations/Action Plan 10–20% As you can see, the emphasis of your presentation should be on analysis. This will probably require you to reorganize the material so that the tools of strategic analysis can be applied.
Be logical and consistent.	A presentation that is rambling and hard to follow may confuse the listener and fail to evoke a good discussion. Present your arguments and explanations in a logical sequence. Support your claims with facts. Include financial analysis where appropriate. Be sure that the solutions you recommend address the problems you have identified.
Defend your position.	Usually an oral presentation is followed by a class discussion. Anticipate what others might disagree with, and be prepared to defend your views. This means being aware of the choices you made and the implications of your recommendations. Be clear about your assumptions. Be able to expand on your analysis.
Share presentation responsibilities.	Strategic management case analyses are often conducted by teams. Each member of the team should have a clear role in the oral presentation, preferably a speaking role. It's also important to coordinate the different parts of the presentation into a logical, smooth-flowing whole. How well team members work together is usually very apparent during an oral presentation.

How to Get the Most from Case Analysis

One of the reasons case analysis is so enriching as a learning tool is that it draws on many resources and skills besides just what is in the textbook. This is especially true in the study of strategy. Why? Because strategic management itself is a highly integrative task that draws on many areas of specialization at several levels, from the individual to the whole of society. Therefore, to get the most out of case analysis, expand your horizons beyond the concepts in this text and seek insights from your own reservoir of knowledge. Here are some tips for how to do that:[9]

- *Keep an open mind.* Like any good discussion, a case analysis discussion often evokes strong opinions and high emotions. But it's the variety of perspectives that makes case analysis so valuable: Many viewpoints usually lead to a more complete analysis. Therefore, avoid letting an emotional response to another person's style or opinion keep you from hearing what he or she has to say. Once you evaluate what is said, you may disagree with it or dismiss it as faulty. But unless you keep an open mind in the first place, you may miss the importance of the other person's contribution. Also, people often place a higher value on the opinions of those they consider to be good listeners.

- *Take a stand for what you believe.* Although it is vital to keep an open mind, it is also important to state your views proactively. Don't try to figure out what your friends or the instructor wants to hear. Analyze the case from the perspective of your own background and belief system. For example, perhaps you feel that a decision is unethical or that the managers in a case have misinterpreted the facts. Don't be afraid to assert that in the discussion. For one thing, when a person takes a strong stand, it often encourages others to evaluate the issues more closely. This can lead to a more thorough investigation and a more meaningful class discussion.

- *Draw on your personal experience.* You may have experiences from work or as a customer that shed light on some of the issues in a case. Even though one of the purposes of case analysis is to apply the analytical tools from this text, you may be able to add to the discussion by drawing on your outside experiences and background. Of course, you need to guard against carrying that to extremes. In other words, don't think that your perspective is the only viewpoint that matters! Simply recognize that firsthand experience usually represents a welcome contribution to the overall quality of case discussions.

- *Participate and persuade.* Have you heard the phrase "Vote early . . . and often"? Among loyal members of certain political parties, it has become rather a joke. Why? Because a democratic system is built on the concept of one person, one vote. Even though some voters may want to vote often enough to get their candidate elected, doing so is against the law. Not so in a case discussion. People who are persuasive and speak their mind can often influence the views of others. But to do so, you have to be prepared and convincing. Being persuasive is more than being loud or long-winded. It involves understanding all sides of an argument and being able to overcome objections to your own point of view. These efforts can make a case discussion more lively. And they parallel what happens in the real world; in business, people frequently share their opinions and attempt to persuade others to see things their way.

- *Be concise and to the point.* In the previous point, we encouraged you to speak up and "sell" your ideas to others in a case discussion. But you must be clear about what you are selling. Make your arguments in a way that is explicit and direct. Zero in on the most important points. Be brief. Don't try to make a lot of points at once by jumping around between topics. Avoid trying to explain the whole case situation at once. Remember, other students usually resent classmates who go on and on, take up a lot of "airtime," or repeat themselves unnecessarily. The best way to avoid this is to stay focused and be specific.

- *Think out of the box.* It's OK to be a little provocative; sometimes that is the consequence of taking a stand on issues. But it may be equally important to be imaginative and creative when making a recommendation or determining how to implement a solution. Albert Einstein once stated, "Imagination is more important than knowledge." The reason is that managing strategically requires more than memorizing concepts. Strategic management insights must be applied to each case differently—just knowing the principles is not enough. Imagination and out-of-the-box thinking help to apply strategic knowledge in novel and unique ways.

- *Learn from the insights of others.* Before you make up your mind about a case, hear what other students have to say. Get a second opinion, and a third, and so forth. Of course, in a situation where you have to put your analysis in writing, you may not be able to learn from others ahead of time. But in a case discussion, observe how various students attack the issues and engage in problem solving. Such observation skills also may be a key to finding answers within the case. For example, people tend to believe authority figures, so they would place a higher value on what a company president says. In some cases, however, the statements of middle managers may represent a point of view that is even more helpful for finding a solution to the problems presented by the case.

- *Apply insights from other case analyses.* Throughout the text, we have used examples of actual businesses to illustrate strategy concepts. The aim has been to show you how firms think about and deal with business problems. During the course, you may be asked to conduct several case analyses as part of the learning experience. Once you have performed a few case analyses, you will see how the concepts from the text apply in real-life business situations. Incorporate the insights learned from the text examples and your own previous case discussions into each new case that you analyze.

- *Critically analyze your own performance.* Performance appraisals are a standard part of many workplace situations. They are used to determine promotions, raises, and work assignments. In some organizations, everyone from the top executive down is subject to such reviews. Even in situations where the owner or CEO is not evaluated by others, top executives often find it useful to ask themselves regularly, Am I being effective? The same can be applied to your performance in a case analysis situation. Ask yourself, Were my comments insightful? Did I make a good contribution? How might I improve next time? Use the same criteria on yourself that you use to evaluate others. What grade would you give yourself? This technique not only will make you more fair in your assessment of others but also will indicate how your own performance can improve.

- *Conduct outside research.* Many times, you can enhance your understanding of a case situation by investigating sources outside the case materials. For example, you may want to study an industry more closely or research a company's close competitors. Recent moves such as mergers and acquisitions or product introductions may be reported in the business press. The company itself may provide useful information on its website or in its annual reports. Such information can usually spur additional discussion and enrich the case analysis. (*Caution:* It is best to check with your instructor in advance to be sure this kind of additional research is encouraged. Bringing in outside research may conflict with the instructor's learning objectives.)

EXHIBIT 13.3 Preparing a Written Case Analysis

Rule	Description
Be thorough.	Many of the ideas presented in Exhibit 13.2 about oral presentations also apply to written case analysis. However, a written analysis typically has to be more complete. This means writing out the problem statement and articulating assumptions. It is also important to provide support for your arguments and reference case materials or other facts more specifically.
Coordinate team efforts.	Written cases are often prepared by small groups. Within a group, just as in a class discussion, you may disagree about the diagnosis or the recommended plan of action. This can be healthy if it leads to a richer understanding of the case material. But before committing your ideas to writing, make sure you have coordinated your responses. Don't prepare a written analysis that appears contradictory or looks like a patchwork of disconnected thoughts.
Avoid restating the obvious.	There is no reason to restate material that everyone is familiar with already, namely, the case content. It is too easy for students to use up space in a written analysis with a recapitulation of the details of the case—this accomplishes very little. Stay focused on the key points. Restate only the information that is most central to your analysis.
Present information graphically.	Tables, graphs, and other exhibits are usually one of the best ways to present factual material that supports your arguments. For example, financial calculations such as break-even analysis, sensitivity analysis, or return on investment are best presented graphically. Even qualitative information such as product lists or rosters of employees can be summarized effectively and viewed quickly by using a table or graph.
Exercise quality control.	When presenting a case analysis in writing, it is especially important to use good grammar, avoid misspelling words, and eliminate typos and other visual distractions. Mistakes that can be glossed over in an oral presentation or class discussion are often highlighted when they appear in writing. Make your written presentation appear as professional as possible. Don't let the appearance of your written case keep the reader from recognizing the importance and quality of your analysis.

Several of the points suggested above for how to get the most out of case analysis apply only to an open discussion of a case, like that in a classroom setting. Exhibit 13.3 provides some additional guidelines for preparing a written case analysis.

LO13.5

How integrative thinking and conflict-inducing discussion techniques can lead to better decisions.

Useful Decision-Making Techniques in Case Analysis

The demands on today's business leaders require them to perform a wide variety of functions. The success of their organizations often depends on how they as individuals—and as part of groups—meet the challenges and deliver on promises. In this section we address three different techniques that can help managers make better decisions and, in turn, enable their organizations to achieve higher performance.

First, we discuss integrative thinking, a technique that helps managers make better decisions through the resolution of competing demands on resources, multiple contingencies, and diverse opportunities. Second, we address the concept of "asking heretical questions." These are questions that challenge conventional wisdom and may even seem odd or unusual—but they can often lead to valuable innovations. Third, we introduce two approaches to decision making that involve the effective use of conflict in the decision-making process. These are devil's advocacy and dialectical inquiry.

Integrative Thinking

integrative thinking a process of reconciling opposing thoughts by generating new alternatives and creative solutions rather than rejecting one thought in favor of another.

How does a leader make good strategic decisions in the face of multiple contingencies and diverse opportunities? A study by Roger L. Martin reveals that executives who have a capability known as **integrative thinking** are among the most effective leaders. In his book *The Opposable Mind,* Martin contends that people who can consider two conflicting ideas simultaneously, without dismissing one of the ideas or becoming discouraged about

EXHIBIT 13.4 Integrative Thinking: The Process of Thinking and Deciding

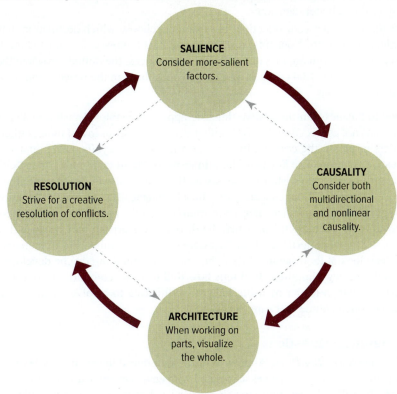

Source: Adaption from Harvard Business School Press from R. L. Martin. *The Opposable Mind*, 2007.

reconciling them, often make the best problem solvers because of their ability to creatively synthesize the opposing thoughts. In explaining the source of his title, Martin quotes F. Scott Fitzgerald, who observed, "The test of a first-rate intelligence is the ability to hold two opposing ideas in mind at the same time and still retain the ability to function. One should, for example, be able to see that things are hopeless yet be determined to make them otherwise."[10]

In contrast to conventional thinking, which tends to focus on making choices between competing ideas from a limited set of alternatives, integrative thinking is the process by which people reconcile opposing thoughts to identify creative solutions that provide them with more options and new alternatives. Exhibit 13.4 outlines the four stages of the integrative thinking and deciding process. Martin uses the admittedly simple example of deciding where to go on vacation to illustrate the stages:

- *Salience.* Take stock of what features of the decision you consider relevant and important. For example: Where will you go? What will you see? Where will you stay? What will it cost? Is it safe? Other features may be less important, but try to think of everything that may matter.
- *Causality.* Make a mental map of the causal relationships between the features, that is, how the various features are related to one another. For example, is it worth it to invite friends to share expenses? Will an exotic destination be less safe?
- *Architecture.* Use the mental map to arrange a sequence of decisions that will lead to a specific outcome. For example, will you make the hotel and flight arrangements first, or focus on which sightseeing tours are available? No particular

decision path is right or wrong, but considering multiple options simultaneously may lead to a better decision.

- **Resolution.** Make your selection. For example, choose which destination, which flight, and so forth. Your final resolution is linked to how you evaluated the first three stages; if you are dissatisfied with your choices, the dotted arrows in the diagram (Exhibit 13.4) suggest you can go back through the process and revisit your assumptions.

Applied to business, an integrative thinking approach enables decision makers to consider situations not as forced trade-offs—either decrease costs or invest more; either satisfy shareholders or please the community—but as a method for synthesizing opposing ideas into a creative solution. The key is to think in terms of "both-and" rather than "either-or." "Integrative thinking," says Martin, "shows us that there's a way to integrate the advantages of one solution without canceling out the advantages of an alternative solution."

Although Martin found that integrative thinking comes naturally to some people, he also believes it can be taught. But it may be difficult to learn, in part because it requires people to *un*learn old patterns and become aware of how they think. For executives willing to take a deep look at their habits of thought, integrative thinking can be developed into a valuable skill. Strategy Spotlight 13.3 tells how Red Hat Inc. cofounder Bob Young made his company a market leader by using integrative thinking to resolve a major problem in the domain of open-source software.

Asking Heretical Questions

In his recent book *The Big Pivot,* Andrew Winston introduced the concept of heretical innovation to help address the challenges associated with environmental sustainability in today's world.[11] He describes the need to pursue a deeper level of innovation that challenges long-held beliefs about how things work. Central to addressing these challenges is the need to pose "heretical questions"—those that challenge conventional wisdom. Typically, they may make us uncomfortable or may seem odd (or even impossible)—but they often become the means of coming up with major innovations. Although the context of Winston's discussion was environmental sustainability, we believe that his ideas have useful implications for major challenges faced by today's managers in a wide range of firms and industries.

Heretical questions can address issues that are both small and large—from redesigning a single process or product to rethinking the whole business model. One must not discount the value of the approach in considering small matters. After all, the vast majority of people in a company don't have the mandate to rethink strategy. However, anyone in an organization can ask disruptive questions that profoundly change one aspect of a business. What makes this heretical is how deeply it challenges the conventional wisdom.

Consider the fascinating story of UPS's "no left turns," a classic tale in the sustainability world that has become rather well known. The catchy phrase became a rallying cry for mapping out new delivery routes that avoided crossing traffic and idling at stoplights. UPS is saving time, money, and energy—about 85 million miles and 8 million gallons of fuel annually.

Also, take the example of dyeing clothing—a tremendously water-intensive process. Somebody at Adidas asked a heretical question: Could we dye clothes with no water? The answer was yes. However, the company needed to partner with a small Thailand-based company, Yeh Group. The DreDye process Adidas is now piloting uses heat and pressure to force pigment into the fibers. The process uses no water and also cuts energy and chemical use by 50 percent!

Finally, in 2010, Kimberly-Clark, the $21 billion firm that is behind such brands as Kleenex and Scott, questioned the simple assumption that toilet paper rolls must have cardboard tubes to hold their shape. It created the Scott Naturals Tube-Free line, which

INTEGRATIVE THINKING AT RED HAT, INC.

How can a software developer make money giving away free software? That was the dilemma Red Hat founder Bob Young was facing during the early days of the open-source software movement. A Finnish developer named Linus Torvalds, using freely available UNIX software, had developed an operating system dubbed "Linux" that was being widely circulated in the freeware community. The software was intended specifically as an alternative to the pricey proprietary systems sold by Microsoft and Oracle. To use proprietary software, corporations had to pay hefty installation fees and were required to call Microsoft or Oracle engineers to fix it when anything went wrong. In Young's view it was a flawed and unsustainable business model.

But the free model was flawed as well. Although several companies had sprung up to help companies use Linux, there were few opportunities to profit from using it. As Young said, "You couldn't make any money selling [the Linux] operating system because all this stuff was free, and if you started to charge money for it, someone else would come in and price it lower. It was a commodity in the truest sense of the word." To complicate matters, hundreds of developers were part of the software community that was constantly modifying and debugging Linux—at a rate equivalent to three updates per day. As a result, systems administrators at corporations that tried to adopt the software spent so much time keeping track of updates that they didn't enjoy the savings they expected from using free software.

Young saw the appeal of both approaches but also realized a new model was needed. While contemplating the dilemma, he realized a salient feature that others had overlooked—because most major corporations have to live with software decisions for at least 10 years, they will nearly always choose to do business with the industry leader. Young realized he had to position Red Hat as the top provider of Linux software. To do that, he proposed a radical solution: provide the authoritative version of Linux and deliver it in a new way—as a download rather than on CD. He hired programmers to create a downloadable version—still free—and promised, in essence, to maintain its quality (for a fee, of course) by dealing with all the open-source programmers who were continually suggesting changes. In the process, he created a product companies could trust and then profited by establishing ongoing service relationships with customers. Red Hat's version of Linux became the de facto standard. By 2000, Linux was installed in 25 percent of server operating systems worldwide and Red Hat had captured over 50 percent of the global market for Linux systems.

By recognizing that a synthesis of two flawed business models could provide the best of both worlds, Young exhibited the traits of integrative thinking. He pinpointed the causal relationships between the salient features of the marketplace and Red Hat's path to prosperity. He then crafted an approach that integrated aspects of the two existing approaches into a new alternative. By resolving to provide a free downloadable version, Young also took responsibility for creating his own path to success. The payoff was substantial: When Red Hat went public in 1999, Young became a billionaire on the first day of trading. And by 2015 Red Hat had over $1.5 billion in annual revenues and a market capitalization of nearly $13 billion.

Sources: Martin, R. L. 2007. *The opposable mind.* Boston: Harvard Business School Press; and *finance.yahoo.com.*

offers this household staple in the familiar cylindrical shape. But it comes with no cardboard core—just a hole the same size. It's been very successful—a key part of the now $100 million Scott Naturals brand. While this product may not save the world, if it became the industry standard, we could eliminate 17 billion tubes that are used in the United States every year and save fuel by shipping lighter rolls. This is a good example of heretical thinking. After all, the product doesn't incrementally use less cardboard—it uses none.

The concept of accepting failure and aiming for deep, heretical innovation is difficult for most organizations to embrace. Ed Catmull, the president and cofounder of animation pioneer Pixar, claims that when you are doing something new, you are by definition doing something you don't know very well, and that means mistakes. However, if you don't encourage mistakes, he says, you won't encourage anything new: "We're very conscientious about making it so that mistakes really aren't thought of as bad . . . they're just learning."

Conflict-Inducing Techniques

Next we address some techniques often used to improve case analyses that involve the constructive use of conflict. In the classroom—as well as in the business world—you will frequently be analyzing cases or solving problems in groups. While the word *conflict* often has a negative connotation (e.g., rude behavior, personal affronts), it can be very helpful in arriving at better solutions to cases. It can provide an effective means for new insights as well as for rigorously questioning and analyzing assumptions and strategic alternatives. In fact, if you don't have constructive conflict, you may get only consensus. When this happens, decisions tend to be based on compromise rather than collaboration.

In your organizational behavior classes, you probably learned the concept of "group-think."[12] *Groupthink,* a term coined by Irving Janis after he conducted numerous studies on executive decision making, is a condition in which group members strive to reach agreement or consensus without realistically considering other viable alternatives. In effect, group norms bolster morale at the expense of critical thinking, and decision making is impaired.[13]

Many of us have probably been "victims" of groupthink at one time or another in our life. We may be confronted with situations when social pressure, politics, or "not wanting to stand out" may prevent us from voicing our concerns about a chosen course of action. Nevertheless, decision making in groups is a common practice in the management of many businesses. Most companies, especially large ones, rely on input from various top managers to provide valuable information and experience from their specialty area as well as their unique perspectives. Organizations need to develop cultures and reward systems that encourage people to express their perspectives and create open dialogues. Constructive conflict can be very helpful in that it emphasizes the need for managers to consider other people's perspectives and not simply become a strong advocate for positions that they may prefer.

Chapter 11 emphasized the importance of empowering individuals at all levels to participate in decision-making processes. After all, many of us have experienced situations where there is not a perfect correlation between one's rank and the viability of one's ideas! In terms of this course, case analysis involves a type of decision making that is often conducted in groups. Strategy Spotlight 13.4 provides guidelines for making team-based approaches to case analysis more effective.

Clearly, understanding how to work in groups and the potential problems associated with group decision processes can benefit the case analysis process. Therefore, let's first look at some of the symptoms of groupthink and suggest ways of preventing it. Then we will suggest some conflict-inducing decision-making techniques—devil's advocacy and dialectical inquiry—that can help to prevent groupthink and lead to better decisions.

Symptoms of Groupthink and How to Prevent It   Irving Janis identified several symptoms of groupthink, including:

- *An illusion of invulnerability.* This reassures people about possible dangers and leads to overoptimism and failure to heed warnings of danger.
- *A belief in the inherent morality of the group.* Because individuals think that what they are doing is right, they tend to ignore ethical or moral consequences of their decisions.
- *Stereotyped views of members of opposing groups.* Members of other groups are viewed as weak or not intelligent.
- *The application of pressure to members who express doubts about the group's shared illusions or question the validity of arguments proposed.*
- *The practice of self-censorship.* Members keep silent about their opposing views and downplay to themselves the value of their perspectives.
- *An illusion of unanimity.* People assume that judgments expressed by members are shared by all.
- *The appointment of mindguards.* People sometimes appoint themselves as mindguards to protect the group from adverse information that might break the climate of consensus (or agreement).

Clearly, groupthink is an undesirable and negative phenomenon that can lead to poor decisions. Irving Janis considers it to be a key contributor to such faulty decisions as the failure to prepare for the attack on Pearl Harbor, the escalation of the Vietnam conflict, and

MAKING CASE ANALYSIS TEAMS MORE EFFECTIVE

Working in teams can be very challenging. Not all team members have the same skills, interests, or motivations. Some team members just want to get the work done. Others see teams as an opportunity to socialize. Occasionally, there are team members who think they should be in charge and make all the decisions; other teams have freeloaders—team members who don't want to do anything except get credit for the team's work.

One consequence of these various styles is that team meetings can become time wasters. Disagreements about how to proceed, how to share the work, or what to do at the next meeting tend to slow down teams and impede progress toward the goal. While the dynamics of case analysis teams are likely to always be challenging depending on the personalities involved, one thing nearly all members realize is that, ultimately, the team's work must be completed. Most team members also aim to do the highest-quality work possible. The following guidelines provide some useful insights about how to get the work of a team done more effectively.

Spend More Time Together

One of the factors that prevents teams from doing a good job with case analysis is their failure to put in the necessary time. Unless teams really tackle the issues surrounding case analysis—both the issues in the case itself and organizing how the work is to be conducted—the end result will probably be lacking because decisions that are made too quickly are unlikely to get to the heart of the problem(s) in the case. "Meetings should be a precious resource, but they're treated like a necessary evil," says Kenneth Sole, a consultant who specializes in organizational behavior. As a result, teams that care more about finishing the analysis than getting the analysis right often make poor decisions.

Therefore, expect to have a few meetings that run long, especially at the beginning of the project, when the work is being organized and the issues in the case are being sorted out, and again at the end, when the team must coordinate the components of the case analysis that will be presented. Without spending this kind of time together, it is doubtful that the analysis will be comprehensive and the presentation is likely to be choppy and incomplete.

Make a Focused and Disciplined Agenda

To complete tasks and avoid wasting time, meetings need to have a clear purpose. To accomplish this at Roche, the Swiss drug and diagnostic product maker, CEO Franz Humer implemented a "decision agenda." The agenda focuses only on Roche's highest-value issues, and discussions are limited to these major topics. In terms of case analysis, the major topics include sorting out the issues of the case, linking elements of the case to the strategic issues presented in class or the text, and assigning roles to various team members. Such objectives help keep team members on track.

Agendas also can be used to address issues such as the timeline for accomplishing work. Otherwise, the purpose of meetings may only be to manage the "crisis" of getting the case analysis finished on time. One solution is to assign a team member to manage the agenda. That person could make sure the team stays focused on the tasks at hand and remains mindful of time constraints. Another role could be to link the team's efforts to the steps presented in Exhibit 13.2 and Exhibit 13.3 on how to prepare a case analysis.

Pay More Attention to Strategy

Teams often waste time by focusing on unimportant aspects of a case. These may include details that are interesting but irrelevant or operational issues rather than strategic issues. It is true that useful clues to the issues in the case are sometimes embedded in the conversations of key managers or the trends evident in a financial statement. But once such insights are discovered, teams need to focus on the underlying strategic problems in the case. To solve such problems, major corporations such as Cadbury Schweppes and Boeing hold meetings just to generate strategic alternatives for solving their problems. This gives managers time to consider the implications of various courses of action. Separate meetings are held to evaluate alternatives, make strategic decisions, and approve an action plan.

Once the strategic solutions or "course corrections" are identified—as is common in most cases assigned—the operational implications and details of implementation will flow from the strategic decisions that companies make. Therefore, focusing primarily on strategic issues will provide teams with insights for making recommendations that are based on a deeper understanding of the issues in the case.

Produce Real Decisions

Too often, meetings are about discussing rather than deciding. Teams often spend a lot of time talking without reaching any conclusions. As Raymond Sanchez, CEO of Florida-based Security Mortgage Group, says, meetings are often used to "rehash the hash that's already been hashed." To be efficient and productive, team meetings need to be about more than just information sharing and group input. For example, an initial meeting may result in the team realizing that it needs to study the case in greater depth and examine links to strategic issues more carefully. Once more analysis is conducted, the team needs to reach a consensus so that the decisions that are made will last once the meeting is over. Lasting decisions are more actionable because they free team members to take the next steps.

One technique for making progress in this way is recapping each meeting with a five-minute synthesis report. According to Pamela Schindler, director of the Center for Applied Management at Wittenberg University, it's important to think through the implications of the meeting before ending it. "The real joy of synthesis," says Schindler, "is realizing how many meetings you won't need."

continued

Not only are these guidelines useful for helping teams finish their work, but they can also help resolve some of the difficulties that teams often face. By involving every team member, using a meeting agenda, and focusing on the strategic issues that are critical to nearly every case, the discussion is limited and the criteria for making decisions become clearer. This allows the task to dominate rather than any one personality. And if the team finishes its work faster, this frees up time to focus on other projects or put the finishing touches on a case analysis presentation.

Sources: Mankins, M. C. 2004. Stop wasting valuable time. *Harvard Business Review*, September: 58–65; and Sauer, P. J. 2004. Escape from meeting hell. *Inc.*, May, *www.inc.com*.

the failure to prepare for the consequences of the Iraqi invasion. Many of the same sorts of flawed decision making occur in business organizations. Janis has provided several suggestions for preventing groupthink that can be used as valuable guides in decision making and problem solving:

- Leaders must encourage group members to address their concerns and objectives.
- When higher-level managers assign a problem for a group to solve, they should adopt an impartial stance and not mention their preferences.
- Before a group reaches its final decision, the leader should encourage members to discuss their deliberations with trusted associates and then report the perspectives back to the group.
- The group should invite outside experts and encourage them to challenge the group's viewpoints and positions.
- The group should divide into subgroups, meet at various times under different chairpersons, and then get together to resolve differences.
- After reaching a preliminary agreement, the group should hold a "second chance" meeting that provides members a forum to express any remaining concerns and rethink the issue prior to making a final decision.

Using Conflict to Improve Decision Making   In addition to the above suggestions, the effective use of conflict can be a means of improving decision making. Although conflict can have negative outcomes, such as ill will, anger, tension, and lowered motivation, both leaders and group members must strive to ensure that it is managed properly and used in a constructive manner.

Two conflict-inducing decision-making approaches that have become quite popular are *devil's advocacy* and *dialectical inquiry*. Both approaches incorporate conflict into the decision-making process through formalized debate. A group charged with making a decision or solving a problem is divided into two subgroups, and each will be involved in the analysis and solution.

devil's advocacy
a method of introducing conflict into a decision-making process by having specific individuals or groups act as a critic to an analysis or planned solution.

With **devil's advocacy,** one of the groups (or individuals) acts as a critic to the plan. The devil's advocate tries to come up with problems with the proposed alternative and suggest reasons why it should not be adopted. The role of the devil's advocate is to create dissonance. This ensures that the group will take a hard look at its original proposal or alternative. By having a group (or individual) assigned the role of devil's advocate, it becomes clear that such an adversarial stance is legitimized. It brings out criticisms that might otherwise not be made.

Some authors have suggested that the use of a devil's advocate can help boards of directors to ensure that decisions are addressed comprehensively and to avoid groupthink.[14] And Charles Elson, a director of Sunbeam Corporation, has argued:

> Devil's advocates are terrific in any situation because they help you to figure a decision's numerous implications. . . . The better you think out the implications prior to making the decision, the better the decision ultimately turns out to be. That's why a devil's advocate is always a great person, irritating sometimes, but a great person.

As one might expect, there can be some potential problems with using the devil's advocate approach. If one's views are constantly criticized, one may become demoralized. Thus, that person may come up with "safe solutions" in order to minimize embarrassment or personal risk and become less subject to criticism. Additionally, even if the devil's advocate is successful with finding problems with the proposed course of action, there may be no new ideas or counterproposals to take its place. Thus, the approach sometimes may simply focus on what is wrong without suggesting other ideas.

Dialectical inquiry attempts to accomplish the goals of the devil's advocate in a more constructive manner. It is a technique whereby a problem is approached from two alternative points of view. The idea is that out of a critique of the opposing perspectives—a thesis and an antithesis—a creative synthesis will occur. Dialectical inquiry involves the following steps:

1. Identify a proposal and the information that was used to derive it.
2. State the underlying assumptions of the proposal.
3. Identify a counterplan (antithesis) that is believed to be feasible, politically viable, and generally credible. However, it rests on assumptions that are opposite to the original proposal.
4. Engage in a debate in which individuals favoring each plan provide their arguments and support.
5. Identify a synthesis which, hopefully, includes the best components of each alternative.

There are some potential downsides associated with dialectical inquiry. It can be quite time-consuming and involve a good deal of training. Further, it may result in a series of compromises between the initial proposal and the counterplan. In cases where the original proposal was the best approach, this would be unfortunate.

Despite some possible limitations associated with these conflict-inducing decision-making techniques, they have many benefits. Both techniques force debate about underlying assumptions, data, and recommendations between subgroups. Such debate tends to prevent the uncritical acceptance of a plan that may seem to be satisfactory after a cursory analysis. The approach serves to tap the knowledge and perspectives of group members and continues until group members agree on both assumptions and recommended actions. Given that both approaches serve to use, rather than minimize or suppress, conflict, higher-quality decisions should result. Exhibit 13.5 briefly summarizes these techniques.

> **dialectical inquiry**
> a method of introducing conflict into a decision-making process by devising different proposals that are feasible, politically viable, and credible but rely on different assumptions and then debating the merits of each.

EXHIBIT 13.5 Two Conflict-Inducing Decision-Making Processes

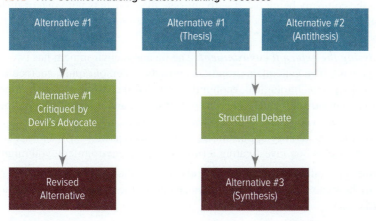

LO13.6

How to use the strategic insights and material from each of the 12 previous chapters in the text to analyze issues posed by strategic management cases.

Following the Analysis-Decision-Action Cycle in Case Analysis

In Chapter 1 we defined strategic management as the analysis, decisions, and actions that organizations undertake to create and sustain competitive advantages. It is no accident that we chose that sequence of words because it corresponds to the sequence of events that typically occurs in the strategic management process. In case analysis, as in the real world, this cycle of events can provide a useful framework. First, an analysis of the case in terms of the business environment and current events is needed. To make such an analysis, the case background must be considered. Next, based on that analysis, decisions must be made. This may involve formulating a strategy, choosing between difficult options, moving forward aggressively, or retreating from a bad situation. There are many possible decisions, depending on the case situation. Finally, action is required. Once decisions are made and plans are set, the action begins. The recommended action steps and the consequences of implementing these actions are the final stage.

Each of the previous 12 chapters of this book includes techniques and information that may be useful in a case analysis. However, not all of the issues presented will be important in every case. As noted earlier, one of the challenges of case analysis is to identify the most critical points and sort through material that may be ambiguous or unimportant.

In this section we draw on the material presented in each of the 12 chapters to show how it informs the case analysis process. The ideas are linked sequentially and in terms of an overarching strategic perspective. One of your jobs when conducting case analysis is to see how the parts of a case fit together and how the insights from the study of strategy can help you understand the case situation.

1. *Analyzing organizational goals and objectives.* A company's vision, mission, and objectives keep organization members focused on a common purpose. They also influence how an organization deploys its resources, relates to its stakeholders, and matches its short-term objectives with its long-term goals. The goals may even impact how a company formulates and implements strategies. When exploring issues of goals and objectives, you might ask:

   - Has the company developed short-term objectives that are inconsistent with its long-term mission? If so, how can management realign its vision, mission, and objectives?
   - Has the company considered all of its stakeholders equally in making critical decisions? If not, should the views of all stakeholders be treated the same or are some stakeholders more important than others?
   - Is the company being faced with an issue that conflicts with one of its long-standing policies? If so, how should it compare its existing policies to the potential new situation?

2. *Analyzing the external environment.* The business environment has two components. The general environment consists of demographic, sociocultural, political/legal, technological, economic, and global conditions. The competitive environment includes rivals, suppliers, customers, and other factors that may directly affect a company's success. Strategic managers must monitor the environment to identify opportunities and threats that may have an impact on performance. When investigating a firm's external environment, you might ask:

   - Does the company follow trends and events in the general environment? If not, how can these influences be made part of the company's strategic analysis process?

- Is the company effectively scanning and monitoring the competitive environment? If so, how is it using the competitive intelligence it is gathering to enhance its competitive advantage?
- Has the company correctly analyzed the impact of the competitive forces in its industry on profitability? If so, how can it improve its competitive position relative to these forces?

3. *Analyzing the internal environment.* A firm's internal environment consists of its resources and other value-adding capabilities. Value-chain analysis and a resource-based approach to analysis can be used to identify a company's strengths and weaknesses and determine how they are contributing to its competitive advantages. Evaluating firm performance can also help make meaningful comparisons with competitors. When researching a company's internal analysis, you might ask:

- Does the company know how the various components of its value chain are adding value to the firm? If not, what internal analysis is needed to determine its strengths and weakness?
- Has the company accurately analyzed the source and vitality of its resources? If so, is it deploying its resources in a way that contributes to competitive advantages?
- Is the company's financial performance as good as or better than that of its close competitors? If so, has it balanced its financial success with the performance criteria of other stakeholders such as customers and employees?

4. *Assessing a firm's intellectual assets.* Human capital is a major resource in today's knowledge economy. As a result, attracting, developing, and retaining talented workers is a key strategic challenge. Other assets such as patents and trademarks are also critical. How companies leverage their intellectual assets through social networks and strategic alliances, and how technology is used to manage knowledge, may be a major influence on a firm's competitive advantage. When analyzing a firm's intellectual assets, you might ask:

- Does the company have underutilized human capital? If so, what steps are needed to develop and leverage its intellectual assets?
- Is the company missing opportunities to forge strategic alliances? If so, how can it use its social capital to network more effectively?
- Has the company developed knowledge-management systems that capture what it learns? If not, what technologies can it employ to retain new knowledge?

5. *Formulating business-level strategies.* Firms use the competitive strategies of differentiation, focus, and overall cost leadership as a basis for overcoming the five competitive forces and developing sustainable competitive advantages. Combinations of these strategies may work best in some competitive environments. Additionally, an industry's life cycle is an important contingency that may affect a company's choice of business-level strategies. When assessing business-level strategies, you might ask:

- Has the company chosen the correct competitive strategy given its industry environment and competitive situation? If not, how should it use its strengths and resources to improve its performance?
- Does the company use combination strategies effectively? If so, what capabilities can it cultivate to further enhance profitability?
- Is the company using a strategy that is appropriate for the industry life cycle in which it is competing? If not, how can it realign itself to match its efforts to the current stage of industry growth?

6. *Formulating corporate-level strategies.* Large firms often own and manage portfolios of businesses. Corporate strategies address methods for achieving synergies among these businesses. Related and unrelated diversification techniques are alternative approaches to deciding which business should be added to or removed from a portfolio. Companies can diversify by means of mergers, acquisitions, joint ventures, strategic alliances, and internal development. When analyzing corporate-level strategies, you might ask:

- Is the company competing in the right businesses given the opportunities and threats that are present in the environment? If not, how can it realign its diversification strategy to achieve competitive advantages?
- Is the corporation managing its portfolio of businesses in a way that creates synergies among the businesses? If so, what additional business should it consider adding to its portfolio?
- Are the motives of the top corporate executives who are pushing diversification strategies appropriate? If not, what action can be taken to curb their activities or align them with the best interests of all stakeholders?

7. *Formulating international-level strategies.* Foreign markets provide both opportunities and potential dangers for companies that want to expand globally. To decide which entry strategy is most appropriate, companies have to evaluate the trade-offs between two factors that firms face when entering foreign markets: cost reduction and local adaptation. To achieve competitive advantages, firms will typically choose one of three strategies: global, multidomestic, or transnational. When evaluating international-level strategies, you might ask:

- Is the company's entry into an international marketplace threatened by the actions of local competitors? If so, how can cultural differences be minimized to give the firm a better chance of succeeding?
- Has the company made the appropriate choices between cost reduction and local adaptation to foreign markets? If not, how can it adjust its strategy to achieve competitive advantages?
- Can the company improve its effectiveness by embracing one international strategy over another? If so, how should it choose between a global, multidomestic, or transnational strategy?

8. *Formulating entrepreneurial strategies.* New ventures add jobs and create new wealth. To do so, they must identify opportunities that will be viable in the marketplace as well as gather resources and assemble an entrepreneurial team to enact the opportunity. New entrants often evoke a strong competitive response from incumbent firms in a given marketplace. When examining the role of strategic thinking on the success of entrepreneurial ventures and the role of competitive dynamics, you might ask:

- Is the company engaged in an ongoing process of opportunity recognition? If not, how can it enhance its ability to recognize opportunities?
- Do the entrepreneurs who are launching new ventures have vision, dedication and drive, and a commitment to excellence? If so, how have these affected the performance and dedication of other employees involved in the venture?
- Have strategic principles been used in the process of developing strategies to pursue the entrepreneurial opportunity? If not, how can the venture apply tools such as five-forces analysis and value-chain analysis to improve its competitive position and performance?

9. ***Achieving effective strategic control.*** Strategic controls enable a firm to implement strategies effectively. Informational controls involve comparing performance to stated goals and scanning, monitoring, and being responsive to the environment. Behavioral controls emerge from a company's culture, reward systems, and organizational boundaries. When assessing the impact of strategic controls on implementation, you might ask:

- Is the company employing the appropriate informational control systems? If not, how can it implement a more interactive approach to enhance learning and minimize response times?
- Does the company have a strong and effective culture? If not, what steps can it take to align its values and rewards system with its goals and objectives?
- Has the company implemented control systems that match its strategies? If so, what additional steps can be taken to improve performance?

10. ***Creating effective organizational designs.*** Organizational designs that align with competitive strategies can enhance performance. As companies grow and change, their structures must also evolve to meet new demands. In today's economy, firm boundaries must be flexible and permeable to facilitate smoother interactions with external parties such as customers, suppliers, and alliance partners. New forms of organizing are becoming more common. When evaluating the role of organizational structure on strategy implementation, you might ask:

- Has the company implemented organizational structures that are suited to the type of business it is in? If not, how can it alter the design in ways that enhance its competitiveness?
- Is the company employing boundaryless organizational designs where appropriate? If so, how are senior managers maintaining control of lower-level employees?
- Does the company use outsourcing to achieve the best possible results? If not, what criteria should it use to decide which functions can be outsourced?

11. ***Creating a learning organization and an ethical organization.*** Strong leadership is essential for achieving competitive advantages. Two leadership roles are especially important. The first is creating a learning organization by harnessing talent and encouraging the development of new knowledge. Second, leaders play a vital role in motivating employees to excellence and inspiring ethical behavior. When exploring the impact of effective strategic leadership, you might ask:

- Do company leaders promote excellence as part of the overall culture? If so, how has this influenced the performance of the firm and the individuals in it?
- Is the company committed to being a learning organization? If not, what can it do to capitalize on the individual and collective talents of organizational members?
- Have company leaders exhibited an ethical attitude in their own behavior? If not, how has their behavior influenced the actions of other employees?

12. ***Fostering corporate entrepreneurship.*** Many firms continually seek new growth opportunities and avenues for strategic renewal. In some corporations, autonomous work units such as business incubators and new venture groups are used to focus corporate venturing activities. In other corporate settings, product champions and

other firm members provide companies with the impetus to expand into new areas. When investigating the impact of entrepreneurship on strategic effectiveness, you might ask:

- Has the company resolved the dilemmas associated with managing innovation? If so, is it effectively defining and pacing its innovation efforts?
- Has the company developed autonomous work units that have the freedom to bring forth new product ideas? If so, has it used product champions to implement new venture initiatives?
- Does the company have an entrepreneurial orientation? If not, what can it do to encourage entrepreneurial attitudes in the strategic behavior of its organizational members?

summary

Strategic management case analysis provides an effective method of learning how companies analyze problems, make decisions, and resolve challenges. Strategic cases include detailed accounts of actual business situations. The purpose of analyzing such cases is to gain exposure to a wide variety of organizational and managerial situations. By putting yourself in the place of a strategic decision maker, you can gain an appreciation of the difficulty and complexity of many strategic situations. In the process you can learn how to ask good strategic questions and enhance your analytical skills. Presenting case analyses can also help develop oral and written communication skills.

In this chapter we have discussed the importance of strategic case analysis and described the five steps involved in conducting a case analysis: becoming familiar with the material, identifying problems, analyzing strategic issues, proposing alternative solutions, and making recommendations. We have also discussed how to get the most from case analysis. Finally, we have described how the case analysis process follows the analysis-decision-action cycle of strategic management and outlined issues and questions that are associated with each of the previous 12 chapters of the text.

key terms

case analysis 416
financial ratio analysis 423
integrative thinking 428
devil's advocacy 434
dialectical inquiry 435

references

1. Bryant, A. 2011. *The corner office:* 15. New York: St. Martin's.

2. The material in this chapter is based on several sources, including Barnes, L. A., Nelson, A. J., & Christensen, C. R. 1994. *Teaching and the case method: Text, cases and readings.* Boston: Harvard Business School Press; Guth, W. D. 1985. Central concepts of business unit and corporate strategy. In Guth, W. D. (Ed.), *Handbook of business strategy:* 1–9. Boston: Warren, Gorham & Lamont; Lundberg, C. C., & Enz, C. 1993. A framework for student case preparation. *Case Research Journal,* 13 (Summer): 129–140; and Ronstadt, R. 1980. *The art of case analysis: A guide to the diagnosis of business situations.* Dover, MA: Lord.

3. Edge, A. G. & Coleman, D. R. 1986. *The guide to case analysis and reporting* (3rd ed.). Honolulu, HI: System Logistics.

4. Morris, E. 1987. Vision and strategy: A focus for the future. *Journal of Business Strategy,* 8: 51–58.

5. Bryant, A. 2011. *The corner office:* 15. New York: St. Martin's.

6. This section is based on Lundberg & Enz, op. cit., and Ronstadt, op. cit.

7. The importance of problem definition was emphasized in Mintzberg, H., Raisinghani, D., & Theoret, A. 1976. The structure of "unstructured" decision processes. *Administrative Science Quarterly,* 21(2): 246–275.

8. Drucker, P. F. 1994. The theory of the business. *Harvard Business Review,* 72(5): 95–104.

9. This section draws on Edge & Coleman, op. cit.

10. Evans, R. 2007. The either/or dilemma. *www.ft.com,* December 19: np; and Martin, R. L. 2007. *The opposable mind.* Boston: Harvard Business School Press.

11. This section draws on Winston, A. S. 2014. *The big pivot.* Boston: Harvard Business Review Press.

12. Irving Janis is credited with coining the term *groupthink,* and he applied it primarily to fiascos in government (such as the Bay of Pigs incident in 1961). Refer to Janis, I. L. 1982. *Victims of groupthink* (2nd ed.). Boston: Houghton Mifflin.

13. Much of our discussion is based upon Finkelstein, S. & Mooney, A. C. 2003. Not the usual suspects: How to use board process to make boards better. *Academy of Management Executive,* 17(2): 101–113; Schweiger, D. M., Sandberg, W. R., & Rechner, P. L. 1989. Experiential effects of dialectical inquiry, devil's advocacy, and consensus approaches to strategic decision making. *Academy of Management Journal,* 32(4): 745–772; and Aldag, R. J. & Stearns, T. M. 1987. *Management.* Cincinnati: South-Western.

14. Finkelstein and Mooney, op. cit.

Financial Ratio Analysis*

Standard Financial Statements

One obvious thing we might want to do with a company's financial statements is to compare them to those of other, similar companies. We would immediately have a problem, however. It's almost impossible to directly compare the financial statements of two companies because of differences in size.

For example, Oracle and IBM are obviously serious rivals in the computer software market, but IBM is much larger (in terms of assets), so it is difficult to compare them directly. For that matter, it's difficult to even compare financial statements from different points in time for the same company if the company's size has changed. The size problem is compounded if we try to compare IBM and, say, SAP (of Germany). If SAP's financial statements are denominated in euros, then we have a size *and* a currency difference.

To start making comparisons, one obvious thing we might try to do is to somehow standardize the financial statements. One very common and useful way of doing this is to work with percentages instead of total dollars. The resulting financial statements are called *common-size statements*. We consider these next.

Common-Size Balance Sheets

For easy reference, Prufrock Corporation's 2014 and 2015 balance sheets are provided in Exhibit 13A.1. Using these, we construct common-size balance sheets by expressing each item as a percentage of total assets. Prufrock's 2014 and 2015 common-size balance sheets are shown in Exhibit 13A.2.

Notice that some of the totals don't check exactly because of rounding errors. Also notice that the total change has to be zero since the beginning and ending numbers must add up to 100 percent.

In this form, financial statements are relatively easy to read and compare. For example, just looking at the two balance sheets for Prufrock, we see that current assets were 19.7 percent of total assets in 2015, up from 19.1 percent in 2014. Current liabilities declined from 16 percent to 15.1 percent of total liabilities and equity over that same time. Similarly, total equity rose from 68.1 percent of total liabilities and equity to 72.2 percent.

Overall, Prufrock's liquidity, as measured by current assets compared to current liabilities, increased over the year. Simultaneously, Prufrock's indebtedness diminished as a percentage of total assets. We might be tempted to conclude that the balance sheet has grown "stronger."

Common-Size Income Statements

A useful way of standardizing the income statement, shown in Exhibit 13A.3, is to express each item as a percentage of total sales, as illustrated for Prufrock in Exhibit 13A.4.

This income statement tells us what happens to each dollar in sales. For Prufrock, interest expense eats up $.061 out of every sales dollar and taxes take another $.081. When all is said and done, $.157 of each dollar flows through to the bottom line (net income), and that amount is split into $.105 retained in the business and $.052 paid out in dividends.

These percentages are very useful in comparisons. For example, a relevant figure is the cost percentage. For Prufrock, $.582 of each $1 in sales goes to pay for goods sold. It would be interesting to compute the same percentage for Prufrock's main competitors to see how Prufrock stacks up in terms of cost control.

---

*This entire appendix is adapted from Rows, S. A., Westerfield, R. W., & Jordan, B. D. 1999. *Essentials of Corporate Finance* (2nd ed.), chap. 3. New York: McGraw-Hill.

	2014	2015
Assets		
Current assets		
Cash	$ 84	$ 98
Accounts receivable	165	188
Inventory	393	422
Total	$ 642	$ 708
Fixed assets		
Net plant and equipment	$ 2,731	$2,880
Total assets	$3,373	$3,588
Liabilities and Owners' Equity		
Current liabilities		
Accounts payable	$ 312	$ 344
Notes payable	231	196
Total	$ 543	$ 540
Long-term debt	$ 531	$ 457
Owners' equity		
Common stock and paid-in surplus	$ 500	$ 550
Retained earnings	1,799	2,041
Total	$2,299	$ 2,591
Total liabilities and owners' equity	$3,373	$3,588

Balance sheets as of December 31, 2014 and 2015 ($ millions).

Ratio Analysis

Another way of avoiding the problems involved in comparing companies of different sizes is to calculate and compare *financial ratios.* Such ratios are ways of comparing and investigating the relationships between different pieces of financial information. We cover some of the more common ratios next, but there are many others that we don't touch on.

One problem with ratios is that different people and different sources frequently don't compute them in exactly the same way, and this leads to much confusion. The specific definitions we use here may or may not be the same as others you have seen or will see elsewhere. If you ever use ratios as a tool for analysis, you should be careful to document how you calculate each one, and, if you are comparing your numbers to those of another source, be sure you know how its numbers are computed.

For each of the ratios we discuss, several questions come to mind:

1. How is it computed?
2. What is it intended to measure, and why might we be interested?
3. What is the unit of measurement?
4. What might a high or low value be telling us? How might such values be misleading?
5. How could this measure be improved?

	2014	2015	Change
Assets			
Current assets			
Cash	2.5%	2.7%	+ .2%
Accounts receivable	4.9	5.2	+ .3
Inventory	11.7	11.8	+ .1
Total	19.1	19.7	+ .6
Fixed assets			
Net plant and equipment	80.9	80.3	− .6
Total assets	100.0%	100.0%	.0%
Liabilities and Owners' Equity			
Current liabilities			
Accounts payable	9.2%	9.6%	+ .4%
Notes payable	6.8	5.5	−1.3
Total	16.0	15.1	− .9
Long-term debt	15.7	12.7	−3.0
Owners' equity			
Common stock and paid-in surplus	14.8	15.3	+ .5
Retained earnings	53.3	56.9	+3.6
Total	68.1	72.2	+4.1
Total liabilities and owners' equities	100.0%	100.0%	.0%

EXHIBIT 13A.2
Prufrock Corporation

Common-size balance sheets as of December 31, 2014 and 2015 (%).

Note: Numbers may not add up to 100.0% due to rounding.

Sales	$2,311
Cost of goods sold	1,344
Depreciation	276
Earnings before interest and taxes	$ 691
Interest paid	141
Taxable income	$ 550
Taxes (34%)	187
Net income	$ 363
Dividends	$121
Addition to retained earnings	242

EXHIBIT 13A.3
Prufrock Corporation

2015 income statement ($ millions).

Sales	100.0%
Cost of goods sold	58.2
Depreciation	11.9
Earnings before interest and taxes	29.9
Interest paid	6.1
Taxable income	23.8
Taxes (34%)	8.1
Net income	15.7%
Dividends	5.2%
Addition to retained earnings	10.5

2015 Common-size income statement (%).

Financial ratios are traditionally grouped into the following categories:

1. Short-term solvency, or liquidity, ratios.
2. Long-term solvency, or financial leverage, ratios.
3. Asset management, or turnover, ratios.
4. Profitability ratios.
5. Market value ratios.

We will consider each of these in turn. In calculating these numbers for Prufrock, we will use the ending balance sheet (2015) figures unless we explicitly say otherwise. The numbers for the various ratios come from the income statement and the balance sheet.

Short-Term Solvency, or Liquidity, Measures

As the name suggests, short-term solvency ratios as a group are intended to provide information about a firm's liquidity, and these ratios are sometimes called *liquidity measures*. The primary concern is the firm's ability to pay its bills over the short run without undue stress. Consequently, these ratios focus on current assets and current liabilities.

For obvious reasons, liquidity ratios are particularly interesting to short-term creditors. Since financial managers are constantly working with banks and other short-term lenders, an understanding of these ratios is essential.

One advantage of looking at current assets and liabilities is that their book values and market values are likely to be similar. Often (though not always), these assets and liabilities just don't live long enough for the two to get seriously out of step. On the other hand, like any type of near cash, current assets and liabilities can and do change fairly rapidly, so today's amounts may not be a reliable guide to the future.

Current Ratio One of the best-known and most widely used ratios is the *current ratio*. As you might guess, the current ratio is defined as:

$$\text{Current ratio} = \frac{\text{Current assets}}{\text{Current liabilities}}$$

For Prufrock, the 2015 current ratio is:

$$\text{Current ratio} = \frac{\$708}{\$540} = 1.31 \text{ times}$$

Because current assets and liabilities are, in principle, converted to cash over the following 12 months, the current ratio is a measure of short-term liquidity. The unit of measurement is either dollars or times. So we could say Prufrock has $1.31 in current assets for every $1 in current liabilities, or we could say Prufrock has its current liabilities covered 1.31 times over.

To a creditor, particularly a short-term creditor such as a supplier, the higher the current ratio, the better. To the firm, a high current ratio indicates liquidity, but it also may indicate an inefficient use of cash and other short-term assets. Absent some extraordinary circumstances, we would expect to see a current ratio of at least 1, because a current ratio of less than 1 would mean that net working capital (current assets less current liabilities) is negative. This would be unusual in a healthy firm, at least for most types of businesses.

The current ratio, like any ratio, is affected by various types of transactions. For example, suppose the firm borrows over the long term to raise money. The short-run effect would be an increase in cash from the issue proceeds and an increase in long-term debt. Current liabilities would not be affected, so the current ratio would rise.

Finally, note that an apparently low current ratio may not be a bad sign for a company with a large reserve of untapped borrowing power.

Quick (or Acid-Test) Ratio   Inventory is often the least liquid current asset. It's also the one for which the book values are least reliable as measures of market value, since the quality of the inventory isn't considered. Some of the inventory may later turn out to be damaged, obsolete, or lost.

More to the point, relatively large inventories are often a sign of short-term trouble. The firm may have overestimated sales and overbought or overproduced as a result. In this case, the firm may have a substantial portion of its liquidity tied up in slow-moving inventory.

To further evaluate liquidity, the *quick,* or *acid-test, ratio* is computed just like the current ratio, except inventory is omitted:

$$\text{Quick ratio} = \frac{\text{Current assets} - \text{Inventory}}{\text{Current liabilities}}$$

Notice that using cash to buy inventory does not affect the current ratio, but it reduces the quick ratio. Again, the idea is that inventory is relatively illiquid compared to cash.

For Prufrock, this ratio in 2015 was:

$$\text{Quick ratio} = \frac{\$708 - 422}{\$540} = .53 \text{ times}$$

The quick ratio here tells a somewhat different story than the current ratio, because inventory accounts for more than half of Prufrock's current assets. To exaggerate the point, if this inventory consisted of, say, unsold nuclear power plants, then this would be a cause for concern.

Cash Ratio   A very short-term creditor might be interested in the *cash ratio:*

$$\text{Cash ratio} = \frac{\text{Cash}}{\text{Current liabilities}}$$

You can verify that this works out to be .18 times for Prufrock.

Long-Term Solvency Measures

Long-term solvency ratios are intended to address the firm's long-run ability to meet its obligations, or, more generally, its financial leverage. These ratios are sometimes called *financial leverage ratios* or just *leverage ratios.* We consider three commonly used measures and some variations.

Total Debt Ratio   The *total debt ratio* takes into account all debts of all maturities to all creditors. It can be defined in several ways, the easiest of which is:

$$\text{Total debt ratio} = \frac{\text{Total assets} - \text{Total equity}}{\text{Total assets}}$$

$$= \frac{\$3{,}588 - 2{,}591}{\$3{,}588} = .28 \text{ times}$$

In this case, an analyst might say that Prufrock uses 28 percent debt.[1] Whether this is high or low or whether it even makes any difference depends on whether or not capital structure matters.

Prufrock has $.28 in debt for every $1 in assets. Therefore, there is $.72 in equity ($1 − .28) for every $.28 in debt. With this in mind, we can define two useful variations on the total debt ratio, the *debt-equity ratio* and the *equity multiplier:*

$$\text{Debt-equity ratio} = \text{Total debt/Total equity}$$
$$= \$.28/\$.72 = .39 \text{ times}$$
$$\text{Equity multiplier} = \text{Total assets/Total equity}$$
$$= \$1/\$.72 = 1.39 \text{ times}$$

The fact that the equity multiplier is 1 plus the debt-equity ratio is not a coincidence:

$$\text{Equity multiplier} = \text{Total assets/Total equity} = \$1/\$.72 = 1.39$$
$$= (\text{Total equity} + \text{Total debt})/\text{Total equity}$$
$$= 1 + \text{Debt-equity ratio} = 1.39 \text{ times}$$

The thing to notice here is that given any one of these three ratios, you can immediately calculate the other two, so they all say exactly the same thing.

Times Interest Earned   Another common measure of long-term solvency is the *times interest earned* (TIE) *ratio.* Once again, there are several possible (and common) definitions, but we'll stick with the most traditional:

$$\text{Times interest earned ratio} = \frac{\text{EBIT}}{\text{Interest paid}}$$

$$= \frac{\$691}{\$141} = 4.9 \text{ times}$$

As the name suggests, this ratio measures how well a company has its interest obligations covered, and it is often called the *interest coverage ratio.* For Prufrock, the interest bill is covered 4.9 times over.

Cash Coverage   A problem with the TIE ratio is that it is based on earnings before interest and taxes (EBIT), which is not really a measure of cash available to pay interest. The reason is that depreciation, a noncash expense, has been deducted. Since interest is most definitely a cash outflow (to creditors), one way to define the *cash coverage ratio* is:

$$\text{Cash coverage ratio} = \frac{\text{EBIT} + \text{Depreciation}}{\text{Interest paid}}$$

$$= \frac{\$691 + 276}{\$141} = \frac{\$967}{\$141} = 6.9 \text{ times}$$

---

[1]Total equity here includes preferred stock, if there is any. An equivalent numerator in this ratio would be (Current liabilities + Long-term debt).

The numerator here, EBIT plus depreciation, is often abbreviated EBDIT (earnings before depreciation, interest, and taxes). It is a basic measure of the firm's ability to generate cash from operations, and it is frequently used as a measure of cash flow available to meet financial obligations.

Asset Management, or Turnover, Measures

We next turn our attention to the efficiency with which Prufrock uses its assets. The measures in this section are sometimes called *asset utilization ratios.* The specific ratios we discuss can all be interpreted as measures of turnover. What they are intended to describe is how efficiently, or intensively, a firm uses its assets to generate sales. We first look at two important current assets: inventory and receivables.

Inventory Turnover and Days' Sales in Inventory During the year, Prufrock had a cost of goods sold of $1,344. Inventory at the end of the year was $422. With these numbers, *inventory turnover* can be calculated as:

$$\text{Inventory turnover} = \frac{\text{Cost of goods sold}}{\text{Inventory}}$$

$$= \frac{\$1,344}{\$422} = 3.2 \text{ times}$$

In a sense, we sold off, or turned over, the entire inventory 3.2 times. As long as we are not running out of stock and thereby forgoing sales, the higher this ratio is, the more efficiently we are managing inventory.

If we know that we turned our inventory over 3.2 times during the year, then we can immediately figure out how long it took us to turn it over on average. The result is the average *days' sales in inventory:*

$$\text{Days' sales in inventory} = \frac{365 \text{ days}}{\text{Inventory turnover}}$$

$$= \frac{365}{3.2} = 114 \text{ days}$$

This tells us that, on average, inventory sits 114 days before it is sold. Alternatively, assuming we used the most recent inventory and cost figures, it will take about 114 days to work off our current inventory.

For example, we frequently hear things like "Majestic Motors has a 60 days' supply of cars." This means that, at current daily sales, it would take 60 days to deplete the available inventory. We could also say that Majestic has 60 days of sales in inventory.

Receivables Turnover and Days' Sales in Receivables Our inventory measures give some indication of how fast we can sell products. We now look at how fast we collect on those sales. The *receivables turnover* is defined in the same way as inventory turnover:

$$\text{Receivables turnover} = \frac{\text{Sales}}{\text{Accounts receivable}}$$

$$= \frac{\$2,311}{\$188} = 12.3 \text{ times}$$

Loosely speaking, we collected our outstanding credit accounts and reloaned the money 12.3 times during the year.[2]

---

[2]Here we have implicitly assumed that all sales are credit sales. If they were not, then we would simply use total credit sales in these calculations, not total sales.

This ratio makes more sense if we convert it to days, so the *days' sales in receivables* is:

$$\text{Days' sales in receivables} = \frac{365 \text{ days}}{\text{Receivables turnover}}$$

$$= \frac{365}{12.3} = 30 \text{ days}$$

Therefore, on average, we collect on our credit sales in 30 days. For obvious reasons, this ratio is very frequently called the *average collection period* (ACP).

Also note that if we are using the most recent figures, we can also say that we have 30 days' worth of sales currently uncollected.

Total Asset Turnover Moving away from specific accounts like inventory or receivables, we can consider an important "big picture" ratio, the *total asset turnover ratio.* As the name suggests, total asset turnover is:

$$\text{Total asset turnover} = \frac{\text{Sales}}{\text{Total assets}}$$

$$= \frac{\$2,311}{\$3,588} = .64 \text{ times}$$

In other words, for every dollar in assets, we generated $.64 in sales.

A closely related ratio, the *capital intensity ratio,* is simply the reciprocal of (i.e., 1 divided by) total asset turnover. It can be interpreted as the dollar investment in assets needed to generate $1 in sales. High values correspond to capital-intensive industries (e.g., public utilities). For Prufrock, total asset turnover is .64, so, if we flip this over, we get that capital intensity is $1/.64 = $1.56. That is, it takes Prufrock $1.56 in assets to create $1 in sales.

Profitability Measures

The three measures we discuss in this section are probably the best known and most widely used of all financial ratios. In one form or another, they are intended to measure how efficiently the firm uses its assets and how efficiently the firm manages its operations. The focus in this group is on the bottom line, net income.

Profit Margin Companies pay a great deal of attention to their *profit margin:*

$$\text{Profit margin} = \frac{\text{Net income}}{\text{Sales}}$$

$$= \frac{\$363}{\$2,311} = 15.7\%$$

This tells us that Prufrock, in an accounting sense, generates a little less than 16 cents in profit for every dollar in sales.

All other things being equal, a relatively high profit margin is obviously desirable. This situation corresponds to low expense ratios relative to sales. However, we hasten to add that other things are often not equal.

For example, lowering our sales price will usually increase unit volume, but will normally cause profit margins to shrink. Total profit (or, more importantly, operating cash flow) may go up or down; so the fact that margins are smaller isn't necessarily bad. After all, isn't it possible that, as the saying goes, "Our prices are so low that we lose money on everything we sell, but we make it up in volume!"[3]

---

[3] No, it's not; margins can be small, but they do need to be positive!

Return on Assets *Return on assets* (ROA) is a measure of profit per dollar of assets. It can be defined several ways, but the most common is:

$$\text{Return on assets} = \frac{\text{Net income}}{\text{Total assets}}$$

$$= \frac{\$363}{\$3,588} = 10.12\%$$

Return on Equity *Return on equity* (ROE) is a measure of how the stockholders fared during the year. Since benefiting shareholders is our goal, ROE is, in an accounting sense, the true bottom-line measure of performance. ROE is usually measured as:

$$\text{Return on equity} = \frac{\text{Net income}}{\text{Total equity}}$$

$$= \frac{\$363}{\$2,591} = 14\%$$

For every dollar in equity, therefore, Prufrock generated 14 cents in profit, but, again, this is only correct in accounting terms.

Because ROA and ROE are such commonly cited numbers, we stress that it is important to remember they are accounting rates of return. For this reason, these measures should properly be called *return on book assets* and *return on book equity*. In addition, ROE is sometimes called *return on net worth*. Whatever it's called, it would be inappropriate to compare the results to, for example, an interest rate observed in the financial markets.

The fact that ROE exceeds ROA reflects Prufrock's use of financial leverage. We will examine the relationship between these two measures in more detail below.

Market Value Measures

Our final group of measures is based, in part, on information not necessarily contained in financial statements—the market price per share of the stock. Obviously, these measures can be calculated directly only for publicly traded companies.

We assume that Prufrock has 33 million shares outstanding and the stock sold for $88 per share at the end of the year. If we recall that Prufrock's net income was $363 million, then we can calculate that its earnings per share were:

$$\text{EPS} = \frac{\text{Net income}}{\text{Shares outstanding}} = \frac{\$363}{33} = \$11$$

Price-Earnings Ratio The first of our market value measures, the *price-earnings,* or PE, *ratio* (or multiple), is defined as:

$$\text{PE ratio} = \frac{\text{Price per share}}{\text{Earnings per share}}$$

$$= \frac{\$88}{\$11} = 8 \text{ times}$$

In the vernacular, we would say that Prufrock shares sell for eight times earnings, or we might say that Prufrock shares have, or "carry," a PE multiple of 8.

Since the PE ratio measures how much investors are willing to pay per dollar of current earnings, higher PEs are often taken to mean that the firm has significant prospects for future growth. Of course, if a firm had no or almost no earnings, its PE would probably be quite large; so, as always, be careful when interpreting this ratio.

Market-to-Book Ratio   A second commonly quoted measure is the *market-to-book ratio:*

$$\text{Market-to-book ratio} = \frac{\text{Market value per share}}{\text{Book value per share}}$$

$$= \frac{\$88}{(\$2{,}591/33)} = \frac{\$88}{\$78.5} = 1.12 \text{ times}$$

Notice that book value per share is total equity (not just common stock) divided by the number of shares outstanding.

Since book value per share is an accounting number, it reflects historical costs. In a loose sense, the market-to-book ratio therefore compares the market value of the firm's investments to their cost. A value less than 1 could mean that the firm has not been successful overall in creating value for its stockholders.

Conclusion

This completes our definition of some common ratios. Exhibit 13A.5 summarizes the ratios we've discussed.

EXHIBIT 13A.5 **A Summary of Five Types of Financial Ratios**

I. Short-term solvency, or liquidity, ratios

$$\text{Current ratio} = \frac{\text{Current assets}}{\text{Current liabilities}}$$

$$\text{Quick ratio} = \frac{\text{Current assets} - \text{Inventory}}{\text{Current liabilities}}$$

$$\text{Cash ratio} = \frac{\text{Cash}}{\text{Current liabilities}}$$

II. Long-term solvency, or financial leverage, ratios

$$\text{Total debt ratio} = \frac{\text{Total assets} - \text{Total equity}}{\text{Total assets}}$$

$$\text{Debt-equity ratio} = \text{Total debt/Total equity}$$

$$\text{Equity multiplier} = \text{Total assets/Total equity}$$

$$\text{Times interest earned ratio} = \frac{\text{EBIT}}{\text{Interest paid}}$$

$$\text{Cash coverage ratio} = \frac{\text{EBIT} + \text{Depreciation}}{\text{Interest paid}}$$

III. Asset utilization, or turnover, ratios

$$\text{Inventory turnover} = \frac{\text{Cost of goods sold}}{\text{Inventory}}$$

$$\text{Days' sales in inventory} = \frac{\text{365 days}}{\text{Inventory turnover}}$$

$$\text{Receivables turnover} = \frac{\text{Sales}}{\text{Accounts receivable}}$$

$$\text{Days' sales in receivables} = \frac{\text{365 days}}{\text{Receivables turnover}}$$

$$\text{Total asset turnover} = \frac{\text{Sales}}{\text{Total assets}}$$

$$\text{Capital intensity} = \frac{\text{Total assets}}{\text{Sales}}$$

IV. Profitability ratios

$$\text{Profit margin} = \frac{\text{Net income}}{\text{Sales}}$$

$$\text{Return on assets (ROA)} = \frac{\text{Net income}}{\text{Total assets}}$$

$$\text{Return on equity (ROE)} = \frac{\text{Net income}}{\text{Total equity}}$$

$$\text{ROE} = \frac{\text{Net income}}{\text{Sales}} \times \frac{\text{Sales}}{\text{Assets}} \times \frac{\text{Assets}}{\text{Equity}}$$

V. Market value ratios

$$\text{Price-earnings ratio} = \frac{\text{Price per share}}{\text{Earnings per share}}$$

$$\text{Market-to-book ratio} = \frac{\text{Market value per share}}{\text{Book value per share}}$$

Sources of Company and Industry Information*

In order for business executives to make the best decisions when developing corporate strategy, it is critical for them to be knowledgeable about their competitors and about the industries in which they compete. The process used by corporations to learn as much as possible about competitors is often called "competitive intelligence." This appendix provides an overview of important and widely available sources of information that may be useful in conducting basic competitive intelligence. Much information of this nature is available in libraries in article databases and business reference books and on websites. This appendix will recommend a variety of them. Ask a librarian for assistance, because library collections and resources vary.

The information sources are organized into 10 categories:

Competitive Intelligence
Public or Private—Subsidiary or Division—U.S. or Foreign?
Finding Public-Company Information
Guides and Tutorials
SEC Filings/EDGAR—Company Disclosure Reports
Company Rankings
Business Websites
Strategic and Competitive Analysis—Information Sources
Sources for Industry Research and Analysis
Search Engines

Competitive Intelligence

Students and other researchers who want to learn more about the value and process of competitive intelligence should see four recent books on this subject. Ask a librarian about electronic (ebook) versions of the following titles.

Rainer Michaeli. *Competitive Intelligence: Competitive Advantage through Analysis of Competition, Markets and Technologies.* London: Springer-Verlag, 2012.

Erik Jannesson, Fredrik Nilsson, and Birger Rapp (Eds.). *Strategy, Control and Competitive Advantage.* Heidelberg: Springer, 2014.

Hans Hedin, Irmeli Hirvensalo, and Markko Vaarnas. *Handbook of Market Intelligence: Understand, Compete and Grow in Global Markets.* Chichester, West Sussex, U.K.: John Wiley & Sons, 2011.

Benjamin Gilad. *Early Warning: Using Competitive Intelligence to Anticipate Market Shifts, Control Risk, and Create Powerful Strategies.* New York: American Management Association, 2004.

Public or Private—Subsidiary or Division—U.S. or Foreign?

Companies traded on stock exchanges in the United States are required to file a variety of reports that disclose information about the company. This begins the process that produces a wealth of data on public companies and, at the same time, distinguishes them from private companies, which often lack available data. Similarly, financial data of subsidiaries and divisions are typically filed in a consolidated financial statement by the parent company, rather than treated independently, thus limiting the kind of data available on them. On the other hand, foreign companies that trade on U.S. stock exchanges are required to file 20F reports, similar

---

*This information was compiled by Ruthie Brock and Carol Byrne, business librarians at The University of Texas at Arlington. We greatly appreciate their valuable contribution.

to the 10-K for U.S. companies, the most comprehensive of the required reports. The following directories provide brief facts about companies, including whether they are public or private, subsidiary or division, U.S. or foreign.

Corporate Affiliations. New Providence, NJ: LexisNexis, 2014.

This eight-volume directory features brief profiles of major U.S. and foreign corporations, both public and private, as well as their subsidiaries, divisions, and affiliates. The directory also indicates hierarchies of corporate relationships. An online version of the directory allows retrieval of a list of companies that meet specific criteria. Results can be downloaded to a spreadsheet. The online version requires a subscription, available in some libraries.

ReferenceUSA. Omaha, NE: Infogroup.Inc.

ReferenceUSA is an online directory of more than 14 million businesses located in the United States. This resource is unique in that it includes both public and private companies regardless of how small or large, as well as educational, medical, and nonprofit organizations. Results can be summarized visually in chart format. Job opportunities are provided in search results when available. Specialized modules include consumer lifestyles, historical records, and health care. Check with a librarian regarding availability of specialized modules at your location.

Finding Public-Company Information

Most companies have their annual report to shareholders and other financial reports available on their corporate website. Note that some companies use a variation of their company name in their web address, such as Procter & Gamble: *www.pg.com.* A few "aggregators" have also conveniently provided an accumulation of links to many reports of U.S. and international corporations or include a PDF document as part of their database, although these generally do not attempt to be comprehensive.

The Public Register Online. Woodstock Valley, CT: Bay Tact Corp.

Public Register Online includes over 5,000 public-company shareholder annual reports and 10-K filings for online viewing. Links are provided to reports on individual companies' websites, official filings from the Securities and Exchange Commission website, stock information from the NYSE Euronext exchange, or some combination of these sources. A link is also provided on this website for ordering personal copies of hard-copy annual reports.

www.annualreportservice.com/

Mergent Online. New York: Mergent, Inc.

Mergent Online is a database that provides company reports and financial statements for both U.S. and foreign public companies. Mergent's database has up to 25 years of quarterly and annual financial data that can be downloaded into a spreadsheet for analysis across time or across companies. Students should check with a librarian to determine the availability of this database at their college or university library.

http://mergentonline.com

Guides & Tutorials for Researching Companies and Industries

Guide to Financial Statements and *How to Read Annual Reports.* Armonk, NY: IBM.

These two educational guides, located on IBM's website, provide basic information on how to read and make sense of financial statements and other information in 10-K and shareholder annual reports for companies in general, not IBM specifically.

www.ibm.com/investor/help/guide/introduction.wss

www.ibm.com/investor/help/reports/introduction.wss

EDGAR Full-Text Search Frequently Asked Questions (FAQ). Washington, DC: U.S. Securities and Exchange Commission.

The capability to search full-text SEC filings (popularly known as EDGAR filings) was vastly improved when the SEC launched its new search form in late 2006. Features are explained at the FAQ page.

www.sec.gov/edgar/searchedgar/edgarfulltextfaq.htm

Ten Steps to Industry Intelligence Research. Industry Tutorial. George A. Smathers Libraries, University of Florida, Gainesville, FL.

> This tutorial provides a step-by-step approach for finding information about industries, with embedded links to recommended sources.
>
> *http://businesslibrary.uflib.ufl.edu/industryresearch*

Conducting Business Research.

> This tutorial provides a step-by-step process for business research.
>
> *www.lib.utexas.edu/services/instruction/learningmodules/businessresearch/intro.html*

Guide to Financial Statements. Armonk, NY: IBM.

> International Business Machines (IBM) created an educational guide for beginners to learn how to understand and interpret a typical financial statement.

How to Read Annual Reports. Armonk, NY: IBM.

> International Business Machines (IBM) created an educational guide to help novices make sense of information that is typically included in annual 10-K and shareholder reports.

Ten Steps to Company Intelligence. Company Research Tutorial. William and Joan Schreyer Business Library, Penn State University, University Park, PA.

> This tutorial provides a step-by-step approach to finding company intelligence information.
>
> *http://businesslibrary.uflib.ufl.edu/companyresearch*

SEC Filings/EDGAR—Company Disclosure Reports

SEC Filings are the various reports that publicly traded companies must file with the Securities and Exchange Commission to disclose information about their corporation. These are often referred to as "EDGAR" filings, an acronym for the Electronic Data Gathering, Analysis and Retrieval System. Some websites and commercial databases improve access to these reports by offering additional retrieval features not available on the official (*www.sec.gov*) website.

EDGAR Database Full-Text Search. U.S. Securities and Exchange Commission (SEC), Washington, DC.

> 10-K reports and other required corporate documents are quickly made available in the SEC's EDGAR database. The 10-K is the most comprehensive disclosure document for company information. Some companies also include the annual report to shareholders as part of the 10-K filing, although it is not required. The SEC made changes to its search engine in 2013, improving visual layout, navigation, and search results. The SEC's legacy search engine is still available.
>
> *www.sec.gov/edgar/searchedgar/companysearch.html*

OneSource. Concord, MA: Avention.

> *OneSource* provides a recent year or so of SEC filings, but it includes a longer history of the shareholder annual reports.

LexisNexis Academic. SEC Filings & Reports. Bethesda, MD: LexisNexis.

> SEC filings are available in *LexisNexis Academic* by selecting "Search by Content Type." A company-name search or an advanced search can be conducted at that point.

Mergent Online—Government Filings Search.

> This database also provides an alternative search interface for SEC filings. *Mergent's Government Filings* search allows searching by company name, ticker, CIK (Central Index Key) number, or industry SIC number. The search can be limited by date and by type of SEC file. Ask a librarian whether your library subscribes to *Mergent Online* for this feature.
>
> *www.mergentonline.com/filingsearch.php?type=edgar&criteriatype=findall&submitvalues*

Company Rankings

Fortune 500. New York: Time Inc.

> The *Fortune 500* list and other company rankings are published in the printed edition of *Fortune* magazine and are also available online.
>
> *http://money.cnn.com/magazines/fortune/fortune500/2014/full_list/index.html*

Forbes Global 2000. Forbes, Inc.

> The companies listed on the Forbes Global 2000 are the biggest and most powerful in the world.
>
> *www.forbes.com/global2000/*

Business Websites

Big Charts. San Francisco: MarketWatch, Inc.

> *BigCharts* is a comprehensive and easy-to-use investment research website, providing access to professional-level research tools such as interactive charts, current and historical quotes, industry analysis, and intraday stock screeners, as well as market news and commentary. MarketWatch operates this website, a service of Dow Jones & Company. Supported by site sponsors, it is free to self-directed investors.
>
> *http://bigcharts.marketwatch.com/*

GlobalEdge. East Lansing, MI: Michigan State University.

> *GlobalEdge* is a web portal providing a significant amount of information about international business, countries around the globe, the U.S. states, industries, and news.
>
> *http://globaledge.msu.edu/*

Yahoo Finance. Sunnyvale, CA: Yahoo! Inc.

> This website links to information on U.S. markets, world markets, data sources, finance references, investment editorials, financial news, and other helpful websites.
>
> *http://finance.yahoo.com*

Strategic and Competitive Analysis—Information Sources

Analyzing a company can take the form of examining its internal and external environments. In the process, it is useful to identify the company's strengths, weaknesses, opportunities, and threats (SWOT). Sources for this kind of analysis are varied, but perhaps the best would be articles from *The Wall Street Journal,* business magazines, and industry trade publications. Publications such as these can be found in the following databases available at many public and academic libraries. When using a database that is structured to allow it, try searching the company name combined with one or more keywords, such as "IBM and competition" or "Microsoft and lawsuits" or "AMR and fuel costs" to retrieve articles relating to the external environment.

ABI/INFORM Complete. Ann Arbor, MI: ProQuest LLC.

> *ABI/INFORM Complete* provides abstracts and full-text articles covering disciplines such as management, law, taxation, economics, health care, and information technology from more than 6,800 scholarly, business, and trade publications. Other types of resources include company and industry reports, case studies, market research reports, and a variety of downloadable economic data.

Business Insights: Essentials. Farmington Hills, MI: Gale CENGAGE Learning.

> *Business Insights* provides company and industry intelligence for a selection of public and private companies. Company profiles include parent-subsidiary relationships, industry rankings, products and brands, industry statistics, and financial ratios. Selections of SWOT analysis reports are also available. The Company and Industry comparison tool allows a researcher to compare up to six companies' revenues, employees, and sales data over time. Results are available as an image, chart, or spreadsheet.

Business Source Complete. Ipswich, MA: EBSCO Publishing.

> *Business Source Complete* is a full-text database with over 3,800 scholarly business journals covering management, economics, finance, accounting, international business, and more. The database also includes detailed company profiles for the world's 10,000 largest companies, as well as selected country economic reports provided by the Economist Intelligence Unit (EIU). The database includes case studies, investment and market research reports, SWOT analyses, and more. *Business Source Complete* contains over 2,400 peer-reviewed business journals.

Hoover's Academic. Short Hills, NJ: Dun & Bradstreet.

> *Hoover's* provides company and industry information for over 85 million public and private U.S. and international companies. The company profiles include the company's history, key financials, and executive information, as well as access to the latest news stories and SEC filings. Over 600 industries are covered in *Hoover's.* Custom reports can be created and downloaded.

OneSource. Concord, MA: Avention, Inc.

> *OneSource* provides a wealth of information about U.S. and international public and private companies. The profiles include key executives, a financial report, and the corporate family structure. Also available are recent analyst reports, company SWOT analyses, industry reports, news and SEC filings information. Custom reports can be created and downloaded.

Thomson ONE Research.

> *Thomson ONE Research* offers full-text analytical reports on more than 65,000 companies worldwide. The research reports are excellent sources for strategic and financial profiles of a company and its competitors and of industry trends. Developed by a global roster of brokerage, investment banking, and research firms, these full-text investment reports include a wealth of current and historical information useful for evaluating a company or industry over time.

International Directory of Company Histories. Detroit, MI: St. James Press, 1988–present. 163 volumes to date.

> This directory covers more than 11,000 multinational companies, and the series is still adding volumes. Each company history is approximately three to five pages in length and provides a summary of the company's mission, goals, and ideals, followed by company milestones, principal subsidiaries, and competitors. Strategic decisions made during the company's period of existence are usually noted. This series covers public and private companies and nonprofit entities. Entry information includes a company's legal name, headquarters information, URL, incorporation date, ticker symbol, stock exchange listing, sales figures, and the primary North American Industry Classification System (NAICS) code. Further reading selections complete the entry information. Volumes 59 to the most recent are available electronically in the Gale Virtual Reference Library database from Gale CENGAGE Learning.

LexisNexis Academic. Bethesda, MD: LexisNexis.

> *LexisNexis Academic* provides access to legal, company, and industry information, news sources, and public records. Industry information is available through the Company Info tab or the "Search by content type" selection. The Company Dossier tool allows a researcher to compare up to five companies' financial statements at one time with download capabilities.

The Wall Street Journal. New York: Dow Jones & Co.

> This respected business newspaper is available in searchable full text from 1984 to the present in the *Factiva* database. The "News Pages" link provides access to current articles and issues of *The Wall Street Journal.* Dow Jones, publisher of the print version of the *Wall Street Journal,* also has an online subscription available at *wsj.com.* Some libraries provide access to *The Wall Street Journal* through the ProQuest Newspapers database.

Sources for Industry Research and Analysis

Factiva. New York: Dow Jones & Co.

> The *Factiva* database has several options for researching an industry. One would be to search the database for articles in the business magazines and industry trade publications. A second option in *Factiva* would be to search in the Companies/Markets category for company/industry comparison reports.

Mergent Online. New York: Mergent Inc.

> *Mergent Online* is a searchable database of over 60,000 global public companies. The database offers worldwide industry reports, U.S. and global competitors, and executive biographical information. *Mergent*'s Basic Search option permits searching by primary

industry codes (either SIC or NAICS). Once the search is executed, companies in that industry should be listed. A comparison or standard peer-group analysis can be created to analyze companies in the same industry on various criteria. The Advanced Search allows the user to search a wider range of financial and textual information. Results, including ratios for a company and its competitors, can be downloaded to a spreadsheet.

North American Industry Classification System (NAICS)

The North American Industry Classification System has officially replaced the Standard Industrial Classification (SIC) as the numerical structure used to define and analyze industries, although some publications and databases offer both classification systems. The NAICS codes are used in Canada, the United States, and Mexico. In the United States, the NAICS codes are used to conduct an Economic Census every five years providing a snapshot of the U.S. economy at a given moment in time.

NAICS: *www.census.gov/eos/www/naics/*

Economic Census: *www.census.gov/econ/census/*

NetAdvantage. New York: S & P Capital IQ.

The database includes company, financial, and investment information as well as the well-known publication called *Industry Surveys.* Each industry report includes information on the current environment, industry trends, key industry ratios and statistics, and comparative company financial analysis. Available in HTML, PDF, or Excel formats.

Business Insights: Essentials. Farmington Hills, MI: Gale CENGAGE Learning.

Business Insights provides company and industry intelligence for a selection of public and private companies. Company profiles include parent-subsidiary relationships, industry rankings, products and brands, industry statistics, and financial ratios. Selections of SWOT analysis reports are also available. The Company and Industry comparison tool allows a researcher to compare up to six companies' revenues, employees, and sales data over time. Results are available as an image, chart, or spreadsheet.

Plunkett Research Online. Houston, TX: Plunkett Research, Ltd.

Plunkett's provides industry-specific market research, trends analysis, and business intelligence for 34 industries.

Search Engines

Google. Mountain View, CA: Google, Inc.

Recognized for its advanced technology, quality of results, and simplicity, the search engine Google is highly recommended by librarians and other expert web surfers.

www.google.com

Dogpile. Bellevue, WA: InfoSpace, Inc.

Dogpile is a metasearch engine that searches and compiles the most relevant results from more than 12 individual search engines.

http://www.dogpile.com/

O

O. R. T. Technologies, 223–224
Oldsmobile, 320
Olympus Corporation, 16, 293
Omega, 171
On the Border, 26
Oracle Corporation, 3, 133, 206, 220, 232, 302, 431, 441
  financial data, 111
Orkut, 388
Orrick, Herrington & Sutcliffe, 121
Otis Elevator, 41
  manufacturing problem, 228
Outboard Marine Corporation, 25
Outdoor Industry Association, 19
Overstock.com, 404
Oxford GlycoSciences, 230

P

Pabst Brewing, 349
Pacific Gas & Electric, 304
Panasonic, 235
  in China, 236
Panera Bread, 341
Patagonia, 18, 19, 26
Paychex, 62
PayPal, 262
PeopleSoft, 206
PepsiCo, 81, 116, 162, 188, 219, 221, 330, 331, 405
Pez, 388
Pfizer, Inc., 48, 92, 99, 195, 223, 224, 288, 385
Phelps Dodge, 183
Pier 1 Imports, 39
Pixar, 431
Pizza Hut, 188
Planning Perspectives Inc., 62
Plum Organics, adaptive new entrant, 262
Plunkett Research, Ltd., 456
Polaris, 184
Polaroid, 131
Pontiac, 320
Porsche, 65, 66, 86, 153, 157, 405
Porsche Cayenne, 86
PPG Industries, 28, 42
  scenario planning, 43
Priceline.com, 204
PricewaterhouseCoopers, 122, 279
Principled Solutions Enterprise, 7

Procter & Gamble, 18, 19, 28, 39, 48, 50, 67, 117, 170, 173, 183, 219, 233, 252, 272, 324, 409, 452
  innovation, 386
Progress Energy, 195
Project: WorldWide, 258, 259
ProQuest LLC, 454
Providence Equity Partners, 102
Pryor Cashman LLP, 256
Pure Digital Technologies, 181
Puritan-Bennett Corporation, 331

Q

Quaker Oats, 168
Qualcomm, 3, 48
Quiznos, 154
  decline, 155
Quora, 40
Qwest Communications, 361

R

Radio Shack, 38
Rainmaker Entertainment, 396
Ralph Lauren, 174
Ralphs, 29, 148
Raytheon, 127, 372–373
Recreational Vehicle Dealer Association, 188
Red Hat, Inc., 430
  integrative thinking, 431
Reebok, 233, 332
Renault, 152, 222
  low-cost policy, 151
Research in Motion, 124, 388
Ricoh Americas Corporation, 225, 226
RightNow Technologies Inc., 156
Rocket Internet, 261
Rockwell Collins, 363
Royal Dutch Shell, 300, 405
Running Press, 265
Ruth's Chris, 153
Ryanair, 163, 270

S

S. C. Johnson, 254
Safeway Company, 300
SAIC, 214
  international strategy problem, 213

Salemi Industries, 37
Salesforce.com, 388
Salomon Smith Barney, 182
Samsung Electronics, 137, 267
Samsung Group, 25
Sanford C. Bernstein, 109
SAP, 50, 113, 441
  accessing knowledge, 135
Sapient Health Network, decision making, 419
Schlumberger, 82
Schmitz Cargobull, 84
  information technology at, 85
Sears, 3, 65, 101, 115
Security Mortgage Group, 433
Sephora.com, 80
Seventh Generation, 29
Shanghai Automotive Industry Corporation, 213
Shaw Industries, 77, 184, 186
Shell Oil Company, 19, 120, 300
ShopRunner, 93
Shutl, 197
Siebel Systems, 232
Siemens, 358
  use of "soft" power, 359
Sikorsky Helicopters, 41
Singapore Airlines, 290
Single Source Systems, 28
Skype, 134
Sleep Health Centers, 40
Slideshare, 40
Sloan-Kettering, 186
Smith Kline, 198
SmithKline Beecham, 198
Smucker's, 252
Sodima, 240
SoftBank, 182, 195
Solectron, 116
Sony Corporation, 6, 20, 397
Southern Alliance for Clean Energy, 369
Southwest Airlines, 3, 5, 9, 84, 92, 111, 269–270, 284, 384
Spanx, adaptive new entrant, 262
Spirit Airlines, 163
Sports Authority, 93
Sprint, 182, 195
Square, 262
SsangYong, 213
Staples, 16
Starbucks, 187, 206–207, 251

Michel, J. G., 277
Michelangelo, 205
Mider, Z., 307
Miles, R. E., 336
Miller, A., 32, 177, 310, 344, 377, 378, 414
Miller, D., 32, 203, 310, 345, 403
Miller, D. J., 209, 412
Miller, F. A., 143
Miller, J., 321
Miller, K. D., 414
Milner, Alex, 224
Minow, Neil, 15, 32, 311, 312
Mintzberg, Henry, 10–11, 12, 31, 32, 280, 310, 440
Misangyi, V. F., 32
Mischkind, L., 310
Mitchell, Margaret, 41
Mitchell, R., 310
Mitsuhashi, H., 211
Mittal, D., 210
Mochari, I., 407
Mohammed, R., 177
Mohr, E., 310
Mol, M. J., 412
Moliterno, T. P., 142
Monahan, J., 276
Monahan, Tom, 262
Monk, N., 107
Monks, Robert, 15, 32, 311, 312
Montes-Sancho, M. J., 33
Montgomery, C. A., 106, 107
Montgomery, D. B., 414
Moon, Y., 171, 179
Mooney, A. C., 440
Moore, Geoffrey A., 405, 414
Moore, J. F., 346
Moran, P., 143
Morison, R., 106
Morita, Akio, 20
Morris, B., 310
Morris, E., 440
Morrissey, C. A., 412
Morrow, J. S., 179
Mors, M. L., 143
Morse, E. A., 106
Morse, G., 210
Moss, S. A., 377
Mottershaw, Heather, 395
Mouio, A., 210
Mowery, D. C., 346
Moynihan, Brian, 109

Moza, M. P., 247
Mozilo, Angelo, 293
Mudambi, R., 71, 211, 247, 277
Muir, Max, 267
Mulally, Alan, 24, 296, 351, 352
Mullaney, T. J., 408
Mumm, J., 312
Murdoch, James, 305
Murdoch, Rupert, 305
Murnigham, J. K., 130, 209
Murphy, D., 377
Murphy, K. J., 312
Murphy, P., 246
Murray, Bill, 52
Murthy, N. R. Narayana, 353
Mussberg, W., 345

N

Nader, Ralph, 304–305
Nagarajan, G., 221
Nagarju, B., 218
Nahapiet, J., 141
Nair, H., 32, 245
Nalebuff, B. J., 62, 71
Narasimhan, O., 106
Narayan, A., 211
Narayanan, V. K., 70
Naughton, K., 71
Ndofor, H., 277
Needham, Charles, 6
Neilson, G. L., 32, 322, 344, 413
Nelson, A. J., 440
Nelson, B., 41, 310
Netessine, S., 85, 106, 310
Neuborne, E., 179
Newbert, S. L., 32, 106
Newman, D., 377
Nexon, M., 142
Ng, S., 177
Ng, T. W. H., 47
Niblack, R. M., 412
Nidumolu, R., 19
Nilsson, Fredrik, 451
Nipper, Mads, 52
Niven, P., 107
Nmarus, J. A., 105
Nobel, Carmen, 372
Nobel, R., 247
Nohria, N., 144, 277, 412
Nonaka, I., 141
Noorda, Raymond, 272
Noot, Walter, 95

Nordstrom, Dan, 80
Norton, David P., 32, 97, 100, 107
Novak, David C., 9, 418
Noyes, K., 276, 385
Nunes, P., 31, 64, 70, 107
Nutt, P. C., 32
Nyberg, A. J., 311

O

O'Brien, Bob, 205
O'Brien, J. M., 142
O'Brien, J. P., 413
O'Brien, William, 363
O'Connor, G. C., 411
O'Connor, M., 224
O'Donnell, J., 177
O'Donnell, S. W., 247
O'Leary-Kelly, A. M., 310
O'Neill, H. M., 344
O'Reilly, B., 377
O'Reilly, C. A., 142, 346
O'Reilly, Charles, 340
Odlyzko, A., 70
Ododaru, O., 34
Oh, H., 143
Ohmae, Kenichi, 245, 346
Okie, Francis G., 24
Oliver, C., 211
Olsen, B., 411
Olsen, Kenneth H., 40–41
Omidyar, Pierre, 388
Ordonez, L., 378
Orey, M., 70
Osawa, J., 23
Oster, S. M., 210
Ostrower, J., 344
Ouchi, William, 310
Ousik, V., 414
Oviatt, B. M., 318n, 345
Ovide, S., 412
Oxley, J. E., 346
Ozzie, Raymond, 96

P

Page, Greg, 322
Page, Larry, 388
Paine, Lynn S., 369–370, 378
Palanjian, A., 262
Palazzo, A., 203
Palazzo, G., 311
Palmer, T. B., 72
Palmeri, Christopher, 177

Cost reduction
  versus adaptation, 229–230
  from diversification, 201
  pressure in global strategy, 232
  for value-chain activities, 220
Costs
  of developing intellectual
      property, 137
  of going green, 21
  hidden in offshoring, 227–228
  legal battles over, 137
  from vertical integration, 190
Cost savings, 186–187
Cost surgery, 173
Counterfeit drugs, 224
Counterfeiting, 223
Country Risk Rating, 221–222
Creative intelligence, 387
Creativity, 89
  enabling, 366–367
  stimulating, 391
Creativity argument for diversity
    management, 122
Cross-functional skills, 333
Cross-functional teams, 337, 340
Crossing the Chasm (Moore), 405
Cross selling strategy, 109
Cross-training, 337
Crowdfunding
  definition, 255
  evaluation of opportunities, 256
  loose rules for, 255–256
  market size, 255
  potential downsides, 255
Crowdsourcing
  definition, 50
  for differentiation ideas, 157
  effects on general environment, 50
  examples of, 50
  at Frito-Lay, 80, 81
  by Lego, 52
  leveraging power of, 86
  perils of
    high demand uncertainty, 86
    hijacking by customers, 86
    strong brand reputation, 86
    too many initiatives, 86–87
  successes, 50
Cultural differences
  advertising mistakes, 224
  challenge for managers, 224–225
  and mergers, 198

Currency fluctuations, 196, 223
Currency risk
  definition, 223
  hedging strategies, 223
  and Israel's shekel, 223–224
  managing, 220
Current ratio, 97, 423, 444–445
Customers
  and balanced scorecard, 100
  and corporate social
      responsibility, 19
  focus on, for information, 366
  integrated into value chain, 85–87
  and perils of crowdsourcing,
      86–87
  prosumer concept, 85–86
Customer service, 80
Customer service organizations,
    155–156
Customer value, from core
    competencies, 185

D

Data analytics, 162
  to enhance control, 291
David C. Lincoln Award for
    Ethics and Excellence in
    Business, 370
Days' sales in inventory, 97,
    423, 447
Days' sales in receivables, 97, 423,
    447–448
Debt-equity ratio, 97
Decision making
  failure for Stroh's Brewing,
      349–350
  intended *vs.* realized strategy,
      10–12
  in multidomestic strategy, 233
  with multiple stakeholders, 9
  using conflict to improve
    devil's advocacy, 434–435
    dialectical inquiry, 434, 435
  with wisdom of employees, 365
Decisions, 8
Decline stage
  definition, 171
  examples, 172
  and new technology, 172
  strategic options
    consolidation, 172
    exiting the market, 172

harvesting strategy, 172
improving price-performance
    trade-off, 173
maintaining, 172
retreating to defensible
    ground, 173
using new to improve the
    old, 173
Dedication, of entrepreneurial
    leaders, 258
Defensible ground, retreating
    to, 173
Defensive actions, 271
Demand conditions
  consumer pressure, 216
  high uncertainty, 86
  in India, 218
Demographics, 45
  Millennials, 116
Demographic segment of the
    general environment
  definition, 45
  impact on industries, 51
  key trends and events, 44
Department of Defense, 172
Department of Justice, 353
Designing the organization,
    351–352, 354
Developing countries
  meeting needs of poor in, 214
  reverse engineering for, 221
Developing human capital
  encouraging widespread
      involvement, 117
  evaluation, 118
  mentoring, 117–118
  monitoring progress, 118
  training, 116
Development teams, 367
Devil's advocacy, 434–435
Devil's Dictionary (Bierce), 283
Dialectical inquiry, 434, 435
Diamond of national advantage
  conclusions on, 218
  definition, 215
  demand conditions, 216
  factor endowments, 215–216
  firm strategy, structure, and
      rivalry, 216–217
  in India, 217–218
  related and supporting
      industries, 216

Era of Lego innovation, 54
Escalation of commitment, 402
Ethical behavior, commitment to, 352–353, 354
Ethical organizations, 15
  in case analysis, 439
  codes of ethics, 372
  corporate credos, 372
  and corporate scandals, 368
  green marketing problem, 369
  individual *vs.* organizational ethics, 368–369
  integrity-based *vs.* compliance-based ethics, 369–371
  JPMorgan Chase problem, 373–374
  key elements, 371
  leaders as role models, 371
  management approaches, 370
  policies and procedures in, 373
  potential benefits, 368–369
  reward and evaluation systems, 372–373
Ethical orientation
  benefit for employees, 369
  of leaders, 368
Ethical values, 368
Ethics
  compliance-based, 369–371
  definition, 368
  individual *vs.* organizational, 368–369
  integrity-based, 369–371
Ethics awards, 370
Ethics management approaches, 370
European Union, 49, 238
  GDP per person growth 2001–2011, 215
Every Business Needs an Angel, 254
Excellence, commitment to, 258, 352–353, 354
Excessive product-market diversification, 302
Executive compensation, 16, 96
Executive leaders, 23
Executives, insight from Melvin Alexander, 7–8
Exit barriers, 57
Exit champions, 398–399
Exiting the market, 172

Expediters, 79
Experience
  versus initiative, 385
  value of, 22
Experience curve, 149
Experimenting, by innovators, 388
Expertise, of directors, 297
Explicit knowledge, 134
  definition, 112
Exporting
  beachhead strategy, 239
  benefits, 239
  definition, 239
  risks and limitations, 239
Expropriation of minority shareholders, 306
Extended value chain, 162–163
  underestimating expenses, 164
External boundaries, 328
External constituencies, 330
External control view of leadership, 6
External environment, narrow focus on, 76
External environment analysis, 12
  in case analysis, 436–437
  checklist, 59
  competitive environment
    five-forces model, 52–58
    strategic groups, 64–67
  competitive intelligence, 39–40
  environmental forecasting, 40–42
  environmental monitoring, 39
  environmental scanning, 39
  general environment
    and crowdsourcing, 50, 52
    demographic segment, 45
    economic segment, 49
    global segment, 49
    impact of trends on industries, 51
    key trends and events, 44
    political/legal segment, 47–48
    relationship among segments, 49–50
    sociocultural segment, 45–47
    technological segment, 48–49
  and informational control, 281
  perceptual acuity, 38
  recognizing opportunities or threats, 37

scenario analysis, 42
SWOT analysis, 42–43
  in turnaround strategy, 173
External governance control mechanisms
  auditors, 302–303
  banks, 303
  definition, 302
  market for corporate control, 302–303
  media, 304–305
  public activists, 304–305
  regulatory bodies, 304
  stock analysts, 303
External information, gathering and integrating, 366
External relationships
  costs, 338–339
  costs and benefits to develop, 338
External staffing, 385–386

F

Factor endowments
  creation of factors of production, 215
  definition, 215, 216
  firm-specific factors, 216
  in India, 217
  industry-specific factors, 216
  resource deployment, 216
Factors of production, 215–216
Failures
  formalize forums for, 367
  and professional development, 367
Financial crisis of 2007–2009
  Bank of America and Merrill Lynch, 109
  effect on General Motors, 357
  Honeywell International in, 138
Financial goals, 101
Financial performance, and corporate governance, 292
Financial perspective, in balanced scorecard, 101
Financial ratios/ratio analysis
  asset utilization/turnover ratios, 97, 447–448
  changes over time, 98
  common-size balance sheet, 441
  common-size income statement, 441

and price competition, 57
  Uber Technologies *vs.* Lyft Inc.,
    57–58
Interest coverage ratio, 446
Interest rate increases, 49
Interlocking directorships, 297
Internal benchmarking, 365
Internal business perspective in
  balanced scorecard, 100
Internal constituencies, 330
Internal corporate venturing, 404
Internal development, 195
  benefits, 203–204
  definition, 203
  example, 203
  potential disadvantages, 204
Internal environment analysis,
    12–13
  in case analysis, 437
  and informational control, 281
  for new business creation,
    250–251
  performance evaluation
    balanced scorecard, 99–101
    financial ratio analysis, 97–99
  resource-based view of the firm,
    88–96
  in turnaround strategy, 173
  value-chain analysis, 76–88
Internal networkers, 23
Internal relationships
  costs, 338–339
  costs and benefits to develop, 338
Internal staffing, 385–386
International Chamber of
  Commerce, 223
International division structure,
    317, 326
International expansion
  ethics of relocation for tax
    purposes, 242
  insights for
    adaptation challenges, 226
    human resource management
      challenges, 226–227
    knowledge transmission, 226
    opportunities and threats, 226
  motivations
    arbitrage opportunities, 219
    enhancing product growth, 219
    increase market size, 218–219
    learning opportunities, 220

optimize value-chain location,
    219–220
  reverse innovation, 220–221
and organizational structure,
    324–327
  geographic-area division, 326
  global start-ups, 326–327
  international divisions, 326
  and multidomestic strategy,
    325–326
  primary types, 325
  worldwide functional
    division, 326
  worldwide product division, 326
potential risks, 221–225
  currency risks, 223–224
  economic risk, 223
  management risk, 224–225
  political risk, 222–223
International Public Relations
  Association, 81
International strategy, 14
  achieving competitive advantage
    cost reduction *vs.* adaptation,
      229–230
    global strategy, 231–232
    global *vs.* regional, 237–238
    international strategy, 230–231
    multidomestic strategy,
      233–234
    transnational strategy, 235–237
  in case analysis, 438
  definition, 231
  diamond of national advantage,
    215–218
  entry modes, 238–241
    exporting, 239
    franchising, 238–240
    joint ventures, 240–241
    strategic alliances, 240–241
    wholly owned subsidiaries, 241
  global dispersion of value chains,
    225–228
  and global economy, 214–215
  motivations for expansion,
    218–221
  multinational companies in, 231
  in orphan drug industry, 230–231
  problem for SAIC in China, 213
  risks and challenges, 231
  risks of expansion, 221–225
  strengths and limitations, 231

International trade
  increases in, 49
Internet
  bots, 61
  effects on five-forces model
    bargaining power of buyers,
      58–60
    bargaining power of suppliers, 60
    intensity of rivalry, 61
    threat of new entrants, 58
    threat of substitutes, 60–61
  legal services on, 61
Internet devices, 408–409
Internet technologies, 337
Interpersonal networks, 127
Interrelationships, 85
Intrapreneuring, 393
Introduction stage
  definition, 169
  first-mover advantage, 169
  late-mover advantage, 169
  strategies for, 169
Inventory costs, hidden in
  offshoring, 227
Inventory management
  continuous replenishment
    program, 79
  just-in-time systems, 77–78, 216
Inventory turnover ratio, 97, 423, 447
Investment decisions
  and agency theory, 401
  and corporate governance, 292
Investments, transaction-specific,
    190
Investors
  and crowdfunding, 255
  and value of acquisitions,
    199–200
Investor's Business Daily, 304
Ironman brand name, 102
Israel, currency strategy, 223–224

J

Japan
  GDP per person growth
    2001–2011, 215
  just-in-time systems, 216
  keiretsus, 306
Jeopardy, 186
Job creation, and immigrants, 48
Job rotation, 337
Jobs, redefining, 121

elusive benefits and greater costs, 227–228

recent explosion of, 225–227

versus reshoring, 228

Older workers

Bureau of Labor Statistics on, 46

research about, 45, 46–47

stereotypes, 46

One-click purchasing, 60

On-the-job consumption, 302

Openness to experience, 258

Open-sourcing model for talent, 120

Operational effectiveness, 8–9

Operational efficiency and effectiveness, 289–290

Operations

at Chipotle, 79

cultural differences, 225

definition, 78

in differentiation strategy, 154

increased from global presence, 218–219

in overall cost leadership, 150

in service sector, 87

Opportunities

entrepreneurial, 250–260

in external environment, 37

misses, 25

Opportunity analysis framework, 251

Opportunity evaluation, 253

Opportunity recognition

definition, 251

deliberate search, 251–253

discovery phase, 251

evaluation phase, 253

qualities for viability, 253

Opposable Mind (Martin), 428

Options, 399

Oral case presentation, 425

Organizational barriers to change, 355–356

Organizational bases of power, 356–357

coercive power, 357

information power, 357

legitimate power, 357

reward power, 357

Organizational boundaries, 15

Organizational capabilities

causal ambiguity, 92

definition, 89

Organizational control, 352–353

Organizational culture

commitment to excellence and ethics, 352–353, 354

consumer-oriented, 285

definition, 283

entrepreneurial, 396

examples, 283

at Ford Motor Company, 352

managerial role models, 292

publications on, 283

role of, 283–284

role of training, 291–292

shared in boundaryless organizations, 337

sustaining

by culture committee, 284

with rallies and pep talks, 284

with storytelling, 284

Organizational design, 15

in case analysis, 439

Organizational flexibility argument for diversity management, 122

Organizational goals and objectives, 9

analysis of, 12

in case analysis, 436

common, 23–24

financial, 101

hierarchy of, 24

rewards aligned with, 292

Organizational integrity, 369

Organizational learning, and informational control, 281

Organizational resources, 89

Organizational structure

benefits, 316

definition, 316

divisional structures, 320–325

dominant growth patterns, 317

functional structure, 318–319

horizontal, 337

international implications

geographic-area division, 326

global start-ups, 326–327

international division, 326

primary types of structure, 325

worldwide functional structure, 326

worldwide product division, 326

and leadership, 351–352

McDonald's, 341

problem at Boeing, 315–316

simple structure, 318

and strategy formulation, 327

strategy-structure relationship, 316–318

types, 316–318

Organizational *vs.* individual rationality, 9

Organization for Economic Cooperation and Development, 218

Organizations; *see also* Companies; Corporations; Ethical organizations; Learning organizations

attracting talent, 110

barrier-free, 328–331

bureaucratic *vs.* decentralized, 124

case for sustainability initiatives, 21–22

changes from social networks, 125

core competencies, 185

egotism and greed in, 205

environmental issues, 19–21

environmentally aware

competitive intelligence, 39–40

environmental forecasting, 40–41

environmental monitoring, 39

environmental scanning, 39

perceptual acuity, 38

scenario analysis, 42

SWOT analysis, 41–42

flatter, 129

gathering and integrating external information, 366

key stakeholders, 17

linking employees to, 120

modular, 331–333

protecting dynamic capabilities, 137–138

protecting intellectual assets, 136–137

redistributing knowledge, 365

setting a direction, 351

social responsibility, 18–19

stakeholders, 17–18

strategic management perspective throughout, 22–23

structural hole, 127

illustration, 78
inbound logistics, 77–78
marketing and sales, 79–80
operations, 78
outbound logistics, 78–79
in overall cost leadership, 150
service, 80
in service organizations, 87–88
Prime Time Live, 304
Principal-agent conflicts, 294, 305
versus principal-principal
conflicts, 306
Principal-principal conflicts, 305–306
Private information, 128
Proactiveness
competitor reactions, 406
definition, 405–406
examples of failure, 405
first-mover advantage, 405
not leading to competitive
advantage, 405
requirements, 407
techniques, 407
Problem identification, 422
Problem-solving argument for
diversity management, 122
Procedures, in ethical
organizations, 373
Process innovation, 382–383
Procurement
definition, 80
in differentiation strategy, 154
at Microsoft, 80–82
in overall cost leadership, 150
Product champions, 397, 439–440
compared to exit champions, 399
definition, 397
Product differentiation, as barrier to
entry, 53
Product division structure,
worldwide, 326
Product expatriates, 333
Product innovation, 382
Production, multinational effort, 225
Productivity, piecemeal
improvements, 173
Product-line extension, brand
identification dilution, 158–159
Product-market diversification,
excessive, 302
Product names, in multidomestic
strategy, 233

Product placement, 79–80
Product pruning, 173
Products
from breakthrough technology, 54
complements, 63
counterfeit, 223
enhancing growth rate, 219
global, 229
luxury brands, 160
substitutes, 56, 60–61
Profit
and employee bargaining
power, 96
and employee exit costs, 96
and employee replacement
cost, 96
and executive compensation, 96
flawed pursuit of, 102
generation and distribution of,
95–96
low, 54
and manager bargaining
power, 96
and shareholders, 96
and stakeholders, 96
Profitability, root causes of, 64
Profitability measures
profit margin, 97, 423, 448
return on assets, 97, 423, 449
return on equity, 97, 423, 449
Profit margin ratio, 97, 423, 448
Profit pool
for airlines, 163
definition, 162
miscalculation, 164
Project definition, 397
Project impetus, 397
Promotion focus, 391
Property rights, 136–137
Prosumer concept, 85–86
Public activists, and corporate
governance, 304–305
Public Company Accounting
Oversight Board, 303
Purchasing power of poorest
people, 214

Strategy implementation
  with action plans, 28
  and contemporary approach to
    strategic control, 281
  definition, 14
  elements of, 14–15
  focus of behavioral control,
    282–283
  in traditional approach to strategic
    control, 280
Strategy/Strategies
  business-level, 14
  corporate-level, 14
  definition, 8
  entrepreneurial, 14
  in health care industry, 7–8
  incremental changes, 280
  indicators for monitoring, 39
  intended *vs.* realized, 10–12
  international, 14
  source of implementation
    problems, 351
  and value of experience, 22
Strengths, not leading to
  advantage, 76
Strike, and Seventh Generation, 29
Structural equation modeling, 335
Structural hole, 127
Structure of Corporation Law
  (Aron & Eisenberg), 283
Stuck in the middle, 148
  for combination strategies, 163
  JetBlue Airways, 173–174
Substitutes
  definition, 56
  identifying, 56
  readily available, 93–94
Super Bowl ads, 81
Supermarkets, problems for, 148
Suppliers
  delayed payments to, 67
  differentiated products, 56
  disintermediation by, 60
  dominated by few companies, 55
  industry unimportant to, 55
  not contending with
    substitutes, 55
  products as important
    inputs, 55
  and reintermediation, 60
  role of, 60

switching costs for buyers, 56
  threat of forward integration, 56
Support activities
  Caterpillar Inc., 104
  definition, 77
  in differentiation strategy, 154
  general administration, 84
  human resource management,
    82–84
  illustration, 81
  in overall cost leadership, 150
  procurement, 80–82
  technology development, 82
Sustainability
  initiatives
    intangible benefits, 22
    return on investment on, 21
  measurable goals, 289
Sustainability report, 114
Sustainable competitive advantage,
  8–9
  and Blockbuster bankruptcy,
    94–95
  Caterpillar Inc., 105
  firm resources
    availability of substitutes,
      93–94
    inimitability, 91–93
    rarity, 91
    value, 90–91
Sustainable global economy, 20
Sustaining innovation, 383
Switching costs
  as barrier to entry, 54
  effect of Internet, 57–60
  faced by buyers, 54
  lack of, 57
SWOT analysis, 90, 91
  and competitive aggressiveness,
    406
  definition, 42
  functions, 42–43
  versus intuition and
    judgment, 43
  limitations, 76
Symbiosis view of stakeholders,
  17–18
Synergos, 183
Synergy/Synergies, 183, 438
  bases of, attained by
    acquisition, 197

  imitated by competitors, 198
  from market power, 187
  from sharing activities, 186
Systemic barriers to change,
  355–356

T

Tacit knowledge, 134
  definition, 112
Tactical actions
  definition, 269
  examples, 270
Takeover premium, 198
Talent
  attracting, 110
  emigration to form start-ups, 124
  Google policies for attracting,
    121
  and green strategies, 113
  open-sourcing model, 120
  worldwide shortage, 121
Talent retention
  and empathy, 361
  by social capital, 124
Tangible resources
  computerized training, 88–89
  definition, 88
  types, 88–89
Target market
  of focus strategy, 148
  isolation from, 232
Taxes, relocation to lower, 242
Taxi industry, 57–58
Teams
  autonomous, 403
  in barrier-free organizations,
    329–330
  in boundaryless organizations,
    336–337
  for case analysis, 433–434
  competition among, 365
  cross-functional, 337, 340
  for development, 367
  leadership exercised by,
    258–259
  in virtual organizations, 335
Technical assistants, 117–118
Technical skills, 358
Technological developments and
  trends, 48–49
Technological resources, 89

Unrelated diversification, 438
  corporate parenting, 184, 191
  definition, 191
  holding company structure, 323
  portfolio management, 184,
    192–194
  restructuring, 184, 191–192
  risk reduction as viable goal,
    194–195
U.S. News & World Report, 372
USA Today, 81, 383

V

Value
  of counterfeit goods, 223
  definition, 77
  of mergers and acquisitions
    2000–2014, 196
  of resources, 90–91
  of unsuccessful innovation,
    392–393
Value chain
  and core competencies, 185
  extended, 162–163
  global dispersion
    Bangalore, India, 227
    from decline in transportation
      costs, 227
    increase in total costs, 227–228
    offshoring, 225–227
    outsourcing, 225–227
    in service sector, 227
    World Trade Organization
      report, 225
  integration of customers, 85–87
  and reintermediation, 60
Value-chain activities
  Caterpillar Inc., 104
  in differentiation strategy, 154
  focus on one or few, 152
  in harvesting strategy, 172
  in international strategy, 231
  interrelationships
    across organizations, 85
    within organizations, 85
  optimizing location of
    cost reduction, 220
    performance enhancement, 219
    risk reduction, 220
  in overall cost leadership, 150
  primary

definition, 77
  inbound logistics, 77–78
  marketing and sales, 79–80
  operations, 78
  outbound logistics, 78–79
  service, 80
  in service organizations, 87
  support
    definition, 77
    general administration, 84
    human resource management,
      82–84
    procurement, 80–82
    technology development, 82
  transnational strategy, 235
Value-chain analysis, 437
  definition, 76
  uses, 76–77
Value-chain concept, 75
Value-creating activities, 75
  underestimating expenses, 164
Value-creating opportunity, 253
Value creation, 77
  contexts of, 250
  from employee development, 136
  from employee retention, 136
  from human capital, 136
  necessary factors, 250
  from social capital, 136
  from technology, 136
Value net concept, 63
Values, shared in boundaryless
  organizations, 337
Vanity Fair, 4
Venture capital, 255
Venture capitalists, 254–255
Vertical boundaries, 328
Vertical integration, 184, 187
  administrative costs, 190
  benefits and risks, 188–190
  definition, 188
  issues to consider, 188–190
  at Nutriva, 189
  transaction cost perspective, 190
Vertical relationships, 191
Vested interest in status quo, 365
Videoconferencing, 337
Virtual, 333
Virtual organizations, 328
  challenges and risks
    building relationships, 334

clarity of objectives, 334
    strategic plan, 334–335
    temporary alliances, 334–335
  characteristics, 334
  compared to modular type, 334
  core competencies, 334
  definition, 333
  internal, 334
  pros and cons, 336
  teams in, 335
Virtual teams, 335
Vision, 436
  definition, 24
  of entrepreneurial leaders, 258
  examples, 25
  identifying with, 120
  at James Irvine Foundation, 27
  of leaders, 350
  leadership trait, 24
  not rooted in reality, 75
  reasons for failure
    elusive, 25
    inconsistent management, 25
    irrelevance, 25
    not anchored in reality, 26
    too much focus, 25
  source of implementation
    problems, 351
  at WellPoint, 26
Vision statement, 25
  compared to mission
    statement, 27

W

Wage costs, hidden in offshoring,
  227
Wage inflation, in developing
  countries, 228
Wall Street Journal, 3, 39, 124,
  200, 268, 269, 304
Watson computer, 186
Web-based storage, 61
Websites, for competitive
  intelligence, 40
Weeds, 385
Whistleblowers, 373
Wholly owned subsidiaries
  benefits, 241
  definition, 241
  risks and limitations, 241
Wikipedia, 50

Win-win solutions, 338
Wisdom of Teams (Smith), 336
Women
  educational attainment, 45–47
  in workforce, 45
Work, challenging, 120
Workforce
  diversity management,
    122–123
  electronic teams, 132–134
  layoffs *vs.* furloughs, 138

percent in manufacturing, 110
percent in service sector, 110
Working Knowledge, 372
Workplace, stimulating
  environment, 120
World Economic Forum Global
  Report, 222
World Trade Organization report on
  production, 225
Worldwide functional division, 317
Worldwide functional structure, 326

Worldwide matrix structure,
  317, 326
Worldwide product division structure,
  317, 326
Written case analysis, 428

Z

Zero-sum game, 62
Zero-sum thinking of
  stakeholders, 17